Cash's Textbook of

Chest, Heart and Vascular Disorders for Physiotherapists

4th Edition

Edited by
Patricia A.Downie

 Mosby

London Baltimore Barcelona Bogotá Boston Buenos Aires Caracas Carlsbad, CA Chicago Madrid Mexico City
Milan Naples, FL New York Philadelphia St. Louis Seoul Singapore Sydney Taipei Tokyo Toronto Wiesbaden

Published by Mosby, an imprint of Times Mirror International Publishers
Limited
Lynton House
7–12 Tavistock Square
London WC1H 9LB

Reprinted 1992, by Butler & Tanner, Frome and London
Reprinted 1995

First published in 1975 by Faber and Faber Limited. Reprinted 1975,
1977. Second edition 1979. Third edition 1983. Fourth edition 1987.

ISBN 0 7234 1848 9

For full details of all Mosby titles please write to Times Mirror
International Publishers Limited, Lynton House, 7–12 Tavistock Square,
London WC1H 9LB, England.

British Library Cataloging in Publication Data

Cash, Joan, E.
Cash's textbook of chest, heart and vascular disorders for physiotherapists
—4th edn.
1. Cardiovascular system—Diseases. 2. Physical therapy.
3. Respiratory organs—Diseases
I. Title II. Downie, Patricia A.
616.1'0024616   RC669

Contents

8 CONTENTS

Mrs A. Percival MCSP
Superintendent Physiotherapist, Cardiothoracic Unit
Harefield Hospital, Middlesex UB9 6JH

Dr J. M. Shneerson MA, DM, FRCP
Consultant Physician, Assisted Ventilation Unit
Newmarket General Hospital, Suffolk CB8 7JG

Miss E. Ward BA
33 Bemish Road
London SW15 1DG

Dr E. Welchew MB, ChB, FFARCS
Consultant Anaesthetist, Northern General Hospital, Sheffield *and*
Honorary Lecturer, Department of Anaesthetics,
University of Sheffield Medical School

R. Whittaker MCSP, DipTP
Senior Lecturer, School of Physiotherapy
Salford College of Technology, Salford M6 6PU

Editor's Preface

The discerning reader will soon appreciate that this radically revised fourth edition has responded positively to the demands of modern technology, which require greater scientific knowledge to relate their effectiveness to the needs of patients. Yet, at the same time, there is a constant reminder of the role of the physiotherapist in establishing good relationships with her patients to enable them (and their families) to co-operate in treatments.

Direct handling of patients cannot be avoided, and physiotherapists, above all paramedical professionals, are taught as an integral part of their training *how* to use their hands to handle patients effectively. Long before the modern talk of 'holistic medicine', touch and handling were well recognised as a means of communication, a recognition of friendship, sympathy and understanding. In 1985, the Annual Congress of the Chartered Society of Physiotherapy was entitled 'Handling the Patient', and all the speakers spoke of the use of their hands to convey definite messages to the patient: resistance to enable muscles respond harder, gentleness in handling the newborn, support and firmness over the incisions of surgical patients, the touch of encouragement and compassion for the very ill. Throughout the physiotherapy chapters in this edition these same points are stressed, indeed there is a quite remarkable unanimity on the subject which is in no way attributable to the editor's direction!

The advances of technology which are well described throughout the book, bring with them wider problems and issues. Nowhere is this more evident than in the area of organ transplantation. Chapter 18 discusses heart and heart-lung transplantations. However much we may marvel at surgical skill we must never forget that for these particular patients the success or failure of the operation really is life or death. Without becoming emotional, subjective or hard, therapists who are involved with these patients (and their families and friends) must fashion for themselves a philosophy and understanding of all the issues so that they can appreciate that person's needs and enable him – with the help of all the others involved in his care – to live each day as it comes, with cautious optimism. For the relatives too, the support of the therapist can be reassuring, and such support must be seen in the context of the total care of the patient. Because I am aware of the increasing interest of many professionals in the whole range of ethical and moral dilemmas found increasingly in medicine, I have included some relevant titles in the Select Bibliography on page 685.

Once again this edition is a blend of tradition and modern thought. There *is* repetition, but this is deliberate to reinforce important points. There is also a sprinkling of opposing views, but this will make for stimulating discussion in staff and common rooms! Always remember that there are no infallible methods, techniques or approaches; patients are individuals and as such must be assessed and treated accordingly. Recognition of this individuality will lead to a more effective treatment plan and satisfaction for both patient and therapist.

I thank all the contributors most warmly, and particularly those who have responded to the invitation to contribute for the first time: Dr S. J. Connellan, Mr P. A. E. Hurst, Dr W. Kinnear, Mr D. B. McHutchison, Dr P. E. Penna, Dr J. M. Shneerson, Dr E. Welchew; Mrs J. Anderson, Mrs L. Brown, Mrs L. Kendall, Mrs A. Parker, Mrs A. Percival and Mr R. Whittaker.

Diana Innocenti and Susan Jackson have been able lieutenants without whose very considerable help much of the advanced material could not have been produced so effectively. I am immensely grateful to them.

To Professor Robin Downie and Miss Edna Ward I offer particular thanks for sharing their experience as patients. Their chapters are highly relevant in the context of the physiotherapist's role in *total* care and I commend both chapters to all therapists for careful reading and considered thought.

And what of the artist, Mrs Audrey Besterman, without whose skill such a textbook might be labelled dull? Once again she has produced some splendid drawings ranging from the 'piggy-back' heart transplant to the simple graph. Her meticulous care and skill are self-evident and rightly earns the gratitude not only of the editor and contributors, but also of the countless hundreds of readers worldwide.

P.A.D., 1987

Glossary: Abbreviations: Normal Values

Although specific terms and abbreviations are explained throughout the text it is thought helpful to provide a composite list for easy reference.

It is also felt that a list of the normal values of the most commonly encountered investigations would be helpful.

GLOSSARY

alkalosis (respiratory) A pathological state of a raised pH resulting from a loss of CO_2 through hyperventilation

anoxia Absence of oxygen in the tissues despite an adequate blood supply

apnoea Cessation of respiration

arrhythmia Disturbance of cardiac rhythm

asphyxia Death due to lack of oxygen

bradycardia Slow heart rate

bruit Turbulence or an abnormal murmur in a vessel heard on auscultation

compliance Change in lung volume for unit change in distending pressure

dyspnoea Laboured, uncomfortable breathing

dysrhythmia Disturbance of rhythm

fibrillation Rapid unco-ordinated contractions of the cardiac muscle

haemodynamics The study of forces governing blood flow

hertz (Hz) SI unit of frequency (of a current). Equals 1 cycle per second

hypercapnia Excess of carbon dioxide in the blood

hypercarbia Excess of carbon dioxide in the blood

hypopnoea Diminution of tidal volume

hypovolaemia Low blood volume

hypoxaemia/hypoxia Reduction of oxygen supply to the tissues

ischaemia Oxygen starvation of the tissues due to a lack of blood supply

joule (J) SI unit of measurement of work, energy, quantity of heat
kilopascal (kPa) 1000 pascals, *q.v.*
myotonia Inability of muscle to relax quickly
orthopnoea Difficulty in breathing when lying
paradoxical movement/breathing Inward drawing of the lower ribs on inspiration with relaxation on expiration
pascal (Pa) SI unit of measurement of pressure (*not* used for blood pressure)
phototherapy Treatment of certain diseases by light rays, e.g. jaundice in the newborn
plethysmography (body) Measurement of changes of body volume related to pulmonary ventilation
polycythaemia An abnormal increase in the volume of red blood cells
stridor Harsh noisy inspiration resulting from airway obstruction
surgical emphysema Air between the subcutaneous tissues following trauma or surgery. When palpated, feels like tissue paper
tachycardia Rapid heart rate
tachypnoea Rapid respiratory rate

ABBREVIATIONS

ARDS   Adult respiratory distress syndrome
BPD   Bronchopulmonary dysplasia
CAO   Chronic airflow obstruction
CFMs   Cerebral function monitors
CO   Carbon monoxide
CO_2 Carbon dioxide
CPAP   Continuous positive airways pressure
CSF   Cerebrospinal fluid
CVP   Central venous pressure
DSA   Digital subtraction angiography
ECG   Electrocardiogram
EEG   Electro-encephalogram
FEV_1 Forced expiratory volume in 1 second
FG   French gauge (sizes for catheter)
FiO_2 Fraction of inspired oxygen
FRC   Functional residual capacity
FVC   Forced vital capacity
GAW   Airways conductance
H_2 Hydrogen
HFJV   High frequency jet ventilation

HFO	High frequency oscillation
HFV	High frequency ventilation
HMEs	Heat and moisture exchangers
Hz	Hertz
IC	Inspiratory capacity
ICP	Intracranial pressure
IHD	Ischaemic heart disease
IMV	Intermittent mandatory ventilation
IPPB	Intermittent positive pressure breathing
IPPV	Intermittent positive pressure ventilation
IVH	Intraventricular haemorrhage
J	joule
KCO	Transfer coefficient
kPa	kilopascal
MEFV	Maximum expiratory flow volume
MIFV	Maximum inspiratory flow volume
mmHg	Millimetres of mercury
MMV	Mandatory minute volume
MRI	Magnetic resonance imaging
MV	Minute volume
NEEP	Negative end-expiratory pressure
NMR	Nuclear magnetic resonance
O_2	Oxygen
$Paco_2$	Arterial pressure of carbon dioxide
Pao_2	Arterial pressure of oxygen
PEEP	Positive end-expiratory pressure
PEFR	Peak expiratory flow rate
RAW	Airways resistance
RDS	Respiratory distress syndrome
RTA	Road traffic accident
RV	Residual volume
SGAW	Specific airways conductance
SRAW	Specific airways resistance
TcO_2	Transcutaneous oxygen
TGV	Thoracic gas volume
TIA	Transient ischaemic attack
TLC	Total lung capacity
T_LCO	Carbon monoxide transfer factor
TV	Tidal volume
VC	Vital capacity
V_T	Tidal volume
V/Q	Ventilation-perfusion
ZEEP	Zero end-expiratory pressure

NORMAL VALUES

Arterial blood gases

P_{CO_2} 4.5–6.1 kPa (34–46mmHg)
P_{O_2} 12.0–15.0kPa (90–110mmHg)
pH 35–45mmol/l (7.35–7.45mg/dl)
base excess – males −2.3 to +2.3mmol/l
              – females −3.0 to +1.6mmol/l
P_{O_2} (capillary) 6.7–10.7 kPa (50–80mmHg)

Blood

Haemoglobin	– males	15.5 ± 2.5g/dl
	– females	14.0 ± 2.5g/dl
Red blood cells	– males	5.5 ± 1.0 × 10^{12}/litre
	– females	4.8 ± 1.0 × 10^{12}/litre
Prothrombin	time	12–30 sec
Urea		3.5–7.4mmol/l
Creatinine	ambulant	up to 110µmol/l
	hospitalised	up to 135 µmol/l

Electrolytes

sodium (Na)	135–150 mmol/l
potassium (K)	3.8–5.5 mmol/l
chloride	95–105 mmol/l

Cardiothoracic Anatomical Illustrations

Basic knowledge of anatomy and physiology of the cardiothoracic systems has been assumed. The following illustrations are included as a means of easy reference and for revision. (A list of suitable books is included on page 27.)

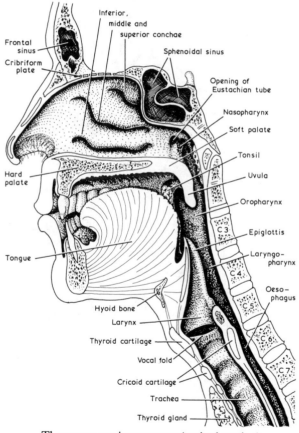

The upper respiratory tract (sagittal section)

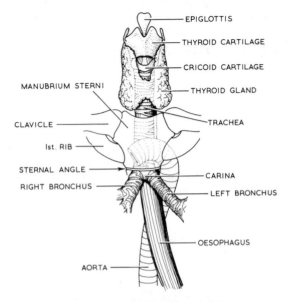

The trachea and its main relations

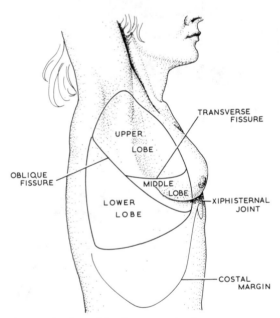

Surface projection of the fissures and lobes of the right lung

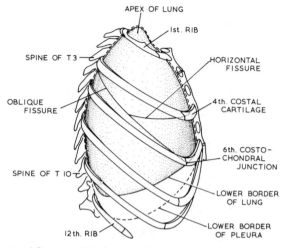

The lobes and fissures of the lungs and pleura in relation to the thoracic cage

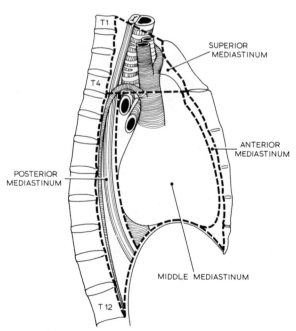

The mediastinum showing its subdivisions

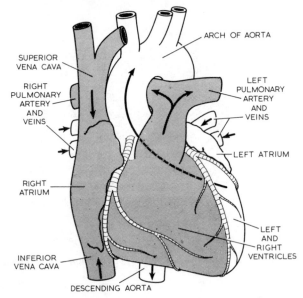

Anterior view of the heart and great vessels

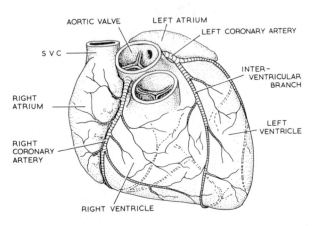

The anterior aspect of the heart showing the coronary vessels

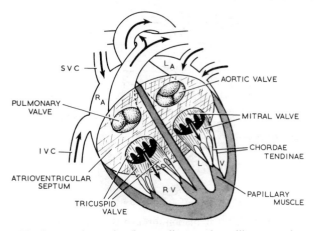

The heart valves, chordae tendinae and papillary muscles

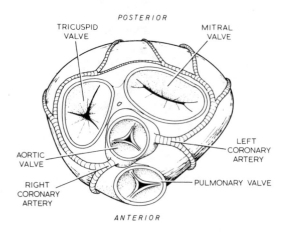

View showing that the 4 heart valves lie in the same plane

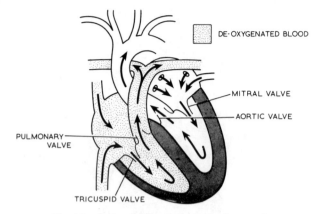

DE-OXYGENATED BLOOD

MITRAL VALVE

AORTIC VALVE

PULMONARY VALVE

TRICUSPID VALVE

The blood circulation through the heart valves

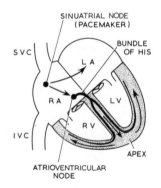

SINUATRIAL NODE (PACEMAKER)

BUNDLE OF HIS

SVC

LA

RA

LV

RV

IVC

APEX

ATRIOVENTRICULAR NODE

The conducting system of the heart

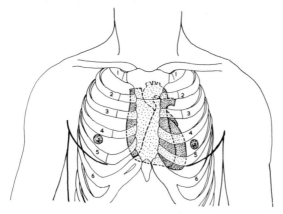

Surface projection of the heart

BIBLIOGRAPHY

The following titles are regularly updated. The current edition is shown, but readers should check with their medical librarian whether there is a more recent edition.

Gray's Anatomy, 36th edition (1980). Churchill Livingstone, Edinburgh.

Green, J. H. (1976). *An Introduction to Human Physiology*, 4th edition. Oxford University Press, London.

Guyton, A. C. (1982). *Human Physiology and Mechanisms of Disease*, 3rd edition. W. B. Saunders, Eastbourne, England.

Keele, C. A., Neil, E. and Joel, S. (eds.) (1982). *Samson Wright's Applied Physiology*, 13th edition. Oxford University Press, Oxford.

(maximum TV) is the vital capacity (VC). The maximum volume of gas in the lungs is the total lung capacity (TLC) (TLC = RV + VC).

DEAD SPACE

Total dead space within the respiratory system is called the *physiological dead space* (to distinguish it from the dead space of any externally applied apparatus, such as a face mask or mechanical ventilator). Dead space is divided into:

Anatomical dead space: The non-respiratory, conducting part of the respiratory system.
Alveolar dead space: The space occupied by gas which is transported to the alveoli but does not meet blood across the alveolar-capillary membrane (Chapter 2, p. 57).

Composition of dead space gas

At the end of a normal expiration, the dead space is occupied by alveolar gas from alveoli which were last to empty. At the next inspiration, alveoli first receive gas from the dead space (alveolar gas), followed by fresh gas. This fresh gas adds to and dilutes the gas of the FRC.

At the end of inspiration, the dead space is occupied by fresh gas. The alveoli contain a gas mixture which is being rapidly converted from fresh gas into alveolar gas as oxygen is removed and carbon dioxide is added.

On expiration, the first gas to leave the lungs is fresh unaltered gas from the dead space, followed by alveolar gas. As expiration

TABLE 1/1 Gas tensions (kPa) at points in the respiratory tract

	Dry air sea level pressure 100kPa	Tracheal air	Alveolar gas	Mixed expired gas
P_{O_2}	21	19	13	15
P_{CO_2}	0	0	5	4
P_{N_2}	79	75	75	75
P_{H_2O}	0	6	6	6

proceeds, the expired gas approaches more and more the composition of alveolar gas until, at the end of a forced expiration to RV, the gas leaving the lungs is pure alveolar gas. It can be collected and analysed. Gas collected throughout expiration (mixed expired gas) is a mixture of dead space (fresh) and alveolar gas (Table 1/1).

Magnitude of the dead space

The anatomical dead space can be divided into intra- and extra-thoracic parts. The extra-thoracic dead space consists of the nose, mouth, pharynx and larynx – those parts of the airways which lie above the thoracic inlet. The conducting airways from the thoracic inlet to the respiratory alveoli constitute the intra-thoracic dead space. The intra- and extra-thoracic parts are approximately equal in volume. Tracheostomy or endotracheal intubation, therefore, decreases anatomical dead space by about half.

The volume of the *anatomical dead space* is influenced by body size and position. The total volume is approximately equal to the body-weight in pounds (1lb = 0.45kg) (Radford, 1955) or 0.05 times the body surface area (m^2) (Engström and Herzog, 1959). The total volume is about 150ml in the sitting adult with normal lungs.

The volume of the *extra-thoracic dead space* is influenced by the position of the head and neck. Protrusion of the jaw and extension of the neck add about 50ml to dead space. Jaw depression decreases it by 25ml. *The intra-thoracic anatomical dead space* is greater in the erect than in the supine position, because it is related to FRC, and FRC increases by 500ml when changing from supine to upright position, due to descent of the diaphragm.

Since Valv = Vt – Vd, at a normal tidal volume, 350ml are added to the FRC at each breath. If the dead space volume remained constant, then, at a TV of 150ml, no alveolar ventilation would occur. Survival is, however, possible when tidal volume is only 60ml. Many patients being weaned from mechanical ventilation have tidal volumes of 250ml or less. A spontaneously breathing anaesthetised patient may have a tidal volume of only 100 – 150ml. In general, as TV decreases, dead space also decreases. The Vd/Vt ratio remains constant. The factors involved are:

1. Laminar flow becomes more marked at low TV.
2. Any fresh gas which does get below the carina is mixed with alveolar gas by the churning effect of the cardiac contractions.

GAS FLOW

Gas will only flow from an area of high pressure to an area of lower pressure. The rate of gas flow ($\dot{V}$) is proportional to the pressure difference (P) and inversely proportional to the resistance to flow (R):

$$\dot{V} \propto P/R$$

The resistance to gas flow along a tube depends on whether flow is laminar or turbulent.

In *laminar* flow, the gas is moving in a series of concentric cylinders (lamellae) within the tube. The layer of gas next to the wall of the tube is stationary. The innermost cylinder is moving fastest. The advancing front of the gas is cone-shaped. All the gas molecules are moving in the direction of flow. Laminar flow is a streamlined, low resistance, silent flow. The radius of the tube is the most important determinant of resistance when flow is laminar. As the radius increases there is a 16-fold increase in gas flow for the same pressure difference.

The alternative to laminar flow is *turbulent* flow. Turbulent flow is higgledy-piggledy flow. Different parts of the gas are moving in different directions and the individual molecules are moving randomly, including some moving at right angles to the direction of flow. Turbulent flow is a high resistance, noisy flow. A noise (bruit) is heard on listening with a stethoscope to blood flowing through a stenosed artery or heart valve. The same blood flowing through a normal artery or valve is silent. The radius of the tube is much less important in turbulent flow; flow only quadruples for an increase in radius. The density of the gas largely determines gas flow rate.

If gas is flowing slowly through a straight, wide tube, flow is laminar. Flow becomes turbulent at high rates of flow, in narrow tubes or where the tube bends, branches or changes in diameter. In quiet breathing, flow in the trachea is partly turbulent. Flow becomes totally turbulent when ventilation is maximal. In the smaller airways, flow is laminar except near branches. It is the noisy, turbulent gas flow through narrow, branching parts of the airways that is heard with a stethoscope applied to the chest.

The overall resistance to gas flow in the normal respiratory tract is 0.1kPa/l/sec – the pressure difference to cause gas to flow at the rate of 1l/sec through the respiratory tract is 0.1kPa. This compares with the resistance to flow of 0.2–0.4kPa/l/sec of any man-made respiratory apparatus, such as a re-breathing bag or mechanical ventilator, which might be attached to the patient.

Since, for a given gas and tube, both the resistance to gas flow and the rate of flow when laminar flow becomes turbulent are influenced by the radius of the tube, any reduction in diameter of the airways will result in an increase in resistance to flow.

Airway diameter is influenced by:

1. Activity of bronchial smooth muscle.
2. Any accumulation of oedema fluid in the wall.
3. The volume of the secretions of the mucous glands in the wall and the effectiveness of the cilia and cough in removing it.

CONTROL OF BRONCHIAL SMOOTH MUSCLE

Bronchial smooth muscle is under both nervous (sympathetic and parasympathetic autonomic nerves) and humoral control and reacts to many non-physiological substances.

Nervous control

Parasympathetic nerves to the bronchial smooth muscle are branches of the vagus (Xth cranial) nerve. Activation of these nerves results in contraction of the muscle and narrowing of the airways. The neuromuscular transmitter is acetylcholine. Parasympathetic blocking (anticholinergic) drugs can be used in the treatment of reversible airways obstruction (asthma). The only drug in common use in this group is ipratropium bromide (Atrovent).

Sympathetic nerves reach the bronchial muscle from plexuses around the hila of the lungs. The cell bodies lie in the lateral horn of the thoracic spinal cord. The transmitter is noradrenaline. Activation of the nerves produces relaxation of the bronchial muscle and an increase in airway diameter.

Liberation of hormones (catecholamines, principally adrenaline) from the medulla of the adrenal glands also causes relaxation of the muscle.

The sympathetic receptors in the lungs are classified as beta-2 (β_2), to distinguish them from alpha (α) receptors in the smooth muscle of blood vessels and beta-1 (β_1) receptors in the heart. Adrenaline, a non-specific sympathetic stimulant, has been used in the treatment of asthma. Modern adrenaline-like (sympathomimetic) drugs, the β_2 stimulants, such as salbutamol (Ventolin) or terbutaline (Bricanyl), are more specific for the pulmonary receptors, to avoid the unwanted changes in heart rate and blood pressure associated with the non-specific agents.

Other agents

Bronchoconstrictor agents may be released directly into the lung following lung injury or infection. In susceptible individuals the inhalation of pollen, dust or other allergens can produce a marked increase in bronchial smooth muscle tone and oedema of the airways. Many of these effects are produced by local liberation of humoral substances, such as 5-hydroxytryptamine and prostaglandins, from the mast cells in the lung.

Effects of gas tensions

LOCAL

Changes in oxygen and carbon dioxide tension in alveolar gas and in pulmonary capillary blood alter bronchial smooth muscle tone by a direct effect on the muscle cells.

REFLEX

Bronchoconstriction occurs if arterial blood carbon dioxide tension is increased or decreased and if oxygen tension is reduced. These are reflex effects brought about partly by stimulation of the chemo-receptors.

These local and reflex changes serve to divert gas away from parts of the lung where gas exchange with blood is deficient. They are deranged by administration of morphine or other narcotic analgesic drugs.

Other reflex effects

There is an increase in bronchial smooth muscle tone:

1. At low lung volumes (stretch receptor reflex).
2. On stimulation of receptors in the nose by cold (diving reflex).
3. By mechanical or chemical stimulation of receptors in the larynx and large airways (cough reflex).
4. On activation of the carotid sinus baroreceptors in systemic arterial hypotension.

THE PRESSURE DIFFERENCE AND THE WORK OF BREATHING

The important factors in getting gas into and out of the lungs are (1) muscle contraction and (2) elasticity.

The pressure difference to enable gas to flow into the alveoli in inspiration is created by contraction of the respiratory muscles, mainly the diaphragm (in quiet breathing) aided by the intercostal muscles. The energy for muscle contraction comes from metabolism of glucose to carbon dioxide and water in the mitochondria of the muscle cells.

Muscle contraction enlarges the thoracic cage. Since the lungs are attached to the chest wall by the moist pleurae, the lungs also expand. Between RV and TLC the lungs expand by a factor of 1.6 in all dimensions. The main expansion occurs in the alveoli and the air passages leading to them.

Of the work done by the respiratory muscles in inspiration, 40 per cent is used in overcoming the non-elastic resistance to ventilation. The most important non-elastic resistance is the resistance to gas flow (60 per cent of the non-elastic resistance). The viscosity of the tissues accounts for 30 per cent and the inertia of tissues and gas for the remaining 10 per cent of the non-elastic resistance.

The remaining 60 per cent of the total work done by the respiratory muscles is used to overcome the elastic resistance. Elasticity is a property of all living tissue, not just the histologically recognisable yellow elastic tissue. The lungs do contain a high proportion of elastic tissue, inserted mostly at the level of the alveoli, but muscle fibres, joint capsules and tendons are also elastic. Enlargement of the thorax stretches all the tissues of the chest wall and lungs.

Since inspiration is an active, energy-requiring process, oxygen is consumed by the respiratory muscles – the oxygen cost of breathing (Fig. 1/3). At rest, the respiratory muscles have an oxygen consumption of 3ml/min. This is less than 2 per cent of the total body oxygen consumption at rest. The actual oxygen consumption is about 0.5ml/l of MV, up to 70l/min. Above this near maximal MV, oxygen consumption rises dramatically so that the extra oxygen delivered to the blood is entirely used up by the respiratory muscles. This is one of the limits to exercise.

In disease, for example emphysema, oxygen consumption is higher at all levels of MV and probably contributes to the reduced exercise tolerance.

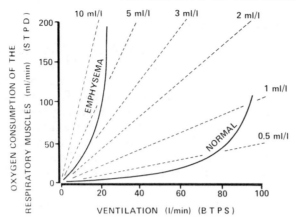

FIG. 1/3 The oxygen cost of breathing. The oxygen consumption by the respiratory muscles increases as ventilation increases, more steeply in disease than in health. In normal lungs, the respiratory muscles consume all the extra available oxygen at maximal ventilation (70 litres/min)

All the work done by the respiratory muscles appears eventually as heat.

Expansion of the lungs reduces intra-alveolar pressure to less than mouth pressure. Mouth pressure is atmospheric pressure. The reduced alveolar pressure is correctly termed subatmospheric, but is more usually referred to as *negative pressure*. Air rushes down the pressure gradient from mouth to alveoli. At the start of inspiration, the pressure difference is large and gas flow is rapid. As inspiration proceeds, the volume of gas in the alveoli increases; alveolar pressure becomes less negative; the pressure gradient and, therefore, gas flow decrease. At the end of inspiration, alveolar pressure equals mouth pressure; there is no gas flow and the lungs contain the full tidal volume.

Expiration occurs when the respiratory muscles relax. The stretched elastic tissue recoils, squashing the alveolar gas and raising its pressure. Alveolar pressure is now greater than mouth pressure. Gas flows down the pressure gradient from alveoli to mouth, at first rapidly and then more slowly as the pressure gradient decreases as the lungs reassume their resting volume. Expiration stops when alveolar and mouth pressures are again equal.

Elastic recoil supplies the work to overcome the non-elastic resistance to gas flow in expiration. Inspiration is an active process (muscle contraction) while expiration is passive (elastic recoil).

ELASTICITY (Fig. 1/4)

Elasticity of the lungs and chest wall can be demonstrated by creation of a pneumothorax. The chest radiograph will show that the lung has shrunk away from the chest wall. Measurement shows that the lung has recoiled to a volume less than RV. The chest wall takes up a position equivalent to about the mid-inspiratory position. These are the resting volumes of the lung freed from the chest wall and the chest wall freed from the lung. In these positions, the elastic tissue in the lungs and in the chest wall is completely relaxed.

In the intact thorax the resting position is FRC (Fig. 1/4B). The lungs are above their resting volume and are trying to contract under the influence of the stretched elastic tissue. The chest wall is at a

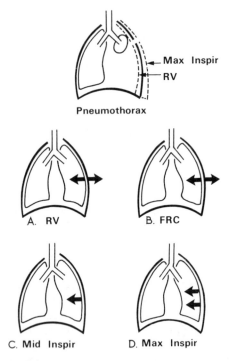

FIG. 1/4 Elasticity. The resting positions of the lung and chest wall are shown (pneumothorax). The elastic forces operating through the intrapleural fluid are shown at: A. residual volume (RV); B. functional residual capacity (FRC); C. mid-inspiration (Mid Inspir); D. at the end of inspiration (Max Inspir)

smaller volume than its resting volume. It is trying to expand under the influence of the 'crumpled' elastic tissue. The inward pull of the lungs is exactly balanced by the outward pull of the chest wall, in the absence of muscle activity. To alter the thoracic volume away from FRC, either through inspiration towards TLC or through forced expiration towards RV, requires muscular activity. At RV (Fig. 1/4A) the elastic tissue of the lungs is still stretched, because it is above its resting length. The chest wall is even further away from its resting volume and trying to expand. The outward pull of the chest wall is greater than the inward pull of the lungs. Residual volume is an unstable position and the respiratory muscles have to do work to maintain this position.

On inspiration from FRC the respiratory muscles contract, enlarging the thorax. The elastic tissue of the lung is stretched further away from its resting position, but the elastic tissue of the chest wall is first brought to its resting position at mid-inspiration (Fig. 1/4C). Up to this point the only elastic resistance to expansion of the chest is that of the lungs. The elastic tissue of the chest wall is aiding expansion. As inspiration proceeds beyond this point, the elastic tissue of both the lungs and chest wall has to be stretched further away from its resting position. At the end of inspiration (Fig. 1/4D) the elastic tissue in both the chest wall and lungs is well above the resting position. The greater the expansion above FRC, the greater the stretch of the elastic tissue.

When the muscles stop contracting at the end of inspiration, all the stretched elastic tissue recoils, creating the expiratory pressure gradient and causing gas to flow.

A consideration of the elasticity of the lungs and chest wall leads to the concept of the negative intrapleural pressure. The inward pull of the lungs is exactly balanced at FRC by the outward pull of the chest wall. There is no intrapleural space in which a pressure can be measured in the intact thorax, because the lungs are tightly stuck to the chest wall by the 'glue' of the thin layer of fluid between the parietal layer of pleura covering the inside of the chest wall and the visceral pleura covering the surface of the lungs. The opposing elastic forces of the lungs and chest wall are trying to pull the glue apart. This distracting force is thought of as being negative in direction. If a small, localised pneumothorax is created, the measured pressure in the pneumothorax is subatmospheric, reflecting the distracting forces.

If, at end-inspiration, the respiratory muscles relax, but expiration is prevented by closure of the glottis, the pressure in the lungs is the pressure exerted on the gas by the stretched elastic tissue attempting to recoil. This pressure is an indication of the elasticity of the lungs and chest wall and is termed *compliance*.

COMPLIANCE

The measurement of compliance is described in Chapter 3. Compliance relates the pressure of the gas in the lungs to the volume of gas inspired (Fig. 1/5). The pressure measured is the pressure due to recoil of the elastic tissue in the absence of:

1. Muscle activity, opposing the elastic recoil; and
2. Gas flow, removing from consideration the non-elastic resistance due to gas flow.

These conditions are met at the change-over from inspiration to expiration in the normal respiratory cycle. Compliance measured at this point is dynamic compliance. An estimate of dynamic compliance in a patient on a mechanical ventilator can be obtained by noting the tidal volume and end-inspiratory pressure.

A *third* condition is imposed on the more usual measurement of static compliance – after gas flow ceases, there is an equilibration period before measurement of gas pressure. This allows fast filling alveoli, containing gas at higher than average pressure, to empty some of their contents into slower filling alveoli, containing gas at lower pressure. This equilibration period is not present in the

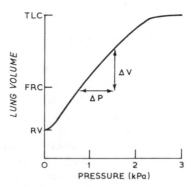

FIG. 1/5 Compliance, pressure/volume, curve. Lung volume is calibrated in functional terms: RV = residual volume; FRC = functional residual capacity; TLC = total lung capacity. Compliance is the slope of the curve, $\triangle V / \triangle P$; the change in volume, $\triangle V$, divided by the change in pressure, $\triangle P$

measurement of dynamic compliance; average alveolar pressure is higher and dynamic compliance is lower than static compliance.

In normal lungs at low respiratory rates, all the alveoli fill with gas at approximately the same rate: static and dynamic compliance are the same. At high respiratory rates, differences in the rate of alveolar filling become exaggerated. In abnormal lungs some alveoli fill more quickly than others – the normal homogeneous structure of the lungs is destroyed. Dynamic compliance is lower than static.

A graph of pressure against volume – the compliance curve – is S-shaped flattening at high and low pressures (Fig. 1/5). The straight part of the curve, where a small change in pressure produces a large change in volume, is in the range of normal tidal volumes. At the extremes (RV and TLC) a large pressure change produces only minimal change in volume. Normal compliance, the slope of the straight part of the curve, is 0.85l/kPa: following inspiration of 850ml of gas from FRC the recoil pressure of the elastic tissue of the lungs and chest wall is 1kPa. Lungs which are stiffened by disease have a low compliance – a greater pressure is required to expand the less elastic lungs.

SURFACE TENSION

Surface tension is a force which exists at the interface between two dissimilar fluids. It is the force which stops the water beetle sinking through the surface of the pond. In the lungs it exists at the gas/liquid interface on the alveolar-capillary membrane.

The theory of soap bubbles has been applied to the lungs. The pressure inside a gas-filled bubble, due to surface tension at the interface between soap and gas, depends on the radius of the bubble. Small bubbles have high internal pressure. When two unequal bubbles are connected together, the smaller empties into the larger under the influence of the pressure difference. Not all the normal lung alveoli have the same radius. If the surface tension in the alveoli behaved like the soap/gas interface, small alveoli would empty into larger ones. In the end there would be only one huge alveolus, quite unsuitable as a gas exchange system (as in emphysema).

The alveolar-capillary membrane is lined with a mixture of lipids (including dipalmitoyl-lecithin and phosphatidyl glycerol) called *surfactant*. This material is produced by the pneumocytes of the alveolar wall and has the amazing property of being able to change its surface tension according to its surface area. At low lung volumes (expiration or small alveoli) the surface tension is reduced. Small alveoli do not empty into larger ones. This serves to stabilise the alveoli. Even at forced expiration – down to RV – surfactant keeps the alveoli open. Surfactant is also responsible for a large part of lung elasticity.

NERVOUS CONTROL OF VENTILATION

Normal breathing is an automatic process – it continues without conscious thought, in sleep and under the influence of drugs which produce unconsciousness. At the very deepest levels of unconsciousness, however, ventilation is depressed or abolished. On the other hand, unlike the reflex knee jerk or the heart beat, it is possible to voluntarily stop breathing or change the rate or depth of ventilation.

The major control centre for rhythmic respiration lies in the hindbrain (medulla oblongata and pons). The activity of the respiratory nerve cells (neurones) is influenced by the following factors (summarised in Figure 1/6):

1. Activity in other parts of the brain (especially cerebral cortex and hypothalamus).
2. Sensory receptors in the lungs (stretch receptors); airways (mechanical or chemical irritation); chest wall (stretch receptors); and in the muscles of respiration (muscle spindles).
3. Chemoreceptor activity.
4. The general state of 'alertness' of the body.
5. Pain and other receptors throughout the body.
6. Head and neck sensory receptors.
7. The state of activity of the skeletal muscles (muscle spindles).

Some respiratory neurones are active only in inspiration and others only in expiration, despite expiration being a passive event (elastic recoil) under normal conditions. Some neurones are inactive in normal ventilation.

The neurones are arranged in 'self-re-exciting' chains. Once activity starts in an inspiratory neurone it spreads to other inspiratory neurones in the chain. At the same time, activity in the expiratory neurones is inhibited. Gradually, the inspiratory neurones become less sensitive to excitation so that activity in one cell no longer spreads to the next member of the chain. Activity in the inspiratory chain is damped down and inhibition of the expiratory neurones is lessened. Freed from inhibition, activity in the expiratory neurones begins to spread throughout the expiratory chain and to inhibit activity in the inspiratory chain. This causes the

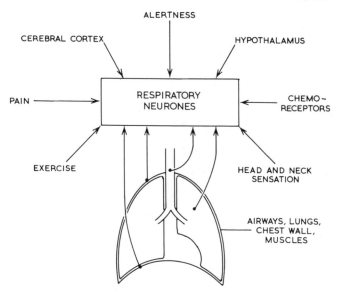

FIG. 1/6 Influences on the respiratory neurones. Rhythmic activity of the medullary respiratory neurones is maintained by activity in other parts of the brain; activity in sensory receptors situated in the lungs, chest wall, airways; sensory receptors in the head and neck; pain receptors throughout the body and activity in the chemoreceptors

inspiratory muscle contraction to cease and allows expiration to commence.

Gradually, in the same way, expiratory neuronal activity ceases and the inhibition of the inspiratory neurones lessens. The inspiratory neurone chain is re-excited and inspiratory muscle activity begins again. This mechanism:

1. Accounts for the rhythmicity of respiration; and
2. Postulates that expiratory neurones are purely 'anti-inspiratory'.

Administration of drugs, such as the narcotic analgesics (morphine, pethidine), depress both brain function and ventilation resulting in either prolonged activity in one group of respiratory neurones or complete absence of neuronal activity. To start an unconscious patient breathing again, a loud shout, a pinch or a slap are often effective. At the end of an operation under general anaesthesia, the endotracheal tube is often moved in the trachea. To encourage a newborn baby to breathe the soles of the feet are slapped or the pharynx is aspirated.

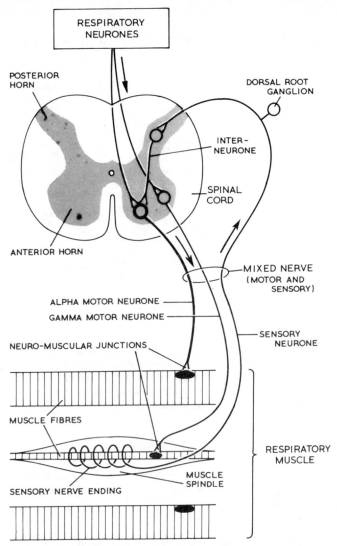

FIG. 1/7 Neuromuscular connections. The respiratory neurones synapse with the large diameter, rapidly conducting alpha motor neurones in the anterior horn of the spinal cord. These neurones join the muscle fibre at the neuromuscular junction. Lying among muscle fibres is the muscle spindle which is fusiform in shape and contains a muscle fibre which in turn is innervated by small diameter, slowly conducting gamma motor neurones arising from cell bodies in the anterior horn, and a sensory nerve ending. The nerve fibre from the sensory nerve ending passes to the dorsal horn of the spinal cord in a mixed peripheral nerve. The cell body is in the dorsal root ganglion. In the spinal cord it synapses with an interneurone which in turn synapses with the cell body of the alpha motor neurone. Impulses also pass along the spinal cord to the brainstem and cortex

These manoeuvres all increase the general level of neuronal activity (the number of nerve impulses) in the brainstem, particularly near:

1. The origin of the vagus nerves which are carrying impulses to or from nearly every organ above the pelvis.
2. The origin of the sensory nerves to the face.
3. The fibre tracts carrying sensory information from all the sensory receptors and motor information to all the muscles of the body below the head and neck.
4. The reticular activating system. This is a network of fine nerve fibres and small nerve cells scattered throughout the brainstem (medulla, pons, hypothalamus and thalamus). It is linked to all the sensory and motor systems in the brain and to the 'higher centres', e.g. sight, smell, memory and intelligence. This system of cells and fibres is involved in consciousness and sleep, and, at least in part, to the attention the brain is paying to any particular part of the body. It is concerned in awareness and alertness.

Impulses in all these systems passing close to the inspiratory and expiratory neurones, help to start and maintain in them their rhythmic activity.

MECHANISM OF SKELETAL MUSCLE CONTRACTION

Activity in the respiratory neurones is transmitted through the spinal cord and peripheral motor nerves (intercostal and phrenic) to the intercostal muscles and diaphragm. Impulses from the muscles, arising in the muscle spindles, are conveyed to the medulla in sensory nerves. The sensory–to–motor connection (via an interneurone) in the spinal cord forms the stretch reflex pathway (Fig. 1/7). Since therapists will be familiar with these pathways and the physiology of muscle contraction, they will not be further discussed.

In the respiratory system, the stretch reflex allows detection of any discrepancy between the desired muscle contraction and the actual contraction produced, as might occur if there was a sudden increase in resistance to breathing. A reflex change in the activity of the motor nerves occurs so that the required tidal volume is obtained. Each inspiration, therefore, contains within itself the mechanism to allow fine adjustments to meet the prevailing conditions. There is no other mechanism which allows such rapid, fine tuning of ventilation. If the reduced tidal volume, following a change in resistance to breathing, had to wait to be corrected until the blood gases had been disturbed, then there would be a delay of up to 90 seconds.

CHEMORECEPTORS

Since ventilation may be said to exist to deliver adequate fresh gas to the alveoli so that oxygen and carbon dioxide can exchange between gas and blood, it is not surprising that there are receptors, *the chemoreceptors*, to detect the blood levels of these gases. These receptors can reflexly alter ventilation to maintain the blood gases within normal limits, despite varying metabolic demands.

There are two main groups:

1. *Central* chemoreceptors which are located in the medulla oblongata. They are either the respiratory neurones themselves or are closely associated with them.

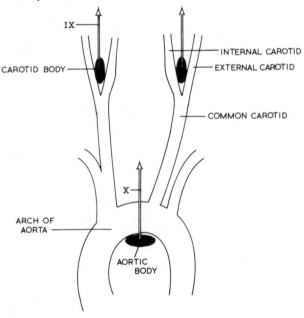

FIG. 1/8 Peripheral chemoreceptors, responding to oxygen, lie in the aortic body, situated in the concavity of the arch of the aorta and in the carotid body, at the bifurcation of the common carotid artery into internal and external branches. The afferent (sensory) nerve from the aortic body is the vagus nerve (X) and from the carotid body is the glossopharyngeal nerve (IX)

2. *Peripheral* chemoreceptors which are groups of specialised cells closely surrounded by specialised blood vessels and sensory nerve fibres. They are found in the carotid body, located in the bifurcation of the carotid artery and in the aortic body, lying within the concavity of the arch of the aorta (Fig. 1/8). Nerve impulses from the carotid body reach the medulla in the glossopharyngeal (IXth cranial) nerve and from the aortic body in the vagus nerve.

The blood supply and metabolic rate of peripheral chemoreceptor cells are, on a weight-for-weight basis, very large (greater even than the cerebral cortex).

Effect of changing inspired gas composition

CARBON DIOXIDE (CO_2)

If the inspired carbon dioxide concentration is increased to 6 per cent there is, after a delay of 90–120 seconds, an increase in ventilation to near the maximal ventilatory capacity (70l/min). This effect is mediated by an increase in arterial blood P_{CO_2} acting via the chemoreceptors. Further increase in inspired carbon dioxide cannot result in any further increase in ventilation and, indeed, ventilation begins to be depressed when arterial blood P_{CO_2} reaches 12kPa. Eventually, unconsciousness results, since carbon dioxide at high tensions is an anaesthetic.

About 80 per cent of the increase in ventilation in response to an increase in inspired carbon dioxide is due to activation of the central chemoreceptors. They also respond to (1) high plasma bicarbonate concentration and (2) acidosis.

The effect of an acidosis is demonstrated by the increase in ventilation in patients with diabetic keto-acidosis, renal failure or shock.

The central chemoreceptors do not respond to hypoxia.

OXYGEN (O_2)

While there is a dramatic and prompt increase in ventilation in response to even a small increase in inspired carbon dioxide concentration, there is little or no change in ventilation until the inspired oxygen concentration is reduced to about 14 per cent. This corresponds to an arterial P_{O_2} of about 7kPa, when cyanosis begins to be noticeable and cerebral function (especially intellectual function) begins to be impaired. Breathing 10 per cent oxygen results in an increase in ventilation of about 1 litre/min. Ventilation is doubled when the inspired oxygen is reduced to 8 per cent and at 4 per cent inspired oxygen ventilation reaches about 30l/min, but the subject is unconscious! Death due to cardiac ventricular fibrillation occurs if 5 per cent oxygen is breathed for any length of time. In other words, hypoxia causes death without much increase in ventilation.

The response to hypoxia is mediated by the peripheral chemo-receptors. Despite the lack of ventilatory response to hypoxia there is activity in the sensory nerves from the receptors even at normal blood oxygen tension. The activity is random and continuous. It is abolished by an increase in arterial blood Po$_2$. If the arterial blood oxygen tension falls to 8kPa or less there is an increase in activity in the afferent nerves, but still no change in ventilation.

Peripheral chemoreceptor activity is also increased by:

1. Acidosis
2. Hypercarbia
3. Hypotension
4. Pyrexia
5. Other chemicals such as nicotine, acetylcholine, carbon monoxide and cyanide.

The response of the peripheral chemoreceptors to hypoxia is enhanced if carbon dioxide is simultaneously elevated, as in asphyxia (strangulation).

Mechanism of chemoreceptor action

The effects of changed blood gases on ventilation, mediated by the chemoreceptors, are produced reflexly by alterations in the motor neurone discharge, resulting in increased contraction of the respiratory muscles.

In the brainstem, the neuronal mechanism is called *recruitment*. The activity of a particular inspiratory neurone in the medulla is unchanged following chemoreceptor activation, but the silent neurones are brought to activity (recruited). Ventilation is increased by recruitment of extra inspiratory neurones which brings into activity extra muscle fibres in the inspiratory muscles.

More expiratory neurones may also be recruited to enhance the motor neurone activity to the expiratory muscles so that expiration may also become an active process.

OTHER REFLEX EFFECTS

Ventilation is altered when other, principally cardiovascular, reflexes are activated. For example, stimulation of the carotid sinus baroreceptors by hypotension causes an increase in ventilation.

VOLUNTARY CONTROL OF VENTILATION

The respiratory muscles are under voluntary control and ventilation can be consciously driven to any level or stopped until breaking point is reached. The chemoreceptors are powerless to prevent this – but will return the system to normal after the voluntary drive is removed.

If voluntary hyperventilation continues for 2–5 minutes then:

1. Alveolar P_{CO_2} is less than 2kPa.
2. Alveolar P_{O_2} is near 20 kPa.

After a period of voluntary hyperventilation, ventilation stops or is depressed because:

1. Chemoreceptor activity is decreased by the low P_{CO_2} and high P_{O_2}.
2. Low P_{CO_2} directly depresses the function of the respiratory neurones.

If ventilation stops, P_{O_2} falls and P_{CO_2} increases; alveolar P_{O_2} may fall to only 4kPa while alveolar P_{CO_2} rises to 5kPa. At this level, the hypoxia drives ventilation to start again. This increases the alveolar oxygen to non-hypoxic levels, but reduces alveolar P_{CO_2}. Ventilation once again stops or is depressed. By a series of such oscillations, the chemoreceptors gradually return the blood gases to normal and rhythmic ventilation then continues at the correct level for the prevailing conditions.

REFERENCES

Engström, C. G. and Herzog, P. (1959). Ventilation nomograms for practical use wtih the Engström respirator. *Acta Chirurgica Scandinavica*, Supp. **245**, 37.

Radford, E. P. (1955). Ventilation standards for use in artificial respiration. *Journal of Applied Physiology*, **7**, 451.

Staub, N. C. (1980). Structural basis of lung function. In *General Anaesthesia* (eds. Grey, T. C., Nunn, J. F. and Utting, J. E.), 4th edition. Butterworths, London.

BIBLIOGRAPHY

See page 82.

ACKNOWLEDGEMENT

Figure 1/3 is reproduced from Nunn, J. F. (1975). *Applied Respiratory Physiology*, Butterworths, London, by kind permission of the publishers. It originally appeared in Campbell, E. J. M. et al (1957). Simple methods of estimating oxygen consumption and efficiency of the muscles of breathing. *Journal of Applied Physiology*, 11, 303.

Chapter 2

Oxygen, Carbon Dioxide and Hydrogen Ion Transport

by P. E. PENNA MA, MB, BChir, FFARCS

COMPOSITION OF ALVEOLAR AIR

While breathing air at sea level (21 per cent oxygen (O_2); Po_2 = 21kPa: zero carbon dioxide (CO_2)) the normal alveolar ventilation of 3.5 litres/min, maintains the alveolar gas composition at 13 per cent oxygen; Po_2 = 13kPa: 5 per cent carbon dioxide; Pco_2 = 5kPa (Table 2/1).

TABLE 2/1   Gas tensions (kPa) at points in the respiratory system

Gas	Dry air, sea level pressure 100kPa	Moist inspired air	Alveolar air	Mixed expired gas
Po_2	21	19	13	15
Pco_2	0	0	5	4
Pn_2	79	75	75	75
Ph_2o	0	6	6	6

The decrease in oxygen tension from air to alveolus is due to:

1. Humidification of the inspired air by the nose. Alveolar gas is fully saturated with water vapour at 37°C (Ph_2o = 6kPa).
2. Dilution of the fresh gas with gas already in the lungs at the end of the previous expiration (alveolar gas).

This decrease in tension is the first stage of the tension gradient for oxygen on its way to the tissues.

A change in alveolar gas composition causes:

1. A change in arterial blood gas tensions:PaO_2 cannot be greater and is usually less than PAO_2; $PaCO_2$ cannot be less than $PACO_2$.
2. Reflex changes in ventilation and circulation to minimise the effects of the changes in blood gas tensions.

Alveolar gas composition is determined by:

1. Alveolar ventilation
2. Inspired gas composition
3. Barometric pressure
4. Oxygen consumption or carbon dioxide production

A decrease in alveolar ventilation causes the alveolar gas concentrations to approach those in mixed venous blood (Table 2/2). If alveolar ventilation is reduced to 1.5l/min, $PACO_2$ rises to 9kPa and PAO_2 falls to 6kPa.

TABLE 2/2   Gas tensions (kPa) in alveolar gas, plasma, arterial and mixed venous blood

Gas	Alveolar gas	Plasma	Arterial blood	Mixed venous blood
PO_2	13	13	12.5	5
PCO_2	5	5	5	6
PN_2	75	75	75	75

Alveolar gas composition approaches the composition of moist inspired air (PO_2 = 19kPa, PCO_2 = zero (see Table 2/1)) when alveolar ventilation is increased. Even in normal lungs at maximal ventilation, carbon dioxide tension cannot fall to less than 2kPa. Lowering arterial PCO_2 causes progressively more severe constriction of the cerebral blood vessels, resulting in progressive respiratory depression and unconsciousness when $PaCO_2$ is 1.3–2kPa.

At high altitude, although 21 per cent of the air is still oxygen, the barometric pressure is much lower. The inspired and alveolar oxygen tensions are reduced. The pressure to drive gas across the alveolar-capillary membrane is reduced.

If oxygen consumption changes, alveolar oxygen also changes at constant alveolar ventilation. In anaesthetised patients, oxygen consumption decreases. Less oxygen is removed from the blood by the tissues; more oxygen remains in the mixed venous blood returning to the lungs and less is taken up from the alveolar gas.

Alveolar oxygen increases. If oxygen consumption increases, as in fever or shivering, alveolar Po_2 will decrease, as more oxygen is removed from arterial blood by the tissues and mixed venous Po_2 is reduced. Usually, a change in oxygen consumption results in a compensatory change in alveolar ventilation.

Increasing the inspired oxygen concentration, at constant alveolar ventilation, results in an increase in alveolar oxygen concentration. This is the reason for increasing the inspired oxygen concentration to compensate for hypoxia in disease. *Decreasing* the inspired oxygen concentration results in a fall in alveolar Po_2.

If the inspired carbon dioxide is increased, there is such a large increase in alveolar ventilation that the effects are complex – carbon dioxide tension may remain constant, increase or decrease depending upon the ventilatory response. If alveolar ventilation is held constant (by mechanical ventilation, for example), then increasing the inspired carbon dioxide concentration produces an increase in alveolar Pco_2.

Barometric pressure and carbon dioxide production also affect alveolar Pco_2, but the major determinant is alveolar ventilation. Any change in alveolar ventilation produces a rapid change in both alveolar and arterial Pco_2.

The patient who presents with hypercarbia (elevated $Paco_2$) is managed initially by encouraging him to increase his alveolar ventilation.

ALVEOLAR FILLING AND GAS DISTRIBUTION

There is bulk flow of gas along the airways, under the influence of the pressure gradient produced by the inspiratory muscles, as far as the alveolar ducts. Mixing of fresh gas with gas already present in the alveolus and presentation of molecules of fresh gas to the alveolar-capillary membrane is brought about by diffusion. Diffusion is adequate to give virtually instantaneous access to the membrane because the distance between the alveolar duct and the membrane is short – comparable with the diameter of the gas molecules. Even in normal lungs, flow of gas by bulk flow or diffusion, to the different parts of the lung is not uniform.

Distribution of gas is determined by:

1. Gravity
2. Time constants
3. Cardiac contraction.

Gravity

The major determinant of gas distribution is gravity. Gravity acts on a column of fluid to increase the weight of the fluid at the base compared with the weight of the same amount of fluid at the top of the column. In the lung, gravity acts on lung tissue, blood and gas.

The effect of gravity accounts for the greater (less negative) intrapleural pressure at the base of the lung compared with the apex. At functional residual capacity (FRC) in the erect lung, pleural pressure is −0.5kPa at the apex but only −0.1kPa at the base. Alveoli at the apex of the lung, therefore, have a larger volume than basal alveoli (Boyle's Law).

On inspiration from FRC, the pressure gradient (mouth-to-alveolus) is greater at the apex of the lung than at the base. The first gas into the lung, therefore, goes preferentially to apical alveoli. These alveoli soon reach the limit of their expansion since they are already at high volume at the start of inspiration. Alveolar pressure in these alveoli will soon reach mouth pressure.

At the start of inspiration, basal alveoli are smaller in volume and have a lower pressure gradient than apical alveoli. These alveoli can continue to receive fresh gas throughout inspiration because their initial volume is smaller and they never reach the limit of their distensibility. Indeed, once they reach a certain volume they become much more distensible and expand greatly, even under the reducing pressure gradient.

In the middle part of the lung, the initial pressure gradient and volume are between those in the apical and basal parts. Some of these alveoli behave like apical ones, becoming full before the end of inspiration; some are more like basal ones, taking gas throughout inspiration.

In addition to these effects of gravity on the pressure/volume relationships in the lung, more fresh gas is presented to basal alveoli because gravity also acts on the inspired gas (see below).

In the supine position the effect of gravity is much less marked because the height of the lung is less (antero-posterior dimension less than base-to-apex) and, in the lateral position, the effect is to distribute most of the gas to the dependent lung.

Time constants

The rate of alveolar filling depends on the time constant (T), which defines the time course of alveolar filling and pressure change. It is proportional to the product of airway resistance (R) and alveolar compliance (C):

$$T \propto R \times C$$

The units are in seconds (sec). 66 per cent of the final alveolar volume and rise in pressure is complete in one time constant.

At a respiratory rate of 10/min, the respiratory cycle (inspiration plus expiration) lasts 6 sec and at the normal inspiratory/expiratory ratio of 1:3 (one part in inspiration, three parts in expiration) the duration of inspiration is 1.5sec. The overall resistance to gas flow in the airways is 0.1kPa/l/sec and the overall compliance is 0.85l/kPa, giving a time constant of 0.085 sec. 95 per cent of the final change in alveolar volume and pressure is complete within three time constants (0.26sec), well within the time available.

There are, even in normal lungs, regional differences in compliance and resistance. Fast alveoli (short T: due to low resistance or low compliance) are found in the perihilar and apical regions. These alveoli fill first on inspiration and empty first on expiration. In disease, compliance and resistance vary much more and the spread of T about the normal value is increased. This accounts for the inability to collect a pure sample of alveolar gas and for the exaggerated difference between static and dynamic compliance (Chapter 1, p. 44).

Cardiac contraction

At each systolic contraction, 60ml of blood are ejected from the heart into the pulmonary and systemic arteries in the thorax. This contributes to the mixing of gas in the lungs and to movement of gas along the airways. This is akin to punching a bean bag to redistribute the beans.

EFFECTS ON GAS DISTRIBUTION

At the end of expiration, the dead space is filled with gas from alveoli which were last to empty. These are the ones in the apex of the lung under the influence of gravity, or the slow alveoli. During the following inspiration, dead space gas goes to fast and apical alveoli, allowing the greater volume of fresh gas to enter basal alveoli under the influence of gravity. The consequences of this gas distribution in relation to blood flow are discussed below.

ALVEOLAR DEAD SPACE

Not all the gas passing the lips on inspiration takes part in gas exchange. Some constitutes the physiological dead space composed of:

1. Anatomical dead space; gas remaining in the conducting tubes.
2. Alveolar dead space; gas reaching the alveoli, but even here, not taking part in gas exchange because blood flow is inadequate.

In the normal alveolus (Fig. 2/1 (1)) blood flow and ventilation are exactly matched. All the deoxygenated haemoglobin delivered to the alveolar-capillary membrane in venous blood is fully oxygenated and the normal amount of carbon dioxide is removed. The tension of oxygen and carbon dioxide in blood leaving this alveolus is the same as the tension of these gases in alveolar gas. All the gas is converted into alveolar gas.

If the airway to an alveolus is patent, but its pulmonary capillary is occluded by, for example, a pulmonary embolus, there is no blood flow, so there can be no gas exchange (Fig. 2/1 (2)). This alveolus contains fresh gas, 'wasted' because it takes no part in gas exchange. It constitutes alveolar dead space.

In normal lungs there are all gradations between complete

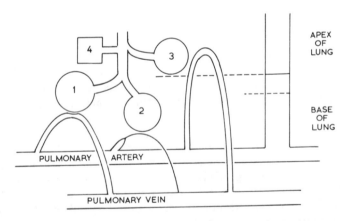

FIG. 2/1 Lung structure at alveolar level. Pulmonary arterial blood pressure is indicated by the height of the vertical column on the right. Alveolus (1) shows normal ventilation and normal blood flow (perfusion). Alveoli (2) and (4) show alveolar dead space, normal ventilation but no perfusion. Alveolus (3) is normal when blood pressure is normal but becomes alveolar dead space when pressure is low

obstruction of the pulmonary capillary, through partial occlusion, to normal patency. In an alveolus where the capillary is only partly occluded, the gas may be thought of as being composed of two fractions:

1. Gas which exchanges with blood to become normal alveolar gas.
2. Gas which is unaltered because there is too much gas relative to the amount of blood. This gas also constitutes alveolar dead space.

In this alveolus there is more than enough oxygen available to completely saturate the limited amount of haemoglobin delivered by the reduced blood flow. Alveolar oxygen tension is increased because oxygen uptake by blood in this alveolus is reduced. There is less carbon dioxide given up by the blood to the alveolar gas than in a normal alveolus because there is less blood flow. Alveolar carbon dioxide tension is low. Alveolar dead space gas composition approaches the composition of fresh gas. The amount of lowering of the alveolar carbon dioxide tension indicates the volume of the dead space.

The normal arterial-to-alveolar (a-A) carbon dioxide tension difference is less than 0.2kPa, indicating that the alveolar dead space is small. Ventilation is almost, but not quite, fully compensated to allow for the effects of the normal dead space. Reflexes exist at alveolar level to decrease the ventilation to non-perfused alveoli and reduce the alveolar dead space. In severe stress these reflexes may not be entirely successful.

Causes of alveolar dead space (Fig. 2/1)

1. In the upright position, there is a relative lack of blood supply to alveoli at the apex of the lung (Fig. 2/1 (3)) because pulmonary artery blood pressure is insufficient to raise blood to the apex against the pull of gravity. Apical alveoli are relatively underperfused. Since these alveoli are relatively well ventilated, they contribute to alveolar dead space. This effect of gravity on blood flow is less marked in the supine position.
2. When pulmonary arterial blood pressure is lower than normal, as in low cardiac output states (severe haemorrhage, myocardial infarction or induction of anaesthesia), there is an increase in alveolar dead space because even fewer apical alveoli are perfused. This is one reason why these patients are nursed in the supine position.
3. Diseases which destroy alveoli, such as emphysema (Fig. 2/1

(4)), result in ventilation of large air spaces which are not surrounded by pulmonary capillaries.

VENTILATION/PERFUSION RATIOS

In terms of the ratio between the volume of gas and the volume of blood delivered to the membrane, the normally ventilated, normally perfused alveolus has a ventilation/perfusion ratio ($\dot{V}/\dot{Q}$) of approximately unity. All the haemoglobin is fully saturated with oxygen and all the fresh gas is converted into alveolar gas. The alveolus with occluded circulation has a $\dot{V}/\dot{Q}$ ratio of infinity (ventilation, one, divided by blood flow, zero). A $\dot{V}/\dot{Q}$ ratio greater than unity indicates alveolar dead space.

MOVEMENT OF SUBSTANCES ACROSS MEMBRANES

Movement of a substance across a membrane may be by:

1. *Active transport*: sodium and potassium, for example, are exchanged across the cell membrane by an energy-requiring process.
2. *Passive diffusion*: the substance moves across the membrane along a gradient, without the need for energy. Passive diffusion may be enhanced by the presence on one side of the membrane of a special receptor.

There may be a trans-membrane gradient in:

1. Tension
2. Concentration
3. Osmotic pressure
4. Electrical charge.

GRADIENTS ACROSS THE ALVEOLAR-CAPILLARY MEMBRANE

Oxygen and carbon dioxide cross the alveolar-capillary membrane by passive diffusion along *tension gradients* between alveolar gas and mixed venous blood. The gradients are maintained by metabolic activity in tissue cells; carbon dioxide is produced and oxygen consumed. Mixed venous blood is in equilibrium with the tissue cells. The oxygen gradient is from alveolar gas to tissue cells and the carbon dioxide gradient is in the opposite direction. Along these gradients oxygen and carbon dioxide diffuse, like water over a waterfall.

There is no tension gradient for nitrogen since it is neither consumed nor produced in the body. At equilibrium, nitrogen tension is the same in alveolar gas, blood and tissues (Table 2/2). Although there is no net transfer of nitrogen, any one particular nitrogen molecule may move from alveolus to blood and to tissues, while another, different, molecule moves in the opposite direction.

If the equilibrium is disturbed, then nitrogen too will diffuse across the membrane, along the tension gradient. The commonest disturbance in nitrogen equilibrium is produced by increasing the inspired oxygen concentration; inspired and alveolar nitrogen tension decrease, because nitrogen in the inspired gas is replaced by the added oxygen. There is now a net loss of nitrogen from the body.

In the resting adult, a red blood cell remains in a pulmonary capillary for about 0.75 sec. Diffusion of oxygen from alveolar gas to blood is complete within this time. During exercise, when cardiac output is higher, the time spent by blood in the pulmonary capillaries is less and the rate of gas diffusion *could* become the limiting factor in determining the amount of oxygen transferred across the membrane.

The diffusion pathway (Fig. 2/2)

The pathway for oxygen from alveolus to blood consists of:

1. The alveolar-capillary membrane which consists of:

   A. *The alveolar cells* (pneumocytes) – flattened cells which bulge into the alveolus around the fatter nucleus of the cell. On the alveolar surface of the pneumocytes is a thin layer of fluid. The first step in diffusion of oxygen from alveolar gas to blood is solution in this water. From then onwards, oxygen is always transferred in solution in water.

   B. *A homogeneous basement membrane* on which the cells are sitting.

   C. *A tissue space* containing (i) extracellular fluid; (ii) lymphatics; and (iii) collagen and elastic fibres.

   D. *Pulmonary capillary endothelial cells* on their basement membrane. The endothelial cells are flattened with bulging nuclei.

   The total width of the membrane is 0.5μm. The pulmonary capillary diameter is 7nm and accounts for 75 per cent of the total width of the membrane. Since the capillary diameter is roughly

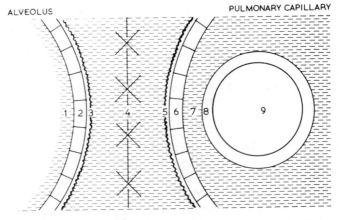

FIG. 2/2 The diffusion pathway: 1. alveolar fluid; 2. alveolar lining cells (pneumocytes); 3. basement membrane; 4. interstitial space containing fluid, lymphatics, collagen and elastic fibres; 5. pulmonary capillary basement membrane; 6. pulmonary capillary endothelial cells; 7. plasma; 8. red blood cell; 9. haemoglobin

the same as the maximum dimension of the red blood cell, the cells are forced to squeeze through the capillary in close contact with the walls.

2. Plasma.
3. The red blood cell.
4. Haemoglobin. The biconvex shape of the red blood cell and the fact that it has to squeeze through the capillary, forces haemoglobin to the periphery of the cell. The diffusion pathway is shortened by these changes in shape.

Movement of gas across the alveolar-capillary membrane

Any liquid exposed to a gas mixture, takes up gas from the mixture. The amount of gas taken up by the liquid depends on:

1. The solubility of the gas in the liquid.
2. The temperature (less gas is in solution at high temperature).
3. The surface area of the gas/liquid interface.
4. Any special feature of the liquid which enhances the solubility of the gas (such as chemical combination with the liquid itself or a component).

At equilibrium, the partial pressure of a gas in the liquid is the same as the partial pressure of the same gas in the gas mixture. At equilibrium, no more gas can flow across the membrane, because the pressures across the interface are equal.

Blood is exposed to alveolar gas across the alveolar-capillary membrane. After equilibration, the tensions of oxygen and carbon dioxide in plasma exposed to alveolar gas are the same as the tension of these gases in alveolar gas (see Table 2/2).

The tension of gas in solution is simply the pressure available to drive it from one compartment to another (alveolar gas to blood and from blood to tissue). The tensions of oxygen and carbon dioxide in blood are easy to measure with special electrodes (the blood gas (Astrup) measurement). Blood oxygen tension is not, however, the most important determinant of survival of tissues. The amount of oxygen in the blood (blood oxygen content) is more important. In clinical practice, oxygen tension is measured and oxygen content is assumed. Since high oxygen tension does not always infer high oxygen content (Table 2/3), blood oxygen content should be measured directly. The reason for the disparity between tension and content is that the measured tension of oxygen is the tension of that small volume of oxygen carried in plasma. Most of the oxygen at the same tension is carried in the red blood cell.

TABLE 2/3 Oxygen tension and corresponding oxygen content. The dependence of oxygen content on the haemoglobin concentration should be noted

Solution	Tension (kPa)	Content (ml/dl)
Air	21	21
Alveolar gas	13	13
Water/plasma	13	0.3
Blood: haemoglobin 15g/dl	13	20.4
5g/dl	13	7.0
Plasma alone	900	20.4

At normal barometric pressure, air contains 21 per cent oxygen at a tension of 21kPa. Water in equilibrium with air also contains oxygen at 21kPa. The oxygen content of air is 210ml/l compared with only 21ml/l in water. At a tension of 13kPa (alveolar oxygen tension) the oxygen content of water or plasma is only 0.3ml/dl (Table 2/3).

HAEMOGLOBIN

Haemoglobin in the red blood cells is responsible for the very large increase in the amount of oxygen carried by whole blood compared with the amount carried by plasma alone exposed to oxygen at the same tension (Table 2/3).

Each gram (g) of haemoglobin can carry 1.34ml oxygen when fully saturated. At a haemoglobin concentration of 15g/dl, the oxygen content of blood in equilibrium with alveolar gas, P_{AO_2} = 13kPa, is 20.4ml/dl, composed of 20.1ml combined with haemoglobin plus 0.3ml dissolved in plasma (Table 2/3). By comparison, in anaemia, haemoglobin 5g/dl, the oxygen content is only 7ml/dl at the same P_{AO_2}, representing 6.7ml combined with haemoglobin and 0.3ml in solution in plasma.

Haemoglobin is a large molecule (molecular weight 65 000) and consists of:

1. *Four globin parts*. Each part is composed of a coiled chain of amino acids. There are two pairs of amino-acid chains, differing from each other in amino-acid composition. One pair contains 141 amino acids in each chain, the other 148.
2. *Four haem elements*. Each haem consists of four nitrogen and carbon (pyrolle) rings, joined together to form a porphyrin compound. An iron atom is attached to each porphyrin ring. One haem is attached to each globin chain.

Haemoglobin synthesis and destruction

Haemoglobin synthesis takes place in the bone marrow, where red blood cells are also formed; it enters the cells before they are released into the circulation. Haemoglobin synthesis depends critically on the amount of iron available.

Red blood cells are destroyed, in the spleen and liver, after about 120 days in the circulation. The globin chains are broken down into amino acids. Haem is first split into iron and porphyrin. The latter is metabolised in the liver to bilirubin. Iron from the worn out red cells is extremely efficiently conserved and re-used in haemoglobin synthesis.

There is, however, an inevitable loss of iron from the body in skin cells, gut lining cells, hair and nails. In males this amounts to 1mg/day. In females there is an additional average daily loss of 1mg in the menses. In pregnancy and lactation the total daily loss is 4mg. These losses have to be made up by dietary intake.

Carriage of oxygen

Oxygen is carried on the iron-containing, haem, part of the haemoglobin molecule. One oxygen molecule is attached by a loose bond to each iron atom. There is no change in the state of the iron atom – no oxidisation from ferrous to ferric form. The process of oxygen carriage by haemoglobin is referred to as *oxygenation of haemoglobin*. Each haemoglobin molecule can carry four oxygen molecules.

The reaction between haem and oxygen is (1) reversible, to allow oxygen to be taken up in the lungs and given up in the tissues; and (2) takes place in four stages.

If haemoglobin is represented as Hb_4, then the reactions are:

$$Hb_4 + O_2 \rightleftarrows Hb_4O_2$$
$$Hb_4O_2 + O_2 \rightleftarrows Hb_4O_4$$
$$Hb_4O_4 + O_2 \rightleftarrows Hb_4O_6$$
$$Hb_4O_6 + O_2 \rightleftarrows Hb_4O_8$$

When all the haemoglobin has been converted into Hb_4O_8, it is fully saturated.

If each of the four reactions took place at the same rate then, as oxygen was taken up to form Hb_4O_2, Hb_4O_4 and Hb_4O_6, the combination of more oxygen with haemoglobin would become slower and slower, because fewer oxygen receptors would remain available. Haemoglobin would never become fully saturated with oxygen and very little Hb_4O_8 would be formed. In fact, the final reaction – the combination of Hb_4O_6 with oxygen – is the fastest reaction in the chain. Thus, each stage in the combination takes place at approximately the same rate.

Overall, it is the combination of oxygen with haemoglobin which is the rate-limiting step in oxygen diffusion from alveolar gas to blood.

As saturation proceeds there is a change in physical properties of the haemoglobin molecule; for example, the absorption of light at certain wavelengths is altered. This provides a relatively easy measure of haemoglobin saturation for calculation of oxygen content:

Content = Haemoglobin saturation × Haemoglobin concentration

Oxygen dissociation curve (Fig. 2/3)

The oxygen dissociation curve of haemoglobin describes the process of oxygenation. It relates blood oxygen content to alveolar gas

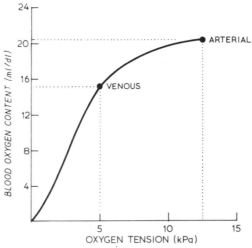

FIG. 2/3 Oxygen dissociation curve of haemoglobin. The S-shaped curve describes the reversible combination of haemoglobin with oxygen

	Arterial	Venous	A-V difference
Tension (kPa)	12.5	5	7.5
Content (ml/dl)	20.4	15	5.4

tension and is S-shaped. Oxygen content is only slightly increased if oxygen tension is greater than 13kPa. Any, even small, decrease in oxygen tension below 13kPa results in a progressively steeper decrease in oxygen content.

The arterial point on the curve corresponds to an oxygen tension of 12.5kPa and content of 20.4ml/dl. The venous point, after the tissues have extracted oxygen, has an oxygen tension of 5kPa and a content of 15ml/dl. There is plenty of oxygen available in venous blood, but the driving pressure (tension) to move it is very low.

Haemoglobin is fully saturated with oxygen after equilibration with alveolar gas containing oxygen at 13kPa. At higher alveolar oxygen tension, there is no further uptake of oxygen by haemoglobin, but there is an extra 0.3ml oxygen dissolved in plasma for each extra 13kPa increase in Pao_2. Hyperbaric oxygen (oxygen at increased pressure) relies for its effect on this increased oxygen in solution. In the absence of haemoglobin, a pressure of nearly nine times normal atmospheric pressure would be required to give a normal arterial oxygen content. The Pa_{O_2} would then be 90okPa (Table 2/3).

From the measured oxygen tension of arterial blood, oxygen content could be calculated from the dissociation curve, if the shape and position of the curve were fixed. While this might be satisfactory in health, such calculations are imprecise in disease because both the position of the curve on the axis and the slope of the straight part can change. For example, the curve moves to the right (haemoglobin has less affinity for oxygen: the oxygen content for a given P_{O_2} is less) when:

1. Blood P_{CO_2} rises
2. pH falls
   (1. and 2. represent a respiratory or non-respiratory acidosis)
3. Body temperature rises
4. Red blood cell content of 2, 3-diphosphoglycerate (2, 3-DPG) falls.

The red cell 2, 3-DPG concentration depends on serum phosphate concentration, which in turn depends on phosphate metabolism and dietary phosphate intake. Patients receiving parenteral nutrition are often phosphate deficient and have abnormal oxygen transport.

The above four factors alter the affinity of haemoglobin for oxygen by opening or closing oxygen pathways from the surface of the molecule to the iron of haem.

VENOUS ADMIXTURE

Table 2/2 (p. 56) shows that there is a small (0.5kPa) difference between alveolar and arterial oxygen tension (the alveolar-arterial (A-a) oxygen tension difference). It is due to venous admixture.

Even under perfect conditions, about 5 per cent of the cardiac output passes from the right ventricle to the left ventricle, and onwards to the systemic arteries, without passing through the capillaries in the alveolar membrane (see Fig. 1/1, p. 32). This blood is 'wasted' blood; it is pumped by the heart, but takes no part in gas exchange. It is the *blood shunt* or *venous admixture*, since it is venous blood which is mixed with oxygenated blood from the alveolar membrane to form the final arterial blood. It is the equivalent, on the blood side of the membrane, of the physiological dead space on the gas side.

As shown by the flat top of the oxygen dissociation curve, there is very little reduction in the arterial blood oxygen content due to this small decrease in oxygen tension.

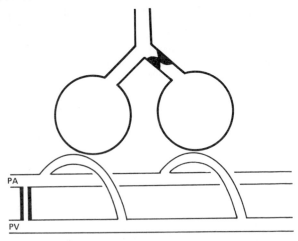

FIG. 2/4 Venous admixture. The normally ventilated, normally perfused alveolus on the left, is contrasted with the non-ventilated, normally perfused alveolus. Other channels carry venous blood directly from the pulmonary artery (PA) and the right ventricle to the pulmonary vein (PV) and the left ventricle and constitute the anatomical shunt

Figure 2/4 compares the normally ventilated, normally perfused alveolus ($\dot{V}/\dot{Q} = 1$) with an alveolus with normal blood supply but no ventilation because the bronchus is blocked. This blood is wasted ($\dot{V}/\dot{Q} = 0$). A $\dot{V}/\dot{Q}$ ratio less than normal indicates venous admixture. Blood leaving the alveolus with blocked airway is venous blood. It mixes, in the pulmonary vein, with oxygenated blood from the normal alveolus. In the pulmonary vein, oxygen equilibrates between fully saturated haemoglobin from pulmonary capillaries ($Po_2 = 13kPa$; content 20.4ml/dl) and the venous blood of the shunt ($Po_2 = 5kPa$; content 15ml/dl). The final mixed arterial blood has an oxygen content between 15 and 20.4ml/dl at a tension between 5 and 13kPa; the exact value depends on the proportions of oxygenated and venous blood mixing together.

If the volume of venous blood mixing with oxygenated blood in the pulmonary vein is greater than 5 per cent of the cardiac ouput, there will be a significant reduction from the normal oxygen tension and content. *Hypoxia exists.*

If the venous blood has a lower than normal oxygen content, because of increased oxygen uptake by the tissues, then, for the same volume of venous admixture, the oxygen content and tension of arterial blood will be further reduced. This becomes a vicious circle

– less oxygen at lower tension in the arterial blood, more oxygen removed by the tissues, lower content and tension in the mixed venous blood, yet lower content and tension when the mixed venous and oxygenated blood mix. *Hypoxia becomes extreme.*

Mechanism of venous admixture

The venous admixture may be divided into:

1. The anatomical shunt – blood passing through anatomical channels.
2. The shunt due to inequalities between ventilation and blood flow to an alveolus.

Pathological processes may affect either shunt.

The *anatomical shunt* consists of:

1. The Thebesian veins, part of the coronary circulation, drain blood from the left heart myocardium directly into the left ventricle. The oxygen content of this blood is extremely low but it accounts for only about 0.3 per cent of the cardiac output.
2. The bronchial veins (about 1 per cent of the cardiac output), drain directly into the pulmonary vein. In coarctation of the aorta, bronchiectasis and emphysema, flow through the bronchial veins may approach 10 per cent of the cardiac output.
3. Any congenital abnormality of the heart, such as the tetralogy of Fallot, where venous blood passes directly from the right side of the heart to the left, causes a marked reduction in arterial P_{O_2} and content (cyanotic congenital heart disease).
4. Collapse of alveoli, due to blockage of their airways by uncleared secretions, may result in perfusion of unventilated alveoli. This condition is common after surgical operations under general anaesthesia, when it is known as *atelectasis*. The administration of anti-sialogogue drugs (atropine) or narcotic analgesics in the pre-operative medication, or inhalation of volatile anaesthetic agents (halothane, enflurane) and ventilation of the lungs with dry gases during a general anaesthetic, results in atelectasis because alveolar ventilation, coughing, sighing and ciliary action in the respiratory tract are depressed or abolished. Pulmonary secretions remain uncleared and block small airways.
5. Lung infection, especially pneumococcal lobar pneumonia, causes a large shunt through the affected area. This area receives no fresh gas because the alveoli are filled with pus, but there is an abnormally high blood flow because inflammation increases the blood supply to the infected area.

Venous admixture due to ventilation/perfusion inequalities

In an ideal lung the volume of gas and the volume of blood reaching each alveolus would be exactly matched to fully saturate all the haemoglobin with oxygen. However, the lung is not a perfect oxygenating structure.

In the upright posture, gravity acts upon the distribution of both blood and gas. The effect of gravity on gas distribution is less marked than on blood distribution, since gas is less dense than blood. This results in unequal distribution of gas and blood.

The erect lung (Table 2/4) may be divided into three horizontal slices (West, 1977). There is an increase in volume of each slice from apex to base. In absolute terms (l/min) there is an increase in both alveolar ventilation and blood flow from apex to base under the influence of gravity. When alveolar ventilation per unit lung volume is considered, basal gas flow is 1.5 times apical flow due to gravity.

TABLE 2/4   Ventilation and blood flow in three horizontal sections of the lung in the upright position. Lung volume, ventilation and blood flow increase from apex to base

Part of lung	Volume	Alveolar ventilation		Blood flow	
		l/min	per unit lung vol	l/min	per unit lung vol
Top	25	1.0	27	0.6	14
Middle	36	1.8	33	2.0	34
Base	39	2.3	40	3.4	52

Blood flow increases from 0.6l/min in the apex to 3.4l/min in the basal slice and, when considered as flow per unit lung volume, basal blood flow is 3.7 times apical flow due to gravity (Table 2/4).

Both ventilation and blood flow increase from apex to base, but the increase in blood flow is more than twice the increase in ventilation.

If all the blood flowing through the lungs came into contact with all the gas, the $\dot{V}/\dot{Q}$ ratio would be approximately unity. Only in the middle section of the lung (Table 2/5) is this $\dot{V}/\dot{Q}$ ratio approached. In the apical slice the $\dot{V}/\dot{Q}$ ratio is 1.7, indicating a considerable excess of gas flow relative to blood flow and forming part of the alveolar dead space. At the base of the lung the $\dot{V}/\dot{Q}$ ratio is low,

TABLE 2/5   Ventilation and blood flow in three horizontal sections of the lung in the upright position, and the ratio between ventilation and blood flow ($\dot{V}/\dot{Q}$)

Part of lung	Alveolar ventilation (l/min)	Blood flow (l/min)	$\dot{V}/\dot{Q}$
Top	1.0	0.6	1.7
Middle	1.8	2.0	0.9
Base	2.3	3.4	0.7
Total	5.1	6.0	0.85

indicating an excess of blood flow over ventilation and forming part of the venous admixture (Table 2/5).

Pathological processes may be superimposed on the effects of gravity, increasing the scatter of $\dot{V}/\dot{Q}$ ratios.

There is an increase in $\dot{V}/\dot{Q}$ inequality:

1. With increasing age.
2. After many years living in towns or cities – an effect related to atmospheric pollution.
3. In smokers.
4. Following induction of general anaesthesia.
5. In pulmonary oedema; the alveoli are flooded with fluid preventing entrance of fresh gas.
6. Following loss of surfactant in the respiratory distress syndrome of the newborn and, possibly, in the adult respiratory distress syndrome following 'shock'.
7. In the crushed chest syndrome.
8. After myocardial infarction, for a variety of reasons, including hypotension and pulmonary oedema.
9. In patients who are being mechanically ventilated because of widespread metabolic, pulmonary and cardiovascular abnormalities.
10. In lung disease (chronic bronchitis with emphysema), because the scatter of $\dot{V}/\dot{Q}$ ratios increases and the absolute number of alveoli with $\dot{V}/\dot{Q}$ ratios of infinity and zero is increased.

EFFECT OF ALVEOLAR DEAD SPACE AND VENOUS ADMIXTURE

Blood leaving normally ventilated, normally perfused, alveoli contains oxygen at a concentration of 20.4ml/dl. No blood leaves alveoli with $\dot{V}/\dot{Q}$ ratios of infinity (alveolar dead space). If blood flow is only reduced, there is more than enough oxygen in the alveolar gas to fully saturate the haemoglobin. Alveolar and blood oxygen tensions will be high, but blood oxygen content will be only slightly increased due to the small extra volume of oxygen dissolved in the plasma.

Blood from alveoli with no ventilation will be venous blood (Po_2 = 5kPa; content 15ml/dl). If ventilation is only reduced there is still insufficient gas to totally saturate the haemoglobin with oxygen. Oxygen content and Po_2 will be between mixed venous and fully arterialised blood.

Blood from the alveolar dead space, with its slightly increased oxygen content, will be unable to fully compensate for the low oxygen content of the venous admixture when all the blood from the different alveoli mixes in the pulmonary vein.

If the inspired oxygen concentration is increased:

1. Alveolar oxygen tension in the normal alveoli will increase, resulting in an increase in arterial Po_2 but only a small increase in arterial oxygen content due to the small extra volume of oxygen dissolved in plasma.
2. There will be an increase in dissolved oxygen in the blood leaving normally ventilated, poorly perfused alveoli.
3. Blood leaving unventilated alveoli will be unchanged.
4. There will be a gradual increase in alveolar oxygen in poorly ventilated alveoli as more of the nitrogen is replaced by the added oxygen. Blood leaving this alveolus will become more like normal arterial blood and less like venous blood.

Provided the venous admixture is less than 30 per cent of the cardiac output, increasing the inspired oxygen concentration will compensate for the reduced oxygen tension and content of blood. No amount of added oxygen at normal atmospheric pressure will compensate for a greater shunt.

In patients with shunts greater than 30 per cent of the cardiac output, mechanical ventilation is required. Despite ventilation with 100% oxygen and the application of positive end-expired pressure (PEEP), hypoxia often persists.

If a patient with an abnormal shunt is disturbed, the shunt may change. Manual hyperventilation and endotracheal suction in a patient on a mechanical ventilator is a common intervention. A good 'bag and suck' will often reduce the shunt by 10 per cent or more, by reducing the imbalance between ventilation and perfusion.

Effect of venous admixture on carbon dioxide

The presence of a blood shunt produces hypoxia. Only if the shunt is very large, are arterial blood carbon dioxide tension and content affected by venous admixture. The reason for this relative lack of effect on carbon dioxide compared with the major effect of shunt on oxygen tension and content lies in differences between the oxygen and carbon dioxide dissociation curves of blood.

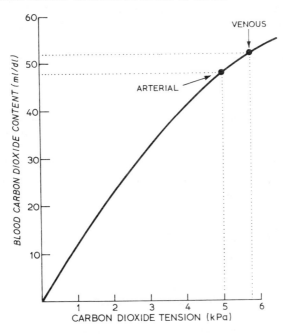

FIG. 2/5 Carbon dioxide dissociation curve

	Arterial	Venous	A-V difference
Tension (kPa)	5.0	5.8	0.8
Content (ml/dl)	48	52	4

The oxygen dissociation curve has a flat top (Fig. 2/3). There is, in effect, a maximum volume of oxygen that can be carried by blood, irrespective of the oxygen tension (haemoglobin is fully saturated and there is only a small extra amount of oxygen in solution). The carbon dioxide dissociation curve (Fig. 2/5) shows a virtually linear relationship between Pco_2 and content – the higher the tension, the greater the amount of carbon dioxide carried.

Blood passing a poorly ventilated alveolus will have a high carbon dioxide content at high tension (mixed venous blood). Even if up to 50 per cent of the cardiac output is shunted away from normally ventilated alveoli, after mixing in the pulmonary vein, the arterial carbon dioxide tension and content are only slightly increased. When this blood returns to a normal part of the alveolar-capillary membrane, more carbon dioxide is removed because the carbon dioxide tension gradient from blood to alveolar gas is increased. This blood, with normal arterial carbon dioxide content and tension can again mix with the shunted blood.

The small rise in arterial Pco_2 due to the shunt causes an increase in alveolar ventilation by chemoreceptor activation. Alveolar carbon dioxide is reduced. A greater than normal amount of carbon dioxide can be removed down the increased tension gradient in normally ventilated, normally perfused alveoli. When this blood mixes with the shunted venous blood, there is complete compensation – arterial carbon dioxide tension and content are normal.

Only if the venous admixture is greater than 50 per cent of the cardiac output does this compensation break down and arterial carbon dioxide content and tension rise.

CARBON DIOXIDE CARRIAGE IN BLOOD

Carbon dioxide is carried in blood:

1. In physical solution. It is very soluble in water and dissolves, not only in plasma water, but in every compartment of body water, including intracellular water.
2. As carbonic acid, produced when carbon dioxide combines with water –

$$CO_2 + H_2O \rightleftarrows H_2CO_3$$

3. As bicarbonate ion, arising by dissociation of carbonic acid –

$$H_2CO_3 \rightleftarrows H^+ + HCO_3^-$$

4. As carbamino-compounds, formed by combination of carbon dioxide with the amino-acid chain of:

(a) Plasma proteins: Very little carbon dioxide is, in fact, carried by the plasma proteins because their physical form prevents it.

(b) Haemoglobin: Each haemoglobin can carry four molecules of carbon dioxide, one on each globin chain. Haemoglobin is a very efficient carbon dioxide carrier.

Deoxygenated haemoglobin is 3.5 times more effective than the oxygenated form as a carbon dioxide carrier. This is very convenient, because, in the tissues, where oxygen is consumed and carbon dioxide produced, more deoxygenated haemoglobin is available to carry more carbon dioxide. Equally, in the lungs, as oxygen is taken up, carbon dioxide is forced out of the haemoglobin.

Arterio-venous carbon dioxide difference

The carbon dioxide content of arterial blood is 48ml/dl. At normal metabolic rate, 4ml carbon dioxide are added to blood as it passes through the tissues. Of this 4ml:

    0.3ml is dissolved in plasma
    0.7ml is carried as carbamino-compounds of haemoglobin
    3.0ml is carried as bicarbonate

Formation of bicarbonate

(1) The reaction
    $CO_2 + H_2O \rightleftarrows H_2CO_3$
is extremely slow. It is catalysed (speeded up) by the enzyme carbonic anhydrase, a zinc dependent enzyme, present only in the red blood cell. Carbon dioxide easily passes the red cell membrane to gain access to the enzyme.

(2) Carbonic acid dissociates into hydrogen and bicarbonate ions –
    $H_2CO_3 \rightleftarrows H^+ + HCO_3^-$.
This reaction does not require an enzyme.

Reactions (1) and (2) are reversible. Together they form a self-regulatory system. If there is an increase in the concentration of one component, the relevant reaction changes in such a way as to prevent further accumulation of the component or to actually decrease its concentration. The dissociation of carbonic acid (reaction 2) would soon stop if hydrogen or bicarbonate ion concentration increased in the red blood cell. To prevent this, hydrogen and bicarbonate ions must be removed.

REMOVAL OF HYDROGEN IONS

Hydrogen ions are mopped up by the amino acids of the globin chains of haemoglobin, allowing the dissociation of carbonic acid (reaction 2) and solution of carbon dioxide in water (reaction 1) to proceed.

In the tissue capillaries, the amount of deoxygenated haemoglobin is increasing. Deoxygenated haemoglobin is a more avid acceptor of hydrogen ions than is oxygenated haemoglobin. Reactions (1) and (2) are speeded up because more hydrogen ions can be removed by deoxygenated haemoglobin in the tissue capillaries.

REMOVAL OF BICARBONATE IONS

Bicarbonate ions do not accumulate in the red blood cell (their principal site of formation). The cell membrane is permeable to bicarbonate ions which leave the cell down a concentration gradient and are carried in plasma. Plasma bicarbonate increases between arterial and venous blood by 2mmol/l.

As bicarbonate leaves the red blood cell, the inside of the cell becomes more positively charged (due to loss of the negatively charged bicarbonate ion) and plasma becomes more negatively charged (gain of the negative bicarbonate ion). To compensate for this, negatively charged chloride ions move from plasma into the red cell along the electrical gradient. This is known as the *chloride shift*.

The functions of the red blood cell

1. Carriage of oxygen.
2. Carriage of carbon dioxide, due to (a) the presence of carbonic anhydrase; and (b) the globin part of haemoglobin which removes hydrogen ions and combines with carbon dioxide to form carbamino-haemoglobin.

As the red blood cell content of oxygenated haemoglobin decreases, the ability of haemoglobin to remove hydrogen ions and form carbamino-haemoglobin increases. More carbon dioxide can be carried in venous blood than in arterial.

The role of plasma

1. Carriage of both oxygen and carbon dioxide in solution.
2. Accepts bicarbonate ions from the red cell in exchange for chloride ions.

3. Despite the presence of plasma proteins, very little carbon dioxide is carried as plasma protein carbamino-compound.

ACID/BASE REACTIONS

Acids

Just as carbonic acid dissociates:
$$H_2CO_3 \rightleftarrows H^+ + HCO_3^-$$
so any acid will dissociate. An acid may be defined as a substance which dissociates to produce hydrogen ions:

Sulphuric acid: $H_2SO_4 \rightleftarrows 2H^+ + SO_4^-$
Hydrochloric acid: $HCl \rightleftarrows H^+ + Cl^-$

Sulphuric and hydrochloric acids dissociate with tremendous gusto for they are strong acids. Carbonic acid is a weak acid. It does dissociate to form hydrogen ions, but not with any great enthusiasm.

The presence of hydrogen ions in a solution makes it acid. The amount of acidity produced by dissociation of an acid may be related to:

1. The amount of hydrogen ions formed
2. The concentration of hydrogen ions
3. The activity of hydrogen ions in solution.

Hydrogen ions themselves react with water to form various compounds. The concentration or activity of any one of these compounds may cause an acid solution to be acid.

Acids are being continuously produced in the body as a result of metabolic activity. They can be divided into:

1. *Fixed acids* including sulphuric, phosphoric and hydrochloric. They can be excreted only through the kidneys
2. *Volatile acids* can be excreted as a gas via the lungs. The only one in this group is carbonic acid.

Buffers

Despite production of all this acid, including 288 litres of carbon dioxide per day, the body is neither acid nor alkaline. There is an equilibrium between acid production and excretion but, between production and excretion, hydrogen ions are *buffered*.

Haemoglobin mops up hydrogen ions produced from carbonic acid. This is a general property of all proteins. Heamoglobin is in the right place, at the right time and in the right concentration to remove hydrogen ions produced by dissociation of carbonic acid. This 'mopping up' is called buffering: the proteins are buffers. When a hydrogen ion is buffered it is no longer producing acidity: its effect is neutralised.

The carbonic acid/bicarbonate system is a very important buffer because:

1. Hydrogen ions from the fixed acids combine with bicarbonate to form carbon dioxide:

$$HCl \rightleftarrows H^+ + Cl^-$$
$$H^+ + HCO_3^- \rightleftarrows H_2O + CO_2$$

2. Ventilation is exquisitely sensitive to carbon dioxide tension and is rapidly adjusted to maintain the arterial P_{CO_2} within normal limits.
3. Bicarbonate is present in high concentration in plasma.
4. Carbonic anhydrase is present in the red blood cell.

The kidneys do excrete hydrogen ions from the fixed acids and from carbon dioxide, but, compared with the ventilatory response to carbon dioxide, it is very slow.

There is only a limited amount of buffer available in the body. It is usually sufficient to mop up the hydrogen ions produced by normal metabolism, without a change in the acidity of the blood. If, however, an excessive amount of acid is produced, or the lungs or kidneys fail to excrete the normal acid load, the buffers become full of hydrogen ions. Further hydrogen ions cannot be buffered so the blood becomes acid. There are actual free, unneutralised, hydrogen ions floating about causing acidity.

Production of ketoacids in large quantities from abnormal glucose metabolism in an uncontrolled diabetic, because of the lack of insulin, may be taken as an example. One of the most obvious features of the illness is increased ventilation. The strong ketoacids dissociate. The hydrogen ions are buffered by haemoglobin, plasma proteins and bicarbonate until they are full. Carbon dioxide is formed from bicarbonate (reactions 1 and 2 (p. 77)) and ventilation is stimulated. The P_{CO_2} may decrease to 3kPa or less.

When there is an acidosis, hydrogen ions diffuse into cells and, in exchange, for reasons similar to the chloride shift (too many positively charged ions inside the cell), positively charged potassium ions diffuse out of the cells. Following loss of intracellular potassium, heart function deteriorates; blood pressure and tissue perfusion decrease; renal function deteriorates and the ability of the kidneys to handle acid is impaired. As tissue perfusion falls, the cells become hypoxic. More acid is produced as metabolism changes to anaerobic. The central chemoreceptors become less responsive to carbon dioxide so that the pulmonary mechanism for acid excretion is also reduced.

INTERPRETATION OF ACID/BASE MEASUREMENTS

When acid/base (Astrup) results are obtained by analysis of arterial blood, acidity of the blood is indicated by pH. pH is the central character in clinical interpretations of acid/base status.

pH has been defined as the negative logarithm of the hydrogen ion concentration, but the form, or forms, of hydrogen ion in aqueous solution causing acidity is in doubt. Total hydrogen ion concentration may not reflect acidity as well as, for example, hydrogen ion activity or the activity of some fraction of the total amount present.

pH is measured by immersion of an electrode made of special glass into blood. An electrode is a device which converts one form of energy (in this case, acidity) into electricity. Electricity is easy to measure. It is not known to what aspect of hydrogen ion, whether concentration or activity, the electrode is responding. The amount of electricity produced when the electrode is immersed in blood is compared with the amount of electricity produced when the same electrode at the same temperature is immersed in a solution of chemicals (the standard buffer solutions) the pH of which is arbitrarily defined. (An easier definition of pH is that it is a number on this arbitrary scale.)

The normal pH range of arterial blood is 7.34–7.43. A pH above 7.43 represents an alkalosis, while one less than 7.34 represents an acidosis. Low pH is acid – despite there being an increase in the amount of hydrogen ion present.

An *acidosis* may be:

1. Respiratory, due to retention of carbon dioxide.
2. Non-respiratory (metabolic), due to accumulation of hydrogen ions from the fixed acids.

In blood with an abnormal pH it is necessary to know the amount of the pH disturbance due to respiratory problems *separately* from the amount due to non-respiratory abnormalities, because each requires a different method of correction. A respiratory acidosis is corrected by increasing ventilation to remove carbon dioxide. A non-respiratory acidosis requires intravenous infusion of an alkali, usually bicarbonate, as sodium bicarbonate solution. An infusion of bicarbonate provides more buffer to mop up hydrogen ions. Carbon dioxide is produced – the patient fizzes like lemonade – and ventilation is stimulated. Bicarbonate infusion corrects the non-respiratory acidosis, but not the cause of the acidosis. This must also be treated.

Many indices have been proposed to separate the respiratory from the non-respiratory pH changes, such as standard bicarbonate, buffer base and base excess.

In practical terms, if the arterial blood Pco_2 is within normal limits, then the whole of any acute pH disturbance is due entirely to non-respiratory abnormalities. Equally, if the $Paco_2$ is elevated above normal, then at least part of the pH disturbance is due to a respiratory problem. If the patient could be encouraged to breathe harder or be mechanically ventilated to a normal Pco_2 then, following this correction of the respiratory acidosis, any remaining pH disturbance must be due to non-respiratory problems and requires bicarbonate infusion for correction.

REFERENCE

West, J. B. (1977). *Ventilation/Blood Flow and Gas Exchange*, 3rd edition. Blackwell Scientific Publications Limited, Oxford.

BIBLIOGRAPHY

Cotes, J. E. (1979). *Lung Function. Assessment and Application in Medicine*, 4th edition. Blackwell Scientific Publications Limited, Oxford.
Nunn, J. F. (1977). *Applied Respiratory Physiology*, 2nd edition. Butterworths, London.
See also page 101.

ACKNOWLEDGEMENTS

The author thanks Mrs S. E. Jackson MCSP, DipTP, for her help, advice and encouragement; Dr G. Jones, Senior House Officer (Anaesthetics), University Hospital of South Manchester for helpful discussions; and Miss S. Grainger for typing the manuscript. He also thanks the Department of Medical Illustration, University Hospital of South Manchester for Figures 1/3, 1/4, and 2/4.

Chapter 3

Clinical Lung Function Testing

by S. J. CONNELLAN MB, MRCP

INTRODUCTION

It is unusual for a specific lung function test to diagnose a disease. At best, a series of tests may place a lung disorder into one of several categories and when other features such as history, physical examination, radiology and pathology are added to the equation, a possible diagnosis is considered. Most requests for tests will include a provisional diagnosis. When the most appropriate tests have been selected, further hurdles must be overcome before any reliable results can be obtained. The patient must be able to co-operate fully and there is no substitute for an experienced, sympathetic but firm technician to ensure that maximum performance has been achieved. A rushed estimate of total lung capacity (TLC) in a claustrophobic and panicking, body-box-bound patient is no use to anyone. The technician must have the right to question the advisability of a test on a particular day as the patient may have become too ill to co-operate or be recovering from fractured ribs or even recent surgery. Finally, it is essential that the equipment used is serviced regularly and reliably calibrated.

The main uses of lung function testing are:

1. To help define more clearly the type of functional disorder.
2. To measure serially natural progression (or regression with therapy) of the disorder.
3. To decide on the feasibility of thoracic surgery.
4. To assess the degree of respiratory failure.

If the brain is functioning normally, a breath begins with contraction of inspiratory muscles enlarging the thorax, lowering intra-thoracic and pleural pressures, enlarging the alveoli and airways, expanding alveolar gas so reducing its pressure below atmospheric. Air at atmospheric pressure must flow into the thorax where it is conducted to, and diffuses out into, the alveoli. At any one moment, approximately 100ml of desaturated blood, with a strong affinity for oxygen, is spread over an area of 70 square metres (area of pulmonary capillary bed) separated from air by a membrane 0.2μ thick. Oxygen from alveolar air diffuses rapidly across the alveolar-capillary membrane and is finally chemically combined with haemoglobin molecules within the circulating red blood cells. Carbon dioxide diffuses in the opposite direction and is eliminated in expired gas.

Appreciation of these steps in respiration is important in helping to understand how a specific lung function test may pinpoint a particular malfunction in the respiratory system.

Three broad categories of testing will be considered:

1. Tests of ventilatory function.
2. Tests of gas exchange.
3. Exercise testing.

TESTS OF VENTILATORY FUNCTION

These measure the 'bellows' action of the thoracic cage and lungs, detecting any abnormal interference in the free flow of air from atmosphere to alveoli and back.

Figure 3/1 shows how the total lung capacity (TLC) is broken

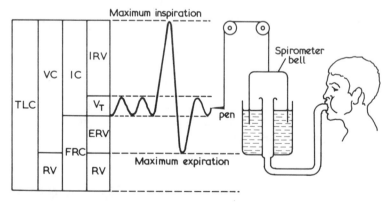

FIG. 3/1 The subdivision of the total lung capacity (TLC) with spirometric recording of tidal volume (V_T) and vital capacity (VC). IC = inspiratory capacity; RV = residual volume; FRC = functional residual capacity; IRV = inspiratory reserve volume; ERV = expiratory reserve volume

down into its various volumes. Their size and relationship to each other give clues to underlying functional disorder. How normal a volume is will depend on what we predict it should be for that person's height, sex and age. If the value obtained is more than 1.7 standard deviations from the predicted it is very likely to be abnormal.

During normal resting ventilation air moves gently back and forth in a tidal manner and the total volume of each breath is called the *tidal volume* (V_T). The largest volume that can be inspired from the endpoint of tidal expiration is called the *inspiratory capacity* (IC) and the largest volume that can be expired after full inspiration is called the *vital capacity* (VC). The lungs cannot collapse to an airless state because of the compliance of the thoracic cage and there is always some residue of gas, the *residual volume* (RV). At the end of a tidal expiration much more air remains in the lungs and this is called the *functional residual capacity* (FRC). This is the neutral position of the respiratory system, at which point the inward recoil of the lungs is exactly balanced by the outward recoil of the chest wall.

All these volumes, apart from RV and FRC can be measured by a spirometer. We can see from Figure 3/1 that the *total lung capacity* (TLC) can be derived by adding IC and FRC.

There are three methods of measuring TLC:

(1) HELIUM DILUTION METHOD

The patient breathes into a closed circuit spirometer containing a mixture of gas with a known concentration of helium. The patient is switched into the system at the end of a normal expiration and this mixture gradually equilibrates with the gas in the lungs. Oxygen is added and carbon dioxide is absorbed, maintaining a stable FRC.

When the helium concentration has stopped falling (having been diluted by the lung volume) the patient takes a full inspiration and this IC is added to the FRC (derived from the equation below) to give the TLC.

$$SV \times He_1 = He_2 \times (SV + FRC)$$

He_1 = helium concentration before equilibration
He_2 = helium concentration after equilibration
SV = spirometer volume

Equilibration between spirometer and lungs is achieved within 5–10 minutes in normal subjects, but in severe airways obstruction mixing is much slower and it may make it more difficult to estimate the point at which equilibration has been achieved.

(2) WHOLE BODY PLETHYSMOGRAPHY

The patient sits in an airtight box (Fig. 3/2) and breathes the air contained within; the flask shape represents alveoli and conducting airways and V_I the unknown volume. The pointers in circles represent pressure gauges – one measuring box pressure (which after calibration gives the alveolar volume) – and the other, airway pressure (which equals alveolar pressure when there is no airflow). In (A), at end expiration, alveolar pressure equals atmospheric pressure and V_I is unknown.

The subject then attempts to inspire against an occluded airway (B) which results in a reduced intrathoracic pressure ($\triangle P$) and a rise in the pressure of gas within the plethysmograph. This latter pressure change is proportional to change in intrathoracic volume ($\triangle V$) which can be estimated. Knowing P_1, P_2 (i.e. $P_1 + \triangle P$) and $\triangle V$ we can derive V_I (initial thoracic gas volume or TGV) using Boyle's Law (assuming a constant temperature):

$$P_I \quad \times \quad V_I \quad = \quad P_2 \quad \times \quad V_2$$

$$\left(\begin{smallmatrix} \text{atmospheric} \\ \text{pressure} \end{smallmatrix} \right) \quad \left(\text{TGV} \right) \quad \left(P_1 + \triangle P \right) \quad \left(\begin{smallmatrix} \text{TGV} + \\ \triangle \text{ alveolar volume} \end{smallmatrix} \right)$$

When the shutter opens the patient inspires fully and this volume is added to the value of V_I to give the total lung capacity (TLC).

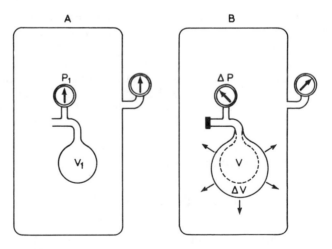

FIG. 3/2 Schematic representation of a patient in a body plethysmograph. In A, breathing from the air within the box; in B, attempting to inspire against a closed shutter

Body plethysmography will measure all gas within the thorax which may include emphysematous bullae, hiatus hernia or pneumothorax. When there is uneven ventilation distribution with generalised airflow obstruction or a large poorly communicating bulla, the TLC estimate by helium dilution may be much less than the plethysmographic estimate; the discrepancy being greater the more severe the disorder.

(3) RADIOLOGICAL

Good postero-anterior and lateral radiographs, at full inspiration, are divided into a series of elliptical slices and the volume of each is calculated. The heart volume is subtracted and the tissue and blood volume are taken into consideration. This is not a widely used technique.

Tests of forced expiration

One of the simplest tests of forced expiration was the Snider match test in which the patient attempted to blow out a lighted match held 15cm from the mouth and, if unable to, was considered to have serious impairment of ventilatory function. All variations on this theme have in common the same manoeuvre, that is, a deep full inspiration followed by expulsion of air from the lungs with the maximum force possible.

(A) PEAK EXPIRATORY FLOW RATE (PEFR)

The peak flow sustained over a 10msec period at the beginning of a forced expiratory manoeuvre can be measured using a Wright's peak flow meter (or the inexpensive mini-Wright meter). From a position of full inspiration, air is forcibly expired across a pivoted vane (Wright's) or a lightweight piston (mini-Wright) both of which are spring-loaded and encased. The displacement of the vane or piston is proportional to maximum flow rate.

This is a highly effort-dependent test but in practice it is very reproducible. It is one piece of equipment which should be available not only to the hospital doctor, nurse and physiotherapist but also to the general practitioner and, of course, the patient. It is one of the simplest ways of measuring lung function. In spite of this, many general medical wards do not have such a meter though they would find it inexcusable to be without a sphygmomanometer.

(B) FORCED EXPIRATORY VOLUME IN ONE SECOND (FEV_1)

This can be obtained by measuring change in expired volume against

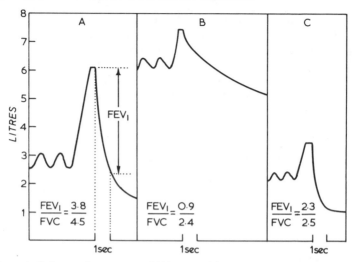

Fig. 3/3 Spirometric patterns of (A) normal forced expiration; (B) airways obstruction; (C) lung restriction

time using a spirometer (see Fig. 3/1). When a forced expiration is started from full inspiration (i.e. TLC) flow rises rapidly to peak value and then, because of progressive airway narrowing due to a combination of (1) high pleural pressure compressing airways and (2) lowering of lung volume with reduction in elastic recoil of lung, there is a rapid fall off of flow rate to zero when residual volume is reached and no more air can be expelled. In normal people this usually takes about 4 seconds and the full volume expired is the *forced vital capacity* (FVC). The volume expired in the first second of the manoeuvre is the FEV_1 and this is usually at least 75 per cent of the FVC (Fig. 3/3A).

The FEV_1 and PEFR are well correlated, but the FEV_1 does measure average flow rate over a larger lung volume than the PEFR. Both FEV_1 and PEFR are the most widely used and reproducible measures of forced expiration.

(C) FLOW-VOLUME LOOPS

If, instead of plotting the FVC manoeuvre as volume against time, we plot maximum flow rate against changing lung volume, it is possible to record the *maximum expiratory flow volume* (MEFV) curve. If this is followed immediately by a full forced inspiration to TLC we can record the *maximum inspiratory flow volume* (MIFV) curve, which completes the *flow volume loop* (Fig. 3/4A). This

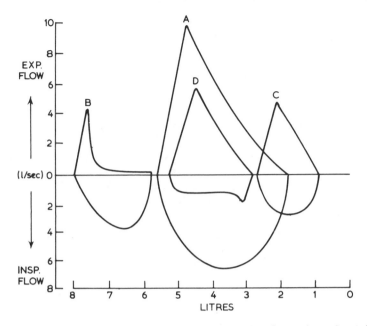

FIG. 3/4 Schematic representation of (A) maximum flow-volume loops in normal people; (B) severe airflow obstruction; (C) lung restriction; (D) upper airways obstruction

enables us to record maximum flow rates not only at large lung volumes near TLC, but also at small volumes near RV at which point flow through smaller airways will predominate. The shape of the MIFV curve is quite different as there is no sudden flow limitation on inspiration in normal people and peak flow occurs about midway up to TLC

Airways resistance

The major site of resistance to airflow during normal breathing is in the larger central airways. Measurement of airways resistance is more sensitive to changes in larger airways and relatively insensitive to changes in smaller airways. It is possible, therefore, for there to be extensive disease present in the peripheral airways before a significant increase in total airways resistance occurs. To measure resistance we need to know the pressure difference between mouth and alveoli (the driving pressure) and the simultaneous flow rate.

$$\text{Airways resistance} \atop (\text{RAW}) = \frac{\text{driving pressure}}{\text{flow rate}}$$

or

$$= \frac{\text{mouth press.} - \text{alveolar press.}}{\text{flow rate}}$$

Flow rate and mouth pressure are measured relatively easily but an indirect estimate of alveolar pressure has to be made using a body plethysmograph. One advantage of this method is that an estimate of thoracic gas volume can be made at the same time. As airways resistance varies with lung volume (airway calibre being greater at larger lung volume) it is useful to know the lung volume at which resistance is measured. *Specific airways resistance* (SRAW) is the product of RAW and the lung volume at which it was measured and corrects for the effect of the latter. The reciprocal of RAW is conductance (GAW) which has a more linear relationship to lung volume and is sometimes used in preference in the form of *specific airways conductance* (SGAW). Measurement of airways resistance is a more sensitive test of airway calibre than FEV_I but is less reproducible. It also avoids the need for a full inspiration or forced expiration which can in itself cause bronchoconstriction in asthmatics and, therefore, is preferred by some workers when assessing dose response studies using bronchodilators or bronchoconstrictors.

Compliance

Compliance is a measure of elasticity or, in the case of the lung, distensibility or stiffness. The stiffer the lungs, the greater the external force (pressure) required to produce a given increase in lung volume. Compliance is measured by plotting changes in intraoesophageal pressure (which is an approximation of intrapleural pressure) against changes in lung volume. This pressure is obtained by positioning a thin-walled balloon in the lower third of the oesophagus connected by a catheter to a pressure transducer. From the FRC position the patient inspires a measured volume at which the breath is held while transpulmonary pressure (mouth pressure-oesophageal pressure) is measured. Several measurements are made between TLC and FRC and a pressure-volume curve constructed, the slope of which gives compliance. The lower the value of compliance the stiffer are the lungs. As with RAW, compliance is related to lung volume. Specific compliance is the ratio compliance/FRC and is independent of age and sex.

TESTS OF GAS EXCHANGE

For efficient respiratory gas exchange, the major processes of lung ventilation, diffusion across the alveolar-capillary memebrane and lung perfusion, should be intact. Normal distribution of the inspired air depends on an adequate thoracic 'bellows' action followed by unimpaired flow through the bronchial tree to the lung periphery where molecular diffusion occurs into the alveolar compartments. The efficiency and uniformity of ventilation can be assessed by measuring nitrogen concentration at the mouth while breathing 100% oxygen. If gas mixing is perfect the expired nitrogen concentration will fall by the same proportion with each breath but, in generalised airways obstruction, wash-out is much slower and more uneven. The single breath nitrogen test or closing volume is a variation in which a single full inspiration of 100% oxygen is followed by a slow full expiration with monitoring of nitrogen concentration at the mouth.

This test and radioactive gas techniques (for estimating topographical inequality of ventilation) will not be discussed further.

Oxygen and carbon dioxide cross the alveolar–capillary membrane by diffusion. Molecules of oxygen have to cross alveolar epithelium, interstitium, endothelium, blood plasma, red cell membrane and then chemically combine with haemoglobin (Fig. 3/5). Carbon monoxide (CO) is also avidly taken up by haemoglobin and serves as

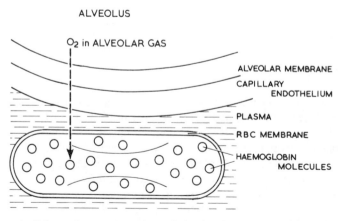

ALVEOLUS

O_2 in ALVEOLAR GAS

ALVEOLAR MEMBRANE
CAPILLARY ENDOTHELIUM
PLASMA
RBC MEMBRANE
HAEMOGLOBIN MOLECULES

FIG. 3/5 Schematic representation of the barriers across which oxygen travels before combining with haemoglobin

a useful inhaled gas in estimating the ease of transfer across these barriers – *carbon monoxide transfer factor* (T_LCO).

The patient takes a vital capacity breath of CO and helium, holds the breath for 10 seconds and then exhales. As helium is not taken up by the pulmonary blood it gives the dilution of the inspired gas with alveolar gas and thus the initial alveolar PCO. It is possible, using a simple equation, to calculate the volume of CO taken up per minute, per mmHg alveolar PCO, i.e. T_LCO. As a bonus, the helium dilution technique also gives an estimate of the alveolar volume or, at least, that volume that the inspired CO 'sees' while the breath is held.

In a patient with generalised airways obstruction this volume will be much less than the true alveolar volume because of the impaired distribution of the inspired volume, and CO transfer will also be reduced because of the reduced area 'seen'. To allow for this reduced volume effect the *transfer coefficient* (or transfer factor divided by the alveolar volume obtained during the test) is estimated. This helps to differentiate between a real reduction in CO transfer or a reduction solely due to the CO being presented to an abnormally small volume or surface area. A patient who has had a pneumonectomy may have a perfectly functioning single lung but his transfer factor will be reduced by about 50 per cent because of the halving of his total lung capacity. The transfer coefficient, or KCO as it is known, corrects for this volume effect.

The transfer factor is determined by the thickness and area of alveolar membrane, the size of the pulmonary capillary volume and how well ventilation is matched to pulmonary perfusion. It will therefore be affected by such diverse disorders as anaemia, pneumonectomy, emphysema and pulmonary embolus.

EXERCISE TESTING

In the same way that any piece of machinery cannot be considered fully tested until maximally stressed, the lungs and heart need to be stressed with exercise to assess their efficiency. Minor dysfunction which is not apparent at rest, may come to light on exercise. Asthma may be induced, known disability graded, myocardial insufficiency diagnosed and on occasions an objective assessment will contrast with the patient's own expectation of exercise performance.

Whatever the choice of exercise, a doctor should be present with resuscitation equipment to hand and the patient should always be able to stop the test if symptoms become distressing.

In those already known to be moderately limited by respiratory disease, a simple walking test will help to grade severity.

The 12-minute walking test (McGavin, 1976)

This is a test of free corridor walking in which the patient is asked to cover as much distance as possible during 12 minutes with stops for a breather when necessary. At least two practice walks are required in order to improve subsequent reproducibility of the test and, like most exercise studies, motivation is an important factor. Free walking can be replaced by treadmill walking at a fixed rate and zero gradient for 12 minutes in a more controlled environment and with continuous ECG monitoring. In more sophisticated testing using a treadmill or cycle ergometer, either during progressive increasing workload or at a steady state of exercise, measurements of tidal volume, ventilation, heart rate, ECG, oxygen consumption and carbon dioxide output, can be monitored continuously. In this way, the overall capacity to perform exercise can be assessed and compared with predicted values. If arterial blood is also sampled during exercise, information on the efficiency of pulmonary gas exchange can be obtained. If dyspnoea on exertion is due to respiratory rather than cardiac disease, the patient will tend to stop near to maximum predicted voluntary ventilation or even exceed this without reaching predicted maximum heart rate. The interpretation of such tests is not always clear.

Running on a treadmill for 6 minutes with regular monitoring of PEFR is one way of diagnosing exercise-induced asthma. The typical response being a slight rise in PEFR during exercise and a marked drop after exercise, usually reaching lowest levels about 4 minutes after stopping. This is one of the few diagnostic tests of lung function.

CLINICAL APPLICATION OF LUNG FUNCTION TESTS

Let us now consider specific examples of respiratory disorder and the associated abnormalities of lung function.

AIRFLOW OBSTRUCTION

Patients with asthma, emphysema (with or without chronic bronchitis), bronchiectasis and cystic fibrosis may all be demonstrated as having variable degrees of airflow obstruction. Asthma is the one condition in which the degree of obstruction may vary spontaneously, or with treatment, by more than 20 per cent. However, any of these conditions may have a reversible component demonstrated by response to a bronchodilator.

Asthma

One of the simplest ways of demonstrating reversible airflow obstruction is by measuring the percentage increase in FEV_1 or PEFR after an inhaled bronchodilator. If this is > 20 per cent (some would accept 15 per cent) asthma is a likely diagnosis. Another approach, particularly in more chronic severe airflow obstruction, is to monitor PEFR during a course of high dose corticosteroids which may result in a mean rise in PEFR of > 20 per cent and may also enhance the acute response to bronchodilator. In some cases of asthma the diagnosis may be missed, unless daily PEFRs are recorded to reveal the typically increased diurnal variation often accompanied by morning 'dips' in PEFR. There may be other 'dips' specifically associated with, for example, exposure to an allergen at work. Typical patterns may also be seen during the recovery from an acute attack of asthma. This is often during a course of high dose

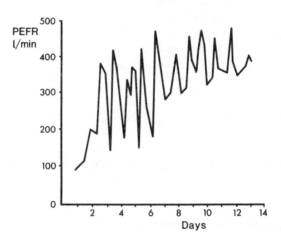

FIG. 3/6 Daily record of peak expiratory flow rates during recovery from an acute exacerbation of asthma. *Note* the tendency to morning 'dips' during the initial recovery period

corticosteroids and the gradual rise in PEFR may be accompanied by transient, troublesome morning 'dips' (Fig. 3/6).

In an acute attack of asthma there is widespread narrowing of airways with bronchospasm, mucosal oedema, inflammation and mucus plugging of small airways. These changes result in reductions in maximum expiratory flow rates ($\downarrow$ PEFR, FEV_I/VC and MEFV flow rates). Airways resistance increases and, because of the tendency for narrowed airways to close off even during tidal expiration, the patient tends to breathe at a higher lung volume to try and keep the airways open for as long as possible during expiration. This results in a higher FRC and RV with some restriction of the VC. Total lung capacity is elevated as a result of widespread air trapping behind closed airways. Ventilation distribution becomes very uneven and poorly matched with perfusion resulting in impaired pulmonary gas exchange. Initially, the increase in total ventilation will offset the fall in Po_2; however, with more severe airflow obstruction the increase in total ventilation may not be maintained. As the patient tires from the exhausting work of breathing, the Po_2 may suddenly start dropping with corresponding rise in Pco_2. Without intensive therapy, including assisted ventilation, death may follow rapidly.

In chronic stable asthma there may be persistent findings of hyperinflation with $\uparrow$ TLC, $\downarrow FEV_I/VC$ and $\downarrow$ VC but T_LCO is usually normal when corrected for lung volume (i.e. KCO).

Many asthmatics will volunteer that certain things, such as cold air, exercise, paint fumes or specific allergens, trigger off their asthma and diagnostic tests may be based on these facts. Exercise-induced asthma can be readily diagnosed as previously described (p. 93). Challenging the patient with increasing amounts of inhaled histamine or cold dry air and noting the point at which the FEV_I falls by 20 per cent will give an estimate of the non-specific bronchial responsiveness of the airways (Cockcroft et al, 1977). The lower the concentration required the more 'twitchy' the airways are.

Under careful supervision, with an overnight stay in hospital, the patient may be challenged with a nebulised solution of suspected allergen; a fall of > 15 per cent being taken as an asthmatic reaction. These latter tests are *not* for the casual, inexperienced investigator.

Chronic airflow obstruction (CAO)

This is an all embracing term which in current usage includes chronic bronchitis with an obstructive element and/or emphysema. It suggests less variability of airflow obstruction, with no periods of

...s can, of course, happen in long-standing asthma but ...lly associated with a long history of smoking.

... *bronchitis* is defined in terms of sputum production and ...cts mucus hypersecretion in the airways. Any associated obstruction can be assessed by using the forced expiratory ...ram or MEFV curve as already described.

(b) *Emphysema* is a pathology diagnosis and at best can only be strongly suspected during life. It is characterised by a breakdown of alveolar walls with consequent dilatation of the distal airspaces and destruction of some of the pulmonary capillary bed. This results in loss of lung elasticity and a reduced area for gas exchange. As in severe asthma there will be reductions in all forced expiratory flow rates (see Figs. 3/3B and 3/4B). This flow limitation, seen early in forced expiration, is the result of dynamic compression of airways which have lost elastic support from surrounding lung and may also be more 'floppy' due to loss of elasticity of airway walls. In addition there may be increased mucus with inflammation and narrowing of small airways. This tendency to early expiratory airway closure may occur during tidal breathing and the patient has to 'climb up' the total lung capacity until tidal breathing is at a point where expiration can be fuller without early airway closure. This results in a higher FRC and RV; TLC is also increased as a result of air trapping. The VC in severe airflow obstruction, particularly in emphysema, is better assessed by avoiding the forced expiration by getting the patient to breathe out slowly from TLC, thus avoiding the much earlier flow limitation due to dynamic airway compression. This is called the relaxed or *slow VC* (SVC) and the difference between this and the FVC gives some indication as to the severity of obstruction.

There is often a large discrepancy between the FRC measured by helium dilution and the body plethysmographic estimate; the former being an underestimate because of poorly ventilated areas. The large RV tends to reduce the 'room' left within the TLC for the VC which becomes more restricted as emphysema worsens.

A recognised response to bronchodilators in emphysema is one of lung deflation (Connellan and Morgan, 1981). The FRC, RV and, possibly, TLC decrease and there may be a small increase in tidal volume. There are greater increases in FVC and *peak inspiratory flow rate* (PIFR) than PEFR and FEV_1 (Fig. 3/7). Although the improvements in FEV_1 and PEFR may be disappointing, the patients may feel less dyspnoeic, presumably as a result of a reduced FRC putting inspiratory muscles at a better mechanical advantage and reducing the work of breathing.

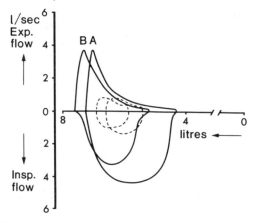

Fig. 3/7 Tidal (dotted lines) and maximum (continuous lines) flow-volume curves in a patient with severe airflow obstruction, before (B) and after (A) treatment with 5mg nebulised salbutamol (Connellan and Morgan, 1981)

Gas exchange is markedly impaired in emphysema contrary to the usual findings of normal or raised T_LCO in stable asthma. The surface area of normal lungs approaches that of a tennis court and in emphysema this may be reduced to the side-lines, particularly if a large non-ventilated bulla is compressing surrounding lung. If, to this, we add damage to the pulmonary capillary bed and poor distribution of ventilation (badly matched with perfusion) we can appreciate how distressing it must be for the emphysematous 'pink puffer' to maintain near normal arterial blood gases at the expense of hyperventilation at high lung volumes and an increased work of breathing. Some patients with chronic bronchitis and airflow obstruction have smaller increases in TLC and tend not to hyperventilate, 'accepting' a high P_{CO_2} and a low P_{O_2} with subsequent drift into pulmonary hypertension and right-sided heart failure. These are known as 'blue bloaters' (i.e. cyanosed and oedematous). The stimulus to breathe in these patients is *hypoxaemia* and this may be removed if the concentration of inspired oxygen delivered to the patient is too high; the result being a reduction in ventilation and a rapid rise in P_{CO_2}, fall in arterial pH, coma and death.

Upper airway obstruction

We have so far considered the effects of generalised airways obstruction but narrowing of the larger more central airways, at any point from the main bronchi up to pharynx, will also cause characteristic functional abnormalities. The flow–volume loop will help to localise the lesion to below (intrathoracic) or above the thoracic inlet (extrathoracic). In the example shown in Figure 3/4D there is a sharp early cut-off of inspiratory flow caused by a narrowing in the upper trachea. The rapid initial flow of air across the narrowing results in a fall in pressure immediately below the lesion, and this negative pressure (Bernoulli effect) tends to suck the walls together, cutting off flow for an instant and setting up a vibration as air forces through. This vibration produces the characteristic noise of stridor. The PEFR is also reduced and often more blunted than shown here. There is usually a high airways resistance with a relatively normal FEV_1 and the VC may be well preserved.

In the *sleep apnoea syndrome*, episodes of upper airway obstruction may occur as a result of loss of tone in the pharynx causing episodic pharyngeal closure during inspiration (the common snore is a less severe form); this effect is accentuated by co-existing narrowing due to excess fat or enlarged tonsils and adenoids. If severe enough it may be associated with transient arterial hypoxaemia, pulmonary hypertension and cor pulmonale. The characteristic features of this syndrome have been discovered by recording the EEG, nasal and oral airflow, oxygen saturation and chest and abdominal wall movement during sleep. Absence of airflow, oxygen desaturation and vigorous, out of phase, chest and abdominal wall movement, suggests obstructive sleep apnoea. If airflow and chest/abdominal wall movement is absent for more than 10 seconds, this suggests central apnoea and results from a transient lack of drive to breathe. Both central and obstructive patterns may occur in the same patient (Guilleminault, 1976).

LUNG RESTRICTION

Diseases which restrict expansion of the lungs are characterised by a reduced VC and TLC. This may result from increased lung stiffness, pleural disease, reduced skeletal mobility or an abnormal neuro-muscular apparatus.

Lung fibrosis

Interstitial and alveolar wall thickening with collagen deposition all serve to stiffen up the lungs. Increased radial traction on the airways may actually increase airway calibre for a given lung volume. Vital capacity and FEV_1 will both be reduced (FEV_1 to a lesser extent) and the $FEV_1/VC\%$ is typically supernormal. The maximum flows as demonstrated by MEFV curve tend to be greater than normal (see Figs. 3/3C and 3/4C). Total lung capacity and RV are reduced (RV to a lesser extent) and the RV/TLC ratio is typically high. Abnormally high pressures are required to distend the lungs (i.e. compliance is decreased). Patchy inequalities in ventilation and perfusion, in addition to thickening of alveolar walls and a reduction in pulmonary capillary bed, result in impaired CO transfer. Estimation of the KCO will help to determine how much of the impairment is a result of the reduced surface area for gas exchange. Arterial blood gases typically show reduced oxygen and carbon dioxide tension. The hypoxaemia is mild at rest but may fall dramatically on exercise. The diffusing capacity for CO may be measured during exercise and usually doubles or trebles in normal people but remains low in interstitial lung disease. The breathing pattern tends to be rapid and shallow in more severe cases and the high resting respiratory frequency achieves a high minute ventilation in spite of the small tidal volume. Dyspnoea tends to be inversely related to VC and the response to a trial of high dose corticosteroids can be assessed by serial measurements of VC.

Chest wall restriction

Anything which limits chest wall expansion will result in a restrictive ventilatory defect with reduction in lung volumes, although TLC may be normal. If there is no associated lung abnormality, gas transfer, although reduced, will be normal or high when corrected for lung volume (i.e. KCO). Skeletal disease (e.g. scoliosis, ankylosing spondylitis), neuromuscular disease (e.g. motor neurone disease, myaesthenia gravis, muscular dystrophy) and pleural disease (e.g. thickening or effusion) will all cause restrictive defects. Long-standing restriction may result in areas of atelectasis which, if widespread, may result in reduced lung compliance. The limited tidal volume, atelectasis and lung stiffness in more severe disease, will result in arterial hypoxaemia and subsequent ventilatory failure with arterial hypercapnia.

Combined restrictive and obstructive pattern

Any disease process of the lung parenchyma which also scars and narrows airways may produce a mixed restrictive and obstructive ventilatory defect with reductions in TLC, FEV_1, FEV_1/VC and T_LCO. Sarcoidosis is a good example of such a condition in which lung fibrosis may be associated with narrowing of small airways and even localised large airway stenoses (the latter may produce an additional feature of upper airway obstruction).

Pulmonary oedema may also result in a mixed picture caused by fluid, narrowing smaller airways and stiffening of the lungs. The phrase, 'all that wheezes is not asthma', reminds us that pulmonary oedema may present with symptoms predominantly of airflow obstruction. In long-standing mitral stenosis with chronic pulmonary venous congestion and ultimate lung fibrosis, there is reduction in lung compliance, VC and FEV_1/VC with a tendency to elevation of RV as a result of airway narrowing and a stiffening of alveolar walls.

RESPIRATORY FAILURE

There is an inverse relationship between arterial CO_2 ($Paco_2$) and alveolar ventilation. The lower the ventilation the higher the $Paco_2$. When the $Paco_2$ rises above normal the patient is in ventilatory failure and there is a concomitant drop in Pao_2. In *acute* ventilatory failure the rise in $Paco_2$ results in a drop in arterial pH (respiratory acidosis). In the *chronic* situation the kidneys will compensate by retaining bicarbonate and this may partially correct the low pH (compensated respiratory acidosis). Other mechanisms which compensate for the low Pao_2 include changes in cardiac output, oxygen dissociation curve and an increase in haemoglobin level. In the acute impairment of gas exchange (as a result of ventilation/perfusion mismatching) as seen in severe asthma, pulmonary emboli or oedema, there will be a lowering, initially, of both the Pao_2 and $Paco_2$. As the patient tires and is unable to maintain an adequate minute ventilation in response to the abnormal gas exchange, alveolar ventilation drops and the $Paco_2$ rises as ventilatory failure supervenes. This sequence of events may follow any sustained and severe impairment of respiratory function whether it be due to severe airflow obstruction or lung restriction.

PRE-OPERATIVE ASSESSMENT

Lung function testing may help in deciding whether to proceed to surgical removal of a lobe or lung. Some patients will be excluded easily on the basis of severe airflow obstruction. In others it may help to have additional information on regional ventilation and perfusion by use of radio-isotope lung scanning. In occasional patients with lung cancer, a surprisingly large defect in both ventilation and perfusion may be found on the side of the tumour. This may indicate mediastinal node involvement and an increased risk of inoperability. It also follows that the effect of a pneumonectomy on overall lung function can be more easily gauged when the lung affected by tumour has already been demonstrated to have little ventilation or perfusion (i.e. contributing little to the existing lung function). An FEV_I of less than 50 per cent of the predicted value or an elevation of $Paco_2$ are indications that, whatever the surgery contemplated, associated risks will be much higher. Lung function is but one of many factors to be taken into consideration in the decision to operate.

Finally, we should always remember that dyspnoea is a very complex sensation, the perception of which may vary greatly from one individual to another. Not only can its awareness be heightened in certain neurotic patients (see Chapter 22) but it can also be precipitated by excess circulating thyroxine in thyrotoxicosis or by progestogenic hormones in pregnancy.

REFERENCES

Cockcroft, D. W., Killian, D. N., Mellon, J. J. A. and Hargreave, F. E. (1977). Bronchial reactivity to inhaled histamine: a method and clinical survey. *Clinical Allergy*, **7**, 235–43.

Connellan, S. J. and Morgan, N. (1981). Acute lung deflation after nebulised salbutamol in patients with severe airflow obstruction. *Thorax*, **36**, 227.

Guilleminault, C., Tilkian, A. and Dement, W. C. (1976). The sleep apnoea syndrome. *American Review of Medicine*, **27**, 465–84.

McGavin, C. R., Gupta, S. P. and McHardy, G. J. R. (1976). Twelve-minute walking test for assessing disability in chronic bronchitis. *British Medical Journal*, **1**, 822–3.

BIBLIOGRAPHY

Gibson, G. J. (1984). *Clinical Tests of Respiratory Function*. Macmillan Press, London.

Pride, N. B. (1971). The assessment of airflow obstruction. Review article. *British Journal of Diseases of the Chest*, **65**, 135.

West, J. B. (1985). *Respiratory Physiology. The Essentials*, 3rd edition. Blackwell Scientific Publications Limited, Oxford.

West, J. B. (1983). *Pulmonary Pathophysiology. The Essentials*, 2nd edition. Williams and Wilkins, Baltimore.

Chapter 4

Percussion and Auscultation

by A. R. NATH MD, MRCP *with* L. H. CAPEL MD, FRCP

The traditional art of physical examination of the chest is based on inspection, palpation, percussion and auscultation. Much can be learned about a patient by simply looking: colour, breathing, posture, deformity and the symmetry of chest movements can be readily observed. In this chapter attention will be on useful aspects of percussion and auscultation.

In the eighteenth century Auenbrugger, son of an Austrian wine merchant, was aware that empty casks of wine were resonant to percussion but when filled with wine the resonance diminished. Later, he applied this knowledge to percussion of the chest which became the most important diagnostic method of chest disorders prior to the introduction of the stethoscope.

Laennec, a French physician, devised the stethoscope in the early nineteenth century. He set out to relate what he could hear (auscultation) to what he found *post mortem*. That is, to relate what he heard to structural changes in the lungs. Nowadays, we have the chest radiograph for the study of structural changes in the lungs, and use auscultation mainly to try to relate what we hear to *functional changes* in the lungs. That is, we use the stethoscope to tell us something of how air moves in and out of the different parts of the lungs, and then speculate on what this might tell us about the condition of the lungs. This chapter presents the modern view of *lung sounds* as developed by Dr Paul Forgacs, perhaps the first advance in the subject for a century and a half.

PERCUSSION

Percussion consists of setting up vibrations in the chest wall by means of a sharp tap. The middle finger of the left hand (pleximeter finger) is placed in close contact with the chest wall in the intercostal space. A firm sharp tap is then made by the middle finger of the right hand (plexor finger) kept at right angles to the pleximeter finger. All areas of the chest are percussed, that is, the front, back and both axillae. Anterior percussion is carried out with the patient reclining; axillary regions are percussed with the arms folded at the back of the head; and when percussing posteriorly the patient leans forward, head flexed and the arms loosely across the chest. The essence of percussion is to compare the note with the corresponding part of the chest on opposite side.

The air containing lung tissue will give a typically resonant note. By contrast solid tissue of the heart and the liver will generate a dull note. In general, increased resonance is more difficult to detect than diminished resonance especially when the pathological process is bilateral. The thin overdistended chest in emphysema will often show increased resonance associated with reduced cardiac and liver dullness. Increased resonance in pneumothorax may be detectable depending upon the size of the pneumothorax. Percussion is most helpful when the impaired note or dullness is detected over normal resonant areas of the chest. Of interest to the physiotherapist will be an underlying consolidated, fibrotic or collapsed segment of the lung. In pneumonic consolidation, normal resonance is restored as

TABLE 4/1 Percussion and ausculatory signs in common lung disorders

Condition	Percussion note	Breath sounds	Added sounds
Consolidation	Dull	Reduced Bronchial breath sounds may be present	Late inspiratory crackles
Collapse	Dull	Reduced or absent	Absent
Pleural effusion	Very dull	Absent	Absent
Emphysema	Increased resonance Diminished cardiac dullness	Uniformly reduced	Early inspiratory crackles
Pneumothorax	Increased resonance	Absent	Absent

the affected segment of the lung re-expands. In pleural effusion the percussion note is typically very dull (stony dull) and associated with absent breath sounds. Occasionally it will need to be distinguished from a paralysed or high diaphragm as the signs are similar. Table 4/1 summarises some of the important findings which might be elicited in these disorders.

In summary, the physiotherapist should observe the following guidelines:

1. Practise percussion systematically.
2. Always compare the corresponding area on the opposite side.
3. Get familiar with normal resonant and dull percussion areas of the chest.
4. Correlate your findings with other observations, for example inspection and auscultation.
5. Discuss your findings with someone more experienced to gain confidence.
6. Look at the chest radiograph and see how your findings relate to it.

AUSCULTATION

LUNG SOUNDS (Fig. 4/1)

Lung sounds are divided into breath sounds and added sounds. *Breath sounds* may be normal or abnormal. *Added sounds* are always abnormal: they are divided into crackles, which are short sharp interrupted sounds, and wheezes, which are usually prolonged and musical.

Breath sounds (Fig. 4/2)

Breath sounds are sounds of a mixture of intensities and frequencies of about 200 to 2000Hz (cycles per second, i.e. just below middle C and four octaves above). These are the sounds heard with a stethoscope placed at the root of the neck. They are generated by turbulent airflow in the pharynx and larger airways. Turbulent airflow, that is airflow disturbed by multitudes of eddies like the swirling seen round the pontoons of a bridge, contrasts with laminar or smooth airflow, which is silent. Airflow in the smaller airways is laminar and silent. The breath sounds generated in the larger airways are transmitted via the alveoli of the lungs to the listening stethoscope on the chest wall. The alveoli damp off the higher

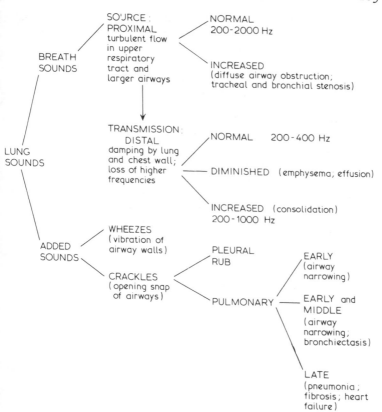

FIG. 4/1 Classification of lung sounds based on the work of Dr P. Forgacs

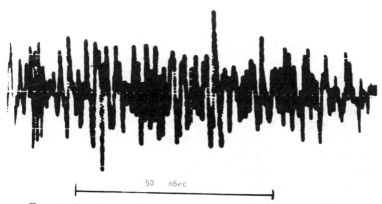

FIG. 4/2 Breath sounds showing random variations in amplitude

frequency sounds, so lower pitched sounds only are heard (about 200 to 400Hz). These lower pitched sounds are normal breath sounds heard at the lung bases. Thus the alveoli are filters and not generators of breath sounds.

Breath sounds may be normal or abnormal in their *generation* and normal or abnormal in their *transmission* through the lungs.

1. Abnormal *generation* of breath sounds occurs in bronchitis and asthma when air flows at increased speed through narrowed airways; this increase in speed increases turbulence and the amount of noise made. This noisy breathing is best heard at the mouth with the ear close by.

2. Abnormal *transmission* of breath sounds can result from an increase or reduction in the damping off of the higher frequencies. Pneumonia consolidates the lung. Consolidated lung is more solid than normal lung and transmits the breath sounds better: high frequency sounds are less damped, and so the bronchial breath sounds of the larger airways are then heard over the pneumonic lung, at the lung bases, for instance. Pleural effusion reflects the breath sounds away from the stethoscope listening over the effusion and the intensity of breath sounds is reduced. Emphysema and pneumothorax increase the damping of all the frequencies, and breath sound intensity is reduced. Effusion is easily distinguished from emphysema and pneumothorax as a cause of reduced intensity breath sounds by percussion: the note is dull with an effusion and resonant with emphysema and pneumothorax.

Added sounds

In the past added sounds were given a variety of names, and there was no agreement. We shall call them crackles and wheezes.

CRACKLES

Crackles are short sharp interrupted sounds. They may be described as fine, medium and coarse according to their loudness, and early, middle and late according to the part of the inspiratory cycle in which they appear. Crackles heard early in inspiration, usually only a few and not loud, are characteristic of patients with severe airway narrowing (Fig. 4/3); crackles heard early and in mid-inspiration are characteristic of patients with bronchiectasis (Fig. 4/4). Crackles heard late in inspiration (late inspiratory crackles), are heard in pulmonary fibrosis, in pneumonia and in heart failure (Fig. 4/5).

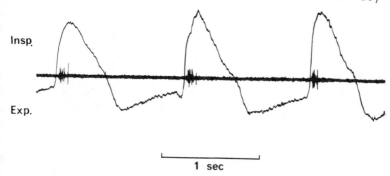

Insp.

Exp.

1 sec

FIG. 4/3 Early inspiratory crackles; the breath sounds and the flow of inspiration and expiration are shown above and below the zero line

Late inspiratory crackles tend to repeat from breath to breath, so the same pattern of crackles will be heard from breath to breath as the same pressure and volume conditions of the lungs are repeated. They persist after coughing.

Early inspiratory crackles in patients with severe airway narrowing originate, we believe, from the opening of larger airways closed by the previous expiration.

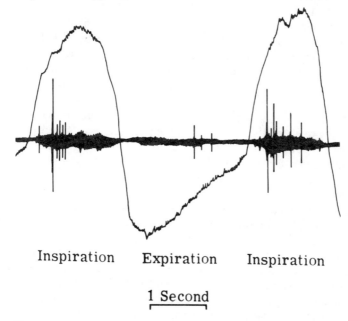

Inspiration   Expiration   Inspiration

1 Second

FIG. 4/4 Early inspiratory combined with mid-inspiratory crackles

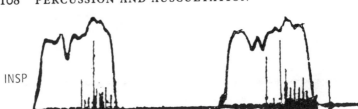

INSP

EXP

FIG. 4/5 Late inspiratory crackles

Early, combined with mid-inspiratory, crackles originate in the more flaccid bronchi and their secretions in bronchiectasis. Unlike early and late inspiratory crackles there is not the same repetitive pattern from breath to breath. The early combined with mid-inspiratory and expiratory crackles are generated by the combination of sounds from the previously closed and flaccid airways and their attendant secretions.

Late inspiratory crackles such as those heard in fibrosing alveolitis (pulmonary fibrosis), pulmonary asbestosis and heart failure originate in the more distant and hence smaller airways. In these conditions the dependent parts of the lungs become partially deflated towards the end of expiration. As the subsequent inspiration inflates the lungs, crackles are heard as each part of the previously dependent lungs are drawn apart again. Each crackle is made by the opening snap of the previously closed airway. So, late inspiratory crackles (but not the others) are heard always over dependent parts of the lungs, for example the lung bases, and they will go with a change in posture which brings the dependent part uppermost; for example, if the patient's right base is listened to while he lies on his right, and then turns on to his left side, the stethoscope remaining in position. When he turns once more so that his right side is again dependent, then the crackles return (Fig. 4/6).

In all crackles the sound arises when the lung expands enough to draw the walls of the airway in question apart and air rushes in.

If the chest radiograph shows evidence of pulmonary fibrosis, pulmonary congestion or bronchiectasis, then crackles will usually, but by no means always, be heard. Further, crackles may be heard though the radiograph is normal.

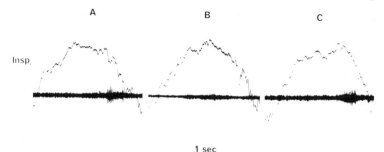

FIG. 4/6 Late inspiratory crackles. A. The patient lying on his right side with stethoscope on the base of his right chest and crackles are heard. B. The patient lying on his left chest with the stethoscope still on his right side and the crackles go. C. The patient again on his right side and the stethoscope on the right as before, and crackles at the right base return

WHEEZE (Fig. 4/7)

A wheeze is a continuous musical sound. It may be of high, medium or low pitch. Wheezes are generated by the vibration of airway walls the faces of which just touch: as air rushes through they vibrate like a reed, or like the sound amusing to children when air from an inflated balloon rushes through the neck if this is held taut. The lung wheezes like a reed instrument and not like an organ pipe. The waxing and waning of wheeze with successful management of

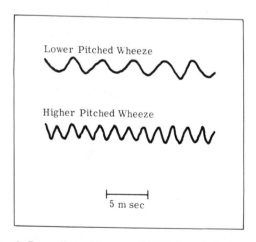

FIG. 4/7 Recording of lower and of higher pitched wheeze

asthma may reflect change in congestion of the wall of the airway and change in bronchospasm.

CRACKLE-WHEEZE (Fig. 4/8)

A crackle-wheeze may be heard, towards the end of inspiration typically in patients with late inspiratory crackles. The airway opens with a crackle and the walls then vibrate with a wheeze. This tends to support the suggestions that this is how crackles and wheezes are generated.

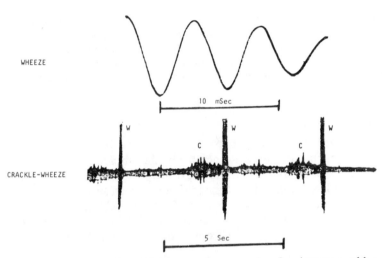

FIG. 4/8 Recording of crackle/wheeze. *Lower tracing*: Inspiratory crackles (C) associated with a wheeze (W) of brief duration in 3 breaths. *Upper tracing*: The same wheeze as in the lower trace recorded at a faster speed. *Note* the regular wave form of the musical wheeze

LISTENING TO THE LUNG SOUNDS

At the mouth

The lung sounds can be heard by listening with the ear at the mouth as well as by auscultation of the chest. This provides information not only about the state of the upper airways, but also about the calibre changes of the larger airways of the chest. This is because sounds generated in the chest can transmit directly to the mouth through the trachea, larynx and pharynx, and so are relatively unfiltered: all high and low frequency breath sounds are heard. By contrast, sounds passing through the lungs and chest wall are filtered by them, so only the lower frequency sounds are heard and not the higher frequency sounds which are filtered off. Therefore, auscultation of the lung should include listening to breath sounds at the mouth as well as at the chest wall through the stethoscope. For this purpose it is sufficient to listen at the mouth with the unaided ear close to the mouth while the patient breathes in and out deeply.

The breathing of healthy subjects at rest is barely audible. The breathing of patients with exacerbation of asthma or bronchitis is often loud at the mouth. In general, the louder the breathing the more severe the airway narrowing. After bronchodilator drugs the breathing can be quieter. (Occasionally noisy breathing occurs where there is localised narrowing by a bronchial tumour or a tumour in the trachea: then there will be no response to bronchodilator drugs.) Wheezing is readily heard at the mouth. Expiratory wheezes in association with noisy breathing are common in asthma and bronchitis. Often wheezing can be brought out by asking the patient to increase the expiratory effort. Several wheezes may then be heard. They are then called polyphonic wheezes. Crackles produced by mucus retention in the large airways are readily heard at the mouth. These mucus crackles arise at random during inspiration and expiration and they can be reduced or abolished by coughing. (In early and mid-inspiration in chronic bronchitis and bronchiectasis these mucus crackles may be heard at the mouth, as well as by the stethoscope.) In pneumonia and alveolitis crackles are heard only via the stethoscope: they originate in the peripheral airways and therefore are not heard at the mouth.

STETHOSCOPE

Laennec's original stethoscope was a simple wooden hollow cylinder. It was replaced by the bin-aural stethoscope in the mid-nineteenth century. The modern version is a lightweght instrument with two chest-pieces and a tubing connected to the two ear-pieces. For good listening the stethoscope should have airtight joints and well-fitting ear-pieces. Of the two chest-pieces, the bell is a better conductor of lower pitched sounds and more suitable for listening to the lung sounds. The diaphragm is used mainly to listen to certain higher pitched heart sounds and murmurs.

At the chest wall

After listening at the mouth, examine the chest systematically. The patient may be standing, sitting on a chair or sitting in bed. The very sick patient may be lying in bed. Stand to the patient's right side if possible. Ensure that the ear-pieces of the stethoscope fit comfortably and snugly into the correct position. Start at the lower axillary zones at the lung bases on the left and then on the right. Then move the stethoscope to the upper chest zones on the right and then on the left. Finally, listen over the front of the chest upper zone first and lower zone last. Listen first while the patient makes a deep *slow* inspiration and expiration. Then listen while the patient makes a deep *forced* inspiration and expiration. This brings out wheezes and crackles, but ensures that the wheezes will not be missed. Compare what you heard on the chest wall with what you heard at the mouth. Wheezes heard with the ear at the mouth may be heard better there than on the chest wall by the stethoscope because with it they are filtered out by the lungs and the chest wall.

If you wish to listen for local abnormalities because of what has been seen on the radiograph, you may then do so. When listening, always apply the stethoscope firmly to the chest. Noise from hairs, subcutaneous emphysema and shivering may confuse auscultation. If you wish to discuss what you have heard with the patient it is better to do so after discussion with the doctor or surgeon in charge to prevent misunderstanding.

It is worth stressing that alterations in breath sounds, wheezes and crackles discovered by auscultation indicate alterations in lung *function*. The radiograph shows only alterations in the lung *structure*. Radiographic changes may in fact precede detectable abnormality on auscultation, while in functional disorders like asthma and chronic bronchitis radiographic abnormalities may be minimal or absent while auscultatory changes are obvious. The findings of the chest radiograph, lung function tests and lung auscultation complement each other and must be judged together.

Terms other than crackles and wheezes are still used by some clinicians. Unfortunately, other terms such as râles, rhoncus and crepitations are, and indeed from their beginnings always were, used differently by different doctors. Many doctors are even unaware of the confusion. Râle is sometimes used to indicate all added sounds, sometimes interrupted sounds only. Crepitation is used mainly to indicate interrupted sounds. Rhoncus commonly means wheeze. The terms fine, medium and coarse may be applied to all. (The nomenclature shown in Fig. 4/1 was introduced in 1970 and then adopted by Dr Paul Forgacs. It is now becoming popular in the United Kingdom.) It brings a sigh of relief to medical students who discover it for the first time! With many of our colleagues we recommend it as a simple and straightforward classification of the auscultation and examination of the lungs.

Regular practice in those with normal lungs brings confidence and helps in the study of the abnormal. Critical use of the stethoscope and discussion with colleagues will add to the interest and success of your work.

BIBLIOGRAPHY

Forgacs, P. (1978). *Lung Sounds*. Baillière Tindall, London.

Chapter 5

Chest Radiographs (x-rays)

by C. A. PARSONS FRCS, FRCR

A very high proportion of the patients treated by physiotherapy will have had a chest radiograph (x-ray) either because their primary disease is pulmonary or there is some long-standing heart or lung illness which should be taken into account during the management of an acute problem. A knowledge of the principles involved in reading the radiograph enables the physiotherapist to understand more clearly what is happening to the patient. There is no intention in this chapter to create a new breed of expert radiologists but rather a hope that some light will be shed on a small aspect of patient care.

TYPES OF CHEST X-RAY

Postero-anterior (PA) (Fig. 5/1, p. 129)

The standard chest film taken in an x-ray department is in the PA position, that is, the front of the patient's chest is against the film so that the x-ray beam passes from posterior to anterior. The x-ray tube is always the same distance from the film, usually 6 feet, so that geometric enlargement is constant. It is important to realise that portable films, even if they are taken in a PA position, will almost always have the x-ray tube closer to the patient – this is the most common cause of a sudden enlargement of the heart shadow on successive films. The PA position can be checked by observing that the medial end of the clavicle overlies the posterior end of the 4th rib.

Antero-posterior (AP) (Fig. 5/2, p. 130)

Many portable chest films are exposed AP when the clavicles are projected above the ribs and anterior structures, such as the heart, appear enlarged. AP films are sometimes used to project the ribs and lungs in different relationships to the PA film, i.e. to uncover small lung lesions. Of course, most chest films are taken with the patient erect but casualty department and intensive care unit x-rays may have to be exposed with the patient supine. In this case the diaphragms are displaced upward by the abdominal contents; this rotates the apex of the heart slightly anti-clockwise and the pulmonary veins are distended. Since it is known that this occurs normally, these features will not be mistaken for pathology.

Lateral (Figs. 5/3(a), p. 128 and 5/3(b), p. 131)

The lateral film presents two slight problems. First, the exposure is longer, with the possibility of movement particularly in the old and very ill. Movement can be reduced simply by seating the patient and, where available, high-powered x-ray equipment will be used to reduce the exposure time. The second problem is positioning the arms out of the x-ray field. Fit patients will hold them above their heads while the more infirm need a hand grip or arm support at an appropriate level. Interpretation of anatomy is difficult on a lateral film since the lungs overlap each other but, assessed with the PA film, it is usually extremely helpful in deciding which lobe or segment of lung is involved by consolidation.

Oblique view: decubitus view

These are two less common projections which are useful. The oblique film is most often used to demonstrate the ribs but may be used also to assess the heart and aorta and in bronchography. The ribs on the side of the pathology are placed against the film since this produces less magnification and so sharper detail. Decubitus films are taken with the x-ray beam horizontal to the floor with the patient lying on the side in a PA position. This is particularly useful to show the flow of fluid when an effusion is suspected but there is some difficulty of interpretation of the PA film.

Children

When x-raying children, much depends on their age and ability to co-operate. The very young are best examined in a supporting chair with the patient's back against the film. The exposure has to be kept brief and this may necessitate moving the x-ray tube closer than the usual 6 feet, so that allowance must be made for magnification. It is helpful to ask the mother, as long as she is not likely to be pregnant, to hold the arms of very young children above their head, as this helps in immobilisation.

Bronchography

There is one practical procedure of particular importance to physiotherapists, that is bronchography. The use of this technique has been declining in recent years so that now it is confined almost completely to the evaluation of bronchiectasis: however, there are two uncommon exceptions. Recently recognised conditions such as adult bronchiolar obliteration provides a small new indication and some physicians inject contrast medium during fibre-optic bronchoscopy to show the peripheral bronchioles beyond their reach.

The standard technique requires the injection of contrast medium, usually oily Dionosil, into the appropriate part of the bronchial tree. This may be done through a catheter passed via the nose or mouth through the anaesthetised larynx. Some experts prefer to pass a needle catheter assembly direct through the skin and cricothyroid membrane, and then advance the catheter into the main bronchus on the side of the pathology. 10ml of Dionosil is injected and the patient positioned, under television control, so that the appropriate area is opacified, and then radiographs are taken. The physiotherapist plays a vital role in the after-care of some patients. If the bronchi are shown to be normal the contrast medium will be cleared by coughing and the normal ciliary action. However, if bronchiectasis or chronic bronchitis is demonstrated then the normal clearing mechanism will be impaired. The radiologist should indicate which lung segment has been injected and then rely on the physiotherapist to accomplish drainage. Occasionally, a similar situation arises when barium enters the bronchial tree in patients who have obstructing lesions of the pharynx or oesophagus. However, the radiologist should be aware that this may occur and make every effort to avoid it.

PRECAUTIONS

On no account should any hospital worker assist in holding a patient during an x-ray exposure, since the dose of radiation throughout life is cumulative and, in the course of years, a biologically significant amount may accumulate. The greatest risk is the induction of leukaemia. X-ray department staff will have devised methods of dealing with very ill or unco-operative patients and that role must be left to them. When a physiotherapist visits an x-ray department to observe procedures she must (1) stand behind the x-ray tube whenever possible, (2) be as far away from the x-ray tube as possible, and, (3) wear a lead rubber apron when necessary.

READING RADIOGRAPHS

When reading a chest radiograph, it is wise to follow some routine order so that no area is missed. A convenient and simple approach is to examine the mediastinum and then the root of each lung followed by the lung itself. Attention is then turned to the heart and, lastly, to what may appear to be minor considerations but are, in fact, areas from which information of enormous value can be obtained, e.g. the diaphragm, the area under the diaphragm, the bony thoracic cage and the surrounding soft tissues. Each of these areas will now be considered in that order.

The mediastinum

The mediastinum is the space between the two pleural cavities, extending from the sternum to the vertebral column. The upper limit is the thoracic inlet and the lower limit, the diaphragm. The space is arbitrarily divided into an upper and lower part by an imaginary line extending horizontally from the lower end of the manubrium sterni to the lower border of the 4th dorsal vertebra. The superior mediastinum is one anatomical unit, but the inferior mediastinum is divided into three parts, anterior, middle and posterior, all of which communicate freely with each other. It is an important radiological step to determine in which of these anatomical divisions an abnormality is located since each characteristically contains different types of pathology.

There are many structures in the mediastinum and it is wise to develop a standard method of examining this part of the film so that nothing is omitted. First, check that the patient is not rotated by noting the distance of the medial end of each clavicle from the vertebral spinous processes. If the patient is rotated to the right, the medial end of the right clavicle will be further from the mid-line than the left. The trachea is the dominant superior mediastinal structure shown on the PA film (Figs. 5/4(a), p. 128 and 5/4(b), p. 132). It usually lies either centrally or just to the right of the mid-line and its walls are parallel to each other. The bifurcation into the major bronchi can usually just be identified. The soft tissues to the left of the trachea contain the great vessels to the head, neck and upper limb and this has a border which is concave to the left as the subclavian artery passes outward over the apex of the lung. At a slightly lower level, the left side of the mediastinum has a convex margin due to the aortic arch. The descending aorta can be traced from the lateral border of the aortic arch downward immediately lateral to the vertebral bodies. Below the aortic arch is the left main pulmonary artery passing into the hilum. The upper part of the left heart border is made up of the appendage of the left atrium and its apex by the left ventricle. On the right side, the soft tissues which lie against the trachea contain the right innominate vein and superior vena cava. Immediately above the right main bronchus, the azygos vein can be identified. Below the bronchus is the right main pulmonary artery and then the lateral surface of the right atrium makes up the right heart border. Occasionally if the patient has taken a very deep inspiration, the inferior vena cava can be identified where it has passed through the diaphragm and is entering the right atrium.

In the elderly, a tortuous innominate artery commonly produces a soft tissue bulge in the right side of the superior mediastinum. At the other end of the age spectrum, the normal thymus of infants frequently extends laterally from the superior mediastinum, particularly on the right, and is said to resemble a sail. However, the normal thymus cannot be identified on the PA film after the age of one. Thymic tumours are uncommon and only the largest protrude laterally far enough to be recognised. This is usually at the level of the manubrium sterni. Small thymic tumours may be apparent on the lateral film where their soft tissue density can be identified immediately posterior to the sternum. A much more common mediastinal mass is the retrosternal goitre. This is most often seen in middle-aged women who may be thyrotoxic. The trachea is usually displaced and may be severely narrowed. Occasionally, the goitre contains calcifications which may be in the form of granules or rings.

Massive lymph node enlargement in the superior mediastinum is a common presentation of lymphoma, particularly in young women (Fig. 5/5, p. 133). This may or may not be associated with lymph node enlargement in the neck. Further lymph node enlargement in the middle mediastinum may splay the main bronchi and projecting posteriorly may cause obstruction to the oesophagus. These patterns of lymph node enlargement are commonly seen in the lymphomas and may accompany carcinoma of the bronchus, particularly of the oat cell variety. Chronic lymphatic leukaemia may present identical appearances. Tuberculosis is still a frequent cause of inflammatory enlargement of mediastinal lymph glands.

Aneurysms of the aorta produce a sharply defined convex opacity anywhere along the course of the vessel. The diagnosis is often obvious because of the calcification contained in the wall of the artery and is easily confirmed by screening the patient and observing pulsations on television or by an aortogram. Dissecting aneurysms, in which blood forces its way between the layers of the wall of the aorta, produce a bulge in the soft tissue opacity of the vessel and are often accompanied by a pleural effusion. In the posterior mediastinum by far the most common mass is a hiatus hernia which can be seen through the cardiac shadow and is recognised because of the air it contains. Generalised distension of the oesophagus, either above a stricture or in achalasia, may become apparent along the lateral border of the mediastinum and usually contains a fluid level. Tumours of the posterior mediastinum frequently arise from neural tissue and may cause erosion of the adjacent ribs or vertebrae.

Lymph node disease below the diaphragm can be demonstrated by *lymphography*. This is a technique in which contrast medium injected into the lymphatics opacifies the lymph nodes. Because lymphatics are so fine and contain clear, colourless liquid they are identified following a subcutaneous injection of blue dye (patent blue violet) into the subcutaneous tissues. The dye is taken up by the lymphatics which can be identified and isolated to allow an injection of contrast medium. The procedure is usually undertaken on the dorsum of the foot and, for an adult of normal size, 7ml of contrast medium is injected on each side. The contrast medium can be demonstrated in the lymph nodes 24 hours later. It will remain in the nodes for, on average, 1 year. Normal lymph nodes are round or oval, up to 3cm in diameter, and show a fine granular internal pattern (Fig. 5/6, p. 134). Lymphomas cause lymph node enlargement and the granular pattern becomes looser (Fig. 5/7, p. 135). Metastases to lymph nodes, which occur commonly in carcinoma of the cervix, uterus, prostate and bladder, are recognised as spherical filling defects within the nodes. By taking plain abdominal films the progress of the disease within the nodes can be followed, or their response to treatment demonstrated. Because some of the oil injected for lymphography will become lodged in the pulmonary capillaries for three or four days following the lymphogram, it is important that the patient has reasonable respiratory function before the test is carried out.

Disease processes in the anterior or superior mediastinum may compress the great vessels causing the superior vena caval syndrome. This most frequently accompanies bronchogenic carcinoma and less often lymphoma and post-radiation fibrosis. It is caused by extrinsic compression of the superior vena cava and other great veins or by thrombosis occurring when blood flow is slowed by compressing masses. The syndrome causes shortness of breath, facial and upper limb swelling with distension of superficial veins in the neck and chest. The abnormality in the veins can be demonstrated by a *superior vena cavagram* in which contrast medium is injected into the antecubital veins on each side (Fig. 5/8, p. 136).

The hila

The opacity of each normal hilum is caused by the pulmonary arteries and veins and to a very minor extent by the walls of the major bronchi (Figs. 5/4(a), p. 128 and 5/4(b), p. 132). Normal lymph nodes do contribute to the hilar opacity but cannot be recognised individually. The density of the two hila is equal and any increase in density on one side suggests that there is a lesion superimposed on the hilum. The centre of the right hilum appears to lie 1–2cm below the left. Anatomically they are actually at the same height, but the upper part of the right hilum comprises the right upper lobe bronchus which does not show on the radiograph, while the upper part of the left hilum contains the left upper lobe artery which is shown. The hilar shadows are of approximately equal size. Rotation of the patient will make one appear larger than the other, this is particularly true when the patient is rotated to the right so that the heart outline no longer covers the left hilum, making it appear more obvious and larger. The lateral border of each hilum is made up of vessels passing to the upper and lower lobes giving it the shape of a Y lying on its side.

Changes in these normal features occur in disease (Figs. 5/9, p. 137; 5/10, p. 138). The most common abnormality is elevation of the hilum usually due to fibrosis in the lung apex caused by tuberculosis or previous radiotherapy; this is sometimes accompanied by deviation of the trachea toward that side. It may also accompany loss of volume due to pulmonary collapse or resection and when this occurs in the lower lobe it may be responsible for depression of the hilum, but this is much less common. The hilum will appear smaller than usual in collapse, since air is lost from the affected segment of lung and the contained vessels become invisible.

Hilar enlargement may be caused by changes in the lymph nodes or blood vessels and unilateral enlargement may be directly due to the development of a primary bronchial tumour. It is essential to decide whether the change is unilateral or bilateral since quite different pathologies are involved in each of these circumstances.

When there is difficulty in deciding whether a hilum is enlarged or not, and whether the enlargement is due to changes in the blood vessels or lymph nodes, tomography in the frontal and oblique planes is used to demonstrate the shape of the mass, vessels being cylindrical and lymph nodes spherical. Bilateral hilar lymph node enlargement is a common presenting feature of sarcoidosis and is occasionally seen in glandular fever. The major differential diagnoses are the lymphomas and chronic lymphatic leukaemia. These diseases are distinguished from each other on their clinical features, blood count, marrow examination and lymph node biopsy. Unilateral hilar lymph node enlargement is usually due to malignant disease. This is most often carcinoma of the bronchus, but sometimes is due to an extra-thoracic primary, such as a renal or testicular tumour. Unilateral hilar lymph node enlargement due to tuberculosis is associated with evidence of a pulmonary lesion and, in the UK, usually occurs in the immigrant population.

It is useful to consider as hilar vessels the right and left main pulmonary arteries and veins and their lobar and proximal segmental branches. When there is a minor degree of dilatation, comparison may have to be made with measurements of normal vessels. This is best done on the right using the basal artery which is easily recognised as it descends from the hilum with the intermediate bronchus on its medial side (Fig. 5/4(a)). The artery is measured half-way along its course and in normal, middle-aged adults, this averages 14mm. On the left, the artery is measured as it arches over the main bronchus and averages 24mm.

The pulmonary vessels may enlarge in lung and heart disease. Bilateral hilar vessel dilatation may occur in emphysema and chronic bronchitis even before pulmonary hypertension has developed, but may be gross after its development when there may also be dilatation of the main pulmonary artery. The same features are seen when pulmonary hypertension is due to multiple small emboli or peripheral arteriolar constriction. There may be associated cardiac enlargement.

Left to right cardiac shunts which produce a high rate of flow at normal pressure, e.g. atrial septal defect, produce considerable hilar vessel dilatation. Shunts which produce high pressure but a low rate of flow, e.g. ventricular septal defect, produce considerably less dilatation. The most gross hilar vessel dilatation is seen when the high rate of flow has caused an increase in pulmonary vascular resistance due to constriction of the peripheral arterioles, this reduces and may even prevent the left to right flow, a circumstance known as the Eisenmenger situation.

Dilatation of the upper lobe vessels alone may be seen in mitral stenosis and left ventricular failure, and is associated with diversion of blood to the upper lobes (Fig. 5/11, p. 139). Increased pulmonary venous pressure in these conditions causes pulmonary oedema which, because of gravity, predominantly affects the lower lobes causing hypoxia and local vasoconstriction with preferential flow to the upper lobes. There may be direct evidence of pulmonary oedema, the features of which are described in the next section.

A very rare, yet interesting, abnormality of the hilar vessels is seen in McLeod's syndrome in which there is hypoplasia and even agenesis of one or other pulmonary artery which is associated with unilateral emphysema. As virtually all of the blood leaving the right side of the heart flows through the contralateral normal lung the pulmonary artery on that side may dilate.

Calcifications in hilar lymph nodes are usually due to previous primary tuberculous infection, but may be associated with histoplasmosis in endemic areas, or, with occupational lung disease particularly coalminer's pneumoconiosis.

The lungs

Before making a detailed examination of any particular area of the chest radiograph, the lungs as a whole should be compared, particularly their relative translucency. Then the upper, middle and lower third on each side is compared with the same area on the other side. If the patient is properly positioned, these should be equal in translucency. The branching opacities passing throughout the lungs are almost solely due to the pulmonary arteries and veins. The size and number of vessels are equal in comparable areas of the two lungs, and they taper as they pass to the periphery. The upper lobe vessels are normally the same diameter or slightly less than those in the lower lobe. Normal peripheral bronchi are not seen, as their walls are so thin and in contact with air on both their internal and external surfaces. However, a bronchus end-on to the x-ray beam will be shown as a ring and this is most commonly seen close to the hilum. Since the right lung contains three lobes and the left only two, there is a difference in the interlobar fissures on the two sides. On the PA film, the fine white line of the horizontal fissure can be identified, in 80 per cent of normal people, extending from the hilum to meet the lateral chest wall between the anterior ends of the 3rd and 5th ribs. Occasional accessory fissures may be seen on the chest film; the most common of these is the azygos fissure at the right apex passing downward to enclose the azygos vein. The oblique, or major fissures are only evident on the lateral film.

Abnormalities in the lung fields become apparent as the normal structures are identified on the film. Little will be missed if the vessels in each lobe are thoroughly inspected. Abnormalities may be found in the size, shape or position of the vessels themselves or in the immediately adjacent lung. Increased diameter of veins in the upper lobes occurs with increase in resistance to pulmonary venous return to the left side of the heart. This is most common in left ventricular failure and mitral stenosis. The distension of these veins when a patient is x-rayed in the supine position must not be mistaken for pathology. A decrease in the diameter of peripheral vessels is seen in emphysema and this can be a relatively localised condition affecting just one lobe. Of course, no vessels at all will be identified in a bulla (Fig. 5/12, p. 140). The vessels are an excellent guide to areas of pulmonary collapse. As a lobe decreases in volume, its contained vessels become crowded together and those in the adjacent lung which expands to fill the space become splayed apart and run in a curved course convex towards the direction of movement (Fig. 5/9, p. 137). This may be a subtle change but is an excellent guide to loss of volume and is, of course, seen following pulmonary resection. There are additional supporting signs of collapse. If the loss of volume is considerable, the interlobar fissures will move towards the collapsed lobe. In the upper lobe, this will cause the horizontal fissure to move upward and vice versa in lower lobe collapse (Fig. 5/9, p. 137). Similar changes will occur in the oblique fissures. Collapse of a whole lung or lobe is accompanied by displacement of the mediastinum towards that side and elevation of the diaphragm. In addition, since the collapsed lobe no longer contains air, it increases in density.

Vessel changes are an essential feature of emphysema. This is a condition in which there is an increase in the size of the air spaces distal to the terminal bronchioles with dilatation and destruction of their walls. This always results in a decrease in the number and calibre of the small blood vessels and is accompanied by an increase in lung volume which causes a barrel-shaped chest with the sternum bowed forward, very low flat diaphragms and narrowing of the mediastinum with a cardiothoracic ratio as low as 1:3. Bullae are a common feature. When the condition is severe, the peripheral vessel changes cause a rise in the pulmonary blood pressure with dilatation of the central arteries and eventually right heart failure and enlargement. Emphysema and chronic bronchitis commonly occur together. There are no specific radiological features of chronic bronchitis and the importance of the chest radiograph is to identify infection and assess the degree of emphysema and associated heart failure. Small ill-defined opacities anywhere in the lung are a common feature of chronic bronchitis and represent consolidation. There may also be small linear opacities due to fibrotic scarring and sometimes to bronchial wall thickening in associated bronchiectasis. These linear and nodular densities may be gross enough to obscure the pulmonary vessels.

Radiologists use the term consolidation to cover all the pathological conditions which replace the air in the lung by tissue or fluid of greater density (Figs. 5/13, p. 141; 5/14, p. 142). Consolidation occupying a whole lobe has distinctive features: as the air in the affected lung is replaced by oedema, pus or tumour, it increases in density. If the bronchi remain patent and air-filled, they now become visible, creating an air bronchogram and is pathognomonic of consolidation (Fig. 5/15, p. 143). This sign is lost if the bronchi also become filled with retained secretions or pus. An air bronchogram is a feature of lobar pneumonia but is not seen in bronchopneumonia which causes small nodular opacities.

Oedema fluid lost into the lung as a result of inflammation or heart failure will descend under the influence of gravity. This is apparent on the chest radiograph as long as the patient spends a proportion of the day upright. The fluid will descend until it reaches a pleural surface, this is most striking in the upper lobe when the fluid is arrested at the horizontal fissure (Fig. 5/10, p. 138). The oedema of heart failure occurs in two patterns, (a) alveolar and (b) interstitial. Alveolar oedema causes multiple small nodular opacities in the perihilar region, usually affecting both lungs and associated with an acute cardiac episode. Interstitial oedema has quite a different distribution causing fine linear opacities 1–2cm long, extending to the periphery of the lung at the bases. These are known as Kerley 'B' lines. Less commonly, similar Kerley 'A' lines will be found in the substance of the upper lobes. Interstitial oedema is also seen in conditions which obstruct the mediastinal lymphatics, the most common being metastases from breast cancer.

Kerley 'B' lines, which in heart failure are caused by fluid accumulating in the interlobular septa, are seen in a number of pulmonary diseases, e.g. sarcoidosis and bronchiectasis and may also be caused by the deposition of heavy metal particles in pneumoconiosis. These conditions may also cause coarser linear opacities due to fibrosis. A network of linear opacities is responsible for the condition known as honeycomb lung. This is seen in two rare conditions, histiocytosis-X and tuberous sclerosis, but a very similar pattern occurs in bronchiectasis, mucoviscidosis and idiopathic interstitial pulmonary fibrosis. In these conditions, the lung tissue is replaced by air spaces, 1–3cm in diameter, enclosed by a fibrous wall. The pulmonary vessels may be obscured by this pattern which can cause pulmonary hypertension with central arterial dilatation and cardiomegaly.

Bronchiectasis is most often a sequel to childhood infection, particularly when there has been some degree of bronchostenosis. It commonly follows collapse associated with whooping cough or measles and is a constant companion of pancreatic fibrocystic disease. The abnormalities are not confined to the bronchi and include evidence of collapse, infection, fibrosis and occasionally emphysema in the surrounding lung. The chest radiograph in mild cases may be normal, so that bronchography is necessary for diagnosis. More often, there is an increase in lung markings due to increased vascularity associated with infection, thickened bronchial walls and occasionally finger-like opacities due to bronchi filled with secretions or pus (Figs. 5/16(a) and (b), pp. 144-5). Cystic dilatation of bronchi may be visible as 1–5cm diameter thin-walled ring opacities, sometimes containing fluid levels (Figs. 5/17(a) and (b), pp. 146-7). These can be very similar in appearance to bullae, but often involve a whole segment or lobe. The changes due to bronchiectasis are most frequently seen at the bases as drainage is more of a problem than in the upper lobes. Evidence of collapse, consolidation and fibrosis will often also be present.

Two common conditions of the pleural cavity, effusion and pneumothorax will be recognised while examining the lung fields. There are many causes of pleural effusion, the fluid may be a transudate caused by an increase in pulmonary capillary pressure or a decreased level of plasma protein, this is seen in heart failure and renal failure. It may be an exudate formed as a result of infection or tumour in the adjacent lung, or it may be frank blood after trauma. The effusion, from whatever cause, obscures the underlying lung and because of gravity, this most often affects the lung bases (Fig. 5/18, p. 148). The outline of adjacent structures such as the diaphragm and the heart outline are lost (Fig. 5/20, p. 150). On a lateral view, the effusion causes the lower vertebral bodies to appear greater in density than those above. The fluid may pass upward along the costal surface of the chest and rarely along the mediastinum. A complex appearance occurs when fluid occupies the oblique and horizontal fissures. Very large effusions displace the mediastinum to the other side; indeed, if the mediastinum remains central, one should suspect that the lung hidden by the effusion has collapsed.

A pneumothorax is the event in which air occupies the potential space between the parietal and visceral pleura. This occurs when a bulla or lung abscess bursts into this space or following trauma when air may enter from the exterior or from a lung pierced by a fractured rib. Endoscopy causing perforation of the trachea or oesophagus is occasionally responsible for a pneumothorax which is accompanied by air in the mediastinum. A broncho-pleural fistula causes a very dramatic pneumothorax and most commonly follows pulmonary resection (Fig. 5/19, p. 149), but may also be associated with pulmonary infection or tumour. On the chest radiograph, air is shown displacing the lung medially. The pleura covering the lung can be recognised as a fine white line and, of course, there is an absence of lung markings in the area occupied by air. The bronchovascular markings in the partially retracted lung are blurred due to the increased transmission of cardiac pulsation. A very large pneumothorax may displace the mediastinum and may so compress the lung, even on the opposite side, that breathing becomes severely embarrassed; this is a tension pneumothorax. When effusions and pneumothorax co-exist, a horizontal fluid level will be present.

The heart

Most cardiac conditions are apparent clinically and it is very uncommon for a diagnosis to become apparent for the first time as a result of a chest radiograph. For instance, an increase in heart size due to hypertension will be due to left ventricular enlargement which is evident clinically and can be confirmed by the ECG. The role of plain films is to demonstrate abnormalities of the heart size and shape which indicate the degree of embarrassment caused by the primary defect and to show the haemodynamic consequences of the lesion on the lung vessels. PA and lateral films provide a base line against which progression of the disease can be assessed. Oblique views, barium swallow and screening have a small specialised role.

The simplest method of assessing the heart size is the ratio between the maximum diameter of the heart and the internal diameter of the rib cage. This is the cardiothoracic ratio and is normally less than 1:2. In an adult, a cardiac diameter greater than 15.5cm is nearly always abnormal. A change of 1.5cm in heart diameter between successive films is usually significant. Of course, measurement must be made in the absence of effusion or consolidation which obscures the heart border. Allowance must be made in children for difficulties of positioning and for the film being exposed during expiration. Allowance must also be made, on serial films, for normal growth.

Several conditions (such as hypertension and aortic stenosis) which cause the heart to do more work than usual cause thickening of the heart muscle without necessarily causing any increase in size. Eventually, cardiac dilatation may occur when the hypertrophied heart muscle fails. Cardiac enlargement can be broadly divided into:

1. Conditions which cause generalised enlargement such as myocardial failure due to rheumatic fever or enlargement due to pericardial effusion.
2. Conditions which cause enlargement of individual chambers, e.g. mitral stenosis causing enlargement of the left atrium.

There are numerous examples of acquired heart diseases causing enlargement of individual chambers. Hypertension causes hypertrophy of the left ventricular muscle which at first retains its normal shape but eventually the apex extends downward and to the left and is often accompanied by unfolding of the aorta. Aortic stenosis produces similar myocardial changes, enlargement only occurring when there is failure. Aortic regurgitation usually produces a much greater degree of enlargement of left ventricular type. Mitral valve disease is usually a combination of both stenosis and regurgitation. This causes enlargement of the left atrium with prominence of the appendage in the upper part of the left heart border, and a double outline to the right heart border. A very large left atrium may elevate and obstruct the left lower lobe bronchus with collapse of the peripheral lung tissue. It may be impossible to tell from the radiograph if one or both atria are enlarged, and this may also apply to the ventricles. Angiocardiography is much more accurate in these assessments than plain films. Pulmonary stenosis often causes no enlargement unless the degree of obstruction is very severe, the most striking feature is usually post-stenotic dilatation of the pulmonary artery. Consideration of congenital heart disease is not appropriate to this chapter and can be found discussed concisely in Simon's *Principles of Chest X-ray Diagnosis*.

Pericardial effusion can be associated with a wide variety of diseases including infection, heart failure, uraemia, myocardial infarction and malignant disease. It causes an increase in cardio-thoracic ratio and a rounded outline with loss of the normal details of shape such as the angle between the atrial appendage and the left ventricle. The two sides of the heart become mirror images of each other. The enlargement often occurs very suddenly. The diagnosis is best confirmed by ultrasound. The radiological diagnosis can be difficult if there is an accompanying pleural effusion or if the differential diagnosis includes cardiomyopathy.

[cont. on p. 153]

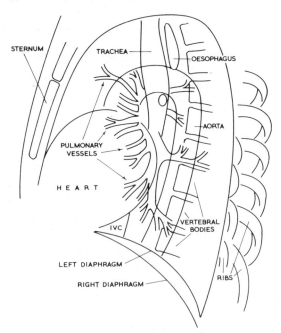

FIG. 5/3 (a) Artist's impression of normal findings on a lateral radiograph, *cf* 5/3b

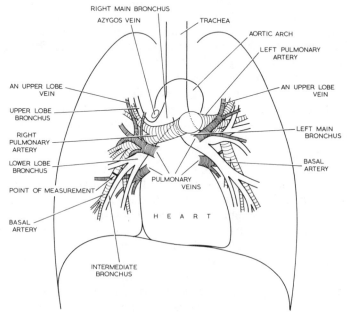

FIG. 5/4 (a) Artist's impression of normal mediastinal anatomy

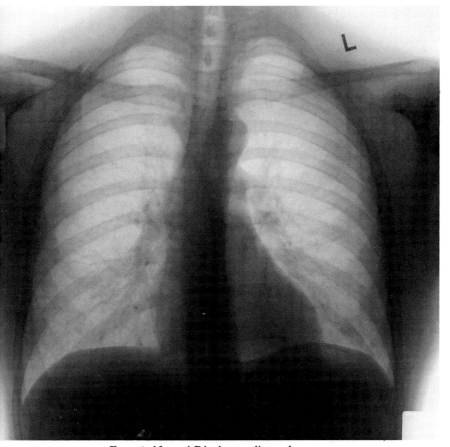

FIG. 5/1 Normal PA chest radiograph

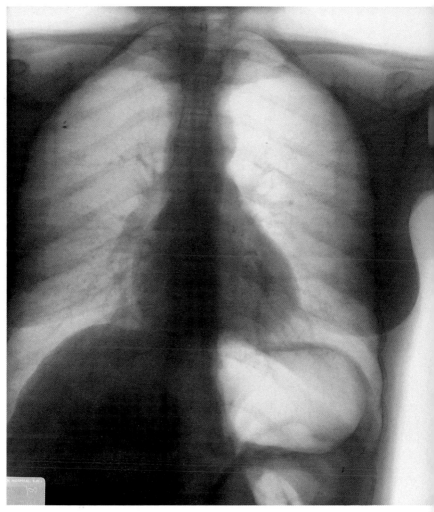

FIG. 5/2 Normal AP chest radiograph

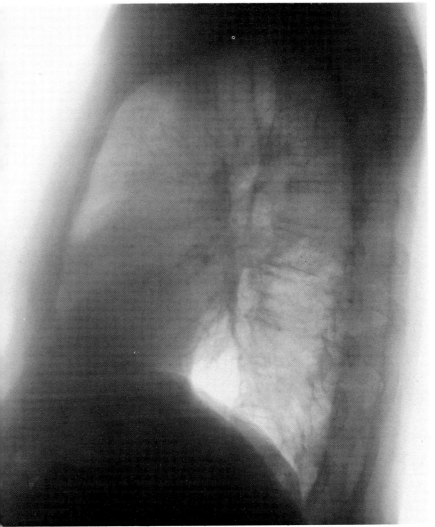

FIG. 5/3 (b) Normal lateral chest radiograph

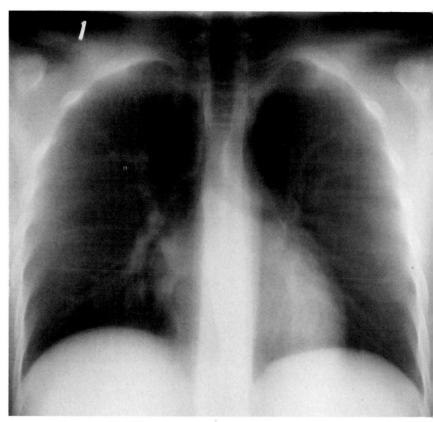

FIG. 5/4 (b) Whole lung tomogram demonstrating normal mediastinal anatomy

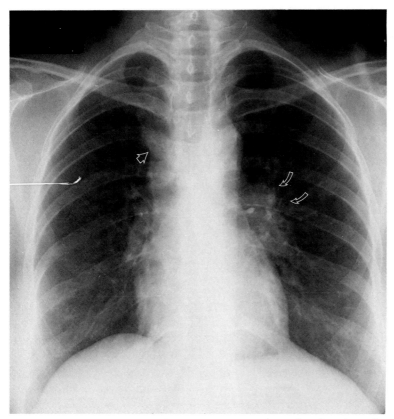

FIG. 5/5 Hodgkin's disease in a young woman causing lymph node enlargement in the right side of the superior mediastinum (broad arrow) and at the left hilum (curved arrows)

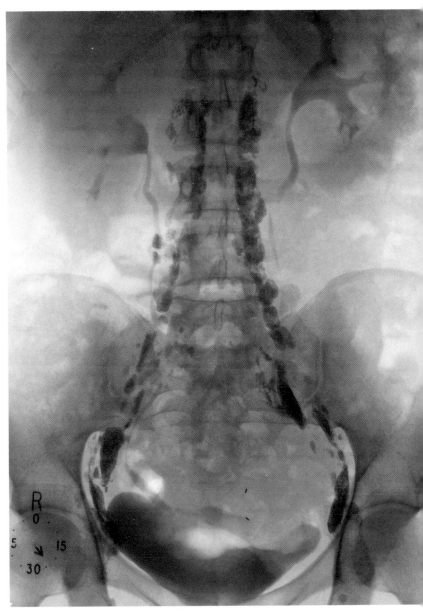

FIG. 5/6 Normal lymphogram showing oval lymph nodes with a fine granular pattern

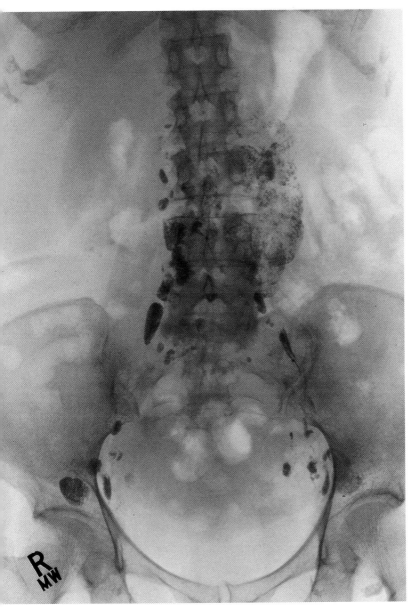

FIG. 5/7 Lymphoma overlying the left side of the vertebral bodies. The
opacified lymph nodes are enlarged and foamy in this area

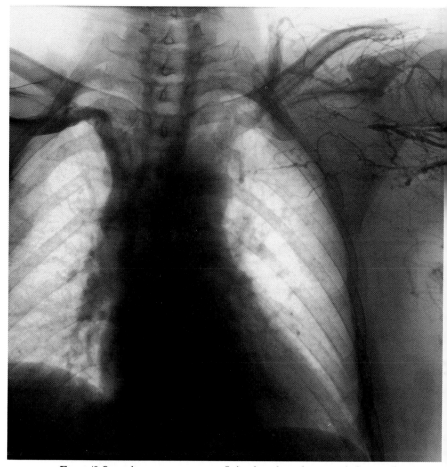

FIG. 5/8 Superior vena cavagram. Injections have been made into each arm. On the right the large veins appear normal, but on the left there is complete obstruction of the innominate vein with multiple collateral vessels demonstrated in the axilla

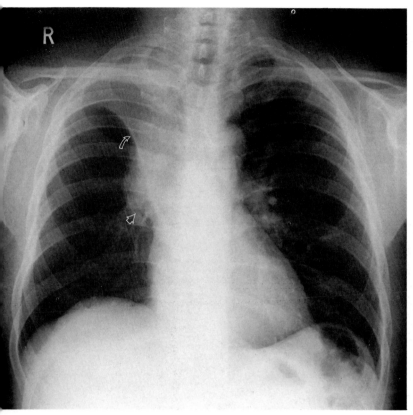

FIG. 5/9 A mass at the right hilum (broad arrow) causing collapse of the right upper lobe with elevation of the horizontal fissure (curved arrows) and displacement of the trachea toward that side

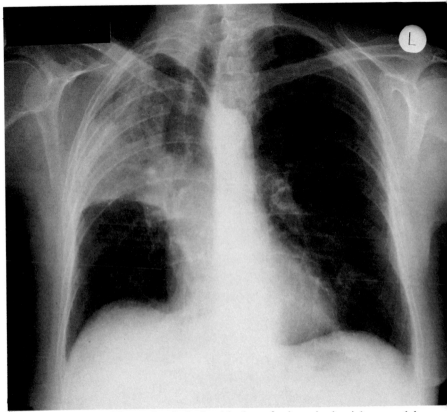

FIG. 5/10 The trachea is deviated by loss of volume in the right upper lobe. The horizontal fissure has maintained its normal position

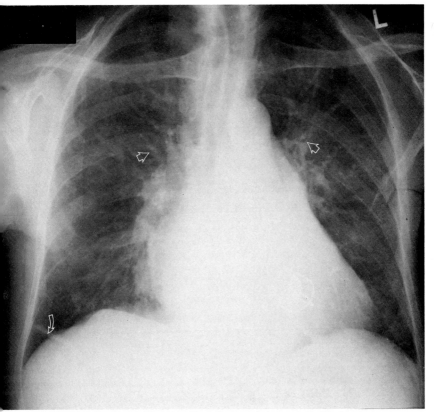

FIG. 5/11 Upper lobe blood diversion (broad arrows) due to left-sided heart failure, in a patient with gross cardiomegaly and a previous aortic valve replacement. There is a small area of atelectasis (curved arrow) at the right base)

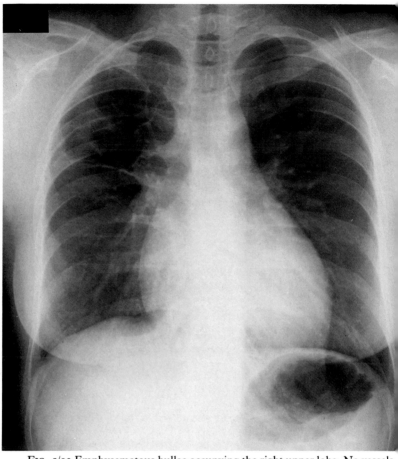

FIG. 5/12 Emphysematous bullae occupying the right upper lobe. No vessels can be identified in the affected area

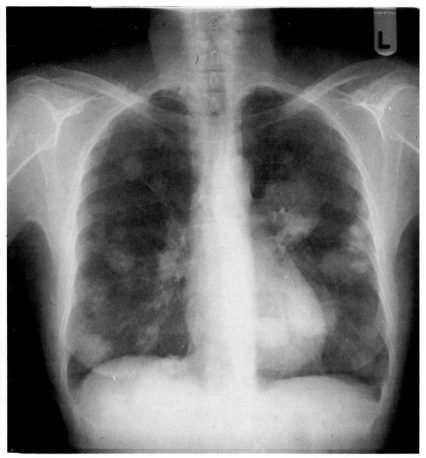

FIG. 5/13 Soft tissue opacities, due to cancer metastases, have developed throughout each lung

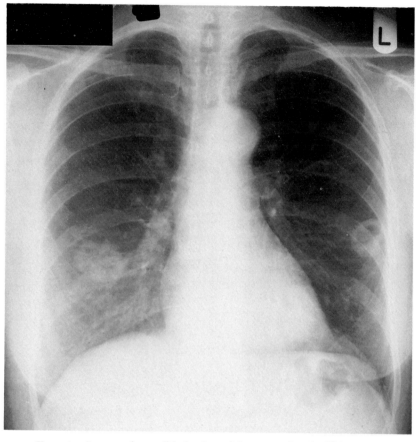

FIG. 5/14 An area of consolidation in each lung contains air. This appearance occurs in lung abscess and, rarely, in metastases, as is the cause here

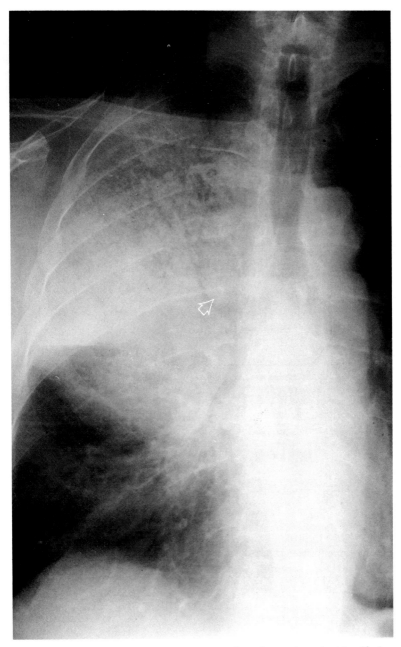

FIG. 5/15 The air-filled upper lobe bronchus (broad arrow) can be identified against the surrounding consolidated lung. An air bronchogram

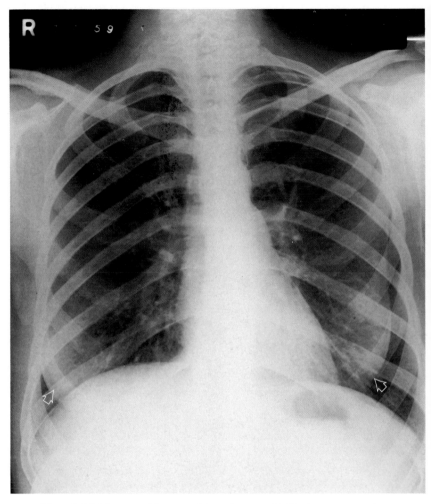

FIG. 5/16 (a) Increased lung markings due to fluid-filled bronchi can be seen at each base (broad arrows)

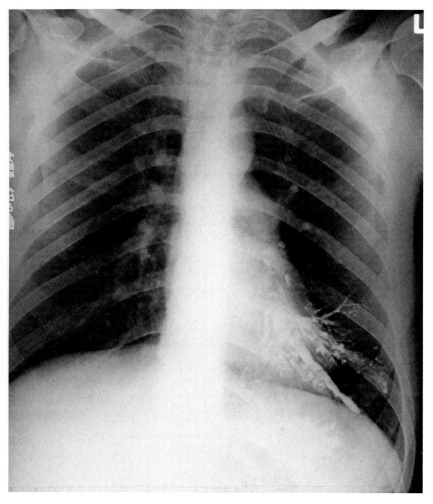

FIG. 5/16 (b) Left lower lobe bronchogram confirms the dilated cylindrical bronchi

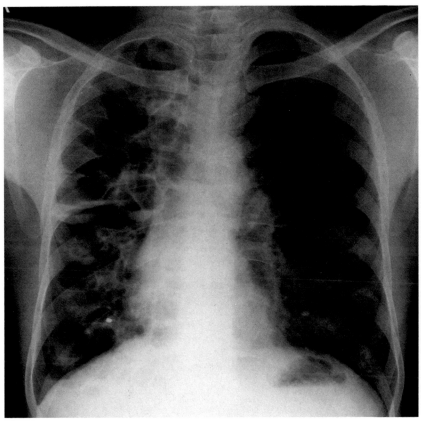

FIG. 5/17 (a) Cystic bronchiectasis, with some fluid levels, occupies virtually all of the right lung. The left lung appears normal

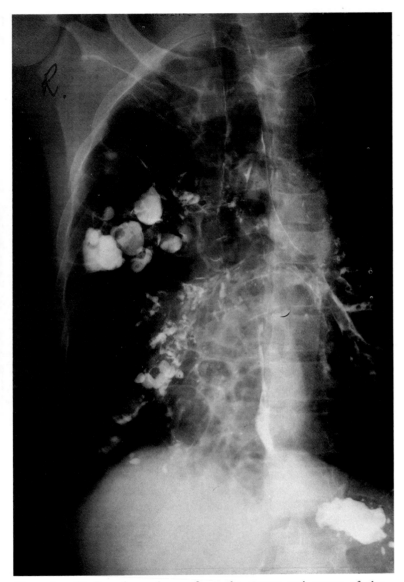

FIG. 5/17 (b) Bronchography confirms the nature and extent of the abnormality and the relative normality on the left

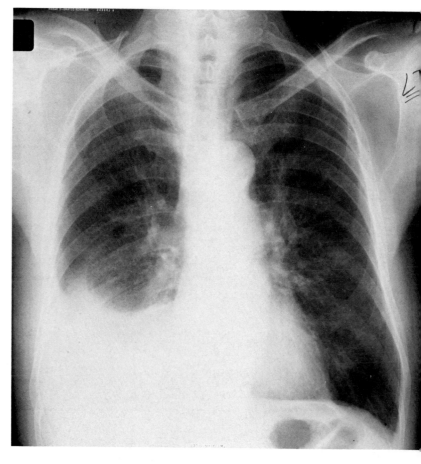

FIG. 5/18 An effusion obscuring the right lung base, diaphragm and right heart border

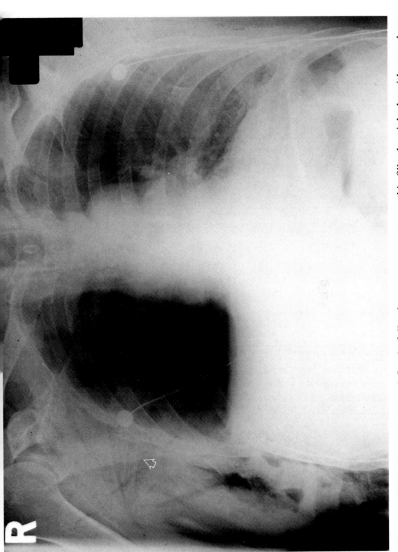

FIG. 5/19 Right broncho-pleural fistula following pneumonectomy. Air fills the right hemithorax above a fluid level. Surgical emphysema is seen in pectoral muscle fibres overlying the right axilla (arrow)

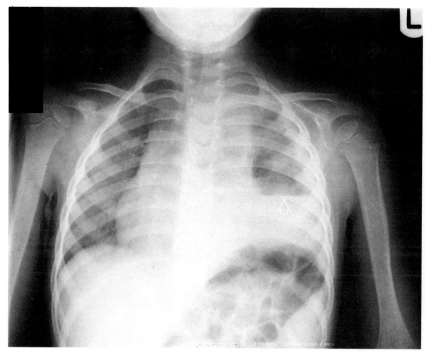

FIG. 5/20 The heart is displaced well to the right by an effusion associated with a staphylococcal lung abscess which itself is responsible for some of the displacement. A fluid level can be seen in the abscess cavity

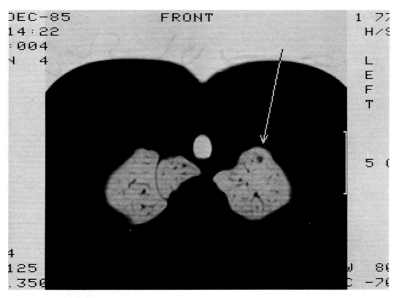

FIG. 5/21 The small white soft tissue density of a metastasis is demonstrated anteriorly in the left lung (arrow)

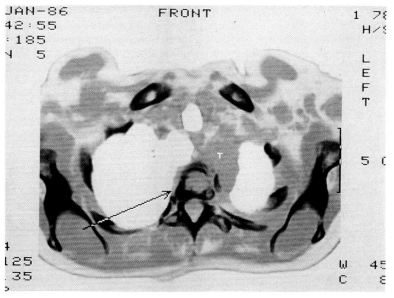

FIG. 5/22 A carcinoma of bronchus (T) is invading the superior mediastinum and the adjacent vertebral body (arrow). This pattern of spread in a bronchial carcinoma is known as a Pancoast tumour

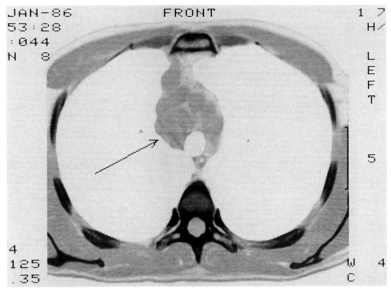

FIG. 5/23 Enlarged lymph nodes (arrow) in the superior mediastinum indicates a lymphoma

The cardiomyopathies are diseases of heart muscle, many of which are of unknown origin. The causes which have been determined are very wide-ranging, including infection, alcoholism, endocrine and malignant disease. The heart muscle may be affected alone or it may be part of a generalised systemic disease. There is usually generalised non-specific enlargement involving both sides of the heart. The degree of enlargement may be trivial but is often gross. The heart's outline is rounded with loss of detail very similar to that of pericardial effusion – indeed the two conditions can occur together. Eventually severe heart failure often occurs producing changes in the pulmonary vessels.

The diaphragm

As a routine, the PA chest film is exposed in full inspiration when, in slim individuals, the right diaphragm lies opposite the posterior end of the right 10th rib. In the obese, the normal position of the diaphragm may be a good deal higher. The left diaphragm usually descends 1 or 2cm further than the right but may in perfectly normal patients lie at a higher level than the right. This is most often due to gas in the underlying stomach or splenic flexure of colon displacing the diaphragm upward. On a lateral film, the right diaphragm can be traced all the way from the posterior to the anterior abdominal wall but the outline of the left diaphragm is lost where it is in contact with the heart shadow.

Movement of the diaphragm during breathing can be demonstrated either by exposing two chest radiographs, one during inspiration and the other during expiration or by screening the patient and watching the movement of the diaphragm on television. There are many reasons for a diaphragm failing to move on breathing. These include inflammatory conditions above the diaphragm such as pneumonia and pleurisy, or below it such as a subphrenic abscess or pancreatitis. Damage to the phrenic nerve by tumour invasion or trauma is another common cause.

The thickness of the diaphragm can be measured when there is air in bowel below the diaphragm and air in the lung above. The normal thickness is 5–8mm. This may be grossly increased when there is an effusion lying between the lung and diaphragm or when there is a subphrenic abscess.

The most common abnormality of the diaphragm on a PA chest film is elevation. This may be unilateral or bilateral and physiological or pathological. Of the physiological causes, unilateral elevation is most often due to gas distension of the gastric fundus or splenic flexure and bilateral elevation to obesity, pregnancy or failure of the patient to take a deep inspiration at the time of the exposure.

The common pathological causes of unilateral diaphragm elevation include:

1. Inflammatory changes in the lung or pleura
2. Subphrenic abscess
3. Pulmonary collapse with the diaphragm rising to fill the space left by the diminished lung volume
4. Pulmonary embolism whether or not this is associated with actual lung infarction
5. Hepatomegaly or splenomegaly
6. Phrenic palsy due to mediastinal tumour or trauma
7. Weakness of the diaphragmatic muscle which, when it involves the whole diaphragm, is known as eventration.
8. Pain due to a fractured rib may prevent full inspiration so that the diaphragm appears raised and this is usually most evident on the side of the fracture
9. Scoliosis of such a degree that it causes thoracic cage deformity.

Bilateral diaphragm elevation occurs most commonly due to pressure from below, either from ascites or a huge abdominal tumour such as an ovarian cyst. It may also be seen in those conditions which make the lungs rigid so that they fail to expand fully on breathing such as lymphangitis carcinomatosa when the rigidity is due to oedema fluid.

The diaphragm may be pushed into a lower level than normal by a large effusion or pneumothorax or by a hyperinflated lung when a bronchus is partly obstructed – this occurs most frequently in children due to inhaling a peanut, but in adults is most often due to a tumour. Very large pulmonary tumours, usually secondary deposits, can also depress the diaphragm.

On a plain film the whole length of the diaphragm outlined by the air above it should be able to be seen; if the silhouette of any part is lost this is due to the air-filled lung being replaced by something of greater density. This is most often a pleural effusion or pulmonary consolidation.

Elevation of the diaphragm compresses the lung at the base so that small 'plate-like' areas of atelectasis will be seen. These are white lines 4 to 5cm in length and 2 to 3mm thick lying horizontally above the diaphragm and usually of only temporary existence, the lung returning to normal when the diaphragm takes up its normal position.

Sub-diaphragmatic area

Reference has already been made to some abnormalities of this area in the section on the diaphragm. There is often a good deal of information about upper abdominal structures on the chest radiograph and some of this is extremely useful in the management of hospital in-patients. The value of ensuring that the tip of a nasogastric tube does actually lie in a position from which gastric fluid can be aspirated is obvious, the same applies to chest and upper abdominal drains. In the erect position, the gastric fundus nearly always contains a small amount of air and larger volumes will be seen in the nervous individual who swallows air and children given a fizzy drink in an inducement to behave for the chest radiograph. Air will normally be seen in the splenic flexure of colon, but the hepatic flexure is usually displaced downward by the liver and does not appear on the chest film. Occasionally, however, the hepatic flexure actually lies between the liver and the diaphragm. The length of an air fluid level in the stomach gives a very good indication of the volume of gastric juice which is retained and is a common feature of upper intestinal obstruction.

Free air in the abdominal cavity is most frequently seen after abdominal surgery, including laparoscopy. Larger amounts of air accumulate under the diaphragm after upper abdominal rather than pelvic surgery, and will be absorbed in the course of the following week. Increasing amounts of air after surgery indicates either perforated bowel or infection by gas-forming organisms. Subphrenic air is easily recognised as a low density area following the smoothly curved lower surface of the diaphragm. Exactly similar features are seen following perforation of the bowel. Perforation of a duodenal ulcer or the caecum produces most gas under the right diaphragm, and a perforated diverticulum of the sigmoid colon most air under the left.

Gas produced in a subphrenic abscess is associated usually with a fluid level, and is loculated rather than following the curve of the diaphragm. This is seen most often following surgery or may occur with any of the conditions causing peritonitis, particularly if this arises in an upper abdominal viscus, such as in pancreatitis. Often the diaphragm is paralysed and elevated and there may be a pleural effusion.

Occasionally, calcification due to hydatid disease, previous tuberculosis or, very rarely, metastases will be found in the liver. Calcification associated with the spleen is rarely shown on a chest film, and then most often is merely due to calcification in the splenic artery. Costal cartilage calcification is extremely common and is considered in the section on the thoracic cage.

Air in the lung occupying the posterior costo-phrenic recess causes the uppermost part of the liver to appear less dense on the PA film than the rest of the liver. This will be lost if an effusion occupies the recess and this can be the only sign of a very small effusion. It is important to look through the diaphragm for lesions, particularly metastases, in the lowermost parts of the lungs.

The thoracic cage

The thoracic cage comprises the dorsal vertebrae and their disc spaces together with the ribs and costal cartilages and the associated ligaments. All of these structures are not evident on every chest film, but there is an opportunity to examine two bony appendages to the thoracic cage, i.e. the clavicle and scapula. The abnormalities of this area can be divided into generalised changes of form and localised changes of individual bones. Of course, any bone in this area is prey to the same conditions such as infection, trauma and tumour as any other bone.

On a properly exposed PA chest film, the dorsal vertebrae are only just visible so that the position of the disc spaces can be recognised but it is usually impossible to make any diagnostic assessment of the vertebrae themselves. However, a scoliosis or kyphosis will be obvious. On the convex side of the scoliosis, the spine will project beyond the outline of the mediastinum and must not be mistaken for a mass in that location. This is less obvious when the convexity is on the left, when the opacity due to the spine may be hidden by the heart and aortic arch. Kyphosis is recognised by the crowding together of the upper ribs. In normal circumstances, the ribs are symmetrical in size and shape and in the spacing between them. The posterior ends of the ribs are approximately horizontal and the anterior ends pass inward and downward parallel to the other ribs on that side. Gross discrepancy in this pattern will be associated with a dorsal scoliosis, the ribs on the convex side of the curve lying higher and spaced further apart than normal, and the ribs on the concave side lower and closer together. These bony changes produce a difference in the volume of each hemithorax, limiting expansion of the lung on the smaller side. Similarly, loss of volume due to pulmonary resection or collapse will be accompanied by secondary changes in the thoracic cage with the ribs lying closer together on the side of the lung lesion.

The costal cartilages which join the anterior ends of the ribs to the sternum are only visible when calcified. This is a common process of ageing. The pattern of calcification is very variable but is usually linear or punctate. The latter, particularly when it lies in the 1st or 2nd costal cartilage, can be mistaken for pulmonary calcification due to previous pulmonary tuberculosis or, when associated with the lower ribs, for biliary or renal calculi. Symmetrical distribution of costal cartilage calcification is extremely helpful in differential diagnosis.

The ribs may be affected by a generalised change in bone density: most often this is a decrease in density due to osteoporosis and is seen in post-menopausal women; less often is it due to osteomalacia. Rarely, there may be an increase in bone density which can be congenital, as in osteopetrosis, or acquired, when the most common cause is metastases due to carcinoma of the prostate. Any assessment of bone density must be made on a properly exposed film since, if the chest radiograph is underexposed, the bones will appear with a greater-than-normal density.

On a PA chest film, the medial end of the clavicle overlies the posterior end of the 4th rib; in the AP projection, which is common for portables, it is projected above the 1st rib. The epiphysis at the medial end of the clavicle is one of the last to fuse and should not be mistaken for a fracture. Laterally, the clavicle articulates with the acromion process of the scapula which is a common site for degenerative change and for subluxation due to trauma. Fracture of the clavicle is the most common pathology seen although the whole variety of bone disease, including agenesis, may be encountered. At its medial end, the articulation of the clavicle with the sternum can be identified on the PA chest film. The lateral margin of the manubrium sterni is projected just lateral to the mediastinal soft tissues. This may be obscured on the left by the density of the aortic arch, but on the right, care must be taken not to mistake this normal structure for mediastinal lymph node enlargement. This feature will be exaggerated if the patient is rotated to the right and, in this position in children, the separate centres of ossification may be identified overlying the lung field. On the lateral film anterior bowing of the sternum will be apparent in emphysematous patients.

The patient positioned for the PA film stands with the shoulders forward to draw the scapula laterally clear of the major part of the lung field. The tip of the blade of scapula presents a rounded outline, which can give the appearance of a lung lesion, but should be recognised by its continuity with the medial border of the scapula passing upward and medially.

Of the localised abnormalities of these bones, the most common is a congenital anomaly in the number of ribs. This is most often recognised when there is an additional rib associated with the 7th cervical vertebra. This may be virtually a complete rib articulating anteriorly with the 1st true rib or there may be a small bony component posteriorly and only a fibrous band anteriorly. Either of these may compress the nerves of the brachial plexus or the vessels passing to the upper limb. Occasionally, instead of additional ribs, there are less than usual on each side, but this is not clinically important. Bifid ribs are Y-shaped, usually with the forked end anteriorly; they are completely incidental findings and never the cause of symptoms.

The most common acquired abnormality of ribs is fracture. If there is no displacement, a recent fracture may be difficult to recognise on the chest film, particularly where the rib is overlaid by pulmonary vessels. At the periphery, where the ribs are in profile, fracture detection is much easier. There is often an accompanying soft tissue swelling due to haematoma. Callus formation due to healing makes the diagnosis straightforward and the rib often shows permanent thickening and distortion when the fracture has occurred in an adult. Remember that not all fractures are caused by direct trauma, stress fractures due to coughing may be seen particularly in the lower ribs and in the first ribs due to pack-carrying.

An interesting, though uncommon, rib abnormality is notching. These are indentations on the inferior surface of the middle third of the rib and must not be confused with the normal irregularity of that surface. There are many causes, the most common being coarctation of the aorta in which the notching is caused by dilated intercostal vessels carrying blood to the dorsal aorta below the area of narrowing. The precise rib involved varies depending on the level of the coarctation and on other associated arterial abnormalities. Dilated intercostal vessels may cause notching in subclavian artery occlusion and in severe congenital reduction in pulmonary blood supply when the intercostals form part of the collateral pathway of blood to the para-hilar tissues. Following thoracotomy, particularly for pleurodesis, the intercostal vessels may dilate enough to cause notching. The only non-vascular cause worth mentioning is neurofibromatosis in which the benign nerve fibre tumours erode the rib by compression.

The detection of destructive lesions, such as metastases, in the ribs is not always easy, particularly if the lesion is purely lytic with no accompanying sclerosis. Small lesions of this type overlaid by lung tissue are easily missed on the chest radiograph, and the patient's complaint of pain or tenderness at a particular point is a very much better guide to the presence of metastases. Views which project the affected portion of rib free of the lung may be valuable. Metastases from carcinoma of the prostate are usually greater in density than the surrounding normal bone and are much easier to detect than purely destructive lesions.

Rib resection at previous thoracotomy will usually be known to the patient and to the physiotherapist, and the radiographic change is obvious. A sub-periosteal approach, retaining the rib, may be the cause of irregularity of the lower margin of a rib and is often accompanied by permanent pleural thickening.

The soft tissues

The breasts often cause easily recognised soft tissue opacities overlaying the lung bases. This is not true in elderly patients with large pendulous breasts which overlie the upper abdomen, nor in those with very small breasts which cause no appreciable opacity. One breast shadow can be made to disappear if that breast is pressed firmly against the x-ray cassette while the film is exposed. One should always look for a change in the pectoral muscles to confirm that a chest radiograph does actually show a mastectomy. Asymmetry in the breast outline may result from previous surgery or from disease, particularly a carcinoma causing a small contracted or ulcerated breast. Silicone prostheses are responsible for very dense rounded opacities usually at a higher level than the normal breast. Heavily built men sometimes have such thick pectoral muscles that they cause a prominent soft tissue density. Neither breast nor pectoral muscle opacities should be mistaken for a pulmonary abnormality.

Soft tissue tumours, particularly benign lesions such as fibromata or warts, may cause very sharply defined rounded opacities when they lie on the anterior or posterior surface of the chest and can easily be mistaken for a pulmonary lesion. The real cause is obvious when the patient is examined.

Delto-pectoral skin flaps, so often used in head and neck surgery, cast a very distinctive tubular shadow across the upper medial part of the thorax.

Air may be seen in the soft tissues of the thorax or neck following surgery. This is most common after thoracotomy, laryngectomy or breast surgery and can also be seen by air tracking upward through the mediastinum after perforation of the oesophagus at endoscopy. This air is known as surgical emphysema and, in trauma, is a particularly important feature when a fractured rib penetrates the lung.

Calcification in the thoracic soft tissues is uncommon. Calcified tuberculous nodes may be seen in the neck and occasionally in the axilla. There are a number of congenital conditions, e.g. myositis ossificans and calcinosis universalis, in which the soft tissues calcify. The cysts of the parasite *Taenia solium* (cysticercosis) may enter muscle and calcify when they die, producing dense oval opacities 1 to 2cm in diameter.

COMPUTED TOMOGRAPHY (CT)

Computed tomography scanning produces cross-sectional images of any part of the body. A conventional *x*-ray source rotates around the patient and the transmitted beam strikes detectors which are 100 times more sensitive than film. The signal produced from the detectors is processed by a computer and reconstituted as a picture which represents a 1cm thick body slice. Enough adjacent slices are imaged to provide the anatomical information required to assess the patient's disease. The advantage of computed tomography over conventional radiography is the ability to distinguish between various soft tissues of near identical density as well as to distinguish fat, bone and air. The pictures produced can be degraded by voluntary and involuntary movement so that in examining the chest the patient is asked not to breathe while each picture slice is being obtained.

Because there is an enormous density difference between air-containing lung and the soft tissue of pulmonary metastases CT is by far the most sensitive way of detecting lung deposits (Fig. 5/21, p. 151). The transverse plane is particularly helpful in identifying deposits which lie anterior or posterior to the heart or mediastinum. Lesions around the edge of the lung are more easily detected by CT than on conventional film. In those malignant diseases which commonly first metastasise to the lung it is reasonable to carry out periodic CT scanning of the chest if the conventional films are normal. With primary bronchial carcinomas CT provides useful information concerning the relationship of the tumour to the chest wall or the mediastinum. If the chest wall is invaded by tumour this may not preclude resection but the surgeon will know that he must expect to excise part of the chest wall. However, invasion of the primary tumour into the mediastinum to any degree may prevent complete removal (Fig. 5/22, p. 151). Because the mediastinum contains a good deal of fat, lymph node enlargement within the mediastinum is easily detected. This is particularly true in the superior mediastinum. This point is of great importance in the pre-operative assessment of patients with carcinoma of the bronchus. Enlargement of lymph nodes at the hila is equally well demonstrated by conventional tomograms as with CT.

Primary mediastinal pathology can be accurately assessed by CT which will not only show the size and shape of any mass but also indicate whether it is composed of fat or soft tissue or whether it contains any calcification (Fig. 5/23, p. 152). Assessment of these features and the position of an abnormal mass are often sufficient for specific diagnosis. Intravenous contrast medium can be helpful in showing the relationship of mediastinal masses to vessels and in the identification of aneurysms.

Bronchiectasis and bullae are accurately demonstrated by CT, but its role in pulmonary fibrosis, emphysema and interstitial oedema are still under investigation.

NUCLEAR MAGNETIC RESONANCE (NMR)

This new imaging technique which is sometimes called *magnetic resonance imaging* (MRI) depends upon the ability of certain atoms to behave as small magnets which spin like wobbling tops. In a magnetic field the atoms line up in one direction. If radio frequency energy is applied, the atoms flip over into the higher energy state. When the energy transmitter is switched off the atoms come back to their resting position giving out signals which are detected and magnified and processed in a computer. The speed at which they do this is related to the way in which they are linked with other atoms in the tissue. This property of atoms can be used clinically by placing the patient within a large magnet. The technique has already been shown to produce very clear pictures of the brain and spinal cord. It can, however, be used to demonstrate any part of the body. The lungs produce a very low signal and there has so far been very little reported work in that field. Masses which do produce a signal can be shown against the 'dark' background of the signal free lung. However, the heart and mediastinal blood vessels have been studied in some detail. The speed at which energised atoms return to their normal state changes following myocardial infarction. The anatomical display will also reveal ventricular dilatation or aneurysm formation. Lack of myocardial contraction can also be demonstrated in the ischaemic area. Thrombus within the cardiac aneurysm or within the aorta is easily demonstrated. In other conditions which produce hypertrophy of the myocardium, such as hypertension and aortic stenosis, the thickness of the individual cardiac chamber walls can be measured with accuracy. This allows differentiation from congestive cardiomyopathy in which the chambers are dilated but the myocardial wall is thin. NMR is capable of demonstrating flow within blood vessels so that vascular structures within the mediastinum are easily differentiated from abnormal masses. The NMR signal allows the characterisation of soft tissue, cystic or fatty pathologies within the mediastinum and chest wall.

BIBLIOGRAPHY

Simon, G. (1978). *Principles of Chest X-ray Diagnosis*, 4th edition. Butterworths, London.

Sutton, D. (ed.) (1980). *A Textbook of Radiology and Imaging*, 3rd edition. Churchill Livingstone, Edinburgh.

ACKNOWLEDGEMENT

The author thanks Dr Basil Strickland of the Brompton Hospital, London for kindly providing the radiographs of bronchiectasis.

Chapter 6

Electrocardiography (ECGs)

by D. BOYLE MD, FRCP

BASIC ELECTROPHYSIOLOGY

Heart cells, when they are not beating, are polarised – that is, the electrical charge on the outside of the cell membrane is positive compared with the inside. Contraction of the heart muscle is triggered off by depolarisation of the cell membrane; that is a movement of ions (initially sodium and later mainly calcium) across the membrane so that the polarity is reversed and the interior of the cell is positive compared with the exterior. Once depolarisation has started it spreads throughout the heart from cell to cell to ensure a synchronised heart beat.

Depolarisation is followed by a recovery phase – repolarisation – and following this the cell membrane remains stable until depolarisation occurs again.

Certain cells in health, e.g. in the sinuatrial (SA) node, will depolarise spontaneously and initiate the heart beat, while other cells will only do so under pathological conditions.

The wave of depolarisation, followed by repolarisation, create voltage changes that can be picked up at the skin and it is a recording of these voltage changes that make up an electrocardiogram.

Once depolarised, muscle cells are incapable of transmitting a further impulse until they are repolarised. During this time when they cannot be stimulated they are said to be refractory.

CONDUCTION IN THE NORMAL HEART BEAT

Normally the cardiac impulse arises from the sinuatrial node, a group of specialised cells in the right atrium near the mouth of the superior vena cava. The impulse spreads from here through the atria rapidly to reach the atrioventricular node. Conduction through the

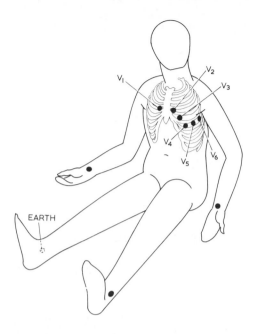

FIG. 6/1 Position of electrodes on the body: left wrist; right wrist; left ankle; 6 leads on the chest wall from the 4th intercostal space to the left mid-axillary line; (right ankle lead is the *earth*)

FIG. 6/2 Leads in the frontal plane

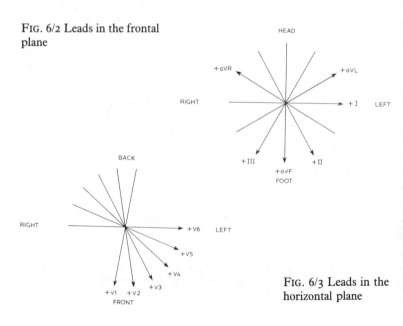

FIG. 6/3 Leads in the horizontal plane

atrioventricular node is slower. The impulse then travels to the ventricle by specialised conduction tissue, the bundle of His, which divides into two branches – the left and right bundle branches supplying the left and right ventricle. The left bundle branch in turn divides into superior and inferior fascicles supplying different areas of the left ventricle. The bundle branches connect to Purkinje fibres which lie on the endocardial surface of the heart. The impulse therefore reaches the endocardial surface of the heart nearly simultaneously. The excitation wave then spreads from endocardium towards the epicardial surface travelling through contractile muscle cells. The anatomy of the conducting tissue ensures that all parts of the ventricle contract at about the same time.

Voltages generated in the sinuatrial node, atrioventricular node and specialised conducting tissue are not large enough to be detected by conventional electrocardiography. The electrocardiogram therefore records voltage changes associated with conduction in the atrium and the ventricle.

LEADS

By convention, electrodes are placed on nine points on the skin (+ one additonal position used to earth the machine) (Fig. 6/1). From these electrode positions it is possible to derive 12 separate tracings. Each of these can be considered to represent a view of the heart's electrical activity from a different direction (Figs. 6/2 and 6/3).

Lead I represents voltage change in the frontal plane pointing to the left (upright on the ECG tracing) and to the right (downwards on the tracing.) Lead aVF represents voltage changes in the frontal plane pointing downwards (upright on the tracing) or upwards (downwards on the tracing). Leads II, III, aVL and aVR also represent voltage changes in the frontal plane as in Figure 6/2, the direction of the arrow being positive, i.e. upright on the tracing. Leads V1 to V6 represent voltage change in the horizontal plane (Fig. 6/3). The direction of the arrows in Figure 6/3 is positive. Leads V1 and V2 look at voltages moving anteriorly and posteriorly. V6 mainly shows voltage moving to the left and right and so is similar to lead I.

TRACING

The changes in voltage are traced on paper running at the speed of 25mm/second. Voltage change is on a scale of 1cm = 1 millivolt. A typical tracing will look like Figure 6/4.

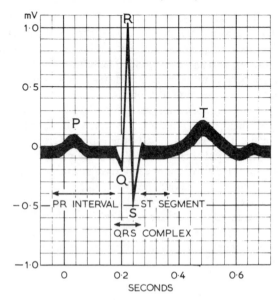

FIG. 6/4 Stylised ECG tracing of one heart beat

By convention the waves are named after the following letters:

P   wave represents atrial activity.
QRS   represents ventricular activity.
R   wave is the first positive wave.
Q   wave is a negative wave not preceded by R.
S   is a negative wave following an R.
T   wave represents electrical changes which occur following the contraction when the muscle 'repolarises' in preparation for the next heart beat.

INTERPRETATION OF THE NORMAL ELECTROCARDIOGRAM

Electrocardiography is not an exact science. The correlation between ECG findings and the anatomical and physiological state is not perfect. Interpretation should be both empirical and deductive. Empirical is purely noting that a certain pattern is associated with a certain condition. Deduction implies analysis of the ECG pattern with regard to the temporal sequence of events and the direction of electrical activity (Fig. 6/5).

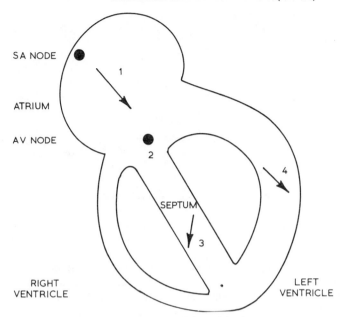

FIG. 6/5 Electrical activity of the heart

Atrial activity spreads from the sinus node to the atrioventricular node (P wave). The effective direction of the impulse is downwards, to the left and to the front (Fig. 6/5, arrow 1). That means that normally the P wave is positive in leads I, aVF and the chest leads. The atrial depolarisation is complete in 0.1sec and the P wave should therefore not exceed $2\frac{1}{2}$ small squares in width.

No electrical activity is recorded as the impulse travels through the AV node to the Purkinje fibres. The QRS deflection of the ventricular depolarisation should not start until 0.12 seconds after the start of the P wave and not later than 0.2 seconds after it (Fig. 6/5, 2).

The effective initial direction of activation in the ventricle is dominated by activation of the septum from the left side to the right. Other electrical forces in the right ventricle and the free wall of the left ventricle cancel each other out. This activation wave moves downwards, to the right, and anteriorly (Fig. 6/5, arrow 3). Therefore usually there is a small initial Q wave in I, V6 and an R wave in V1.

After septal activation, the dominant contribution to the depolarisation wave arises in the free wall of the left ventricle (Fig. 6/5, arrow 4). The force is downwards to the left and posteriorly.

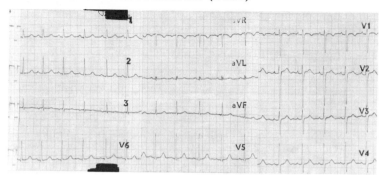

FIG. 6/6 A normal electrocardiogram (ECG)

Therefore, usually there is an R wave in I, aVF, V6 and a deep S in V1.

Ventricular activation is complete within 0.10 seconds and the width of the QRS complex should not exceed $2\frac{1}{2}$ small squares.

The ventricular repolarisation wave roughly follows that of depolarisation, but moves more anteriorly. Therefore, the T wave in leads I, aVF and V6 is similar in positivity to the QRS complex, but it may be positive in the anterior chest leads where the dominant QRS is negative.

The time interval from the beginning of the QRS complex to the end of the T depends on heart rate but is usually not more than 0.42 seconds ($10\frac{1}{2}$ small squares).

If the T wave becomes abnormal its direction is generally away from the anatomical site of abnormality. Figure 6/6 is typical of a normal electrocardiogram.

INTERPRETATION OF THE ABNORMAL ECG

1. Since the P wave represents atrial activity and the QRS ventricular activity the electrocardiogram can be used to determine heart rhythm.
2. Damage to the conducting tissue will alter the pathways of activation and may alter the QRS morphology.
3. Increased muscle mass will alter the amplitude and duration of P and QRS waves and this allows recognition of hypertrophy of the muscle in different chambers of the heart.
4. Loss of muscle mass alters the QRS and allows recognition of myocardial infarction.

5. Many factors can alter the patterns of repolarisation and these can be suspected from changes in the ST-segment and T waves.

Arrhythmias

ECTOPIC BEATS (Fig. 6/7)

A beat arising from a focus in the ventricle occurs prematurely. Since its activation route does not initially involve the specialised conducting tissues the complex is wide and of a different shape to the sinus beat. Since it makes the ventricle refractory to the following sinus beat the next conducted sinus beat occurs after a 'compensatory pause'.

A supraventricular ectopic beat (arising in the atria or in the atrioventricular node) is also premature but generally has the same QRS morphology as the sinus beat, and the following pause is less long.

TACHYCARDIAS

A rapid series of beats – ventricular (Fig. 6/8) or supraventricular – produces paroxysmal or sustained tachycardia. This can be dangerous as cardiac function is less efficient and the oxygen and metabolic needs of the heart are increased.

The QRS complexes are wide and different in shape to the sinus beats. The end of the paroxysm is followed by the 'compensatory pause'.

VENTRICULAR FIBRILLATION (Fig. 6/9)

Ventricular fibrillation occurs with completely chaotic electrical activity in the heart. No coherent contraction occurs and this is the commonest cause of cardiac arrest. The tracing shown was taken from a man in the early phase of acute myocardial infarction in 1972. Sinus rhythm was obtained by electric shock. He survived this incident and remains well.

Ventricular fibrillation may occur without warning, follow a ventricular ectopic beat, especially if it is very premature, or degenerate from ventricular tachycardia.

ATRIAL FIBRILLATION (Fig. 6/10)

Atrial fibrillation occurs with chaotic electrical activity of the atrial muscle with no coherent atrial contraction. The P wave disappears and the base line shows irregular deflections. Refractory cells in the atrioventricular node prevent very rapid stimulation of the ventricle. The ventricle response is irregular.

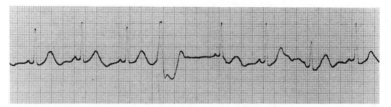

FIG. 6/7 Ventricular ectopic beats. The 4th complex is wide and followed by a compensatory pause

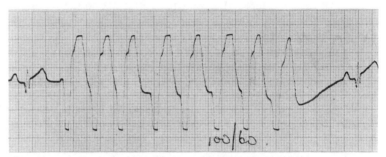

FIG. 6/8 Ventricular tachycardia

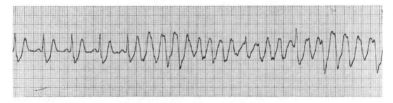

FIG. 6/9 Ventricular fibrillation

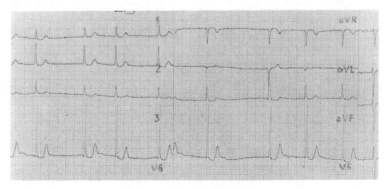

FIG. 6/10 Atrial fibrillation

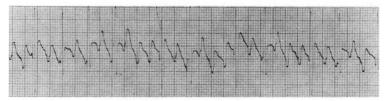

Fig. 6/11 Atrial flutter

ATRIAL FLUTTER (Fig. 6/11)

Atrial flutter occurs when there is 'circus movement' in which an activation wave moves around in a circle of atrial tissue. The tail of the activation wave leaves behind it refractory cells, but these are repolarised by the time the head of the waves reaches them again. This is described as re-entry mechanism. The characteristic 'saw-tooth' pattern of the base line seen in atrial flutter is seen in the illustration.

SUPRAVENTRICULAR TACHYCARDIA

This is associated with a very rapid atrial rate and is usually due to a re-entry circuit within the atrioventricular node itself.

Heart block

Heart block, or atrioventricular block occurs when a lesion interferes with the conduction from atrium to ventricle. Figure 6/12 is an example: the initial complex shows PR interval of 0.22 seconds –

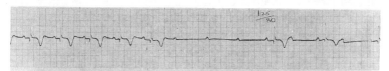

Fig. 6/12 Varying atrioventricular block (see text description)

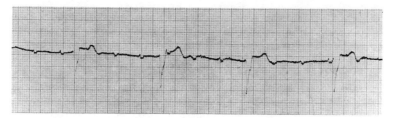

Fig. 6/13 Complete heart block

longer than normal – and this is called *first degree block*. PR interval of the 5th beat shows increased block, a PR interval of 0.28 seconds. This is followed by three P waves where the impulses are totally blocked and no ventricular activation occurs. The next P wave is followed by a QRS with a long PR interval. The next P wave is lost in the end of the T wave and is blocked.

In complete heart block (Fig. 6/13) the atria and ventricles beat independently of each other and the ventricular rate is typically low.

BUNDLE BRANCH BLOCK

If the *left bundle branch* is blocked, activation of the left ventricle follows that of the right. The early activation pattern is completely changed so that no Q wave is seen in I, V6 and no R in V1. The complex is wide (Fig. 6/14).

If the *right bundle branch* is blocked, initial activation of the left (and dominant) ventricle is unchanged but there is delay in activation of the right ventricle. The right ventricle is at the front and the right of the heart so that the terminal part of the QRS shows activation to the right and anteriorly, i.e. there is a late S in I and R in V1 (Fig. 6/15).

Pre-excitation (Fig. 6/16)

Some hearts, in addition to the AV node, have an accessory pathway joining the atria to the ventricle. The PR interval is short – the delay of the impulse in the atrioventricular node is by-passed. Activation begins in non-specialised tissue with a slow conduction giving a slurred start to the QRS called a delta wave. Simultaneously, the impulse reaches the ventricle through the atrioventricular node and bundle branches and the latter part of the QRS complex is therefore normal. The presence of two pathways joining atria and ventricle facilitate the re-entry mechanism and paroxysmal tachycardia is common. Atrial fibrillation with pre-excitation can be dangerous when the accessory pathway allows rapid impulses to reach the ventricle and precipitate ventricular fibrillation.

Changes in the ST-segment and T wave

ST-segment and T wave reflect repolarisation of the cell. They are easily altered and represent the most non-specific of ECG changes. It will be noted that changes occur in ST-segment and T wave in ventricular hypertrophy and infarction. Changes also occur with ischaemia, hypothyroidism, abnormal levels of electrolyte concen-

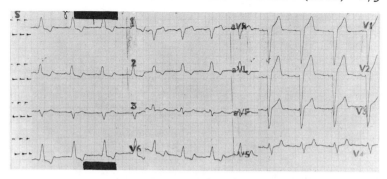

FIG. 6/14 Left bundle branch block

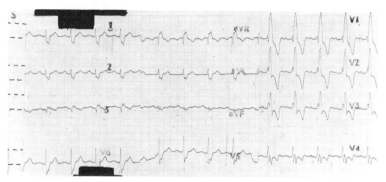

FIG. 6/15 Right bundle branch block

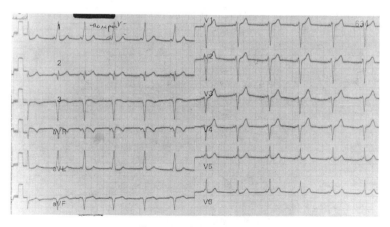

FIG. 6/16 Pre-excitation

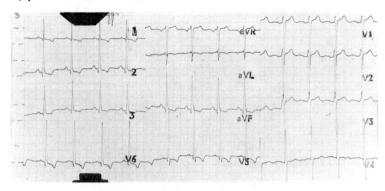

FIG. 6/17 Left ventricular hypertrophy

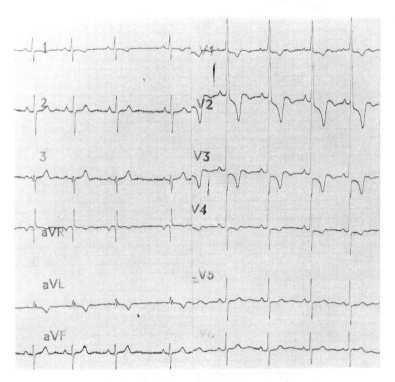

FIG. 6/18 Right ventricular hypertrophy

trations in the blood, inflammation of the heart, change in the temperature of the heart and certain drugs. For example, T wave abnormality in Figure 6/10 is probably due to digitalis.

Chamber hypertrophy

In left atrial hypertrophy the P wave is wide and in right atrial hypertrophy the P wave is tall. In left ventricular hypertrophy the free wall of the left ventricle is thickened and the R wave in leads looking to the left (I, V6) and the S wave in leads looking to the front are increased. The tall R can be seen in Figure 6/10 in a patient with mitral regurgitation. When left ventricular hypertrophy increases in severity there is also an abnormality in repolarisation giving ST depression, T wave inversion, the repolarisation wave moving away from the left (Fig. 6/17). In right ventricular hypertrophy the normally thin right ventricle is thick and contributes forces to the QRS moving towards the right and anteriorly. This shows as an S wave in I and an R wave in VI (Fig. 6/18). There is some similarity between this and right bundle branch block, but in right ventricular hypertrophy the QRS is not abnormally prolonged.

Myocardial infarction

The first ECG evidence of acute myocardial infarction is marked elevation of the ST-segment – the electrical forces moving towards the direction of the site of infarct (Fig. 6/19). This is followed typically with the loss of electrical forces in the direction of the site of the infarct and T wave forces moving away from the infarct. In anterior infarction (Fig. 6/20) there is a loss of R wave in VI-4 giving a QS pattern in leads VI-3 with T wave inversion.

In inferior infarction (Fig. 6/21), the loss of the R waves is in the leads looking at the inferior surface of the heart, i.e. II, III and

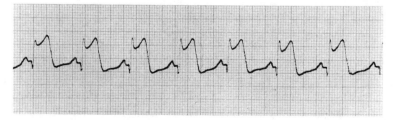

FIG. 6/19 Early myocardial infarction

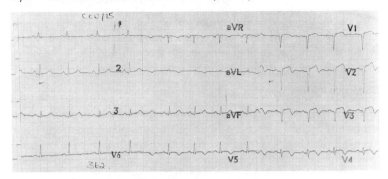

FIG. 6/20 Anterior myocardial infarction

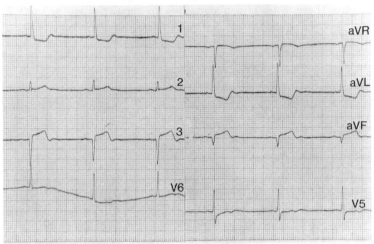

FIG. 6/21 Inferior myocardial infarction

aVF. There is ST-segment elevation in the same leads and T wave inversion has appeared in lead 3. ST-segment depression is also present in leads I, and aVF. This so-called reciprocal depression generally means a more extensive infarction.

FURTHER ECG INVESTIGATIONS

In addition to the routine ECG taken at rest, more complex procedures can be used.

Exercise ECG

ECG taken during and following exercise may show abnormalities not seen in the resting ECG. Rhythm disturbance can be provoked. In suspected coronary disease the exercise tolerance is established by measuring the time the patient can exercise on a fixed bicycle or on a treadmill.

Patients with coronary disease are more likely to develop ST-segment depression in some leads during exercise than those with normal hearts. However, interpretation of exercise tests must include the clinical and haemodynamic response to exercise and even with this, false positive and false negative results occur.

Ambulatory monitoring

A normal resting ECG looks only at about 50 ECG complexes whereas in a day a normal person has over 100 000 heart beats. By wearing a tape recorder connected to a small portable ECG carried on a belt, all the heart beats in 24 hours can be recorded. This often allows the detection of paroxysmal arrhythmia and ST-segment displacement that would be otherwise missed. Ambulatory monitoring helps in diagnosis and in assessing a patient's response to treatment.

Ambulatory monitoring can also be carried out using radio telemetry. A small portable radio transmitter sends the ECG to a receiver where rhythm disturbance can be seen in real time.

Intracardiac monitoring

ECG tracings can be taken using electrodes attached to catheters that can enter the cavities of the heart. They can be of assistance in determining the site of origin of an arrhythmia. Using the intracardiac technique, ECG complexes from the bundle of His can be recorded, and this can assist in elucidating complex arrhythmias.

Averaging techniques

If the sensitivity of the ECG is increased, the surface ECG may show small waves of very low voltage following the QRS wave which are called 'after potentials'. Experimental work suggests that these are associated with increased risk of lethal arrhythmia. Random disturbance of the base line 'electrical noise' makes the technique difficult since the 'noise' swamps the after potentials. This problem is overcome by electronically averaging a large number of complexes. The random fluctuations of the 'noise' cancel out leaving the undistorted after potential. This, however, remains an experimental technique.

Electrophysiological studies

Using an intracardiac electrode on the end of a catheter it is possible to stimulate the heart. By varying the intensity, timing and number of impulses, arrhythmia can be provoked in susceptible patients. This not only identifies a group of patients at particular risk of lethal arrhythmia, but, by repeating the test after drug intervention, allows an assessment of the efficacy of treatment.

SUMMARY

Voltage changes recorded on the skin reflect electrical activity in the heart. Variation from normal patterns are associated with certain pathology. However, to be of value clinically, the ECG must be considered in the context of history, clinical findings and other investigations. It is important to remember that a normal ECG does not necessarily mean a normal heart and that an abnormal ECG can have many possible explanations.

BIBLIOGRAPHY

Campbell, R. W. F. (1985). 24-hour tape monitoring. *Medicine International*, 2, 17, 717–21.

Guide to Cardiac Arrhythmias. A *Nursing Times* publication obtainable from Macmillan Journals Limited, Basingstoke RG21 2XS.

Hampton, J. R. (1980). *The Electrocardiogram Made Easy*, 2nd edition. Churchill Livingstone, Edinburgh.

Hampton, J. (1985). The electrocardiogram. *Medicine International*, 2, 17, 703–10.

Joy, M. (1985). Exercise electrocardiography. *Medicine International*, 2, 17, 711–16.

Ward, D. and Camm, A. J. (1985). Cardiac electrophysiology. *Medicine International*, 2, 17, 722–9.

ACKNOWLEDGEMENT

The author thanks Mrs P. McCoy MCSP for her help and contribution to this chapter.

Chapter 7

Drugs used in the Cardiovascular and Respiratory Systems

by D. B. McHUTCHISON BPharm, MPS

THE CARDIOVASCULAR SYSTEM

Angina

Drugs may be used to prevent angina, or to treat it symptomatically when it occurs. Angina occurs when the myocardium suffers an inadequate oxygen supply, and may therefore be treated by drugs which reduce the oxygen requirement of the heart.

Beta blockers, such as propranolol, are used to prevent attacks, and act by slowing the heart and preventing the rise in blood pressure that follows exercise, and thus reduce the oxygen requirement of the myocardium.

Nitrate vasodilators are widely used to treat attacks as they occur. Glyceryl trinitrate acts very rapidly when taken sublingually, within a minute or two, but is of short duration. The more recently introduced drugs, isosorbide dinitrate (Cedocard) and isosorbide mononitrate (Mono-Cedocard), are slower in onset but longer in effect. They also avoid the unpleasant headaches commonly occurring after glyceryl trinitrate. The latter drug is also of interest in that it is readily absorbed through the skin. This has led to the formulation of novel preparations, such as ointments (e.g. Percutol) and adhesive patches (e.g. Transiderm-Nitro) which allow constant uptake of drug through the skin, and help to prevent attacks.

Calcium antagonists – drugs which inhibit the transfer of calcium ions in cardiac muscle, reducing cardiac workload and oxygen demand – are also used. They must be taken regularly to prevent angina, and have comparatively few side-effects, other than headache and flushing associated with their peripheral vasodilator action. Examples of drugs in this group are nifedipine (Adalat), verapamil (Cordilox), lidoflazine (Clinium) and diltiazem (Tildiem).

Cardiac glycosides

These drugs are used in the treatment of heart failure and cardiac arrhythmias. An important consideration is that their therapeutic doses are very close to their toxic dose, and that side-effects such as nausea, vomiting and headaches, are very common. More important side-effects such as arrhythmias and bradycardia are usually associated with too high a dose and necessitate withdrawal of treatment.

Drugs within the group all have similar action, though varying in their rate of onset and duration of action. They increase the strength of contraction of heart muscle and slow the heart rate, and probably act by increasing the concentration of calcium ions in the myocardium. The slowing of conduction through the atrioventricular node makes these drugs of particular value in the treatment of atrial fibrillation.

Digoxin (Lanoxin) is the main drug in this group and is available as injection, tablets and oral solution. The injection is used if initial emergency digitalisation is necessary, and the tablets (or oral solution in small children) for maintenance therapy. Digoxin is excreted unchanged via the kidneys, thus renal function is important in determining the optimum dose in each patient. In the elderly this will often mean a reduced dose.

Other drugs in this group are digitoxin (Digitaline Nativelle), lanatoside (Cedilanid), medigoxin (Lanitop) and ouabain.

Cardiac glycosides may sometimes be referred to as digitalis glycosides, as originally treatment was with preparations made from dried leaves of the foxglove, *Digitalis purpurea*. Though effective, such natural products vary in potency and are now rarely used, though tablets of digitalis, made from dried leaves, may still be encountered. Digoxin is the pure glycoside and is extracted from a related plant, *Digitalis lanata*.

Diuretics

These are drugs used to increase the excretion of water and electrolytes via the kidneys, and may be used in the treatment of conditions such as heart failure, hypertension and pulmonary oedema. Diuretics fall into several categories, dependent upon how they exert their action on the kidney.

Loop diuretics are the most potent, acting by preventing the resorption of water in the renal tubules at the ascending loop of Henle. As these drugs increase the excretion of potassium ions, a potassium supplement is usually given as well. Drugs in this group include frusemide (Lasix) and bumetanide (Burinex), both of which have a very wide dosage range, orally or by injection. For example, frusemide is given orally at 20 to 80mg per day or by injection at 20 to 50mg per dose, in the treatment of heart failure or pulmonary oedema. In renal failure, and following renal transplantation, very much larger doses may be used, up to 4g orally or continuous intravenous (IV) infusions at 4mg per minute.

Thiazide diuretics constitute the largest group in this class. They are less potent than the loop diuretics, and act on the distal convoluted tubule, inhibiting the resorption of sodium and chloride. As with the loop diuretics they increase the excretion of potassium, so supplementation may be necessary. Single daily doses are often adequate, with their onset of action in 1 to 2 hours and duration of effect from 12 to 24 hours. Some examples of drugs in this group are shown in Table 7/1.

TABLE 7/1 Diuretics

Approved name	Oral daily dose range (adults)	Proprietary name
(a) LOOP DIURETICS		
bumetanide	Normal 1mg	Burinex
	High dose 5mg	
ethacrynic acid	50 to 150mg	Edecrin
frusemide	Normal 20 to 80mg	Lasix: Diuresal
	High dose 2g	Dryptal: Frusid
piretanide	6 to 12mg	Arelix
(b) THIAZIDE DIURETICS		
bendrofluazide	2.5 to 10mg	Aprinox: Berkozide
		Centyl: Neonaclex
chlorothiazide	0.5 to 1g	Saluric
cyclopenthiazide	0.5 to 1mg	Navidrex
hydrochlorothiazide	50 to 100mg	Esidrex
hydroflumethiazide	25 to 50mg	Hydrenox
indapamide	2.5mg	Natrilix
mefruside	25 to 50mg	Baycaron
methyclothiazide	2.5 to 10mg	Enduron
polythiazide	1 to 4mg	Nephril
xipamide	20 to 40mg	Diurexan
(c) POTASSIUM SPARING DIURETICS		
amiloride	5 to 10mg	Midamor
spironolactone	50 to 200mg	Aldactone
triamterene	50 to 200mg	Dytac

Potassium sparing diuretics, as their name implies, lead to retention of potassium (Table 7/1c). Some, such as the aldosterone antagonist spironolactone, are most effective when used with a loop or thiazide diuretic, since they potentiate the action of the latter. Others, such as amiloride (Midamor), or triamterene (Dytac) may be given alone, but again to strike the right balance of treatment, combined therapy with loop diuretics or thiazides is often employed.

TABLE 7/2   Potassium sparing combined products

Proprietary name	Potassium sparing component	Other component
Aldactide 25	spironolactone 25mg	hydroflumethiazide 25mg
Aldactide 50	spironolactone 50mg	hydroflumethiazide 50mg
Amilco	amiloride 5mg	hydrochlorothiazide 50mg
Dyazide	triamterene 50mg	hydrochlorothiazide 25mg
Dytide	triamterene 50mg	benzthiazide 25mg
Frumil	amiloride 5mg	frusemide 40mg
Frusene	triamterene 50mg	frusemide 40mg
Kalspare	triamterene 50mg	chlorthalidone 50mg
Lasilactone	spironolactone 50mg	frusemide 20mg
Moduret 25	amiloride 2.5mg	hydrochlorothiazide 25mg
Moduretic	amiloride 5mg	hydrochlorothiazide 50mg
Synuretic	amiloride 5mg	hydrochlorothiazide 50mg

Any patient given more than one drug to take is likely to experience compliance problems, such as taking doses at the right time, failing to take the correct dose, failing to take two drugs at the same time. While it has always been considered best to take each drug separately

TABLE 7/3   Combined diuretic preparations with potassium

Proprietary name	Diuretic constituent	Potassium (millimoles (mmol))
Brinaldix-K	clopamide 20mg	12
Burinex-K	bumetanide 500 micrograms	7.7
Centyl-K	bendrofluazide 2.5mg	7.7
Diumide-K	frusemide 40mg	8
Esidrex-K	hydrochlorothiazide 12.5mg	8.1
Hygroton-K	chlorthalidone 25mg	6.7
Lasikal	frusemide 20mg	10
Navidrex-K	cyclopenthiazide 250 micrograms	8.1
Neo-Naclex-K	bendrofluazide 2.5mg	8.4

at a dose suitable for the particular condition, many drug manufacturers are now producing combined preparations, and diuretic therapy is a common area where these may be encountered (Tables 7/2, 7/3). While they may reduce flexibility of therapy they do ease compliance problems, for example with fewer tablets to take and the certainty that where two drugs are essential they will both be taken. Physiotherapists, particularly when seeing patients at home, can help in this matter, by discussion and reminder of the importance of following prescribed dose and time schedules as closely as practical.

Antihypertensive agents

Raised blood pressure may lead to increased likelihood of heart failure, stroke or kidney failure. It is usually considered that patients with a diastolic pressure above 100mmHg should be treated with antihypertensives. A range of drugs, either alone or in combination is available, the most important groups being the beta blockers and thiazide diuretics (q.v.). Alternatively, or in combination with the above two groups, specific antihypertensive agents may be employed. These fall into several types and some are only used in emergency treatment, for example by injection during surgery. Some of these drugs are perhaps best regarded as reserve agents for use where other treatments have failed. Common problems with their use include a significant incidence of side-effects and their interaction with other drugs.

Vasodilator antihypertensives act by reducing peripheral resistance, examples being hydralazine (Apresoline) and minoxidil (Loniten) which may be given by mouth; sodium nitroprusside (Nipride) and diazoxide (Eudamine) which may be used by IV injection to treat severe hypertensive crisis.

Prazosin (Hypovase), indoramin (Baratol) and phenoxybenzamine (Dibenyline) are examples of alpha receptor blockers; prazosin gives such a rapid onset of action when first used that it can lead to hypotensive collapse, and subsequently postural hypotension may be a problem.

A recent addition to the specific agents is the angiotensin-converting enzyme inhibitors, captopril (Capoten) and enalapril (Innovace). Both are active by mouth and, like prazosin, may cause hypotension with the initial dose. They are recommended for use only where other treatments have failed.

The older centrally acting agents such as methyldopa (Aldomet) and clonidine (Catapres) are now used less frequently, though methyldopa still has an important place in therapy in that it is safe to use in pregnancy and in asthma. Side-effects, particularly drowsiness, are common, particularly with high doses.

Anti-arrhythmic drugs

Disturbances in heart rhythm can result from several causes, and successful drug treatment requires the use of the electrocardiograph (ECG) to determine the precise type of arrhythmia. In many cases the initial treatment is the use of synchronised DC shock rather than drugs.

Supraventricular tachycardia may be treated with digoxin, beta blockers (*q.v.*), by verapamil (Cordilox) orally or by injection, or by amiodarone (Cordarone X). The latter is also effective orally or by injection and its use is associated with side-effects of particular concern to physiotherapists. Photosensitivity may occur, requiring the use of sun screens, and peripheral neuropathy has also been reported, reversible on withdrawal of the drug.

Bradycardia following myocardial infarction may be treated with atropine sulphate injection. Bradycardia may also occur as a side-effect of beta blocking agents, and again this is treated with atropine injection.

Ventricular arrhythmias following cardiac infarction may need urgent treatment by IV injection, for which several drugs are available. Lignocaine is probably the drug of choice, given by bolus IV injection from a pre-filled syringe (e.g. Xylocard) or by IV infusion in 5% glucose. (*Note:* lignocaine is also widely used as a local anaesthetic.) It is not absorbed from the gastro-intestinal tract so for maintenance therapy other agents are used, for example disopyramide (Rythmodan), mexiletine (Mexitil), flecainide (Tambocor), procainamide (Pronestyl) or quinidine. The latter is a long established drug, being the stereo-isomer of the antimalarial agent quinine, its main drawback being the possibility of hypersensitivity, so it is usual to use a test dose before treatment is established. It is available in sustained release formulations, such as Kinidin Durules or Kiditard.

Beta blocking drugs

These drugs play a major role in the treatment of cardiovascular disease. They act by blocking the action of catecholamines at the β_1 adrenergic receptors in the heart and the β_2 adrenergic receptors in the lungs. Because of this latter effect their use in patients with obstructive airway disease requires caution, with adjustments to dosage of β_2 stimulants such as salbutamol (*q.v.*). ◼ blockers show a reduced effect on the β_2 receptors and are the◼ often termed cardioselective. Blockade of the β_1 receptors slo◼ heart rate, reduces the force of contraction of the heart muscle, improves tolerance to stress and reduces myocardial oxygen demand.

Given in equivalent dosage the therapeutic effects of all drugs in this group are similar, and their properties provide for their use in treating angina (*q.v.*) and cardiac arrhythmias. They are of particular value in supraventricular tachycardia, where they act by prolonging conduction at the atrioventricular node. The reduction in cardiac output following beta blockers allows these drugs to be used to treat hypertension. Other factors are involved as well, such as the blocking of peripheral receptors, and their full mode of action in hypertension is not yet fully elucidated. In many patients control of hypertension can be achieved by beta blockers alone. Following myocardial infarction use of beta blockers has been shown to reduce the incidence of further attacks, though the effects of β_2 suppression in the lungs may be a limiting factor in some patients.

TABLE 7/4   Beta blocking drugs

Approved name	Proprietary name	Forms available
acebutolol	Sectral	Injection 5mg/ml Capsules 100mg, 200mg and 400 mg
atenolol	Tenormin	Injection 500 microgram/ml Tablets 50mg and 100mg
betaxolol	Kerlone	Tablets 20mg
labetalol	Trandate	Injection 5mg/ml Tablets 100mg, 200mg and 400mg
metoprolol	Betaloc Lopresor	Injection 1mg/ml Tablets 50mg, 100mg and 200mg
nadolol	Corgard	Tablets 40mg and 80mg
oxprenolol	Trasicor Laracor Apsocox	Injection 2mg Tablets 20mg, 40mg, 80mg and 160mg
propranolol	Inderal: Angilol Berkolol: Apsolol Bedranol: Sloprolol	Injection 1mg/ml Tablets 10mg, 40mg, 80mg, 160mg
sotalol	Beta-Cardone Sotacor	Injection 2mg/ml Tablets 40mg, 80mg, 160mg and 200mg
timolol	Betim Blocadren	Tablets 10mg

...igs in this group used at present in the UK.
...are Prescription Only Medicines (POM).
...y in different conditions, details should be
...*National Formulary* (BNF) or manufacturers
...anufacturers provide slow release preparations
...ily dosage.

...nstrictors, vasodilators and sympathomimetics

...ood flow in peripheral vessels may result from spasm of the v.... physical blockage by an embolus. Blood flow may be increased by the use of peripheral vasodilators, relieving some symptoms, for example, in Raynaud's disease. Because of their effect on peripheral resistance and blood flow they must be used with caution where other cardiovascular problems also exist. Drugs commonly used include cinnarizine (Stugeron), thymoxamine (Opilon) and nicotinic acid derivatives. Some drugs in the group such as cyclandelate (Cyclospasmol) and naftidrofuryl (Praxilene) are also used for their vasodilator effect on cerebral vessels, after stroke and in an attempt to improve mental ability in the elderly.

Vasoconstrictors may be used by injection to restore blood pressure in emergencies such as may arise during use of general anaesthetics. Their use is short term and requires careful medical supervision, as they will also restrict blood flow to important organs such as the kidneys. Examples of drugs used in this way are metaraminol (Aramine), noradrenaline and phenylephrine.

In such conditions as septic shock and cardiogenic shock sympathomimetic agents with cardiac stimulant action are used. Isoprenaline increases both contractility of heart muscle and heart rate, while the newer agents dopamine (Intropin) and dobutamine (Dobutrex) increase muscle contractility only. The latter are, therefore, of particular value in cardiac shock and following cardiac surgery.

Anticoagulants and haemostatics

These are drugs used to prevent the development of the formation of blood clots – thrombi – in the venous circulation. The two principal agents used are heparin and warfarin.

Heparin is present in mammalian tissue and is extracted from the intestinal mucosa of sheep or pigs (mucous heparin) or from the lungs of cattle (lung heparin). It can only be given by injection and either form may be presented as the sodium or calcium salt. As with other natural products, e.g. insulin, the activity varies with different batches and the extract is therefore compared to a known standard preparation, and the potency defined in terms of units. After injection the drug is bound to plasma proteins and is thought to act by increasing the activity of anti-thrombin factors, preventing the formulation of thrombin and thus ultimately preventing clotting. It follows therefore that control of dosage is important; too much heparin can cause haemorrhage.

In the prophylaxis or treatment of venous thrombosis in patients undergoing heart surgery or during dialysis heparin is given intravenously, by infusion or bolus injection. Laboratory control of bleeding time is normally necessary. In the prophylaxis of deep vein thrombosis postoperatively, or in less mobile patients (e.g. pregnancy), smaller doses are given by subcutaneous injection. The calcium salt is usually used and preparations are now available, such as pre-filled syringes, which enable patients to self-administer the drug at home. Laboratory monitoring is not necessary for low dose therapy. In hospitals it is common, though questionable, practice to use very small doses of heparin to flush IV cannulae at intervals to prevent clots forming in the lumen. Flushing with saline is probably just as effective.

If necessary, the effects of heparin may be reversed by the intravenous injection of protamine sulphate.

In oral anticoagulant therapy the drug of choice is *warfarin*; some patients are still treated with phenindione (Dindevan) or nicoumalone (Sinthrome) where they have been stabilised on these drugs and have not suffered haemorrhage.

Warfarin antagonises vitamin K in the synthesis of clotting factors such as prothrombin. It is used in treatment and prophylaxis of pulmonary embolism, deep vein thrombosis, and in patients with prosthetic heart valves. Tablets are available of 1, 3, or 5mg and the dose required is determined by laboratory measurement of prothrombin time. All patients on this therapy are recommended to carry an anticoagulant card. A particular point with warfarin is its interaction with aspirin, which increases the risk of haemorrhage and patients are advised not to use aspirin containing preparations concurrently. Many other drugs are known to inhibit or potentiate the action of warfarin, details of which will be found in the BNF.

Prevention of thrombus formation may also be achieved by using drugs which reduce platelet adhesion in the arterial circulation. This treatment may be used in patients with prosthetic heart valves and may be of value prophylactically following myocardial infarction. Drugs used for this purpose include aspirin, dipyridamole (Persantin) and sulphinpyrazone (Anturan).

Haemostatics are drugs which increase the ability of blood to clot. Ethamsylate (Dicynene) is thought to act by decreasing platelet adhesion and is used, for example in ENT work, to treat haemorrhage in small blood vessels. Antifibrinolytic drugs inhibit the breakdown of fibrin and may thus be used to treat haemorrhage after surgery. Aminocaproic acid (Epsikapron) is used orally, while the newer agent tranexamic acid (Cyclokapron) can be given either orally as tablets or syrup, or by intravenous injection.

Atherosclerosis may develop in patients with raised serum lipid levels, which may be treated in one of several ways. Colestipol (Colestid) and cholestyramine (Questran) reduce the absorption of cholesterol from the gut; probucol (Lurselle) increases the metabolism of lipoproteins; clofibrate (Atromid) and bezafibrate (Bezalip) lower plasma cholesterol levels. Any of these treatments must be used in association with other measures, such as strict diet and reduction in smoking, if they are to have any lasting effect.

THE RESPIRATORY SYSTEM

Treatment of cough

Many products, some single agents, many compound preparations, are available for the treatment of cough.

Cough suppressants act centrally by depressing the cough centre in the brain, and have some use in suppressing dry unproductive cough, which can be distressing. Most are presented in linctus formulation, a viscous sweet liquid based on sugar or glycerin. They, therefore, give a brief soothing effect when taken, as well as the central action of the active ingredient. They must be used with caution as they can lead to retention of sputum and inhibition of ventilation. Several drugs in this group are derived from, or have similar action to, the opium alkaloids, hence constipation is a common side-effect. Examples include the linctus formulations of codeine, diamorphine, methadone and pholcodine. Apart from the cough suppressants many products are available, claiming to sooth the throat and act as expectorants.

Expectorants are drugs which are claimed to increase the expulsion of bronchial secretions, but there is no evidence that any drug can exert such an effect. Other than simple formulations, such as simple linctus which will give a brief soothing effect, the majority of products in this group were withdrawn from prescribing on the NHS by the limitations introduced in April 1985.

Inhalations

Inhalation therapy is a traditional treatment in chronic asthma and bronchitis. Preparations such as menthol and eucalyptus and benzoin tincture in hot water are used, but it is most likely that it is the inhalation of the warm moist air which reduces the viscosity of the mucus in the lungs. Steam inhalations together with postural drainage can facilitate expectoration.

Mucolytics

Mucolytics, drugs intended to reduce the viscosity of sputum, can be given by inhalation, e.g. acetylcysteine (Airbron) or tyloxapol (Alevaire). Other agents, which can be given by mouth, are thought to alter the composition, and increase the flow, of mucal secretions. Carbocisteine (Mucodyn) and bromhexine (Bisolvon) are examples, but their value has been questioned and most oral forms have been withdrawn or restricted in use in the NHS by the prescribing limitations mentioned above. Bromhexine can also be given by injection, as an IV bolus or by infusion.

Respiratory stimulants and oxygen

Respiratory stimulants are drugs which act centrally to increase the rate and depth of respiration, and may be used in conjunction with active physiotherapy in patients with chronic obstructive airway disease which results from CO_2 retention. These drugs are given by intravenous injection or infusion; their use requires expert medical supervision, and blood gas and pH measurements may be necessary to ensure correct dosage. In the case of nikethamide the therapeutic dose is close to the toxic level, at which convulsions can occur. Nikethamide and the similar drug, ethamivan (Clairvan), must be given by repeated injection, while the other agent in the group, doxapram (Dopram) can be given by continuous infusion. In respiratory failure not associated with retention of CO_2, such as drug overdose, asthma or neurological disease, respiratory stimulants are of no value.

Oxygen therapy may often be used in association with respiratory stimulants. Low oxygen concentrations up to 28% are used in chronic obstructive airway disease. Blood gas measurements are needed to determine the correct concentration, since too high an input can lead to CO_2 retention and respiratory acidosis. In some conditions such as pulmonary embolism and pneumonia much higher concentrations may be used for short periods.

Oxygen may be supplied to the user in one of three ways. In large hospitals it is stored in bulk as liquid oxygen, and piped via an evaporator to wall outlets at the bedside or operating theatre. Alternatively, it is supplied as compressed gas in cylinders, which is flexible in that the cylinders can be moved with the patient. Their disadvantages are the high cost and weight, particularly of the larger cylinders. For home use smaller cylinders are available, including lightweight types which can be carried. The third source of supply is the recently developed oxygen concentrator – a small machine which extracts oxygen from the atmosphere. They are very economical and are proving very convenient for home use.

All fittings used to connect administration equipment to cylinders or wall outlets are specific to the particular gas. Besides oxygen, air, carbon dioxide and nitrous oxide will commonly be encountered in cylinders or pipelines. It is an unfortunate fact that patients have died by being given the wrong gas to inhale. All personnel using gas therapy should be aware of the hazards and must ensure that any repairs or modifications to such equipment are carried out and tested only by specialist technical staff.

Allergy

Allergy can result from a variety of causes, such as skin contact, food or insect bites. In the context of this chapter, however, consideration is given only to the response to inhaled allergens, in particular the seasonal form, hay fever. This condition, characterised by severe rhinorrhoea and sneezing, is treated with H_1 antagonists, commonly called antihistamines. Many drugs are available (Table 7/5) and the choice is often one of trial and error, as patients vary very widely in their response. The major side-effect, particularly of the earlier drugs, is sedation which can be of particular importance in patients who drive or have to operate machinery at work. Some of the newer drugs cause less sedation, probably because they penetrate the blood/brain barrier to a much smaller extent than the older agents. (*Note*: the sedative effect of some antihistamines, e.g. promethazine, is actually used for premedication and night time sedation, particularly in children.) Severe sudden allergic reaction, for example following an insect bite, or administration of vaccine, can cause anaphylactic shock. This may be treated by adrenaline to restore blood pressure, and an injectable antihistamine, e.g. chlorpheniramine, to control the response. Intravenous cortico-steroids and IV electrolyte replacement may also be needed.

TABLE 7/5   Antihistamines

Approved name	Daily adult dose range	Proprietary name
*astemizole	10 to 30mg	Hismanal
azatadine	2 to 4mg	Optimine
brompheniramine	12 to 32mg	Dimotane
chlorpheniramine	12 to 16mg	Piriton
clemastine	1 to 2mg	Tavegil
cyproheptadine	4 to 20mg	Periactin
diphenhydramine	25 to 75mg	Benadryl
diphenylpyraline	10 to 20mg	Histryl
mebhydrolin	150 to 200mg	Fabahistin
mequitazine	5 to 10mg	Primalan
*oxatamide	60 to 120mg	Tinset
phenindamine	25 to 200mg	Thephorin
pheniramine	75 to 150mg	Daneral SA
promethazine	20 to 75mg	Phenergan
*terfenadine	120mg	Triludan
trimeprazine	30 to 100mg	Vallergan
tripolidine	7.5 to 20mg	Actidil: Proactidil

*newer drugs causing less sedation

Some products are available in sustained release form to reduce the number of doses needed each day.

Asthma

In an asthma attack the bronchi contain thickened mucus, their walls are oedematous and the bronchial muscle is constricted. Asthma may be of two types: *intrinsic* or inherent, treated with corticosteroids; or *extrinsic*, triggered by some external stimulus or allergen, treated with β_2 stimulants.

Asthma may be treated prophylactically with sodium cromoglycate (Intal) or ketotifen (Zaditen). These must be taken regularly and it is important to bear in mind that they cannot be used to treat an attack. Ketotifen is given orally as tablets but its onset of action is slow, perhaps up to 4 weeks before full effect is obtained. Sodium cromoglycate has the disadvantage of acting only by inhalation, but where this therapy is acceptable to the patient it is probably the drug of choice. Its precise mode of action is not fully understood. It is thought to act by stabilising sensitised cell membranes, thus preventing the release of histamine and other trigger substances which cause bronchospasm.

Aminophylline and theophylline were once widely used as prophylactics, but suffer from a high incidence of side-effects. They have regained some acceptance in recent years with the development of sustained release preparations, which have reduced the incidence of side-effects. They are often used at night to control nocturnal asthma and wheezing. Intravenous aminophylline is widely used to treat severe asthma attacks.

Corticosteroids

Corticosteroids have a well established place in the treatment of intrinsic asthma. Oral treatment was originally used, e.g. with prednisone tablets, but this has the disadvantage of dangerous side-effects such as adrenal suppression, development of diabetes, osteoporosis and retardation of growth in children. All patients on oral therapy should carry a *Steroid Treatment Card*.

The problems of corticosteroid therapy in asthma have been largely overcome by the development of inhalation therapy, using dry powder inhalations, pressurised aerosols or suspensions for use with nebulisers. The drugs and forms available are shown in Table 7/6. When given by inhalation the dose administered is sufficiently small to exert only a local action in the lung, thus avoiding side-effects from systemic action. Though their precise mode of action is not fully

TABLE 7/6 Corticosteroids used for inhalation

Approved name	Proprietary name	Forms and strengths used
beclomethasone	Becotide	Pressurised inhaler, 50 micrograms per dose Dry powder insufflation capsules, 100 and 200 micrograms Nebuliser suspension 50 micrograms per ml
betamethasone	Bextasol	Pressurised inhaler, 100 micrograms per dose
budesonide	Pulmicort	Pressurised inhalers (adult), 200 micrograms per dose Paediatric 50 micrograms per dose

understood, they are thought to exert an anti-inflammatory effect, reducing oedema, and affecting capillary permeability thus reducing the flow of mucus.

Bronchodilators

These drugs are used in the treatment of extrinsic asthma, bronchitis, and other diseases causing bronchospasm. Drugs having non-specific alpha and beta agonist properties such as adrenaline, isoprenaline and ephedrine were used and are still available. They do, however, have unwanted side-effects on the heart, gastro- intestinal tract and bladder which limits their usefulness. The selective β_2 stimulants are now the drugs of choice (Table 7/7). They produce prompt bronchodilation, relieve bronchospasm and reduce bronchial secretions. All drugs in the group have similar action, though they may vary in their rate of onset and duration of action. Anticholinergic bronchodilators have been used in the past, but their side-effects largely preclude their use. A recent drug in the group, ipratropium bromide (Atrovent), has a much reduced incidence of side-effects and is used in patients who may be resistant to treatment with β_2 stimulants.

As with corticosteroids, inhalation therapy is preferred, as it produces the most prompt response and minimises side-effects. Oral or injected doses, which may be necessary in some patients may produce side-effects from the β_1 agonist activity shown by these drugs. The commonest side-effects are tachycardia and tremor and, in addition, night cramps, increased insulin and free fatty acid levels have been reported. The aerosol is not without its drawbacks. Patients must receive careful instruction in their use, and the manual aptitude needed to use them may be a problem in arthritics, the very old or the very young. Problems of synchronising breathing with the activation of the inhaler can be overcome by the use of additional devices such as the Spacer or Nebuhaler (see p. 357) or, alternatively, by use of the dry powder insufflator products.

Respiratory solutions and suspensions are commonly used in hospital and may be encountered in the home as well, being preferable to injections in some cases. They may be used in status asthmaticus, severe bronchospasm resulting from bronchitis or bronchial asthma, or where bronchial infections are present. Undiluted solutions, for example 2ml of salbutamol (2mg/ml) or 1ml of terbutaline (10mg/ml) may be given up to 4 times a day, over a period of about 3 minutes in oxygen-enriched air. A suitable intermittent positive pressure ventilator such as the Bird respirator is used. Alternatively, these solutions may be given continuously using

TABLE 7/7 β_2 selective bronchodilators

Approved name	Proprietary name	Form and strengths used
fenoterol	Berotec	Pressurised inhaler 180 micrograms per dose Nebuliser solution 5mg/ml
isoetharine	Numotac	Tablets 10mg
pirbuterol	Exirel	Pressurised inhaler 200 micrograms per dose Capsules 10 and 15mg Syrup 7.5mg in 5ml
reproterol	Bronchodil	Pressurised inhaler 500 micrograms per dose Nebuliser solution 10mg/ml Tablets 20mg Elixir 10mg in 5ml
rimiterol	Pulmadil	Pressurised inhaler 200 micrograms per dose
salbutamol	Ventolin Asmaven Cobutolin Salbulin	Pressurised inhaler 100 micrograms per dose Dry powder insufflation, capsules 200 and 400 micrograms Respiratory solution 5mg/ml (and 1mg/ml in single doses) Tablets 2 and 4mg Syrup 2mg in 5ml Injection 250 and 500 micrograms and 5mg
terbutaline	Bricanyl	Pressurised inhaler, 250 micrograms per dose Respiratory solution 2.5mg/ml, and 10mg/ml Tablets 5mg Syrup 1.5mg in 5ml Injection 500 micrograms

equipment such as the De Vilbis or Wright's nebuliser and the Ventimask. In these cases the above solutions are diluted in sterile water or saline to a concentration of 100 micrograms per ml and given at the rate of 1 to 2mg per hour. To avoid contamination and infection, solutions in nebulisers should be replaced with fresh material at least every 24 hours.

It is important to remember that all drugs in this group are POM and may therefore only be administered by the physiotherapist *when prescribed by a physician*. After treatment the appropriate details, such as dose and time given must be recorded by the physiotherapist in the appropriate section of the patient's case notes or treatment card.

Infections

Infections are often encountered in patients suffering from respiratory tract disease. Viral infections such as the common cold or influenza cannot be treated with antibiotics, but the patient's reduced resistance may make him susceptible to bacterial infection, perhaps leading to pneumonia. A wide range of antibiotics is available to treat infections, the successful prescribing of which is an onerous task for the physician in determining the appropriate drug and correct dose and frequency; the assistance of the microbiology laboratory to indicate sensitivities is often vital. The physiotherapist can be of particular assistance, especially with home patients, in reminding them of the importance of taking the correct dose at the prescribed interval, adhering to special instructions such as before and after food, and in particular completing the full course of treatment supplied.

BIBLIOGRAPHY

Hopkins, S. J. (1983). *Drugs and Pharmacology for Nurses*, 8th edition. Churchill Livingstone, Edinburgh.

Hopkins, S. J. (1985). *Principal Drugs: An Alphabetical Guide to Modern Therapeutic Agents*, 8th edition. Faber and Faber, London.

Martindale: The Extra Pharmacopoeia, 28th edition (1982). The Pharmaceutical Press, London.

Wilkes, E. (ed) (1982). *Long-Term Prescribing: Drug Management of Chronic Disease and Other Problems*. Faber and Faber, London.

British National Formulary is published 6-monthly by the British Medical Association and the Pharmaceutical Society of Great Britain. Available through book shops. All pharmacy departments receive a supply to be distributed free to specific personnel in the hospital.

MIMS (Monthly Index of Medical Specialists). Only lists proprietary products, and is distributed free to GPs, pharmacy departments and selected medical personnel. It may be supplied on subscription to others who write. Published monthly by MIMS, Haymarket Publishing, 38/42 Hampton Road, Teddington TW11 0JE.

Chapter 8

Cardiac Arrest and Resuscitation

by E. WELCHEW MB, ChB, FFARCS

INTRODUCTION

The leading causes of sudden death before old age, in people over the age of 44, are ventricular fibrillation from asymptomatic ischaemic heart disease or non-traumatic accidents such as drowning and poisoning. In people under the age of 38, the commonest causes are traumatic, due to accident or violence. In such instances death may be prevented if airway obstruction can be reversed, apnoea or hypoventilation avoided, blood loss prevented or corrected and the person not allowed to be pulseless or hypoxic for more than 2 or 3 minutes. If, however, there is circulatory arrest for more than a few minutes, or if blood loss or severe hypoxia remain uncorrected, irreversible brain damage may result.

Immediate resuscitation is capable of preventing death and brain damage. The techniques required may be used anywhere, with or without equipment, and by anyone, from the lay public to medical specialists, provided they have been appropriately trained.

Resuscitation may be divided into three phases:

1. *Basic Life Support* using little or no equipment.
2. When equipment and drugs become available *Advanced Life Support* may start, in which a spontaneous circulation is restored.
3. *Prolonged Life Support* which is usually conducted in an intensive therapy unit and is directed towards salvaging cerebral function in the comatose patient, maintaining a stable circulation, restoring oxygenation to normal and other aspects of intensive care.

When confronted by an apparently unconscious patient, first establish that they are unconscious by *shaking* him and *shouting* at him. Then *call for help without leaving the patient.* Immediately check that he has a patent airway, and, if not, provide one. If the patient is

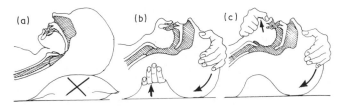

FIG. 8/1 Head positioning to prevent airways obstruction.
(a) *Wrong*: on a pillow the head is flexed forward causing pharyngeal obstruction by the tongue. (b) *Correct*: tilting the head backward and lifting the back of the neck upward stretches the anterior neck structure bringing the base of the tongue off the pharyngeal wall. (c) *Correct*: tilting the head backward and pulling the chin upward also prevents the tongue obstructing the pharynx

unconscious but is breathing through a patent airway, then he should be rolled into a stable position on his side with the face pointing slightly downwards. The head should be tilted backwards and the jaw supported to keep the airway patent (Fig. 8/1). In this position, it will be less likely that the tongue will fall backwards to obstruct the pharynx, and saliva, blood and vomitus will be able to

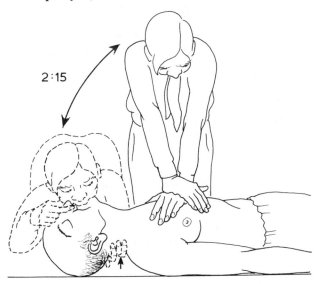

FIG. 8/2 Artificial ventilation and external cardiac massage with one operator only. 15 sternal compressions are alternated with 2 inflations of the lungs. The chest should be compressed at a rate of about 80 per minute; the return of a spontaneous pulse should be checked every 2 minutes or so

drain forwards out of the mouth instead of being aspirated into the lungs. If the patient is not breathing then, while keeping the airway patent, he should be put on to his back and artificial ventilation started. Finally, his pulse should be palpated – preferably at the carotid artery in the neck. If no pulse can be felt and the patient is unconscious, it must be assumed that he is in cardiac arrest. While continuing to provide artificial ventilation, external cardiac massage should also be given to maintain the patient's circulation (Fig. 8/2).

Where a patient is already in hospital having his ECG monitored when he has a cardiac arrest, and it is known that he went into witnessed ventricular fibrillation during the last 30 seconds, then the treatment of choice would be to first attempt to defibrillate him using 200 joules (J). If this did not succeed, then one should immediately proceed to Basic Life Support with the maintenance of a patent airway and ventilation as well as keeping the patient's circulation going with external cardiac massage as described below.

THE ABC OF RESUSCITATION

Basic Life Support

A.   AIRWAY

1. Ensure that the patient has a patent airway (Fig. 8/1).
2. Remove fluid and debris from the mouth using fingers and suction as necessary.
3. Insert a pharyngeal airway if necessary and available.

B.   BREATHING

1. Maintain a *patent airway.*
2. If the patient is breathing *roll him on to his side* into a stable position with the head tilted back. Maintain a patent airway and *check that breathing does not stop.* Check his pulse.
3. If the patient is not breathing leave him on his back and;
4. *Inflate the patient's lungs* rapidly 3 to 5 times using one of the following methods:
    (a) Use mouth to mouth or mouth to nose ventilation.
    (b) Insert a Brook airway, give mouth to airway ventilation.
    (c) Ventilate the patient using a bag and mask.
5. *Look for the rise of the patient's chest* with each ventilation. If this is not seen there may be (a) an obstruction in the airway,
    (b) a poor seal with the patient's airways during inflation, or
    (c) simply not enough air being blown into the patient.
6. Feel for the carotid pulse.

7. If the pulse is present, but no spontaneous ventilation, then continue 12 lung inflations per minute.

C. CIRCULATION

1. If the pulse is present and there is obvious external haemorrhage, control bleeding by applying pressure to the bleeding point and elevating it if appropriate.
2. If the pulse is absent, and
3. If there is no spontaneous breathing or gasping, then
4. Transfer the patient to the floor, if he is not already on a hard surface, and start external cardiac massage:

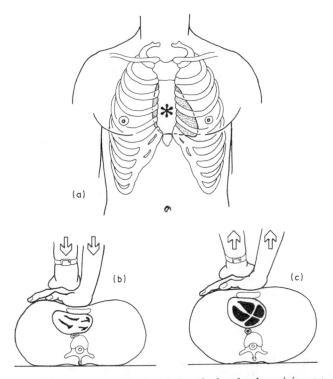

FIG. 8/3 (a) The correct position for placing the hands when giving external cardiac massage. (b) Compression of the chest with the heel of the hand on the sternum, and the second hand on it. The heart and major vessels in the chest are compressed between the sternum and the vertebral body. (c) Without losing contact with the patient's chest, the pressure on the chest should be released for 50 per cent of each cycle to allow the heart and blood vessels to fill with blood

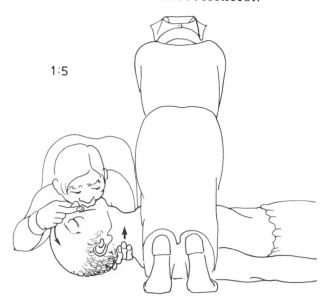

1:5

FIG. 8/4 Artificial ventilation and external cardiac massage with two operators. The first operator compresses the chest at one per second, the second operator inflates the lungs once every fifth compression

Single operator: Alternate 2 quick lung inflations with 15 sternal compressions (Fig. 8/2). Compress the sternum at a rate of 80/min (Fig. 8/3).

Two operators: Alternate 1 lung inflation with 5 sternal compressions (Fig. 8/4). Compress at a rate of 60/min.

The lower third of the sternum should be compressed about 5cm (2in) each time.

Resuscitation should be continued until a spontaneous pulse returns.

Advanced Life Support (The restoration of a spontaneous circulation)

D. DRUGS

1. Cardiac compression and ventilation of the lungs should not be interrupted.
2. A central or peripheral intravenous catheter or needle should be inserted if not already in place.

3. The trachea should be intubated (when possible this should be done by someone appropriately skilled in the procedure). Not only will this make maintenance of the patency of the airway much easier, it will also protect the airway to some extent from contamination by fluid or vomitus, and make artificial ventilation much easier to perform effectively.

4. The following drugs may be used:
   (a) adrenaline 0.5–1mg, repeated every 3–5 minutes as necessary.
   (b) sodium bicarbonate 1mEquiv/kg body-weight. This is repeated every 10 minutes of arrest time. For adults an 8.4% bicarbonate solution is used (this contains 1mEquiv/ml); however, this solution is generally too concentrated for small children, for whom a 4.2% solution should be used.
   (c) intravenous fluids as required, e.g. blood or plasma.

5. If intravenous access is not established, drugs may be given down the endotracheal tube directly into the patient's airway, where they work as quickly as when given intravenously. The exception to this is bicarbonate solutions, which must only be given intravenously.

6. As a last resort, drugs such as adrenaline may be given directly into the heart through the chest wall, though this may damage the heart muscle or cause a pneumothorax.

E. ECG (ELECTROCARDIOGRAM) (Fig. 8/5) (*see also* Chapter 6)

As soon as possible the ECG of the patient should be monitored:
Ventricular fibrillation should be treated by defibrillation.
Asystole should be treated with adrenaline and then defibrillation.
Ventricular tachycardias may be treated by defibrillation or verapamil.
Bradycardias may be treated with atropine.

F. FIBRILLATION TREATMENT (Fig. 8/6)

If coarse ventricular fibrillation or ventricular tachycardia are seen then clear the area and DC defibrillate the patient. Cardiac massage and ventilation should not be interrupted for more than a few seconds.

1. External defibrillation using 100–400J. Repeat shock as necessary.
2. Convert fine fibrillation to coarse fibrillation using adrenaline.
3. Lignocaine 1–2mg/kg intravenously as necessary. If a defibrillator is not available, then lignocaine intravenously or via the endotracheal tube may convert to a sinus rhythm.

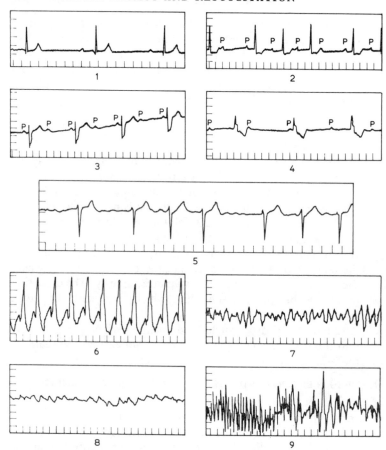

FIG. 8/5 Stylised ECG patterns:

1. The fixed, prolonged P-R interval of first degree atrioventricular block
2. A gradually increasing P-R interval, followed by a dropped beat, typical of the Wenckebach type of second degree heart block
3. Fixed 2:1 type of second degree heart block (2 P waves for each QRS complex)
4. Complete atrioventricular heart block with total dissociation of P waves and QRS complex
5. Atrial fibrillation with irregularly spaced QRS complexes, no visible P waves and a finely irregular baseline between QRS complexes
6. Ventricular tachycardia with wide and rapid QRS complexes
7. Coarse ventricular fibrillation with no normal features visible at all
8. Fine ventricular fibrillation
9. Artefact due to patient movement, with completely irregular, narrow, high voltage complexes overlying normal, regular QRS complexes

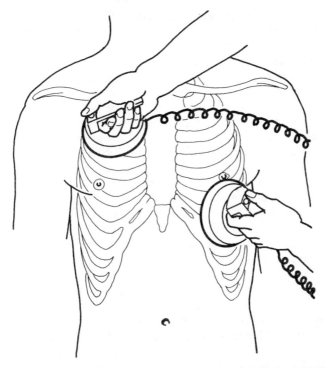

Fig. 8/6 External electrical defibrillation. After connecting the defibrillator to the power supply and switching on, it should be charged to give 200 joules (J), or roughly 3J/kg body-weight. The electrodes should be well lubricated with conductive jelly, and placed one just below the patient's right clavicle and the other over the cardiac apex. Clear the immediate area, ensure that *no one* is touching the patient or the bed, apply firm pressure on to the patient's chest with the paddles and press the defibrillator button. Wait 5 seconds to confirm the resultant ECG and resume external cardiac massage and artificial ventilation as necessary. The latter should not be interrupted for more than 30 seconds for defibrillation

Prolonged Life Support (on intensive therapy unit)

G. GAUGING

1. Gauge the likely outcome of resuscitation.
2. Gauge the cause of the cardiorespiratory arrest and treat it.

H. HUMAN MENTATION

1. Preserve cerebral function by maintaining normal cerebral blood flow and oxygenation.

This may necessitate prolonged mechanical ventilation via a tracheal tube, or even the insertion of a tracheostomy tube in order to facilitate this.

The patient may require oxygen to be added to the respiratory gas mixture in carefully controlled amounts, with repeated estimations of the oxygen content of the patient's blood.

2. Reduce and control intracranial pressure.

This may necessitate the insertion of devices through the patient's skull to measure intracranial pressure continuously so that therapy may be modified accordingly.

Mechanical ventilation is one of the most important ways to reduce and maintain stable the patient's intracranial pressure. If the intracranial pressure is allowed to rise due to swelling or bleeding, this will reduce the blood flow to the brain and, hence, also reduce the oxygen supply to it. The patient may also be given steroids and diuretics to reduce the swelling.

3. Monitor cerebral function.

The electrical activity of the brain may be monitored continuously with a variety of cerebral function monitors (CFMs). More specific information may be obtained with repeated electro-encephalograms (EEGs).

Repeated neurological examinations by the doctors and careful observation of the patient by *all* members of staff will provide invaluable information on the degree of neurological damage or recovery exhibited by the patient.

I.   INTENSIVE CARE

1. Provide intensive therapy.
2. Intensive nursing.
3. Intensive monitoring.

Patients who have undergone cardiorespiratory resuscitation need careful monitoring and care afterwards. They may have a further cardiac or respiratory arrest from the same cause as the original insult or as a result of its consequences. This will necessitate intensive monitoring of the patient's condition at all times and provision of immediate skilled resuscitation within seconds. He may require cardiac, as well as respiratory, support in order to maintain adequate tissue oxygenation. This cardiac support may be pharmacological, using drugs such as dopamine to increase cardiac output, or vasodilators such as sodium nitroprusside to reduce the work done by the heart. On the other hand, the support may be mechanical using the aortic balloon pump (see p. 391).

In a similar way, support for the patient who has had a respiratory arrest may be either pharmacological or mechanical. Pharmacological support may be provided with respiratory stimulants such as doxapram or, in the case of narcotic overdoses by the narcotic antagonist naloxone. Mechanical support may be provided with ventilators.

One of the commonest problems encountered in these patients is acute renal failure, but with careful management function may be restored to normal. Patients with renal failure will require careful monitoring of their fluid input and urine output, serum and urinary electrolytes and osmolality. Fluid restriction, diuretics and, possibly, peritoneal or haemodialysis will be required.

Figure 8/7 summarises action and management following cardiac arrest.

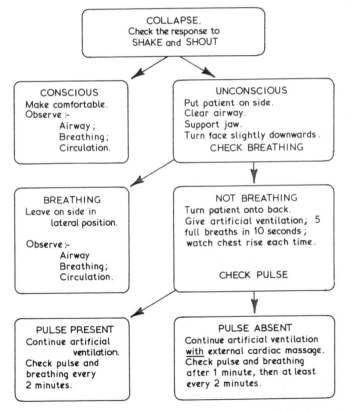

FIG. 8/7 Flow chart summarising action and management following cardiac arrest

INFANTS AND CHILDREN

In this context, *infants* are aged less than 1 year and *children* aged 1 to 8 years. Over the age of 8, resuscitation may proceed as for a small adult. The most common causes of cardiorespiratory arrest in these groups are:

1. Asphyxia due to foreign bodies, near drowning or upper airway infection.
2. Trauma, burns or poisoning.
3. Sudden infant death syndrome.

In these groups, prevention of accidents will have the greatest effect on the overall mortality.

There are certain key differences in the methods used to resuscitate infants and children compared with the scheme proposed so far. The overall 'ABC' plan, however, remains the same.

A.   AIRWAY

1. The neck should not be hyperextended, nor the head tilted, as far back as the adult as this will obstruct the upper airway.
2. Infants and small children are obligatory mouth breathers. During resuscitation the mouth should be kept open, using a pharyngeal airway if necessary.

B.   BREATHING

If the infant is not breathing begin artificial ventilation.

1. The infant's mouth and nose should be encircled with one's own mouth.
2. Small, gentle inflations should be given, puffing from the checks to avoid damaging the infant's lungs.
3. Watch the chest rise with each inflation and take the mouth off the face in between inflations to allow passive expiration.
4. An infant should be ventilated at a rate of 30/minute, and children at a rate of 20/minute.

Give 3–5 inflations of the lungs, then feel for a pulse.

C.   CIRCULATION

If no pulse can be felt, then give external cardiac compressions.

1. In infants, press the *mid-sternum* with 2 or 3 fingers. It should be depressed about 1.25cm($\frac{1}{2}$in) at a rate of about 100/min.

2. In children, using the heel of one hand, press slightly *below the mid-sternum*. It should be depressed about 2.5cm(1in) about 80 times per minute.
3. Ventilation should be continued at a rate of 1 inflation every 5 sternal compressions.

D. DRUGS AND E. ECG

Drugs and fluids used are essentially the same as those for adults except that the doses and volumes are scaled down to roughly 1/60th of the total adult dose per kilogram of the child's body-weight.

F. FIBRILLATION TREATMENT

1. Much smaller defibrillator paddles should be used than in adults.
2. In infants, 4.5cm diameter electrodes should be used and in children 8cm diameter ones should be used.
3. DC counter-shock should be applied using 2J/kg body-weight, repeating this, if necessary, with 4J/kg while taking steps to improve oxygenation, and giving adrenaline and bicarbonate as necessary.

Prolonged Life Support is similar to that of adults.

BIBLIOGRAPHY

Brophy, T. (1978). *Resuscitation in the Electrical Industry.* Handbook of the Brisbane Electrical Commission of Queensland, Australia.

Carden, N. I. and Steinhaus, J. E. (1956). Lidocaine resuscitation from ventricular fibrillation. *Circulation Research*, 4, 640.

Jennett, B. and Bond, M. (1975). Assessment of outcome after severe brain damage. A practical scale. *Lancet*, 1, 480.

Kirimli, B., Harris, L. C. and Safar, P. (1966). Drugs used in cardiopulmonary resuscitation. *Acta Anaesthesiologica Scandinavica*, 23, 255.

Redding, J. S., Asuncion, J. S. and Pearson, J. W. (1967). Effective routes of drug administration during cardiac arrest. *Anaesthesia and Analgesia*, 46, 253.

Safar, P. (ed) (1981). *Cardiopulmonary Cerebral Resuscitation.* W. B. Saunders, Philadelphia.

Tacker, W. A. (Jr) and Wey, G. A. (1979). Emergency defibrillation dose: Recommendations and rationale. *Circulation*, 60,223.

Winchell, S. W. and Safar, P. (1966). Teaching and testing lay and paramedical personnel in cardiopulmonary resuscitation. *Anaesthesia and Analgesia*, 45, 441.

Chapter 9

Intensive Therapy – Clinical Management

by B. R. H. DORAN MB, BS, FFARCS

THE INTENSIVE CARE UNIT

An intensive care unit (ICU) is an area set aside for the care of patients who are either critically ill or who are in danger of becoming so if deprived of continuous care and attention.

It may go under a variety of names according to its specific purpose and the degree of dependency of the patient. For example, a renal care unit (RCU) cares for patients on chronic renal dialysis and the level of patient monitoring is relatively low (but still higher than the general ward) as these cases are usually stable; a coronary care unit (CCU) looks after patients with ischaemic heart disease, such as angina and myocardial infarction, and, while a continuous readout of the electrocardiogram (ECG) is required, more invasive techniques are relatively infrequent; a special care baby unit (SCBU) handles neonatal problems often requiring intermittent positive pressure ventilation (IPPV) and invasive monitoring techniques; a high dependency unit (HDU) is akin to the recovery area of an operating theatre and will have a low level of monitoring but a high level of nursing attendance; an intensive therapy unit (ITU) has the highest level of patient dependency and the most aggressive treatment and monitoring protocols. Cardiac surgery units (CSUs) are good examples, as are the major ITUs which look after the most serious cases from many disciplines such as trauma and orthopaedics, general surgery, neurosurgery; and various medical specialties among which respiratory medicine will figure prominently.

There is some confusion as, for example, the terms 'ICU' and 'ITU' are often used interchangeably, but while a CCU could be called an ICU it would not usually qualify as an ITU – it usually has a 'watching' brief rather than an aggressively therapeutic one.

This chapter, and the next concern the highest level of dependency, active intervention and therapy. The other types of unit will use the same protocols to a lesser or greater degree. [The term ITU is being used throughout the book – Editor.]

Logistics

An ITU requires space, personnel and equipment to a degree not found outside the operating theatre. Each bed requires 20m² of space plus similar back-up space in terms of equipment and 'ready use' storage, 'stat' labs, workshops, offices and staff rest rooms. Facilities for patients' relatives are not included, but clearly, on a humanitarian basis, adequate waiting, rest and refreshment and interview rooms should be available.

In the most acute situation even more space (perhaps 40m², or the size of a respectable operating theatre) is required to allow access to the patient for several attendants and the multitude of apparatus. In the latter regard, 16 electrical, 3 oxygen, 2 vacuum and 1 air outlets are essential, and a nitrous oxide outlet is desirable.

In terms of staffing, a 1:1 nurse:patient ratio is required at all times and this means four nurses to every patient over the 24 hours to allow for leave and sickness, plus 24-hour medical cover. A nurse to patient ratio of 4.25 to 1 has been suggested (Tinker, 1976), i.e. for a six-bed unit a total of 25.5 nurses (or nurse equivalents) are needed, and for 10 beds 42.5. To be viable and manageable it has been found that ITUs should be of between four and 10 beds. As each bed requires some £40,000 worth of apparatus (at 1986 prices) plus the staff and the space outlined above, ITUs are thus expensive of technology, space and manpower.

For the best care, an efficient service is required from a multitude of other disciplines, for example, biochemistry, haematology, bacteriology, physiotherapy, pharmacy, radiology, dietetics, and medical physics – not forgetting, and perhaps most importantly, the goodwill and efficient co-operation of clerical, telephone and portering services.

Because results of certain investigations are critical to the continued well-being of the patient it is essential that a swift service is available from the laboratories. If this is not possible for reasons of distance and communication then a small local laboratory for the estimation of blood gas, sodium and potassium, blood sugar and haematocrit is needed. In this case machines that are robust and easy to use, with automatic calibration and cleansing facilities, should be provided. Unit staff must ensure that proper quality controls are carried out to ensure accuracy.

Intensive therapy brings together many branches of medicine and surgery, and several specialties are commonly involved in the treatment of one case. Not the least of ITU functions is to liaise between the admitting team and any other specialist team who might be asked to advise, to ensure that a co-ordinated effort is directed towards the recovery of the patient. The 'Intensivist' is the co-ordinator and final common pathway for these services, as well as being the final arbiter should disagreement arise either with regard to treatment or to treatment priorities. The consultant in charge can be from any discipline (e.g. physician, surgeon or anaesthetist) but in the UK he is commonly an anaesthetist, because the care of patients on life-support machines is closely akin to the practice of anaesthesia.

The role of the physiotherapist in all this is vital. These patients can often do little or nothing for themselves, and so are prone to all the disorders of immobility, such as hypostatic pneumonia, muscle wasting and limb contractures, and pressure sores. Frequently the patient is in a poor nutritional state, engendered by the disease and exacerbated by the difficulties of providing adequate nutritional intake to the seriously ill.

All such problems are multiplied by infections, and patients intubated on an ITU are very prone to chest infections in particular. Frequently they have a microbial overgrowth caused by antibiotic therapy. It is often the case that good chest physiotherapy can prevent or treat chest complications without recourse to antibiotics, and its frequent application is vital. The physiotherapist is often required in 'out-of-office' hours. This is *not* to say that she *must* be on call all night; nurses are trained in basic chest care, and the patient does need sleep too.

PATIENT MONITORING

The essence of an ITU is the ability to assess the status of patients quickly and accurately, and to follow their progress for better or worse. This is accomplished as follows:

Electronic measurement

It should be stated at the outset that a great deal of ITU monitoring is invasive, and carries with it a definite risk of morbidity, not to say mortality, and so should be instituted only where clear indications exist. There is still no substitute for close clinical observation by trained medical and nursing staff.

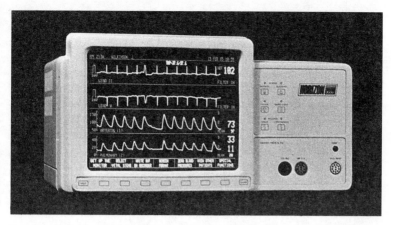

FIG. 9/1 Mennen bedside patient monitor (*courtesy* Mennen Medical Ltd)

Bedside monitoring units should be capable of displaying four waveforms simultaneously, and two temperatures as digits (Fig. 9/1). The reasons for this are discussed below. The latest monitors contain powerful microprocessors which can store data for future recall and examination, and perform a certain amount of data handling and manipulation. It is becoming possible to relieve the nurses of a lot of the charting and paperwork they have to do at present, thus allowing them to concentrate more on direct patient care.

Many ITUs will have a central station where staff can observe all beds while performing administrative tasks.

The requirements of a monitoring system include:

ELECTROCARDIOGRAM (ECG)

This is essential on one channel, and a digital rate meter should be incorporated so that the nurse can observe the patient's heart rate easily and quickly. It is used for the more general rate and rhythm disturbances rather than the finer more academic cardiological diagnoses. The ECG electrodes are commonly positioned on the chest, and are very subject to interference, so that it should not come as a surprise if the ECG trace goes peculiar or the alarms sound during chest physiotherapy. Of course, close watch on the clinical condition is vital, because it is all too easy to ignore alarms in these circumstances, perhaps fatally.

PRESSURE

This can be:

Arterial pressure. Systemic blood pressure, popularly known as the 'BP' can be measured conventionally by a nurse with a stethoscope or may be taken automatically by a machine; the latter could be a device that performs as an automatic stethoscope or it could be one that is directly connected to a cannula placed in an artery (a transducer). In the latter case blood sampling is made very easy. The radial artery at the wrist is commonly used.

Central venous pressure (CVP). Measured either by transducer or by simple water manometer, the CVP allows the 'filling' or 'driving' pressure to the heart to be assessed. No pump can work without an adequate supply of fluid (blood) and any pump can fail if the supply is too great for its capacity – there is a build-up behind the pump causing in the human subject the signs and symptoms of congestive cardiac failure.

A catheter is placed in or close to the right atrium, usually by percutaneous puncture of the median basilic vein of the arm or of one of the great veins of the neck – internal jugular or subclavian. The latter carry the risk of pneumothorax or worse, being in close proximity to the pleura and the great vessels and nerve trunks. However, a CVP line does allow the administration of potent drugs and hypertonic solutions relatively safely, and the latter include the parenteral nutrition solutions and other hyperosmolar fluids. Given peripherally such concentrated drugs and solutions (these include sodium bicarbonate used for the treatment of acidosis) can cause tissue necrosis.

Multilumen CVP lines are now in common use (Fig. 9/2), allowing separation of the many drugs and solutions administered so that accidental over- or underdosage is less likely to occur.

Pulmonary artery pressure and pulmonary wedge pressure. Pressure in the pulmonary artery, and in particular the wedge pressure (where the catheter is jammed ('wedged') into a small pulmonary vessel so as to occlude it, thereby recording pressures transmitted back via the pulmonary circulation from the left atrium), can be measured by means of a balloon catheter (Swan et al, 1970), the balloon of which can be released or inflated at will so as not to occlude the vessel permanently. The wedge pressure reflects the function of the left side of the heart – and hence the output of blood to vital organs such as brain and kidney – more accurately than does the CVP and

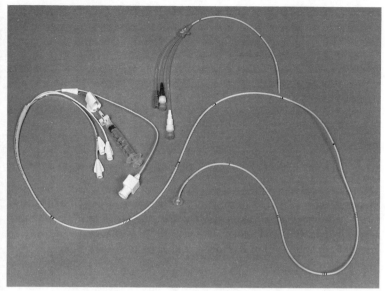

FIG. 9/2 *upper*: Arrow triple lumen CVP line (*courtesy* Kimal Scientific Products Ltd). *lower*: Swan Ganz Thermodilution Catheter VIP model (*courtesy* American Hospital Supply (UK) Ltd)

thereby more closely monitors how well the heart is performing, and the effects of treatment such as transfusion, drug therapy to improve cardiac output (digoxin, dopamine, dobutamine, adrenaline, calcium), and therapy to reduce the work of the heart (nitroglycerine, nitroprusside).

Intracranial pressure (ICP). Raised ICP occurs after head injury; other causes are cerebral tumour and hypoxic brain damage. As ICP rises towards systemic blood pressure then clearly blood flow to the brain must be reduced (and along with it the supply of nutrients such as oxygen and glucose); the bony skull cannot expand, and with the onset of cerebral oedema ICP rises sharply. The ICP can be measured by means of a transducer connected to either the extradural space or to the ventricles and can provide early warnings of impending disaster, or testify to the adequacy of treatment. The electro-encephalogram (see below) is a complementary investigation.

TEMPERATURE

It is important to know the patient's temperature as part of the general assessment. For instance, fever is found in cases of sepsis and subnormal temperature may be a sign of brain damage. Skin temperature as well as central or core temperature is measured, because if the skin (usually measured at the big toe) is warm then the blood supply to vital organs such as brain, liver and kidneys is probably adequate.

High temperatures are associated with high oxygen consumption, and make it all the more important for the lungs to be working well. In such cases the patient may be treated by deliberate cooling, by fanning or by placement on a blanket which circulates cold water to accomplish cooling in a controlled manner.

ELECTRO-ENCEPHALOGRAM (EEG)

A simple single channel device is frequently used during open heart bypass and on ITUs because it is reasonably cheap, can provide useful information as to gross cerebral function, and can demonstrate trends in conscious level. It is not, nor was ever claimed to be, more than a crude tool. It can show gross changes, and demonstrate the occurrence of such events as post-traumatic epilepsy when they may be masked by intercurrent treatment with, for instance, muscle relaxant drugs.

Diagnostic quality EEGs are required for the assessment of coma and expert neurological opinion must be sought for their interpretation.

OTHER MEASUREMENTS

Fluid balance is the difference between input and output, and while the normal person regulates this automatically, the sick patient is often unable to. Input must be meticulously controlled by accurate delivery systems such as volumetric pumps (the normal ward infusion set is very difficult to regulate accurately), and the exact recipe and route of administration is decided by results of laboratory tests and clinical observations. Output is more difficult, as allowances have to be made for immeasurable losses such as sweating, and water in exhaled breath, or in faeces. Nasogastric aspirate is easily collected, but fluid from fistulae may not be so. All that can should be collected and measured; in particular the urine as this gives a measure not only of simple fluid and electrolyte balance and the efficiency of the kidneys, but also of protein metabolism and muscle breakdown, because this is related to the output of urea in the urine, and forms the basis of the science of nutrition in the critically ill.

Weight is a guide to nutritional status and water balance, and is important as a guide to the dosage of some potent drugs. Patients on renal dialysis are usually weighed continuously during treatment so that sudden excessive changes in water balance, which could result in dehydration, or in circulatory overload and pulmonary oedema, may be avoided.

Respiration is monitored for volume and frequency using a respirometer, which may be a simple wind vane such as a Wright's respirometer, or a more complicated device such as a pneumotachograph which senses the pressure drop across a known resistance and relates this to gas flow. Newer ventilators have respirometers built in to automatically register the information.

Gas analysers may also be put into a breathing circuit, and are usually of the fuel cell or polarimetric type for oxygen, and infra-red type for carbon dioxide. The latter are placed very close to the patient to measure peak CO_2 concentration at the end of expiration (end-tidal CO_2) which relates to alveolar CO_2 and thus arterial Pco_2 so providing a useful index of ventilation without the need for an arterial puncture.

Respiratory monitors can be interfaced with ventilators (e.g. the Engstrom Erica) to work out the patient's metabolic rate from the rate of oxygen consumption and carbon dioxide production. This is important in the calculation of nutritional needs; it seems that it is very easy to over-feed sick patients who simply turn calories into carbon dioxide and water and then have problems in disposing of these by-products. Excessive carbon dioxide production from feeding will clearly be an embarrassment to, say, a chronic bronchitic who needs to be weaned from IPPV.

Laboratory investigations include haematological (e.g. blood counts for the detection of anaemia and the raised white cell count of infection); biochemical (e.g. serum electrolytes for the detection of such conditions as hypokalaemia which can produce life-threatening cardiac arrhythmias; hypoglycaemia which may result from disease or insulin therapy; and levels of poisonous substances in overdose cases); and bacteriological (e.g. sputum, urine and blood cultures, and sensitivities of offending organisms to antibiotic therapy).

Radiology is mainly confined to chest radiographs, but other types may be needed, notably computerised axial tomography (CT scan) in head injuries. Portable radiographs are notoriously of poor quality, and in spite of transportation problems in patients on life-support systems, when high quality results are necessary the patient must be moved to the machine rather than vice versa. Such a case might be suspected cervical spine fracture or CT scan.

In addition to portable x-ray machines there are now portable diagnostic machines based on ultrasound and isotope techniques. The diagnosis of intra-abdominal sepsis (a particularly lethal condition), cardiac lesions and embolic episodes (such as pulmonary embolus) should hopefully become easier for the ITU patient.

THE AIRWAY

A patent airway is central to the practice of intensive care. If the patient cannot maintain his own airway then some form of endotracheal tube is used (see p. 230), or at the least a simple oropharyngeal airway which might be enough to allow suction.

Endotracheal tubes can be passed via the mouth (oral) or the nose (nasal), or a tracheostomy (an operation to create an opening or stoma into the trachea) can be performed. Oral intubation is usually the easiest to perform but is the least comfortable. In addition, a patient may occasionally clamp his teeth on the tube and thus totally obstruct his airway. Nasal intubation overcomes this particular problem but a longer tube of smaller diameter has to be used (except in small children) and it is thus more difficult to keep patent. There is also the risk of sinusitis as the tube may block the nasal sinuses.

It is our practice to perform tracheostomy at about 7 days. The patient is much more comfortable than with either oral or nasal tube, and mouth hygiene is much simpler. We do insist that an experienced surgeon performs the operation, and we prefer to ask the ENT team.

The functions of an endotracheal or tracheostomy tube are:

1. To facilitate access to pulmonary secretions.
2. To prevent substances from the mouth entering and soiling the lungs.
3. To help to maintain positive pressure ventilation by preventing air from escaping round the tube.
4. To by-pass an obstruction preventing ventilation.

All endotracheal and tracheostomy tubes reduce the anatomical dead space by about one half but this gain is usually negligible in comparison to the increased physiological dead space present in the patient with pulmonary disease. There is therefore some doubt as to whether intubation significantly facilitates spontaneous ventilation in these patients.

Tracheostomy and endotracheal tubes are sized from 2.5mm (neonatal) increasing by 0.5mm to 11.0mm (large adult male).

The silver tracheostomy tube cannot be used easily for connection to a ventilator and is used in the intermediate stage before finally closing the tracheostomy. It is sometimes a permanent feature for patients following laryngectomy. It usually has an inner tube which can be removed for cleaning. Some have a valve which allows the patient with a larynx to speak.

The disadvantages of tracheostomy (and of endotracheal intubation by any route) are the increased danger of infection and the loss of humidification. Dry gases entering the trachea can cause crusts to form and a blockage of one of the respiratory passages may occur.

Passage of any sort of endotracheal tube also prevents the patient developing spontaneous positive end-expiratory pressure (PEEP). You will have noticed how a chronic bronchitic breathes out through pursed lips in an attempt to develop PEEP and improve his oxygenation – an effective manoeuvre. Having bypassed the lips with a tube, where necessary one must provide a PEEP valve in the breathing circuit. One can augment spontaneous PEEP and avoid intubation in some cases using a CPAP mask (see Chapter 10).

Opinions differ as to the frequency with which tracheostomy tubes should be changed. Within a few days of operation there is a firm track from the skin to the trachea and after this there is usually no difficulty in changing the tube; prior to this the route from skin surface into the trachea may be lost, with lethal results.

Occasionally it may be necessary to use an airway to facilitate suction through the mouth. All physiotherapists should be familiar with the airway, which is frequently in position when a patient returns from theatre. It is a simple tube, usually made of rigid plastic, flattened vertically, with a flange to prevent it from slipping past the teeth and into the mouth completely. It has a right-angled curve so that the tube fits over the tongue and down into the pharynx. Airways vary in size. An airway facilitates artificial ventilation when used in conjunction with an anaesthetic bag and mask during resuscitation but cannot be used for intermittent positive pressure ventilation (IPPV). It serves the simple purpose of preventing the tongue falling backwards and suffocating the unconscious patient; it also gives a clear pathway for suction in both the conscious and the unconscious patient. In some centres individual physiotherapists after tuition are allowed to insert them without supervision. The usual method of doing this is to put the airway into the mouth with the curved end pointing upwards. Once in the mouth it is rotated through 180°. It is then in position to restrain the tongue, protect the suction catheter from being bitten and direct it into the pharynx.

HUMIDIFICATION

Humidification is the moistening of the air or gases we breathe. This is normally one of the functions of the upper respiratory tract. Artificial humidification is necessary for patients in the following circumstances:

When breathing through endotracheal or tracheostomy tubes (see Fig. 10/4, p. 236)

The natural humidification and warming function of the upper respiratory tract is by-passed if a patient is breathing through either an endotracheal or tracheostomy tube. Dry air at lower than body temperature passing over secretions in the bronchial tree extracts moisture from them causing crusts to be formed. These crusts may partially block the trachea or main bronchus or occlude one of the smaller airways. They are very difficult to remove. Ciliary action is diminished and eventually destroyed in the absence of adequate humidification. Artificial humidification is therefore essential for the maintenance of adequate ventilation. The vast majority of ventilators incorporate some form of humidification. Patients who need a permanent silver tracheostomy tube eventually acclimatise themselves to the lack of humidification and provided the inner tube is cleaned regularly suffer no gross ill-effects.

When breathing air to which gases have been added (O_2 masks)

Medical gases are completely dry and will require considerable humidification and it may be considered advantageous to the patient to augment the natural humidification process.

When secretions are abnormally thick

Humidification will facilitate their removal.

There are several methods of achieving humidification, but the majority have the same two problems to a greater or lesser extent.

Condensation in the tubes ('rain out') is one of these and when using apparatus where this pertains, care must be taken to ensure that the tubes are emptied at regular intervals. It is very distressing for the patient if water spills into the airways. Additionally, the tubes may become so full of water that they become effectively blocked, performing efficient iatrogenic suffocation. The other problem is that humidifiers are liable to become infected by bacteria and introduce this infection into the patient's respiratory system. Careful sterilisation of the apparatus is essential, and the introduction of single use disposable apparatus has largely overcome this problem. Types of humidifier are discussed in Chapter 10, page 235.

VENTILATION AND OXYGENATION

Inadequate gas exchange can result from a multitude of causes, ranging from central nervous system depression (head injury, drug overdose) through neuromuscular disorders (myasthenia gravis, poliomyelitis, ascending polyneuritis) and musculoskeletal malfunction (flail chest, ruptured diaphragm) to problems with the lungs and airways themselves (pneumonia, bronchitis, asthma, shock lung). It is important to recognise impending problems early so that they may be treated swiftly before complications ensue (e.g. inability to cough adequately postoperatively leading to bronchopneumonia).

Impending respiratory failure from most causes can be recognised clinically by the syndrome of anxiety, restlessness, sweating, confusion, and (excepting perhaps the chronic bronchitics) cold extremities, in a patient with tachycardia and tachypnoea. Very often the accessory muscles of respiration are being used. Whether or not there is cyanosis present will to some extent depend on whether oxygen therapy is being given, and on how alkalotic the patient has become (alkalosis can allow the patient to remain pink in spite of very low arterial oxygen levels).

Biochemically the initial response is a respiratory alkalosis due to hyperventilation in an attempt to gain more oxygen; therefore a low Pco_2 is found, and (except again in the case of the severe chronic bronchitic) a higher than normal Pco_2 is a late and ominous finding. Even the severe bronchitic will initially lower his Pco_2, but as his resting level was already high it may still be above normal. In both groups of patients when the Pco_2 eventually rises a respiratory acidosis will appear, often with a metabolic element secondary to release of lactic acid from hypoxic tissues.

Some of the clinical findings may be masked by the administration of drugs, particularly the narcotic analgesics such as morphine and pethidine.

Mechanical intervention is a medical decision, but the opinion of the physiotherapist is invaluable. An overall view of past history and present illness is necessary, with particular attention being paid to the trend of events. A patient who is becoming exhausted should not have to await deterioration of his blood gas status before ventilation is considered. Equally, the chronic bronchitic who normally has a low Po_2 and high Pco_2 might not be ventilated even when he has blood gases that would automatically mean ventilation for a previously normal subject.

Probably the best guide to the problem is the arterial Po_2 when taken in conjunction with the inspired oxygen concentration. As a rule of thumb a previously healthy patient should be considered for ventilation if he cannot maintain a Po_2 of 9.31kPa (70mmHg) on 40% oxygen.

Oxygen prescription

Oxygen should be regarded as a drug and it can produce toxic effects. Retrolental fibroplasia in neonates was described by Petz (1958) and pulmonary abnormalities in patients who died after prolonged IPPV were greater in patients receiving over 90% oxygen in one series (Nash et al, 1967); 70% inspired oxygen is often regarded as the upper safe limit. However, if this does not produce an adequate arterial Po_2 then one may be forced to use a higher concentration. Many units regard an achieved arterial Po_2 of 10kPa (75mmHg) a reasonable compromise between adequate oxygen delivery and high inspired oxygen concentrations.

Oxygen therapy can produce depression of respiration in those patients who have lost their sensitivity to the normal CO_2 drive, and who thus rely on the stimulus of hypoxia to maintain breathing. Oxygen therapy may then cause a cessation of breathing and a build-up of CO_2 to levels which have a narcotic effect within minutes. Such patients are the 'blue-bloater' type of chronic bronchitic, and oxygen therapy where necessary must be carefully delivered and monitored. Venturi-type masks are the safest because they deliver accurate concentrations with high total gas flows so that there is no danger of CO_2 build-up within the mask itself. Low O_2 concentrations (e.g. 24–28%) are used and low arterial Po_2 may have to be accepted in such cases if they are to be kept breathing for themselves.

Having noted some of its dangers, it must be realised that oxygen is essential for life, and that the above effects are of secondary importance in the critical case. Only the effect on the 'blue-bloater' type of patient can be dangerous in the very short term, and these patients are not common anyway. The widespread fear of such cases has caused low concentrations of oxygen to be administered to many patients who could not only tolerate, but in fact desperately need, higher doses. Trauma cases should be given high concentrations *de novo*, and if such problems arise then the treatment is intubation and ventilation.

Once the patient is artificially ventilated the physiotherapist has a very important role to perform. Often such cases are heavily sedated and may be paralysed with muscle relaxant drugs, and as such will be unable to move, cough or co-operate in any way. Limb movements then become even more vital, and strict attention to optimal position for chest physiotherapy and the use of manual hyperventilation is of paramount importance.

Artificial ventilation

Starting with experiments by the Humane Society in 1774, and progressing via the inflation of a donkey's lungs using a pair of bellows in a tracheostomy during Charles Waterton's experiments with curare in 1825, artificial ventilation has become a complex art involving the latest microprocessor technology today. Real advances were made in the poliomyelitis epidemics of 30 to 50 years ago, and the 'iron lung' or tank respirator was designed by Drinker in 1929. Over the last 20 years the science has advanced rapidly and today it is an everyday procedure in operating theatres and intensive care units the world over. Nowadays the 'iron lung' is seldom used (but still *is* used (see Chapter 23)) and artificial ventilation is by means of positive pressure rather than negative. Whereas the tank respirator *sucked* air into the patient's lungs (by creating a negative pressure around the patient's thorax) the vast majority of machines today *blow* gas via an endotracheal tube into the lungs. The process has obviously to be intermittent, to allow the patient to breathe out, and we now speak of intermittent positive pressure ventilation, or breathing, abbreviated to IPPV or IPPB.

The number of machines available to perform IPPV is legion, ranging from machines that are little more than the bellows of 150 years ago that kept a donkey alive to complex electronic marvels of the 1980s. It should be said that many patients can be treated perfectly well using the simpler models, and that complexity for its own sake has no virtue. There is no need for the microchip in everyday anaesthesia. However, sick patients require more, and it is necessary for the intensive care ventilator to be extremely reliable, extremely accurate in terms of what it is instructed to do by the operator, adaptive to the changing needs of the patient, and capable of providing information as to patient status and machine status; that is, if the condition of the patient changes and the machine is suddenly required to do more work (e.g. bronchospasm or kinking of the tube) or less (as in accidental disconnection), or part of the mechanics fails (electrical or gas supply failure for instance) then the machine should let the staff know via a comprehensive alarm system. In a busy and often noisy unit there is seldom the staff available to simply stand and monitor the performance of machines. Alarm systems are hence very necessary. It is thus not surprising that ITU ventilators cost more than ordinary ones, and today upwards of £12,000 is not unusual.

Conversely, the complex machines should also remain simple in that the control of their various functions should be immediately obvious to a reasonably experienced operator. The acid test of a new machine is the ability of staff to understand it quickly. In the same vein, it is possible to design a machine that can take care of most problems by itself, so that the various settings will be automatically adjusted to accommodate changing compliance, changing blood gases, or changing cardiovascular state. Clearly this moves into the realms of computation and servo (feedback) mechanisms, but such machines are becoming available.

The initiation of IPPV can be a time of considerable hazard in the ill patient. It may be that clumsy intubation will cause severe bronchospasm, that the administration of drugs such as sedatives, relaxants and narcotics to facilitate intubation will cause cardiovascular collapse as well as respiratory depression, or that there is a mechanical failure – involving not only the ventilator but also such items as powerful suction (quite vital), electricity and gas supplies, intravenous lines (for drug administration), laryngoscope failures, tube failures and monitoring failures. While everyone should clearly know their job, and all the equipment should have been checked at the assembly stage, the whole system should be double checked before embarking upon intubation and ventilation.

Ventilation is initiated manually, so that adaptation to a swiftly changing situation is possible – machines are not that good yet! When things are stable then the machine is attached (having been checked out previously), and the initial settings made on it, both of frequency, volume and sensitivity, and of alarm settings appropriate for the particular patient. Then, after a stabilisation period of half to one hour, or sooner if the situation warrants it, a blood gas measurement will be made to ensure adequate ventilation and oxygenation are being accomplished.

THE PHYSIOLOGY OF IPPV

This description will necessarily be brief. Much work continues to be done on the subject: opinions on the finer points vary enormously. It is hoped that a concise review of generally accepted principles will be useful.

Positive pressure breathing itself is totally unphysiological as we normally draw gas into the lungs using negative pressure. However, negative pressure ventilators (e.g. iron lungs) have not been proven practicable propositions in the vast majority of ventilator applications and are now rarely used.

With the introduction of IPPV it was feared that the development of a positive pressure within the thorax would dangerously interfere with venous return to the heart (giving rise to hypotension) and also overdistend the lungs with the possibility of rupture and pneumothorax. This is why ventilators were built to be capable of developing a negative or subatmospheric phase during expiration, so that blood prevented from returning to the heart during inspiration could be assisted in its passage during expiration; and there was frequently a very limited amount of positive pressure available, with a red line drawn across the pressure scale at the supposed safe limit of around 0.29–0.39kPa (30–40cmH$_2$O), with a blow-off valve set at a pressure somewhat higher making it impossible to develop high pressures.

These fears have proved largely unfounded. Normal lungs will withstand very high pressures – up to 11.76kPa (120cmH$_2$O) for short periods, and fall in venous return is largely compensated for by increased tone of the venous system – blood is virtually squeezed back to the heart by a reduction in the size of the venous side of the circulation. However, it must be said that it *is* possible to rupture lungs with IPPV, and it *is* possible to embarrass the heart from lack of venous return, particularly if the blood volume is low (e.g. shock states and relative hypovolaemia) as in patients on antihypertensive therapy or if there is a lack of sympathetic response (e.g. Guillain-Barré syndrome, or therapeutic epidural block affecting the thoracic region whence the sympathetic nerves leave the spinal cord). Over-enthusiastic manual hyperinflation can cause serious falls in blood pressure, and the physiotherapist is warned against it. It is usual for some fall in blood pressure to occur with the institution of IPPV – there is frequently vasodilatation associated with the simultaneous administration of analgesics and sedatives to allow intubation – but usually a swift intravenous infusion restores the situation.

This is not to say that very high pressures are at all desirable – in fact the opposite is true. However, there are occasions when pressures in excess of 6.86kPa (70cmH$_2$O), and even in excess of 9.8kPa (100cmH$_2$O), are necessary. A very severe status asthmaticus, for example, may require such pressures until therapy takes effect.

The problems have re-emerged more recently with the discovery that the use of *PEEP* and *inspiratory hold* is sometimes invaluable in the treatment of pulmonary disorders. Both manoeuvres cause an increase of intrathoracic pressure, and may have deleterious circulatory effects.

PEEP increases the functional residual capacity (FRC), and can swiftly bring about an improvement in arterial oxygenation. Inspiratory hold allows ventilation of alveoli that would otherwise remain unventilated and eventually collapse, without the use of excessive pressures. When a pressure is applied to the lungs, the parts of the lung with the best compliance get ventilated preferentially. Increasing the pressure so that poorly compliant areas are ventilated overdistends the normal areas, and may collapse the capillaries in their alveolar walls so that no blood passes, thus ventilating without perfusing, or increasing physiological dead space. If, however, the pressure is held relatively low but constant, then the 'slower' alveoli may eventually become ventilated without detriment to the 'faster' ones.

Thus both PEEP and inspiratory hold are 'good' but not if the cost in terms of blood pressure and cardiac output is too great. Better oxygenation but worse cardiac output may not be so good for delivery of oxygen to the tissues where it is needed as worse oxygenation with better cardiac output. It is possible to measure the oxygen delivery using Swan-Ganz catheters, and in spite of the added complications of this invasive technique it can prove of great value where the balance of oxygenation of the blood versus cardiac output is in doubt. It may be possible to improve oxygenation simply by increasing inspired concentration, but this too has dangers and long-term high oxygen concentrations are widely considered undesirable for their possible deleterious effects on lung function.

Raised intrathoracic pressures affect venous pressures in several organs, including liver, kidney and brain, to the possible detriment of the functions of all three. Circulation may become stagnant, and this has been incriminated in the causation of gastric ulceration. Certainly where there is pre-existing raised intracranial pressure, as in head injuries, then the institution of PEEP has caused worries. However, it can be shown that the amount of PEEP transmitted to the great veins and hence to these vital organs is not very great, especially in the presence of lung disease, and airway pressures are not effectively transmitted to the veins in cases of severe asthma, for example. It is rare for PEEP to affect either central venous pressure (CVP) or intracranial pressure (ICP) by more than one-fifth of its value, especially if there is a slight head-up tilt on the bed; a PEEP value of 0.98kPa (10cmH$_2$O) will usually raise ICP by only 1–2mmHg (0.13–0.26kPa). The improvement in oxygenation is usually of the greater benefit. Hypoxia is a potent cause of worsening of cerebral status, for instance.

The I:E ratio is simply the ratio of inspiratory to expiratory time. In normals this is 1:2, and usually this ratio is adhered to during IPPV if possible. However, to ventilate very stiff lungs without excessive peak ventilatory pressure a longer inspiratory time can be necessary. The I:E ratio may become reversed, that is, inspiration longer than expiration, causing eventually over-distension of the lungs, and a raised mean intrathoracic pressure across the respiratory cycle, which could cause some of the above mentioned effects. Some ventilators prevent the operator from choosing an 'inverse' ratio, others will let him know that that is the result of his machine settings for this particular patient.

Very often the institution of IPPV causes an ileus and gastric dilatation; part of the reason is the use of morphine-like sedatives, and air-swallowing. Inadvertent inflation of the stomach by bad technique with a face mask prior to intubation is also a factor. Often several days are needed for the gastro-intestinal tract to return to normal, and a nasogastric tube is a great relief for the patient.

ANALGESIA

Pain relief is not only humanitarian from the patient's point of view, it is also of assistance to those treating him. From the particular point of view of the physiotherapist a patient who is in pain or anxious or both will be unwilling to move either limbs or chest, and it is known that chest movement can be restricted by pain (causing a reduction in FRC and a rise in closing volume) and that this can be relieved by adequate analgesia.

Analgesia, however, can frequently of itself cause respiratory complications, particularly with regard to the respiratory depressant effects of the narcotic analgesics such as morphine and pethidine, and the multitude of synthetic and natural analogues and derivatives.

The difference between adequate analgesia and respiratory depression is sometimes so close as to overlap. This creates a problem that is only solved with the active assistance of IPPV on an ITU.

Routes for analgesia

While it is possible to create analgesia by making a patient so unconscious that he feels nothing, this is only a feasible situation in the context of the operating theatre and general anaesthesia.

For ward or ITU application, where the aim is to maintain maximum co-operation and analgesia with minimal side-effects, a number of options are available.

SYSTEMIC ANALGESIA

This may be delivered intravenously, intramuscularly, or orally, and the difference is the speed of onset, depth of analgesia, and the duration of effect. Intravenous administration is fast and profound but short acting (and this includes side-effects), whereas oral is slow, rather variable and long acting. Intramuscular is in between.

All morphine-type analgesics (including morphine antagonists such as pentazocine (Fortral)) are respiratory depressants, and will cause respiratory failure in overdose. Such drugs are morphine itself, diamorphine (heroin), papaveretum (Omnopon), pethidine, piritramide; the powerful short-acting drugs such as phenoperidine and fentanyl, and many others. The effects can be reversed by the antidote naloxone (Narcan) but the analgesia is also reversed. The dosage of these drugs is therefore a matter of good clinical judgement and experience.

INHALATION

Some anaesthetic agents are analgesic, but again in overdose they produce respiratory, and even cardiovascular, depression. For many years inhaled nitrous oxide (N_2O) has been used in obstetrics (and is now in the 50:50 mixture $N_2O:O_2$ (Entonox)) as has trichloroethylene (Trilene). These techniques may be useful for short-term pain relief during painful physiotherapy procedures, e.g. chest physiotherapy in chest injuries.

REGIONAL LOCAL ANALGESIA

Local nerve blocks with agents such as lignocaine or bupivacaine can be valuable in pain relief. Unless the block is performed epidurally, and there is a catheter in situ for 'topping up', then repeated injections are required and this is stressful for the patient. For instance, for fractured ribs multiple intercostal blocks may need to be performed at 6- to 8-hourly intervals. The better technique would seem to be epidural with a catheter in situ (as in the relief of pain during obstetric delivery) but again there are complications. First, with a catheter left in place there is risk of infection which, while negligible with good technique over short periods, can become significant for the longer term, e.g. 10 days for a flail chest. Second, the higher the delivery of local anaesthetic up the spinal column, the more the side-effect of hypotension and for the high epidural needed for fractured ribs this can be serious, especially in the elderly.

EXTRADURAL AND INTRATHECAL INJECTIONS

Recently the technique of extradural and intrathecal injection of opiates has re-emerged. This involves the administration of morphine or a similar drug into the extradural or intrathecal space, where it seems to be taken up by the receptor sites for the natural agents, endorphins and encephalins. The drug must be specially prepared, as the regular preservatives can be neurotoxic. The extradural route seems to be moderately effective, and the intrathecal route very effective. The pain relief can last for up to 4 days, but there are side-effects, e.g. itching and nausea, and also respiratory depression. With the intrathecal route this latter effect seems to be reversed by naloxone (Narcan) and the analgesic remains – unlike systemic above. However, it does mean that patients so treated should be very closely observed, and preferably be on an ITU.

SEDATION

Some patients will not be in pain and so will not need analgesia as such, but they may be upset by their surroundings or unco-operative for one reason or another. For these cases a powerful sedative with no side-effects and a swift elimination from the body (to allow easy reassessment) would be ideal.

There is, however, no such agent presently available. Two intravenous anaesthetic agents, etomidate (Hypnomidate) and the steroid mixture alphaxolone/alphadolone (Althesin) were both good, but it has been found that the former reduced the patient's own corstisol levels, and the latter has been withdrawn by the manufacturers because of the relatively high incidence of allergic-type responses to the solvent used (Cremophor EL), the active agents being insoluble in water.

Benzodiazepines such as diazepam (Valium) and midazolam (Hypnovel) are used, but have an unpredictable length of action. When benzodiazepine antagonists become available their use may be easier to control.

Many units have reverted to the use of narcotic analgesics, in particular morphine, not for the analgesic effect but for the associated sedation. Of course, a danger of addiction exists and must be guarded against.

PSYCHOLOGICAL ASPECTS

Considerable psychological trauma can be suffered by ITU patients, particularly if heavily sedated for long periods. They may become disorientated in time and space, and are sometimes totally confused as to their circumstances. An especial danger arises if they are paralysed with muscle relaxants as an aid to IPPV, as any remarks they do happen to hear they may well assume apply to themselves; being totally unable to communicate with the staff they are liable to become very distressed. Another common finding is that patients are amnesic for much of their stay (sometimes permanently), only realising their circumstances when they near recovery, at which stage they might well have to suffer the indignity of being unable to speak to the staff because of an endotracheal tube or tracheostomy. Some staff learn to lip read remarkably well, and there are devices such as the Possum communicator and artificial voice generators which may help. However, most patients are too unwell to use them.

All staff must learn to practise sound bedside manners. Never discuss the patient across the bed (and be careful to stay out of hearing of his neighbour); *always* tell the patient exactly what you plan to do to him and why – even if you are 'sure' that he cannot hear you. Do not disturb him unnecessarily – simply because he is where he is he will be assaulted for large parts of the day (and night) and suffer very considerable auditory input from the various monitors and machines, and alarm signals from all parts of the unit. There is much coming and going, ringing of telephones, clattering of trolleys and so on, all contributing to a high noise level.

As an aid to re-orientation it is a good idea to have large and prominently displayed clocks and calendars. The less severely ill and the recovering patient will appreciate a radio or television (bearing in mind the noise factor for the others), or a cassette recorder, perhaps containing messages from relatives and friends. At all times a sympathetic approach by the staff is of paramount importance.

REFERENCES

Nash, G., Blennerhassett, J. B. and Pantoppidan, A. (1967). Pulmonary lesions associated with oxygen therapy and artificial ventilation. *New England Journal of Medicine*, **276**, 368.

Petz, A. (1958). Retrolental fibroplasia. *Pediatric Clinics of North America*, 239.

Swan, H. J. C., Ganz, W., Forrester, J. et al (1970). Catheterisation of the heart in man with use of a flow-directed balloon-tipped catheter. *New England Journal of Medicine*, **283**, 447.

Tinker, J. (1976). The staffing and management of intensive care areas. *British Journal of Hospital Medicine*, **10**, 399.

BIBLIOGRAPHY

See end of Chapter 11.

ACKNOWLEDGEMENT

The Swan Ganz Thermodilution Catheter VIP model shown in Figure 9/2 (lower catheter) is reproduced by permission of American Hospital Supply (UK) (Ltd). Its full description reads: 'S-G (plus "R" trademark) venous infusion port (VIP) (plus "TM" trademark) flow directed thermodilution catheter. S-G (plus "R" trademark) is a registered trademark of American Edwards Laboratories, American Hospital Supply Corporation. 1985 American Edwards Laboratories, American Hospital Supply Corporation. Reprinted with permission.'

Chapter 10

Intensive Therapy – Apparatus

by B. R. H. DORAN MB, BS, FFARCS

ENDOTRACHEAL TUBES, TRACHEOSTOMY TUBES AND AIRWAYS (Fig. 10/1)

The purpose of these tubes is to maintain a clear airway. They were originally made of red rubber, but now plastic tubes are universal.

The endotracheal tube is one which passes either through the mouth (oral) or the nose (nasal), the pharynx, the larynx and into the trachea. They vary in size and design. There are two basic tubes, the plain and the cuffed. The nasal endotracheal tubes are made of much thinner materials than the oral tubes: this allows the lumen to remain almost as large as for the oral tube but the overall diameter is less. The cuffed oral tube is usually the type chosen for adult patients, especially those on ventilators, whereas the plain nasal tube is that most commonly used for small children and babies. To maintain the endotracheal tube in place a piece of cotton tape is tied firmly round the tube. For easy release this is tied in a bow at the side of the neck. The use of endotracheal tubes can only be a temporary measure as prolonged intubation may cause inflammation and ulceration of the larynx. It is usually considered that 3 to 4 days is the time for safe use. However, plastic tubes may be used for a week or more without adverse effect.

Tracheostomy

Tracheostomy is an operation, usually performed under a general anaesthetic, in which a short horizontal incision is made in the neck and a small opening or stoma fashioned in the trachea. To ensure that the tracheostomy tube will be parallel with the walls of the trachea it is necessary for the surgeon to perform a high tracheostomy at the level of the 2nd and 3rd, or 3rd and 4th tracheal rings. If the tracheostomy is too low the tube may extend beyond the carina,

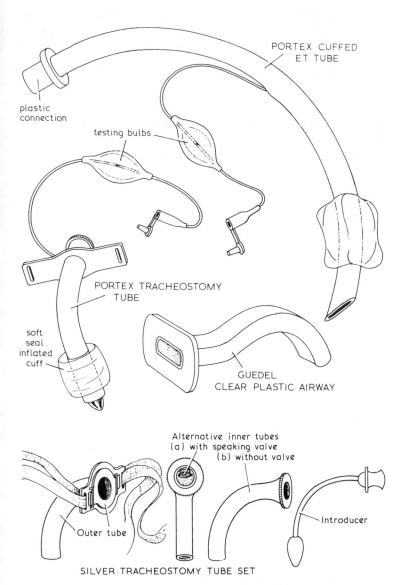

PORTEX CUFFED
E.T. TUBE

plastic
connection

testing bulbs

PORTEX TRACHEOSTOMY
TUBE

soft
seal
inflated
cuff

GUEDEL
CLEAR PLASTIC AIRWAY

Alternative inner tubes
(a) with speaking valve
(b) without valve

Introducer

Outer tube

SILVER TRACHEOSTOMY TUBE SET

FIG. 10/1 Endotracheal, tracheostomy and airway tubes

enter the right main bronchus and thus prevent air from entering the left lung. If higher than this subglottic tracheal stenosis may result. It is normal practice for an endotracheal tube to be in place during this operation. It is withdrawn to just above the operation site to enable the surgeon to insert the tracheostomy tube.

The tracheostomy tube should provide a clear airway with a low resistance to the flow; it should be well-fitting to prevent damage to surrounding structures, and the possibility of accidental displacement should be reduced to a minimum. A right-angled cuffed rubber tube with a metal connecting piece for use with a ventilator was designed by Spalding and Smith in 1959. The plastic cuffed tube is now in common use. This tube has a straight arm lying in the trachea, parallel to the walls so that no pressure is exerted on the tissues, and a short section at right angles to this lying in the tracheostome (Fig. 10/2). The tube is secured in position by a piece of cotton tape fastened round the patient's neck, again in the form of a bow for easy release.

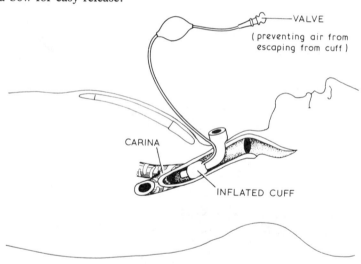

FIG. 10/2 Cuffed tracheostomy tube in situ

CUFFED TUBES

The cuffed form of endotracheal and tracheostomy tube is designed to ensure a good seal between the tube and the trachea. A cuff is a band of thin plastic bonded to the outside of the tube. It can be inflated by a syringe via a small tube running in the wall of the main tube to the exterior where there is a small pilot balloon which allows judgement of inflation. Care must be taken not to over-inflate the cuff as pressure on the adjacent structures can cause ulceration and erosion by impairing the circulation. Only enough air should be used to create a seal. It is possible, with practice, to judge the correct amount by listening, if necessary with a stethoscope. There should be no audible hissing sound when the patient is receiving artificial ventilation. When the patient is off the ventilator, no air should escape from the mouth or around the tube. Devices are available, sometimes incorporated into the inflating tube, which limit the pressure in the tracheal cuff; it is wise in any case to check the pressure using a cheap portable pressure gauge (e.g. Portex or Mallinckrodt) and to try to remain well under 3.3kPa (25mmHg). Pressure-limiting devices will inevitably allow escape of ventilator gas if the ventilator is forced to develop high pressures, e.g. in asthmatics. There is one device (the OMP Cuff Pacer) which attempts to overcome this problem by increasing the cuff pressure during the inspiratory phase, but releasing it to a residual pressure (say 0.66–1.33kPa (5–10mmHg)) to prevent aspiration of fluids collected above the cuff during the expiratory phase. A patient with an inflated cuff cannot speak as no air is passing over the vocal cords. In an attempt to overcome this problem, the Pitt tube allows diversion of gas through the cords, but most patients are too weak or ill to allow good results.

Most tubes now in use have a large-volume low-pressure cuff which ensures a larger area of contact and reduces the possibility of undue pressure being exerted at any one point. Such cuffs tend to make better seals at lower pressures when faced with excessive ventilator pressures. With these soft-seal cuffs, some centres feel that it is necessary to release the cuff at intervals. However, there is evidence to suggest (Ching et al, 1971) that prolonged use of these tubes may lead to tracheal stenosis if the cuffs are reduced at regular intervals due to progressively higher inflationary pressures. In addition, unless great care is taken, accumulated secretions above the cuff will enter the tracheobronchial tree, which is not only distressing to the patient but may also cause inhalational pneumonia.

HUMIDIFICATION

Methods by which humidified air can be introduced into the respiratory system

Humidification is effectively delivered to the patient only by wide-bore tubing, because too much condensation will occur in narrow-bore tubing and block it.

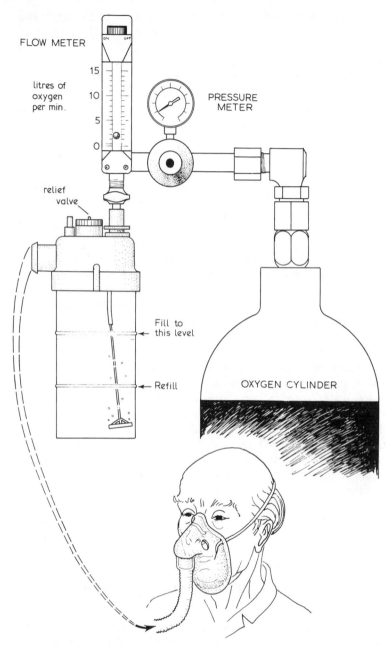

FLOW METER

litres of
oxygen
per min.

15

10

5

0

PRESSURE
METER

relief
valve

Fill to
this level

Refill

OXYGEN CYLINDER

FIG. 10/3 A patient receiving humidified oxygen via a face mask

A FREE BREATHING PATIENT WHO IS NOT INTUBATED

(a) A face mask (Fig. 10/3).
(b) A mouthpiece which the patient has to hold. This method is frequently used with a nebuliser as a method of giving a short period of humidification prior to chest clearance.

A FREE BREATHING PATIENT WITH A TRACHEOSTOMY TUBE (Fig. 10/4)

(a) A tracheostomy humidifying T-tube (Brompton tube). This is made of plastic and fits directly on to the wide-bore tubing and the tracheostomy. This method of delivery is also suitable for patients with an endotracheal tube.
(b) Tracheostomy mask. These are now usually disposable and made from flexible plastic though some rigid plastic boxes are still in use.

A PATIENT ON INTERMITTENT POSITIVE PRESSURE
VENTILATION (IPPV)

It is essential that patients receiving IPPV receive humidification. A humidifier is usually incorporated into the ventilator. The majority of humidifiers used for this purpose are heated. The ideal temperature at the entrance to the endotracheal or tracheostomy tube is thought to be $34°C \pm 2°C$.

Types of humidifier

Boys and Howells (1972) classified humidifiers into suppliers and conservers of water, and subdivided the former group.

SUPPLIERS

Ambient temperature vapour suppliers. Gas is bubbled through room temperature water; if passed through a very fine sieve so that the bubbles are very tiny then some useful humidification can perhaps be obtained.

Heated vapour suppliers. Gas is passed *across* (Cape; East Radcliffe) or, preferably, *through* hot water (Bennett Cascade). Alternatively it may be dripped onto a very hot plate (Kontron). The patient tubing may be lagged, or heated as in the Fischer-Paykell device, to prevent temperature loss and 'rain out'. It is vital that no danger of burning the patient exists, and these devices must not be capable of delivering gas at over $39°C$ to the patient end of the circuit; some sort

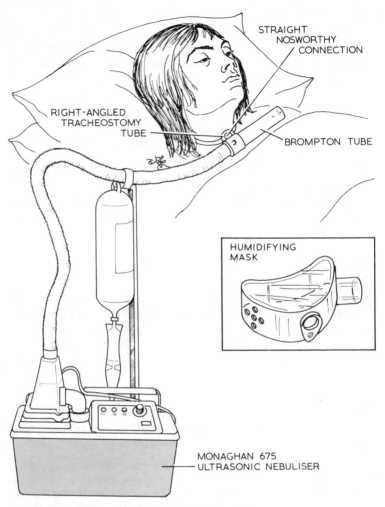

FIG. 10/4 A patient with a tracheostomy receiving humidification via an ultrasonic humidifier. *Inset*: the polythene box which can be used instead of the Brompton tube

of safety feed-back cut-off mechanism from a thermometer close to the patient will probably become mandatory shortly.

Ambient aerosol suppliers. These produce a mist of liquid water, either by breaking up water entrained by a high pressure gas jet (Bernouilli principle) on an anvil (Bird; Ohio; Bard Inspiron), or by generating the mist with a high speed spinning disc or an ultrasonic vibrating crystal. These latter (Mistogen; Corona) produce a very dense mist and there is a real danger of overloading the patient with water. A recently available device (Solosphere, McGaw Ltd) uses the Babington principle, whereby air is forced through a fine film of water, and this produces a particularly dense mist.

Many of these devices are oxygen driven, and entrain room air (using a venturi) in varying amounts according to the oxygen percentage ($O_2\%$) required. The total gas flow varies with the entrainment, and they become rather noisy when low O_2 concentrations (and hence high rates of air entrainment) are used. The relative amount of vapour also falls at these high flows.

Heated aerosol suppliers. The water to be nebulised is heated, and in particular the Bernouilli-type devices are often made to take a heating element or 'hot rod'. Thermal safety again is essential.

Installation. Water may be simply added to the airway by direct instillation from a syringe, drip set or pump.

CONSERVERS

These heat and moisture exchangers (HMEs), or condenser-humidifiers, trap expired heat and water in a mesh, and return it to fresh inspired gas. They can be reasonably efficient but are prone to blockage by secretions. Disposable examples are available (Portex; Siemens; Engstrom).

Choice of humidifier

Although often dictated by availability and cost, the choice should be made with the following factors in mind.

As has been said, dry gases are harmful to the respiratory tract, not only reducing ciliary action (and eventually destroying it altogether), but also drying secretions, making them harder to remove and even causing total blockage of an endotracheal tube. Where secretions are already thick, droplet humidity is better at loosening them than vapour. (Attention to adequate hydration of the patient is also important.) Ultrasonics are the best for this purpose, and they are also irritant and promote coughing.

Cold droplets, however, cause bronchoconstriction and are therefore unsuitable for asthmatics, patients with chronic obstructive airways disease, and some forms of heart disease, notably mitral valve disease. Cold droplets may also cause hypothermia as water deposited in the airways uses body heat in order to vapourise. As mentioned, the ultrasonics may cause a water overload in a susceptible patient and should probably be avoided altogether in small children.

Totally disposable humidifiers are convenient and clean, but at present there is no model available which can conveniently deliver less than 28% oxygen together with warm humidity such as might be needed by the respiratory failure patient with chronic bronchitis, asthma and emphysema, although the Kendall model can be persuaded to do so with some considerable difficulty. A system driven by a gas blender as mentioned below is preferable.

Because they are oxygen driven and entrain room air (and are thus open to atmosphere), venturi devices (Fig. 10/5) are very subject to back pressure if there is any blockage in the patient tubing (usually water); entrainment is prevented and the O_2 concentration rises to close to 100% whatever the nominal setting. The condition is easy to diagnose as the back pressure causes them to spit water over the

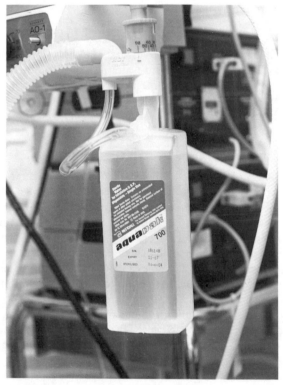

FIG. 10/5 Kendall Aquapak venturi nebuliser (*courtesy* The Kendall Company (UK) Ltd)

floor from the venturi. This phenomenon also makes it very awkward to include a CPAP device for the spontaneously breathing patient without recourse to cumbersome arrangements of reservoir bags and one-way valves. Where CPAP is needed it is better to set the device to 100% (no entrainment) and to drive it using an air/oxygen blender which can then be set to the required concentration.

CLASSIFICATION OF VENTILATORS

It is worth spending a little time familiarising oneself with a certain amount of the nomenclature and classification of ventilator types, that has been generated by the practice of IPPV.

Four phases of ventilation are described:

1. Inspiratory phase
2. Cycling, or changeover, to expiration
3. Expiratory phase
4. Cycling to inspiration.

These will be described, together with the nomenclature applicable to each.

Inspiratory phase

Ventilators produce, or generate, either a flow or a pressure.

Pressure generators expose the lungs to a pressure, produced in the simplest case by the use of a weight resting on a bellows. Gas flows into the lungs until the pressure within the patient is equal to the ventilator pressure, or until the cycling mechanism interrupts the process.

Flow generators expose the lungs to a flow of gas, often developed by passing a very high pressure source (e.g. pipeline supplies) through a narrow orifice, thus making the flow virtually constant when faced with the much lower pressures within the chest. Gas enters the lungs for as long as the flow continues, and the pressure and volume rise accordingly.

Nowadays, few machines can be classified exclusively as one type or the other, but the concept is useful. Many flow generators are adjustable so that the flow can be made of increasing or decreasing rate as well as constant. *Inspiratory hold* can be added during this phase, whereby the lungs can be held inflated for a period of time, usually up to two seconds; this manoeuvre can improve gas distribution in the lungs.

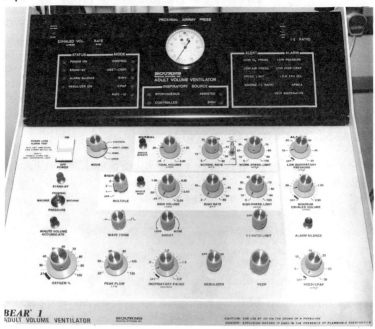

FIG. 10/6 Bourn's Bear 1 ventilator (*courtesy* Penlon Inter Med)

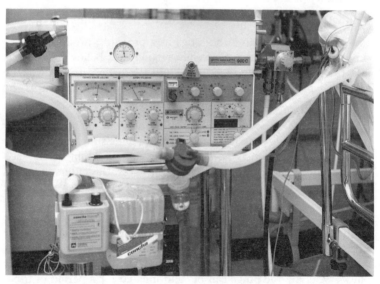

FIG. 10/7 Siemens 900C ventilator (*courtesy* Siemens Ltd) fitted with Kendall Conchapak heated humidifier (*courtesy* The Kendall Company (UK) Ltd)

Cycling to expiration

Ventilators may be:

Pressure cycled, when the development of a pre-set pressure within the system terminates inspiration. Examples are Bird; Blease; Harlow; Cyclator.

Volume cycled, when the machine cycles after a pre-set volume has been delivered, e.g. Bear (Fig. 10/6); Bennett; Monaghan; Brompton (volume mode).

Time cycled, cycling after a set length of time, e.g. Servo (Fig. 10/7); Cape; Phillips; Engstrom; Brompton (time mode).

On the ITU, volume-cycled machines (volume ventilators) are often preferred, as the pressure-cycled variety copes poorly with changing compliance, needing frequent re-adjustments; and the time-cycled machines will continue to cycle whether or not they have delivered gas to the patient. As seen above in the case of the Brompton, some machines can be used in more than one mode.

If *inspiratory hold* is used, then a time element is added to the basic cycling mechanism, so that a machine could be volume-plus-time cycled.

Expiratory phase (PEEP; NEEP; ZEEP)

During expiration, ventilators are normally open either to atmosphere, and the patient is allowed to exhale by normal physiological process so that at the end of expiration the airways pressure has returned to zero (zero end-expiratory pressure (ZEEP)); or else a predetermined pressure is applied to the airway. This is usually positive (PEEP), but may rarely be negative (NEEP) with respect to atmosphere. The use of PEEP and NEEP is explained below.

Some ventilators allow an expiratory restriction or choke to be used, so that expiration is slowed in a manner analogous to that of an asthmatic. This is potentially highly dangerous, because if all the gas does not escape before the next inspiration then that which was left stays in the lungs, and with the next regular inspiration the lung volume will be increased, and so on until, eventually, a dangerous hyperinflation occurs.

Cycling to inspiration (trigger/assist)

This is accomplished by a simple pre-set time switch, which may be labelled as 'expiratory time' or as I:E ratio (inspiratory to expiratory time (see p. 225)), so that the machine adjusts the expiratory time to fulfill the pre-set I:E ratio. It may also be a function of the machine rate-per-minute setting, so that expiration simply takes up that part of the total cycle not already used by inspiration.

On ITU machines a triggering device allows the patient to initiate the next inspiration himself, and over-ride the machine. Such a system is essential on intermittent mandatory ventilation (IMV) and mandatory minute volume (MMV) machines (see below).

TIDAL VOLUME (TV); MINUTE VOLUME (MV); RATE

These are the basic machine settings. Tidal volume equals minute volume divided by rate:

$$\left(TV = \frac{MV}{rate} \right)$$

The rate, and either TV or MV is set, the remaining variable naturally being resultant upon the above equation.

Measurement of ventilation is made on the expiratory side, so that gas leaks from the circuit will not be included, and modern machines have built-in respirometers connected to alarms.

SIGH

Some machines have a built-in facility for giving the patient one or several deep breaths analogous to the sigh of the normal subject. It has been shown that this can improve compliance and gas exchange. The sigh may be varied as to rate and depth (volume), and be single or multiple. There is usually a 'compensatory' pause, to allow the circulatory system time to recover from the effects of the increased intrathoracic volume and pressure generated transiently by the sigh, before the machine returns to normal mode.

VENTILATOR MODE (CONTROL; TRIGGER/ASSIST; IMV, MMV, CPAP)

Simpler and older machines performed their set function no matter what the patient did – this was (and is) called *controlled ventilation*, but might better be called forced ventilation, in that the machine attempts to force its 'will' on the patient no matter whether that patient accepts it or fights against it.

TRIGGER/ASSIST

The first attempt to overcome both this problem, and the problem of weaning a patient from a ventilator, was the development of the patient trigger or assist, a device that allowed the patient to initiate the inspiratory phase by his own effort. This meant that the machine could deliver an extra breath when the patient required it. By decreasing the trigger sensitivity, so that the patient had to work harder and harder for this extra breath, and at the same time reducing the frequency of the set machine breaths, it was thought that a patient could be retrained in the art of breathing normally and gradually build up his strength. Unfortunately, in most cases, it does not work, and it is better to disconnect the patient altogether and allow free spontaneous respiration for increasing intervals in order to wean from the machine.

INTERMITTENT MANDATORY VENTILATION (IMV)

More recently the trigger mechanism has been used not to initiate a full machine breath but to open a gas supply to the patient so that he can take whatever sized breath he wishes and is able to. The machine still gives him a pre-set number of breaths each minute, but in between these he can breathe for himself. The IMV system can be adjusted so that machine breaths become gradually less frequent until the patient is breathing entirely for himself with no machine breaths, i.e. he is effectively weaned. Machine breaths can be synchronised with the patient's own efforts (SIMV) so that the machine breath coincides with the patient's own inspiration rather than otherwise; and the machine can be made to add up the patient's own minute volume and deliver extra if it is deemed insufficient – mandatory minute volume (MMV). Both IMV and MMV systems can be made to give the patient some slight assistance to his own spontaneous efforts – not true ventilation, but assisted IMV.

Such systems mean that a difficult case can be taken from complete full ventilation to totally spontaneous without changing any machinery. Therefore, a full alarm system, controlled oxygen and humidity, and controlled PEEP is available throughout the weaning process, including total spontaneous ventilation where it is usually called continuous positive airways pressure (CPAP). It is definitely easier, safer and quicker than older methods, and if expense prohibits the use of such machines on every ventilated patient then every unit should have at least one available. It will be found that it is rarely out of use, even when a simpler machine would do.

ALARMS

Ventilator alarms have become accepted and are now usual on ITUs. It could be that in the future they will become mandatory on all new ventilators.

An alarm signal should be both audible and visible, but not overpowering or the staff will simply disconnect it. It should be possible to silence it, but only for a very limited period, e.g. long enough to perform endotracheal suction. The whole system should be reliable, not producing false alarms, so that the staff will act on it rather than ignore it.

The single most important aspect is a *disconnect* or *low-pressure* alarm, as low pressure in the circuit during inspiration means that the system has developed a major gas leak, i.e. is disconnected from the patient. Other very useful ones are *high pressure* (tube kink or sudden bronchospasm usually), *low exhaled volume* (inadequate ventilation, especially useful on IMV or MMV), *low oxygen percentage* (oxygen line failure), and *mains failure* – this is operated by a battery or a capacitor when the electricity supply fails. It is possible to build alarms into every aspect of IPPV, but the operator must be able to see the wood for the trees, and it can be overdone.

HIGH FREQUENCY VENTILATION

Over the last few years the technique of high frequency ventilation (HFV) has emerged as a serious proposition. The frequencies used are from 60/min up to even 3000/min, as against the normal 12–16/min.

There are two main types, jets and oscillators.

High frequency jet ventilation (HFJV) consists of the application of a high pressure jet to the airways via a special cannula or endotracheal tube, the jet being interrupted at the selected frequency, usually up to 250/min but sometimes up to 600/min. A special ventilator (Fig. 10/8) is required (one cannot simply increase the rate on a standard machine) as the valve mechanism must cycle very quickly or else it will intrude into the time allowed for expiration.

In the case of the HFJ, expiration is passive, using the natural elastic recoil of the lungs as in normal IPPV. Because the expiratory time for each breath is relatively short, some gas is trapped and the system develops PEEP automatically, the level of which rises with rate. CO_2 retention occurs simultaneously.

High frequency oscillation (HFO) usually uses a reciprocating piston, and in this case expiration is active – the piston will aid expiration on its return stroke. For this reason PEEP is not developed and rates can go up to 3000/min, at least experimentally.

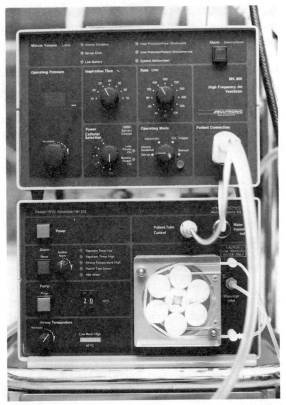

FIG. 10/8 Accutronic high frequency jet ventilator and humidifier (*courtesy* Primary Medical Aid Limited)

The main advantage of either system is that peak pressures in the airways are less than in conventional ventilation, so that barotrauma is less likely and less gas is lost through any lung leak, such as a bronchopleural fistula.

Other advantages have been quoted as less effect on the heart (Klain and Smith, 1977) and intracranial pressure (Todd et al, 1981), but as this seems to depend on mean, rather than peak, pressure such may not be the case (Froese, 1984). Oxygenation is similar to conventional ventilation as this also depends on mean airway pressure, but as it is possible to raise mean airway pressure using HFV without causing the high peak inspiratory pressures that may be found in conventional ventilation then some benefit in oxygenation may be available.

As it is possible to insert a jet cannula very quickly through the cricothyroid membrane the jet system may be useful for emergency resuscitation. It is also said to prevent aspiration of stomach contents or other debris (Klain et al, 1983).

A very real problem is the provision of adequate humidification in either HFJV or HFO because of the high gas flows involved. It has been our own experience with the Acutronic device that endotracheal tubes become encrusted with secretions and block not infrequently. Any entrained gas must be humidified, and the installation of extra water into the endotracheal tube is a wise precaution.

DIFFERENTIAL VENTILATION

When a patient has bilateral lung pathology (such as generalised bronchopneumonia) and needs IPPV, then, using a conventional machine, gas from the ventilator is distributed preferentially to the more compliant, non-dependent (uppermost) regions of the lung. Perfusion of the lungs with blood, however, is affected by gravity. The result is that most gas goes to the uppermost parts of the lung and most blood to the lowermost, so creating a ventilation-to-perfusion ($\dot{V}/\dot{Q}$) mismatch.

If a patient were to be put in the lateral position, and PEEP applied to the lower lung only, then more gas should go to the lower lung and more blood to the upper, hopefully correcting this mismatch. This might be accomplished by the use of a double-lumen endobronchial tube and two ventilators, one for each lung.

The hypothesis has been tested (Baehrendtz and Hedenstierna, 1984) and it does seem that it could work. It requires two synchronised ventilators, master and a slave (to my knowledge only Siemens and Engstrom provide this facility), and a double-lumen tube to separate the two lungs. Such treatment is expensive as two ventilators are needed.

CPAP MASKS

The use of a tight-fitting face mask and a PEEP valve has been advocated in the treatment of mild to moderate acute respiratory insufficiency (Smith et al, 1980), and in other situations such as following median sternotomy for coronary artery bypass grafting (Stock et al, 1984). These studies have shown it to be an efficient way of increasing functional residual capacity and improving oxygena-

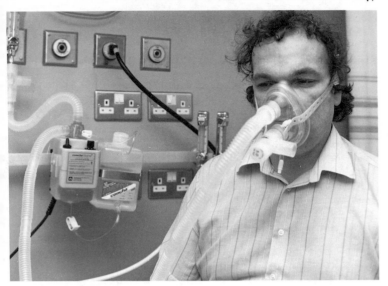

FIG. 10/9 Down's CPAP mask and flow generator (*courtesy* Medic-Aid Ltd)

tion. In many cases the need for intubation and ventilation has been avoided.

Such masks cannot be run off ordinary flow meters and venturi-type humidifiers because of the high flows needed and the back pressure caused by the PEEP valve. A system of one-way valves and a reservoir bag has been used, but it is better to use the Down's flow generator which can provide the necessary flow without recourse to cumbersome plumbing (Fig. 10/9).

A considerable degree of patient co-operation is needed if the tight mask is to be tolerated, so clearly such systems are better used early before any cerebral hypoxia occurs.

REFERENCES

Baehrendtz, S. and Hedenstierna, G. (1984). Differential ventilation and selective positive end-expiratory pressure: effects on patients with acute bilateral lung disease. *Anaesthesiology*, **61**, 511–17.

Boys, J. E. and Howells, J. H. (1972). Humidification in anaesthesia: a review. *British Journal of Anaesthesia*, **44**, 8, 879.

Ching, N. P. H., Ayres, S. M., Paegle, R. P. et al (1971). The contribution of cuff volume and pressure in tracheostomy tube damage. *Journal of Thoracic and Cardiovascular Surgery*, **62**, 402.

Froese, A. B. (1984). High-frequency ventilation: a critical assessment. In *Critical Care State of the Art*, Vol. 5 V(A) 1–55. The Society of Critical Care Medicine.

Klain, M. and Smith, R. B. (1977). High frequency percutaneous transtracheal ventilation. *Critical Care Medicine*, 5, 280–7.

Klain, M., Keszler, H. and Stool, S. (1983). Transtracheal high frequency ventilation prevents tracheal aspiration. *Critical Care Medicine*, 11, 170–2.

Smith, R. A., Kirby, R. R., Gooding, J. M. and Civetta, J. M. (1980). Continuous positive airway pressure (CPAP) by face mask. *Critical Care Medicine*, 8, 483–5.

Stock, M. C., Downs, J. B. and Corkran, M. L. (1984). Pulmonary function before and after prolonged continuous positive airway pressure by mask. *Critical Care Medicine*, 12, 973–4.

Todd, M. M., Toutant, S. M. and Shapiro, H. M. (1981). The effects of high-frequency positive-pressure ventilation on intracranial pressure and brain surface movements in cats. *Anaesthesiology*, 54, 496–504.

BIBLIOGRAPHY

See end of Chapter 11.

ACKNOWLEDGEMENTS

The author acknowledges the help of the University Department of Medical Illustration, Manchester Royal Infirmary in providing the photographs, to whom the copyright belongs. He also thanks the secretaries of the Anaesthetic Department, Manchester Royal Infirmary.

Intensive Therapy – Physiotherapy Management of the Adult Patient

by L. KENDALL MCSP *with* S. E. JACKSON MCSP, DipTP

The physiotherapist working in an intensive therapy unit (ITU) has an important role to play both as an individual and as a team member.

Individual role

The most overwhelming impression when walking into an ITU for the first time is that the room is full of equipment coupled with a certain amount of mechanical noise. When this is associated with very ill patients and seemingly ultra-efficient staff it can be, for some people, a rather alarming experience. However, the physiotherapy techniques are straightforward and there are many people on hand should an emergency arise, which is more than can be said when a cardiac arrest occurs in the street.

It is important for the physiotherapist entering an ITU for the first time to familiarise herself with the equipment in that unit. Standard pieces of equipment such as ventilators, monitors, humidifiers (see Chapter 10) and suction apparatus will be present in all units; but the design and operation will vary, although the basic principles will often follow a common pattern.

The physiotherapist will need to be competent in the handling of some of the equipment and should be able to interpret and analyse the recorded data relevant to her assessment before treatment of the patient.

The role of the physiotherapist is the care of the whole patient: this includes his respiratory care as well as his postural care by maintenance of full joint mobility, muscle extensibility and correct positioning wherever possible.

Team role

As a team member liaison with other disciplines and continual consideration of the overall management of the patient is vital. It cannot be stressed too often that the patient is an individual who, underneath all the technology and equipment, can often hear, see and feel everything that is happening to him, and around him, even though this may not be apparent. The ITU can be a terrifying experience for the patient and it is the duty of everyone involved to try to minimise this feeling.

It is the aim of this chapter to familiarise the reader with the basic principles of intensive therapy, patient assessment, aims of treatment and the techniques available to the physiotherapist. Once these are understood the physiotherapist should be able to apply this knowledge to any patient in any ITU.

CLINICAL ASSESSMENT

Each patient in the ITU is an individual and even though 'conditions' may be the same, the treatment programme must be planned for each person. Routine treatments are to be avoided; the patient should be assessed thoroughly at each visit and the treatment given accordingly.

Case notes

These will provide a history of the present condition, related past medical history, operation notes if relevant and often a report on the progress of the patient since admission to the ITU.

Intensive care charts

Important information is to be obtained from the recordings on these charts. Each unit records the data differently but whether it be on one large chart or several small charts the information will have been documented somewhere. To some extent the detailed recordings depend on the pathology of the patient, e.g. intracranial pressure readings for a patient suffering from a head injury.

The physiotherapist should work systematically through the information so that a complete picture of the condition of the patient is obtained. The following will be included:

RESPIRATION

Is the patient ventilated? If so, is it via an endotracheal tube or tracheostomy tube? The latter way indicates that the patient had needed, or is likely to need, ventilatory assistance for some time.

What mode of artificial ventilation is being used?

Full – is PEEP being applied?
Assisted – e.g. IMV (see Chapter 10).
None – the patient is breathing spontaneously.

A full respiratory assessment should be made, whether the patient is ventilated or not, noting the following:

Minute volume
Inflation pressures (if ventilated)
Respiratory rate
Breathing pattern
Presence of cough or wheeze
Secretions – (amount, colour, consistency, and whether produced by coughing and expectoration or obtained by suction).

ARTERIAL BLOOD GASES

These are usually frequently recorded; blood samples often being taken from a cannula sited in a convenient artery, commonly the radial artery at the wrist. Levels of Pao_2, $Paco_2$, pH, base excess and oxygen saturation of haemoglobin should be noted and reasons for abnormal levels determined (a useful tip is to keep a list of normal values and causes of common deviations in a pocket notebook). Occasionally a transcutaneous oxygen (TcO_2) electrode (see Chapter 12, p. 306) may be used giving continuous Pao_2 recordings displayed on a monitor. Careful observation of these recordings should be made during treatment of patients requiring a high percentage of inspired oxygen (FiO_2). Most techniques of physiotherapy drop the Pao_2 in acutely ill patients but it returns to the pre-treatment level in approximately 15 minutes (personal communication, see p. 430).

CARDIOVASCULAR STATUS

The following should be noted and reasons for any instability ascertained, e.g. temporary pacemaker or prescribed drugs:

Heart rate
Heart rhythm
Blood pressure.

CONSCIOUS LEVEL

Check whether the patient is conscious. If not, is it a natural state or drug induced? If conscious, is he alert, moving all limbs, drowsy or confused?

FLUID BALANCE

A large positive balance may produce overloading and wet lungs (pulmonary oedema). Patients suffering from cardiovascular instability are particularly at risk of this. If the patient is dehydrated he may have difficulty expectorating secretions because of their increased viscosity; he may also be confused.

DRUGS

Take note of the drugs prescribed, the dosages and the times they have been administered with particular reference to:

Analgesics – small doses will indicate that they have been given for pain relief but large doses may have been given to depress the respiratory centre in the medulla to inhibit spontaneous respiration. This will prevent the patient from breathing out of phase with the ventilator or 'fighting' the ventilator.

Respiratory drugs, such as bronchodilators and mucolytics.

Muscle relaxants – these are neuromuscular blocking agents so rendering the patient immobile. He cannot therefore move to express any emotion and it is vital that prior to any procedure which may be uncomfortable that the patient is given some analgesia so suppressing the sensation of pain.

Drugs stabilising vital systems, such as supporting heart activity, e.g. dopamine, are often delivered by continuous infusion into a major vein. It is important that these infusion lines are not obstructed during treatment as this may seriously affect the patient's condition.

TEMPERATURE

The presence of a pyrexia should be noted. In some units skin temperature as well as central or core temperature (see Chapter 9, p. 214) is recorded. When a patient is in 'shock', widespread peripheral vasoconstriction occurs in order that the available blood flow be directed to the major organs. A difference of more than 5°C between the two readings will therefore demonstrate this serious state.

Other related recordings that should be noted are (a) time of last feed; and (b) times when the patient is turned.

Radiographs

The most recent chest radiograph and the previous film should be viewed and compared with the latest normal radiograph if possible (see Chapter 5). Patients who have suffered a road traffic accident (RTA) may also have had radiographs taken of their limbs, pelvis and skull. These should be looked at and note taken of any fractures which may affect the positioning and movement of such patients.

Drains

Observation should be made of any drainage tubes sited in the chest, the amount and type of fluid draining and/or the existence of an air leak noted.

The presence of drainage tubes in the abdomen may indicate that the patient is undergoing peritoneal dialysis. This treatment for renal failure involves filling the peritoneal cavity with an alkaline solution into which acid waste products in the intestines pass by osmosis; the fluid is then drained out of the abdomen. Physiotherapy treatment should coincide with the 'out' cycle in these patients as treatment with the abdomen full of fluid is neither comfortable nor effective.

Patient

In addition to the information already obtained the patient's appearance should be carefully observed and the following noted:

Colour – normal, indicating a well oxygenated patient.
– blue, which may be evidence of cyanosis (indicating hypoxaemia and/or hypercapnia).
– yellow, which may be an indication of renal and/or liver failure.

Expansion of the chest – observe the breathing pattern, abnormal chest movements, e.g. paradoxical movement of the ribs with a flail segment of the chest.

Evidence of other injuries – for example a Thomas's splint for a fractured shaft of femur or skull traction for a neck injury.

AUSCULTATION

Listen to the patient's chest with a stethoscope noting whether the breath sounds are normal, reduced, absent, or whether there are any added sounds (see Chapter 4). It is advisable to listen both before and after treatment.

HUMIDIFICATION

All patients receiving mechanical ventilation will receive humidified inspired gases (see Chapter 10, p. 233). Patients who are breathing unaided may not be receiving humidification and should be assessed as to their need of it.

Nurse

The nurse looking after the patient will be able to give a good 'up-to-the-minute' report on the patient and will often fill any gaps caused by misplaced data.

The clinical assessment of the patient is completed by a collation and synthesis of all the information obtained, for only then can aims of treatment and priorities be ascertained.

The treatment selected should provide the most effective means of achieving those aims.

Continual reassessment is vital to monitor the effects of treatment both during the treatment by careful observation of the patient and his physiological measurements and after its completion.

TREATMENT

The frequency of treatment will be determined by the assessment and it may be as little as once or twice a day or as frequently as at 2-hourly intervals. Occasionally a patient will require treatment at intervals throughout the night.

In a number of centres the nursing sisters will have been taught the basic physiotherapy techniques during a postgraduate intensive therapy course and can therefore carry out routine treatments during the night. Anything more than routine, for example a patient requiring IPPB or the treatment of a collapsed lobe of a lung, would need the skills of the physiotherapist on call.

AIMS OF TREATMENT

1. To assist in the removal of excess bronchial secretions.
2. To ensure adequate ventilation of all areas of the lungs and to help prevent atelectasis and/or consolidation.
3. To maintain full joint range and muscle length by passive movements – if the patient is unable to perform active exercise.
4. To maintain mobility and blood circulation by free active exercises, when possible.
5. To ensure the maintenance of a good posture by accurate positioning and advice.
6. To help rehabilitate the patient to as full and independent a life as possible by always considering the overall team approach to his management.

Before considering the techniques available for selection comprising a treatment it is important to consider two points.

1. Always treat the patient as if he were awake and rational. As previously mentioned the administration of drugs may make him appear comatose but that may not be the case. Talk to him, explain the procedure you are about to embark on and the rationale behind it. *Never* talk about the patient or his condition *within* his hearing.
2. The site and function of all infusions and cannulae should be noted prior to handling the patient, so that if one accidentally becomes disconnected it can be speedily reconnected. Particular attention should be paid to the arterial line which may cause considerable loss of blood if left disconnected for any length of time. In the event of an accident occurring, firm pressure should be applied immediately proximal to the cannula to prevent further loss of blood while attracting help from someone. Continuous infusion lines which are obstructed or disconnected during treatment can seriously affect the condition of the patient.

TREATMENT TECHNIQUES

Postural drainage

Every physiotherapist working in the respiratory field must be familiar with the standard postural drainage positions (see Chapter 14). The patient is positioned so that gravity assists the drainage of secretions from specific bronchopulmonary segments, the positions being determined by the anatomy of the bronchial tree.

In the ITU, however, it is often difficult to position the patient accurately as either his condition or the presence of tubes, such as endotracheal or drainage, may prevent it. A patient who has undergone a neurosurgical procedure may not be able to lie tipped head down because of the possibility of raising the intracranial pressure. The advice of the neurosurgeon should be sought in this case. The patient may have had a bone flap removed, in which case it may not be desirable to turn him on to that side. A compromise may be reached whereby, for the period of treatment, his body is turned as far as possible while his head remains in the supine position.

It may not be possible to position a patient with a flail chest, caused by multiple rib fractures, into side lying and a modified position may have to be used.

If one considers a patient receiving IPPV with no contra-indications preventing accurate postural drainage, the presence of an endotracheal or tracheostomy tube will not allow him to lie prone. Collapse of the posterior segments should be prevented by regular turning of the patient from side to side every 2 hours, allowing him to lie supine only for 2 hours in every 6. The normal 2-hourly turning programme, which is the rule for most patients, may be modified to a 2- and 1-hourly regime, if indicated by the condition of the chest. The simple fact of moving the patient may have the effect of loosening secretions.

An ITU should be equipped with tipping beds which work from a central fulcrum. This enables the bed to be tipped from side to side as well as from end to end. Patients who are unable to be positioned in side lying may be tilted to one side on the bed so altering the line of gravity.

It is essential that all moves are carefully planned by the physiotherapist, bearing in mind all the factors of the patient's condition. It is important, too, not to forget the general contra-indications to postural drainage (see p. 350)

The worst affected area of the lungs should be treated first and the following techniques may be used in combination with the drainage position when appropriate.

Manual techniques

PERCUSSION

Chest percussion or clapping is performed with slightly cupped hands applied alternately to the chest wall with a quick, relaxed flexion and extension of the wrists. Percussion should always be applied over a blanket or towel. It is thought that the mechanical effect of percussion is to loosen secretions from the bronchial walls. For the medical patient in the ITU this technique may be most effective; however, for many patients it is either not appropriate or should be used with the utmost caution.

In the presence of rib fractures or surgical incisions percussion is avoided. Other contra-indications include haemoptysis, acute pleuritic pain, osteoporosis or metastatic deposits in the ribs or spine and active pulmonary tuberculosis. Possible adverse affects of chest percussion include the onset of cardiac arrhythmias, with a subsequent fall in cardiac output and Po_2, and a possible increase in bronchospasm especially with rapid percussion.

SHAKING

Chest shaking also transmits mechanical energy through the chest wall to loosen secretions. In the ITU it is often a more appropriate technique to use than percussion, and is the technique most commonly employed in the treatment of a ventilated patient. The physiotherapist places her hands suitably on the chest wall with her elbows slightly bent, but with her body well positioned over the patient, if necessary kneeling up on the bed. If the patient is in supine lying the physiotherapist places her hands on the anterior aspect of the chest or one hand anteriorly and the other posteriorly. For large patients it is often more effective to place both hands anteriorly. When the patient is in side lying the hands may be placed either together on the lateral wall of the chest or anteriorly and posteriorly.

As the patient pauses at maximum inspiration the physiotherapist should vigorously shake the chest using her body-weight and continue to shake through expiration. On inspiration the physiotherapist should relax and repeat the manoeuvre through each expiration.

Coarse, vigorous shakings may be used to dislodge very thick tenacious secretions unless the condition of the patient dictates otherwise. As always, the patient's condition determines how vigorously the technique is applied. Factors such as pain, and the frailty and size of the patient should be taken into account and the technique moderated accordingly. Contra-indications include osteoporosis or metastases in the ribs and spine, haemoptysis and acute pleuritic pain.

VIBRATIONS

This technique works on the same principle as percussion and shaking but has a finer action and tends to be used in the ITU when other techniques are contra-indicated. Vibrations are not as effective as coarse shakings in loosening tenacious bronchial secretions, but for some patients with fractured ribs or a painful surgical incision they may be the only procedure tolerated.

As with shakings, vibrations are applied throughout the expiratory phase, but the movement is brought about by contraction of the pectoral muscles and biceps. As the muscles contract to bring the hands towards each other vibration takes place; it is not a smooth compression of the chest wall. This technique is contra-indicated in the presence of metastases of the ribs or spine.

BREATHING EXERCISES

Controlled deep breathing exercises, which increase the length and diameter of the airways above that of normal tidal volume, may help to loosen bronchial secretions. Not all patients in the ITU will be receiving mechanical ventilation and most of those who are not, will be capable of carrying out breathing exercises, for example patients who have undergone open heart surgery, or those who have recently been weaned from the ventilator. Breathing exercises may be combined with positioning and shakings or vibrations as appropriate, plus coughing and huffing in order to maximise clearance of bronchial secretions.

COUGH/HUFF

The optimum method of clearing bronchial secretions from the lungs is a cough followed by expectoration. Coughing and huffing are forced expiratory manoeuvres which, by producing a rapid flow of air combined with a narrowing of the airways, dislodge secretions and move them towards the pharynx.

The patient in an ITU will often need help in order to huff and cough effectively, for example by having his surgical incision and/or rib cage supported, or by applied pressure to the abdomen for a patient with weak abdominal muscles.

Manual hyperinflation

Many patients in an ITU require mechanical ventilation via a tracheostomy or endotracheal tube (see Chapter 10). Some patients will have very few bronchial secretions – those who have been electively ventilated following open heart surgery; for such patients adequate humidification and good sterile suction techniques are usually sufficient to deal with any secretions. However, many patients do develop large quantities of sputum which need to be mobilised and removed.

Any patient receiving IPPV is at risk of developing an increase in the amount of bronchial secretions and possible subsequent chest infection for the following reasons:

1. The presence of an endotracheal or tracheostomy tube causes irritation of the tracheal mucous membrane resulting in an increase in the secretion of mucus.
2. Secretions may become dry and crusted within the endotracheal or tracheostomy tube because the upper respiratory tract, which normally provides the humidification of inspired gas, has been by-passed.
3. The patient is unable to cough effectively due to the presence of a tube.
4. There is reduction and/or paralysis of normal ciliary action.
5. Loss of normal sigh mechanism.

The longer a patient is receiving IPPV the more likely is the possibility of developing a problem with secretions and infection.

During the treatment of a patient with copious secretions who is breathing spontaneously, the physiotherapist would ask the patient to take deep breaths prior to coughing. A fully ventilated patient cannot do this and so is given deep breaths manually to fully expand his lungs and loosen secretions. This technique is known as bag-squeezing or, more accurately, *manual hyperinflation.*

Usually an anaesthetic re-breathing bag (Fig. 11/1) is used; alternatively, the bag incorporated into some ventilator circuits could be used. The self-inflating Ambu bag should only be used when an anaesthetic bag is unavailable. Various sizes of anaesthetic bags are available and it is usual to use the 2-litre bag for adults.

The adjustable expiratory valve in the circuit (Fig. 11/1) is to control the gas flow and thereby the pressure generated to the patient. This valve needs continuous adjustment during treatment as the compliance of the lungs changes. If the valve is fully open the majority of gas escapes to the atmosphere. When the valve is fully closed all the gas is delivered to the patient but this does not allow for the gas to escape during expiration. The skill of this technique lies to a large extent in the correct adjustment of this valve so that effective inflation occurs without a build-up of an excessive inflationary pressure.

The bag is supplied with gas, air, oxygen, or Entonox; commonly one of the two latter. The circuit may incorporate a soda lime (Water's) canister to prevent the build-up of CO_2 (a real and

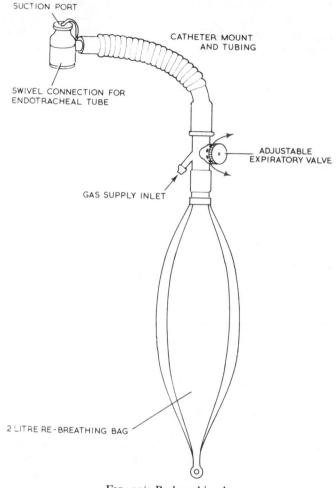

SUCTION PORT

CATHETER MOUNT
AND TUBING

SWIVEL CONNECTION FOR
ENDOTRACHEAL TUBE

ADJUSTABLE
EXPIRATORY VALVE

GAS SUPPLY INLET

2 LITRE RE-BREATHING BAG

FIG. 11/1 Re-breathing bag

dangerous problem when these bags are used) – this is essential if
the flow rate of gas cannot reach 10l/min. If a good flow of gas,
10–15l/min, is used and the bag squeezed completely empty from
time to time all stale gas will be removed.

Ideally, three people are required to treat a ventilated patient with
manual hyperinflation: one to hyperinflate the patient – depending
on the unit this will be an anaesthetist, physiotherapist or nurse; one
to perform the appropriate manual technique; and one to perform
the suction. A treatment can be carried out with only two operators,

one performing both latter techniques but this is not ideal as the manual technique cannot be carried out during suction.

METHOD

The patient is positioned, disconnected from the ventilator and attached to the bagging circuit. Using both hands the bag is squeezed at a steady rate, building up over two to three breaths to maximal inflation of the lungs; the aim being to fully aerate the alveoli. Attention should be paid to the frequency of inflations per minute as the inexperienced operator, realising that the patient's life 'is in her hands', will tend to inflate the bag at far too rapid a rate so making effective treatment impossible and hyperventilating rather than hyperinflating the lungs of the patient. The operator may time the squeezing with her own rate of breathing. Maximum inspiration is held momentarily before the bag is rapidly released to produce a high expiratory flow rate which assists the removal of secretions towards the carina. Maximal effect of this technique is achieved when the physiotherapist, with hands suitably positioned, compresses the chest wall at the peak of inspiration, fractionally before the release of the bag. Vibrations or shakings are then given throughout the expiratory phase to supplement the fast expiratory flow rate and help move the secretions from the smaller peripheral airways to the larger, central bronchi. Accurate co-ordination between the two parties is essential for effective treatment.

After approximately six to eight inflations of this nature, suction is applied both to stimulate a cough and aspirate the loosened secretions. The physiotherapist should continue to shake the chest and encourage the patient to assist coughing (if able to do so) during the suction, to facilitate the removal of secretions. Suction may have been indicated earlier in the procedure by a spontaneous cough from the patient or by wet sounds produced on inflation indicating the presence of loose secretions in the large airways. If the secretions prove stubborn 2–3ml of normal saline (0.9%); may be instilled into the airway prior to hyperinflation. However, if the patient is known to have tenacious secretions the saline may be instilled prior to positioning as the fluid will fall to the most dependent bronchi, to mix with the secretions.

The treatment should be continued until the chest is clear; this may include a change of the patient's position midway through the treatment, the worst affected area of the lung being drained first. At the end of the procedure the patient is reconnected to the ventilator and a vital check is made to ensure that the ventilator is working properly and that the humidifier and alarm systems are switched on.

The frequency and duration of the treatment is entirely dependent on the condition of the individual patient. It may need to be performed hourly as in the case of a collapsed lung (Fig. 11/2) in order to reinflate the lung as quickly as possible (Fig. 11/3), 2-hourly in the case of a severe chest infection or as infrequently as once or twice a day. Actual change of drainage positioning should coincide with the nursing routine for turning and pressure care in order to reduce patient discomfort.

The main effects of manual hyperinflation are:

1. The deep inflation recruits alveoli by re-expanding alveoli 'unused' during the tidal volume of IPPV and so helps both to prevent and to reverse atelectasis and promotes full aeration of alveoli. If secretions are not excessive, this technique alone may be useful in helping to maintain lung compliance.
2. The fast expiratory flow rate generated, enhanced by the vibrations and shakings, loosens and moves secretions towards the main airways.

It should be remembered that as this is a very unpleasant procedure for the patient, he should be informed of what is to happen and the reasons for the routine. Analgesia by drugs is usually necessary before treatment; Entonox may be used if more appropriate.

SPECIAL PRECAUTIONS

Manual hyperinflation, if performed inappropriately, can cause major problems and, therefore, should be used with caution, especially on very sick patients. The technique should not be used unless there is a valid indication to do so, and the bag-squeezing should not be performed by inexperienced staff unless under close supervision.

Hyperinflation of the lungs can result in:

Fall in cardiac output and PaO_2. Bagging can produce a fall in the cardiac output and arterial oxygen tension (Gormezano and Branthwaite, 1972). It is thought that the increased intrathoracic pressure causes a decreased venous return, due to compression of the great veins, and so results in a fall in blood pressure and cardiac output; in extreme cases cardiac arrest may ensue. The patient's monitors must always be carefully observed during the procedure, watching in particular for a significant fall in blood pressure and/or a slowing of the heart rate (bradycardia), if either occurs, the treatment must be stopped *immediately*.

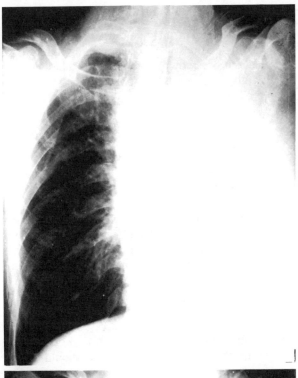

FIG. 11/2
Radiograph of a
collapsed left lung

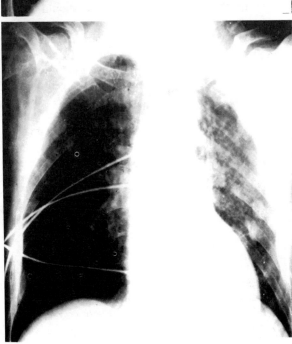

FIG. 11/3
Radiograph to
show the left lung,
now re-expanded,
following
treatment

Barotrauma. This may be caused by overzealous bagging, leading to scarring and possible fibrosis of lung tissue. It is possible to cause a pneumothorax by over-inflating the chest especially in patients with chronic lung disease or lung bullae.

CONTRA-INDICATIONS

This technique is contra-indicated in patients who present any of the following:

1. An unstable cardiovascular system, e.g. low cardiac output, certain arrhythmias.
2. Pneumothorax: whether or not a drain is in situ, or in the presence of surgical emphysema. Bagging with a chest drain in situ will have little effect – the gas taking the line of least resistance and leaking down the drain. When no drain is sited, manual hyperinflation may increase the size of the pneumothorax possibly causing the lung to collapse and may increase the surgical emphysema.

   The technique should be avoided in at-risk patients likely to develop pneumothoraces, e.g. those suffering from cystic fibrosis, emphysema, or stiff fibrotic lungs. If its use is essential in these patients, treatment should only be carried out in the presence of medical staff.
3. Hypoxia. Patients with severe hypoxaemia and few secretions, e.g. those suffering from the adult respiratory distress syndrome (ARDS)/shock lung or pulmonary oedema, usually require a high PEEP (see p. 244) from the ventilator; this would be lost if manual hyperinflation was used. By careful adjustment of the expiratory valve and a high gas flow rate the very experienced operator can maintain PEEP while bagging but this should not be attempted by the inexperienced physiotherapist.
4. Severe bronchospasm. Bagging sometimes increases broncho-spasm so where this symptom is the main problem, as in the asthmatic patient, this must be dealt with first. There is a very real risk of causing a pneumothorax by bagging a wheezy patient.

Suction

Airway suction is frequently required for the patient on an ITU, in order to facilitate the removal of bronchial secretions.

Some patients will be capable of coughing at either a voluntary or reflex level, others will not. While the very sick, spontaneously breathing patient may indeed be able to co-operate during treatment, and to cough and expectorate, this may not always be effective due to weakness and exhaustion; suction is then needed to supplement his efforts and gain full clearance of secretions. Other patients, breathing spontaneously, may be unwilling or unable to cough effectively due to confusion, pain or fear and suction is required to stimulate the cough reflex and aspirate secretions. There is a group of patients who will have no cough reflex either because they are so deeply unconscious or because their respiratory muscles have been paralysed by disease or drugs; these patients will require postural drainage, and manual techniques to mobilise and move the secretions towards the upper airways followed by suction to aspirate them. All intubated patients require suction whether receiving ventilatory assistance or not.

Suction should be given:

1. Whenever secretions can be heard in an intubated patient.
2. For retained secretions in the spontaneously breathing patient who is unable to cough and expectorate efficiently.
3. Before and during the release of the cuff on a tracheostomy tube.
4. If the inflation pressure of the ventilator suddenly rises. This may indicate the presence of a large plug of mucus in one of the larger bronchi or even within the endotracheal or tracheostomy tube.
5. If the minute volume (MV) drops, this may indicate retained secretions.

SUCTION EQUIPMENT

Suction pumps: various types of apparatus are available to produce the vacuum or suction force necessary to aspirate substances.

1. Suction apparatus designed to work from a vacuum point close to the patient's bed (Fig. 11/4). The power is provided by a large motor situated at some convenient site within the hospital grounds. This is the type of apparatus most commonly found in ITUs and on wards in modern hospitals. In addition to an on/off switch, there is a control dial, which allows the applied negative pressure to be increased or decreased as desired, a manometer displays the pressure used. The control usually has low, medium and high settings, these will vary with different pieces of apparatus but will correspond roughly to −50mmHg, −100mmHg and −300mmHg.
2. Electrical suction apparatus is powered from the mains. This type has its own small motor, with an on/off switch and a control

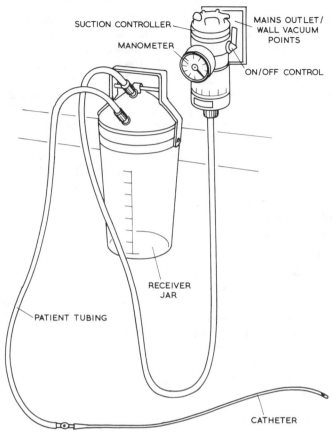

FIG. 11/4 A wall-mounted vacuum suction unit which is available at the bedside

dial (Fig. 11/5). This is the equipment most commonly used on wards where a vacuum point is not available.

3. Portable suction apparatus is available powered by rechargeable batteries. This too has a small motor and on/off switch. The machine should be tested at frequent intervals to check the batteries.

4. Foot pump: As the name suggests the power is provided by the operator. This pump was the only type available in the period when intensive care was developing. Modern versions are available and, like the battery operated pumps, these are suitable for use in the community or for an emergency resuscitation team.

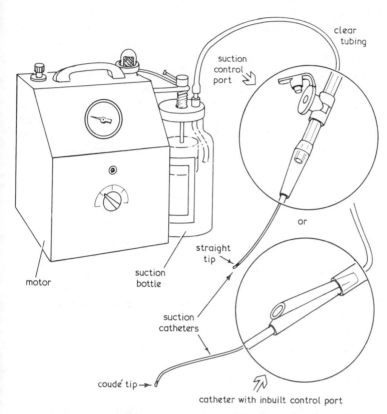

FIG. 11/5 Suction apparatus, also showing different types of control ports and suction

All suction pumps have at least one suction bottle, the electrically operated pumps often have two. These act as a receiver for the aspirate and should be partially filled with some antiseptic solution. The most modern suction bottles contain a disposable inner bag with which to collect the secretions.

Suction tubing:
This leads from the suction bottle to the connection for the suction catheter. Usually the tubing is made from clear plastic for easy viewing of secretions, and is disposable, but sometimes rubber tubing is used still.

Connections: These are usually plastic and either clear or semi-transparent. A clear connector must be used with rubber tubing in order to view the secretions being aspirated. Most connections have three holes, or in the case of the Y-connector, three arms; one at either end and a third at the side used as the control port. Some catheters have in-built control ports (see Fig. 11/5). The catheter and tubing fit on to opposite ends leaving the open aperture for the operator to use. This opening offers less resistance to the suction force than does the catheter and when unblocked the suction takes the line of least resistance and air is taken in through the hole. To apply the suction force to the catheter the operator places a finger or thumb over the opening.

Catheters: Many makes of suction catheter are available but all come in standard sizes. Most are made from soft, clear plastic and are disposable. Commonly used sizes for the adult patient are 10, 12, 14 and 16 French Gauge (FG) and are usually colour coded for size. It is vital that the correct size of catheter is used for each patient – it should not exceed half the diameter of the endotracheal or tracheostomy tube. Too large a catheter may cause alveolar collapse when suction is applied, since insufficient air will be able to enter the lungs to neutralise the negative pressure being produced.

Soft rubber catheters are still used in some hospitals, these are not disposable and must be sterilised after use. They are particularly useful for nasopharyngeal suction as they cause less trauma because they are softer and more flexible than the plastic catheters. They may be too short for some endotracheal tubes.

Coudé catheters, sometimes known as bronchoscopy or Pinkerton's catheters, should be available in the ITU. These are extra long catheters with a curved tip (see Fig. 11/5) used for selective suctioning of the left main bronchus. A straight catheter passed beyond the carina will almost certainly enter the right main bronchus which is an almost direct continuation of the trachea. Using a coudé catheter with the head side flexed to the right gives a greater chance of the catheter entering the left main bronchus.

For some patients even minimal trauma caused by airway suctioning would be dangerous, as, for example, those having had laryngeal or tracheal surgery, because of the danger of perforating or damaging the suture line; or for patients undergoing anti-coagulation therapy. In these instances it may be necessary to use Argyle Aero-Flo catheters which have a specially designed tip to minimise mucosal trauma. These catheters have a bead surrounding the distal hole at the end of the catheter, and there are four small holes just proximal to this bead. The effect of this construction is to alter the airflow, and on movement up or down of the catheter the air is buffered around this bead forming an air-cushion to prevent the tip of the catheter from coming into contact with the walls of the trachea. Because the bead tip is larger than the shaft of the catheter sometimes it may be necessary to use a smaller size catheter, and if the secretions are very thick the smaller size may not be adequate to remove them. Some studies have shown that using Aero-Flo catheters for nasopharyngeal suction may cause, on insertion, trauma from the bead tip when there is no air cushion effect to protect the mucous membrane (Link et al, 1976; Jung and Gottlieb, 1976).

All catheters should be used once only and then thrown away if disposable or if rubber collected for sterilisation.

When bronchial secretions need to be sent for laboratory investigations a sputum trap must be used. This is a small specimen container which fits between the catheter and connection for the collection of sputum. Various types are available.

Suction trolley: All the equipment needed for airway suction should be set out on a trolley for ease of access:

Sterile plastic gloves – disposable.
Suction catheters – appropriate sizes for the patient.
Lubricating jelly – water-based only, not oil-based, for use in nasopharyngeal suction.
Sterile gauze swabs – to transfer jelly to tip of catheter.
Bowl of sodium bicarbonate or sterile water – to flush the secretions through the catheter and tubing. Sodium bicarbonate acts as a solvent of the secretions.
Forceps (if used).
Plastic bag for the collection of disposables.
Bowl of antiseptic solution for the collection of items to be sterilised (if required).

SUCTION TECHNIQUE

Because there is a high risk of introducing infection into the respiratory tract a sterile suction technique must always be carried out using either sterile plastic gloves or forceps to introduce the catheter (the former needs less skill). This applies particularly to the intubated patient.

Before use, the equipment should be checked for efficient suction, and the appropriate vacuum pressure selected, probably −100 to

−120mmHg is ideal for most patients although pressure up to −200mmHg may be needed for thick secretions. If the suction is not adequate it is wise to check the lids of the bottles to see that they are correctly screwed down and that the sealing washers are in position. Inspect all the tube connections and it is even possible that the on/off switch could be in the wrong position.

The physiotherapist should wash her hands, thoroughly, explain to the patient the procedure to be carried out, and then select the appropriate size of catheter.

Mode of entry: A suction catheter may be introduced into the respiratory tract via the nose, the mouth or a tube. Suction for the conscious patient, especially via the nose or mouth, is a very uncomfortable experience. It must be done with the correct combination of gentleness and firmness which is the direct product of the attitude of mind of the operator. Fear or distaste for the job in hand will result in either ineffective or over-vigorous use of the catheter. If possible, it is advisable to make one's first attempt at suction in this way on an unconscious patient. He will not be distressed and the operator can gain that confidence which is necessary to use any form of apparatus efficiently.

1. *Nasopharyngeal suction.* When introducing a suction catheter via the nose it is helpful if the patient's neck is extended so that the head is tilted backwards resting on a pillow. If the patient can co-operate the tongue should be protruded, as this helps when attempting to pass the catheter between the vocal cords and into the trachea, especially if the catheter is advanced on inspiration only.

The lubricated catheter is held between the fingers and thumb of the gloved hand and introduced into the nose. It is directed slightly upwards and backwards until the tip reaches the posterior naris where a little resistance may be felt. Gentle rolling of the catheter at this point usually allows the advancement of the catheter into the pharynx. If the patient has a nasogastric tube in situ it has, occasionally, been found easier to use the same nostril. The catheter seems to slide along the first tube and through the posterior naris more easily.

Once in the pharynx, the route of the catheter cannot be guaranteed. The aim is to stimulate a cough reflex and by advancement of the catheter on inspiration only with the mouth open, a fair degree of success is achieved. If the patient retches, the wrong reflex has been stimulated, the catheter should be withdrawn a little way, the patient encouraged to take some deep breaths and the catheter advanced again. If unsuccessful again the catheter should be withdrawn. Even in the unconscious patient, by using this method of advancement on inspiration only, success is achieved in the majority of cases.

It must be remembered that nasopharyngeal suction is a very unpleasant experience for the conscious patient and should only be used when absolutely necessary. If the patient is well prepared beforehand and able to co-operate he will usually tolerate the procedure very well. In a minority of cases where the patient is unco-operative or confused, assistance will be needed to hold the patient still in order to minimise trauma.

Nasopharyngeal suction should not be used for patients with head injuries where there is a leak of CSF into the nasal passages.

2. *Oropharyngeal suction.* Although the nose is the preferred mode of entry in the non-intubated patient it may be necessary on occasions to use the mouth. A lubricated plastic airway is usually needed to prevent the patient biting the catheter and it is difficult to direct the catheter accurately into the pharynx and beyond.

3. *Suction via tube.* Most commonly the catheter is introduced into an endotracheal, tracheostomy or mini-tracheotomy tube, which present no difficulties. However, it should be remembered that if the patient is dependent upon a ventilator, the time available for suction is limited. To get some idea of the patient's tolerance of this, the physiotherapist should breath hold from disconnection to reconnection of the ventilator; if the need to breathe is felt then it is likely that the patient also needs to take a breath.

Mini-tracheotomy: This is a relatively new technique for the treatment of sputum retention in the spontaneously breathing patient (Matthews and Hopkinson, 1984). Early use of the technique avoids use of the more hazardous conventional methods such as bronchoscopy, endotracheal intubation or tracheostomy.

A size 4.0mm paediatric uncuffed, endotracheal tube is inserted into the trachea through the cricothyroid membrane. Once in place, tracheal suction, via the tube, can be performed using a size 10FG catheter. Saline may be administered via this tube, which is only minimally invasive and is usually tolerated by the conscious patient without the need for sedation. Since the tube is of small diameter the upper respiratory tract is unobstructed and the patient, therefore, retains spontaneous breathing, natural humidification and a cough reflex as well as the ability to talk, eat and drink normally. Due to the small size of catheter available with the mini-tracheotomy, suction may need to be extended in order to remove thicker secretions.

Suction. Whatever the mode of entry, the physiotherapist must ensure that no suction pressure is applied while the catheter is being introduced. It has been shown that severe mucosal trauma may be caused by airway suction (Sackner et al, 1973; Kuzenski, 1978); minimal trauma will take place if no suction force is applied during insertion of the catheter. This is easily practised if a three-hole connection is used; if one is not available then the catheter itself may be pinched or disconnected from the tubing during introduction. The catheter should be advanced until either a cough reflex is elicited or some resistance in the trachea is met, the length of catheter inserted is a guide to the proximity of the carina; suction is then applied by occluding the open hole of the control port. Simultaneously, the catheter is slowly withdrawn, while gentle rolling of the catheter between finger and thumb ensures a continual rotation to minimise tracheal trauma. Interrupted suction should always be used to avoid a maximum build-up of negative pressure (Young, 1984a). If a pool of secretions is reached, there may be a pause to clear them, while continuing to rotate the catheter and keep an eye on the time taken. *Under no circumstances* should the tromboning method be used, that is, a vigorous up and down movement of the catheter. If the catheter blocks with secretions it may be possible to clear it by rapidly moving the thumb on and off the open hole of the connection.

At all times during this procedure it is important to observe the patient for signs of hypoxia, and, should this occur, administer oxygen or ventilation immediately. Patients at risk of suffering from hypoxia – those with an already low PaO_2 – may benefit from pre-suction oxygenation and manual hyperinflation if intubated (Young, 1984a).

If, during nasopharyngeal suction, the patient becomes cyanosed and the catheter was difficult to insert, it is acceptable to disconnect the suction, leaving the catheter in situ, while administering oxygen until the patient recovers and suction can be resumed.

No longer than 15 seconds should elapse between the disconnection and reconnection of the patient to the ventilator, more than adequate time for effective removal of secretions by the experienced operator.

Where possible, the patient should be suctioned in side lying or with the head rotated to one side to avoid aspiration of gastric contents should vomiting occur.

After suction the patient must be reconnected immediately to the ventilator or oxygen supply. The physiotherapist should flush the catheter through with sodium bicarbonate or sterile water, remove the glove over the catheter and discard both. The suction pump should be switched off and any bowls re-covered.

SUMMARY OF HAZARDS OF AIRWAY SUCTION

The actual technique of airway suction, once mastered, may be relatively straightforward. It is a very unpleasant experience for the patient and there are adverse effects which are well documented (Young, 1984b). They include:

1. Risk of infection which can be avoided by a good, sterile technique.
2. Trauma which can be minimised by the correct choice of catheter and negative pressure combined with good technique.
3. Hypoxia which may occur during nasopharyngeal as well as endotracheal suction (Petersen et al, 1979). The effects are minimised by the accurate use of the applied negative pressure, and accurate timing – not too powerful or too long.
4. Cardiac arrhythmias which may occur as a secondary response to hypoxia; usually bradycardia is noted, but breathing higher concentrations of oxygen prior to suction may help to counteract this problem should it occur. It is also possible for arrhythmias to occur as a result of vagal inhibition. Afferent vagal nerve fibres are present in the walls of the pharynx, oesophagus and respiratory tract, stimulation of these fibres may cause a triggering of reflexes resulting in arrhythmias. It is also possible for respiratory arrhythmias to occur on suction, for example apnoea possibly initiated by the same mechanism, as strong vagal stimulation may cause inhibition of respiration.
5. Atelectasis may be caused by too powerful and prolonged suction. It is also possible to cause obstruction of the airway by repeated, traumatic suction techniques resulting in bleeding, crusting and eventually fibrosis of the mucous membranes. Careful, correct technique should minimise this.

INTERMITTENT POSITIVE PRESSURE BREATHING (IPPB)

This is a form of assisted breathing which can provide a valuable adjunct to chest physiotherapy. The ventilator will provide more

FIG. 11/6 Close-up of Bird Mark 7 showing controls

effective aeration of the alveoli and can aid the removal of retained secretions; it is also a means of delivering drugs and humidification directly into the bronchial airways; when used correctly and the patient relaxes, the work of breathing may be reduced.

Several types of IPPB machines are suitable for use with physiotherapy. The Bird and the Bennett are commonly used, each having a number of models available. These are pressure-cycled ventilators, with a patient-triggering mechanism, and are usually driven by compressed gas (oxygen or air). Electrically powered ventilators are also available and these are suitable for use in the home. The Bird Mark 7 machine (Figs. 11/6, 11/7) is the type often used in the hospital. Whichever machine is used, each should have several breathing-head assemblies so allowing one machine to be used to treat several patients each day. The breathing-head assembly is sterilised at the end of the course of treatment (or at least once a week); the machine may be moved from patient to patient.

Sterilising. After each treatment, the mouthpiece must be washed in warm soapy water and dried, the nebuliser must also be washed and dried. The breathing-head assembly should be disconnected from

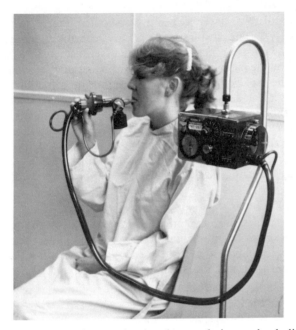

Fig. 11/7 Bird Mark 7 in use, showing the mouthpiece and nebuliser

the ventilator and stored in a plastic bag or clean pillow case until it is needed for the next treatment. After the completion of the course of treatment, the breathing-head assembly is completely sterilised. All the parts are dismantled, washed and then soaked in a suitable disinfectant, such as Milton, Cidex or Eusol, for the appropriate length of time. Following this, the parts must be thoroughly rinsed in clean water to remove the taste of the disinfectant. The components must be carefully dried before reassembly and storage in a bag ready for future use. In some hospitals, the sterilisation of such equipment is undertaken by the CSSD or the clinical physics department. The machine itself is sterilised with ethylene oxide gas. If a patient is infected with a resistant strain of bacteria, then the ventilator should not be moved to other patients and must be sterilised immediately the particular patient has finished the course of IPPB.

Controls

The controls will vary slightly according to the make of the ventilator, but basically are as follows:

INSPIRATORY PRESSURE CONTROL

Most ventilators have a positive pressure range of at least 0–40cmH$_2$O. The inspiratory pressure control determines the maximum pressure generated by the ventilator. The pressure received by the patient should equal the pre-set pressure and may be read on the gauge on the machine. This pressure will not be reached if there is a leak anywhere in the circuit, such as may occur around the mouthpiece or mask, or if the patient breathes through his nose; if this occurs, the machine will not cycle into expiration. If the patient exhales before the ventilator has reached the pre-set pressure, the needle on the gauge will swing up to a very high pressure, indicating that the machine is not being used correctly.

SENSITIVITY CONTROL

This determines the inspiratory effort required by the patient to trigger the machine into the inspiratory cycle. Usually, the control is set so that the slightest effort to breathe in on the part of the patient is sufficient to trigger the machine into the inspiratory phase.

MANUAL CONTROL

Most machines have a hand triggering device which is useful on occasions.

FLOW-RATE CONTROL

This is the rate at which the gas is delivered to the patient and is measured in litres per minute. In machines such as the Bird the flow rate may be pre-set by a control knob which also acts as the on/off switch. A low rate is usually preferred but if the patient is short of breath, and has a fast respiratory rate, then the flow rate may be increased so that the pre-set inspiratory pressure is reached more quickly. No adjustment is required on machines such as the Bennett for they have an automatic variable flow already incorporated – it is known as 'flow sensitivity' with the rate of flow of the gas adapting to the individual patient's airway resistance.

AIR-MIX CONTROL

When the machine is driven by oxygen it is necessary to entrain atmospheric air, by using the air-mix control, in order to deliver a mixture of oxygen and air to the patient; it is not advisable to deliver 100% oxygen to the patient (see Chapter 19, p. 471). The percentage of oxygen obtained will vary according to the type of machine used. Some manufacturers state that 40% oxygen, 60% air is delivered but in practice the mix is very variable. Any patient requiring oxygen therapy, especially those with severe hypoxia, should *never* use an IPPB machine driven by air alone. When the machine is driven by compressed air, an attachment called an 'oxygen blender' may be used to give a controlled amount of oxygen. If the Bird Mark 7 is driven by compressed air, 24% oxygen may be obtained by entraining oxygen via a hypodermic needle, connected to an oxygen flowmeter running at 2 litres per minute, inserted into the inlet port of the micro-nebuliser.

EXPIRATORY TIMER

This dial controls the expiration time for a ventilated patient after which the machine will automatically cycle into the inspiratory phase. This dial should be turned off for IPPB.

Preparation for treatment

1. Fill the nebuliser with the required solution, commonly either normal saline or a bronchodilator. The nebuliser should *never* be used dry. Any drug used must always be prescribed by the physician or surgeon in charge of the patient. Most nebulisers hold up to 5ml of solution; depending on the unit, 3–5ml are used which takes 10–15 minutes to be nebulised. If using a bronchodilator, the prescribed dose of the drug is combined with normal saline; for example, a 2.5mg dose of salbutamol (0.5ml of 0.5% respirator solution) may be combined with 4.5ml of normal saline to make a 5ml solution. Occasionally the mucolytic acetylcysteine (Airbron) may be prescribed, but for this the machine should be powered by air, since oxygen renders the substance less effective. Glycerols are not usually suitable for use in IPPB nebulisers.
2. Connect the breathing-head assembly to the ventilator and connect the ventilator to the driving gas.
3. Check that the air-mix selector is pulled out to entrain air (unless the machine is being powered by air).
4. Check that the expiratory timer control is turned off.
5. Set the controls of the ventilator according to the individual patient's requirements. Usually, with the Bird Mark 7, sensitivity needs to be set at a low figure, 5–7, so that minimal effort triggers the machine. The pressure is likely to be between 10–15 and the flow rate between 6–10 initially. The aim is to provide slow, deep, assisted ventilation which is comfortable for the patient and this will be achieved by adjusting the controls

accordingly. With the Bennett, the only control to be set is the pressure (the flow rates and sensitivity being automatically adjusted) and the nebuliser is switched on separately.

6. Turn on the ventilator to check that the nebuliser is functioning correctly and that there are no leaks in the breathing head assembly.

Treatment of the patient

The patient should be well supported in a comfortable position that enables him to relax the upper chest and shoulder girdle. The position chosen depends upon the reason for giving IPPB; but it may be used effectively in the sitting, half-lying, high side-lying or side-lying positions. The patient places the mouthpiece in his mouth and is told to close his lips firmly around it and breathe in through his mouth (it is often necessary to use nose clips until the patient is accustomed to the machine). Minimal inspiratory effort will 'trigger' the machine and the patient should then be instructed to relax throughout inspiration, allowing the ventilator to inflate his lungs. The gas flow will stop when the pre-set pressure has been reached at the mouth and the patient should then breathe out gently, pausing slightly before breathing in again and recycling the machine into its inspiratory phase. If there is a leak in the circuit, for example around the mouthpiece or through the patient's nose, or if the patient attempts to assist inspiration, then there will be a delay in the machine cycling into expiration. Expiration should always be relaxed. If the patient exhales before the machine has cycled into expiration, then the needle on the pressure gauge will be seen to swing much higher than the pre-set pressure while, at the same time, the machine cycles prematurely into expiration. Observing the movement of the needle provides a useful indication as to whether the patient has a correct or faulty technique.

When the patient has taken a few breaths in a relaxed manner he should be encouraged to breathe using the lower chest. To encourage this the physiotherapist should place her fingers over the chest as in diaphragmatic breathing.

The treatment should continue in this manner until the contents of the nebuliser have been used.

INDICATIONS FOR IPPB

In some countries IPPB is used instead of physiotherapy but, really, it should be used only as an adjunct to treatment when other measures have failed.

Indications include:

1. *Respiratory failure*, as for example in patients who develop an acute exacerbation of chronic bronchitis with sputum retention and hypercapnia. The patient is often at the stage of impending coma; confused, drowsy and unable to cough effectively; treatment with IPPB can be invaluable and often intubation may be avoided. With this type of patient it is often necessary to use a face mask and have another physiotherapist or nurse to assist with the treatment. If possible, the patient should be turned on to his side and, if tolerated, the foot of the bed elevated. One physiotherapist or nurse should hold the mask over the patient's face, elevating the jaw and ensuring an air-tight fit, while the other physiotherapist shakes the chest on expiration. It may be necessary for the person holding the mask to use the manual control on the machine in order to effect deep breathing on the patient. After about 10 minutes of treatment the patient may become more rational and start to cough spontaneously but it may be necessary to continue the treatment for longer. If effective coughing is not stimulated then nasopharyngeal suction should be attempted. Initially, treatment may be necessary 2-hourly, each session lasting approximately 20 minutes; as the condition of the patient improves, the frequency of treatment is reduced until the IPPB may be discontinued altogether. The patient should be observed for signs of increasing drowsiness during, and for a short time following, treatment, and care with oxygen therapy is needed. Studies have shown that increased drowsiness during IPPB is not so much caused by the low oxygen concentration of the driving gas but by inadequate tidal volume (Starke et al, 1979). It is vital that the physiotherapist adjusts the pressure and flow controls to give adequate ventilation to the patient; particular care is needed in those patients with a rigid thoracic cage; they will need a higher pressure setting in order to obtain an adequate tidal gas exchange.

2. *Sputum retention in medical and surgical conditions*: If a patient with, for example, bronchitis or a chest infection or who has undergone surgery fails to breathe and cough adequately then he will retain sputum. In such cases, IPPB may assist the physiotherapist in the removal of bronchial secretions during postural drainage. Normal saline is used in the nebuliser for humidification unless bronchospasm is a problem, in which case, a bronchodilator should be given before attempting to make the patient cough; such drugs are usually given 4-hourly. It is

possible that only two or three treatments with IPPB may be necessary but a bronchoscopy may well be avoided if the secretions can be cleared. The treatment should be discontinued as soon as the patient can breathe deeply enough to loosen secretions and cough effectively.

3. *Relief of bronchospasm*, for example in severe acute asthma. For such patients IPPB is a useful way of delivering bronchodilators while also reducing the work of breathing for the patient. It may also benefit some patients with bronchospasm who have thick, tenacious secretions, for example those with aspergillosis or chronic bronchitis; in this instance physiotherapy to assist the removal of secretions must not be attempted until broncho-dilation has been attained. It is important to try and estimate the efficacy of such treatments; recording the PEFR or FEV_1 and FVC before and after treatment may be useful. IPPB should not be used purely to administer bronchodilators if a simpler method, such as a nebuliser, works just as efficiently (Webber et al, 1974). IPPB is usually only necessary for the near exhausted, severe, acute asthmatic and only then if the patient is comfort-able using the machine.

4. *Inability to perform effective breathing*: Several factors may lead to a patient being unable to breathe and/or cough effectively, for example:
   - 'weaning' from the ventilator, the patient may easily become fatigued and unable to clear his airways effectively.
   - laryngeal or phrenic nerve dysfunction may lead to difficulty with ventilation and coughing.
   - chest deformity and respiratory muscle weakness, for exam-ple following acute poliomyelitis, especially during periods of chest infection.
   - brain damage, when such patients may be unable to co-operate with the physiotherapist and IPPB using a face mask may be helpful.

5. *Re-education of paralysed respiratory muscles*, for example patients with acute polyneuritis. In such cases, IPPB is used initially with the sensitivity on a low setting so that minimal inspiratory effort triggers the machine. The sensitivity is then gradually increased so that a greater inspiratory effort is required to trigger the machine. In this manner IPPB machines may be used to 'wean' patients from non-triggered positive pressure ventilators.

CONTRA-INDICATIONS TO IPPB

1. *Pneumothorax*: IPPB would tend to increase a pneumothorax and

should not be used. If the patient has an intercostal drain to control the air leak, IPPB may increase the leak and should only be used if absolutely necessary with pressures being kept low.

2. *Large bullae or cavities in the lung*: Patients with emphysematous bullae are at risk of developing a pneumothorax with the use of IPPB as are those with cystic fibrosis. It is unwise to use IPPB for a patient with a lung abscess since air trapping may occur in the cavity.
3. *Haemoptysis*.
4. *Active tuberculosis*.
5. *Bronchial tumour in the proximal airways*: If a tumour is partly occluding a large bronchus the use of IPPB may cause air trapping; this would not be a problem if the tumour was in the peripheral airways.

IPPB used correctly, and in appropriate circumstances, provides a valuable adjunct to physiotherapy treatment, but the patient should *not* be allowed to become *dependent* on the machine and its use should be withdrawn as soon as it no longer serves a genuine purpose. IPPB apparatus is expensive and should not be used unnecessarily, particularly when simpler methods produce equally beneficial results (Webber, 1981)

MAINTENANCE OF EQUIPMENT

The ventilators should be overhauled and cleaned internally by a specialist engineer every three months. It is advisable to keep a supply of spare parts for the breathing-head assembly so that washers and such like may be replaced quickly.

CPAP

The use of a continuous positive airway pressure (CPAP) system in the spontaneously breathing patient may be effective in the treatment of certain respiratory conditions (Branson, 1985). CPAP may be used (with either a mask or mouthpiece) as an adjunct to the physiotherapy treatment of, for example, postoperative atelectasis. The aims of using CPAP in this way are the same as when applied via an artificial airway (see Chapter 10). The main goals being to increase functional residual capacity (FRC) accompanied by an increased Pao_2 and to decrease the work of breathing and oxygen consumption.

MOVEMENT

Some form of movement will be a part of the treatment of any patient requiring intensive care. Occasionally the patient will be capable of doing routine maintenance exercises as instructed, for example following cardiac surgery; others will be able to perform active assisted movements of their limbs; however, a percentage of patients in the ITU will be unconscious or paralysed and will require passive movements.

The aims of passive movments are to (a) maintain full joint range movements; (b) maintain full muscle extensibility; (c) aid venous return; and (d) maintain the sensation of movement patterns.

Particular care should be given to the maintenance of full mobility of the hip, shoulder girdle and glenohumeral joints which seem particularly susceptible to progressive limitation of movement. Muscles acting over more than one joint need special attention to ensure that full muscle length is maintained, the long flexors and extensors of the fingers being particularly vulnerable. This problem is easily overcome by passively moving the limbs in the patterns used in facilitation techniques – this also helps to maintain the sensation of normal movement. Care should be taken to maintain full range passive and accessory movements in all the joints of the hands and feet; particularly the range between the thumb and index finger. The hand loses considerable function if the thumb is fixed in adduction.

Accurate positioning is also of great importance to the unconscious or paralysed patient; ideally, the joints should be rested in the mid-range or 'neutral' position to avoid stress, but in some cases the patient's general condition will prevent this. The majority of conscious patients with voluntary movement will recover in a relatively short time and there is little chance of contractures developing. Very occasionally, a patient still requiring ventilation may be ready to progress from maintenance exercises to an exercise programme and this situation should not be overlooked.

The unconscious or paralysed patient may well require prolonged care; if possible he will be nursed in side lying and turned 2-hourly. Accurate positioning for such patients is essential, the full side-lying position allowing for chest and pressure area care as well as accurate joint positioning. Pillows and sandbags should be suitably placed to stop the patient from rolling on to his back, the lower leg should be extended and the upper leg placed on pillows with the hip and knee comfortably flexed. Both feet should be kept at right angles using sandbags and/or pillows. The lower shoulder should be positioned comfortably so that the patient is not lying on the point of the shoulder and the forearm rests on a pillow. The upper hand and forearm rest either on the patient's thigh or on a pillow. The fingers and wrists should be maintained in a good position using, for example, a roll of gamgee, so that the wrist is extended, the fingers semiflexed and the thumb abducted. The positions of the limbs will be regularly reversed as the patient is turned 2-hourly throughout the 24 hours.

Problems of spasticity will have to be accommodated in the best way possible using one of the many methods available.

Positioning of the patient is the joint responsibility of the nursing and physiotherapy staff. It is also advisable to seek the assistance of the nursing staff in giving simple passive movements which should be performed at each turn and, for the conscious, paralysed patient, whenever he becomes uncomfortable.

Since most ITU patients will have several infusions and drains in situ, great care is needed during either active or passive movements not to dislodge them. A patient requiring the intra-aortic balloon pump (see p. 391) should not flex the hip, where the catheter is inserted into the femoral artery, beyond 50° because of the risk of 'kinking' the balloon.

GENERAL CARE

Although the general care of the ITU patient is primarily the responsibility of the nursing staff, everyone must be willing to assist when necessary, and the physiotherapist who works in an ITU must be aware of this and the need to liaise closely with the nursing staff and other disciplines. Everyone working in an ITU needs to be closely observant not only of the patient but also the equipment (ventilator, monitor, infusions and drains). It cannot be stressed too often that at *all* times the patient must be treated as though he were fully awake by talking *to* him and not *about* him. It may be helpful to talk to the patient about his surroundings, the weather, his family, job and so on to try and maintain some 'normality' in his life. Certainly, it is not unusual for conscious patients in the ITU to suffer from sensory deprivation and develop the so-called 'ITU syndrome'. An intensive therapy unit *is* a frightening place for the patient, and this should be remembered at all times.

The patient is nursed in the ITU without clothes and the temperature of the room is such that he is covered only by a sheet, making for ease of access and nursing procedures. Good nursing care will prevent the development of pressure sores and strict turning routines should be adhered to, ensuring that good techniques are used to lift the patient clear of the bed. Nursing the patient on special mattresses or sheepskins also helps to prevent pressure sores.

Care must be taken to prevent the eyes and mouth from damage. He may be unable to close the eyes properly (facial palsy) or there may be sensory loss affecting the cornea; it is possible for corneal ulceration to occur as a result of pressure from bed linen or foreign bodies causing irritation. This can be prevented by using eye pads or tape to protect the eyes. Some patients will dribble from the mouth and sores may develop; to prevent this the patient's head should be placed on an absorbent pad and the mouth aspirated as necessary – this also protects the bed linen.

The two procedures concerning nursing care of which the physiotherapist should be most aware are turns and feeds. These will be precisely timed and the physiotherapist should fit in her treatments accordingly. Many patients will be tube fed; if this is given continuously the feed should be turned off prior to treatment; it is not advisable to tip any patient head down following a feed.

Turning the patient is part of the physiotherapy care and should always coincide with the turning regime when it may be necessary to change sheets at the same time. It is desirable to have three, but essential to have two, people to turn a patient who is unable to help himself. Speed and efficiency are essential especially for the ventilator dependent patient. The lifting technique will to some extent depend upon the patient's condition and his various 'attachments' but the most experienced person should be responsible for co-ordinating the lift. Generally, the bed should be cleared as far as possible and equipment moved accordingly. One person looks after the patient's head and tubes, the other operator(s) stand at the side of the bed facing the patient at the level of the hips and legs. The operators place their arms as far as possible under the patient's body, pressing down into the mattress to avoid hurting the patient. He is then disconnected from the ventilator, lifted clear of the bed and turned to the opposite side. He is immediately reconnected to the ventilator and pillows replaced. All infusions, tubes, drains should be checked and his chest will usually need aspirating due to the change of position.

The physiotherapist must always be aware of the basic nursing procedures and the team approach to the patient. This knowledge must be constantly applied both in the general care of the patient and in co-operation with the nursing staff.

APPLICATION OF ASSESSMENT AND TECHNIQUES

There are numerous conditions which may require intensive respiratory care but it is neither practical nor possible to cover them all. The aim here is to outline how the physiotherapist may utilise the techniques and equipment available in certain circumstances and the assessment by which she can decide what needs to be done and how often.

Major trauma

A patient involved in a road traffic accident (RTA) may often suffer multiple injuries; he may have a head injury, crushed chest injuries and limb fractures. The physiotherapist must take account of all during treatment. Crush injuries can present major problems for the patient if there is extensive damage to the chest wall.

FLAIL CHEST

Severe chest injuries involving multiple rib fractures, often bilateral, lead to instability of the chest wall and flail segments. Paradoxical breathing will occur: on inspiration the flail part of the chest wall will be sucked in and *vice versa* on expiration. Lung function is impaired because of the paradox and also because air in adjacent bronchi is shunted ineffectually to and fro. Added to this there may be lung contusion, pneumothorax and/or haemothorax, the latter two instances requiring the insertion of an underwater seal chest drain (see p. 368). Serious impairment to ventilation results and the patient frequently requires intubation and IPPV. The IPPV will also act as a form of internal splintage thus helping to prevent paradoxical breathing. Ventilation (full or assisted) may be continued for approximately 10 days or until the ribs stabilise. Good pain control for these patients is essential. Obviously, the physiotherapist cannot exert direct pressure over the damaged areas of chest wall. Such patients need good humidification to keep secretions as loose as possible. Accurate positioning to drain specific areas of lung may be limited, if possible at all, and may simply consist of tilting the bed or mattress from side to side (particularly if the patient also has spinal injuries); tilting the bed head up and head down may also be helpful provided there are no contra-indications. Gentle manual hyperinflation may be helpful in loosening secretions especially if used with Entonox, since the patient's pain threshold may be increased. The physiotherapist may use her hands to help stabilise the chest wall during this procedure; suction is necessary to remove the blood and secretions which will accumulate in the bronchial tree. Many of these patients will be conscious with a good cough reflex and suctioning will stimulate coughing which will be extremely painful for the patient, again, the physiotherapist should use her hands to stabilise the rib cage as much as possible. If analgesia is ineffective, intercostal nerve blocks or a morphine infusion may help control pain. Once the rib cage becomes stable, the physiotherapist may begin to apply chest vibrations to help loosen secretions but great care is needed for there is a risk of re-fracturing

FRACTURED RIBS

Rib fractures often occur close to the angle of the rib and are usually caused by direct violence. One or two rib fractures will be acutely painful for the patient and he will be unwilling either to breathe deeply or cough effectively, this could prove dangerous if he has any underlying medical chest disease such as chronic bronchitis, or was confined to bed. The patient will need breathing exercises and assisted coughing; provided the pain control is sufficient, this should not present any problems.

Patients with moderate chest injuries – several fractured ribs on one or both sides – may not be able to breathe and cough adequately enough to maintain their own airway and so may need intubation and assisted ventilation. If, however, good control of pain is achieved this may be avoided. Pain control is the key factor in the management of patients with rib fractures and a regime to suit the individual must be found. Good humidification is required together with as accurate a positioning as the overall condition allows, combined with breathing exercises and assisted coughing. If the majority of the ribs on one side are fractured, the patient would tend to rely on the unaffected side, which would result in hypo-inflation and eventual collapse of part, or all, of the lung on the affected side unless treatment is given to prevent this happening. If the chest wall is stable, IPPB may help loosen secretions and old blood clots, the machine may be driven by Entonox to help with pain relief. However, before IPPB is used any possibility of a pneumothorax must be eliminated. Some units advocate the use of vibrators over the chest wall in the treatment of patient with rib fractures.

In addition to the respiratory care of a patient with major trauma, attention should also be paid to the limbs and passive or active assisted movements given as appropriate.

Chronic pulmonary disease

Occasionally patients with chronic lung disease will require IPPV, for example, some patients suffering from respiratory failure in an acute exacerbation of chronic bronchitis. Such patients rely on their high Pco_2 for respiratory drive and IPPV tends to reduce the Pco_2; if this occurs too quickly, the patient may find difficulty in breathing spontaneously following artificial ventilation. However, it is thought that if the Pco_2 is lowered *slowly* then, in time, the blood and CSF levels for CO_2 and bicarbonate will also adjust and the patient should be able to breathe spontaneously following IPPV (Branthwaite, 1978).

Such patients usually need vigorous physiotherapy since the main problem is usually sputum retention. The secretions are often copious and tenacious so good humidification is essential. Mucolytic agents may be required if humidification alone is not sufficient to loosen the secretions. Instillation of saline (1–5ml) into the endotracheal tube during treatment may also be required. If bronchospasm is present bronchodilators must be given *before* attempting treatment. Provided there are no contra-indications, postural drainage, manual hyperinflation with chest shaking/percussion and suction should be used in order to clear the secretions. These patients often have a 'rigid' thoracic cage and care is needed not to cause pneumothoraces if bullae are present. Initially, treatment may be needed 2-hourly but the frequency will be dictated by the condition of the patient, and it should be remembered that he will need some rest. The patient should also be encouraged to perform simple maintenance exercises.

Paralysis of the muscles of respiration

This will include patients suffering from myasthenia gravis, tetanus, drug overdose or a polyneuropathy, such as Guillain-Barré syndrome. Tetanus is only occasionally seen in Britain nowadays but it is quite commonly seen in the Third World countries, particularly among children. The use of the paralysing drug curare to control the spasm, in conjunction with IPPV, has proved to be the most successful form of treatment. With the exception of the drug overdose, the patients in this category are usually conscious and must be treated as such; it might be easy to forget this since the paralysed patient is unable to move or respond and may appear to be unconscious.

These patients are prone to develop chest infection and/or lobar collapse. Their treatment is time consuming, all areas of lung need attention with adequate time spent in each position to allow drainage to occur. Unless a particular lobe is a problem, drainage usually begins with the patient in the side-lying position in which the physiotherapist finds the patient. The patient is then tipped head up to drain the upper zone of the chest. The techniques of manual hyperinflation with coarse chest shakings and suction are applied until the area is clear. The patient is then tipped head down to drain the lower zones and the techniques applied again; following this the patient is positioned to drain the middle or lingula lobes and the chest clearance procedures repeated. Once that side of the chest is clear, the bed is returned to the horizontal and some of the pillows and sandbags are removed to allow for full range passive movements of the uppermost limbs in the side-lying position. The patient may be reconnected to the ventilator during the passive movements. The patient is then turned on to the opposite side and aspirated as soon as possible. Passive movements to the second side are given and then the pillows/sandbags are replaced in a comfortable position before the chest clearance pattern is repeated on the second side. This treatment is usually required at least three times daily.

Unconscious, free breathing patient

Such patients may include those suffering from a cerebrovascular accident, a head injury, drug overdose or who have undergone recent neurosurgery. Many will have normal lungs but it is not always possible to stimulate a cough reflex. It is unlikely that the patient will be breathing deeply enough to ensure good air entry to all segments of the lungs. These patients may or may not have a tracheostomy. Tipping these patients head down (with the exception of those who have taken an overdose) may well be contra-indicated as this could cause a rise either in the blood pressure or in the intracranial pressure; some head injury/neurosurgical units do allow tipping provided there is intracranial pressure monitoring and a valid indication for using the position. Commonly, though, these patients are nursed and treated in alternate side lying. If the patient has a cough reflex the most effective method of moving secretions is to stimulate a cough. The best results are achieved by repeatedly vibrating or shaking the chest on expiration with the patient in side lying – this may loosen secretions sufficiently to stimulate spontaneous coughing, or it may be necessary to use suction to stimulate a cough and aspirate secretions. As well as assisting in chest clearance, shaking during expiration tends to increase the rate and depth of respiration thus improving the ventilation of the lungs. The procedure should then be repeated for the opposite side of the chest. If the secretions are still present following this, the position of the patient should be adapted as far as possible to the standard postural drainage position for the affected area.

If the patient is so deeply unconscious that a cough reflex cannot be stimulated, the physiotherapist will have to rely upon positioning and the squeezing effect of chest shaking. In this case, suction without an endotracheal or tracheostomy tube will be relatively ineffective as the secretions will remain in the large airways and trachea, and the likelihood of the suction catheter reaching this level via the nose or the mouth is debatable. IPPB using a face mask may be helpful. These patients are at risk of developing a chest infection and/or atelectasis and may need treatment at frequent intervals.

Patients with either an endotracheal or tracheostomy tube in situ will need humidification; they may also benefit from combining gentle manual hyperinflation with the treatment. Full range passive movements and careful joint positioning will also be required.

Postoperative IPPV

These patients usually fall into one of three categories:

1. Elective IPPV following major surgery, e.g. open heart surgery. These patients do not usually suffer from a primary chest condition.
2. Elective IPPV following major surgery for a patient with a known chest condition such as chronic bronchitis (or a heavy smoker). In both these categories the patients may be ventilated only overnight or for 24 hours.
3. Emergency IPPV for the patient in postoperative respiratory failure due to areas of lung collapse.

In group (1) many patients will have few secretions and will need no physiotherapy treatment prior to extubation (which is often done within a few hours of the patient returning from theatre), their treatment commencing on the first postoperative morning by which time they are usually breathing spontaneously. If treatment is indicated earlier, the techniques of manual hyperinflation, chest shaking and suction should be employed in combination with appropriate postural drainage positions. Following cardiac surgery, particular attention should be paid to the cardiovascular status and the patient's condition discussed with the surgeon before considering tipping head down. Treatment must be discontinued immediately if any alteration to the cardiac rhythm occurs. The physiotherapist must also take care not to cause undue pressure on the sternal incision by positioning her hands more posteriorly than laterally and supporting the incision during coughing. Should these patients require IPPV for longer than the overnight period, preventive treatment may be required provided the patient's condition is stable enough.

In groups (2) and (3) chest clearance procedures will need to be performed as vigorously and frequently as the patient's general condition will allow, in order to clear secretions and prevent further areas of atelectasis developing.

Patients in all groups should be encouraged to perform active assisted exercises.

WEANING FROM A VENTILATOR

As the condition of the patient improves, so the process of 'weaning' from the ventilator begins under supervision of the medical staff. Before attempting to wean the patient, several factors should be considered and the process carefully explained. The patient should not be under the effect of any respiratory depressive drugs. The chest radiograph should be reasonably clear and the chest should be as clear of secretions as possible (although it is not wise to try him off the ventilator immediately following physiotherapy since he may be tired with the exertion of coughing). The arterial blood gases should be relatively normal without the need for high inspired concentrations of oxygen.

Most patients find the half-lying position the most comfortable for the first attempts at breathing spontaneously. In this position the patient will be disconnected from the ventilator and a humidifier connected in its place, probably with added oxygen. It is important that a member of staff stays with the patient at this stage talking to him and reassuring him, as well as encouraging him to deep breathe, since he will undoubtedly feel anxious and uncomfortable no matter how well prepared he has been. He needs to be closely observed and the pulse, respiration rate and, intermittently, arterial blood gases, recorded. If there are signs of respiratory distress, the doctor must be informed and the patient reconnected to the ventilator. If the patient is comfortable, the observations and blood gas results satisfactory, then the patient may be extubated. The length of time that this process takes is very variable; for the patient requiring a short period of IPPV, for example after open heart surgery, extubation can usually be done at the first attempt off the ventilator;

those who have received prolonged ventilation may take several days to be weaned, starting with short periods of spontaneous breathing which will be lengthened progressively as the patient gains strength and confidence. It is always the decision of the doctor as to how long the patient spends off the ventilator and whether or not he is ready for extubation.

During the initial periods of spontaneous breathing vigorous chest clearance procedures should *not* be used as this could distress and tire the patient – so shortening his time off the ventilator. Instead, he should be encouraged to do breathing exercises and cough spontaneously, any secretions being aspirated. When the patient can manage longer periods of spontaneous breathing – several hours each day – then breathing exercises, huffing and coughing may be carried out in alternate side lying using percussion, shakings, vibrations as necessary supplemented with endotracheal/tracheal suction to remove secretions. If necessary, manual hyperinflation may be continued, but should be discontinued as soon as the patient can huff and cough effectively himself. IPPB may be useful in helping to wean the patient from the ventilator.

Once a patient with a tracheostomy tube has been weaned off the ventilator, the cuffed, plastic tube may be changed for an uncuffed silver tube (see p. 231) which has an inner speaking tube enabling him to talk. Before this tube is finally removed the physiotherapist must ensure that the patient is capable of clearing his own secretions by huffing and coughing, and chest clearance procedures should be carried out to facilitate the removal of secretions. Once the doctor is sure the patient will no longer need suction to remove the secretions, the silver tube will be removed and a dry dressing placed over the stoma, which should heal in a few days. Although the dressing over the stoma should be as airtight as possible, the patient must be taught how to hold the site of the tracheostomy with his hand during coughing so that secretions are coughed into the mouth and not through the stoma. If pressure is not applied, the high pressure of the cough will cause air and secretions to leak through the stoma and the full force of the cough is lost. Application of pressure may be reduced as the stoma heals until it may be stopped when the wound has sealed completely.

REFERENCES

Branson, R. D., Hurst, J. M. and de Haven, C. B. (1985). Mask CPAP: state of the art. *Respiratory Care*, **30**, 10, 846–57.

Branthwaite, M. A. (1978). *Artificial Ventilation for Pulmonary Disease*, pp. 32–3. Pitman Medical, Tunbridge Wells, Kent.

Gormezano, J. and Branthwaite, M. A. (1972). Effects of physiotherapy during intermittent positive pressure ventilation. *Anaesthesia*, **27**, 3, 258–63.

Jung, R. C. and Gottlieb, L. S. (1976). Comparison of tracheobronchial suction catheters in humans. *Chest*, **69**, 179–81.

Kuzenski, B. M. (1978). Effect of negative pressure on tracheobronchial trauma. *Nursing Research*, **27**, 4, 260–3.

Link, W. J. et al (1976). The influence of suction catheter tip design on tracheobronchial trauma and fluid aspiration efficiency. *Anaesthetics and Analgesia*, **55**, 290–7.

Matthews, H. R. and Hopkinson, R. B. (1984). Treatment of sputum retention by minitracheotomy. *British Journal of Surgery*, **71**, 147–50.

Petersen, G. M. et al (1979). Arterial oxygen saturation during nasotracheal suctioning. *Chest*, **76**, 3, 283–7.

Sackner, M. A. et al (1973). Pathogenesis and prevention of tracheobronchial damage with suction procedures. *Chest*, **64**, 284–90.

Starke, I. D. et al (1979). IPPB and hypercapnia in respiratory failure: the effect of different concentrations of inspired oxygen on arterial blood gas tensions. *Anaesthesia*, **34**, 283–7. [Misprint, p. 286, para. 4, '125mmHg' should read '12.5mmHg']

Webber, B. A., Shenfield, G. M. and Paterson, J. W. (1974). A comparison of three different techniques for giving nebulised albuterol to asthmatic patients. *American Review of Respiratory Disease*, **109**, 293–5.

Webber, B. A. (1981). Use and abuse of inhalation equipment. *Physiotherapy*, **67**, 5, 130–3.

Young, C. S. (1984a). Recommended guidelines for suction. *Physiotherapy*, **70**, 3, 106–8.

Young, C. S. (1984b). A review of the adverse effects of airway suction. *Physiotherapy*, **70**, 3, 104–6.

BIBLIOGRAPHY

Brewis, R. A. L. (1985). *Lecture Notes on Respiratory Disease*, 3rd edition. Blackwell Scientific Publications Limited, Oxford.

Keen, G. (1984). *Chest Injuries*, 2nd edition. John Wright and Sons Limited, Bristol.

Mackenzie, C. F., Ciesla, N., Imle, C. and Klemic, N. (1981). *Chest Physiotherapy in the Critical Care Unit*. Williams and Wilkins Company, Baltimore.

Preston, I. M., Matthews, H. R. and Ready, A. R. (1986). Minitracheotomy: A new technique for tracheal suction. *Physiotherapy*, **72**, 10, 494–7.

Sherwood Jones, E. (1978). *Essential Intensive Care*. MTP Press Limited, Lancaster.

Sykes, M. K., McNichol, M. W. and Campbell, E. J. M. (1986). *Respiratory Failure*, 3rd edition. Blackwell Scientific Publications Limited, Oxford.

West J. B. (1981) *Pulmonary Pathophysiology: The Essentials*, 2nd edition. Williams and Wilkins Company, Baltimore.

Zagelbaum, G. L. and Pare, J. A. P. (1982) *Manual of Acute Respiratory Care*, 4th edition. Longmans, London.

ACKNOWLEDGEMENTS

The author thanks her colleagues at Killingbeck Hospital for their help and advice. She thanks Mr E. Wall for providing the photographs, and Mrs G. Watkin for typing the manuscript.

Chapter 12

Paediatric and Neonatal Intensive Therapy

by A. PARKER MCSP

The general principles of intensive therapy for neonates (0–1 month), infants (1–12 months) and children are the same as those for adults, but with some important additions:

1. The general state of an infant or child will fluctuate *much more quickly* than an adult. This means extreme diligence on behalf of attendant staff.
2. Physiotherapy can cause a deterioration in the patient's condition so it is *essential* that a full assessment is carried out before *each* treatment to ascertain whether treatment is necessary.
3. Infants and children are unable to tolerate lengthy, vigorous physiotherapy sessions, so short, frequent treatments should be given. Treatment may need to be given 2-hourly throughout the day and, at times, the night, although in a 24-hour period it is important that the patient gets at least one period of 3–4 hours rest, if not longer.
4. Sick children should be handled as little as possible; treatment should, therefore, be timed to coincide with turning and other nursing care, whenever possible.
5. Young children who are conscious in an intensive care unit will have little or no understanding of the situation and will, therefore, be very frightened.

Sympathetic, caring handling is required to achieve an effective treatment while causing minimal distress to the child. Parents should be allowed to stay with the child most of the time, and favourite toys should be given.

MANUAL TECHNIQUES

Percussion, shaking and vibrations can all be used in the treatment of children; older children can be treated in a similar manner to adults, and the same contra-indications apply. Where the patient is being fed orally or nasogastrically, sufficient time should be given following a feed before treatment is commenced to avoid aspiration of stomach contents.

All techniques should be applied firmly, physiotherapists inexperienced in handling children may be too gentle and, therefore, ineffective. Care should be taken, however, with children with dietary deficiencies, or with babies who have been born very prematurely, as rickets may be present. If this is the case then manual techniques may be contra-indicated and the paediatrician in charge of the patient should be consulted.

Percussion

In small children percussion may applied with one hand. In neonates and premature infants the first 3 or 4 fingers of one hand may be used, slightly elevating the middle finger (tenting), or the thenar and hypothenar eminences (contact-heel percussion). Percussion can also be applied using various cup-shaped objects, e.g. a medicine pot padded with lint or a small face mask with a soft plastic or foam cuff (Fig. 12/1).

The amount of pressure applied when percussing will depend on the age of the child and the medical condition.

Percussion should always be applied over something like a towel or a dressing gown, not over the bare skin. It should not be

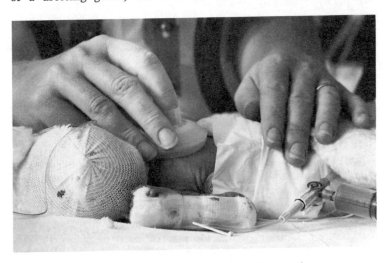

FIG. 12/1 Chest percussion using a face mask

performed over recent incisions, drainage tubes, open wounds or bony prominences.

Shaking and vibrations

These should be applied to the chest wall, using the fingertips in premature infants, or whole fingers for infants and small children. The size of the child will determine how much of the hand is used.

The chest wall of neonates and small children is very compliant so shaking and vibrations can be very effective in removing secretions. It is often easier to vibrate rapidly breathing infants every second or third exhalation rather than on each breath.

Postural drainage

Postural drainage positions can be used for children in the same way as for adults, providing that there are no specific contra-indications, for example cardiac failure. Care should be taken with neonates as they are predominantly diaphragmatic breathers, due to weak intercostal muscles and horizontally positioned ribs, and so may not tolerate the head down position.

Some severely ill infants, especially those who are premature, will not tolerate any change in position, and so have to be treated in situ.

Manual hyperinflation

This is a technique used to expand areas of lung which are not inflated during the inspiratory cycle of the ventilator, thereby helping to prevent atelectasis and aiding removal of secretions. It is a technique which is particularly useful postoperatively.

A 500ml bag, with valve, should be used for babies; a 1 litre bag, with valve, for children. Some units have bags which are open-ended thereby giving an extra outlet for excess pressure when the bag is squeezed. The amount of gas expelled through this opening is controlled by the operator's fingers.

Self-inflating bags are often used in neonatal units but these are mainly for resuscitation purposes, when they are rapidly squeezed with the fingertips.

The flow rate of gas into the bag will depend on the size of the patient: 2 litres per minute for babies; up to about 8 litres per minute for children. One or two hands may be used to empty the bag depending on its size. A manometer may be added into the bag's circuit in order to show how much pressure is being generated.

PRECAUTIONS

The same precautions should be considered when treating a child with manual hyperinflation as when treating an adult: low blood pressure, surgical emphysema, pneumothorax and bronchospasm.

A further consideration is that premature infants, babies and small children have very delicate lung tissue which can be damaged easily by high inflation pressures causing hyperinflated alveoli, pneumothorax or both, and can eventually lead to permanent lung damage. These patients may be receiving their maximum inspiratory pressure from the ventilator, so manual hyperinflation using a higher inspiratory pressure can cause lung damage; manual hyperinflation using a lower inspiratory pressure than the ventilator will be ineffective.

Manual hyperinflation, therefore, should only be carried out by members of staff experienced in its use who have carefully assessed the patient before commencing treatment.

An anaesthetic bag and mask may be used to facilitate chest clearance in small children who are not intubated. The child must be accurately positioned with the neck extended, an airway in situ and the mask held tightly over the face. The bag should be compressed in time with the patient's inspiration otherwise the stomach may become inflated causing respiratory embarrassment. Only experienced staff should use this technique.

Breathing exercises

It is possible to teach deep breathing to children from the age of 18 months upwards, with the aid of bubbles, paper windmills, etc. Older children can be taught specific exercises in the same way as adults. Most children find diaphragmatic breathing quite simple – encouraging them to 'fill up their tummy with air, like a balloon' works quite well, providing they are reminded not to use their abdominal muscles.

Coughing

It is very difficult to teach critically ill children how to cough. Where an effective cough cannot be produced tracheal compression may be used – gentle pressure with a sideward motion is briefly applied to the trachea below the thyroid cartilage. This causes apposition of the tracheal walls, which are soft and pliant in young children and infants, stimulating the cough reflex. Great care must be taken when applying this technique as the patient may become bradycardic. In the presence of copious secretions with no effective cough suction will have to be used.

SUCTION

Suction can be used to remove secretions from intubated patients and from infants and children who are unable to cough and expectorate.

General principles

The technique should be as quick, clean and gentle as possible. Suction is very traumatic to delicate mucosal tissue and it is very easy to introduce infection, especially in intubated patients.

Suction should only be carried out *as and when necessary*, rather than on a routine basis.

Equipment

Vacuum suction. This should be checked prior to each treatment to ensure that it is working effectively, and that it is set at the correct negative pressure for the patient. Recommended values are between 9.5–13.5kPa for infants and small children, although the pressure may need to be increased when secretions are particularly thick. The maximum pressure for premature infants is 10.5kPa.

Interrupting the suction pressure on withdrawing the catheter can help to minimise trauma.

Catheters. These should be of a material soft enough to reduce trauma yet strong enough to avoid collapsing on the application of negative pressure. They should be of the correct size, that is small enough to pass easily down endotracheal and tracheostomy tubes, but large enough to remove copious, thick secretions. Size 6 FG and 8 FG are the most useful catheters; size 5 FG and below are often too small to remove thick secretions effectively and size 10 FG and above are too large for anyone other than older children.

Small children and infants should not be suctioned nasally with any catheter larger than a size 8 FG as this may cause unnecessary trauma and upset.

Suction catheters with control valves or Y-connections should preferably be used to prevent a build-up of negative pressure.

Gloves or forceps should be used for handling the catheter in order to maintain a clean technique. Gloves and catheters should be discarded after single use to prevent introduction of infection.

Mucolytics and diluents. These are used to loosen thick secretions in intubated patients and should be sterile to avoid introduction of infection.

The most commonly used diluent is normal saline but an alkaline sodium bicarbonate solution may be used. A mucolytic such as n-acetylcysteine can be used to remove very thick secretions but bronchial bleeding and bronchospasm can follow its use. The amount to be instilled prior to passing each suction catheter is dependent on the size of the baby/child. The following is only a guide:

Premature (pre-term) infants   0.3–0.5ml
Babies (full term)   0.5–1.0ml
Small children   1.0–2.0ml

Care must be taken when the mucolytic has been instilled as this may cause complete blockage of the very small bore tracheal tubes used in premature infants and neonates; in which case the solution should be aspirated immediately. This event can be avoided by instilling the mucolytic via a suction catheter which also ensures that the solution reaches further down into the bronchi. A catheter is filled with saline or mucolytic from a syringe which is left attached as the catheter is passed into the tracheal tube. The required amount of solution is then delivered from the syringe into the lungs via the suction catheter. The catheter is then removed without applying suction.

Risks and complications of suction

Trauma. Mucosal haemorrhage and erosion frequently occur in the patient who has been suctioned, leading eventually to the formation of granulation tissue. The amount of trauma depends upon the frequency of suction, the amount of negative pressure applied, the size and type of catheter used and the vigour of insertion.

Hypoxia. This can occur following suction. To avoid this the suctioning time should be kept to a minimum, particularly in those patients who are dependent on a ventilator, and the inspired oxygen and/or ventilation may be increased prior to suction providing there are no contra-indications.

Cardiovascular effects. Cardiac arrhythmias and hypotension can occur during suction due to hypoxia and/or vagal stimulation from direct pharyngeal and tracheal irritation. Particular care should be taken with neonates as bradycardia and apnoea can follow nasopharyngeal suction in these patients (Cordero and Hon, 1971).

Atelectasis. Too large a suction catheter in too small an airway will prevent room air from entering around the catheter during suctioning and atelectasis, in varying degrees, may occur. Too high a negative suction pressure may also cause atelectasis and airway collapse.

Pneumothorax. This can occur primarily in premature infants with severe underlying lung disease due to perforation of segmental bronchi by a suction catheter (Vaughan et al, 1978).

Suction for intubated patients

This method applies to those patients who have tracheostomy tubes, endotracheal tubes, nasotracheal tubes or nasopharyngeal tubes in situ.

1. Wash hands.
2. Prepare equipment:
   – turn on vacuum, check pressure
   – attach suction catheter
   – prepare saline or mucolytic solution
   – prepare gloves/forceps.
3. Prepare patient – if conscious the patient should be swaddled in a blanket being aware of infusions, drains, tubes, etc; or he should be held firmly by an assistant. The procedure should be explained to the child and constant reassurance given while suctioning is taking place.
4. Instil mucolytic/saline solution into tracheal tube.
5. Physiotherapy may be carried out at this point if indicated.
6. Place glove on the hand that is to hold suction catheter.
7. Withdraw catheter from its sterile pack with the gloved hand.
8. Disconnect ventilated patient from ventilator.
9. Insert catherter into tube *without* applying suction.
10. Push catheter gently and quickly down tube until a slight resistance is met.
11. Withdraw catheter 0.5cm.
12. Apply suction.
13. Withdraw catheter quickly, rotating gently between thumb and first finger and interrupting the suction pressure every few seconds.

14. Reconnect patient to ventilator.
15. The same catheter can then be used to clear secretions from the mouth and nose.
16. Discard both the glove and the catheter.
17. Repeat until secretions are cleared.

Suction for non-intubated patients

Children and infants should always be suctioned in side lying to prevent aspiration of vomit.

Follow the above instructions for *Suction for Intubated Patients* from No. 1 to No. 7 omitting No. 4. Then proceed as follows:

NASAL SUCTION

It is very important to keep the nasal passages clear in neonates as they are nose breathers and may become apnoeic if their noses are blocked.

8. Gently insert catheter into the nose using an upward motion until the nasal septum is passed, then using a downward motion. If a slight resistance is met, withdraw catheter slightly and try again.
9. Insert catheter to the back of the throat until a cough has been stimulated.

    It is possible to pass a catheter into the trachea by inserting the catheter during inspiration, but an effective cough can be elicited merely by stimulating the pharynx.
10. Apply suction.
11. Withdraw catheter, rotating slightly between thumb and first finger and interrupting the suction every few seconds.
12. Repeat procedure via other nostril.
13. Discard both the glove and the catheter.
14. Repeat until secretions are cleared.

ORAL SUCTION

8. Pass suction catheter to the back of the throat until a cough has been stimulated. Ensure that the catheter is not curling up in the mouth.
9. Apply suction.
10. Withdraw catheter.
11. Repeat until secretions are clear.
12. Discard both the glove and the catheter.

NB: Great care must be taken when suctioning the oro/nasopharynx of patients who have recently been extubated as this may cause laryngospasm. Suction should not be carried out on patients with laryngospasm which is causing stridor unless absolutely necessary.

EXERCISES

Passive movements should be given regularly to the unconscious child in the ITU to maintain full range of movement in all joints. Frequent turning and careful positioning are important to prevent pressure sores and, in the case of the child with spasticity, to avoid positions which encourage abnormal reflexes.

Care should be taken when handling children and infants who are hypotonic in order to avoid soft tissue damage. Premature infants are generally hypotonic and should have minimal handling, therefore passive movements are not usually necessary.

Conscious infants and children in the ITU will usually move around the bed adequately without assistance from the physiotherapist. Older children may need specific exercises and posture correction particularly following cardiothoracic surgery.

When treating children in the ITU the physiotherapist should at all times be aware of the patient's vital signs – heart rate, respiratory rate, skin colour and movement. Should any change in these signs occur treatment must be stopped immediately.

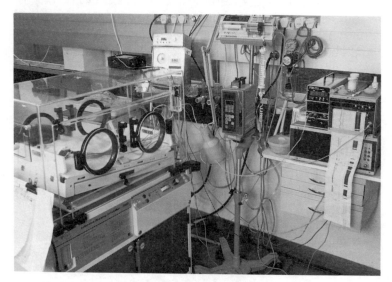

FIG. 12/2 Equipment used in a neonatal intensive therapy unit

Infants, especially if premature, can be hypoxic without appearing cyanosed; pallor, staring, worried expression and sweating are all signs of hypoxia in infants.

Intercostal and sternal recession, and nasal flaring are signs of respiratory distress in the infant and young child.

EQUIPMENT USED IN NEONATAL AND PAEDIATRIC INTENSIVE CARE (Fig. 12/2)

Physiotherapists working in an intensive care unit should have a basic knowledge of all equipment used on that unit. They should be able to respond when a problem is indicated by the equipment, and be able to ascertain when the problem is with the patient or the machine.

Mechanical ventilators

These may be specifically designed paediatric ventilators, such as the Sechrist and Bourne Ventilators, or adult ventilators adapted for paediatric use. Ventilators may be pressure cycled or volume cycled.

Pressure-cycled ventilators are used for neonates; *volume-cycled ventilators* are usually used for older children. Young children can be ventilated using either pressure- or volume-cycled machines.

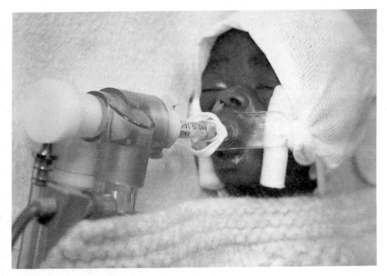

FIG. 12/3 Oral intubation of a premature infant

Premature infants and neonates may be intubated with either nasal or oral uncuffed endotracheal tubes (Fig. 12/3); older children are usually intubated using nasal endotracheal tubes as these are less easily dislodged and allow easier mouth care. The use of uncuffed tubes reduces the risk of tracheal stenosis but means that foreign material such as vomit may be aspirated into the lungs around the tracheal tube.

Care must be taken when positioning the ventilator tubing as its weight may cause displacement of the tracheal tube, also condensation from humidified gases may drain into the lungs.

Paediatric ventilators are capable of ventilating premature infants and neonates at very fast rates, up to 200 breaths per minute. Some ventilators, such as the Sechrist, can give *high frequency positive pressure ventilation* at rates of up to 2000 per minute. Paediatric ventilators are also capable of providing *intermittent mandatory ventilation* (IMV) and *continuous positive airways pressure* (CPAP) using the same ventilation circuit as for IPPV.

IMV is used to wean patients from the ventilator when IPPV is no longer necessary – the intubated patient is able to breathe spontaneously but also receives a predetermined number of breaths/minute at a pre-set pressure or volume. The number of breaths/minute given by the ventilator will be gradually reduced until the patient is weaned on to CPAP or extubated.

CPAP is used as a means of weaning patients off a ventilator but can also be used primarily as a means of treating hypoxia, as in premature infants with *respiratory distress syndrome* (RDS). The patient breathes spontaneously against a continuous positive pressure which may help in keeping the airways patent. CPAP can be delivered by an endotracheal tube, nasopharyngeal tube, or nasal prongs. One complication of these methods, excepting the endotracheal tube, is gaseous abdominal distension.

Maximum pressures used in all forms of assisted ventilation (IPPV, IMV or CPAP) will depend on the size of the patient and the condition. Regular blood gas measurement will ensure that the minimal amount of assisted ventilation is given to produce satisfactory blood gas levels.

Incubators and radiant warmers

Neonates, that is premature infants and full term infants who have undergone surgery, will be nursed in incubators or under radiant warmers.

Incubators are enclosed units of transparent material with portholes in the sides for access. They can be warmed, and humidified air or oxygen can be delivered to the infant inside. The temperature inside an incubator is kept in the thermo-neutral range – this is the environmental temperature at which oxygen consumption is minimal in the presence of a normal body temperature. It will vary according to the patient's gestation and weight.

Perspex heat shields can be placed over infants in an incubator to help minimise heat loss.

Portholes should be opened only when necessary and never left open, to prevent draughts.

The mattress in an incubator can be tipped up or down for postural drainage, if indicated.

A *radiant warmer* consists of an open-topped unit with a radiant heating device above it. It allows free access to the infant and space for tubes, infusions and drains. Disadvantages are convective heat loss and insensible fluid loss. The whole unit can be tipped up or down, if necessary.

Headbox (Fig. 12/4)

This is a clear plastic box placed over an infant or small child's head to deliver oxygen and/or humidification.

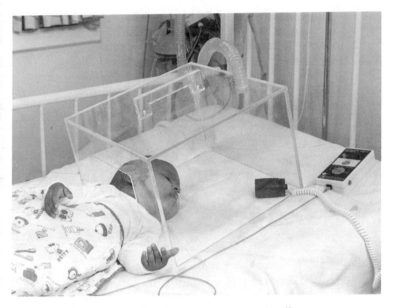

FIG. 12/4 Child receiving humidified oxygen via a headbox

Phototherapy unit

This consists of white or blue lamps which emit light waves between 400–500nm. Light of these wavelengths oxidises unconjugated bilirubin into harmless derivatives and so is very important in the treatment of jaundice in neonates.

Infants receiving phototherapy have to be nursed naked which can cause problems of temperature control. There is also increased insensible fluid loss, and a theoretical risk of eye damage so eye shields should be worn.

ECG, respiratory rate and blood pressure monitors

These are similar to those used on adults although normal values vary according to the age of the patient:

Age	HR (beats/min)	RR (breaths/min)	BP (mmHg)
Premature infants	120–140	35–40	70/40
Full-term neonate	100–140	30–40	80/40
1–4 years	80–120	25–30	100/65
Adolescence	60–80	15–20	115/60

Transcutaneous oxygen monitors (TcO$_2$)

These monitors provide a non-invasive means of measuring the partial pressure of oxygen in arterialised capillaries through the skin. TcO$_2$ monitors have electrodes which, when placed on the infant, heat up a small area of skin and produce a superficial erythema. The partial pressure of arterial oxygen (Pao$_2$) in the dilated capillaries can be assessed by the machine and displayed on a visual monitor; normal values are between 8–12kPa. The electrodes are moved to a different position on the skin every 4–6 hours to prevent the skin becoming burned. Transcutaneous carbon dioxide monitors are also available which work on a similar principle.

Humidification

Humidification is extremely important in the infant and young child as their small bore tracheal tubes and narrow airways can easily be blocked off by plugs of thick sputum. Heated humidifiers, such as the Bennett cascade, should be used for infants but care should be taken that they do not overheat and burn the patient.

REASONS FOR ADMISSION TO A PAEDIATRIC INTENSIVE CARE UNIT

1. Trauma, e.g. accidents on the road, at home.
2. Postoperatively, e.g. cardiac surgery, neurosurgery.
3. Life-threatening medical conditions such as (a) respiratory, e.g. asthma, whooping cough; or (b) neurological, e.g. encephalo- pathy, meningitis.

Trauma

Accidents rank as the commonest cause of child death after the first year of life. Children of all ages may be admitted to an ITU following accidents on the road or at home.

ROAD TRAFFIC ACCIDENT (RTA)

About half of all accidental deaths of children are due to traffic accidents. The most common need for intensive care following a RTA is head injury. The major effect of head injury is cerebral oedema leading to an increase in intracranial pressure (ICP). In infants and young children where fusion of the cranial sutures is incomplete some compensation for increased ICP can be seen by skull expansion.

Children with severe head injuries may need to be ventilated until the acute phase of cerebral oedema is over; this will take varying amounts of time depending on the severity of the injury. During this phase any handling will cause a rise in ICP possibly leading to further brain damage. Chest physiotherapy and suction are particu- larly likely to cause a rise in ICP so should not be performed unless absolutely necessary. However, hypoxia can cause further cerebral oedema so it is important that the patient's chest is kept clear.

When treatment is indicated, drugs, such as mannitol, to reduce the ICP, may be given prior to chest physiotherapy and suction; treatment should be discontinued immediately if there is any change in the patient's vital signs. Postural drainage with the head tipped downwards is always contra-indicated in these patients, and turning and positioning will depend on their condition and any other injuries they may have sustained.

ACCIDENTS AT HOME

These include accidental poisoning with a variety of substances, accidental strangulation and drowning. Intensive therapy will be indicated when the patient is in a comatose state, and mechanical ventilation may be necessary. Regular assessment of the patient's condition should be made, and chest physiotherapy and suction given as necessary.

BURNS

Children with severe burns should be nursed in specialised burns units, but some patients with only minor burns may be suffering from the effects of smoke inhalation and may be admitted to a paediatric or adult intensive therapy unit. Chest physiotherapy will be needed to remove the thick black secretions which are produced following smoke inhalation, but precautions must be taken where there are burns to the chest and when bronchospasm is present.

Intensive physiotherapy will be needed to prevent contractures from scar tissue following severe burns to the skin.

Postoperatively

Children and infants will need intensive care following major surgery of any kind. Particular points to remember are:

1. Patient and parents should be seen by the physiotherapist pre-operatively, unless the operation is done as an emergency. Whenever possible the physiotherapist should visit the patient more than once pre-operatively in order to build up a relationship. Where the child is old enough to co-operate, breathing exercises and coughing should be taught and their necessity explained to the child and the parents. It is important that the parents fully understand the need for postoperative physiotherapy as they can play an important role in encouraging exercise.

   A full chest assessment should be carried out pre-operatively in case chest clearance is necessary.
2. Postoperatively the patient should be regularly assessed by the physiotherapist but treatment should only be given as necessary and *not* as a routine.
3. It is important that analgesia should be given prior to treatment, especially in the first few days, as children will not co-operate if they are in pain. If infants are treated without adequate analgesia

they may become tachycardic and tachypnoeic and an effective treatment is not possible.

4. Children often prefer not to have their wounds supported by the physiotherapist and may not want to support the wounds themselves. They may prefer to press a pillow to the area.

5. Early mobilisation should be encouraged as soon as the patient's condition allows it.

CARDIAC SURGERY

Most patients undergoing cardiac surgery will have congenital cardiac defects. They are usually nursed in specialised cardiothoracic units, but may be in a paediatric ITU or, in the case of the newborn, in a neonatal ITU.

Infants with cardiac problems often have pulmonary hypertension which may be associated with excessive secretions leading to repeated chest infections. It is important that the lung fields are as clear as possible prior to surgery so chest physiotherapy may be necessary pre-operatively. The condition of the infant will determine what treatment can be tolerated but all manoeuvres should be carried out with care. Postural drainage, in particular, may need to be modified.

Postoperatively, chest physiotherapy will begin when the patient's condition has stabilised; in some units treatment will be on the day of operation, in others the day after. Depending on the type of operation the patient may or may not be ventilated. The patient should be assessed and physiotherapy given as necessary. Treatment may need to be in situ at first but alternate side lying will be possible as the patient's condition improves. A careful watch must be kept on the patient's vital signs at all times.

IMV and CPAP may be used to wean the patient off the ventilator and physiotherapy, if necessary, can still be applied as for the ventilated patient. Some patients only have a small amount of clear secretions which are easily removed by suction alone so, if the chest radiograph is clear, chest physiotherapy is not needed. Regular assessment of the patient's chest by the physiotherapist is essential, however, as the situation can rapidly change.

Once the patient has been extubated regular physiotherapy may be necessary to clear the chest. Much encouragement will be needed to persuade children to cough and expectorate. Early mobilisation is very important to stimulate deep breathing and coughing, the timing of this will depend on the cardiac condition. If it is not possible to clear the chest this way then the bag and mask technique may be used as previously described, or the child may be temporarily intubated in order to facilitate efficient bronchial toilet.

In patients who are not ventilated after surgery gentle physiotherapy in situ, or in alternate side lying can be given as necessary.

Nasopharyngeal suction may be used in infants and children who are unable to expectorate.

Some patients, especially older children, may develop a poor posture and be reluctant to move, so shoulder girdle and thoracic exercises should be given in the form of games.

NEUROSURGERY

Following any surgery to the brain the same precautions apply as for treating a patient following a head injury.

GENERAL SURGERY

Following major abdominal surgery, children will be nursed in a paediatric or adult ITU; the newborn will be nursed in a neonatal ITU. Operations which will necessitate intensive care postoperatively are:

Oesophageal atresia with or without tracheo-oesophageal fistula. This is a congenital malformation in which the upper end of the oesophagus finishes in a blind pouch. There may also be a fistula from the lower part of the oesophagus into the trachea. The infant presents shortly after birth with respiratory distress due to the inability to swallow oral secretions which then overflow and may be aspirated into the trachea. The acid stomach contents may also be regurgitated through the distal fistula into the lungs – atelectasis and pneumonia can result. Surgical treatment consists of primary anastomosis where this is possible, and tying off the fistula.

Postoperatively the patient may need to be ventilated and regular chest physiotherapy may be needed for several days. The patient will be nursed head up and treatment should only be given in this position for the first few days. In some cases care must be taken not to extend the neck as this may put stress on the anastomosis. In the non-intubated patient pharyngeal suctioning should only be carried out with extreme caution to avoid passing the catheter into the oesophagus and damaging the anastomosis.

Diaphragmatic hernia. This is a congenital abnormality where loops of bowel herniate through the diaphragm into the thoracic cavity. The infant presents with signs of respiratory distress and a chest radiograph shows abdominal viscera present in the thoracic cavity. Surgical repair is often done as an emergency – the viscera are returned to the abdomen and the defect in the diaphragm sutured. The patient may still show signs of respiratory distress after surgery as hypoplastic lungs are often associated with this condition.

Chest physiotherapy may be required postoperatively when tenacious secretions are present. The infant will be nursed in the head-up position and treatment should be given in this way.

Older children may be admitted to the ITU following major abdominal surgery, such as removal of a liver tumour; or if there are other factors which may complicate postoperative recovery, for example a child with sickle cell anaemia having a cholecystectomy, or a child with cystic fibrosis having a splenectomy.

Children who have had liver surgery should not have vigorous physiotherapy postoperatively as there is a risk of haemorrhage.

Children with sickle cell anaemia will need intensive chest physiotherapy postoperatively as they are prone to atelectasis and pneumonia.

Children with cystic fibrosis will need vigorous and intensive chest treatment postoperatively but techniques may need to be modified to take into account incisions, pain or other factors.

Life-threatening medical conditions

RESPIRATORY

Occasionally children suffering from respiratory problems such as asthma, bronchiolitis and whooping cough may need to be admitted to an ITU for ventilation.

Asthma. Children of any age may need ventilation during an asthma attack. Physiotherapy will be contra-indicated where there is severe bronchospasm.

When bronchospasm has been relieved by drug therapy there may be mucus plugs blocking the smaller airways causing areas of lung collapse – percussion with instillation of saline, followed by suction may help to remove these.

Manual hyperinflation is often contra-indicated in these patients as there may be areas of alveolar hyperinflation between areas of collapse. It is possible in these cases that manual hyperinflation, rather than expanding areas of collapse, will over-expand the hyperinflated areas with the risk of pneumothorax. Manual hyper-inflation can also aggravate bronchospasm, as can vibrations to the chest, so these techniques should be avoided if possible.

Bronchodilators can be given prior to physiotherapy treatment in order to reduce bronchospasm. Should bronchospasm become worse during treatment, then treatment should be stopped.

Bronchiolitis. This is a viral illness occurring mainly in infants under one year. The disease presents with acute dypsnoea, coughing and wheezing, sometimes with areas of lung collapse on the chest radiograph. Initial treatment is for the infant to be nursed head up in high humidity with added oxygen. Physiotherapy is contra-indicated at this stage although suction may be required to clear nasal secretions.

If the infant needs to be intubated and ventilated physiotherapy is contra-indicated until the acute stage of wheezing is over, unless there are copious secretions. Treatment should be given as for the asthmatic patient and discontinued if wheezing worsens. Following extubation treatment should continue, providing there is no wheezing, until the chest radiograph is clear.

Whooping cough. This is a disease caused by the organism *Bordetella pertussis*. It is characterised by paroxysms of coughing which may be followed by the inspiratory 'whoop'. The patient then usually vomits. Whooping cough can be very severe especially in infants; bronchopneumonia is a serious complication of this disease and the patient may need to be ventilated. The symptoms of the disease can last for many weeks. Vigorous physiotherapy will be needed when the patient is ventilated to remove the very thick, tenacious secretions which can easily block the bronchi. If the patient is not intubated and ventilated, physiotherapy is often ineffective in the acute stage of the disease and, in fact, it is usually contra-indicated in infants as treatment can initiate paroxysmal coughing leading to apnoea.

Following extubation, physiotherapy is often needed for persistent lobar collapse.

Epiglottitis; acute laryngotracheobronchitis. These illnesses may cause acute respiratory obstruction needing intubation. They usually affect children between the ages of 1–5 years. When the child is intubated chest physiotherapy may be needed if there are copious secretions, but the endotracheal tube usually only needs to be in situ for a couple of days. Following extubation the child often needs no treatment.

NEUROLOGICAL CONDITIONS

Children of all ages may need ventilation for neurological problems such as (a) coma and respiratory depression; (b) respiratory muscle weakness; (c) following sedation or anticonvulsant therapy; or (d) management of increased intracranial pressure.

The patient should be regularly assessed and chest physiotherapy given as necessary. Passive/assisted active movements will need to be given daily.

REASONS FOR ADMISSION TO A NEONATAL INTENSIVE CARE UNIT

1. Pre-term, that is less than 37 completed weeks of gestation. Some infants may be born after a pregnancy lasting only 24 weeks.
2. Low birth-weight, that is 2500g (5½lb) or less. This can be due to several reasons including intra-uterine fetal malnutrition. Some infants may weigh less than 700g.
3. Perinatal problems, such as birth asphyxia, meconium aspiration.
4. Congenital abnormalities, such as congenital heart disease, diaphragmatic hernia.

Problems of the pre-term or low birth-weight infant

RESPIRATORY DISTRESS

The main cause of respiratory distress in the pre-term infant is respiratory distress syndrome (RDS) (hyaline membrane disease). This is a disease related to lack of surfactant in the immature lung. Surfactant is the phospholipid alveolar lining which lowers surface tension and allows the lungs to expand more easily. Surfactant appears in the lungs at about 20 weeks' gestation, the amount present increasing slowly until, following a surge at 30 to 34 weeks, the lungs become functionally mature.

RDS presents within a few hours of birth with sternal and costal recession, grunting and tachypnoea. Treatment includes avoidance of hypoxia, which hinders sufactant production, by giving added oxygen. This may be done simply by adding oxygen to the atmosphere that the infant is breathing or it may be necessary to give assisted ventilation in the form of CPAP or IPPV. Recovery time varies considerably; some infants, especially more mature ones, recover after 36 to 48 hours, but others may need assisted ventilation for much longer.

Secretions are not a problem in RDS, so physiotherapy is not required unless there is also a chest infection or the infant has been intubated for more than 36 to 48 hours when secretions due to the presence of an endotracheal tube may become a problem.

The treatment of RDS by oxygen and ventilation can, however, cause complications. The PaO_2 of neonates should be between 8–12kPa. Too low a level leads to hypoxia and bradycardia. Too high a level – above 16kPa – especially if for prolonged periods (for example, more than 1 hour), can cause retrolental fibroplasia, a condition in which the delicate capillaries in the retina proliferate leading to haemorrhage, fibrosis and scarring of the retina, causing permanent visual impairment. It is therefore essential that PaO_2 levels are constantly monitored, either with arterial lines or transcutaneous oxygen (TcO_2) monitors, or both.

Prolonged ventilation, especially with high peak pressures and high inspiratory oxygen, can lead to bronchopulmonary dysplasia (BPD). In this condition, there is widespread destruction of alveoli which are replaced by areas of collapse, emphysema and fibrous tissue. Infants suffering from BPD may need supplementary oxygen for many months until the lung has had a chance to recover and grow new alveoli. During this time there is an increased risk of developing viral chest infections and obstructive airways disease, which must be vigorously treated with physiotherapy. Secretions can increase the extent of lung damage in BPD and regular physiotherapy may be required. Infants may take months to improve. A minority may never recover and will need increasing amounts of oxygen until they develop cor pulmonale and eventually die.

Other causes of respiratory distress include meconium aspiration. This can occur during prolonged or difficult labour when the infant may become hypoxic. Hypoxia causes the infant to pass meconium into the amniotic fluid and to make gasping movements so that some of the meconium is inhaled into the lungs. If the mother's liquor is meconium stained the infant's airway should be sucked out as soon as the mouth is free to prevent further aspiration when the first breath is taken. The infant may need to be intubated so that meconium can be sucked out from the lungs. Physiotherapy is indicated to assist removal of meconium and any excessive secretions.

TEMPERATURE CONTROL

Pre-term infants have great difficulty in maintaining their body temperature. They have a large surface area for a small body mass and easily lose heat through the skin by evaporation and radiation. To counteract this, these babies are nursed in incubators and the ambient room temperature is kept at 27–28°C. It is extremely important that infants are not allowed to become cold.

FEEDING

The very pre-term infant cannot suck satisfactorily and has impaired swallowing and imperfect gag and cough reflexes. Most infants are, therefore, fed frequent small amounts of milk via nasogastric or nasojejunal tubes. Regurgitation and inhalation of milk can be a problem so the infants should be handled only as necessary following a feed and, so far as possible, physiotherapy should be done before feeds.

JAUNDICE

Many normal full-term babies develop jaundice in the first week of life, but the pre-term infant is more susceptible to this and there is a risk of developing kernicterus. This is a rare condition in which bilirubin is laid down in the brain tissue, particularly the basal ganglia, causing permanent brain damage or even death.

To prevent this, infants are given phototherapy from a phototherapy unit or they may even need an exchange transfusion in which some of their blood is replaced by fresh blood from a donor.

INFECTION

The pre-term infant is particularly vulnerable to infection – the skin is very thin, easily damaged and infected, and the cellular and humoral defences are impaired. Physiotherapists must be scrupulous about hand-washing before and after treatment.

INTRAVENTRICULAR HAEMORRHAGE (IVH)

This is the main cause of death and long-term handicap in pre-term and low birth-weight infants. The haemorrhages arise from the fragile capillaries of the extremely vascular germinal layer in the floor of the lateral ventricle. Fluctuations of PaO_2, $PaCO_2$ and blood pressure lead to marked variations in cerebral blood flow causing the capillaries to burst and bleed into the ventricles.

There are several grades of IVH. Minor ones may have no neurological sequelae, but moderate to severe ones, especially associated with hydrocephalus, or areas of infarction, may lead to cerebral damage or death.

HANDLING

Handling and disturbing a sick neonate *in any way* will cause his condition to deteriorate. As physiotherapy is a form of fairly vigorous handling, it can be seen that there should be definite indications, and no definite contra-indications, before treatment is carried out.

Physiotherapy

Indications for physiotherapy include:

1. Presence of secretions due to (a) long-term intubation, i.e. 36 to 48 hours; (b) meconium aspiration; (c) operations, such as diaphragmatic hernia repair; or (d) pneumonia.
2. Lung collapse due to mucus plugging.

Contra-indications to physiotherapy:

1. Severely ill, unstable infant.
2. Untreated tension pneumothorax.

Contra-indications to postural drainage:

1. Intraventricular haemorrhage.
2. Cardiac failure.
3. Recent cranial surgery.
4. Abdominal distenstion.

Important note: Inappropriate physiotherapy and suction can cause hypoxia, hypercarbia and bradycardia leading to IVH, cerebral damage or death.

TREATMENT

1. Check the infant's charts and obtain an oral report from the attending nurse before beginning treatment.
2. Prepare suction equipment for use.
3. Check the monitors and note the normal, stable values for that infant.

    It is not advisable to begin physiotherapy if the Pao_2 is below 8kPa. The inspired oxygen (FiO_2) or ventilation can be increased until the Pao_2 reaches an acceptable level, although this must be done with great care so that the infant does not become hyperoxic.
4. If the infant is intubated, instil saline into the endotracheal tube, using between 0.3ml and 0.5ml depending on the size of the infant.
5. Posturally drain the infant, if this is indicated.
6. Percussion and vibrations may be applied.

While applying these techniques, the physiotherapist must be constantly aware of any changes in the baby's condition. Once treatment has begun, the TcO_2 monitor will register the falling Pao_2, the length of the physiotherapy treatment depending on how quickly this falls to an unacceptable level. Physiotherapy should be discontinued when the Pao_2 reaches 7.5kPa and suction should then be carried out as quickly and gently as possible. This will cause a further fall in the Pao_2 to 7kPa or below and the infant must then be allowed to recover until the Pao_2 has reached the pre-treatment level or above. If the infant is slow to recover, the FiO_2 or ventilation may be carefully increased.

Instillation of saline followed by postural drainage if advisable, percussion and vibration should then be repeated until all secretions have been cleared, always allowing adequate recovery time.

Oral and nasal suction should also be carried out.

REFERENCES

Cordero, L. and Hon. E. H. (1971). Neonatal bradycardia following nasopharyngeal stimulation. *Journal of Paediatrics*, **78**, 441–7.

Vaughan, R. S., Meuke, J. A. and Giacoia, G. P. (1978). Pneumothorax – A complication of endotracheal suctioning. *Journal of Paediatrics*, **92**, 633–4.

BIBLIOGRAPHY

Young, C. S. (1984). Airway suction – review of adverse effects and recommended guidelines. *Physiotherapy*, **70**, 3, 104–8.

Chiswick, M. L. (1978). *Neonatal Medicine*. Update Publications, London.

Crane, L. (1981). Physical therapy for neonates with respiratory dysfunction. *Physical Therapy*, **61**, 12, 1765–73.

Chapter 13

Assessment of Chest Function by the Physiotherapist

by J. M. ANDERSON MCSP

Before starting any treatment for a patient with a chest condition, the physiotherapist should carry out an assessment. There are occasions when an extremely ill patient is unable to co-operate with a full assessment and treatment has to be instituted at once. Where patients are known to be admitted from time to time, such an assessment becomes very helpful in noting any deterioration.

The suggested form of assessment outlined in this chapter can be used for both medical and surgical conditions, although in each case the stress may be placed on different headings.

GENERAL ASSESSMENT

The patient's name, age and sex are noted. The following information is gained from the medical notes, or from questioning the patient:

Occupation: Note the patient's present job and, if he is retired, whether this was premature due to ill-health. Note should be made if there has been any exposure to asbestos or coal dust (as these can cause fibrosing lung disease later in life), or if the patient has worked in a bakery or on a farm (as yeasts and spores can produce allergic responses).

Social history: If the patient is married, note the health of the spouse. Note the type of living accommodation and whether there are stairs to encounter: whether there is dampness; and how far he lives from shops and social amenities. The patient should be asked whether he has pets – as there may be an allergy problem; and about his hobbies, as the physiotherapist may be able to advise on suitable breathing patterns for gardening or swimming, etc., each depending on the patient's disability.

Family history: If there is a history of allergy, such as hay fever or skin problems, the patient should be asked whether there is any relevant family history.

Smoking habits: The patient must be questioned carefully as to how many cigarettes are smoked, whether they are home-made and, if he has given up, when he did so.

Past medical history: Note any operations, accidents or illnesses such as rheumatic fever which can cause heart problems; pulmonary tuberculosis which leaves scarring and possible cavities (apparent on the chest radiograph); whooping cough and measles which can cause bronchiectasis through plugging of the small airways.

Physiotherapy: This information applies especially for the patient with a chronic chest condition; he will probably know which techniques have helped him in the past.

Drug therapy: Relevant drugs should be listed and the technique for the use of inhalers or Rotahalers checked.

SPECIFIC ASSESSMENT

The patient should be questioned regarding his symptoms, and any signs observed and examined, where applicable.

Dyspnoea: If there has been an increase in breathlessness, does it vary with position or change of position and has it affected the patient's lifestyle?

Orthopnoea: How many pillows does the patient require in order to sleep or lie comfortably? (This may influence the choice of starting position for the treatment session.) If the patient suffers from paroxysmal nocturnal dyspnoea which may be caused by slipping down the bed, the physiotherapist can suggest types of back rest or, perhaps, seek advice from the occupational therapist.

Wheeze: Ask whether this has increased recently. Is it so bad as to be audible from the foot of the bed?

Sputum: Ask if there has been any change in the colour, quantity, viscosity or presence of blood. Sputum may be *mucoid* (clear or white) or *flecked* with black or grey particles as with cigarette smoking or atmospheric pollution. *Purulent* sputum contains pus cells and is usually yellow; with severe infections, such as pseudomonas, it may become green and foul-smelling. *Rusty* sputum is usually associated with a resolving lobar pneumonia. Varying quantities of *blood* may be present in the sputum, from streaking to gross haemoptysis. Blood in the sputum should be reported to the doctor in charge and treatment may need to be discontinued.

Cough: Any change in the type, frequency, duration or timing of cough should be noted. Many patients have paroxysms of coughing, causing dizziness or collapse (cough syncope).

Pain: The type and position of any pain should be noted. Are there any irritating factors? How can it be relieved? It may be necessary to arrange analgesia prior to treatment. Alternatively, there may be occasions when regular analgesia will be sufficient to remove the need for prophylactic treatment after minor surgery, or in some cases of pleurisy or pneumonia.

Weight: If there is an increase in weight it may be associated with fluid retention, in which case the patient may present with ankle or sacral oedema and extreme dyspnoea. On auscultation there will be late inspiratory crackles (see p. 108). A decrease in weight may signify inability to eat due to increasing dyspnoea, the presence of a carcinoma; or pulmonary tuberculosis.

CHEST ASSESSMENT

Deformities which may be congenital or acquired, should be noted:

Congenital

(1) Pectus carinatum (pigeon chest) where the sternum projects forward and is held in a prominent position by the ribs and costal cartilages.
(2) Pectus excavatum (funnel chest) where the sternum is depressed in its lower end and, with the in-turning costal cartilages, forms a depression of varying degree. Ventilatory and cardiac function may be impaired.

Acquired

(1) Barrel chest where the thorax is held high in inspiration and with an increased antero-posterior diameter.
(2) Scoliosis or kyphosis; either of which may be idiopathic or secondary to disease, trauma or operation.

(3) Asymmetry due to impaired movement from an underlying chest disease.

Skeletal mobility: The movement of the cervical and thoracic spine and the shoulder girdle should be assessed and recorded.

Respiratory muscles: The physiotherapist should observe whether the patient is using his diaphragm or accessory muscles of respiration. Is his musculature wasted or hypertrophied?

Respiratory pattern: Thoracic movement should be equal both laterally and posteriorly. Look to see whether the movement is upper or lower costal; whether the diaphragm is used normally or paradoxically; and whether there is an abdominal bounce. Note if the patient has a long or forced expiration; whether he is purse-lip breathing or has a Cheyne-Stokes pattern.

Audible noises: Listen for any audible wheeze or stridor.

Anaemia: If the patient appears pale and has a low haemoglobin he may be short of breath and lethargic.

Cyanosis: If the blood contains a high proportion of reduced haemoglobin (that is haemoglobin not attached to oxygen) certain parts of the body will appear blue. 5g reduced haemoglobin produces a detectable blue colour which will be most obvious in those parts with thin mucosa or overlying tissues, such as the lips and conjunctivae. Cyanosis can be described as central and/or peripheral.

Central cyanosis is due to the inadequate uptake of oxygen secondary to pulmonary disease, or to a right to left cardiac shunt. It is seen in the mouth and tongue as well as the extremities (fingers and toes) which will be warm.

Peripheral cyanosis is due to the stagnation of the blood and is seen best in the extremities which will be cold.

To assess the patient properly nail varnish must be removed. Assessment of dark-skinned patients can be very difficult. Sometimes the skin appears matt, but this is not reliable.

Clubbing: This is the filling in of the angle at the base of the fingernails, and, in severe cases, of the toenails. It can be graded into five stages. In the worst case (grade 5), the whole end of the finger is misshapen, the nail is curved and the pulp enlarged, so that the finger resembles a 'club'. The actual cause is still unknown, but this sign is seen in patients who have congenital cyanotic heart disease, cor pulmonale, infective endocarditis, carcinoma of the bronchus, chronic lung infections such as bronchiectasis, and cirrhosis of the liver.

Oedema: The physiotherapist should look at the patient's ankles for any oedema; this is a sign of water retention. If the patient has been lying in bed for any length of time there may be evidence of sacral oedema.

Auscultation: See Chapter 4.

Measurements: Chest expansion may be measured using a tape measure although it is not regarded as being fully accurate. The flat tape should be placed around the chest; the patient is then asked to breathe out as far as possible while the measuring tape is drawn taut; he is then asked to breathe in as deeply as possible, at the same time allowing the tape measure to be released. The two measurements are recorded. Measurements are usually taken at three levels: (1) the 4th costal cartilage; (2) the xiphisternum; and (3) the anterior end of the 9th costal cartilage.

INTERPRETATION OF MEDICAL INVESTIGATIONS

The patient's blood pressure, temperature, pulse and respiratory rates should be recorded. The chest radiograph should be studied and any abnormalities noted (see Chapter 5). Some patients will have respiratory function tests and these results will indicate to the physiotherapist the type of lung condition, lung volumes and alveolar gas transfer (see Chapter 3).

Several blood tests will be carried out and the results of these should be noted by the physiotherapist as it may affect her treatment:

White blood cell count (WBC): A *high* WBC indicates an infection which is being overcome; a *low* WBC suggests that an infection is not being overcome or, possibly, that the patient may have leukaemia.

Haemoglobin (Hb): If this is *low* the patient may be short of breath and lethargic. If it is *raised* the patient may have cyanotic heart disease or is a 'blue bloater' with chronic hypoxia. In either case the patient will be very dyspnoeic as there is reduced haemoglobin. The doctor may perform a venesection and remove a unit of blood, often giving instant relief to the patient.

Platelet count: If the count is low the patient may have problems with blood clotting. He may bruise easily and may bleed excessively with minimal trauma caused by suction.

Prothrombin time: If this is very long, the physiotherapist must take great care when suctioning as the patient may bleed profusely.

Sodium: If the patient has *hyponatraemia* (low sodium) then he will be 'dry'; this will also affect his sputum, making it tenacious. If the patient has *hypernatraemia* (high sodium) then he will retain water and, possibly, be dyspnoeic with the presence of late inspiratory crackles on auscultation.

Potassium: If the patient has *hypokalaemia* (low potassium) then he will be lethargic and, in extreme cases, may suffer a cardiac arrest. The latter is slightly more likely when the patient has *hyperkalaemia* (high potassium).

Urea and creatinine: If these are increasing it is a sign of renal failure and the patient may be confused and show signs of water retention.

Blood gases: See Chapter 2.

The physiotherapist should note the cerebral function of the patient, as problems, such as hypoxia or arterial disease, may cause confusion. Some patients have no understanding of their disease or are unco-operative regarding the administration of drugs. The physiotherapist may well be able to help with explanations.

APPLYING THE ASSESSMENT

This explanation of the clinical assessment has, of necessity, been comprehensive; with experience the physiotherapist can assess the patient quickly. If she is to take care of the whole patient, then she should be aware of all the points mentioned, but in practice may not have time to record all the results. From the assessment findings the physiotherapist should compile a problem list, covering each point that requires treatment or advice. Each problem should be numbered and sub-divided, for example:

> (1)   Airflow obstruction
> (a) Bronchospasm
> (b) Mucosal hypertrophy

The physiotherapist will then decide on the treatment necessary for each problem. Items on the problem list should correspond to the same numbered items in the treatment plan, for example:

Problem list	Treatment plan
(1) Airflow obstruction	(1) (a) Organise adequate
(a) Bronchospasm	bronchodilators
(b) Mucosal hypertrophy	(b) Teach relaxed expiration
	(c) Avoid forced expiratory
	patterns
(2) Retained secretions	(2) (a) Deep breathing exercises
	(b) Teach huffing
(3) Decreased exercise	(3) (a) Teach relaxed breathing
tolerance	pattern
	(b) Teach diaphragmatic
	breathing
	(c) Show relaxation positions
	(d) Exercise programme

With this type of problem list and treatment plan, the daily notes need only record any changes. If other problems arise they can be added to the list with the appropriate treatment; when a problem resolves, it can be deleted.

BIBLIOGRAPHY

Coates, H. and King, A. (1982). *The Patient Assessment*. Churchill Livingstone, Edinburgh.

Crofton, J. and Douglas, A. (1981). *Respiratory Diseases*, 3rd edition. Blackwell Scientific Publications Limited, Oxford.

Parry, A. (1985). *Physiotherapy Assessment*, 2nd edition, pp. 20–41. Croom Helm, London.

Chapter 14

Techniques used in Chest Physiotherapy

by J. M. ANDERSON MCSP *and* D. M. INNOCENTI MCSP

The physiotherapist will be asked to see many different types of chest problems, acute and chronic, medical and surgical; having assessed the patient, she will decide on the best techniques appropriate to that patient and use them accordingly.

In hospital, the physiotherapist will be working as a member of a team and should co-ordinate her treatment with the nurses, for example, treatment in side lying can be done when the bed linen is changed; or breathing exercises and coughing arranged after regular analgesia or bronchodilators.

The patient, and his relatives, will be anxious regarding the stay in hospital, the treatments and tests, and most of all his symptoms. The physiotherapist can help by careful explanation of her techniques, by answering questions and by giving suitable encouragement.

Chronic chest conditions may be treated in hospital during an acute episode, or at home in the long term. The physiotherapist is a key person in encouraging independence and self-care, in teaching the patient and his relatives how to use and care for equipment (e.g. nebulisers and air compressors) and to ensure that his living environment is as suitable as possible.

BREATHING EXERCISES

There are several techniques of teaching breathing exercises. The term 'breathing exercises' is often misleading as it implies that the patient is physically exerting himself. Many patients suffering from respiratory disease are already expending far too much effort on respiration and need to be taught a more relaxed and economical pattern of breathing. Even today there is still controversy about the precise action of certain respiratory muscles and the mechanics of breathing (Campbell et al, 1970).

Moxham et al (1980) studied the sternomastoid muscle function and fatigue in man and suggested that if fatigue of this accessory muscle of respiration were to develop in patients with pulmonary disease, it could have important consequences for the onset of respiratory failure.

The patient's position is important in order to achieve relaxation, concentration and freedom of thoracic and abdominal movement. The positions most commonly used are (a) half lying; (b) side lying with the upper arm supported on a pillow; (c) high side lying with the arm supported on a pillow and (d) sitting in a comfortable upright chair.

When the patient is in the half-lying position in bed, it is preferable for the physiotherapist to sit on the side of the bed, as this facilitates communication with the patient as well as being able to observe the control of the thorax and abdomen. When breathing exercises are practised in the side-lying or high side-lying positions, the physiotherapist should stand behind the patient as this enables her to see the face and be able to give resistance and assistance during breathing. It also allows her to more easily help the patient to alter his position without being encumbered by his arms. When the patient is sitting in a chair the physiotherapist should sit facing and to the side of him.

Very often patients are quite unaware of the relationships between thoracic and abdominal movements and airflow. A short explanation of these mechanics should be given and the factors kept in mind by the patient and the physiotherapist, as increased movement does *not* always mean increased function.

When the patient is aware of chest, abdominal and air movements during quiet breathing and is relaxed, attention is directed towards the specific exercises. Although costal and diaphragmatic movements occur simultaneously they are considered separately for treatment purposes.

'Diaphragmatic' breathing

One method of 'diaphragmatic' breathing concentrates on forward movement of the whole abdominal wall. Another technique combines forward movement of the upper abdominal wall with some lateral movement of the lower ribs. The diaphragm is the main muscle of respiration, but it must be remembered that the diaphragm also plays an important part in lower costal breathing exercises. The term 'diaphragmatic breathing' is therefore misleading.

POSITION OF THE PATIENT

'Diaphragmatic' breathing is usually taught in a relaxed half-lying or sitting position. The patient should be sitting straight and upright with the head and back fully supported, and the abdominal wall relaxed. If he is in bed relaxation of the abdominal wall is helped by slightly flexing the knees (provided it is removed after treatment, a small pillow may be used). When teaching breathing exercises out of bed, a high-backed chair without arms is preferable.

There are two schools of thought concerning the teaching of diaphragmatic breathing: the first concentrates on epigastric and lower rib movement (Gaskell and Webber, 1980). The second concentrates on allowing the whole abdomen to swell as the diaphragm descends (Innocenti, 1966).

1. The physiotherapist places her hands on the anterior costal margins and upper abdomen to feel the movement occurring. At a later stage the patient can feel this movement himself (Fig. 14/1A). He starts by gently breathing out, while relaxing the shoulders and upper chest, and feeling the lower ribs sink down and in towards the mid-line. When the patient is ready to breathe in, he is told to breathe in gently and to 'feel the air coming in around the waist'. If done correctly, the upper abdomen will bulge forward slightly and the anterior costal margins will move up and out.

2. The physiotherapist places both hands over the abdomen. The patient starts by gently breathing in and concentrating on allowing the abdominal wall to swell, gently not forcibly, under the slight pressure of the physiotherapist's hands. On breathing out he feels his abdomen slowly sinking back to rest. The patient can practise by resting both hands over the abdomen to feel the gentle movement which occurs as a result of diaphragmatic movement not abdominal muscle contraction (Fig. 14/1C). The upper chest and shoulders should remain relaxed throughout. The emphasis should be on gentle breathing with the minimum of effort. If the patient takes too deep a breath he will expand the apical areas of his chest. The patient should breathe at his own rate and no attempt should be made to slow this until a more controlled pattern of breathing is achieved. It is *vital* to remember that the expiratory phase is completely passive; any forced or prolonged expiration may increase airways obstruction. In normal expiration the airways shorten and become narrower, so if the airways are already partly obstructed and the patient forces expiration the flow of air will be further reduced. Forced

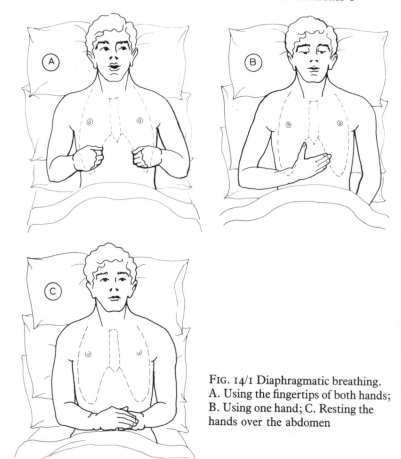

FIG. 14/1 Diaphragmatic breathing.
A. Using the fingertips of both hands;
B. Using one hand; C. Resting the
hands over the abdomen

expiration (huffing) must not be used when teaching breathing control.

After careful instruction emphasis needs to be placed on the importance of regular practice. Sufficient progress will not be made if the patient only does his exercises during his physiotherapy sessions.

Localised basal expansion

Localised breathing exercises are useful for assisting in the removal of secretions and improving movement of the thoracic cage. It is unlikely that individual lobes of the lung are ventilated by these exercises. They should not be performed during attacks of breathlessness. It has been stated that localised basal expansion utilises the 'bucket-handle' movement of the ribs. Although there is a certain amount of controversy about this, it seems to be agreed that the movement is caused by the contraction of the outer fibres of the diaphragm when the central tendon is fixed. When treating most conditions it is preferable to teach unilateral basal expansion, otherwise the patient is unable to relax the shoulder girdle adequately and this tends to exaggerate the movement of the upper chest.

POSITION OF THE PATIENT
The patient should be in a half-lying position with the knees flexed over a pillow, or sitting in an upright chair.

TECHNIQUE
The physiotherapist places the palm of her hand in the mid-axillary line over the 7th and 8th ribs; her fingers should be relaxed and well round the posterior aspect of the thorax. The patient is instructed to relax and breathe out, allowing the lower ribs to sink down and in: this movement must not be forced. At the end of expiration the

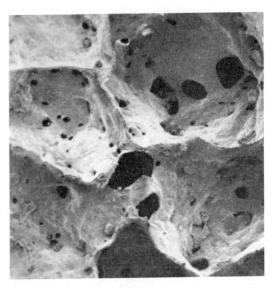

FIG. 14/2 Cross-section of the alveoli under great magnification showing the thin walls and the alveolar pores (pores of Kohn)

physiotherapist should apply firm pressure against the chest and instruct the patient with the next inspiration to expand the lower ribs against her hand. Pressure should be released at the end of inspiration and the weight of the hands follow the chest back to rest. Pressure is re-applied when the patient is ready to breathe in again. If the aim of the treatment is to expand lung tissue, the emphasis should be on holding the maximum inspiration for 3 seconds (Ward, 1966) and then 'sniff' in a little more air. Where there is a region of lung which has partially obstructed airways or decreased compliance, the alveoli will fill at a slower rate than the unaffected areas (i.e. increased time constant). Patients with airways disease or scattered areas of atelectasis have local variations of time constants. These areas need more time to expand than unaffected areas, therefore slow deep breathing with a hold on inspiration allows them more chance of gaining ventilation. Holding the breath also allows time for the air to diffuse through the pores of Kohn (Fig. 14/2). There is collateral air drift at alveolar level and hence a 'sniff' will provide a little more expansion.

Once the patient has learned the correct technique, he is taught to give pressure himself. Some patients who have limited wrist extension will find it easier to apply pressure with the back of the fingers or the palm of the opposite hand (Fig. 14/3). When using any

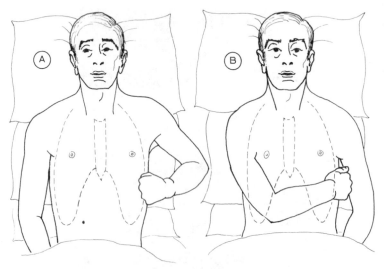

FIG. 14/3 Localised lateral costal breathing with self-pressure (in bed). A. With the back of the fingers of the same side; B. With opposite hand across the rib cage

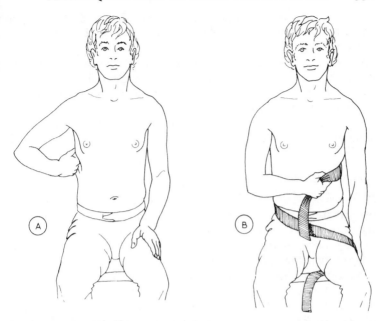

FIG. 14/4 Localised lateral costal breathing (in sitting). A. By self-pressure; B. With a webbing belt

of these methods the patient should not elevate his shoulder girdle, or achieve costal expansion by side flexion of the spine. The use of a wide belt made of webbing or some other strong, non-extensible material may be helpful (Fig. 14/4).

When helping to remove secretions from the lungs, or when trying to stimulate increased ventilation in a chronic condition or after abdominal or thoracic surgery, it is often helpful to concentrate on one phase of breathing at a time, as full range costal exercises may be tiring.

Full inspiration can be encouraged verbally and manual resistance given to encourage expansion. Full inspiration is held for about 3 seconds, the expiratory phase is naturally passive in this exercise.

Expiratory costal exercises may be practised to encourage maximum costal movement and to stimulate coughing. The patient gently breathes out fully, actively contracting the expiratory muscles. The physiotherapist may assist with increased gentle pressure at full expiration. The inspiration will not be emphasised in this exercise. As full expiration narrows the airways, this exercise should be avoided if bronchospasm is present.

Care must be taken to give enough rests between the efforts of the breathing exercises. Each deep breath should be done slowly and paced for the individual, to prevent breathlessness or dizziness.

Incentive spirometry is widely used in the United States (Dull and Dull, 1983; Iverson et al, 1978; Oulton et al, 1981) and research is presently (1986) being carried out at King's College Hospital, London to assess its value. There are several choices of equipment, but they all involve the patient breathing in deeply, through a mouthpiece, to move coloured balls or a plunger. These give a visual stimulus to the patient.

Apical expansion

It is necessary to teach apical expansion exercises if there is underlying disease in the upper lobe. When there is involvement of the upper lobes, as in cystic fibrosis or emphysema, the patient is already over-inflating the upper chest and needs to concentrate on relaxed diaphragmatic breathing and localised basal expansion. In certain cases after thoracic surgery, for example residual apical pneumothorax following lobectomy, or when there is restricted movement and deformity of the chest wall caused by extensive pleural thickening, apical expansion exercises are useful. They should be taught unilaterally.

TECHNIQUE

Pressure is applied below the clavicle using the tips of the fingers. The patient is instructed to breathe in and expand the chest upwards against the pressure of the fingers. Full inspiration may be held for a moment but the shoulders must remain relaxed. The patient should be in a well supported half-lying or sitting position and can be taught to give pressure himself with the opposite hand.

Posterior basal expansion

This exercise is useful if movement is restricted in this area. Pressure is given unilaterally over the posterior aspect of the lower ribs and the patient can be taught to apply this pressure himself.

Raising the resting respiratory level

The *resting respiratory level* is the point at which the tidal volume (TV) rests within the vital capacity (VC) (see p. 85). The natural expiratory level is that point at which natural expiration ends and is usually constant. It is the point at which the elasticity or recoil of the rib cage is in balance with the elasticity of the lung tissue (*Handbook of Physiology*, 1966). As a result of respiratory disease, especially in emphysema, portions of the lung shut down sooner than others. In these instances of gross expiratory obstruction, there is a sharp decrease in air flow early in the expiratory phase; continuing with expiration only increases muscle work and takes up time, while an ever decreasing amount of air is being moved.

If the breathing cycle is lifted between 200–300ml from the obstructed point, the ventilation will be more efficient – greater air flow for less work (Innocenti, 1966). Therefore, improved function and exercise tolerance can be achieved without altering the course of the disease.

The technique is taught as part of diaphragmatic breathing. The relaxed expiratory phase is watched by the physiotherapist who directs the patient to begin inspiration a little sooner in the respiratory cycle, thus avoiding prolonged expiration. The tidal volume is maintained, thus it is not just the expiratory level which is raised but the whole respiratory level.

Although this technique was designed to help patients with airways obstruction due to emphysema, it is also useful in helping to improve airflow during an episode of reversible airways obstruction.

Relaxation positions for the breathless patient

If patients can be taught how to control their breathing during an attack of dyspnoea, this can be of great benefit to them. The patient should be put into a relaxed position, and encouraged to do 'diaphragmatic' breathing at his own rate. The *rate* of breathing does not matter at this stage; it is the pattern of breathing that is important. As the patient gains control of his breathing he should be encouraged to slow down his respiratory rate.

Any of the following positions will assist relaxation of the upper chest while encouraging controlled diaphragmatic breathing. They can be adapted to various situations in everyday life (Fig. 14/5).

HIGH SIDE LYING (Fig. 14/5 A)

Five or six pillows are used to raise the patient's shoulders while lying on his side. One pillow should be placed between the waist and axilla, to keep the spine straight and prevent slipping down the bed. The top pillow must be above the shoulders, so that only the head and neck are supported. The underneath forearm can be placed under the head pillow, or resting on the bed underneath the pillow in the waist. It is more comfortable if the knees are bent and the top leg

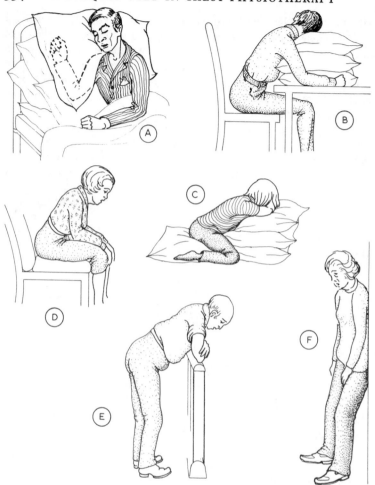

FIG. 14/5 Positions of relaxation suitable for the breathless patient

placed in front of the one beneath. This position is helpful for patients in acute respiratory distress or those who suffer from acute breathlessness during the night.

FORWARD LEAN SITTING (Fig. 14/5 B, C)
The patient sits at the table leaning forward from the hips with the head and upper chest supported on several pillows. The back must be kept straight, so that diaphragmatic movement is not inhibited. Children can sit or kneel with the head and upper chest resting against pillows.

RELAXED SITTING (Fig. 14/5 D)

This is an unobtrusive position that can be taken up easily. The back should be kept straight, with the forearms resting on the thighs and the wrists relaxed.

FORWARD LEAN STANDING (Fig. 14/5 E)

If there is nowhere to sit many breathless patients find this position beneficial. The patient should lean forward with the forearms resting on an object of suitable height, such as the windowsill or banisters.

RELAXED STANDING (Fig. 14/5 F)

The patient can lean back against a wall with the feet placed slightly apart and approximately 30cm away from it. The shoulders and arms should be relaxed.

Breathing control on walking

When the patient is able to control his breathing in the necessary relaxed positions, progression can be made to the control of breathing while walking on the level, up stairs and on hills. Many patients tend to hold their breath and find it difficult to breathe economically when taking exercise. The tendency to hold the breath only increases the feeling of breathlessness. Breathing in rhythm with their steps can be helpful; for example, breathing out for two steps and in for one step, out for three steps and in for two steps, or out for one step and in for one step. The correct breathing pattern will vary with each individual.

The physiotherapist can help to find the optimum pattern by walking with the patient and helping him, initially, by counting the synchronised walking-breathing pattern with him.

Functional activities

Some patients tend to become distressed when bending forward (e.g. to tie shoe laces). Many of them breathe in before bending down and experience discomfort due to the upward pressure of the abdominal contents against a flattened diaphragm. This discomfort is less if breathing out is encouraged while bending down. The next breath in takes place during the return to an upright position.

Many patients will need advice and help with daily activities such as bathing and dressing; often simple aids can help in making everyday tasks easier. A high walking frame can be helpful for patients who are severely breathless, or are suffering from osteo-porosis of the spine because of prolonged steroid therapy.

A home visit, prior to discharge, by the physiotherapist and/or occupational therapist can be helpful; this is particularly important if the patient has been prescribed home oxygen. The home will need to be assessed and the relatives taught how to handle the oxygen cylinders. Although the cylinders are supplied on prescription and delivered to the patient's home, the domiciliary flow head will have to be changed as the cylinder becomes empty. It is sometimes necessary also to supply the patient with a portable oxygen cylinder. These portable cylinders can be filled from the larger domiciliary cylinders and often allow the patient to become slightly more ambulant.

EXERCISE FOR THE BREATHLESS PATIENT

Many patients with chronic bronchitis and emphysema become increasingly disabled and frustrated by breathlessness on exertion. As breathlessness is uncomfortable the patient tends to avoid becoming breathless by curtailing his daily activities. With this gradual reduction of general activity he also becomes less fit and any exercise that he does take becomes more of an effort.

The encouragement of the patient by the doctor and the physiotherapist are important factors in exercise training as there is probably a psychological aspect in improved exercise tolerance. After training it is also possible that the same amount of exercise requires less oxygen.

Exercise tolerance tests

Because the patient's spirometry does not correlate with his exercise performance this does not give an accurate prediction of how far he can walk; subjective methods of asking the patient how far he can walk may also be unreliable. The objective 6-minute walking test can give an accurate assessment of the patient's condition and his response to treatment.

SIX-MINUTE DISTANCE (SMD) TEST

This is simple, easily reproducible and requires no apparatus. The SMD is the distance a subject can walk in 6 minutes along a level enclosed corridor. The subject may stop for a rest during the 6 minutes if necessary, but on completing the test he should feel that he could not have walked any further (Butland et al, 1981). A practice walk to learn the test procedure is essential and the two walks should be done either on the same day with at least 20 minutes rest between them, or on two consecutive days. As the SMD is a self-paced exercise test it is important that the patient should perform this test alone. If the test is used at intervals to assess the patient's response to treatment it should, if possible, be carried out at the same time of day and at the same time in relation to the administration of any prescribed bronchodilator drugs (Webber, 1981a). Walking is familiar to all and the SMD is a useful method of assessing sub-maximal exercise tolerance. Many patients are less familiar with exercising on either a bicycle ergometer or treadmill.

Exercise programme

A programme scheme of walking on the stairs or on the flat can be adapted to suit the individual's disability. The exercise programme should be undertaken at least once a day and a diary card given to the patient so that he can record the number of stairs or lengths accomplished at each exercise session. If illness interrupts the training scheme, the exercise grading is reduced by two or three weeks on re-starting the programme.

If a staircase is not available, a suitable programme can be worked out over a measured distance on the flat. In the first week for example he should walk for 2 minutes, then rest until he has recovered his breath before walking briskly for a further 2 minutes. The length of time that the patient walks can be gradually increased each week or as necessary. When undertaking either exercise programme, the patient must make himself moderately breathless for the exercise to be worthwhile, but this should not be so excessive that he has to stop.

It is essential that the patient understands the difference in walking for exercise training and walking at all other times. Breathing control using relaxed diaphragmatic breathing should be used before, between and at the end of the exercise periods. It is also hoped that the patient will use this controlled breathing in his daily activities, when he is walking on the flat, up hills, or stairs to try and avoid breathlessness and achieve further distances comfortably.

Contra-indications for patients using the exercise scheme are: ischaemic heart disease; intermittent claudication; disabling musculo-skeletal disorders and malignant pulmonary disease (McGavin, 1977). If the patient experiences *any* chest pain while exercising he *must* contact his doctor.

THE STAIRCASE EXERCISE PROGRAMME

Week 1 Climb up and down 5 steps for 2 minutes
Week 2 Climb up and down 5 steps for 2 minutes
Week 3 Climb up and down 5 steps for 5 minutes
Week 4 Climb up and down 5 steps for 5 minutes
Week 5 Climb up and down 10 steps for 5 minutes
Week 6 Climb up and down 10 steps for 6 minutes
Week 7 Climb up and down 10 steps for 8 minutes
Week 8 Climb up and down 10 steps for 10 minutes

COUGHING AND HUFFING

Coughing is a forced expiration against a closed glottis causing a rise in intrathoracic pressure. As the glottis opens, there is a difference in pressure between the smallest airways and the upper trachea, causing a rapid flow of air. This rapid flow, combined with the narrowing of the airways, increases the force of the air, which dislodges mucus and foreign particles into the pharynx. Since a high intrathoracic pressure diminishes the return of blood to the heart, a prolonged bout of coughing may cause a fall in the cardiac output and the patient may faint (cough syncope). Patients must be taught to avoid this.

A forced expiratory manoeuvre (cough or huff) produces compression and narrowing within the airways from a point dependent on lung volume. The compression point is adjacent to the equal pressure point, where the pressure within the airways is equal to the pleural pressure. At high-lung volume this point lies in the trachea and main bronchi, and secretions in this area can normally be cleared by coughing or huffing at high-lung volume. At mid-lung volume these points are in the lobar and segmental bronchi. If the lung volume further decreases, the point at which this compression takes place moves a little further down the bronchial tree towards the alveoli. Throughout this forced expiratory manoeuvre there is a vibratory movement in the posterior wall of the trachea and upper bronchi.

This concept of the equal pressure point was described by Mead et al (1967). A cough or huff is only effective from the point downstream (nearer the mouth) of the compression point. Mead advocated a series of coughs without intervening inspirations to clear progressively deeper portions of the lungs. Many patients find this can be exhausting and, clinically, it seems that a single continuous huff down to the same lung volume is as effective and less exhausting. To produce a huff, a forced expiratory effort is made but the glottis remains open and the intrathoracic pressure does not rise to such high levels as with a cough. Nevertheless, the pressure generated again produces compression and narrowing of the trachea and bronchi and secretions are moved up the bronchial tree.

The forced expiration technique (FET)

The forced expiration technique has been shown to increase the efficiency in the clearance of bronchial secretions, without causing or increasing bronchospasm (Pryor and Webber, 1979). When the technique is correctly taught with relaxed diaphragmatic breathing between huffs, there should be no increase in airways obstruction and the patient should not feel exhausted.

It consists of one or two huffs from mid-lung volume to low-lung volume followed by a period of relaxed diaphragmatic breathing. This period of relaxed diaphragmatic breathing is an essential part of the technique to prevent the aggravation of any bronchospasm. Breathing out with a partially closed glottis does not produce an effective huff. After taking a breath in, the patient breathes out forcefully through the mouth contracting the abdominal and chest wall muscles at the same time. When secretions are present in the upper airways a huff or cough from a high-lung volume will clear them. It is necessary to take a deeper breath in and contract the abdominal muscles during the huff or cough. Short bouts of coughing should be interspersed with relaxed diaphragmatic breathing; paroxysms of uncontrolled coughing can be exhausting and must be discouraged. Children as young as three years can be taught to huff, but may need to practise by blowing down a tube.

The forced expiration technique is combined with correct drainage positions, breathing exercises, percussion and shaking. The correct technique must be taught before including percussion and shaking. Self-percussion and shaking can be taught but this can be difficult and ineffective when draining the posterior areas of the lungs. When proficient in the technique, the patient can reinforce the huff by self-compression of the chest wall. A brisk adduction of the upper arm from an angle of $45°$ abduction is combined with the forced expiration. This compression is not essential and the vibrating action within the airways is possibly more effective than external shakings and vibrations. Many patients prefer to be given a programme for their postural drainage sessions. This programme will need to be adapted to each patient, but the following outline may be useful: the patient takes three or four deep, slow breaths combined with percussion either by an assistant or the patient; this is followed by a short period of controlled diaphragmatic breathing; then two or three huffs from mid-lung volume to low-lung volume accompanied by assisted chest shaking or self-compression. In some people this programme may drop the Pco_2 to the point of stimulating unpleasant symptoms such as dizziness. In these cases a breath hold for 2–3 seconds will be helpful at the point of expiration. This is then followed by a further period of relaxed diaphragmatic breathing.

When secretions reach the upper airways, another cough or huff will clear them. This is followed by diaphragmatic breathing and the cycle is repeated until the area being drained is clear. To complete the treatment, the patient can sit on the side of the bed or on a chair and clear any remaining secretions from the upper airways by using the huff with self-compression of the chest by both upper arms.

Vibratory chest shaking

Shaking is performed only during the expiratory phase of breathing and therefore reinforces the expiratory flow of air from the lungs.

The relaxed hands are placed over the appropriate area of chest and, beginning immediately as the patient exhales, the physiotherapist shakes the chest wall in towards the main bronchus. This technique mechanically shifts sputum from the smaller to the larger airways.

Shaking can be performed unilaterally or bilaterally depending on the type of patient. If there is no incision, with the patient in half lying or sitting, the hands can be placed on the lower lateral aspect of the chest wall and the movement made in and upwards toward the main bronchi. Shaking over the sternum during expiration often stimulates a cough, by shifting the sputum further up the respiratory tract.

For the patient following thoracotomy, (either in half lying or side lying), the hands are placed on the anterior and posterior aspects of the chest, below the incision and not over the intercostal drains. If the patient then coughs, the physiotherapist can apply firmer pressure to support the patient and make coughing more comfortable.

A patient with a sternotomy must always be supported over the sternum. If the patient is in sitting, lying or side lying, one hand and forearm are placed along the length of the sternum and used purely as support. The other hand is placed posteriorly and, as shakings are performed, there is no movement of the sternum. If, after cardiac surgery, patients develop a pulmonary complication, it is likely to be atelectasis of the lower lobes, and the physiotherapist is thus perfectly placed to encourage full expansion between her shakings.

The pressure applied to the thorax must be modified according to the build of the patient as well as the underlying condition. A patient with osteoporosis or rib metastases must be treated with great care. Rib fractures can occur with over-vigorous treatment. Shaking may increase bronchospasm with some patients, therefore percussion may be more useful if sputum is very tenacious.

Shaking should not be used in cases of severe haemoptysis, acute pleuritic pain and active pulmonary tuberculosis.

POSTURAL DRAINAGE

Postural drainage consists of positioning the patient to allow gravity to assist the drainage of secretions from specific areas of the lungs.

The length of time spent in each position, and the total treatment time will depend on the quantity of secretions in each area and the number of areas that have to be drained. It may be necessary to spend an average of 15 to 20 minutes in each position to allow adequate drainage and this may mean that different areas will require draining at alternate treatments. The worst areas should be drained first. A recent radiograph, or bronchogram if available, is a useful adjunct in isolating the affected areas. Postural drainage should never be carried out immediately before or after a meal, for the patient will feel either too tired to enjoy his meal, or nauseated and perhaps vomit.

Postural drainage can only be carried out effectively if the patient takes an active part in his treatment. The treatment becomes ineffective if the patient just lies in the appropriate drainage position. Therefore, a selection of the preceding techniques is chosen and used in the programme. It must be remembered that not all patients who have to carry out regular postural drainage can be independent. Additional help from an assistant will be necessary during periods of infection and exacerbations of their disease. Very frail patients or small children will probably need assistance.

Anatomy of the bronchial tree (Figs. 14/6, 14/7)

The following illustrations show the divisions of the bronchial tree and their respective segments. This knowledge is essential to enable the patient to be placed in the correct position for drainage.

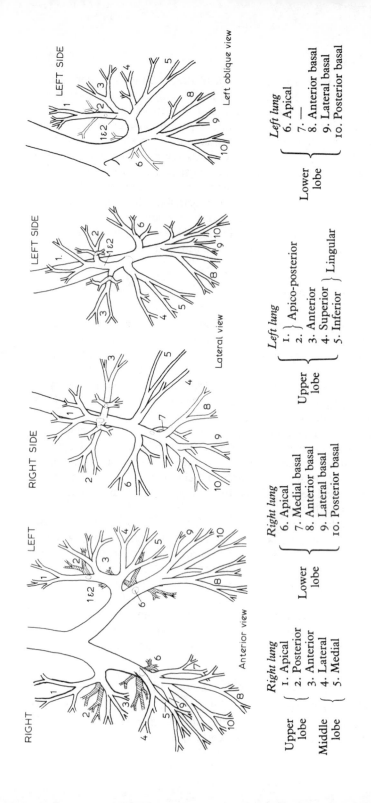

Fig. 14·6 The bronchial tree with the nomenclature as approved by the Thoracic Society

RIGHT   LEFT

Anterior view

RIGHT SIDE

LEFT SIDE

Lateral view

LEFT SIDE

Left oblique view

Right lung

Upper
lobe
{
1. Apical
2. Posterior
3. Anterior
}

Middle
lobe
{
4. Lateral
5. Medial
}

Right lung

Lower
lobe
{
6. Apical
7. Medial basal
8. Anterior basal
9. Lateral basal
10. Posterior basal
}

Left lung

Upper
lobe
{
1. } Apico-posterior
2. }
3. Anterior
4. Superior } Lingular
5. Inferior }

Left lung

Lower
lobe
{
6. Apical
7. —
8. Anterior basal
9. Lateral basal
10. Posterior basal
}

343

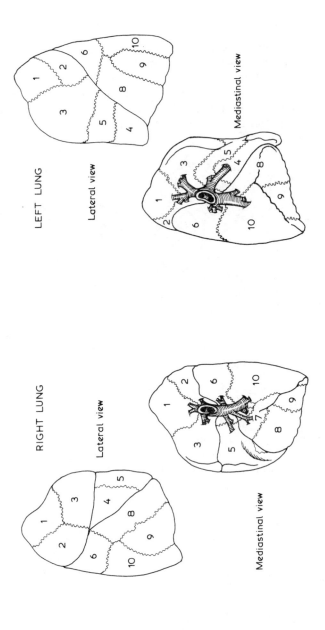

LEFT LUNG

Lateral view

Mediastinal view

RIGHT LUNG

Lateral view

Mediastinal view

FIG. 14/7 The bronchopulmonary segments. The numbers correspond to those in Fig. 14/6

Postural drainage positions

Upper lobe

APICAL SEGMENTS (Fig. 14/8)

The patient should sit upright, with slight variations according to the position of the lesion which may necessitate leaning slightly backward, forward or sideways. The position is usually only necessary for infants or patients being nursed in a recumbent position, but occasionally may be required if there is an abscess or stenosis of a bronchus in the apical region.

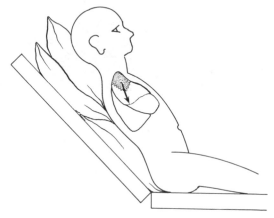

FIG. 14/8 Draining the apical segments of both upper lobes

POSTERIOR SEGMENT

(a) Right (Fig. 14/9)

The patient should lie on his left side and then turn 45° on to his face, resting against a pillow with another supporting his head. He should place his left arm comfortably behind his back with his right arm resting on the supporting pillow; the right knee should be flexed.

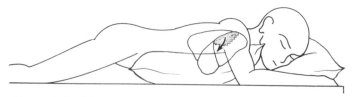

FIG. 14/9 Draining the posterior segment of the right upper lobe

(b) Left (Fig. 14/10)
The patient should lie on his right side turned 45° on to his face with three pillows arranged to raise the shoulder 30cm (12in) from the bed. He should place his right arm behind his back with his left arm resting on the supporting pillows; both the knees should be slightly bent.

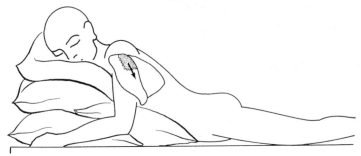

FIG. 14/10 Draining the posterior segment of the left upper lobe

ANTERIOR SEGMENTS (Fig. 14/11)
The patient should lie flat on his back with his arms relaxed to his side; the knees should be slightly flexed over a pillow.

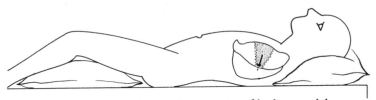

FIG. 14/11 Draining the anterior segments of both upper lobes

Middle lobe

LATERAL SEGMENT: MEDIAL SEGMENT (Fig. 14/12)

The patient should lie on his back with his body quarter turned to the left maintained by a pillow under the right side from shoulder to hip and the arms relaxed by his side; the foot of the bed should be raised 35cm (14in) from the ground. The chest is tilted to an angle of 15°.

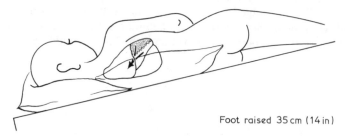

Foot raised 35 cm (14 in)

FIG. 14/12 Draining the lateral and medial segments of the middle lobe

Lingula

SUPERIOR SEGMENT: INFERIOR SEGMENT (Fig. 14/13)

The patient should lie on his back with his body quarter turned to the right maintained by a pillow under the left side from shoulder to hip and the arms relaxed by his side; the foot of the bed should be raised 35cm (14in) from the ground. The chest is tilted to an angle of 15°.

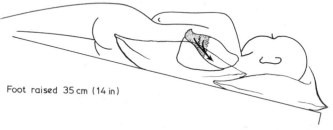

Foot raised 35 cm (14 in)

FIG. 14/13 Draining the superior and inferior segments of the lingula lobe

Lower lobe

APICAL SEGMENTS (Fig. 14/14)

The patient should lie prone with the head turned to one side, his arms relaxed in a comfortable position by the side of the head and a pillow under his hips.

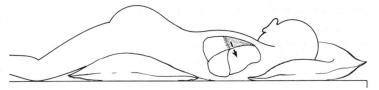

FIG. 14/14 Draining the apical segments of both lower lobes (arm removed for clarity)

ANTERIOR BASAL SEGMENTS (Fig. 14/15)

The patient should lie flat on his back with the buttocks resting on a pillow and the knees bent; the foot of the bed should be raised 46cm (18in) from the ground. The chest is tilted to an angle of 20°.

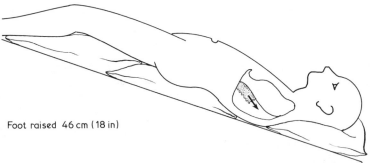

Foot raised 46 cm (18 in)

FIG. 14/15 Draining the anterior basal segments of both lower lobes

POSTERIOR BASAL SEGMENTS (Fig. 14/16)

The patient should lie prone with his head turned to one side, his arms in a comfortable position by the side of the head and a pillow under his hips. The foot of the bed should be raised 46cm (18in) from the ground. The chest is tilted to an angle of 20°.

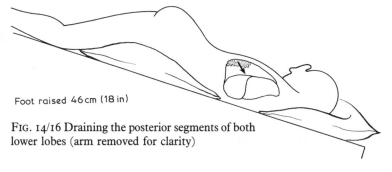

Foot raised 46 cm (18 in)

FIG. 14/16 Draining the posterior segments of both lower lobes (arm removed for clarity)

MEDIAL BASAL (CARDIAC) SEGMENT (Fig. 14/17)

The patient should lie on his right side with a pillow under the hips and the foot of the bed should be raised 46cm (18in) from the ground. The chest is tilted to an angle of 20°.

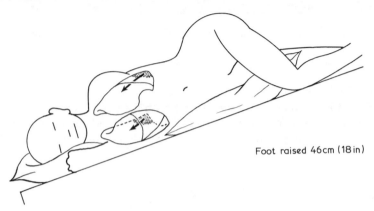

Foot raised 46cm (18in)

FIG. 14/17 Draining the lateral basal segment of the left lower lobe and the medial (cardiac) basal segment of the *right* lower lobe

LATERAL BASAL SEGMENT (Fig. 14/18)

The patient should lie on the opposite side with a pillow under the hips and the foot of the bed should be raised 46cm (18in) from the ground. The chest is tilted to an angle of 20°.

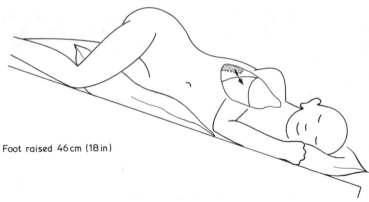

Foot raised 46cm (18in)

FIG. 14/18 Draining the lateral basal segment of the *right* lower lobe

ALTERNATIVE METHOD OF POSTURAL DRAINAGE FOR LOWER
LOBES (Fig. 14/19)

If it is not possible to raise the foot of the bed, an alternative position
can be used. Two or three pillows are placed over a 15cm (6in) pile of
newspapers or magazines and the patient can lie over this so that the
chest is tilted downwards. It is important that the shoulders do not
rest on the pillow supporting the patient's head. This method can be
used for drainage of the lower lobe segments when necessary and is
often a useful method of home postural drainage.

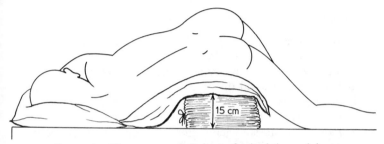

FIG. 14/19 Home postural drainage for both lower lobes

Modified postural drainage

Some patients cannot lie flat without becoming dyspnoeic. If a
patient is likely to become more breathless by conventional postural
drainage it is better to position him in a high side-lying position or as
flat as possible. The foot of the bed can then be elevated as the
patient's condition improves.

Bronchography (see Fig. 5/17, p. 146)

If the patient has a productive cough postural drainage should be
given prior to bronchography. The accumulation of excessive
secretions could prevent adequate outlining of the bronchi by the
radio-opaque medium. After a bronchogram the majority of the
contrast is sucked into the peripheral airways and is absorbed into
the bloodstream. Any remaining medium in the upper airways is
removed by the action of the cilia and effective huffing and
coughing. Although postural drainage is not essential for a patient
with normal airways, they are often more comfortable if physiotherapy is given following the bronchogram. Postural drainage

should always be carried out on patients suffering from bronchiectasis, as the cilia are damaged and the contrast is not removed in the normal way.

It is important that the patient has nothing to eat or drink for 3 hours following a bronchogram, until the local anaesthesia has worn off. If the bronchogram has been performed through the cricothyroid membrane, the patient must be instructed to give pressure with a finger over the cricothyroid cartilage when he huffs or coughs. This is to avoid surgical emphysema.

Contra-indications to postural drainage

1. Head injuries including cerebral vascular accidents because intracranial pressure would be increased.
2. Severe hypertension as venous return is increased with tipping and this can overload the heart.
3. Following oesophagectomy there can be undue stress on the anastomosis and tipping may cause regurgitation.
4. Severe haemoptysis, when all forms of physiotherapy should be discontinued until there has been discussion with the doctors.
5. Aortic aneurysms which would be put under tension if the patient is tipped.
6. Pulmonary oedema which collects in the dependent areas; postural drainage would cause extreme dyspnoea and probably worsen the situation.
7. Surgical emphysema which might track toward the face if the patient is tipped and might result in dyspnoea.
8. Tension pneumothorax without an intercostal drain. This condition should not require physiotherapy, but must never be tipped as the cardiac embarrassment may lead to a cardiac arrest.
9. Cardiac arrhythmias which can be worsened by postural drainage; in some positions the myocardial oxygen demand would be greater and so its sensitivity to abnormal rhythms is increased.
10. Hiatus hernias should not be tipped as the patient may regurgitate gastric juices.
11. The filling cycle of peritoneal dialysis. The descent of the diaphragm is impeded during this phase and tipping may cause more respiratory distress.
12. Facial oedema from burns will be increased with tipping.
13. Eye operations where there may be some associated oedema which could be increased with tipping.

Sometimes it is vital for a patient with one of the above contra-indications to have postural drainage. Care must be taken and the case discussed with the doctors. Generally it is unnecessary to tip the elderly, as they find it very distressing.

Postural drainage at home

Many patients who require postural drainage at home are able to carry out their treatment effectively and independently by using the forced expiration technique (see p. 339). Those who are more disabled may need percussion or shaking from an assistant in conjuction with the forced expiration technique. In fact many patients can clear their secretions effectively with a correct huffing technique and do not always need percussion or shaking of the chest wall. Assistance may be needed if there is an increase in their daily sputum production, or secretions become more difficult to clear. When teaching relatives or friends percussion and shaking, it is important that they understand the necessity for periods of relaxed diaphragmatic breathing.

Any patient who needs to continue postural drainage at home often benefits from carrying out his own treatment for one or two days prior to discharge from hospital. The physiotherapist having carefully instructed the patient then only supervises his treatment. In this way the patient is made to realise that he can manage his physiotherapy independently at home.

The areas requiring drainage and the time needed for treatment must be discussed individually with each patient. In most cases treatment will be required for at least 15 to 20 minutes twice daily.

A suitable drainage position will have to be discussed with the patient. Many patients will find it difficult to elevate the foot of the bed at home. Some patients have a bed permanently tipped in a spare room, while others have a portable frame to lie on at the correct angle. Another method is to place a 15cm (6in) pile of newspapers or magazines tied tightly together, in the centre of the bed and place pillows on top (Fig. 14/19). The patient can lie over this in various positions to drain several areas of the lung. If these methods do not provide an efficient drainage position it may be necessary to provide the patient with a hospital tipping bed.

The drainage position in which the patient lies prone over the side of the bed is unsuitable. It is uncomfortable, cannot usually be tolerated for very long, and only drains the posterior segments of the lower lobes. Babies and small children can be given postural drainage over their mother's knee (Fig. 14/20). It is usually advisable to give the treatment before a feed.

FIG. 14/20 Postural drainage for the apical segments of the upper lobes of a child being treated on mother's lap

Percussion

Most secretions can be removed by the previously mentioned techniques. If the sputum is particularly tenacious, percussion (clapping) may be of benefit.

Percussion is carried out over the appropriate area of chest wall which is covered by a towel to prevent skin stimulation; with the hands slightly cupped, the wrists are quickly flexed and extended. Percussion is thought to send sound waves through the chest wall, causing compression and rarefaction of air within the airways, thus setting up a vibration and consequently loosening secretions.

Patients who suffer from chronic lung disorders, such as cystic fibrosis, and who benefit from percussion can be taught to percuss themselves. There are several mechanical percussors available, but at present there is no evidence to suggest that bronchial secretions are more effectively cleared when using one of these devices (Pryor et al, 1981).

As with shaking, percussion should be avoided in cases of haemoptysis, pleuritic pain or acute pulmonary tuberculosis. Also patients with osteoporosis or rib metastases must be treated carefully. It is unlikely that these types of patients would require percussion.

MECHANICAL AIDS AS AN ADJUNCT TO PHYSIOTHERAPY

As in other fields of medicine there is an ever increasing range of equipment for the treatment of respiratory conditions (see Chapter 10). Physiotherapists who work with patients suffering from chest conditions may have to assist in the selection of equipment such as nebulisers, compressors, suction machines and IPPB machines, all of which, if used correctly, can enhance the efficacy of other techniques. There is no doubt that some forms of inhalation therapy used with physiotherapy can be helpful. It should, however, be remembered that simple methods may be as beneficial as expensive equipment (Webber, 1981b).

It becomes essential that individual patients are assessed carefully and objectively as to their response to various forms of treatment. This has become particularly important because patients are being prescribed regular drugs by inhalation for use when they return home. Home equipment must then be considered: treatment may require a nebuliser which would need an electrical compressor or oxygen source to drive it – this could be costly, cumbersome and unnecessary if it is shown that the patient gets an equally good response from using a pressurised aerosol or Rotahaler. Such factors are important and fall well within the role of the physiotherapist.

When comparing different methods of delivery of the same drug, the patient's response can be assessed by measurements of FEV_1 and FVC (see below). When comparing the response of a patient to salbutamol by pressurised aerosol and by a nebulised solution, measurements are made until the maximal response is reached after inhalation using the pressurised aerosol; this is followed immediately by the inhalation of the drug in a simple nebuliser. Any further increase is shown in the post-nebuliser recordings.

If the response to one method is assessed on one day and the other on the following day, it is impossible to compare the results accurately because the baseline recordings and the time of testing may be different. It is essential that the complete bronchodilator test is carried out on the same day and this method must be followed also when comparing the response to two different drugs. Although time consuming, these comparative tests are important when assessing the necessity of more sophisticated equipment for the inhalation of drugs.

SIMPLE SPIROMETRY TO ASSESS RESPONSE TO BRONCHODILATOR THERAPY

Although formal lung function tests will be carried out in the respiratory laboratory, the physiotherapist can assess the patient's response to treatment by measuring the FEV_1 and FVC on a Vitalograph. In addition the PEFR can be measured using a Wright peak flow meter or the mini-Wright peak flow meter. These meters record the maximum flow over 10 milliseconds at the beginning of expiration.

If the FEV_1 and PEFR improve following the administration of a bronchodilator, this is known as reversible airways obstruction – asthma and chronic bronchitis with an asthmatic component. In emphysema, severe chronic bronchitis and bronchiectasis there is often irreversible airways obstruction. Although the FEV_1 and PEFR do not improve, some patients feel relief following the bronchodilator drug. This is because of an increase in the FVC due to some deflation of the over-distended lungs with slight reversibility in the airways obstruction. It is important therefore to assess the patient's reversibility by recording the FEV_1 and FVC on a Vitalograph, as the PEFR does not show this minimal change in the airways obstruction. Bronchodilator drugs should not be given for 6 hours prior to the test.

The best result of two or three baseline recordings is taken. These are repeated allowing a 30-second pause between them, at 5-minute intervals until a maximum pre-treatment level is recorded. Some patients will continue to improve over several minutes, while others will reach a plateau, or the recordings will start to decrease. The bronchodilator drug is then inhaled and the post-treatment readings are taken at the required time interval. This will vary with the particular drug. After salbutamol (Ventolin) or terbutaline (Bricanyl), readings can be taken at 15- and 30-minute intervals. Following the administration of the slower acting ipratropium bromide (Atrovent), recordings are made 40 and 60 minutes after the inhalation. In either case the recordings must be continued until the maximum response is obtained. If a greater response to the drug is shown at the second reading, further spirometry is taken at 10-minute intervals until a plateau or fall in the FEV_1 or FVC is recorded (Gaskell and Webber, 1980). Any drug irrespective of whether it is given in conjunction with physiotherapy must be prescribed by the doctor on the patient's drug chart. The policy for recording and administration of this drug by the physiotherapist or the nurse will differ in various hospitals. Every physiotherapist involved in using drugs for IPPB, nebulising, etc, must be fully conversant with her hospital's policy as to the responsibility for this recording of drug usage.

METHODS OF USING PRESSURISED AEROSOLS, ROTAHALERS, SPINHALERS, SPACERS AND NEBUHALERS

Pressurised aerosol

Instruction in the correct use of an inhaler is often necessary to ensure that the maximum amount of the drug enters the lungs and is not lost to the atmosphere. Approximately 10 per cent of the drug actually reaches the bronchi, the rest being swallowed, therefore a good technique is essential (Fig. 14/21).

The patient should breathe out quietly, and having placed the aerosol to the mouth, should press the actuator firmly while

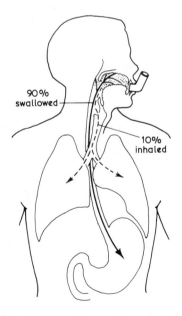

FIG. 14/21 Distribution of drug with pressurised aerosol

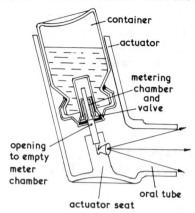

FIG. 14/22 Section through a pressurised aerosol

inhaling deeply. To be effective the drug should be released at the very beginning of inspiration. After inhaling, the patient should hold his breath for approximately 10 seconds if possible, before breathing out quietly through his nose. The patient should allow 1 minute before taking the next puff (Fig. 14/22).

If the patient is having both bronchodilator and steroid therapy via aerosols, then the bronchodilator should be taken first to allow the airways to dilate. The steroid inhaler is then used 15–20 minutes later if following salbutamol or terbutaline, or 30–60 minutes later if following ipratropium bromide.

Rotahaler

The patient must be shown how to insert the capsule into the Rotahaler, that is, the *coloured end* first. He is then shown how to

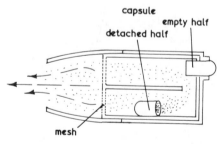

FIG. 14/23 Section through a rotahaler

twist the Rotahaler to break the capsule and then to inhale deeply to get the powder into the major airways. Several breaths may be needed to inhale all the drug. This device does not require the co-ordination of the aerosol (Fig. 14/23).

Spinhaler

This device is similar to the Rotahaler, except that the outer sleeve slides down the inhaler to pierce the capsule and there is a propellor inside to disperse the drug (Fig. 14/24). A placebo Spinhaler incorporating a whistle can be useful, particularly when teaching the technique to children.

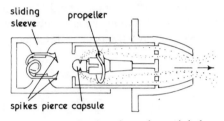

FIG. 14/24 Section through a spinhaler

Spacer

This is another device designed for patients who could not co-ordinate inspiration with the depression of the actuator on the pressurised aerosol. With the unit extended (Fig. 14/25) the patient

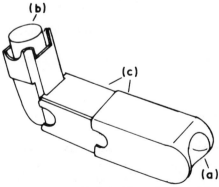

FIG. 14/25 Spacer in the extended position, showing (a) mouthpiece, (b) actuator and (c) middle section

seals his lips around the mouthpiece (a) and depresses the actuator (b) whence the mist is then trapped in the middle section (c), allowing him a little more time to inhale without losing the required drug.

Nebuhaler

The mist from a pressurised aerosol is emitted in the shape of a pear and so the Nebuhaler was designed along the same lines (Fig. 14/26). The aerosol slots into one end (a), the mouth at the other end next to a one-way valve (b). The patient seals his lips around the mouthpiece, depresses the actuator the required number of times and then takes several breaths in to clear the trapped mist. Some consultants prefer one puff to one breath. Again this device overcomes the lack of co-ordination and also slows down the speed of the mist, so that less drug hits the back of the mouth.

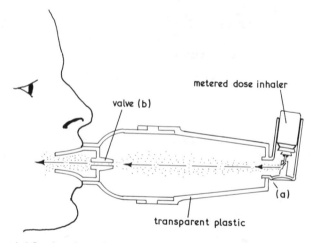

FIG. 14/26 Section through a nebuhaler, showing the trapped mist from the aerosol

NEBULISERS

Some patients with severe reversible airways obstruction, require larger doses of a bronchodilator to achieve maximum lung function. This can be administered in the form of a nebuliser.

There are many forms of nebuliser, but the majority work on the venturi effect. If a stream of gas is passed through a small hole it creates a lower pressure as it emerges from that hole. In the case of nebulisers, there is a small tube, with one end immersed in the bronchodilator solution and the other end near the area of low pressure. Consequently, the liquid is drawn up the tube and it is then pushed on to a baffle, which splits the liquid into tiny particles, hence nebulising (Fig. 14/27). The small hole can become blocked with saline and the nebuliser should be rinsed after use.

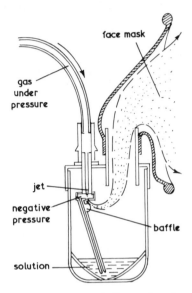

FIG. 14/27 Section through a nebuliser using the venturi effect

There is another, more expensive, type of nebuliser that works on the piezo-electric effect (Fig. 14/28). It still incorporates a baffle, but the liquid is set into motion by the vibrating crystal. This nebuliser is suitable for home use and is much quieter. The larger models are very useful for delivering high humidity to patients with tenacious sputum to aid expectoration.

For most patients' nebulisers, the driving gas can be oxygen. However, if the patient is hypercapnoeic and is using his hypoxic drive, then compressed air should be used. This can be in the form of an air compressor or an air cylinder.

In many hospitals the physiotherapist is responsible for each patient's bronchodilator therapy and must be aware of her hospital's policy. She can give advice for each patient, especially regarding the

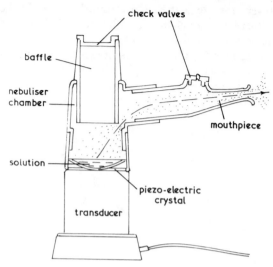

FIG. 14/28 Section through an ultrasonic nebuliser using the piezo-electric effect

use of a mask or mouthpiece, and relaxed positioning during the inhalation.

The bronchodilator drug should be diluted with a solution of sodium chloride (saline), itself a mild bronchodilator, to make 4ml. This amount delivers the maximum drug without an unnecessary length of time for the patient and the residual liquid is not purely drug; for example, 1ml salbutamol with 3ml saline; or 2ml ipratropium bromide with 2ml saline. If both drugs are prescribed, they can be delivered together. It is probably advisable to add 2ml of saline to the 1ml of salbutamol and the 2ml of ipratropium bromide, so that the residue is still diluted.

Some patients will require inhaled antibiotics or antifungal agents. As these drugs are thicker than bronchodilators, it is important to have a powerful compressor to drive the nebuliser. The nebuliser must have a mouthpiece and a one-way valve attached to a piece of wide bore tubing which must be placed leading out of the window. If antibiotic or antifungal drugs are allowed to circulate in the room not only will the organisms become resistant to them, but also other patients, or the family, will become resistant to them. Drugs, such as carbenicillin, also damage the surface of furniture.

OXYGEN AND EXERCISE TOLERANCE

Oxygen can improve both breathlessness and exercise tolerance but before domiciliary oxygen is prescribed for any patient, it is advisable to carry out a simple 6-minute walking test with the patient breathing oxygen and air. The patient does a practice 6-minute walk carrying the cylinder only, followed by two further single blind walking tests breathing oxygen and air. There should be a 20-minute interval between each walk. If it is impossible to complete the test on the same day, the walks should be carried out at the same time on consecutive days. If the patient walks significantly further when breathing oxygen, it can be assumed that his exercise tolerance is likely to be increased if he has portable oxygen for home use.

The weight and inconvenience of the present portable systems can be a problem for some patients. Portable oxygen may therefore prove more useful if lighter cylinders and simpler valves are available in the future.

A paper in the *Lancet* described how a study of 'pink-puffers' showed that they were less breathless and walked further when breathing oxygen. This was true whether the cylinder was carried by an assistant or by the patient. Breathing oxygen for 5 to 15 minutes before exercise but not during exercise resulted in a similar improvement in exercise tolerance (Woodcock, Gross and Geddes, 1981).

DOMICILIARY EQUIPMENT

Some patients may benefit from domiciliary equipment. An electrical compressor may be necessary for the inhalation of nebulised bronchodilators or for the inhalation of antibiotics and antifungal drugs in the home.

The majority of compressors are powered by a mains electrical supply and some have adaptors so that the machine can run off a car battery or cigarette lighter; battery-driven compressors are now available.

The normal domiciliary flow head supplied with an oxygen cylinder is unsuitable as the driving source for a nebuliser because the maximum output is only 4 litres per minute. Although many nebulisers function at 4 litres per minute, when the oxygen cylinder becomes half empty, the output falls, making the driving force inadequate for efficient nebulisation. If a nebuliser is being run off oxygen a flow meter permitting higher flows of oxygen must be supplied.

Both the patient and his relatives will need to be taught the correct use and care of the equipment before discharge. Any electrical equipment must be serviced at least once a year *by the hospital which supplied it.* The patient should be taught how to draw up the drug and fill the nebuliser as well as understanding the dosage of the drug and the number of inhalations to be taken each day. The need for safe disposal of all used needles, syringes, and empty drug containers must be most carefully explained. (A small tin with a tight fitting lid can be used for disposing sharp pointed materials.)

REFERENCES

Butland, R. J. A., Pang, J. A., Gross, E. R. et al (1981). 2-, 6-, and 12-minute walks compared. *Thorax.* **36**, 3, 225.

Campbell, E. J. M., Agostini, E. and Newsom Davis, J. (1970). *The Respiratory Muscles: Mechanics and Neural Control.* Lloyd-Luke (Medical Books) Limited, London.

Dull, J. L. and Dull, W. L. (1983). Are maximal inspiratory breathing exercises or incentive spirometry better than early mobilisation after cardiopulmonary bypass? *Physical Therapy*, **63**, 655–9.

Gaskell, D. V. and Webber, B. A. (eds) (1980). *The Brompton Hospital Guide to Chest Physiotherapy*, 4th edition. Blackwell Scientific Publications, Oxford.

Handbook of Physiology, section 3, volume 1, 391–3. (1966). American Physiological Society, New York.

Innocenti, D. M. (1966). Breathing exercises in the treatment of emphysema. *Physiotherapy*, **52**, 437.

Iverson, L. I. G., Ecker, R. R., Fox, H. E. et al (1978). A comparative study of IPPB, the incentive spirometer and blow bottles: the prevention of atelectasis following cardiac surgery. *American Thoracic Surgery*, **25**, 197–200.

McGavin, C. R. (1977). A place for physical rehabilitation in the management of chronic bronchitis. *Chest, Heart and Stroke Journal*, **2**, 19.

Mead, J., Turner, J. M., Macklem, P. T. and Little, J. B. (1967). Significance of the relationship between lung recoil and maximum expiratory flow. *Journal of Applied Physiology*, **22**, 95.

Moxham, J., Wiles, C. M., Newham, D. and Edwards, R. H. T. (1980). Sternomastoid muscle function and fatigue in man. *Clinical Science*, **59**, 463.

Oulton, J. L., Hobbs, G. M. and Hicken, P. (1981). Incentive breathing devices and chest physiotherapy: a controlled trial. *Canadian Journal of Surgery*, **24**, 638–40.

Pryor, J. A. and Webber, B. A. (1979). An evaluation of the forced expiration technique as an adjunct to postural drainage. *Physiotherapy*, **65**, 10, 304.

Pryor, J. A., Parker, R. A. and Webber, B. A. (1981). A comparison of mechanical and manual percussion as adjuncts to postural drainage in the treatment of cystic fibrosis in adolescents and adults. *Physiotherapy*, **67**, 140.

Ward, R. J. et al (1966). An evaluation of postoperative manoeuvres. *Surgery, Gynecology and Obstetrics*, **123**, 1, 51–4.

Webber, B. A. (1981a). Living to the limit: exercise for the chronic breathless patient. *Physiotherapy*, **67**, 5, 128.

Webber, B. A. (1981b). Use and abuse of inhalation equipment. *Physiotherapy*, **67**, 5, 130.

Woodcock, A. A., Gross, E. R. and Geddes, D. M. (1981). Oxygen relieves breathlessness in 'pink puffers'. *Lancet*, **1**, 907.

BIBLIOGRAPHY

The following additional sources are offered for those physiotherapists who may wish to read more deeply on specific points made in this chapter.

Belman, M. J. and Mittman, C. (1980). Ventilatory muscle training improves exercise capacity in chronic obstructive pulmonary disease patients. *American Review of Respiratory Disease*, **121**, 273.

Bradley, M. E. and Leith, D. E. (1978). Ventilatory muscle training and the oxygen cost of sustained hyperpnoea. *Journal of Applied Physiology: Respiratory Environment: Exercise Physiology*, **45**, 6, 885.

Cochrane, G. M., Webber, B. A. and Clarke, S. W. (1977). Effects of sputum on pulmonary function. *British Medical Journal*, **2**, 1181.

Langlands, J. (1967). The dynamics of cough in health and in chronic bronchitis. *Thorax*, **22**, 88.

Leggett, R. J. E. and Flenley, D. C. (1977). Portable oxygen and exercise tolerance in patients with chronic hypoxic cor pulmonale. *British Medical Journal*, **2**, 84.

McGavin, C. R., Gupta, S. P., Lloyd, E. L. and McHardy, G. J. R. (1977). Physical rehabilitation for the chronic bronchitic: results of a controlled trial of exercises in the home. *Thorax*, **32**, 307.

McGavin, C. R., McHardy, C. J. R. and Lloyd, E. L. (1976). *Exercise Can Help Your Breathlessness*. Chest, Heart and Stroke Association, London.

Parvia, D., Thomson, M. L. and Clarke, S. W. (1978). Enhanced clearance of secretions from the human lung after administration of hypertonic saline aerosol. *American Review of Respiratory Disease*, **117**, 199.

ACKNOWLEDGEMENT

The authors are indebted to Miss D. V. Gaskell MBE, FCSP and Miss A. J. Davis MCSP for the continued use of material from their original chapters in the previous editions. This has been used extensively in the presentation of this chapter.

Chapter 15

Pulmonary Surgery

by J. R. PEPPER MChir, FRCS, J. M. ANDERSON MCSP
and D. M. INNOCENTI MCSP

Clinical

INDICATIONS FOR SURGERY

The commonest indication is bronchial carcinoma which accounts for around 90 per cent of all resections.

1. *Malignancy*: Primary bronchial carcinoma, bronchial carcinoid, isolated secondaries arising from kidney or large intestine.
2. *Inflammatory*: Lung resection is occasionally required for the following conditions: lung abscess, tuberculosis, bronchiectasis, aspergillosis, hydatid disease.
3. *Trauma*: Stab wounds, gunshot wounds.
4. *Degenerative*: Large lung bullae in selected patients where there is compression of normal lung.
5. *Congenital*: Arterio-venous fistula, sequestrated lobe, lobar emphysema.

TYPES OF PULMONARY RESECTION

Pneumonectomy

The entire lung is removed. Operative mortality in the UK is around 7 to 10 per cent but rises to 20 per cent over the age of 70. In a radical pneumonectomy, mediastinal lymph nodes and part of the chest wall may also be removed. The resulting cavity is filled by protein-rich fluid and fibrin. The cavity size is reduced by lateral shift of the trachea and heart, upward shift of the diaphragm, and reduction of the intercostal spaces on the operated side. Occasionally, and later, a scoliosis may develop.

Lobectomy

Any of the five lobes may be removed; on the *right* side the middle and lower lobes are often removed together because of their common lymphatic drainage. If a tumour in an upper lobe protrudes into the main bronchus a cuff of main bronchus can be removed with the lobe and the remaining lung and bronchus is joined to the trachea. This is termed a *sleeve lobectomy*.

Segmental resection

A bronchopulmonary segment is removed with its segmental artery and bronchus. This used to be indicated for tuberculosis but is now rarely performed.

Wedge resection

This non-anatomical resection is used for diagnosis in open lung biopsy and treatment of well-localised peripheral carcinomas in patients with reduced lung function.

PRE-OPERATIVE INVESTIGATIONS (Fig. 15/1)

These investigations are designed to answer two questions:

1. Can the carcinoma be removed?
2. Is the patient fit for thoracotomy?

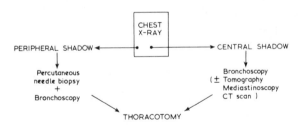

FIG. 15/1 Scheme for investigating patients with bronchial carcinoma

Bronchoscopy

This is carried out by two separate techniques: (a) via a flexible fibre-optic instrument in a conscious patient or (b) via a rigid instrument in a patient under a general anaesthetic. Technique (a) allows the operator to see further into subsegmental bronchi while technique (b) allows a better assessment of operability in central lesions. The two methods can be used together under a general anaesthetic.

Mediastinoscopy

A small transverse incision is made 1cm above the suprasternal notch. The strap muscles are separated and the pre-tracheal fascia entered. Abnormal paratracheal and carinal nodes can then be felt. A mediastinoscope is inserted and a biopsy taken. Not all lymph node groups in the mediastinum can be reached by this technique, in particular those nodes on the left below the aortic arch (Fig. 15/2). Many surgeons, therefore, prefer to use an *anterior mediastinotomy* in which a mediastinoscope is passed through the 2nd or 3rd intercostal space and a biopsy taken.

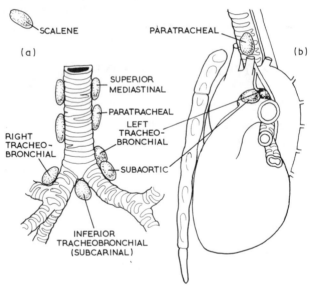

FIG. 15/2 Mediastinal lymph nodes: (a) antero-posterior view; (b) left lateral view

CT scan

Computerised tomographic scanning of the thorax and upper abdomen to include the adrenals is becoming a part of the routine clinical work-up. It is particularly useful for identifying metastatic deposits in the liver or adrenals. It will also detect enlarged mediastinal lymph nodes but cannot identify whether carcinoma is present in the node. Therefore, if the CT scan demonstrates abnormally large mediastinal nodes this should be confirmed by mediastinoscopy or mediastinotomy.

Other investigations

In some centres radionuclide scans of bone and liver, and ultrasound examination of the liver are performed routinely to screen for distant metastases. Unfortunately, bone and liver scans may be positive when no malignancy exists. Liver ultrasound is a more reliable test.

Many patients will also have coronary artery disease which will require careful investigation. Recent myocardial infarction (less than 3 months), is an indication to postpone thoracotomy.

Lung function

Clinical assessment alone may be sufficient. For example, if the patient is able to hold a conversation while walking the length of a corridor then he will be able to withstand a pneumonectomy. Respiratory function tests are helpful in borderline cases. If the FEV_1/FVC ratio is less than 40 per cent of the predicted value, or the $Paco_2$ is greater than 5kPa (40mmHg) then operation is definitely contra-indicated. Ventilation-perfusion scans may also be helpful particularly where abnormal lung is perfused but unventilated and therefore shunting deoxygenated blood from right to left. Under these conditions removal of the abnormal lung can be expected to improve overall lung function.

INCISIONS IN THORACIC SURGERY (Fig. 15/3)

Most thoracic operations are performed through a postero-lateral incision. This divides the lower fibres of trapezius, latissimus dorsi, serratus anterior and the external and internal intercostal muscles. A high posterior extension of the incision also divides rhomboid major and the erector spinae group. An antero-lateral thoracotomy is the standard approach for a closed mitral valvotomy and is used by some surgeons for pleurectomy.

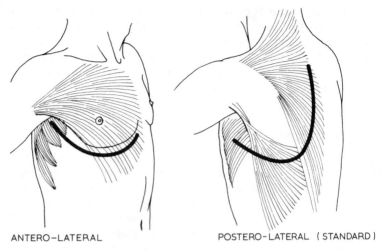

ANTERO–LATERAL   POSTERO–LATERAL (STANDARD)

FIG. 15/3 Incisions for thoracic surgery, including closed heart surgery

DRAINAGE OF THE CHEST (Figs. 15/4 and 15/5)

The purpose of drains in thoracic surgery is to remove fluid or air which is expected to accumulate. Drainage may be open or closed.

Closed drainage

A tube with end and side holes is introduced into the thorax via an intercostal space. It is connected to a closed bottle via a transparent tube which ends under water (Fig. 15/4). A second short tube left unconnected maintains atmospheric pressure within the bottle. This arrangement provides a simple one-way valve. If the short tube is connected to a suction apparatus the air pressure within the bottle will be reduced below atmospheric. If sufficient suction is applied the negative pressure which exists between the lung and the chest wall will be increased. The calibrated bottle allows for easy measurement of blood loss (Fig. 15/5).

On free drainage (Fig. 15/4) the water level in the long tube will rise on inspiration and fall on expiration due to the change in intrathoracic pressure. If the fluid level ceases to swing this means that the lung is fully expanded or that the tube is blocked. If the drainage is connected to suction there should be no swing.

The drainage bottle should be kept at a lower level than that of the

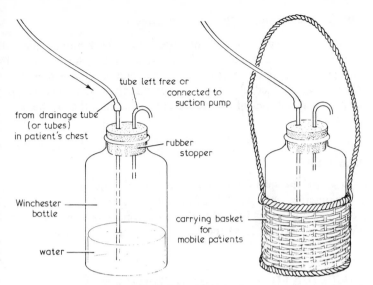

FIG. 15/4 Closed drainage of the thoracic cavity by means of an underwater drain; also showing a carrying basket

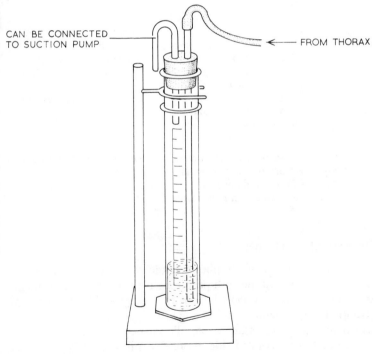

FIG. 15/5 A calibrated underwater drainage bottle

patient's chest to prevent the siphoning of fluid back into the pleural cavity. The drains should not be clamped except during difficult changes in the patient's position. After a pneumonectomy intercostal drains are rarely used. After other types of lung resection two drains, one placed at the apex of the pleural cavity and the other at the base, are used.

Open drainage

A tube in the pleural cavity connects directly with air. This arrangement is only safe when the pleural cavity has become rigid and immovable. This is used to drain a chronic empyema where the infection is localised from the rest of the pleura by fibrosis.

COMPLICATIONS OF LUNG SURGERY

	Local	General
Early (0–2 weeks)	Haemorrhage Atelectasis/lobar collapse Wound infection Surgical emphysema Pleural effusion Empyema Broncho-pleural fistula Nerve damage, e.g. recurrent laryngeal, phrenic	Ventilatory insufficiency Atrial fibrillation Myocardial infarction Pulmonary embolus/deep vein thrombosis Cerebrovascular accident
Late	Thoracotomy wound pain Recurrence of carcinoma Chest wall deformity Restricted arm movements	Distant spread of carcinoma

Broncho-pleural fistula

A broncho-pleural fistula implies breakdown of the bronchial stump and it occurs around the 10th postoperative day, although if small it may not be noticed until much later. It is recognised by dyspnoea, an irritating cough and possible expectoration of dark fluid. An associated empyema is inevitable. The patient should be sat up or turned on to the operated side to prevent spill-over of infected fluid into the remaining lung.

Recurrent laryngeal nerve damage

Damage to the recurrent laryngeal nerve may occur during *left* pneumonectomy, or upper lobectomy due to its course around the arch of the aorta. Such damage seriously impairs the ability to cough.

PNEUMOTHORAX

A collection of air under atmospheric pressure in the pleural cavity. As a result the lung will collapse and *if air continues to accumulate* shift of the heart and trachea to the opposite side of the chest will occur. This will result in compression of the opposite lung and kinking of the orifice of the superior and inferior vena cavae leading to cardiac arrest. This situation is called a *tension pneumothorax* and is an emergency requiring prompt insertion of a chest drain.

Pneumothorax is classified into open or closed.

Open pneumothorax

This results from trauma, usually gunshot. It results in a 'sucking' chest wound, with air rapidly accumulating into the open pleural cavity. A large dressing pad is placed over the wound and the patient transferred to the operating theatre.

Closed pneumothorax

Spontaneous: The commonest type of pneumothorax due to rupture of the visceral pleura. It most frequently occurs in young men aged between 20 and 40 but the precise cause is not known. Less commonly it occurs in an older group due to rupture of an emphysematous bulla, in association with obstructive airways disease, lung cancer, lung abscess, or tuberculosis.

Traumatic: (a) Accidental, e.g. blunt trauma to the chest or perforation of trachea or oesophagus; (b) iatrogenic, e.g. insertion of central venous lines, operations on the neck or abdomen, artificial ventilation especially if positive end-expiratory pressure (PEEP) is used.

MANAGEMENT OF CLOSED PNEUMOTHORAX

Pneumothoraces occupying less than 25 per cent of the pleural cavity do not require drainage. Larger pneumothoraces in otherwise fit patients are treated by simple aspiration with a needle, or intercostal tube drainage. If, despite aspiration, air continues to accumulate in the pleural space, tube drainage connected to an underwater seal is mandatory.

Recurrent pneumothorax is treated by one of these methods:

1. *Pleurodesis*: A chemical pleurisy is produced by the insertion of an irritant such as tetracycline into the pleural cavity. Other irritants are iodised talc or silver nitrate.
2. *Pleurectomy*: Via a small posterior thoracotomy, the parietal pleura over the lateral wall is removed leaving a raw surface to which the visceral pleura and lung will adhere. At the same time the area on the visceral pleura which is leaking air is oversewn.

EMPYEMA (Fig. 15/6)

This is a localised collection of pus in the pleural cavity. It may be associated with lung abscess, broncho-pleural fistula, subphrenic abscess, trauma, septicaemia or osteomyelitis of the spine.

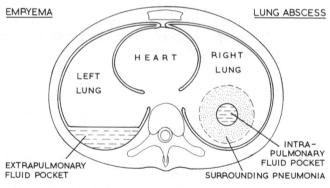

FIG. 15/6 The distinction between empyema and lung abscess

Treatment

The aims of treatment are to abolish infection; obtain full lung expansion, and prevent development of a rigid chest wall.

METHODS

1. Daily pleural aspiration, instillation of antibiotic, physiotherapy. This is very successful in infants and children.

2. Intercostal tube drainage and irrigation with antiseptic solution.
3. Rib resection and open drainage.
4. Thoracotomy and decortication. This is reserved for chronic empyemas of many months duration. The principle is to peel the thickened fibrotic layer of visceral pleura (cortex) off the surface of the lung. This allows the lung to expand fully and adhere to the parietal pleura.

OPERATIONS ON THE CHEST WALL

Individual ribs or parts of a rib may be resected during excision of a neoplasm or for drainage of an empyema.

Fractured ribs

Operation is performed only if the lungs are damaged. Pinning of fractured ribs is practised in some centres. The rib ends are approximated and fixed with medullary pins.

Major injuries

Injuries of the chest wall occur frequently in road traffic accidents. Multiple rib fractures may result in a flail chest. If a segment of the chest wall becomes detached (flail) paradoxical breathing occurs which seriously compromises ventilation. During inspiration when intrathoracic pressure becomes more negative the flail segment moves inwards while the remainder of the chest wall expands. During expiration when intrathoracic pressure becomes less negative the flail segment moves outwards.

TREATMENT

The first essential is to maintain adequate ventilation. In the presence of a flail chest IPPV via an endotracheal tube is established. This may be required for up to 3 weeks or until the thoracic cage has become mechanically stable.

Recently the use of epidural morphine delivered via a thoracic epidural catheter has enabled the patient to be weaned off the ventilator more easily. It has also enabled the patient with less severe injuries not requiring artificial ventilation to cough effectively while receiving adequate analgesia.

CONGENITAL DEFORMITIES

Pectus carinatum (pigeon chest)

The sternum projects forward and is held in a prominent position by the ribs and costal cartilages. Operation is performed mainly for cosmetic reasons. The prominent costal cartilages are removed and the sternum split horizontally and depressed. Fixation is established by suturing together both pectoralis major muscles in the mid-line.

For physiotherapy see page 386.

Pectus excavatum (funnel chest)

This deformity is probably caused by overgrowth of the lower costal cartilages and ribs which is compensated for by depression of the lower end of the sternum, presumably due to pull of the diaphragm. Ventilatory and cardiac function may be impaired but operation is performed usually for cosmetic reasons.

The lower costal cartilages are resected on both sides and the sternum is split horizontally. The position is maintained by a metal bar which is removed later. An alternative method is to place a preformed silastic prosthesis subcutaneously to improve the contour of the chest wall.

For physiotherapy see page 386.

THORACOPLASTY

This operation is now uncommon. It used to be performed in some cases of pulmonary tuberculosis before effective chemotherapy was available. An extensive resection of ribs is performed; this allows the chest wall, having no scaffolding, to fall inward and obliterate the pleural cavity and/or lung tissue. Infected pneumonectomy spaces are sometimes closed in this manner. The 1st rib may or may not be removed.

For physiotherapy see page 384.

Physiotherapy

In the following section, certain treatments will be discussed but it must be stressed that it is only possible to generalise. Each patient must be assessed individually, and at each treatment. Techniques and regimes will vary with the patient's condition, from hospital to hospital (indeed from consultant to consultant within a single hospital) and according to the country. It is essential to know and abide by the surgeon's wishes and special routines, as well as ensuring that the patient has adequate analgesia before treatment starts.

Subsequent sections will consider specific operations.

THORACOTOMY (excluding pneumonectomy)

The following plan is suitable for wedge, segmental and sleeve resections, lobectomy or simple thoracotomy (as in the case of an inoperable tumour). Initially, the patient should be given an explanation of the likely operation, including the incision used (see p. 367), drains, intravenous infusion, the need for oxygen and the importance of physiotherapy.

Pre-operative period

Pre-operatively, the physiotherapist may be involved in the overall assessment of the patient, particularly exercise tolerance testing from which a decision can be made as to whether surgery is possible. Patient assessment will follow the outline discussed in Chapter 13. Pre-operative chest clearance is sometimes required.

Objectives

The objectives of pre-operative physiotherapy will be that:

1. Full joint range and adequate circulation are maintained by teaching active or active/assisted exercises of arms, legs and trunk. Special attention will need to be given to the shoulder on the operation side, because the thoracotomy incision divides latissimus dorsi and full range of movement at the shoulder can be quickly lost. Active assisted shoulder elevation through flexion is taught.
2. Correct posture is maintained by teaching postural awareness and a correct sitting position. After a thoracotomy, the tendency is to side flex towards the affected side, that is, to drop the shoulder and raise the hip because this is less painful (Fig. 15/7).
3. Adequate ventilation is maintained by teaching breathing exercises to help the remaining lung tissue to hyperinflate, and to aid removal of secretions.

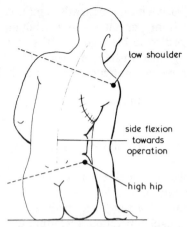

FIG. 15/7 Postural deformity after a thoracotomy

4. General mobility is encouraged by showing the patient how best to move around in bed. A rope tied to the foot of the bed is a helpful aid (Fig. 15/8).
5. The patient will cough effectively by learning how to support himself as well as understanding how the physiotherapist will encourage and support him (Fig. 15/9).
6. Excess secretions will be removed by practising huffing and coughing techniques.

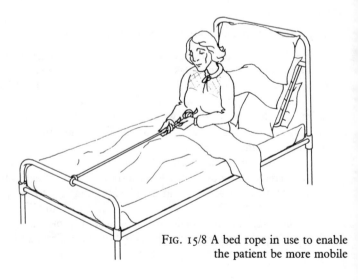

FIG. 15/8 A bed rope in use to enable the patient be more mobile

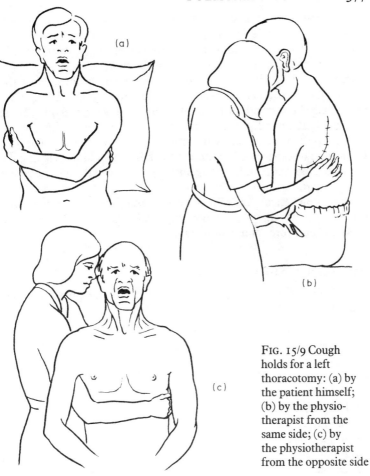

(a)

(b)

(c)

FIG. 15/9 Cough holds for a left thoracotomy: (a) by the patient himself; (b) by the physiotherapist from the same side; (c) by the physiotherapist from the opposite side

The costal exercises are taught with emphasis on one phase at a time as described on page 328. The 'diaphragmatic' breathing should also involve concentration on full range movement of the diaphragm to prevent pleural adhesion formation.

The patient must understand the importance of coughing and be assured that it will do no damage postoperatively. To ease the obviously painful manoeuvre the physiotherapist can assist by manual support. The thoracotomy incision can best be supported in the sitting, lying, half-lying or side-lying positions by firm pressure of the physiotherapist's hands on the anterior and posterior aspect of the affected side of the thorax. Probably the forward-sitting position is the most effective for coughing and the physiotherapist should stand on the unaffected side of the patient. The anterior and posterior aspects of the affected side of the thorax can be supported with the hands, while at the same time the forearms will stabilise the whole chest and create a 'bear-hug' hold (Fig. 15/9c). The patient should also be shown how to stabilise the chest when coughing alone by placing the hand of the unaffected side as far round the affected ribs as possible and applying firm pressure with the hand and forearm. The other hand reinforces the hugging hold by clasping the opposite elbow and pulling it against the chest wall during the cough (Fig. 15/9a).

Some units encourage the patients to exercise together in a class. Often patients enjoy the fellowship and interest of these group sessions, both pre- and postoperatively.

Postoperative period

Following surgery and before each treatment the physiotherapist should check the following:

1. Type of operation.
2. Incision.
3. Chest radiograph.
4. Temperature.
5. Pulse rate.
6. Respiratory rate.
7. Blood pressure.
8. Drug chart.
9. Fluid chart.
10. Oxygen therapy.
11. Drains – the amount of fluid drained
    – whether or not there is an air leak
    – whether on or off suction
    – if off suction, whether or not the drain is swinging (see p. 368).

Postoperative problem list

Problems which may arise post-surgery can be considered under the following headings:

1. Pain.
2. Intercostal drains in situ.

3. Decreased air entry.
4. Retained secretions.
5. Decreased movement – especially the shoulder on the operation side.
6. Decreased mobility.
7. Poor posture.

Other problems, such as bronchospasm or a peripheral neuropathy, must be included and, where appropriate, treatment instituted.

Postoperative treatment plan

1. Ensure that the patient has adequate analgesia.
2. Ensure patency of drainage tubes, 'milking' them as necessary. To do this the drainage tube is compressed between the finger and thumb of one hand. The tube distal to this occlusion is then squeezed between rollers specially designed for the purpose, or between the finger and thumb of the dominant hand (talc or soap is necessary to allow the tube to be drawn smoothly through the finger and thumb). This manoeuvre dislodges any clots, which then drain into the drainage bottle.

   Do *not* clamp drains, unless lifting the bottle above the level of the patient's chest. The reason for this is that intercostal drains are only in situ because air and/or fluid needs to be removed from the pleural cavity. If the tube is clamped it prevents free drainage and the air and/or fluid is retained. This prevents the visceral pleura from adhering to the parietal pleura. It is especially so if there is an air leak from the cut surface of the lung as a pneumothorax will be formed.
3. Deep inspiratory breathing exercises (costal and diaphragmatic) with inspiratory holds and sniffs in lying and side lying, with the operated side *uppermost*. Also, from side lying, quarter turn to both prone and supine positions (see p. 380).
4. (a) Lateral costal shakings below the incision (see p. 340).
   (b) Elevation of the foot of the bed to aid drainage of secretions and pleural fluid and/or air as necessary.
   (c) Huffing and coughing with good support in forward lean sitting or over the edge of the bed (Fig. 15/9).
5. Full range active/assisted arm exercises.
6. Active leg, foot and ankle exercises, and early mobilisation, that is, as soon as the drains are off suction. The patient should be encouraged to walk around carrying his own drainage bottle(s) in a holder (see Fig. 15/4).
7. Trunk, shoulder girdle exercises and postural correction.

Postoperative regime

DAY OF OPERATION

Oxygen therapy is usually administered for the first few hours after the patient's return to the ward. Although the patient will still be drowsy from the anaesthetic full range active/assisted shoulder movements should be carried out. As the incision cuts through latissimus dorsi these exercises must begin immediately to prevent muscle shortening and adhesions.

The patient should be able to co-operate with the breathing exercises and cough with support. The physiotherapist should support the operation side firmly, but gently, taking care not to press directly on the incision or drainage tube sites. The patient should be reminded that the exercises should be continued each time he wakes from the sedation.

DAY I

The treatment plan should be followed, first ensuring that the patient is in a comfortable position when in side lying. To achieve this position, the patient should sit forward with the physiotherapist on the operation side, who should re-arrange the pillows, leaving only one on the bed. The patient turns into side sitting toward the unaffected side; the patient's body-weight must be supported at the shoulder as he lowers on to his elbow and then into side-lying. Figure 15/10 shows the positioning of the pillows for maximum comfort of the patient and support of the drains. If the patient is rolled back on to the pillow (quarter turn up from supine) it 'opens up' the anterior chest wall and facilitates bilateral costal movement while still draining the affected lung. If the patient rolls forward on to the pillow (quarter turn up from prone) it allows unrestricted posterior chest movement.

Three treatment sessions through the day will probably be necessary, all with adequate analgesic cover. The patient will probably sit out of bed that morning for as long as he wishes. He should be encouraged to practise the breathing, coughing, limb and shoulder girdle exercises and correct his posture, regularly during the day.

When the patient is sitting in bed, the pillows should be arranged to support the patient in a good posture without undue pressure on the site of the incision and drainage tubes. Five pillows should be used: one placed crossways at the bottom; the next two are placed vertically; and the other two cross-ways at the shoulder and head level. The two vertical pillows should be placed to support the

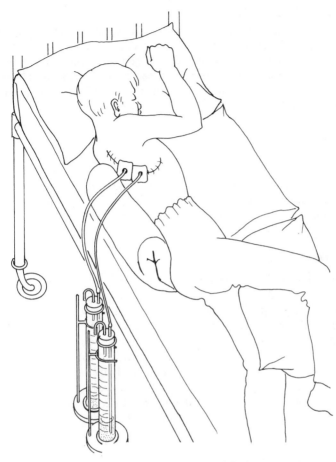

FIG. 15/10 Positioning of a patient following thoracotomy. *Note* the placing of the pillows and the support of the drains to prevent them 'dragging'

lumbar area, yet be contoured so that the pressure is relieved over the incision. The body-weight is then supported bilaterally at shoulder level.

DAY 2

Chest treatment should be given two or three times, depending on the chest radiograph and auscultation. With the patient sitting on a firm chair trunk exercises can be added to the regime. As soon as the drains are off suction, mobilisation is increased quickly and stair climbing added as soon as possible.

DAY 3 TO DISCHARGE

The patient needs to be assessed on a day to day basis during the following week, treating his chest as necessary. Postural exercises and general activities should be progressed. The patient will probably go home 8–10 days postoperatively; follow-up physiotherapy should not be necessary, unless the shoulder has been a particular problem.

PNEUMONECTOMY

Although this operation is performed through a thoracotomy incision, the postoperative problems will be slightly different and consequently the treatment plan will change.

Pre-operative

The patient will be given simple details of the operation and told not to lie on his good side for approximately 10 days after the operation. This will prevent the fluid in the pneumonectomy space from covering the bronchial stump thereby decreasing the risk of any breakdown of the suture line with possible development of a broncho-pleural fistula. In all probability the patient would find that his respiratory pattern is embarrassed by lying on his remaining lung. Because coughing creates a back pressure which can traumatise the bronchial stump, huffing must be taught and encouraged, to move secretions prior to a final gentle clearing cough.

Postoperative problem list

1. Pain.
2. Decreased air entry on the good side.
3. Retained secretions.
4. Decreased shoulder movement on the operation side.
5. Decreased mobility.
6. Poor posture.
7. Decreased exercise tolerance.

Postoperative treatment plan

1. Ensure that the patient has adequate analgesia.
2. Deep breathing exercises (unilateral costal on the good side and

diaphragmatic) with inspiratory holds and sniffs in sitting or half lying.

3. (a) Unilateral shakings on the good side during expiration.
   (b) Huffing with good support of the incision.
4. Full range active/assisted shoulder exercises.
5. Active leg, foot and ankle exercises.
6. (a) Bilateral costal and diaphragmatic breathing exercises.
   (b) Trunk and shoulder girdle exercises and postural correction.
7. Early mobilisation with controlled breathing pattern designed to improve exercise tolerance.

Postoperative regime

When the patient returns from theatre he will be given oxygen for the first few hours and have an intravenous infusion.

Depending on the surgeon, he may have a drain which will be clamped and, probably, released for a short period every hour. The patient must *not* cough when it is unclamped because too much fluid will be expelled which may cause a mediastinal shift, resulting in cardiac embarrassment.

The treatment will be as in the plan, starting on the day of operation. Apart from the general observations, the physiotherapist must also check if there is a deficit between the apex and the radial pulse, as these patients can have atrial fibrillation if there is a large mediastinal shift.

It is only necessary to position the patient in side lying if the remaining lung requires drainage. As drainage necessitates lying *on* the incision the positioning must be carefully carried out as described on page 380.

Generally, these patients are discharged about 10 days postoperatively, but they may need further support at home. The social worker should be kept fully informed about such patients so that suitable arrangements may be made, when necessary, *before* the actual discharge takes place.

PLEURODESIS, PLEURECTOMY AND DECORTICATION

The immediate postoperative period is particularly painful and adequate analgesia must be given to achieve a satisfactory treatment. The intercostal drainage tubes must *never* be clamped as retention of air and/or fluid in the chest will prevent the lung from adhering to the chest wall.

Postoperative regime

This will follow that described on page 379 and will be started on the day of the operation. Care of the drainage tubes together with costal and diaphragmatic breathing exercises and coughing will be carried out with the patient in the side-lying position and the affected lung uppermost; the foot of the bed will be elevated. Special efforts must be made to regain maximum rib and diaphragmatic movement. There may have been very limited chest movement prior to decortication of an empyema and every effort should be made to increase the local movement postoperatively. The patient will sit out of bed on the first day and commence walking as soon as possible. All exercises are increased and postural drainage continued until intercostal tubes and/or all excess secretions are removed. Walking, stair climbing and general exercises should continue until discharge, when all movements should be unrestricted and the posture free and upright. Vital capacity and exercise tolerance should show improvement on the pre-operative assessment. If the patient is young and has undergone pleurectomy for pneumothorax, and thoracic movement, lung function and exercise tolerance are not satisfactory he should attend for outpatient physiotherapy.

Tetracycline pleurodesis

Some patients with recurrent malignant pleural effusions will require a pleurodesis. This can be achieved by instilling diluted tetracycline into the pleural cavity via an intercostal drain, which is then clamped. The physiotherapist should be present and immediately carry out breathing exercises with the patient in all positions. The treatment should take 30 minutes, allowing at least 3 minutes in each position, including a full tip in lying, alternate side lying and, if possible, prone lying to allow the tetracycline to reach all areas of the pleura. Some surgeons will leave the drain clamped for up to 24 hours and others will release it immediately.

It must be realised that these patients are generally much more disabled than the previous type of patient, and therefore they should not be 'pushed' as hard.

THORACOPLASTY

The particular postoperative problem is postural due to lack of structural support. Due to overcompensation the patient will develop a position opposite to that after thoracotomy, i.e. the posture will be that of a long lean *away* from the incision side. The hip will drop, the shoulder will be raised and the head and neck will lean towards the operation side to correct equilibrium (Fig. 15/11).

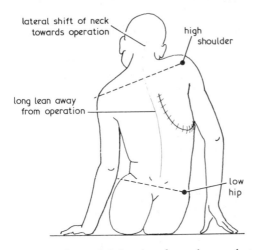

lateral shift of neck towards operation

high shoulder

long lean away from operation

low hip

FIG. 15/11 Postural deformity after a thoracoplasty

Treatment commences on the day of operation. If there is paradoxical movement of the upper chest it should be prevented by the application of a firm 'paradoxical pad' which should extend from below the clavicle and into the axilla. Deep breathing exercises, huffing and coughing, full range active assisted shoulder movements and correction of posture must be practised as soon as possible after the patient returns to the ward. The upper chest must be well supported during coughing to prevent the paradoxical movement of the chest wall. The best position for coughing is forward-sitting. The physiotherapist must hold the chest very firmly, with one hand on the back and the other over the upper part of the front of the chest.

All breathing exercises, huffing and coughing, leg, arm, shoulder girdle and head and neck movements must continue through the following days. The patient will sit out of bed and walk around as soon as possible. Trunk exercises will begin on the second or third day. The posture exercises and correction should be done in front of a mirror as soon as the therapist feels that the patient can tolerate seeing himself. The intensive postural re-training is essential, especially in cases when the first rib has been removed. It may be necessary for the patient to attend for outpatient physiotherapy until postural control has been achieved.

PECTUS CARINATUM AND PECTUS EXCAVATUM

Postoperative physiotherapy follows the routine procedure for maintaining clear airways and lung expansion and preventing lung collapse and/or consolidation. It is advisable to nurse the patient in the lying position for one to three days to prevent the tendency to 'kyphose'. Side lying should also be avoided. Shoulder girdle and arm exercises should be practised bilaterally to maintain symmetry. Postural correction is of particular importance and, when not walking about, the patient should either be flat in bed or sit in an upright chair preferably with a lumbar pillow to prevent kyphosis.

PHYSIOTHERAPY BEFORE AND AFTER REPAIR OF HIATUS HERNIA AND OESOPHAGEAL RESECTIONS

Patients with oesophageal obstruction at any level are at risk from overspill of the oesophageal contents into the lung which will cause an aspiration pneumonia and/or reactive bronchospasm. The areas which are most commonly affected are the apical segments of the lower lobes and the 'axillary' parts of the upper lobes, these being the areas of the lung which are most dependent during sleep, as the two common sleeping positions are lying and side lying.

The pre-operative physiotherapy will follow that described on page 375 and include localised treatment, including postural drainage, for any affected lung area. Fortunately, the commonly affected areas do not require tipping the end of the bed, for in so doing one may precipitate further overspill.

Postoperatively the patients having had extensive resection and reconstruction will probably be returned to the intensive care unit and their treatment is described on page 289. Those patients having extensive thoraco-abdominal incisions may have a great deal of pain and administration of Entonox during physiotherapy may be beneficial. (Entonox is a mixture of 50 per cent oxygen and 50 per cent nitrous oxide which is used in the immediate postoperative period for its analgesic and sedative effect.)

Patients who have undergone repair of a hiatus hernia or a Heller's operation (for achalasia of the cardia) will be returned to the ward and will need treatment following that described for a thoracotomy. Care should be taken not to force coughing and to avoid tipping the foot of the bed if possible, as there may be regurgitation of gastric juices.

BIBLIOGRAPHY

Brewis, R. A. L. (1980). *Lecture Notes on Respiratory Disease*, 2nd edition. Blackwell Scientific Publications Limited, Oxford.

Waldhausen, J. A. and Pierce, W. S. (jt. eds.) (1985). *Johnson's Surgery of the Chest*. Year Book Medical Publications Inc, Chicago.

Chapter 16

Cardiac Surgery

by J. R. PEPPER MChir, FRCS, J. M. ANDERSON MCSP
and D. M. INNOCENTI MCSP

Clinical

Despite the sophistication of modern cardiac investigations, the history and examination of the cardiac patient remains extremely important. The cardiac surgeon seeks to fit the clinical data with the data he obtains from invasive and non-invasive investigations. He must look for an overall picture and be alert to any features that do not fit. Good postoperative results can only be achieved by properly planned and well executed operations.

Pre-operative investigations also enable the surgeon to assess the risk of operation which is then discussed openly with the patient or parents. This discussion will include a realistic appraisal of the benefits of the operation and is probably best done in outpatients. Once admitted for operation most units now organise a brief counselling session supported by an explanatory booklet.

PRE-OPERATIVE INVESTIGATIONS

ECG (see Chapter 6)

Exercise ECG

This provides an objective assessment of the patient's ability to exercise and the degree of ischaemia and haemodynamic disturbance which this exercise produces. The patient is connected to an ECG machine while he walks on a treadmill. The gradient and speed of the treadmill are gradually increased according to a standard protocol. Patients who develop chest pain, ST or T wave changes at a low workload are at an increased risk of developing myocardial infarction or sudden death. A poor blood pressure response indicates impaired left ventricular function.

Echocardiogram

A non-invasive investigation whereby a beam of sound is projected into the heart from a probe held on the skin of the anterior chest wall. Two-dimensional echocardiography can now provide excellent pictures of all chambers of the heart and is used in the diagnosis of congenital heart disease especially in the neonate and even in the fetus. In acquired heart disease ECHO can accurately predict the aetiology and severity of valvular disease and detect abnormalities of ventricular wall motion in ischaemic heart disease.

Cardiac catheterisation

In experienced hands this invasive procedure has a very low morbidity and can be completed in less than 30 minutes. It provides three sets of data: intracardiac pressures, intracardiac saturation and, after injection of contrast medium, images of the heart and great vessels.

To obtain information on the right side of the heart a balloon-tipped catheter is passed via an antecubital vein into the right atrium. The balloon is inflated to allow the catheter to 'float' into the right ventricle and pulmonary artery. For left-sided heart studies a catheter is introduced into the arterial system either via the brachial or femoral artery. By use of a stylette within the catheter it can be passed, under radiographic control, across the aortic valve and into the cavity of the left ventricle. Selective catheterisation of the coronary arteries is performed by the use of special pre-formed catheters designed to slip into the orifice of left and right coronary arteries.

Recently the technique of percutaneous transluminal angioplasty (PTCA) of the coronary arteries has been developed. During this procedure a balloon catheter is passed across a stenosed coronary artery so that the balloon lies within the stenosed segment. The pressure of CO_2 gas in the balloon is raised to about 750mmHg (1 atmosphere). This significantly reduces the degree of stenosis in approximately 80 per cent of patients. The early results are encouraging but as the technique is still evolving the long-term results remain uncertain.

INCISIONS (Fig. 16/1)

For operations on the heart or mediastinum the approach is usually from the front:

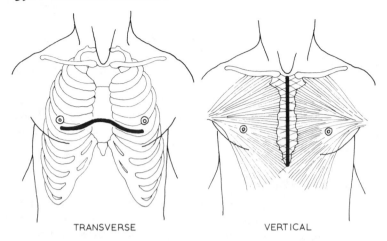

TRANSVERSE   VERTICAL

FIG. 16/1 Incisions used in open heart surgery

VERTICAL APPROACH

Median sternotomy is probably the most commonly used anterior incision. The sternum is divided longitudinally and retracted. No muscles are divided but the action of the pectoralis major is affected because the pre-sternal aponeurosis is cut.

TRANSVERSE APPROACH

This is submammary and bilateral, through the 4th intercostal spaces and a transversely divided sternum. The pectoralis major is divided together with the external and internal intercostal muscles. This approach is used rarely as both pleural cavities are opened. It is sometimes preferred for cosmetic reasons.

CARDIOPULMONARY BYPASS

The great majority of procedures are carried out with the aid of cardiopulmonary bypass whereby the circulation through the heart is interrupted so that the surgeon can see the internal defect. It is a technique by which the pumping action of the heart and the gas-exchange functions of the lung are temporarily replaced by a mechanical device. Venous blood is siphoned from the right atrium via clear plastic tubing to an oxygenator, and then filtered and pumped back into the aortic arch. A heat exchanger which will cool or warm the blood is included in the circuit. The pump and oxygenator are mounted together on a movable frame close to the ground beside the operating table.

Oxygenators are disposable and can be of two types: bubble or membrane. Bubble oxygenators are most commonly used. They work on the principle of bubbling oxygen into a column of venous blood. The blood is arterialised as the oxygen bubbles rise. Excess bubbles are removed and the blood filtered before being returned to the patient.

Membrane oxygenators are also available as disposable items. They work on the principle of a semi-permeable membrane which separates a stream of oxygen gas from a film of blood. These latter oxygenators cause less damage to blood products (mainly red cells and platelets) than the bubble type but the difference only becomes clinically significant for long bypass times, i.e. over 3 hours. Cardiac units that specialise in infant surgery often use membrane oxygenators.

INTRA-AORTIC BALLOON COUNTERPULSATION
(Figs. 16/2, 16/3, 16/4)

The relationship between the *supply* of oxygen to the myocardium and the *demand* by the energy processes of the myocardium for oxygen becomes critical in low cardiac output states. Drugs which increase the contractility of the myocardium and thus the cardiac

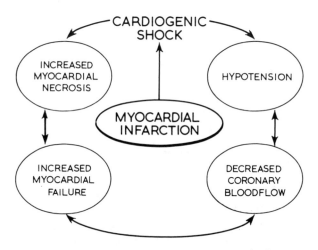

FIG. 16/2 Indications for balloon counterpulsation

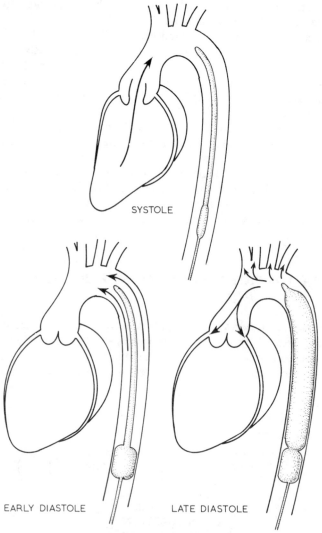

SYSTOLE

EARLY DIASTOLE   LATE DIASTOLE

FIG. 16/3 Balloon counterpulsation. *Upper*: Systole – balloon collapsed; *Lower*: *left*: early diastole; *right*: late diastole – balloon inflated

output tend to do so at the expense of increased demand by the myocardium for oxygen. Such drugs may increase demand beyond the available supply and thus build up an oxygen debt. Counterpulsation provides a way of improving the ratio between supply and demand.

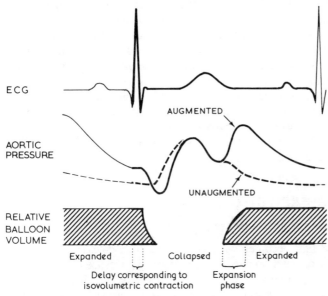

ECG

AORTIC
PRESSURE

AUGMENTED

UNAUGMENTED

RELATIVE
BALLOON
VOLUME

Expanded   Collapsed   Expanded

Delay corresponding to   Expansion
isovolumetric contraction   phase

FIG. 16/4 The effect of counterpulsation on the arterial pressure wave

The concept of counterpulsation is based on the finding that myocardial oxygen consumption is dependent upon the pressure generated by the left ventricle. Counterpulsation does two things: first it increases the diastolic perfusion pressure and second it reduces the systolic pressure against which the left ventricle contracts (a similar effect to that of a vasodilator drug).

A special balloon catheter is introduced into the descending thoracic aorta via a femoral artery. When the balloon inflates blood is displaced and the diastolic pressure in the aorta is increased. When the balloon deflates the systolic pressure is reduced and the capacity of the aorta for blood increases.

The catheter is attached to an electronically controlled actuator. The R wave of the ECG (see Chapter 6) is the trigger which is picked up by the control unit. The effect is delayed so that the balloon is inflated during diastole when the aortic valve is closed. Since the majority of coronary blood flow occurs during diastole and is dependent upon diastolic perfusion, the selective elevation of diastolic pressure by the balloon will increase coronary blood flow. Shortly before the onset of left ventricular systole the balloon is deflated. This reduces the systolic pressure against which the left ventricle ejects its blood and so reduces work and hence myocardial oxygen consumption by the left ventricle (Fig. 16/3).

The counterpulsation pump is used in two clinical instances. First, in the operating theatre to enable a struggling heart to take on the load of the circulation and so come off cardiopulmonary bypass. Second, to assist a patient in low cardiac output, either following open heart surgery or as a means of holding a severely ill patient with coronary artery disease for a limited period before emergency coronary artery vein bypass surgery is done.

Physiotherapy for patients having counterpulsation is discussed on page 429.

ACQUIRED DISORDERS

Ischaemic heart disease (IHD)

This has become, with cerebrovascular disease, the commonest cause of death in the Western world. It is caused by a degenerative process, atherosclerosis, the hallmark of which is the lipid-filled plaque in the intima of an artery. Important risk factors in coronary artery disease are raised plasma lipoproteins, high blood pressure, cigarette smoking, lack of exercise and a strong family history. Although the peak incidence of this disease is between 40 and 50 it may occur at any age.

IHD occurs in three clinical settings: angina pectoris, myocardial infarction and sudden death.

Myocardial infarction is a pathological event in which an area of ventricular muscle dies due most frequently to thrombosis in a major coronary artery. This has given rise to an increased awareness of the role of thrombolytic drugs in acute myocardial infarction. It raises the exciting possiblity of being able to reverse the natural history of myocardial infarction and so prevent myocardial damage.

Coronary bypass grafting

First performed in 1967, this has become a common operation for a prevalent disease. The aim of the operation is to relieve the symptoms of angina and in certain groups of patients to prolong life. Patients with severe stenosis of all three coronary arteries or severe stenosis of the main stem of the left coronary artery survive longer (over 5 years) with surgery than with medical treatment. The most important predictor of long-term survival is the extent of damage of the left ventricle.

Once accepted for operation the patient is admitted to hospital 48 hours in advance. Pre-operative medical treatment with beta blockers, calcium antagonists and nitrates is designed to reduce cardiac work and reduce the incidence of coronary spasm. A careful anaesthetic technique is used to prevent hypoxia, tachycardia or hypertension which may otherwise precipitate a myocardial infarction. The operation is performed using cardiopulmonary bypass. Reversed segments of the long saphenous vein are used to form bypass grafts from the ascending aorta to the coronary artery distal to the stenosis. Up to five or six grafts may be required.

Postoperative care occurs in an intensive care ward for the first 24 hours. The majority of patients are fit to leave hospital 1 week after operation. Operative mortality is now less than 2 per cent and at 1 year after operation over 85 per cent of patients are symptom free. Re-operation can be carried out at a low risk but the results are less satisfactory than the initial procedure. Because of the attrition rate of vein grafts, surgeons are now using the internal mammary artery on one or both sides. The patency of the internal mammary at 7 years (95 per cent) is superior to that of saphenous vein grafts (70 per cent). Three complications of myocardial infarction are amenable to surgical correction:

1. Ventricular aneurysm.
2. Mitral regurgitation due to papillary muscle infarction.
3. Ventricular septal defect due to infarction of the septum.

Multiple coronary bypass grafts may be performed at the same time.

POSTOPERATIVE COMPLICATIONS

In the current era the number of postoperative complications is small. They may be early or late.

EARLY

1. Haemorrhage with or without cardiac tamponade. Tamponade describes the situation in which blood accumulates within the pericardial cavity and compresses all chambers of the heart. It is recognised by a rise in right (or left) atrial pressure associated with a fall in arterial pressure and in urine output.
2. Peri-operative myocardial infarction occurs in approximately 5 per cent of patients. This may or may not be clinically significant. Usually it is not associated with a fall in cardiac output, but if extensive it will obviously increase the risk of death.
3. Dysrhythmia: usually supraventricular tachy-arrhythmias, e.g.

atrial fibrillation. This is common but is easily treated and well tolerated by the patient.

4. Cerebrovascular accident is now the most serious complication after coronary artery surgery particularly in the elderly. Two broad types of neurological insult are recognised. The first is the discrete neurological deficit associated with emboli such as thrombus, atheromatous plaque or surgically introduced air. This type of deficit is now rare. The second type of insult is a diffuse injury usually associated with delayed return of consciousness, impaired intellect and loss of memory. Fortunately these changes are usually transient.

5. Acute renal failure is now a rare complication. It is caused by low arterial pressure producing renal hypoperfusion, haemolysis, septicaemia, disordered coagulation.

LATE

Recurrence of angina due to either occlusion of vein grafts or progression of disease in native coronary arteries.

AORTIC VALVE DISEASE

The aortic valve may be involved in congenital, rheumatic, bacterial, atherosclerotic and syphilitic changes. Stenosis and regurgitation may occur as isolated lesions but are often combined. Calcification of the cusps may occur and is responsible for the stenosis which occurs in congenitally bicuspid valves.

Aortic stenosis

This is usually the result of disease of the valve cusps but may be due to narrowing of the outflow tract below the valve (subvalvar) or, rarely, above the valve (supravalvar).

AETIOLOGY

Aortic valve stenosis may be congenital, rheumatic or sclerotic. It most commonly presents in middle age with no involvement of other valves. Aortic stenosis is often associated with regurgitation.

PATHOPHYSIOLOGY

Stenosis becomes serious when the area of the orifice is reduced to 25 per cent of normal. The left ventricle responds to the pressure load by contracting more forcibly and left ventricular systolic pressure increases. A systolic pressure difference develops between the left ventricle and the aorta. The left ventricular muscle thickens progressively as the valve orifice narrows.

PROGNOSIS

Once symptoms of breathlessness, angina or syncope have developed, death is likely to occur suddenly at any time or within 3 years from the onset of heart failure.

TREATMENT

Medical treatment has little to offer. Surgery is indicated for all patients.

Aortic regurgitation

AETIOLOGY

Aortic regurgitation is usually due to rheumatic heart disease. It may be congenital but the associated lesion, such as ventricular septal defect, is usually more important. Other causes are hypertension, aortic dissection, endocarditis, Marfan's syndrome, ankylosing spondylitis, Reiter's disease, syphilitic aortitis.

PATHOPHYSIOLOGY

In aortic regurgitation a large volume of blood leaks across the valve into the left ventricle during each diastole. As a result the left ventricle dilates and left ventricular output may be more than doubled. The dilated left ventricle contracts more forcefully in accordance with Starling's law but because the ventricle is large there is increased tension in the wall and therefore increased oxygen consumption by the myocardium. The heart is therefore working hard to produce a normal cardiac output.

PROGNOSIS

Minor degrees of aortic regurgitation are compatible with a normal life span. In the moderate to severe case disability progresses slowly and the patient remains well until the age of 40 to 50 years. Increasing breathlessness and an enlarging heart suggests that the patient is unlikely to survive beyond a few years.

TREATMENT

For severe cases, symptomatic improvement by standard treatment of cardiac failure. When symptoms and heart size increase surgery is usually indicated.

MITRAL VALVE DISEASE

Chronic mitral valve disease is usually due to rheumatic endocarditis and commonly takes the form of mitral stenosis with little or no regurgitation. Combined stenosis and regurgitation is well recognised but pure mitral regurgitation due to rheumatic diseases is rare.

Mitral stenosis

This is usually the result of recurrent rheumatic inflammation. The two leaflets adhere at their commissures leaving a small central orifice. The chordae may thicken and shorten to produce a funnel-shaped orifice.

PATHOPHYSIOLOGY (Fig. 16/5)

In the normal heart the pressure in the left atrium is similar to that of the left ventricle during ventricular diastole. As mitral stenosis develops the pressure in the left atrium rises and this rise is transmitted to the pulmonary veins, capillaries and arteries. When pulmonary vascular disease develops, the pulmonary arterioles narrow which leads to a rise in pulmonary arterial and right ventricular systolic pressure.

If pulmonary capillary pressure rises rapidly above 25mmHg pulmonary oedema develops. If the process takes place slowly, fluid leaks into the alveolar wall and a barrier develops between capillaries and alveoli. Under these conditions patients can tolerate high pulmonary capillary pressure without developing pulmonary oedema. As a result of the increased interstitial fluid, the lymphatics become enlarged.

As pulmonary capillary pressure rises there may be a disproportionate rise in pulmonary artery pressure producing pulmonary hypertension. This in turn leads to right ventricular hypertrophy and eventually right heart failure. The pulmonary vascular congestion typical of mitral stenosis leads to increased rigidity in the lungs. As a result patients with severe mitral stenosis may have to double the work of breathing.

COMPLICATIONS

The earliest complication is atrial fibrillation which eventually develops in nearly all patients with mitral stenosis. It leads to atrial stasis and therefore the risk of thrombosis and embolism. Systemic embolism is common and often follows the onset of atrial fibrillation.

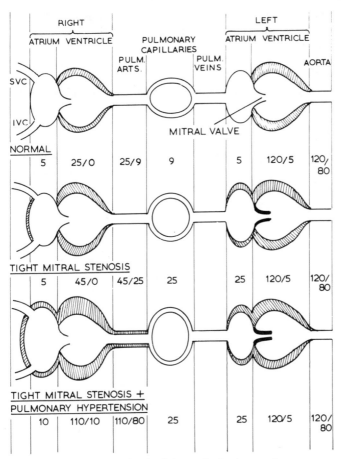

FIG. 16/5 Pathophysiology of mitral stenosis

The raised pulmonary capillary pressure makes the patient liable to attacks of acute bronchitis and likely to develop chronic bronchitis.

A late complication is pulmonary embolism and infarction.

PROGNOSIS

For those patients in whom complications do not develop there is a steady deterioration over years and without treatment the majority will die in their 40s. In women, pregnancy is often associated with the onset of breathlessness but is usually well tolerated unless mitral stenosis is severe. Rapid deterioration may occur due to pulmonary infarction or infection associated with the onset of atrial fibrillation. Once right ventricular failure has developed the prognosis without operation is poor.

TREATMENT

Some form of medical treatment will be required for most patients. Initially, control of atrial fibrillation and anticoagulation to prevent emboli are required. Infections should be treated promptly, and prophylactic antibiotics given for any potentially septic hazards (e.g. dental extraction) in order to prevent endocarditis. Surgical treatment takes two forms – either mitral valvotomy or mitral valve replacement. Mitral valvotomy can be performed either as a closed procedure (the surgeon *feels* but does not *see* the valve and cardiopulmonary bypass is not required), or, more commonly, as an open operation using cardiopulmonary bypass. The mortality for mitral valvotomy is around 1 per cent. If there is severe calcification of the valve, valve replacement will be required which carries a mortality of around 5 per cent. Where there is severe pulmonary hypertension or right ventricular failure the risk may rise to 10 per cent.

Mitral regurgitation

Mitral regurgitation may be due to rheumatic endocarditis, infective endocarditis, papillary muscle dysfunction from myocardial infarction, left ventricular dilatation from any cause such as aortic regurgitation or severe coronary artery disease. Other causes include mitral valve prolapse, rupture of chordae tendinae and congenital mitral regurgitation.

PATHOPHYSIOLOGY

The severity of mitral regurgitation depends upon the pressure relationship between left ventricle and left atrium, the cardiac output and the size of the mitral valve orifice. Therefore, an increased cardiac output or raised systemic vascular resistance will increase mitral regurgitation.

The left atrium is usually very enlarged in chronic mitral regurgitation.

Pulmonary capillary pressure does not rise until late in the natural history of the disease in association with left ventricular failure.

PROGNOSIS

Patients with mild regurgitation and without an enlarged heart may live a normal life-span. Those with rheumatic mitral regurgitation deteriorate slowly over a period of 10 to 20 years unless a complication supervenes. Mitral regurgitation due to ruptured chordae, or papillary muscle dysfunction, tends to progress more rapidly and carries a worse prognosis.

TRICUSPID VALVE DISEASE

Significant tricuspid stenosis develops in around 5 per cent of cases of rheumatic heart disease. Very often mitral stenosis is also present and dominates the clinical picture. Most patients with tricuspid stenosis do not require surgery; but if symptoms are severe valvotomy or valve replacement will be required. Organic tricuspid regurgitation is less common and is nearly always of rheumatic origin. Functional tricuspid regurgitation is a common sequel to right ventricular failure from whatever cause.

Patients with functional tricuspid regurgitation often improve with diuretic treatment and bed rest. If surgery is required for associated mitral valve disease, the tricuspid regurgitation often resolves. However, in severe tricuspid regurgitation valve repair or replacement will be required.

PULMONARY VALVE DISEASE

This is uncommon. Pulmonary valve stenosis is usually congenital and is discussed on page 412. Pulmonary regurgitation is usually secondary to pulmonary hypertension and associated with right ventricular hypertrophy. The treatment of pulmonary regurgitation is that of the associated pulmonary hypertension.

VALVE REPAIR

Conservative operations for obstructed valves

CLOSED MITRAL VALVOTOMY

This operation, first successfully performed in 1948, brought great benefit to many patients with rheumatic mitral stenosis. Due to the falling incidence of rheumatic heart disease in Europe and North America it is now uncommonly performed in these areas but remains a common operation elsewhere, notably India.

The approach is via a left antero-lateral thoracotomy (see Fig. 15/3, page 368) through the 4th or 5th intercostal space. The valvotomy is termed 'closed' because the mitral valve is not seen but only felt with the index finger inserted into the left atrium via the appendage. The commissures of the valve are then split by the use of an expandable dilator inserted into the left ventricle via the apex.

The postoperative routine follows the same course as for a thoracotomy. A good valvotomy will last for 10 to 20 years at which time a valve replacement will probably be required.

OPEN VALVOTOMY

This is done using cardiopulmonary bypass to relieve the stenosis under direct vision. It is performed in children for pulmonary or aortic valve stenosis. In adults the aortic valve is not suitable for conservation but the mitral and less commonly the tricuspid valves are.

Conservative operations for leaking valves

It is sometimes possible using cardiopulmonary bypass to repair a leaking valve. The commonest valves to be repaired are the mitral and tricuspid. A good repair will offer the patient freedom from the complications of prosthetic devices.

Valve replacement

The devices available fall into two broad categories: mechanical and biological.

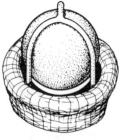

STARR-EDWARDS
AORTIC VALVE

from above – open

BJÖRK-SHILEY VALVE

from the side — open

FIG. 16/6 Mechanical prostheses

MECHANICAL PROSTHESES (Fig. 16/6)

(a) Ball and cage type, e.g. Starr-Edwards: a silastic ball moves inside a metal cage.
(b) Tilting disc type, e.g. Bjork-Shiley, Lillehei-Kaster, and many others: a free-floating disc moves around an ingenious hinge.

BIOLOGICAL PROSTHESES (Fig. 16/7)

(a) Porcine valves, e.g. Carpentier-Edwards, Hancock: these are made from aortic valve tissue taken from a pig. The tissue is preserved in glutaraldehyde and sewn on to a flexible stent.
(b) Bovine pericardium, e.g. Ionescu-Shiley: this is made from ox pericardium also preserved in glutaraldehyde and sewn on to a flexible stent.

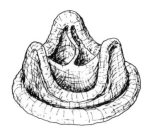

CARPENTIER-EDWARDS
VALVE

FIG. 16/7 A biological prosthesis

HOMOGRAFTS

This is a human valve obtained from a cadaver within 48 hours of death and treated with antibiotics. It is most commonly used in the aortic position and is sewn directly into place without a stent.

COMPLICATIONS OF VALVE REPLACEMENT

Patients who receive a mechanical prosthesis must take an anti-coagulant for the rest of their lives to avoid developing emboli or thrombosis on their valves. Patients with a biological prosthesis or homograft may not need to take anticoagulants but the durability of biological valves is less certain than the mechanical prostheses.

All patients after valve replacement should receive antibiotics for any dental or other surgical procedure in order to protect them against the risk of infection of the valve.

OUTLOOK AFTER VALVE REPLACEMENT

The early complications after cardiac valve replacement are similar to those after coronary artery surgery outlined above. The late results are determined by the following factors:

1. Pre-operative disability of the patient.
2. Type of valve prosthesis.
3. Long-term anticoagulation.
4. State of the myocardium.
5. Endocarditis.

OPERATIONS ON THE GREAT VESSELS

Pulmonary embolectomy

A massive embolus may obstruct so much of the pulmonary tree that the right ventricle fails and the heart arrests. Few of such patients survive long enough but for those who do an urgent operation can be very successful.

Closed operation: The chest is opened quickly via a mid-line sternotomy. The superior and inferior vena cavae are clamped and the pulmonary artery opened. The embolus is removed by forceps and suction. The circulation is restored after 1 minute to prevent irreversible brain damage.

Open operation: Cardiopulmonary bypass is first established via the iliac or femoral vessels. Thus closed cardiac massage can be performed continuously until bypass is established. The pulmonary artery is opened and the embolus removed.

Dissection of the aorta

If the innermost layer of the aorta (intima) develops a tear blood can track into the middle layer (media) to form a haematoma which extends both around and along the aorta. This is called an aortic dissection and is an uncommon and lethal condition. These tears are of two types arising in the ascending or descending aorta.

In the *ascending type* blood spreads retrogradely beneath the commissures of the aortic valve making it incompetent. Blood may also spread (1) forwards around the arch and down to the aortic bifurcation, compressing branches which supply the spinal cord, kidneys, and gut on the way; (2) into the pericardium causing tamponade and (3) around the coronary ostia causing compression and infarction.

In the *descending type* a tear develops just distal to the origin of the left subclavian artery and extends down the thoracic aorta. The aortic valve is not damaged.

MANAGEMENT

1. Control of hypertension by vasodilator drugs and beta blockers.
2. Aortogram to confirm diagnosis and identify site of tear.
3. Urgent operation for *ascending type*.
4. Continued medical treatment for *descending type*.

PERICARDECTOMY

This is performed to relieve the symptoms of constrictive pericarditis. The pericardium is fibrotic and often calcified due to previous viral or tubercular infection. The heart is encased in a rigid shell which restricts the flow of blood into the heart. The operation aims to remove enough of the rigid pericardium to enable the heart to expand and allow free flow of blood into both atria.

CARDIAC MYXOMA

This is a rare condition of specific tumour formation within the cardiac chambers: it arises most commonly in the left atrium. It is mobile and obstructs the mitral valve. The signs and symptoms are those of intermittent mitral valve disease. It may throw off embolia.

A median sternotomy or left antero-lateral thoracotomy is used. The heart is entered through the left atrium and the myxoma resected away from its root on the atrial wall. Alternatively, the right atrium is entered and the septum divided and removed with the pedicle and myxoma. The septum will be repaired or patched with Dacron.

HEART BLOCK

This is a condition where there is interference in the normal conducting system of the heart. There are various degrees of the condition which may be due to coronary artery disease, myocarditis, valve disease, rheumatic fever, diphtheria, congenital disorder, or surgical interference.

In complete heart block the atria and ventricles work independently. The pulse rate is slow usually between 30/40 beats per minute. There is risk of attacks of unconsciousness during which the patient's pulse stops. Convulsions may occur if unconsciousness is prolonged. When the pulse returns the patient regains consciousness and may have a characteristic flush. Such periods of unconsciousness are termed Stokes-Adams attacks.

Pacemakers

An electrical device which artificially paces the heart is being increasingly used to correct the condition of heart block. There are two methods of inserting a permanent internal artificial pacemaker system:

Transvenous system. A cardiac catheter with a wire core and electrode tip is passed transvenously and embedded into the myocardium at the apex of the right ventricle. The pacemaker box is implanted subcutaneously in the axilla or epigastrium and connected to the electrode wire.

Epicardial system. Should the previous method be unsuccessful, it is necessary to perform a left thoracotomy and pericardotomy. Small electrodes are sutured to, or screwed into, the epicardium and connected by screened wires to the pacemaker box, implanted subcutaneously as above.

A *temporary pacing system* may be necessary and will be fixed transvenously through the basilic vein or subclavian vein. The wires will be attached to an external pacemaker box.

Internal and external pacemaker systems may work on a fixed rate, on demand, or be atrial triggered.

Fixed rate pacemakers discharge at regular fixed intervals. The atrial and ventricular contractions will not be synchronised.

Demand pacemakers may operate in two ways. One type is linked to the interval between ventricular contractions. A ventricular contraction is sensed by the pacemaker, but should the next contraction be delayed the pacemaker will produce an impulse. The second type produces stimuli regularly. A spontaneous ventricular contraction will be sensed and the stimulus superimposed upon it (this will be ineffective as the myocardium will have depolarised). Should a ventricular contraction not take place the impulse will produce a contraction.

Atrial triggered pacemakers produce a near normal situation. An electrode situated in the right atrium relays the atrial impulse via a lead to the pacemaker box. The pacemaker then produces a stimulus which is relayed via a second wire and electrode to the right ventricle. As the atrial rate varies, so will the ventricular rate.

Postoperative physiotherapy. For transvenous implants – routine chest care with complete mobilisation after 24 hours. For epicardial implants – routine post-thoracotomy care (p. 379).

Surgical treatment of tachycardias

Certain ventricular tachycardias and some cases of Wolf-Parkinson-White syndrome can be effectively treated by an operation when drug treatment has failed. Some patients who have recurrent attacks of ventricular tachycardia and who have left ventricular aneurysm may be cured of their tachycardia by excision of their aneurysm.

In recent years with the development of electrical mapping of the epicardium in the operating theatre it has been possible precisely to identify the course of a re-entry circuit in W-P-W syndrome. The surgeon can then interrupt a part of this circuit by cutting myocardial fibres and thus prevent development of a tachycardia.

Patients who have had this procedure usually experience more pain than those who have had valve or vein graft surgery. Care must be taken to give them sufficient analgesia.

CONGENITAL DISORDERS

In order to help to understand these, a brief outline of the development of the heart is given here.

Development of the heart

The heart is formed between the 21st and 40th days of embryonic life. Two symmetrically developing endothelial tubes fuse, commencing at the bulbar or arterial end, to form a tubular heart. As the tube grows in length, two grooves appear in the surface, which subdivide it into three primitive sections or chambers. The arterial end is called the bulbous cordis, the central chamber the ventricle, and the venous end the sinuatrial chamber. The groove between the ventricle and the sinuatrial chamber indicates the position of the atrioventricular canal.

The tube continues to increase in length. The middle portion grows more rapidly than the ends, resulting in the formation of a U-shaped loop, termed the bulboventricular loop (the right limb of the loop is formed by the bulb and the left limb by the ventricle).

The venous end of the tube (the common atrium) is pushed into an S-shaped curve and so lies above and behind the ventricular portion. A fold appears at the venous end of the atrium, dividing the chamber, to form the sinus venosus. Meanwhile, paired endothelial tubes arise to form the dorsal aortae, which grow down to the pericardium and join with the bulbus to form the truncus arteriosus.

The venous drainage is established by the union of an anterior cardinal vein from the head end of the embryo with a posterior cardinal vein from the tail end. This vessel then opens into the sinuatrial chamber by draining into the sinus venosus. The umbilical arteries and veins develop. These veins terminate in the sinuatrial chamber and will eventually drain into the right atrium.

The atria are formed from the common chamber.

The communication between the atrium and the ventricle (the atrioventricular canal) becomes divided by the formation of the atrioventricular endocardial cushions. These swellings grow from the centres of the ventral and dorsal walls of the canal, join together (thus forming the septum intermedium of His) and leave the right and left atrioventricular orifices, within which the mitral and tricuspid valves form.

The division between the right and left atria is formed by the growth of two septa (Fig. 16/8).

The first septum, or septum primum, grows from the upper and dorsal part of the atrial wall down towards the endocardial cushions. It is necessary in the fetal heart for the two atria to communicate. The free passage of blood is maintained below the advancing edge of the septum. This communication is termed the ostium primum, and is low down, near to the atrioventricular canal. This hole decreases in size and finally closes as the septum encroaches on the endocardial cushions. To maintain an inter-atrial communication the dorsal part of the septum breaks down. This communication is termed the ostium secundum (foramen ovale) and is high up in the septum.

The second septum, or septum secundum, is formed by inflection of the muscular atrial wall, and it overlaps the septum primum at its periphery, leaving the centre free.

While the septum is developing, a pulmonary vein opens into the left atrium and subsequently expands into the four pulmonary veins. The ventral walls of the atria bulge forwards one on each side of the bulbus cordis, to form the atrial chambers.

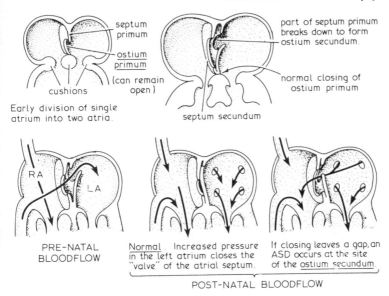

FIG. 16/8 The development of the atrial septa, also showing how an atrial septal defect can occur

The separation of the ventricles and of the truncus arteriosus into the aortic and pulmonary trunks are interrelated. Four endocardial cushions grow at the distal end of the bulbus (ventral, dorsal, right and left). The right and left cushions join to form the distal bulbar septum, which divides the orifice into ventral or pulmonary and dorsal or aortic sections. The four cushions eventually form the aortic and pulmonary valves.

Right and left spiral ridges appear within the truncus arteriosus and fuse together forming the spiral aortopulmonary septum (thus dividing the truncus arteriosus into the pulmonary trunk and the aorta). The proximal end of the septum fuses with the distal bulbar septum. The distal end of the aortopulmonary septum fuses with the aortic arches; thus one pair of arches fuse with the pulmonary trunk and the others with the aorta.

The separation of the ventricles occurs in three stages:

1. A muscular ridge projects into the ventricle to form the muscular septum, and fuses with the dorsal atrioventricular endocardial cushion, at its right extremity.
2. Right and left bulbar ridges fuse to form the proximal bulbar

septum and divide the bulbus cordis into pulmonary and aortic channels, which will continue up into the truncus arteriosus. The proximal bulbar septum fuses with the ventricular septum and the right extremity of the fused atrioventricular cushions.

3. The atrial septum fuses with the centre of the atrioventricular cushions and the ventricular septum with the right extremity. Hence, there is a portion of cushion dividing the right atrium from the left ventricle. It is this tissue which forms the membranous portion of the ventricular septum.

The mitral and tricuspid valves develop at the atrioventricular orifices by proliferation of endothelial tissue. The aortic and pulmonary valves develop from the four endocardial cushions at the distal end of the bulbus cordis.

The heart rotates to the left before birth and this rotation affects the final positions of the aorta, pulmonary trunk and valves, relative to each other. The normal anatomy of the heart is shown in Figure 16/9.

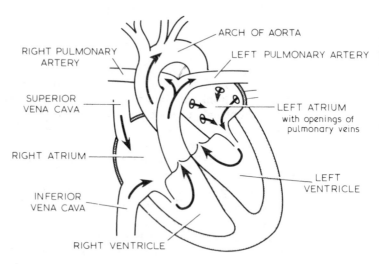

FIG. 16/9 Normal anatomy of the heart

At the bedside it is often useful to divide congenital cardiac disorders into three main physiological groups:

	Haemodynamic problem	*Examples*
Group 1	Hypoxaemia (Decreased pulmonary blood flow)	Tetralogy of Fallot Transposition of great vessels (complicated forms) Pulmonary atresia
Group 2	Volume overload (Increased pulmonary blood flow)	Ventricular septal defect Atrial septal defect Persistent ductus arteriosus Transposition of great vessels Total anomalous pulmonary venous drainage
Group 3	Pressure overload (Increased pressure in heart chambers behind obstruction)	Pulmonary stenosis Aortic stenosis Coarctation of aorta

Corrective operations for most of the above conditions are open procedures on cardiopulmonary bypass. The two exceptions are persistent ductus arteriosus and coarctation of the aorta. All conditions may be isolated lesions or they may be combined with other defects. Each lesion will be considered separately in this text.

COARCTATION OF THE AORTA (Fig. 16/10)

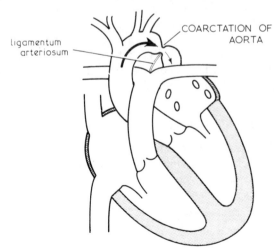

FIG. 16/10 Coarctation of the aorta

This is a constriction located at any site but most commonly just distal to the origin of the left subclavian artery; many tortuous collateral vessels develop chiefly over the scapular region. It may be due to contraction at the time of obliteration of the ductus arteriosus, or more possibly to embryonic malformation at the junction of the 3rd, 4th and 6th aortic arches.

Haemodynamics. Proximal hypertension: the blood pressure in the head and arms is elevated and increases on exercise. There is distal hypotension and reduced femoral pulses. Blood flow to the lower half of the body is maintained through collateral vessels.

Symptoms. Patients may be asymptomatic or there may be headache, dizziness, tinnitus, epistaxis and palpitations due to increased blood pressure in the head and neck. Cold feet and possible claudication in the lower limbs are the result of decreased blood flow to the lower part of the body.

Incision. A left postero-lateral thoracotomy through the 4th intercostal space.

Closed procedure. The coarctation is dissected and the ligamentum arteriosum or persisent ductus is ligated and divided. Due to the presence of large collaterals, care is required to prevent haemorrhage. The aorta is opened longitudinally over the constriction and a Dacron onlay patch anastomosed to its margin.

Pre- and postoperative physiotherapy. Routine post-thoracotomy regime (see p. 379). The incision may extend very high posteriorly and special attention must be paid to posture and arm movements. Physiotherapy must not be vigorous and tipping avoided. The blood pressure must not rise excessively, as it will put undue strain on the anastomosis site. Discharge is during the 2nd or 3rd week. Vigorous exercise should be avoided for a few months.

PULMONARY STENOSIS

This is a congenital defect of fusion of the valve commissures, possibly in association with infundibular stenosis. It is probably due to failure of complete rotation of the left dorsal ridge during separation of the aorta and pulmonary artery.

Haemodynamics. The pulmonary circulation is decreased and the work of the right ventricle increased. This may result in right ventricular hypertrophy and diminished cardiac output, which is the main problem in severe cases.

Symptoms. Exertional dyspnoea, fatigue and possibly systemic venous congestion; hypoxaemia and cardiac failure in infants.

Incision. A median sternotomy.

Open procedure. The valve is exposed via the anterior aspect of the pulmonary artery and the commissures are cut. If the annulus is constricted it is cut through vertically and a Dacron or pericardial gusset inserted. It may be necessary to replace the valve.

Infundibular resection. The right ventricle is entered and the obstructing infundibular muscle and fibrosis are resected or the infundibulum is incised and a Dacron or pericardial gusset inserted.

Pre- and postoperative physiotherapy. Routine bypass scheme with discharge after 10 days (see p. 423).

AORTIC STENOSIS

Left ventricular outflow obstruction may be caused at three levels: (a) valvular, (b) subvalvular or (c) supravalvular. The majority of patients with valvular stenosis do not develop symptoms until the valve becomes calcified around the age of 40 to 50.

Haemodynamics. The narrowed valve orifice subjects the left ventricle to a pressure overload. As a result, left ventricular hypertrophy develops.

Symptoms. Mild – asymptomatic; severe – fatigue, syncope, effort dyspnoea and angina.

Incision. A median sternotomy.

Open procedures

Valvular stenosis. Valvotomy is performed by entering the ascending aorta and incising the commissures.

Subvalvular stenosis. If the obstruction is due to a fibrous diaphragm arising from the ventricular septum, it may be approached through a low aortic incision and a through-valvular excision will be undertaken. When muscular sub-aortic stenosis is present, it may be corrected by selective myomectomy through an aortic or left ventricular incision.

Supravalvular stenosis. This is relieved by suturing an elliptical Dacron gusset into a vertical incision through the constricted portion of the aorta.

Pre- and postoperative physiotherapy. Routine bypass scheme with discharge after 10 days (see p. 423).

PERSISTENT DUCTUS ARTERIOSUS(Fig. 16/11)

The ductus arteriosus, which connects the left pulmonary artery to the descending thoracic aorta just beyond the origin of the left subclavian artery, should have contracted, closed and fibrosed into the ligamentum arteriosum in a few days from birth. Occasionally it persists and blood will flow from the aorta into the pulmonary system.

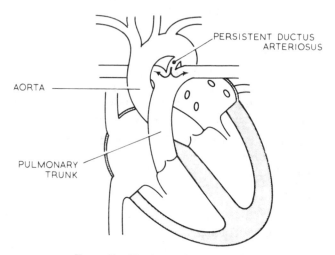

PERSISTENT DUCTUS ARTERIOSUS

AORTA

PULMONARY TRUNK

FIG. 16/11 Persistent ductus arteriosus

Haemodynamics. As a result of recycling of the shunted blood, the left side of the heart eventually becomes overloaded.

Symptoms. Asymptomatic or exertional dyspnoea. There is risk of subacute bacterial endocarditis and pulmonary hypertension.

Incision. A left postero-lateral thoracotomy through the 4th intercostal space.

Closed procedure. Ligation of ductus arteriosus.

Pre- and postoperative physiotherapy. Routine thoracotomy scheme with discharge at about the 11th day.

ATRIAL SEPTAL DEFECT (see Fig. 16/8)

Ostium secundum. This is a defect in the middle area of the septum. It is due to failure of fusion of the septum secundum to the septum primum to obliterate the foramen ovale. This is the most common and simplest to correct.

Ostium primum. The defect occurs low down in the septum and is sometimes associated with malformed mitral and tricuspid valves. It is due to defective formation of the interatrial septum as it fuses to the endocardial cushions. The operation is more complicated, because of the proximity of valves, coronary sinus, and the atrioventricular node.

Sinus venosus. This is a defect occurring high in the septum near to the orifice of the superior vena cava.

Haemodynamics. There is a left to right shunt and if the defect is large it may function as a common atrium.

Symptoms. Secundum lesions may be asymptomatic or show mild exertional dyspnoea as the blood flows from the left to the right atrium, thus overloading the pulmonary system. Primum defects may produce extreme dyspnoea due to left ventricular failure if the mitral valve is involved.

Incision. A median sternotomy or an anterior right thoracotomy, through the 4th intercostal space.

Open procedure. The heart is entered through the right atrium.

The secundum type is closed by direct suture. The primum type is repaired by insertion of a Dacron patch. If the mitral valve is involved it will be repaired first. Great care is taken to avoid damage to the atrioventricular bundle, which runs near to the operation site.

The sinus venosus type is associated with anomalous drainage of the pulmonary veins from the right upper lobe into the right atrium. The defect is repaired with a Dacron patch which redirects the venous drainage into the left atrium.

Pre- and postoperative physiotherapy. Routine bypass scheme with discharge after 10 days (see p. 423).

VENTRICULAR SEPTAL DEFECT (Fig. 16/12)

This is perhaps the most common form of congenital heart disorder and involves the muscular or membranous portions of the septum.

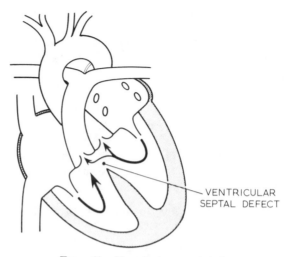

FIG. 16/12 Ventricular septal defect

The defect may occur independently or be associated with other lesions.

Haemodynamics. The size of the shunt depends upon the size of the defect and the ratio between the resistance to flow into the aorta and pulmonary artery. In small defects the pulmonary blood flow may be only 1.5 × systemic flow. In larger defects the ratio increases until eventually pulmonary hypertension develops and the flow across the defect begins to fall. In extreme pulmonary hypertension the flow will reverse as the right ventricular (RV) pressure is now greater than the left ventricular (LV) pressure. Both ventricles are subjected to a volume overload.

Symptoms. Patients with small defects may be asymptomatic. Large defects may cause exertional dyspnoea and right ventricular failure with systemic venous congestion.

Relief may be temporary in infants or complete after the age of three or four years.

Temporary operation

Relief is obtained by pulmonary artery banding (Muller and Damman, 1952).

Incision. A median sternotomy or left thoracotomy through the 4th intercostal space.

Closed procedure. The pulmonary artery is identified and its lumen restricted by a Teflon band. If the ductus arteriosus is persistent it is ligated.

Repair of the defect

Incision. Median sternotomy.

Open procedure. The heart is entered through the right ventricle, or the right atrium. If the defect is small it can be repaired by primary suture. Larger defects are repaired with a Dacron patch.

Pre- and postoperative physiotherapy. Routine bypass scheme with discharge between 11 and 21 days (see p. 423)

TETRALOGY OF FALLOT (Fig. 16/13)

This is perhaps the most common form of congenital heart disease with cyanosis. There is (1) a high ventricular septal defect, (2) a pulmonary stenosis, which may be valvular, infundibular or a combination of the two, (3) an anomalous position of the aorta and (4) hypertrophy of the right ventricle.

The anomaly results in a right to left interventricular shunt due to the right outflow tract obstruction and high right ventricular

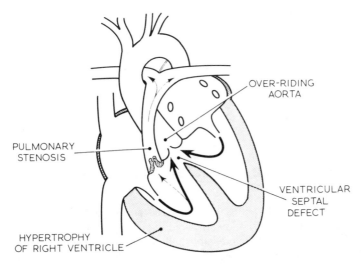

PULMONARY STENOSIS

OVER-RIDING AORTA

VENTRICULAR SEPTAL DEFECT

HYPERTROPHY OF RIGHT VENTRICLE

Fig. 16/13 Tetralogy of Fallot

pressure. There is systemic cyanosis and risk of syncope. The child is usually undersized, has clubbing of fingers and toes, exertional dyspnoea and a spontaneous desire to squat. There is an acyanotic group of patients with the same anatomical abnormalities, but without severe pulmonary stenosis and therefore minor shunting.

The condition is probably due to the misalignment of the spiral ridges in the embryonic heart. This would account for the dextraposed aorta, small pulmonary trunk and abnormal valves and ventricular septal defect. The secondary hypertrophied right ventricle is due to outflow obstruction.

Correction may be palliative in the early years. Total correction is preferred before school age.

Anastomotic palliative treatment

Blalock's anastomosis. Anastomosis of the pulmonary artery to the left subclavian artery (Blalock, 1945).

Incision. A left postero-lateral thoracotomy through the 4th intercostal space.

Waterston's anastomosis. Anastomosis of the ascending aorta and the right pulmonary artery (Waterston, 1962).

Incision. A right antero-lateral thoracotomy through the 4th intercostal space.

Palliative or first stage correction by closed pulmonary valvotomy

An expanding dilator (Brock, 1948) or valvulotome is introduced into the outflow tract of the right ventricle and the pulmonary valve is dilated.

Total correction

Incision. This depends on previous palliative surgery. A median sternotomy or submammary incision will be used following a Waterston or Blalock procedure, and if there has been no previous intervention.

Open procedure. Existing anastomoses are closed prior to the intracardial total correction to avoid 'flooding' of the lungs when cardiopulmonary bypass is established. The right ventricle is opened and a pulmonary valvotomy and/or infundibular resection carried out. The ventricular septal defect is repaired either by primary suture or by the insertion of a Dacron patch. The position of the Dacron patch will correct the position of the over-riding aorta.

Pre- and postoperative physiotherapy. Routine bypass scheme (see p. 423). After correction there may be considerable alveolar oedema. It may be necessary to prolong artificial ventilation with the use of PEEP (see p. 224), and to wean the patient off the ventilator with the use of CPAP (see p. 304). Breathing exercises with emphasis on inspiration are particularly important. Fine shakings and percussion seem to be helpful in the resolution of the peripheral lung involvement. Discharge is between 2 and 3 weeks.

COMPLETE TRANSPOSITION OF THE GREAT VESSELS (Fig. 16/14)

The aorta arises from the right ventricle, the pulmonary artery arises from the left ventricle. The two circulations, pulmonary and systemic, instead of being in series are in parallel. Thus venous blood circulates round the body while oxygenated blood circulates round the lungs. For the child to survive there must be a communication between the two circulations. Possible communications are persistent ductus arteriosus, atrial septal defect or ventricular septal defect.

Symptoms. There may be cyanosis, syncope and dyspnoea.

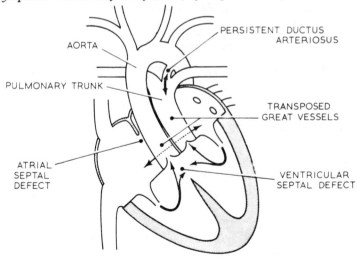

FIG. 16/14 Transposition of the great vessels

Palliative operations

Incision: A right lateral thoracotomy through the 5th intercostal space.

(a) The atrial septum is excised (Blalock and Hanlon, 1950), or ruptured (Rashkind and Miller, 1966), to create an atrial shunt.

(b) The pulmonary artery may be banded to protect the pulmonary system from overloading, if there is a large ventricular septal defect (Sterne et al, 1965).

Corrective operations

Physiological. All inflow and outflow tracts may be retained but the venous return is redirected by excising the existing atrial septum and creating an artificial atrial septum fashioned from the pericardium. The pulmonary venous return in the left atrium is directed towards the tricuspid valve and right ventricle. The systemic venous return in the right atrium is entrained to the mitral valve and the left ventricle. Ventricular septal defects and anastomosis will be corrected (Mustard, 1964). An alternative method to achieve a similar result is to use a portion of the right atrial wall instead of pericardium (Senning procedure) (Senning, 1959).

Anatomical. The pulmonary artery and aorta are switched round so that oxygenated blood now enters the systemic circulation. The coronary arteries are re-implanted (Jatene, 1976).

Pre- and postoperative physiotherapy. Routine bypass scheme (see p. 423). Discharge is between 2 and 3 weeks.

The following conditions are improved by reconstructive or palliative surgery:

PULMONARY ATRESIA

The pulmonary valve or trunk is malformed or deficient. The pulmonary blood flow is maintained by other communications, e.g. atrial and ventricular septal defects and a persistent ductus arteriosus.

TRUNCUS ARTERIOSUS COMMUNIS (Fig. 16/15)

A common pulmonary systemic trunk arises from the ventricles. There will be a ventricular septal defect and the trunk may or may not have two valves.

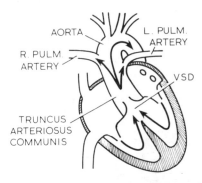

FIG. 16/15 Truncus arteriosus communis

TRICUSPID ATRESIA

The tricuspid valve is deficient and the right ventricle may be malformed. The pulmonary flow is maintained through atrial and ventricular septal defects and a persistent ductus arteriosus.

SINGLE VENTRICLE

This is a chamber which receives blood either from a common AV valve or from both AV valves. Both arterial trunks arise from this single chamber. Frequently there is an appendage to the chamber which is rudimentary and is called an outlet chamber. It is now possible in some patients to insert an artificial septum made of Dacron or pericardium and thus separate the pulmonary and systemic circulations.

Total correction of some cases of pulmonary atresia, tricuspid atresia, truncus arteriosus, and single ventricle can be achieved by the use of a valved conduit. This is a Dacron tube with a homograft or heterograft valve sewn into it. Depending on the site of obstruction the conduit is anastomosed between the right atrium or right ventricle and the pulmonary artery.

ANOMALOUS PULMONARY VENOUS DRAINAGE
(Fig. 16/16)

All or some of the pulmonary veins may drain into the superior vena cava, the coronary sinus or directly into the right atrium. Sometimes the veins join behind the left atrium and are channelled into the brachiocephalic vein. Rarely drainage is into the inferior vena cava.

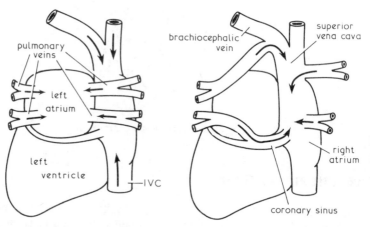

FIG. 16/16 Pulmonary venous drainage to show (a) the normal and (b) some of the possible anomalies

Physiotherapy

CLOSED HEART SURGERY

Following a closed procedure such as mitral valvotomy, the patient will return directly to the ward. The regime is similar to that for a thoracotomy (see p. 375). The lung secretions will probably be less, but general progress may be a little slower.

OPEN HEART SURGERY

This section describes the pre- and postoperative regimes for patients undergoing surgery for coronary artery grafting, valve repair, valve replacement, ventricular aneurysmectomy, repair of ascending aortic aneurysm, surgical intervention for ventricular tachycardia and other adult corrective surgery.

Pre-operative

During this time the physiotherapist should get to know the patient and his relatives thereby achieving a good rapport and understanding with them; this makes the postoperative period much easier.

The pre-operative assessment will follow that outlined in Chapter 13. In addition it will include testing the mobility of the hips, knees and ankles.

The patient should have explained to him, in words that he can understand, simple details of the operation and about his stay in the intensive therapy unit (ITU). If the 'pipes and drains' are explained carefully, the patient will be far less frightened and will be able to co-operate more effectively after the operation. The following attachments should be mentioned very briefly, as they will affect his physiotherapy:

Endotracheal tube: This is probably the tube which most affects the patient; he should know the reason for ventilation and particularly he should be told that he will not be able to speak while intubated.
Central lines
Nasogastric tube
ECG leads
Drains
Peripheral lines
Urinary catheter
Rectal temperature probe
Peripheral temperature probe.

Most patients are a little bewildered by all the information but are grateful to have it explained. ITUs vary but a brief description of the particular unit is useful and whether there is a facility for the spouse to stay overnight. The ITU nurse and the anaesthetist may visit the patient, so enabling further questions to be asked and answered.

The general routine for the first postoperative week should be explained, according to the individual surgeon's preferences. This is also a good time to introduce other patients on the ward – by indicating their progress this will help to allay more fears.

Objectives

The objectives of pre-operative physiotherapy will be that:

1. Full joint range and adequate circulation are maintained by teaching active or active/assisted exercise of arms, legs and trunk.
2. Correct posture is maintained by teaching postural awareness and correct sitting position; after a mid-line incision there is a tendency to stoop and to drop the chin.
3. Breathing exercises are practised to improve ventilation and, if necessary, to clear secretions prior to surgery.
4. General mobility is encouraged by showing the patient how best to move around in bed. A rope tied to the foot of the bed is a helpful aid (see Fig. 15/8, p. 376).
5. The patient will learn to cough effectively both when supporting himself and when assisted by the physiotherapist (Fig. 16/17).
6. Excess secretions will be removed by practising huffing and coughing techniques.

As coughing will be an important part of the postoperative therapy each patient is taught how to support the chest by holding both hands across the sternum. Instruction should be given in the judicious use of a pillow to support the chest wall as it is particularly

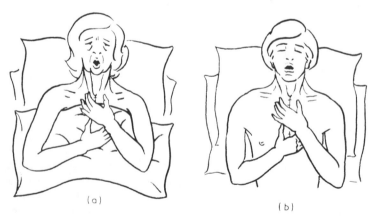

(a)

(b)

FIG. 16/17 Cough holds for a median sternotomy: (a) with a pillow; (b) with both hands and no pillow

effective after cardiac surgery. It improves coughing effectiveness by increasing confidence and decreasing pain (Fig. 16/17).

The physiotherapist will best support the sternal incision by placing both hands on the anterior aspect of the chest and maintaining equal pressure to minimise sternal movement.

As in some thoracic units, patients are encouraged to exercise together in a class. Many enjoy the fellowship and interest of these sessions, both before and after their operations.

The patient will have been asked to absorb much information and will often ask questions. Time should be taken to answer these, as well as those of relatives, who will probably see the patient fully ventilated (see Chapter 11).

Postoperative

Generally, the first treatment will take place in the ITU; as indicated previously the following points and charts should be noted or looked at:

Type of operation
Incision, including any leg wounds if vein grafts have been taken
Temperature, both central and peripheral
Blood pressure and arterial trace
Pulse rate
ECG (see Chapter 6)
Respiration: (a) artificial (see Chapter 11); (b) spontaneous, e.g. rate, depth
Colour – is there cyanosis, anaemia?
Blood gases including pH, inspired oxygen %
Packed cell volume and haemoglobin
Electrolytes
Fluid chart: if oral fluid is allowed sips of water may be given to help moisten the mouth and this will aid expectoration
Drug chart: analgesia will be required before treatment, as will bronchodilators if bronchospasm is present
Chest radiograph
Drainage tubes: there are usually two – pericardial and anterior mediastinal; occasionally there is a pleural drain. A check should be made as to how much drainage there is and whether they are on suction.

The position of other lines should also be noted. These could include any or all of the following: central lines, nasogastric tube, left atrial line, arterial line, pulmonary arterial line, ECG leads, pacemaker wires, endotracheal tube, urinary catheter, intra-aortic balloon pump and electrodes, temperature probes.

Postoperative problem list

The problems that may arise after surgery can be listed under the following headings:

1. Pain.
2. Decreased air entry.
3. Retained secretions.
4. Reduced arm and leg movements
5. Decreased mobility.

There may be other problems such as bronchospasm, peripheral neuropathy, haematoma, wound infection or delayed healing; these should be listed as appropriate together with any treatment required or change of management.

Postoperative treatment plan

1. Ensure that the patient has adequate analgesia.
2. Unilateral and bilateral deep breathing exercises including inspiratory holds and sniffs in half lying, lying or alternate side lying as necessary. IPPB may be given if necessary (see p. 273).
3. Unilateral posterior basal shakings, huffing and coughing with sternal support. Percussion after 48 hours if sputum is very tenacious.
4. Unilateral active/assisted arm and leg exercises; active ankle exercises.
5. Increase mobility and progress to stair climbing and exercise class.

Postoperative regime

This will vary from patient to patient and from surgeon to surgeon. Some will request physiotherapy as soon as the patient is co-operative and others will ask that the patient is not rolled for 24 hours. The regime which is described is the one which the authors use. Readers should also refer to Chapter 11, pages 289–90.

No treatment is given on the day of operation.

DAY I

The *first treatment* is given in the ITU. Analgesia should be arranged and any relevant information gained by observing the charts and the radiograph. If the patient's condition is stable with a good blood pressure, acceptable ECG and pulse rate, a normal potassium and steady drainage from the pericardial and anterior mediastinal drains, then the treatment plan can be followed.

Arm and leg exercises are given in half lying. If vein grafts have been taken from a leg it will be bandaged, but care must be taken to obtain good movement. The physiotherapist should assess for any possible neurological damage while carrying out the exercises, as there can be peripheral nerve damage. The possibility of cerebral damage also exists.

The chest should be auscultated before changing position and starting chest therapy. The patient should be placed in a lying position. The movement can be made more comfortable if he holds himself across the chest and flexes his hips and knees to relieve some strain from his abdominal muscles. Breathing exercises are then practised according to the plan (2) and (3). Suitable rest periods must be given.

If the patient is returning to the ward shortly after physiotherapy, he can be rolled to allow the stretcher canvas to be inserted. He should then be sat up and given a drink of water if allowed, as this will aid expectoration. Encouragement in huffing and coughing with adequate sternal support should be given as necessary.

Oxygen therapy should be continuous throughout the treatment session with the mask being removed *only* for expectoration (personal communication, see page 430). The effectiveness of the chest treatment should then be assessed by auscultation.

The *second treatment* will usually be given on the ward. Analgesia should be given and the charts checked. On the ward the nurses will record the apex beat and the radial pulse to ensure that the patient remains in sinus rhythm. If there is an apex/radial deficit, the patient has atrial fibrillation and may not tolerate a lot of treatment. If everything is stable then the treatment plan can be followed.

The patient should be positioned in side lying with the help of the bed rope, to practise his breathing exercises. The procedure is repeated on his other side and then, with the help of a nurse (if necessary) the physiotherapist should help the patient back to a sitting position against pillows.

Most patients will need a *third treatment* and it is usually sufficient to treat them according to the plan, but in sitting.

DAY 2

Prior to the *first treatment* any necessary analgesia should be organised, and the charts and chest radiograph checked. The patient will probably be sitting out in a chair and unless there are severe chest problems, treatment can be carried out in the chair. Oxygen therapy will probably have been discontinued by this stage.

At the *second treatment* the patient will probably have his first walk with the nurses and be weighed. Most patients gain up to 1kg after the operation, but it should be lost over the next one or two days. (This increase in weight is due to the raised circulating volume achieved in the ITU to maintain a good cardiac output.) If the weight gain is more than 1kg then the patient may feel short of breath, have swollen ankles and late inspiratory crackles may be heard on auscultation.

The patient is treated in alternate side lying as before.

DAY 3

If all observations remain stable, walking can be increased. If vein grafts have been taken from a leg, a well applied bandage or firm stocking should be worn until good healing has occurred. The chest is treated according to the findings on auscultation and the chest radiograph.

DAY 4

If the patient can walk about 100 yards with no shortness of breath, then stair climbing can begin. It is advisable to climb only 1 flight at first to ensure that there are no adverse effects.

DAY 5

Stair climbing and walking should be increased and the patient advised to continue exercising on his own. Trunk exercises can be included at this stage and he can join the ward exercise class (if there is one).

DAY 7

The patient will probably go home with advice to continue his walking and exercises. A list of home exercises which includes neck, shoulder girdle, arm and trunk movements together with reminders concerning the breathing exercises and coughing is useful. The walking should be increased gradually each day until 1–2 miles a day is achieved by the time he attends for his 6 weeks' post-discharge appointment.

The patient will be advised that he should not drive for 6 weeks, and that sexual relations should be avoided for 4 weeks after leaving hospital. Generally, he will be able to resume light or part-time work after 2 months and heavy work after 3 months.

PHYSIOTHERAPY FOR THE PATIENT ON AN INTRA-AORTIC BALLOON PUMP

If the patient's condition is stable, physiotherapy may be carried out. Special care must be taken with the following points:

Electrodes: The whole mechanism of the balloon pump is triggered by the electrodes connected to it. Any interference such as shaking over, or close to, the electrodes, will trigger the machine and severely disturb the synchronisation.

Catheter: The balloon catheter enters at the femoral artery. Severe damage can be done if the hip is hyperextended or flexed more than 50°.

REFERENCES

Blalock, A. and Hanlon, C. R. (1950). The surgical treatment of complete transposition of the aorta and the pulmonary artery. *Surgery, Gynaecology and Obstetrics*, **90**, 1.

Blalock, A. and Taussig, H. B. (1945). The surgical treatment of malformations of the heart in which there is pulmonary stenosis or pulmonary atresia. *Journal of the American Medical Association*, **128**, 189.

Brock, R. C. (1948). Pulmonary valvulotomy for the relief of congenital stenosis. Report of three cases. *British Medical Journal*, **1**, 1121.

Jatene, A. D., Fontes, V. F., Paulista, P. P. et al (1976). Anatomic correction of transposition of the great vessels. *Journal of Thoracic and Cardiovascular Surgery*, **72**, 364.

Muller, W. H. and Damman, J. F. (1952). The treatment of certain congenital malformations of the heart by the creation of pulmonic stenosis to reduce pulmonary hypertension and excessive pulmonary flow. A preliminary report. *Surgery, Gynaecology and Obstetrics*, **95**, 213.

Mustard, W. T. (1964). Successful two-stage correction of transposition of the great vessels. *Surgery*, **55**, 469.

Rashkind, W. and Miller, W. W. (1966). Creation of atrial septal defect without thoracotomy. A palliative approach to complete transposition of the great arteries. *Journal of the American Medical Association*, **196**, 991.

Senning, A. (1959). Surgical correction of transposition of the great vessels. *Surgery*, **45**, 966.

Sterne, L. P., Ferlie, R. M. and Lilleheic, W. (1965). Cardiovascular surgery in infancy. Ten years results from the University of Minnesota Hospitals. *American Thoracic Surgery*, **1**, 519.

Waterston, D. J. (1962). Treatment of Fallot's tetralogy in children under one year of age. *Rozhledy v Chirurgii*, **41**, 181.

Personal communication mentioned on pages 251 and 427 refers to recent work which has not yet been published. It relates to the following paper, and further information may be obtained by direct application to Miss D. M. Innocenti MCSP.

Adams, A. P., Broadbent, M., Innocenti, D. M. and Thompson, M. (1984). Arterial oxygen saturation during chest physiotherapy.

BIBLIOGRAPHY

Anderson, R. H. and Shinebourne, E. A. (eds.) (1978). *Paediatric Cardiology*, vol. 1. Churchill Livingstone, Edinburgh.

Braimbridge, M. V. (1981). *Postoperative Cardiac Intensive Care*, 3rd edition. Blackwell Scientific Publications Limited, Oxford.

Emery, E. R. J., Yates, A. K. and Moorhead, P. J. (1984). *Principles of Intensive Care*. Hodder and Stoughton, London.

Fleming, J. S. and Braimbridge, M. V. (1985). *Lecture Notes on Cardiology*, 3rd edition. Blackwell Scientific Publications Limited, Oxford.

Gibbon, J. H. (jr.), Sabiston, D. C. (jr.) and Spencer, F. C. (eds.) (1983). *Surgery of the Chest*, 4th edition. W. B. Saunders Eastbourne.

Lefrak, E. A. and Starr, A. (1979). *Cardiac Valve Prosthesis*. Appleton-Century-Crofts, New York.

Munro, J. L. and Shaw, G. (1982). *Surgery of Acquired Heart Disease*. Wolfe Medical and Scientific Publications Limited, London.

Chapter 17

On Being a Coronary Bypass Patient

by ROBIN DOWNIE

Even the most robust and optimistic of us must occasionally anticipate ill-health, whether the annual few days of influenza or more serious afflictions. In my own case my gloomier anticipations were mainly of cancer, mining unseen, but never of heart disease. For one thing, I am slightly underweight and have been for years, and I have never been a smoker. Again, while I do not take vigorous exercise every week I am fortunately able to walk to and from my work. Both my parents lived till they were over 80 and I have aunts still alive at 90. Against this background the first onset of chest pains did not seem particularly worrying. I was walking along the street in a leisurely way when they occurred, and I attributed them to indigestion or a virus infection. They recurred over a period of about 10 days, with no particular pattern, except that I usually had them when I got up in the morning. What finally decided me to call my GP was a bout of pain in the middle of the night. This was really quite severe, and moved down my arms as well as across the whole area of my chest. For the first time I found the pain a bit frightening.

The GP was everything that was helpful and sympathetic, pointing out that it was about 15 years since I had last called on him. The whole consultation took about 5 minutes, the time required to refer me to a hospital for an ECG. I had an appointment quite soon, and did not need to wait very long at the hospital for my turn. After the ECG test I had to wait a further 20 minutes until I was handed a sealed envelope with the results to take back to my doctor.

The envelope presented the first of my psychological problems. It was undoubtedly about me, but undoubtedly addressed to someone else – my GP – and sealed. After much soul-searching I opened it, feeling in a contradictory way that I had a right to know what was being said about me, but that I had no right to open someone else's letter. I resented being put in this position. The general point coming out of this is that while the idea of informing patients about their problems is widely accepted, the detailed application of the principle is harder to bring about. For example, during a later visit to the hospital after my operation I was waiting to be seen by the consultant. To while away the time, I took my chest radiograph out of its envelope and tried to understand it. While I was doing this I was glared at by one senior nurse, and mildly rebuked by another, who told me that I wouldn't under-stand it, that it would alarm me, and that it belonged to the doctor. There was no sign that my GP or the consultant minded in the slightest, or even noticed, that I had looked at the ECG and the later radiograph, but the clerical staff and some of the nursing staff clearly felt that what I had done was contrary to good order and discipline. It was all a little like being back at school.

Anyway, the ECG report, apart from the graph which I did not expect to understand, contained the comment 'marginal evidence of hypertrophy of left ventricle'. My GP was frank, pointing out that the ECG gave no clear indications and that we could either do nothing for a bit, or, if I preferred, I could request further examination. It so happened that I was at a quiet period in my work, so I chose to have further investigation in the hospital.

The hospital investigations were of two kinds – functional ones and a structural one. The functional ones were of the treadmill and bicycle types. I really did work at these, with the irrational aim of trying to show that there was nothing much wrong with me. And I must say that I did not experience any pain, and did not feel myself to be more than normally out of breath. I was therefore a bit disappointed to be told that there was evidence of a problem and that I had to have a structural investigation called an angiogram in the afternoon. A local anaesthetic was administered in the groin and a thin tube inserted to enable a dye to be poured into my coronary arteries. I was given the opportunity of observing this myself on a screen, and although most people to whom I have related this episode regard it as gruesome I found it most interesting and did not experience any pain or even discomfort. When the dye was inserted I felt a strange sensation of warmth spreading all over my body. Although this was not painful it would have been alarming if I had not been warned about it. And this is the moral I continually had to draw: when I was warned or informed about what to expect most things were easier to put up with.

This investigation was of course an invasive one, involving an insertion into an artery, and I already knew that I would need to spend the night in the hospital. I was therefore prepared for that. But I wasn't prepared for what happened after an hour or so. I was visited by the cardiologist and another physician who had both examined me previously. They drew the curtains round my bed and said they wanted to chat about their findings. The tests indicated a serious problem in a coronary artery, and they strongly urged me to stay in, for there was a prospect of a coronary artery bypass operation the following week. This was difficult for me to accept. In the case of many bypass patients the need for the operation is more clearly perceived, as there has been a history of discomfort and pain. In my case, however, I had had pain for only a few weeks, and wild thoughts kept going through my head that it was all unnecessary, or that medical treatment would do just as well as surgical. Gently but firmly the possibilities were outlined – yes, there could be medical treatment, but it would not be nearly so effective as the operation. The operation had excellent prospects of success ... I was finally able to decide without too much agony to accept the possibility of an operation whenever there was a gap, possibly around the middle of the following week.

The weekend was a period of psychological adjustment for myself and family. As far as I was concerned the problem was that of coming to terms with the fact that I had something seriously wrong with me, and that I was going to be out of commission for a bit. To begin with I kept worrying about various things I had to do in my work and who would now do them. Gradually, over a few days, those worries began to fade and the life of the hospital began to dominate. Indeed, I began to have some understanding of what I had heard about but had never believed – that many people actually enjoy their time in hospital. I was fortunate in being in a medium-sized ward with about 10 patients who were very congenial. Most of them were there for the same or related reasons, and I found that *their* views and advice made more impression on me than that of the doctors and nurses. The atmosphere in the ward was very cheerful, and this may reflect the fact that coronary bypass operations and heart surgery generally represent a successful side to medicine. The vast majority of the patients were in the ward for only a short period – about 10 days – and they were clearly getting better. The nursing and medical staff shared in this atmosphere and altogether it was a hopeful place to be, if one had to be in hospital.

I was told on the Monday that there had been an unexpected gap and that my operation was to be on Tuesday morning. Thereafter things happened fast – blood tests, further radiographic examination, and a visit from the physiotherapist. The physiotherapist took some time over explaining to me the importance of proper breathing and coughing, and I was given some practice in these. One important side to this was the psychological one – I felt that I was being given the chance to help in my own recovery, and that there were things that I could do. Indeed, as I shall later stress, this side of my treatment was the weakest. In our efforts to avoid any suggestion that there is moral blame attached to illness we perhaps underplay the individual's responsibility for taking certain steps to assist his own health.

During the day I had visits from the surgeon and the anaesthetist, who were both very helpful in explaining what would happen and gave me every opportunity to ask questions. On reflection this seems to me to be the important side to the doctrine of informed consent. There has been much recent debate about consent, and the problem seems to be that the greater the legal involvement the less satisfactory the psychological side. Legally, what is important is presumably to get the patient to sign a document on which is stated what is to be done. For example, the doctrine of informed consent is part of the law in the United States and I have heard US lawyers say to doctors 'Don't explain anything, just get them to sign it!' But I believe that what most patients want when they talk of 'consent' is not legal involvement but rather that medical, nursing and paramedical staff should take time and trouble to explain what is happening and to get the patients involved in their own care. The legal consent form I signed was quite undetailed and was brought to me on the eve of the operation by a doctor I had never seen before or saw after, but on the other hand I did find that a lot of trouble was taken by everyone to explain what was going on.

The evening before the operation was more relaxed than I could have imagined. The nursing staff did not fuss me and I was allowed to read until late and finished a novel before turning in. I was able to shave and shower in the morning and can still remember these events, but thereafter everything is quite blurred. I have vague impressions of being wheeled out of the ward, but I cannot be sure. I have also the vaguest memories of stirring in the intensive care ward after the operation and of a nurse speaking to me and easing me over to one side, but what was dream and what was reality is hazy.

The physiotherapist visited me soon after I was back in the ward to resume the breathing exercises. These were no problem, but I did have problems over coughing and spitting. Never having smoked and having good lungs I had great difficulty in spitting, unlike most of the other patients, who seemed to be smokers and who suffered dreadfully as a result – to cough after one's sternum has been split is a very painful business.

I recovered very quickly and was allowed home about a week after my operation. My own reactions to myself were not what I expected. In the first place, I did not particularly want to meet people. I was given a leaflet telling me to take exercise every day, and I was able to do this, but I had a great dread of encountering neighbours. I am told that prisoners leaving prison have the same sort of reaction, but it is less clear why I should have felt like that after such a short and successful stay in hospital. A second and connected point was that I found my perceptions of myself and my body began to alter. As I said to begin with, I have always been healthy, but I now came to think of my physical integrity as having been violated in some way, and that my body was flawed. Some months later this feeling is still with me. It is irrational for I do not know of any physical activity which I cannot now perform. For a month or two after the operation my psychological vulnerability was increased by the wearing of white elastic stockings to help bring down the swelling in my leg and ankle caused by the removal of the vein for the bypass. I am still very conscious of the beating of my heart after exertion, or before going to sleep, and do not know how much of this is just a sharpened perception of what I had always noticed a little and how much it is an awareness of some actual change in my physical condition. I have been assured by my cardiologist that everything is normal, but I am not fully convinced. No doubt with the passage of time I shall stop noticing these things so much.

My treatment by doctors, nurses and paramedical staff was everything that was excellent insofar as I was what can be called an 'acute' patient. *But* not enough attention was devoted to the question of how I came to have the problem or of how my lifestyle should be changed. A month or two after the operation the cardiologist suggested that my cholesterol level was on the high side of normal, and set me as an objective the reduction of it. I have responded in a positive way to this, because it has involved me personally in my own health care. But more could have been done in this direction. For example, the physiotherapist who suggested breathing exercises before the operation did not give me any programme of exercises to carry out when I was home again. It was as if he saw himself as entirely ancillary to the acute medicine specialty, when perhaps a physiotherapist has a function independently, as part of community medicine or preventive medicine.

In conclusion, I should like to say that I was all the time conscious of the advantages of living near a large teaching hospital. Had I lived in a village or small town then I do not doubt that there would have been many more delays in my treatment. The distribution of health care is not one of the respects in which the justice of the welfare state is shown to best advantage. But wherever there is health care I am convinced from my own experience of two things: that the more the patient is told about and involved in his own treatment the less frightened he will be, and the more positively he will respond; and that the more the medical team and its patients (or all of us) see ill-health and its treatment as part of the total life of the individual and the community (as distinct from acute episodes) the healthier we shall all become.

Chapter 18

Cardiac Transplantation

by A. PERCIVAL MCSP

In 1967 the first successful heart transplant was achieved in South Africa (Barnard, 1968), although research had been taking place during the previous years in America as well as South Africa. The first patient survived for 18 days; the second operation was performed in January 1968, also in South Africa, and the patient lived for 18 months. Between then and the middle of 1969, 135 further cardiac transplants were carried out in 60 centres throughout the world. Unfortunately, due to the immense problems of infection and rejection, the survival record did not improve as fast as had been hoped. The programme therefore suffered a lack of confidence, and only five centres continued with their clinical research programmes; Dr Shumway of Stanford performed the greatest number of operations using the orthotopic technique (heart of recipient replaced by heart of donor).

In 1974, Barnard and his associates in South Africa started to concentrate on the heterotopic technique (heart of donor placed to the right of recipient's heart in 'piggy-back' fashion) (Wolpowitz et al, 1978). Since then the life expectancy of survival following heart transplantation has steadily improved, and graft survival rates have become comparable with those achieved in cadaveric kidney transplantation.

Clinical heart transplantation re-started in Britain in 1979 at Papworth Hospital (English et al, 1980), and in January 1980 at Harefield Hospital. It is interesting however to note that the longest surviving heart transplant recipient is a Frenchman who underwent his operation in 1968.

THE RECIPIENT

The main indication for heart transplantation is end-stage heart disease which is totally incapacitating and may be secondary to widespread coronary disease or to idiopathic or rheumatic cardio-myopathy (Russell and Cosimi, 1979). These conditions cannot be remedied by any further conventional medical or surgical treatment. Patients with incorrectable congenital abnormalities may also benefit.

In order to undertake transplantation it is essential that the recipient be assessed before acceptance into the transplant prog-ramme. In addition to this assessment other criteria must be taken into account:

1. There is no upper or lower age limit when considering a patient for heart transplantation even those aged over 60 years.
2. The patient should have no active infection (nor recent pulmon-ary infarction, although this is not an absolute contra-indication).
3. The patient should have a strong motivation to survive, be psychologically stable, and, if possible, be from a supportive background.
4. A raised pulmonary vascular resistance is an absolute contra-indication for an orthotopic heart transplant, although in this situation a heterotopic transplant, or heart/lung transplant, would be appropriate.
5. With the advent of cyclosporin A, insulin dependent diabetes mellitus is no longer a contra-indication but such patients should be free from other complications of diabetes.

THE DONOR

Any potential donor must have suffered irreversible brain damage – this is due usually to an intracranial haemorrhage or may be the direct result of a road traffic accident. The diagnosis of brain death is made by doctors who are independent of the transplant team.

Other points to be considered include:

1. Any donor over 35 years of age must undergo coronary angiography to preclude any possibility of undetected coronary disease (De Bakey, 1969).
2. Compatability of size of the heart may be a consideration between recipient and donor, but smaller hearts may be used for heterotopic transplantations in adults.
3. ABO blood group compatibility is essential.
4. Cross-matching of donor lymphocytes and recipient serum is necessary only in patients with cytotoxic antibodies (detected at assessment).

5. Tissue typing is performed on all recipients and donors but a match is not essential.
6. There must be no history of heart disease, systemic infection, or malignancy other than a primary cerebral tumour. The donor should not have been on long-term medication which could adversely affect the performance of the heart.

TRANSPORTATION OF THE DONOR HEART

Quick and easy transportation is essential for a successful operation. The donor heart is plunged into ice-cold Hartmann's solution to cool it from the outside. The aorta is clamped and a Medicut is inserted into the aorta and connected to a litre of Hartmann's containing 1 ampoule of Cardioplegia Infusion (St Thomas's Hospital Formula). This is infused into the aortic root causing the heart to stop suddenly. The heart is then examined.

The donor heart is transported in Hartmann's solution, packed in three sterile bags, and put into a cool box filled with ice. Rapid transportation to the recipient hospital then takes place in order to keep the total ischaemic time as short as possible.

TECHNIQUES FOR CARDIAC TRANSPLANTATION

Orthotopic technique (Fig. 18/1)

The patient is placed on to cardiopulmonary bypass. Cardectomy of the recipient heart is carried out by division of the atria at their mid-level plane and of the great vessels immediately above the semilunar valves. This leaves the walls of the recipient's right and left atria and intra-atrial septum in situ, and they are anastomosed to the correspondingly prepared structures of the donor heart. The sinuatrial node in the recipient's right atrium is retained and care is taken to preserve the integrity of the donor's sinuatrial node.

Heterotopic technique ('piggy-back') (Fig. 18/2)

The recipient's heart is left in situ and the donor heart is placed to the right of it, within the right pleural cavity. The superior and inferior venae cavae of the donor heart are ligated, and the pulmonary artery is anastomosed to that of the recipient heart. An end-to-side anastomosis is performed between the aorta of the donor and the aorta of the recipient, and the donor left and right atria are

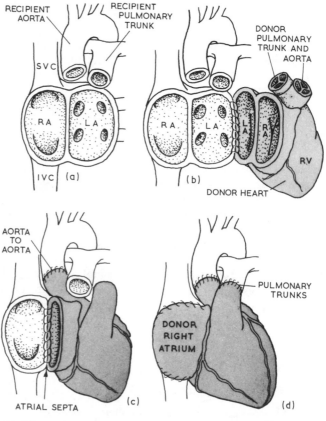

FIG. 18/1 The orthotopic technique for heart transplant: (a) large cuffs of atria are left after most of the recipient's heart is removed; (b) the left atria are joined; (c) the two aortas and atrial septa are joined; (d) the right atria and pulmonary trunks are joined

anastomosed to the respective atria of the recipient. Haemodynamically the heterograft assists the failing left ventricle of the recipient.

IMMEDIATE POSTOPERATIVE CARE

This differs little from that received routinely by cardiac surgical patients except for the use of immunosuppressive drugs and reverse barrier nursing techniques. Due to the failing heart and circulatory deficiencies the desperately ill patient undergoing transplantation is prone to pulmonary infections and the use of immunosuppressive

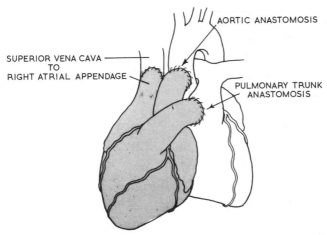

AORTIC ANASTOMOSIS

SUPERIOR VENA CAVA
TO
RIGHT ATRIAL APPENDAGE

PULMONARY TRUNK
ANASTOMOSIS

FIG. 18/2 The heterotopic (piggy back) technique for heart transplant

drugs increases the high risk of postoperative infection. It is mandatory therefore to provide an atmosphere as free as possible from bacteria. Nursing is considered in three stages and the length of time each patient spends at each stage depends on the individual's postoperative progress.

In some patients mechanical respiratory assistance is required for several days but most patients are extubated less than 12 hours after the operation. Orthotopic patients will have the usual pericardial and mediastinal drains but a heterotopic transplant patient will have a right pleural drain also. These patients may also have undergone repair of their own heart at the same time, for example an aneurysmectomy or bypass grafts, in which case the long saphenous vein will have been removed from one or both legs to provide the grafts. Most of the other peri-operative attachments are much the same as for any cardiac surgery except that all heart transplant patients have pacing wires in situ on return from the theatre. Orthotopic patients have three wires (two atrial, and one ventricular) and heterotopic patients have six wires (two atrial wires and a ventricular wire for the donor heart, and the same for the recipient's own heart). These pacing wires are connected to a pacemaker which works on demand.

First stage barrier nursing

The patient is returned from the operating theatre into an isolation room which is self-contained, individually ventilated, and has temperature controlled filtered air at a positive pressure. Before entering the cubicle the staff must, in the airlock, put on a plastic apron, cap, mask, and sterile gown and overshoes as they pass through the sliding doors into the room. Hands must be washed prior to donning sterile gloves, and then the patient may be approached. This stage may last only 24 hours.

Second stage barrier nursing

Only a plastic apron, mask and overshoes are required with washing of hands prior to treating the patient.

Third stage barrier nursing

No barrier nursing techniques are required and by this time the patient is usually in an ordinary single hospital room.

PHYSIOTHERAPY

Pre-operative physiotherapy

When the patient attends the hospital for assessment for cardiac transplant surgery he will be seen by a multidisciplinary team including the physiotherapist. Her role is:

1. To gain the patient's confidence and to explain the reasons for the course of postoperative physiotherapy.
2. To teach correct breathing control and effective coughing in order to improve and maintain efficient ventilation and to clear the lung fields if necessary.
3. To reinforce the general peri-operative routine, with regard to infusions and drains, given by the nursing staff.

Many patients may be assessed at other hospitals or in other countries, so it is difficult for the unit physiotherapist to see every patient before operation. Once accepted on to the list for transplant surgery, an explanatory pre-operative booklet is sent to each patient. This does help the patient to become familiar with the likely pre- and postoperative routine, but does not replace the direct contact between patient and therapist. Additionally, some patients are admitted at night for the operation and in such cases pre-operative physiotherapy will not be possible.

Postoperative physiotherapy

Individual programmes are designed depending on the patient's age, pre-operative condition and postoperative progress, but the aims of treatment are consistent throughout:

1. To clear and maintain the lung fields in order to prevent pulmonary infection.
2. To prevent circulatory complications.
3. To encourage and improve exercise tolerance, range of movement, and muscle power.
4. To achieve early independence and a return to normal life.

DAY OF OPERATION

If the period of ventilation of the patient is to be continued then treatment will be given as and when requested, similar to other ventilated patients; but in general the patient only requires to be ventilated for less than 12 hours after surgery. Physiotherapy treatment commences within an hour of extubation of the patient.

1. Breathing exercises, especially diaphragmatic and unilateral basal, are encouraged. The latter are important in all patients but particularly for the right side of 'heterotopic' patients as the new heart may cause some compression of the right base (Fig 18/3).
2. The patient will be encouraged to cough, the physiotherapist supporting in the mid-axillary line (as all drains are still in situ). The patient can support himself around the lower chest.
3. Active leg exercises: (a) plantar and dorsiflexion of feet; (b) knee flexion and extension; and (c) isometric quadriceps exercises.

Due to the pre-operative condition of most patients it is unlikely that they will have been able to manage more than a small amount of exercise or mobility. Early mobilisation, therefore, is of the utmost importance. On the first treatment only three of each exercise may be possible. Assistance may be necessary at first.

The number of treatments on the operation day is dependent upon the condition of the patient. Routine evening treatments are not required but emergency physiotherapy should be available.

FIRST POSTOPERATIVE DAY

The mediastinal and pericardial drains are removed during the first day, and breathing and leg exercises continue as before with an increase in the latter to five or eight times depending on the individual patient. The patient will be treated two or three times during the day.

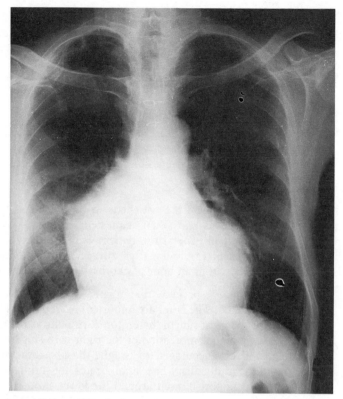

FIG. 18/3 Radiograph showing heterotopic transplant

Under normal circumstances breathing exercises are continued twice a day, but may be modified if the patient is producing sputum, or the blood gas measurements, radiographic appearances or lung expansion are unsatisfactory. Leg exercises continue to be increased according to the patient's exercise tolerance until he is allowed out of bed.

SECOND POSTOPERATIVE DAY

If most of the infusion lines, drains, and other attachments have been removed the patient is allowed out of bed to sit in a chair for short periods.

1. Breathing exercises may be given either in the bed or in a chair.
2. The use of a 'pedal machine' (Fig. 18/4) is started for 1 or 2 minutes to stimulate the patient's circulation and encourage

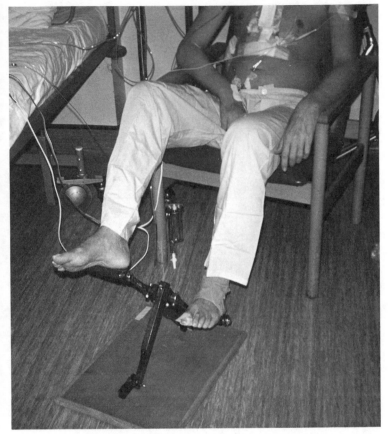

FIG. 18/4 A 'pedal machine' in use

gentle mobility. This machine can be used a number of times during the day and the time will be increased as the patient is able.

3. If the patient is unable to stand from a chair without using his hands on the sides, the first short-term goal is to encourage this activity. Knee flexion in a standing position and heel raises encourage general leg muscle movement. These three exercises (stand-ups, knee-bends and heel-raises) plus the breathing and leg exercises are recorded on an exercise progression chart which is filled in during the patient's stay in hospital (Fig. 18/5).

Note: The denervated human heart is able to provide a normal cardiac output at rest and yet respond appropriately to exercise by

NAME: Mr. X.   OP. DATE: 9/10. 11. 85   O /AT
HA

EXERCYCLE

1985

DATE	BR. EXS.	LEG EXS.	STAND UPS	KNEE BENDS	HEEL RAISES	PEDALS	WARM UP	TIME	RESIS.	SPEED r.p.m.	COOL DOWN	WALK	STAIRS
								WORKLOAD					
10.11	✓	×5											
11.11	✓	×8											
	✓	×10											
12.11	✓		×2	×3	×3	2'							
	✓		×3	×4	×4	3'							
13.11	✓		×4	×5	×5	4'						✓	
	✓		×4	×6	×6	4'						✓	
14.11	✓		×5	×7	×7		—	2	0	35	—	✓	
	✓		×5	×8	×8		—	2	0	35	—	✓	
15.11	✓		×6	×9	×9		—	3	0	35	—	✓	
	✓						—	3	0	35	—	✓	
16.11	✓		×7	×10	×10		—	4	0	35	—	✓	
17.11	✓		×8	×11	×11		2 @35	1	5	50	2 @35	✓	
18.11	✓		×9	×12	×12		2	2	5	50	2	✓	✓
19.11			×10	×14	×14		2	3	5	50	2	✓	✓

FIG. 18/5 An exercise progression chart for transplant patients

increasing its output. In contrast to the normal heart the extra cardiac output results primarily from an increase in stroke volume, the elevated heart rate having a relatively minor role (De Bakey, 1969). The pulse rate of a heart transplant patient is *not*, therefore, a reliable measure to gauge the effect of exercise in the early stages. A gentle steady routine is therefore required with constant consideration of the patient's overall condition. When treating a heterotopic patient it must be remembered that the patient has two hearts to be exercised. It is important that the 'old' one is not overtaxed, yet, at the same time, ensuring that the 'new' one is being stimulated sufficiently.

If the patient is feeling unwell this may be a sign of rejection and physiotherapy treatment will be adapted accordingly.

PROGRESSION FROM THE THIRD DAY

As soon as all attachments are removed the patient starts to walk within the room. Once all heart support (dopamine) is discontinued the exercycle programme commences in place of the 'pedal machine'. Breathing and general exercises continue.

EXERCYCLE PROGRAMME (Fig. 18/5)

At first no resistance is used and the patient builds up to 4 minutes at 15kph or 35 revs per minute (rpm) depending on the exercycle used. This constitutes the 'warm-up' and 'cool-down'. A work load is then introduced at 20kph or 50rpm. The first treatment with a work load would be:

> warm-up 2 minutes at 15kph
> work load 1 minute at 20kph
> cool-down 2 minutes at 15kph

The warm-up and cool-down are kept constant but as the patient becomes stronger the work-load time is increased or resistance may be added, the aim being to encourage both the endurance and strength without overtaxing the patient.

When barrier nursing is no longer required the patient may walk, wearing a mask while in the hospital corridor or attending departments such as x-ray or cardiology. At about five days postoperatively the patient will be able to go for short walks in the grounds accompanied at first by a member of staff and a relative. He is encouraged to negotiate stairs as soon as his physical condition allows, and should be able to climb a flight of about 17 stairs with ease by the time of discharge.

Note: If the patient is having an infusion of HATG or RATG (see p. 452) he will only have breathing exercises if indicated, as exercises at this time tend to increase muscle pains which are one of the side-effects of these drugs.

A chart showing the rate of perceived exertion (RPE) is introduced to the patient at about seven days postoperatively so that the patient is able to gauge at what level he is to work at his exercise programme (Fig. 18/6). After any walk, set of exercises, or exercycle session, the patient should feel that the exercise has been fairly light, that is between 11 and 12. The numerical scale used allows for easy transfer to the Toronto Rehabilitation Research Project where this scale (8–20) is also used.

8

9   VERY LIGHT

10

11   FAIRLY LIGHT

12

13   SOMEWHAT HARD

14

15   HARD

16

17   VERY HARD

18

19   VERY VERY HARD

20

FIG. 18/6 A rate of perceived exertion (RPE) chart

Relatives should be involved at all times and should be made aware of how important it is for the patient to reach successive short-term goals. This not only stimulates the patient but also increases the confidence of both patient and relative by the time comes for discharge and a return to their normal environment, away from the constant attention of the hospital staff.

In order to continue the exercise programme and walking routine, home advice will be given.

At about 10 days postoperatively, if the patient shows no signs of rejection, is coping well and lives locally, he will be discharged home. If he lives a long distance away from the unit at which the author works, he is moved to one of the half-way flats in the village for two or three weeks.

HEART-LUNG TRANSPLANTATION

More recently, it has become evident that some patients require heart and lung transplants, and the first successful cardiopulmonary transplant was performed by Reitz and Shumway at Stanford University Medical Centre in 1981 (Reitz, 1982).

Indications for this procedure are:

1. Primary pulmonary hypertension.
2. Secondary pulmonary hypertension due to heart disease, embolic disease, multiple pulmonary emboli, or high altitude.
3. Absent connections between heart and lung.
4. Primary lung disease.

The recipient may have varied reasons for both the heart and lungs to be transplanted together. Other reasons include:

1. In single lung transplantation there is an imbalance between ventilation and perfusion.
2. The procedure is easier technically.
3. Tracheal anastomosis heals better than bronchial anastomosis.
4. The coronary-bronchial to trachea blood supply is left intact. (Blood supply to the trachea is better than that to the bronchi and collateral vessels between the coronaries and bronchioles become well developed in time.)

For the procedure the donor must have:

1. Irreversible brain damage with medical and legal brain death.
2. ABO compatibility.
3. Negative lymphatic cross-match.
4. Comparable thoracic volumes.
5. Clear chest radiograph.
6. Acceptable blood gases.
7. Acceptable lung compliances.
8. Absence of gross pulmonary infection.

Where possible the transplant team will assess the donor before acceptance, and the potential donor and recipient's radiographs are superimposed to ascertain the compatibility of thoracic volumes.

Present methods of transportation of the donor are:

1. The donor may be taken to the recipient's hospital, so that the removal and re-implantation procedures can take place in adjoining theatres.
2. If the organs only are to be removed the donor body is cooled to 10°C by connection to a portable heart-lung machine to minimise damage to the delicate lung tissues. The heart and lungs are then removed and transported, floating in the donor's blood (2–300ml), in layers of sterile plastic coverings in a cool box packed with ice to the recipient's hospital.

Treatment of the donor

If the *donor* has been moved to the recipient hospital he will be attached to a ventilator and may require treatment prior to the operation to ensure that the lungs are in the best possible condition for transplantation. On a request from the medical staff, treatment will be undertaken including, if necessary, postural drainage, percussion, and vibrations to the specific areas of the chest to be cleared. Bag-squeezing may also be requested.

Pre-operative treatment of the recipient

The same aims are followed as for a heart transplant patient but, again, few may be seen prior to surgery.

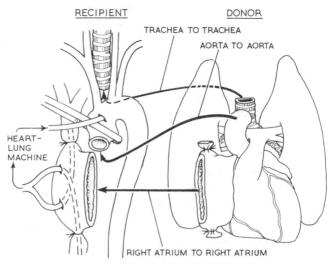

FIG. 18/7 Heart-lung transplant

Operative technique (Fig. 18/7)

The recipient's heart is removed, leaving a cuff of right atrium and ascending thoracic aorta just distal to the semilunar valve for anastomosing to the respective parts of the donor heart. A cuff of left pulmonary artery is left in place to preserve the integrity of the left recurrent laryngeal nerve. Both lungs are then dissected, dividing the pulmonary ligament and the hila except the bronchi. The trachea is exposed and divided just above the carina, and the lungs removed. Implantation of the donor organs starts with the tracheal anastomosis followed by union of the two aortas and then the right atrial anastomosis.

The most critical part of the operation hinges on the removal of the recipient's heart and lungs without injury to the surrounding nerves (vagus, recurrent laryngeal and phrenic) and bronchial arteries.

Postoperative treatment

All heart and lung transplant patients have right and left pleural drains in addition to the other attachments required for heart transplant surgery, including two atrial and one ventricular pacing wires attached to a pacemaker on demand. A longer time is spent in stage one barrier nursing conditions and some patients may require a longer time on a ventilator.

Generally the first few days follow the same pattern as for heart transplants but with greater emphasis on the general condition of the lungs. Most of these patients have been ill for a considerable length of time, some since birth, and their progression will be according to their individual capabilities.

POSTURAL DRAINAGE

This is started early, at about four days, because of the denervation below the tracheal anastomosis which causes lack of sensitivity to the presence of secretions in the base of the lungs. Even if the pleural drains are in situ the patient will be turned from side to side, at first in high side lying, progressing to side lying, and finally to the tipped position. All heart/lung transplants in the author's unit are encouraged to posturally drain themselves once a day on discharge, as well as while in the ward, in order that any secretions which may be formed can be mobilised to above the desensitised area. For the younger children who are unable to co-operate with breathing exercises, gentle percussion and vibrations in the required postural drainage position are carried out from the beginning. Parents are shown how to continue this treatment at home.

Progression of all exercises including use of the pedal machine and exercycle continues as for a heart transplant patient.

The average length of stay inside the hospital is approximately three weeks, and the only difference in home advice is the continuation of the postural drainage routine.

ROUTINE DRUG REGIME FOR HEART TRANSPLANT PATIENTS

All patients require immunosuppressive drugs so that the graft is not rejected (Yacoub et al, 1985).

Azathioprine (Imuran) is a drug widely used for all transplant patients. It is taken daily according to blood results and the heart transplant officer's prescription.

Cyclosporin A is a fungal metabolite and is also a potent immuno-suppressant (Oyer et al, 1983). The patient takes it twice a day according to blood results.

Antithymocyte globulin (HATG; RATG) (H=horse; R=rabbit). Either drug is given only if there are signs of rejection. They are usually given in an infusion over 4–6 hours in a course of 3–5 days depending on the degree of rejection. Panadol (to reduce pain) and piriton (to control any allergic response) are given 1 hour prior to the intravenous ATG and during the infusion if necessary.

Prednisone may be given to certain patients for anti-rejection purposes.

Dipyridamole (Persantin) is an anti-platelet drug which is taken for life.

Nu-Seals Aspirin is given every third day for life. This particular brand is used because it is enteric coated, slow release, thus reducing gastric irritation.

Acyclovir is an anti-viral drug which is active against herpes simplex and varicella/zoster viruses. It is given four times a day for three months.

Nystatin is an anti-fungal drug which is given 4-hourly for one month.

Multivite, vitamin C and *Ferrograd C* are all given daily for one month.

TRANSVENOUS ENDOMYOCARDIAL BIOPSY

Serial biopsies of the graft have been found to be a very valuable investigation. It enables the physician to make an objective diagnosis of rejection in patients who have no clinical signs or symptoms and to see how the immunosuppressive drugs are controlling the heart and the rejection process. In order to perform the biopsy a catheter sheath is introduced into the right internal jugular vein and a bioptome is then passed through the sheath into the vein and advanced into the right atrium. Under radiographic control the biopsy forceps are guided to the apex of the right ventricle where the biopsy specimen is obtained from the myocardium. After removal of the first specimen from the forceps the bioptome is reintroduced and a second specimen obtained.

Routine for endomyocardial biopsies

1. During the first postoperative month after a heart transplant operation, biopsy is performed once a week, and then once a fortnight in the second month. Between 3 and 6 months a biopsy is required once a month, and then at 2-monthly intervals until the end of the first year. After a year a biopsy is performed as needed.
2. After a heart/lung transplantation patients only require a biopsy every 3 months unless otherwise indicated (the chest radiograph is a better indicator of the possibility of rejection) for the first year and thereafter every 6 months.

MONITORING OF PATIENTS AFTER CARDIAC TRANSPLANTATION

1. *From discharge up to 3 months after surgery*
   (a) The patients are reviewed twice a week for a full blood count and a 12-lead ECG (looking for rhythm disturbance, atrial arrhythmias, and total voltages).
   (b) If the patient is on cyclosporin A liver function tests are obtained once a week and the cyclosporin level in the blood is measured.

(c) For a heart transplant patient a chest radiograph will be taken once every 2 weeks, or more often if the patient develops a fever. For the heart/lung transplant patient, a chest radiograph is performed once a week.

2. *From 4 months postoperatively up to a year.*
Full blood count, serum urea and creatinine, cyclosporin levels and an ECG are taken once a week. Liver function tests and a chest radiograph once a fortnight.

3. *One year after surgery and onwards.*
Full blood count, blood chemistry, cyclosporin levels and an ECG are taken once a week; liver function tests once a fortnight. A chest radiograph is taken once a month for heart transplant patients, but every 2 weeks for heart/lung patients until 18 months is reached when they will be reduced to once a month. Respiratory function tests and echocardiography are required once a month for the first year and thereafter 3-monthly for heart/lung transplant patients.

LONG-TERM REHABILITATION

Current research indicates that long-term rehabilitation is beneficial, and a Canadian research team from the Toronto rehabilitation centre, in association with Mr Yacoub, has been carrying out a research programme into the effects of long-term rehabilitation. Patients are put on to the programme 3 months postoperatively after full assessment of their cardiorespiratory state; this will include physical examination and static multi-stage exercise testing on a bicycle ergometer to measure oxygen consumption and aerobic threshold. An exercise prescription is then made up of a walking programme of 5 sessions a week carried out over a specific distance in a stated time. Exercycle and swimming programmes are also given when required. Consequent upon results of the research programme a long-term rehabilitation project will continue based on exercycle, walking and jog routines.

Many patients have shown the benefit of long-term rehabilitation and a team attends the British transplant games every year participating in many sports including track events, basket ball, badminton, tennis and swimming. Two patients have also completed marathons.

All everyday activities, hobbies, and social events are encouraged as it is important that the additional time gained by the operation is used meaningfully by the patient. Most patients who were previously employed return to work within 6 months, and the younger ones return to school or college.

At first it may be very difficult for the patient and family to adjust and that is why active involvement from the patient's partner and family is encouraged from a very early stage. Almost all recipients have an intense sense of personal accomplishment and an awareness of another chance to enjoy their lives.

PSYCHOLOGICAL/EMOTIONAL ASPECTS

It is important that the physiotherapist understands the feelings of patients who are admitted for transplantation, and those of their relatives. Some patients may have heard details from others who have undergone major heart surgery, such as coronary bypass operations, but no doubt any descriptions will be over-dramatised. As well as the natural fear of surgery, patients for a transplant will have been told that the operation is a 'last hope' procedure. While this will add to their apprehension, it may also give them a greater incentive to fight, for the desire to live can be a potent force. This may account for the occasional aggressive attitude which some patients may show at the start of treatment.

Sufficient time should be allowed for getting to know the patient and his family and friends; during this period, thorough explanations of all procedures should be given. While most of this will be done by the medical and nursing team, the physiotherapist is in a good position to reinforce these explanations and be certain that the patient does understand. Simple language should be used, avoiding medical or pseudo-medical jargon.

While the patient and his family are delighted and 'relieved' that something is being done, they are likely to be concerned that any restoration of health is now dependent on another's death; there is also the fear at the back of the mind that a suitable donor will not be available in time.

Postoperatively, questions may arise about the donor heart, and patients may be anxious to know the age and sex; these are matters which should be discussed with the doctors.

Following the operation, the patient's moods often change; confidence is gained as survival becomes cautiously evident, allowing a new lease of life. With such a background, the patient becomes eager to work toward the goal of returning home to a normal life at the earliest opportunity. The physiotherapist can capitalise on this eagerness, while at the same time tempering over-eagerness with sensibility. While some patients are excited as they appear to improve each day, others will need time and care to be weaned off oxygen, continuous treatment, or dependency on relatives or staff.

Relatives may remain over-protective; because of this, participation by the relatives *at all stages* is essential. With the patient, they must learn a new pattern of life and the physiotherapist will need to discuss and explain these factors with them, together. Care must be taken not to rush the relatives, for habits learned during the months or years of critical illness and deterioration of activity will need to be adjusted. Some relatives may feel that the physiotherapist is driving the patient too quickly, and they cannot understand the patient's keenness to improve. Major surgery has been undertaken and this change seems too sudden. Discussion and counselling with, or by, the members of the team must be available at all times for both the patient and his family.

With the patient's improvement, the changing role within the family means that the husband may return to work and the wife will have time on her hands. All these matters need to be considered and the physiotherapist, social worker, nursing staff and chaplain (where applicable) should liaise closely.

When the patient is discharged, communication is essential and he should be given a telephone number that he can ring, at any time, if problems arise.

Moral and ethical problems can, and do, arise, and the physiotherapist, as indeed all members of the team, should take time to consider the implication of such medical advances. Discussion groups, counselling facilities or the availability of sympathetic 'listeners' should be available for all professionals. As with the care given to the dying patient, the yardstick of the physiotherapist's role is the improvement of the quality of life for the individual patient. Undoubtedly, she is able to help provide this following heart transplantation.

Heart/lung transplantation

There may be occasions when the physiotherapist is asked to treat the *donor* as well as the *recipient*. In such cases, a *different* physiotherapist should treat *each* person. The *donor* is likely to be being maintained on a ventilator and the therapist may feel unhappy about the procedure. Careful counselling and advice from the hospital chaplain, or some other experienced person, should be available.

This situation is less likely to arise in the future as a portable heart/lung machine is now available.

REFERENCES

Barnard, C. N. (1968). Human cardiac transplantation. *American Journal of Cardiology*, **22**, 584–6.

De Bakey, M. E. (1969). Human cardiac transplantation – clinical experience. *Journal of Thoracic and Cardiovascular Surgery*, **58**, 303–17.

English, T. A. H., Cooper, D. K. C. and Cory-Pearce, R. (1980). Recent experience with heart transplantation. *British Medical Journal*, **281**, 699–702.

Oyer, P. E., Stinson, E. B., Jamieson, S. W. et al (1983). Cyclosporin in cardiac transplantation: a 2½ year follow-up. *Transplantation Proceedings*, **15**, 4 Suppl. 1, 2546–52.

Reitz, B. A. (1982). Heart and lung transplantation. *Heart Transplantation*, **1**, 1, 80–1.

Russell, P. S. and Cosimi, A. B. (1979). Transplantation. *New England Journal of Medicine*, **301**, 9, 470–9.

Wolpowitz, A., Losman, J. G., Curcio, C. A. et al (1978). Human heterotopic cardiac transplantation: current status. *South African Journal of Surgery*, **16**, 2, 99–102.

Yacoub, M., Alivizatos, P., Khaghani, A. and Mitchell, A. (1985). The use of cyclosporin, azathioprine and antithymocyte globulin with or without low dose steroids for immunosuppression of cardiac transplant patients. *Transplantation Proceedings*, **12**, 1, 221–2.

BIBLIOGRAPHY

Buxton, M., Acheson, R., Caine, N. et al (1985). *Costs and Benefits of the Heart Transplant Programmes at Harefield and Papworth Hospitals*, DHSS Research Report No. 12. HMSO, London.

Mai, F. M., McKenzie, F. N. and Kostuk, W. J. (1986). Psychiatric aspects of heart transplantation: pre-operative evaluation and postoperative sequelae. *British Medical Journal*, **292**, 311–13.

ACKNOWLEDGEMENTS

The author thanks her many colleagues at Harefield Hospital who have helped in the preparation of this chapter. In particular: Mr M. Yacoub FRCS, consultant cardiac surgeon; Mr P. Mankad FRCS, senior registrar in cardiac surgery; and Miss P. M. Walker MCSP and Miss S. Boardman MCSP, physiotherapists.

Chapter 19

Clinical Aspects of Medical Chest Disease
1. Asthma: Chronic Airways Obstruction: Occupational Lung Diseases

by J. V. COLLINS MD, FRCP

BRONCHIAL ASTHMA

Bronchial asthma is a common disease marked by breathlessness and wheezing caused by generalised narrowing of intrapulmonary airways which varies in severity spontaneously or as a result of treatment. Symptoms may be episodic or chronic but the pattern may vary considerably from time to time in individual patients. The changes causing airways obstruction in asthma include hypertrophy and hyperplasia of bronchial smooth muscle, thickening of the epithelial basement membrane of the airways, oedema and eosinophilic infiltration of the bronchial wall and hypertrophy of the bronchial mucous glands with increase in the number of goblet cells. This leads to narrowing of larger bronchi and plugging of bronchi and bronchioles with viscid mucus which contains eosinophils and shed respiratory epithelial cells. The lungs of patients dying from asthma show overinflation with widespread mucus plugs in airways of all sizes.

Aetiology

The pathological changes characteristic of asthma may result from a number of different pathogenic mechanisms. Hitherto, patients have been subdivided into polar groups labelled extrinsic and intrinsic but this is an over-simplification, for patients of either group may be susceptible to the same aggravating factors and will usually respond to similar treatments.

EXTRINSIC ASTHMA

This generally begins earlier in life and is associated with atopy – the presence of immediate hypersensitivity to external allergens associated with positive skin-prick tests. These patients show a high incidence of seasonal rhinitis and flexural eczema. There is usually a strong family history of asthma, hay fever or eczema. In patients with extrinsic asthma episodes may be precipitated by exposure to antigenic materials including pollens, house dust, animal furs and feathers. Foodstuffs including milk, eggs, fish and chocolate may, very occasionally, be incriminated. Patients with extrinsic asthma may also react adversely to non-allergic provoking factors including air temperature changes, emotional disturbance, exercise, laughter and respiratory tract infection.

INTRINSIC ASTHMA

This tends to occur later in life and recognisable allergic features are usually absent so that skin tests to common allergens are negative. This later onset type of asthma is commoner in women than men. Non-specific precipitating factors leading to acute exacerbations or generalised worsening of symptoms for asthma of both types include bronchial irritation by strenuous exercise, exposure to cold air, dust, tobacco smoke, fumes, emotional stress and respiratory infections.

Clinical types

Episodic asthma. Typically, episodic asthma may occur at any time and is usually of sudden onset preceded by a feeling of tightness in the chest with breathlessness and wheezing. Expiration becomes difficult with short gasping inspiration, and the wheezes are usually expiratory and often audible without the aid of a stethoscope. A troublesome cough is common with scanty viscid mucus. In severe episodes there will be tachycardia, pulsus paradoxus and central cyanosis. Such acute episodes may last as little as 30 to 60 minutes although the patient is usually left with cough productive of viscid mucus and persisting breathlessness for 24 hours or so. Prolonged severe episodes of asthma and status asthmaticus will be described later.

Chronic asthma. Here paroxysms of symptoms are usually less conspicuous and there is persistent wheezing with breathlessness. Cough may be a prominent feature with mucoid sputum and recurrent episodes of frank respiratory infection are common.

Childhood asthma. Wheeziness is common in infancy with minor respiratory infections but it may also be present in acute bronchiolitis. Non-asthmatic wheeziness usually resolves as the child grows.

The earlier the onset of wheezing in childhood and the longer it persists, the more likely is the child to continue with typical asthma after the age of 10 years. Childhood asthma is commoner in boys than girls and usually accompanies atopy. Allergic factors commonly precipitate acute episodes but exercise, respiratory infections and emotional factors are also frequent causes of exacerbations.

Adult asthma. Asthma may persist into adult life from childhood and about 90 per cent of males with asthma have their first episode before the age of 35 years but onset after this age occurs in about 25 per cent of women with asthma. Adult asthma is episodic with a background of good health where intermittent acute episodes are precipitated by respiratory infection, vigorous exercise or sudden exposure to irritants including smog, cigarette smoke, and pollens. More commonly, chronic asthma with persistent wheezing and breathlessness without good remission may occur and here there may be superimposed episodes of more severe airways obstruction provoked by precipitating factors.

Status asthmaticus. This term which has been superseded by *severe acute asthma* refers to episodes of severe wheezing and breathlessness lasting more than 24 hours not responding to normal medication and potentially life threatening. Such patients may have central cyanosis and be too breathless to walk about or speak. In very severe episodes restlessness and disturbance of consciousness develop. Other important signs are a pulse rate greater than 100 per minute, pulsus paradoxus and very quiet breath sounds on auscultation.

Physical signs

During an episode of asthma the chest will be overinflated and hyper-resonant with loss of the cardiac and liver areas of dullness to percussion. The breath sounds are usually obscured by high pitched musical wheezes with prolonged expiration. When asthma is very severe, airflow in the trachea and main bronchi may be insufficient to produce breath sounds leading to a 'silent chest' – an ominous physical sign. Between paroxysms of asthma, especially in the episodic variety, there may be no abnormal physical sign although forced expiration may elicit wheezes on auscultation. In patients with asthma beginning early in life chest deformity is common with increase in the antero-posterior diameter and sometimes pigeon chest deformity.

Symptoms of exacerbation

The main complaint is of breathlessness with wheezing often accompanied by troublesome cough which may be paroxysmal and may aggravate the breathlessness. Sputum production is usually of small quantities of viscid mucoid sputum with plugs. In an acute episode exercise tolerance is limited and the patient may be chair or bed bound. Sleep is characteristically disturbed by acute paroxysms of cough, breathlessness and wheezing in the early hours of the morning. Episodes vary considerably in their duration lasting from a few hours to several days or longer.

Clinical signs

The patient usually sits upright or leans forward using accessory muscles of respiration to assist expiration which is unduly prolonged. The respiratory rate is usually increased. Wheezing may be audible at the bedside with prolonged expiration and overinflation of the chest.

Physiological changes in asthma

The characteristic features of airways obstruction may not be detectable between attacks but are often present in the absence of symptoms or abnormal signs. Simple measurements such as PEFR, FEV_1 and FVC will be impaired and the ratio of FEV_1 to FVC will be reduced. During acute episodes and in some instances during remission the total lung capacity and residual volume may be increased above the predicted levels without apparent distress. In the presence of airways obstruction there is usually alveolar overventilation leading to hypocapnia but during severe exacerbations carbon dioxide retention may occur when overventilation no longer compensates for the effects of the under ventilated alveoli. Hypercapnia is a grave sign.

Investigations

1. *Blood:* An absolute eosinophil count can be helpful. Counts above 0.5×10^9/litre in the absence of parasitic infestation supports a clinical diagnosis of asthma. Counts in excess of 1.0×10^9/litre are common with pulmonary eosinophilia with or without asthma.
2. *Sputum:* The presence of eosinophils is helpful in diagnosis and

Charcot-Leyden crystals and Curschman's spirals of inspissated mucus may also be present.

3. *Chest radiograph:* This is usually normal but a radiograph is always advisable especially in acute exacerbations to search for signs of overinflation, pneumothorax, pneumo-mediastinum, pulmonary infiltrates and signs of bronchial wall thickening.

4. *Pulmonary function tests:* Simple measurements of airways obstruction including PEFR, FEV_1 and FVC before and after inhalation of a bronchodilator aerosol are helpful. An increase of more than 20 per cent in PEFR or FEV_1 after a bronchodilator is suggestive of asthma but in severe episodes and with more persistent asthma there may be no such change. Between episodes in the asymptomatic patient there may be no detectable airways obstruction. More complex measurements of lung function including total lung capacity and gas transfer indices are only necessary in a minority of patients.

Tests for hypersensitivity

Skin-prick tests with common allergens are useful in identifying those patients who are atopic, but only in a minority of patients will this lead to important changes in therapeutic measures adopted. Inhalation challenge tests are occasionally indicated especially where occupational asthma is suspected. These must be done in hospital under carefully controlled conditions because of the dangers of severe delayed asthmatic reactions.

Treatment

Avoidance of allergens. In a few instances particular allergens may be identified as a cause of episodes of asthma, especially likely are grass pollens, the house dust mite, and *Aspergillus fumigatus*. Here obvious measures to reduce the concentration of house dust within the home, avoidance of pollens or moulds during the particular season may be helpful in the control of asthma.

Prophylactic treatment with sodium cromoglycate (Intal) may be useful particularly in children with extrinsic asthma. An initial trial of four weeks' duration with a standard dose of 1 capsule 4 times daily is necessary and in some instances it may also be effective in intrinsic asthma. Intal has proved very useful in the management of exercise-induced asthma. Many affected individuals can be successfully protected by inhalation of Intal 20 to 30 minutes before exercise.

Bronchodilator therapy. In general, wherever possible, this should be given by aerosol as the doses used are very much smaller than when tablets of the same drug are prescribed and there are many effective selective beta$_2$-adrenoceptor antagonists such as salbutamol, terbutaline, fenoterol and rimiterol. In episodic asthma where mild infrequent symptoms occur the bronchodilator aerosol should be used when symptoms occur. With more persistent asthma regular use of an aerosol is indicated. For exercise-induced asthma prior use of the aerosol before exercise will often control symptoms adequately. In chronic asthma it may sometimes be helpful to add an oral bronchodilator as tablets to the aerosol. With chronic asthma not responding to bronchodilator therapy alone addition of a corticosteroid aerosol such as beclomethasone dipropionate, betamethasone valerate or budesonide may be very helpful in controlling symptoms; the introduction of steroid aerosols has allowed considerable reduction and often withdrawal of systemic steroids in patients who previously were dependent upon these drugs.

In chronic asthma it may be necessary to resort to long-term medication with systemic steroids, and prednisolone is well tried and the preparation of choice. The dose chosen should be the lowest which will control the patient's symptoms. To minimise side-effects and adrenal suppression, if possible it should be below 7.5 to 10mg daily.

Management of the severe attack

When an acute attack of asthma becomes severe and life threatening the major danger is of hypoxia leading to cardiac dysrhythmias. Such patients should be admitted to hospital as quickly as possible. Treatment should start as soon as possible with oxygen, intravenous bronchodilators and large doses of corticosteroids by intravenous injection and by mouth. In hospital most patients respond to such treatment together with an aqueous aerosol of a sympathomimetic bronchodilator delivered by a nebuliser or with IPPB. Rarely is it necessary to proceed to tracheal intubation and mechanical ventilation or bronchial lavage.

Physiotherapy

See Chapter 21, page 507.

CHRONIC AIRWAYS OBSTRUCTION

The commonest respiratory disorder in the United Kingdom is chronic airways obstruction caused by chronic bronchitis and emphysema. These are two distinct pathological entities which frequently occur together in the same patient in varying proportions. It is often difficult to establish in life the relative contributions of each process to disability in an individual patient. Some patients appear to have predominantly bronchitis while a much smaller group show features suggesting that their problem is emphysema; most patients fit into a middle group with mixed defects.

Aetiology

Epidemiological studies have demonstrated a number of relevant factors in the aetiology of chronic bronchitis and emphysema although the initiating and propagating mechanism for the development of these diseases are still unclear. Disability usually only becomes apparent when the processes of destruction have been in progress for 20 years or more, so that patients present with symptoms in middle to old age. Smoking, especially of cigarettes, is a major causative factor and urban industrial air pollution and dusty occupations are also associated with increased incidence of these diseases. Lower respiratory tract infection, once thought to be a major causative factor, is now regarded as of lesser importance. Many patients, especially of the bronchitic type, are susceptible to recurrent infections which produce worsening of dyspnoea and cough with recognisable additional temporary impairment of pulmonary function. These episodes can be fatal, but, with recovery, measurable respiratory function usually recovers to previous levels and sequential records of lung function in these patients do not usually show sustained worsening following acute episodes. In many episodes of sudden deterioration with increased symptoms, features of infection may be unidentifiable. There remain some patients in whom none of these factors appear relevant and yet all the features of chronic airways obstruction develop. In some cases there may be a possible inherited predisposition to the disease. Certainly in a few patients who develop severe emphysema in the third and fourth decade there appears to be a genetically linked deficiency of alpha one (α_1)-antitrypsin in the serum. This is a protein produced by liver cells which inactivates proteolytic enzymes such as leucocyte collagenase and elastase. The normal serum level of serum α_1-antitrypsin is governed by a series of alternative genes known as the Pi protease inhibitor system. About 30 phenotypes have been distinguished by serum electrophoresis and labelled alphabetically by their electrophoretic mobility. Of the normal population about 90 per cent have the M.M. phenotype, and the M.S. or M.Z. phenotypes with slightly diminished α_1-antitrypsin levels account for the remainder. The phenotype Z.Z. occurs in about 1:2500 of the population and is associated with gross deficiency in α_1-antitrypsin. Affected individuals show a greatly increased liability to pulmonary emphysema of early onset usually affecting mainly the lower lobes of the lung. On present evidence, partial deficiency of α_1-antitrypsin associated with phenotypes M.S. or M.Z. does not seem to be associated with an increase in susceptibility in the development of chronic airways obstruction.

Chronic bronchitis

Various definitions of chronic bronchitis have been formulated. The useful one which has found wide acceptance is that of the Medical Research Council (MRC) (1965): 'Chronic bronchitis is a disease characterised by cough productive of sputum on most days for at least three consecutive months of each year for at least two successive years'. The sputum may be mucoid or mucopurulent and subdivisions of chronic bronchitis into simple mucopurulent and obstructive were previously popular. This definition assumes that other causes for sputum production including bronchiectasis and tuberculosis have been excluded. Chronic bronchitis has been used without qualification to indicate a wide range of disability from patients with regular production of small quantities of sputum with hardly any abnormality of lung function or impairment of health to those with severe airflow obstruction at the other extreme in whom little or no sputum is produced. More recently, studies have suggested that mucus hypersecretion of itself is a harmless condition which is not always accompanied by airways obstruction. Emphysema has been defined (CIBA Symposium, 1959) in pathological terms as 'a disease in which there is an increase beyond the normal size in the air spaces distal to the terminal bronchioles due to destruction of tissue and not simply overinflation'.

PATHOLOGY – CHRONIC BRONCHITIS

The main morphological feature in chronic bronchitis is hypertrophy of mucous gland tissue in the trachea, bronchi and bronchioles. There is considerable increase in the mucous gland content in the submucosa of the airways and a great increase in the number of goblet cells especially in the bronchioles. Associated with this mucous gland hypertrophy there is thickening of the mucous membrane and excessive mucus production together with some bronchial wall muscle hypertrophy. The end result of these changes is impairment of removal of inhaled particles and infection in mucus within the tracheo-bronchial tree leading to sputum retention and increase in airways obstruction. Culture of sputum from patients with chronic bronchitis usually yields a growth of *Haemophilus influenzae* or *Streptococcus pneumoniae*. The number of these organisms is often increased during acute exacerbations.

Emphysema

The presence of emphysema leads to airways obstruction by loss of the elastic recoil properties of the lungs. With the loss of alveolar tissue, structural support to the airways, especially bronchioles, is diminished and on expiration premature closure of airways occurs due to lack of this support.

Clinical features – chronic airways obstruction

The characteristic symptoms of chronic airways obstruction are wheezy breathlessness with or without productive cough. Most patients with sputum production have a slight cough between exacerbations usually with sputum production in the early morning. With infection or other causes of exacerbation sputum becomes more copious and often purulent, rarely there may be some streaky haemoptysis. The severity of breathlessness varies considerably and many patients do not complain spontaneously of dyspnoea unless asked about their ability to walk on inclines or stairs. In others breathlessness is a major symptom which develops rapidly over two to three years into early respiratory crippledom. There may be orthopnoea mostly due to limitation of diaphragmatic movement by abdominal contents.

CLASSIFICATION

Patients have been classified into two polar groups according to their tendency to develop carbon dioxide retention and underventilation but the majority show mixed features of these conditions.

'*Blue-bloater*': This is the commoner of the two polar groups. The patient is usually obese, with copious sputum production and in whom exacerbations of breathlessness and wheezing are accompanied by infected sputum. Because of an associated tendency to underventilation and insensitivity to carbon dioxide such patients are commonly hypoxaemic with hypercapnia especially during acute exacerbations. They frequently develop secondary polycythaemia, and renal bicarbonate retention, due to the chronic hypercapnia, leads to peripheral oedema because of the associated sodium retention often in the absence of right heart failure. This type of patient will show moderately severe airflow obstruction with relatively normal total lung capacity but increased residual volume. Carbon monoxide diffusing capacity may be little impaired.

'Pink-puffers' Type A: This uncommon type of patient is usually thin, and severely breathless at rest with little or no sputum production. They may show little or no arterial oxygen desaturation at rest but develop marked desaturation on effort. Their sensitivity to carbon dioxide remains normal and hypercapnia only develops as a pre-terminal event. In these patients peripheral oedema or right heart failure is a late development and usually heralds impending death. Here there is severe airways obstruction with increased total lung capacity and marked reduction in diffusing capacity for carbon monoxide. It is quite common for the chest radiograph of this type of patient to show radiolucent areas at the lower zones indicating the presence of panacinar emphysema.

CLINICAL SIGNS

In a patient with predominant symptoms suggestive of chronic bronchitis noisy breath sounds may be audible at a distance with the unaided ear. Inspiration may be aided by contraction of the accessory muscles of respiration including the infrathyroid strap muscles. The wide swings in intrathoracic pressure associated with airways obstruction cause indrawing of the supraclavicular fossae and intercostal spaces during inspiration. Exaggerated jugular venous emptying on inspiration and distension on expiration also occur. Chest expansion may be poor with an increase in the anteroposterior diameter of the chest making the apex beat impalpable and reducing the areas of cardiac and liver dullness. In bronchitic patients (Type B) wheezes and crackles are usually present and when right ventricular hypertrophy develops there may be a parasternal heave with a loud pulmonary second sound. Again these symptoms may be masked by overinflation. In emphysematous Type A patients the breath sounds are usually very quiet because the increased thoracic volume and the loss of lung tissue serve to diminish the transmission of breath sounds.

RADIOLOGY

In patients with advanced chronic bronchitis a simple postero-anterior chest radiograph often shows no abnormality but there may be overinflation producing low flat diaphragms, elongation of cardiac shadow and prominence of the hilar vessels due to enlargement of the proximal pulmonary arteries. There may be upper lobe blood diversion leading to dilatation of the upper lobe pulmonary veins. Patients with extensive panacinar emphysema usually show increased radiolucency of the lung fields with areas where reduction in the vascular markings result from loss of the vessels with destruction of lung tissue. There may also be bullae visible.

FUNCTIONAL ABNORMALITIES

The dominant feature is generalised airways obstruction. Simple measurements of FEV_1, PEFR and FVC are useful. Once chronic airways obstruction is established all will be reduced but the reduction in FEV_1 and PEFR is usually greater than the fall in FVC so that the FEV_1/FVC ratio will be low. Some patients may still show a reversible component of their airways obstruction but if this amounts to more than about 20 per cent the presence of co-existent asthma should be considered. Overinflation of the lungs indicated by increase in the total lung capacity and residual volume is usually present especially with emphysema. The diffusing capacity for carbon monoxide (T_LCO) is not seriously affected in chronic bronchitis until the disease is advanced. In contrast in emphysema the most striking features are the marked reduction in the T_LCO with overinflation of the lungs.

Cause and complications

Chronic airways obstruction usually develops over a prolonged period of time perhaps starting, when the patient is in the twenties or thirties, as a smoker's cough and early morning expectoration. At this time minor respiratory tract infections may lead to episodes of acute bronchitis. Any impairment of the patient's exercise tolerance may pass unnoticed until a severe episode of bronchitis prevents work. These episodes begin to occur at more frequent intervals and working capacity deteriorates leading finally to loss of employment, especially in physically demanding jobs. Episodes of pneumonia and pleurisy are another recognised complication but spontaneous pneumothorax is a relatively uncommon occurrence.

INVESTIGATIONS

Sputum culture usually grows *H. influenzae* and *S. pneumoniae*. A blood count may show a polymorphonuclear leucocytosis during infective exacerbations and secondary polycythaemia may develop in those patients with chronic hypoxaemia.

COMPLICATIONS

Pulmonary hypertension and right ventricular failure may occur due to increase in pulmonary artery pressure. This results from pulmonary vasoconstriction mediated by the effects of the hypoxia on pulmonary arterioles and ultimately from destruction of the pulmonary vascular bed. When hypoxia is aggravated by the increase in airways obstruction from bacterial infection or other causes, right ventricular hypertrophy may ensue.

Bullae may develop in association with emphysema. These are thin-walled inflated spaces created by the rupture of alveolar walls. They are most often subpleural in position and can rupture to form a spontaneous pneumothorax. They may develop progressively in size becoming large enough to interfere with pulmonary ventilation compressing surrounding lung.

Treatment

Patients should be urged to give up smoking and obese patients should be advised to lose weight as this should improve exercise tolerance. Breathing exercises may bring additional relief and several studies have shown that exercise training can be valuable (see p. 336).

INFECTION

Polyvalent influenza vaccine can be given at the start of each winter as this may help to reduce the incidence of secondary bacterial bronchitis. Patients should be instructed to treat minor infections such as colds or sore throat with antibiotic therapy which they can hold in reserve. The infecting organism is usually *H. influenzae* or *S. pneumoniae* and suitable oral antibiotic regimes would be a 5–7-day course of any of the following:

1. Co-trimoxazole, two tablets twice daily.
2. Ampicillin, 500mg 6-hourly.
3. Amoxycillin, 250mg three times a day.
4. Oxytetracycline, 250–500mg 6-hourly.

BREATHLESSNESS

Bronchodilator therapy is often helpful to a limited degree. These are probably best given as aerosols of the sympathomimetic type such as salbutamol, terbutaline, rimiterol or fenoterol. Additional benefit may be obtained with oral preparations of the theophylline group. Aminophylline suppositories may be very useful for the control of nocturnal breathlessness. Any patient with severe, seemingly irreversible airways obstruction should be given the benefit of a trial of systemic corticosteroids but this should be covered by careful observation, preferably in hospital. A dose of prednisolone, 30mg a day for 10 to 14 days should be monitored by frequent measurements of PEFR or FEV_1, three or four times a day and only if there is objective evidence of improvement should corticosteroid treatment be continued. If there is no response this can be stopped without serious risk of adrenal suppression.

ACUTE RESPIRATORY FAILURE

Severe exacerbations of chronic airways obstruction usually begin with increase in the quantity and purulence of the sputum. The patient becomes exhausted by persistent coughing and is unable to clear the airways causing further deterioration in ventilatory function. This leads to a fall in arterial oxygen tension often accompanied by a rise in carbon dioxide tension. The resultant hypoxia leads to further pulmonary hypertension and congestive cardiac failure. Hypoxia and hypercapnia can both cause drowsiness and further inability to cough up secretions. Treatment is aimed to reduce hypoxia by improving alveolar ventilation. A search should always be made for a pneumothorax as a cause for sudden deterioration and this is excluded by a chest radiograph. Note should be made of the state of consciousness, ability to cough, presence of cyanosis, congestive heart failure and the level of carbon dioxide tension. Sputum specimens should be sent for culture.

The two fundamental principles of treatment are (1) to relieve the airways obstruction and (2) to keep the patient alert. Coughing should be encouraged at frequent intervals with help from nursing and physiotherapy staff and postural drainage may be helpful. If there is any dehydration, intravenous therapy may be necessary and inspired gases can be humidified with a suitable humidifier. Bronchodilator therapy should be given although it may only make a marginal contribution to improvement, aminophylline by intravenous injection or by continuous infusion can be combined with use of IPPB and a bronchodilator solution such as salbutamol.

clubbing. Physical signs are usually restricted at this stage to fine basal crepitations.

Respiratory function tests reveal a typical restrictive ventilatory defect and loss of total lung capacity with marked and progressive impairment of gas transfer.

The other dangers of exposure to asbestos include the development of pleural plaques with fibrosis and calcification of the pleura. These look quite dramatic on chest radiographs, but may lead to relatively little functional disturbance. More serious are bronchial carcinoma, of which asbestos workers have a greatly increased incidence especially if they are smokers, and the development of pleural and peritoneal mesotheliomata which usually develop after a latent period of 20 years or more. It seems that only transient minimal exposure to asbestos is necessary to initiate the development of mesotheliomata

EXTRINSIC ALLERGIC ALVEOLITIS

This group of diseases share a common pathogenesis of pulmonary hypersensitivity caused by inhalation of organic dusts leading to a Type III hypersensitivity reaction and lung damage with fibrosis. The commonest agent in the UK is a thermophyllic mould *Micropolyspora faeni* causing *farmer's lung*, but other examples include *bird fanciers' lung, pituitary snuff takers' lung, malt workers' lung*, and *mushroom workers' lung*. In most of the extrinsic alveolitides the causal agents are antigens of thermophyllic fungi which grow readily under conditions of high humidity and temperature. When inhaled, they induce lung reactions with an allergic alveolitis. Typically, in *farmers' lung* acute episodes following exposure occur with fever, muscle aches and acute breathlessness. These begin 8–24 hours after exposure and last a few days. Examination of the chest reveals widespread crackles but little else. The chest radiograph may show typical fine 'ground glass' shadowing. With repeated exposures, widespread pulmonary fibrosis may develop with typical clinical, radiological and physiological effects. *Bird fancier's lung* usually presents with a more insidious onset without recognisable acute episodes.

In allergic alveolitis the Type III precipitin reaction occurs about 4–6 hours after exposure and results in systemic upset with fever, muscle aches and acute breathlessness. If exposure ceases, this usually recovers spontaneously. After recurrent exposure to mouldy hay an insidious onset of diffuse pulmonary fibrosis resulting in progressive breathlessness with finger clubbing is common. The other types of extrinsic alveolitis show a more insidious pattern without the acute alveolitic phase. Histological examination of the lungs in fibrosing extrinsic allergic alveolitis shows thickening of the alveolar walls by oedema, plasma cells, lymphocytes and the formation of epithelioid granulomata. This process may also affect the respiratory bronchioles. In the chronic diseases, widespread diffuse interstitial fibrosis develops. The physiological changes are similar to other causes of diffuse pulmonary fibrosis and include a restrictive ventilatory defect, the reduction of FEV_I and VC, together with loss of total lung volume presenting as reduced total lung capacity and severe impairment of gas transfer indices. In extrinsic alveolitis in the acute phase the chest radiograph may show fine 'ground glass' shadowing which, if exposure ceases, will recover. In the chronic disease, nodular shadows develop and a typical pattern of interstitial pulmonary fibrosis may develop, showing a predominant upper zone distribution.

IRRITANT REACTIONS TO GASES AND FUMES

Occupational exposure to ammonia, chlorine, sulphur dioxide, phosgene, and nitrogen dioxide, may result in acute inflammation of the respiratory tract and conjunctivae. Typical symptoms are an acute onset of cough with breathlessness and choking respiration immediately after exposure followed by the development of acute pulmonary oedema within 4–6 hours. Permanent bronchial damage can occur resulting in breathlessness with widespread airways obstruction. Similar reactions may occur with the fumes of some inorganic compounds including nickel, platinum, tungsten and vanadium. The acute treatment of all these conditions is with oxygen and corticosteroids to combat the acute inflammatory condition.

OCCUPATIONAL ASTHMA

Asthma may arise as a result of occupational exposure to a wide variety of substances which may act as non-specific stimuli precipitating asthmatic reactions in individuals whose airways are already hyper-reactive or they may act by inducing the onset of asthma as hyper-reactivity in previously unaffected individuals.

The term occupational asthma is generally restricted to asthma induced by hypersensitivity to an agent inhaled at work. Reactive chemicals which provoke asthma in individuals who are already hyper-reactive are more readily dealt with by control of atmospheric concentrations so that inhaled concentrations are insufficient to induce asthma. Sensitising agents which provoke the development of hyper-reactivity through specific reactions present a greater problem since asthma will continue to develop unless further exposure to the causative agent can be prevented. In the last five years an increasing number of agents provoking occupational asthma have been recognised for statutory compensation in the UK. Among the commoner examples are:

1. Sensitivity to the *wheat weevil* (*Sitophilus granarius*) from exposure to contaminated wheat grain.
2. Reactions to *Western red cedar* and other wood dusts.
3. Reactions to *pine resins* (*colophony*); this is a particular problem in the electronics industry where soldering, using soft fluxes including colophony, is the cause.
4. Reactions to a number of drugs in their manufacture, including antibiotics, especially the penicillins and cephalosporins; reactions to bacterial enzymes such as those of *Bacillus subtilis* in enzyme detergent manufacture. Di-isocyanates in polyurethane foam manufacture and a number of other synthetic processes.

Where the development of occupational asthma is suspected, careful history taking and investigation, including if necessary challenge testing to suspected agents, are the province of specialist units and such patients should be referred for further investigation, evaluation and occupational counselling.

BIBLIOGRAPHY

Godfrey, S. and Clark, T. J. H. (1983). *Asthma*, 2nd edition. Chapman and Hall, London.
Parkes, W. R. (ed.) (1982). *Occupational Lung Disorders*, 2nd edition. Butterworths, London.
See also Bibliography on pages 506, 534 and 685.

Chapter 20

Clinical Aspects of Medical Chest Disease
2. Bronchiectasis: Cystic Fibrosis: Pneumonia: Tumours: Pleural Problems

by J. V. COLLINS MD, FRCP

BRONCHIECTASIS

Bronchiectasis is chronic dilatation of bronchi with impaired drainage of bronchial secretions leading to persistent infection of the affected segments or lobes. Bronchiectasis most commonly forms in childhood but the onset of symptoms may be delayed to later life. It usually follows inadequately treated pneumonia and may arise especially in association with whooping cough (pertussis) or measles when the presence of thick tenacious, viscid mucus obstructs bronchi with distal collapse of the lung. During the subsequent inflammatory process there is destruction and alteration of the structure of the bronchial mucosa. When the lung re-inflates, the bronchus then becomes dilated and the lining is usually changed from a normal columnar ciliated epithelium to a more cuboidal or even squamous epithelium with fewer or absent cilia.

ASSOCIATED CONDITIONS

1. Congenital: In Kartagener's syndrome of dextrocardia, sinusitis and bronchiectasis, structural abnormalities of cilia have been demonstrated with functional impairment of muco-ciliary clearance. Sequestrated lung segments and bronchomalasia may also be associated with bronchiectasis.
2. Cystic fibrosis: In association with bronchial obstruction by mucus and secondary bacterial infection most patients with cystic fibrosis develop extensive bronchiectasis.
3. Pertussis (whooping cough), measles, tuberculosis and pneumonia in childhood and adult life may be complicated by the development of bronchiectasis.

4. Immunodeficiency: Congenital or acquired immunodeficiency, including hypogammaglobulinaemia or immunodeficiency in association with leukaemias and lymphomas, may lead to recurrent lung infections and the development of bronchiectasis.

The examples so far cited produce bronchiectasis mainly affecting the more distal bronchi.

5. Allergic bronchopulmonary aspergillosis: In contrast to the first four associated conditions this affects the more proximal medium-sized bronchi and a Type III immune response to *Aspergillus fumigatus* occurs, with mucus plugs lodged in the more central bronchi. The associated inflammatory process leads to destruction and distortion of the walls of the large and medium-sized bronchi resulting in proximal bronchiectasis when the plugs containing the aspergillus are subsequently coughed up.

Pathology

Following the initial inflammatory process with the development of bronchiectasis there is destruction of the cartilage and in the bronchial wall a change from the normal ciliated columnar epithelium to a cuboidal form with absent or fewer cilia. The mucous gland content of the bronchial walls is increased and at the same time the ciliary function is diminished. This leads to poor clearance of the mucus and a tendency to recurrent infections. In addition, there may be marked changes in the bronchial arterial circulation within the walls of the bronchi with many anastomoses with the pulmonary circulation as a result of which haemoptysis is a common clinical feature. Because of the effects of gravity bronchiectasis most commonly forms in the right middle and lower lobes and the left lingular lobe.

Clinical features

The amount of clinical disturbance depends upon the extent of the bronchiectasis. Where only one or two segments are affected there may be few clinical signs or symptoms except with ensuing respiratory infections. In most instances cough is a prominent feature and may be present all the time but worsening at times of infection. Sputum, if present, is usually purulent and may be copious. On waking in the morning there is usually a paroxysm of coughing on change of posture leading to the discharge of secretions accumulated overnight. Haemoptysis which results from bleeding from the bronchopulmonary arterial anastomoses is common especially during infective exacerbations. Rarely, it may lead to anaemia or become life threatening. Breathlessness is usually associated only with widespread bilateral bronchiectasis.

SYSTEMIC SYMPTOMS

With extensive bronchiectasis and copious purulent sputum there may be malaise, anorexia, weight loss and fever, which in children may lead to a failure to thrive with stunting of growth.

The *clinical* signs usually consist of coarse crackles over the affected segments and an associated wheeze. During episodes of infection there may be signs of consolidation and collapse. With extensive bronchiectasis and suppuration, finger clubbing is common and central cyanosis may occur. Very rarely, secondary amyloidosis may develop with long-standing severe infection.

Investigations

Chest radiograph. This can be normal with very limited bronchiectasis but it usually shows crowding and haziness of the vascular markings in the affected areas, and thickening of the bronchial walls may be visible as parallel line shadows in the affected segments. In more extensive bronchiectasis cyst-like shadows form and fluid levels are often visible within them. *Bronchography* is rarely necessary unless surgical resection is being considered. This will show pooling of the contrast medium within the dilated bronchi (Fig. 5/17, pp. 146–7)

Sputum culture commonly grows bacteria including anaerobic organisms and in long-standing cases, especially with cystic fibrosis, *Pseudomonas aeruginosa.*

Serum immunoglobulin levels. These should be measured to identify patients with immunodeficiency in whom treatment with hyperimmune gammaglobulin replacement may be helpful.

Sweat test is advisable to exclude the presence of cystic fibrosis.

Complications

1. Recurrent pneumonia and pleurisy.
2. Chronic bronchitis.
3. Empyema.
4. Lung abscess.

to a surrounding inflammatory reaction. These transient pulmonary infiltrates are associated with fever, wheezing and a blood eosinophilia. The repeated attacks lead to the development of proximal bronchiectasis and may cause diffuse pulmonary fibrosis.

3. Simple aspergilloma. This may be discovered by chance on a chest radiograph as a round shadow within a cavity already present. The classical radiological sign is of an opacity with a cresent of air above it (the 'halo' sign). Many aspergillomas may be asymptomatic while others are associated with repeated infections with purulent sputum and recurrent haemoptysis which can be life threatening.

Investigations

The chest radiograph may show the characteristic appearance of an aspergilloma. For invasive aspergillosis the appearances are non-specific with patchy coarse shadowing in the lung fields. In allergic bronchopulmonary aspergillosis the characteristic finding is of transient patches of infiltration in the lung which change position over the course of the disease.

The presence of serum precipitins to aspergillus may be confirmed by agar gel precipitin tests. In patients with aspergillomas, over 90 per cent have a strongly positive reaction; weaker reactions occur with allergic aspergillosis when precipitins are present in about 75 per cent of patients. In patients with invasive aspergillosis there are often no demonstrable precipitins, usually because of the associated immunosuppression.

Skin tests, both immediate Type I and delay Type III reactions are usually demonstrable in allergic aspergillosis but they are uncommon with aspergillomas unless there is co-existent bronchopulmonary aspergillosis.

Treatment

For allergic bronchopulmonary aspergillosis prompt treatment with corticosteroids will suppress the inflammatory reactions and thereafter the plugs containing the aspergillus will usually be coughed up. It is often necessary to maintain such patients on long-term systemic steroids in a low dose to prevent destructive recurrences. *For invasive aspergillosis* treatment is with oral amphotericin or other antifungal agents and inhalation of anhydroxystilbamidene. *For simple aspergilloma* no treatment may be necessary. Surgical resection is indicated if severe recurrent haemoptysis becomes a problem and the aspergilloma enlarges and becomes invasive. Secondary bacterial infection of aspergilloma cavities are not uncommon and may present a major problem requiring potent antibiotic therapy or even surgical resection which is hazardous and difficult.

CANDIDIASIS

Lung infection with *Candida albicans* usually only happens with severe pre-existing disease or in the presence of immunosuppression. Bronchial candidiasis which may arise as a complication of aerosol steroid therapy causes scanty mucoid sputum and an irritating cough. Invasive pulmonary candidiasis is a severe illness, with cough, fever, haemoptysis, breathlessness and chest pain. Treatment is with amphotericin by inhalation and by intravenous infusions of amphotericin, or 5-fluorocytosine.

NOCARDIOSIS

Infection with *Nocardiasteroides*, an aerobic organism, leads to a granulomatous disease affecting the lungs and other organs. This soil saprophyte is thought to infect through skin damage or by inhalation. Clinical features include high fever, cough, breathlessness and haemoptysis and the mortality rate is high. Treatment is with high doses of sulphadimidine.

ACTINOMYCOSIS

Actinomyces israeli is a branching filamentous anaerobic Gram-positive organism which is found in the mouth. Inhalation leading to lung infection usually follows dental extractions or other surgical procedures. The onset of the illness is usually insidious with fever, cough with sputum containing the fungus and haemoptysis with pleuritic pain. An empyema may occasionally develop. If chest wall involvement occurs there may be skin sinuses discharging pus containing the typical 'sulphur granules' of the mycelium of *A. israeli*. Treatment with benzyl penicillin in high doses may be necessary for several months. Rarely, surgical excision may be necessary to eradicate lung damage once infection has been controlled.

CRYPTOCOCCOSIS (TORULOSIS)

Cryptococcus neoformans is a yeast found in soil and pigeon droppings. Individuals affected usually have severe underlying debilitating disease. The commonest presentation is an acute meningo-encephalitis, and a respiratory infection may develop as a mild self-limiting influenza-like illness or a typical pneumonia with fever, productive cough and haemoptysis and pleuritic pain. Chest radiographs show a variety of changes including solitary opacities, lung abscesses or diffuse pulmonary infiltration. The diagnosis is made by demonstrating the organism in the sputum and treatment is with amphotericin, 5-fluorocytosine or other antifungal agents by intravenous infusion.

Pneumonia

Pneumonia is an acute inflammatory process involving the lung alveoli and surrounding airways. It is usually caused by infection with micro-organisms but can also be induced by chemical injury, by gases, vapours, fatty or oily material and by allergic processes. The injury produced by infection or other causes sets up an inflammatory reaction with vasodilation leading to an outpouring of exudate into the alveoli containing red blood cells, leucocytes, macrophages and fibrin.

Causative organisms

Most pneumonias are caused by bacteria, and although viruses can cause primary pneumonia these are relatively rare; more commonly, secondary bacterial infection gives rise to pneumonia as a complication of preceding respiratory virus infection such as influenza.

PNEUMONIA IN PREVIOUSLY HEALTHY PEOPLE

The commonest causes are bacteria: *Streptococcus pneumoniae* and less often, *Staphylococcus pyogenes* and *Klebsiella pneumoniae*, especially during influenza epidemics. *Mycoplasma pneumoniae* is probably the most common cause of pneumonia in previously healthy young people. Less common causes of pneumonia include *Chlamydia psittaci* or *Coxiella burnetii* (the agent of Q-fever) and Legionnaire's disease caused by *Legionella pneumophila*.

PNEUMONIAS WITH PRE-EXISTING DISEASE

The commonest causes are *Streptococcus pneumoniae* and *Haemophilus influenzae*. Other causative organisms include *Klebsiella pneumoniae*, *Streptococcus pyogenes*, *Mycobacterium tuberculosis* and the Gram-negative bacteria *Pseudomonas aeruginosa*, *Escherichia coli* and *Proteus mirabilis*.

Factors which predispose to pneumonia

1. *Viral infections.* Respiratory viruses including the influenza and respiratory syncytial virus (RSV), rhinoviruses, adenoviruses, varicella (chickenpox), measles, and smallpox may all rarely cause primary pneumonia. More commonly, pneumonia occurs through secondary bacterial invasion following a preceding viral respiratory infection.

2. *Chronic airways disease.* Chronic bronchitis, bronchiectasis and cystic fibrosis all predispose to pneumonia caused by bacteria such as *Haemophilus influenzae*, *Pseudomonas aeruginosa* and *Proteus mirabilis*.

3. *Bronchial obstruction.* Pneumonia may arise secondary to obstruction of the main airways by carcinoma, benign tumours, foreign bodies or from the retention of secretions following unconsciousness from general anaesthesia, drug or alcohol abuse.

4. *Aspiration pneumonia.* This arises secondary to oesophageal disorders such as hiatus hernia, achalasia of the cardia, systemic sclerosis (scleroderma), oesophageal diverticuli and carcinoma. The cause is overspill of oesophageal and gastric contents into the trachea during sleep, or coma from drug overdose or alcohol excess.

5. *Impaired resistance.* Pneumonia is much more common in patients with immunodeficiencies whether primary or secondary to treatment with immunosuppressive drugs. It is also more common in patients suffering from malnutrition, uncontrolled diabetes mellitus, rheumatoid arthritis and chronic renal disease.

LOBAR PNEUMONIA

This is still most commonly caused by infection with *Streptococcus pneumoniae* and presents as a homogeneous consolidation of one or more lobes or segments of the lung. It is commonest in early and middle adult life but can occur at any age. The highest incidence is in the winter months.

Clinical features

The onset is sudden with high fever (39 to 40 °C), rigors, vomiting or even convulsions in children. Malaise, anorexia, headache and generalised aches and pains are common and there may be pleural pain. Coughing is usually painful and dry at first, later becoming productive of tenacious sputum which is often rust-coloured or frankly bloodstained. Respiration is rapid, shallow and painful. The pulse is rapid and the skin hot and dry. Central cyanosis occurs in severe cases.

Physical signs

These include reduced respiratory movement on the affected side with diminished percussion note and a pleural rub. When consolidation is established breath sounds become bronchial.

As resolution occurs coarse crackles become audible as the consolidated tissue re-aerates and the fluid infiltrate is coughed up via the airways. Radiological examination at first shows a homogeneous opacity localised to an affected segment or lobe of the lung.

Treatment

Many patients are not very ill and can be treated at home by antibiotic therapy for those cases where a bacterial cause or suprainfection is suspected or proven and rest in warm surroundings with an adequate fluid intake and control of pain with analgesics. The decision to admit the patient to hospital depends upon the severity of the disease and the social conditions of the patient.

BRONCHOPNEUMONIA

Bronchopneumonia is much commoner than lobar pneumonia, especially in the elderly. It is frequently associated with chronic obstructive lung diseases and is a common postoperative complication. There is acute inflammation of the bronchi and bronchioles with collapse and consolidation of associated groups of alveoli scattered irregularly through the lungs, more often in the lower lobes. The lesions are usually distributed bilaterally in small patches but can become more confluent. The alveolar exudate contains neutrophils, lymphocytes and a small amount of fibrin. There is interstitial oedema with cellular proliferation in the alveolar walls.

Clinical features

Following an episode of acute bronchitis when bronchopneumonia develops, there are further rises in temperature, pulse rate and respiration rate with dyspnoea and often central cyanosis. A profuse cough with purulent sputum is common but pleural pain is much less frequent than with lobar pneumonia. In the early stages the signs are of acute bronchitis with wheezes, but crackles develop later. There may be no signs of consolidation such as dullness to percussion or bronchial breathing.

OTHER TYPES OF PNEUMONIA

Staphylococcal pneumonia

Primary pneumonic infection with *Staphylococcus pyogenes* is uncommon but secondary invasion is common in pneumonias in patients with chronic lung disease, especially cystic fibrosis and bronchiectasis, where previous antibiotic therapy has altered the bacteria flora.

Secondary staphylococcal pneumonia also occurs during influenza epidemics and in the presence of immunosuppression and malnutrition. Drug addicts are especially susceptible to infection from contaminated intravenous injections.

Klebsiella pneumonia

This is caused by *Klebsiella pneumoniae* (Friedlander's bacillus); it is a rare disease with massive consolidation and excavation of one or more lobes of the lung especially in the upper zones. There is profound systemic disturbance with large amounts of thick, greenish purulent sputum. The diagnosis can be suspected from the radiological appearances and is confirmed by the isolation of the causative organism in the sputum. It has a high mortality. The treatment of choice is streptomycin with chloramphenicol.

Mycoplasma pneumoniae infection

This was previously known as 'primary atypical pneumonia'. Mycoplasma are small organisms which are a common cause of minor upper respiratory and lower respiratory tract infections. Cases of pneumonia are usually found in epidemics of infection especially in institutions such as schools or barracks, the young being most often affected. Marked constitutional upset is common with a relatively low fever and few clinical signs on examination of the chest. By contrast, the radiological changes may be quite extensive and usually present a 'ground glass' appearance most often unilateral with a patchy distribution. A minority of patients develop maculopapular rashes, arthropathy and rarely meningo-encephalitis. Although cold agglutinins develop in about 50 per cent of patients these cause a haemolytic anaemia in only about 5 per cent of patients.

Coxiella burnettii

Although this organism is usually found in cattle and sheep it can give rise to an atypical pneumonia with marked headache and muscle pains and constitutional upset. Endocarditis sometimes occurs.

Chlamydia psittaci

This disease is primarily an infection of birds transmitted to humans by inhalation of dust from the faeces of an infected bird. The pneumonia caused by these organisms may be extensive with severe toxaemia and headache.

Legionnaire's disease or pneumonia

This is caused by a coccobacillus (*Legionella pneumophila*) which gives rise to severe respiratory illness often occurring in epidemics. This is characterised by pneumonia with gastro-intestinal symptoms, confusion, hyponatraemia and proteinuria. Sputum is scanty and not usually purulent. The white blood count may be normal or slightly raised. Chest radiograph shows patchy consolidation which is unilateral in about half of the cases. Death has occurred in 20 per cent or more of cases from cardiovascular collapse and renal failure. At post-mortem the lungs show changes of bacterial pneumonia with alveolar damage. At present the most simple reliable means of confirming the diagnosis is the demonstration of a four-fold or greater rise in titre of serum immunofluorescent antibody to the legionella.

Legionnaire's disease should be suspected in any patient with severe pneumonia which fails to respond to conventional antibiotic therapy. Erythromycin, rifampicin or tetracycline are suitable antibiotics for treatment.

Physiotherapy

Treatment for the pneumonias by physiotherapy is described in Chapter 21, page 526.

Miscellaneous conditions

PULMONARY TUBERCULOSIS

The management and outlook of pulmonary tuberculosis has changed dramatically since the introduction of adequate chemotherapy but it is still a major cause of morbidity and mortality especially in underdeveloped countries. There are still about 10 million cases of active tuberculosis throughout the world and it causes three million deaths each year.

Natural history

On initial exposure to *Mycobacterium tuberculosis* infection occurs by spread from an infected individual who has positive sputum. When a susceptible individual inhales the bacilli, a primary infection may develop if bacilli are deposited in the alveoli. This is characterised by a small inflammatory lesion usually in the middle or lower zones of the lungs with a hilar and paratracheal lymph node reactive hyperplasia: this combination is referred to as a *primary complex*. The primary lesion is often asymptomatic but in early life symptoms and complications are common. The enlarged lymph nodes may cause bronchial compression, and rupture of caseous nodes into the bronchus may lead to tuberculous bronchopneumonia. The primary infection usually heals uneventfully and this results in hypersensitivity to tuberculin and subsequent improved immunity. Thereafter, further inhalation of tubercle bacilli will not result in infection and post-primary disease is almost always caused by dissemination of bacilli from the site of the primary complex. The majority of primary complexes heal without subsequent symptoms but the bacilli within the primary lesion are not killed and viable bacilli can be recovered from dormant lesions unless anti-tuberculous chemotherapy has been given.

POST-PRIMARY TUBERCULOSIS

This may develop as a result of inadequate immunity or loss of immunity with breakdown of dormant lesions. Improvement in nutrition and housing has played a part in the decline in the incidence of tuberculosis in the UK, and other developed countries. Conditions of overcrowding, malnutrition and stress account for the continued greater prevalence of tuberculosis in underdeveloped countries. Debilitating diseases such as diabetes, immunosuppression, malnutrition, chronic alcoholism and total gastrectomy, are all factors which may predispose individuals to the development of post-primary tuberculosis.

Post-primary disease usually involves the upper lobes or apex of the lower lobe where it is thought that a combination of increased ventilation and reduced pulmonary blood flow encourages bacterial multiplication. Hilar lymphadenopathy is not usually a major feature in post-primary lesions which show a more fibrotic cavitating development. Pleural effusion which occurs very early with primary infection develops much later in post-primary disease and is usually associated with haematogenous spread to the pleura.

Infants are highly susceptible to tuberculosis and in this group there is considerable mortality from miliary tuberculosis and tuberculous meningitis. The risk again increases in adolescence but in adult life relative immunity persists until late middle or old age.

Prevention

Political programmes aimed at improvement in housing and nutrition in underdeveloped countries are important and prompt diagnosis and treatment of infectious individuals with positive sputum are essential. BCG vaccination giving hypersensitivity to tuberculin improves immunity to tuberculosis and reduces the incidence of the more serious complications of the primary complex. It is a cheap and easily administered measure which is of greatest efficacy where the incidence of the disease is high. Its value in countries such as the UK where the incidence of tuberculosis is low is now questionable.

Diagnosis

This is based upon clinical features, radiology, microbiology, the tuberculin test and sometimes histology. It is essential to keep the possibility of tuberculosis in mind in cases of pneumonia in spite of the falling incidence of the disease, otherwise cases will be missed.

CLINICAL FEATURES

Uncomplicated primary pulmonary tuberculosis may be symptomless but in younger children constitutional symptoms are usual.

Erythema nodosum may develop within a few weeks of infection. Compression of the trachea or main bronchi from lymph node enlargement may cause breathlessness, stridor or paroxysmal cough, and erosion of a lymph node may lead to tuberculous bronchopneumonia with typical physical signs. In older subjects with post-primary tuberculosis the commonest presentations are persistent cough, sputum, unexplained haemoptysis, unresolved pneumonia and non-specific symptoms including fever, malaise and weight loss. These are particularly likely to occur in Asian immigrants and the elderly. Any of the above conditions may give rise to typical physical signs.

RADIOLOGICAL FEATURES

Common patterns observed are:

1. A patchy solid lesion of part of one lobe or lung especially in the upper zones.
2. Areas of streaky fibrosis.
3. Cavitated solid lesions.
4. Irregular areas of calcification suggestive of previous tuberculous infection. However, it is often not possible to discount active infection without further investigation.
5. Solitary round shadows present a frequent diagnostic problem. The differentiation between a tuberculoma and a neoplasm may only be possible after resection of the lesion.
6. Hilar lymph node enlargement associated with a lung lesion is characteristic of tuberculosis but again differentiation from bronchial carcinoma or lymphoma may require extensive investigation.
7. Pleural effusion. This is rare in the UK.

MICROBIOLOGY

Ideally, the diagnosis is based upon the finding of tubercle bacilli in the sputum. At least three sputum smears, laryngeal swabs or gastric aspirates should be examined by direct smear, fluorescent microscopy or Ziehl-Neelson staining. Culture examination is still necessary to recognise atypical mycobacteria which account for 1–2 per cent of infections and the incidence of primary resistant strains which has increased since the arrival of Asian immigrants.

Biopsy. Where suitable biopsy material is available the diagnosis can be made more rapidly. With fibre-optic bronchoscopy it is easy to obtain mucosal or lung tissue for histology and culture.

TUBERCULIN TESTING

Within 3 to 4 weeks from the onset of the primary infection hypersensitivity to proteins of the tubercle bacillus develops and can be demonstrated by an intradermal injection of a purified protein derivative (PPD) of the bacilli. The test may be carried out as a Mantoux test using the 1:10000 solution of PPD; the result is read 48 to 72 hours later. A positive reaction, evidence of present or past infection with *M. tuberculosis*, is an area of induration of at least 10mm diameter to five tuberculin units (5 TU) (i.e. 0.5ml of 1:10000 solution of PPD). Lesser degrees of reaction are regarded as non-specific. The multiple puncture Heaf test and Tine test each using 5 TU are widely used and more convenient, but may be less reliable. The Heaf test is read at three to five days and a confluent disc of induration is equivalent to a positive reaction to a Mantoux test. With the Tine test, two to four papules each of at last 2mm in diameter constitute a positive reaction.

Symptoms

Malaise with persistent fever, although common with extensive disease, is often absent in post-primary infections encountered in the United Kingdom. A persistent cough in a middle-aged smoker should never be attributed to cigarette smoking without a chest radiograph and clinical examination. With more extensive disease gastro-intestinal symptoms including anorexia and dyspepsia may occur and increased susceptibility to pulmonary tuberculosis is common following total gastrectomy. Long-term corticosteroids and immunosuppressive therapy may lead to reactivation of quiescent tuberculous lesions. Such patients should have reguar chest radiographs throughout such treatment.

MILIARY TUBERCULOSIS

Haematogeneous spread of tuberculosis is especially likely to occur in very young children, in the elderly and with immunosuppression.

Treatment

It is not necessary to segregate patients with infectious smear-positive tuberculosis; most patients in the UK are admitted to hospital for the start of chemotherapy, although the risk of infecting contacts is minimal. Hospital treatment remains essential for:

1. Very ill patients needing rest.
2. Drug resistant tuberculosis with hypersensitivity reactions or drug toxicity.
3. Unco-operative patients with bad domestic or social circumstances, mental disturbance or alcoholism where close supervision of treatment is essential.

ANTI-TUBERCULOUS CHEMOTHERAPY

Combined drug therapy is obligatory in tuberculosis. Bacterial multiplication is slow, and protracted treatment is essential because resistant mutant bacilli develop naturally. Drugs used singly produce immediate clinical improvement, but there is a high incidence of relapse as resistant organisms develop. Few drugs have bactericidal action against the tubercle bacillus, the majority are bacteriostatic. An ideal drug regime combines at least two bactericidal drugs although one bactericidal drug may be combined with bacteriostatic drugs to offer a reasonable prospect for cure. The use of bacteriostatic drugs alone will arrest clinical progress of the disease but will not cure.

The most bactericidal drugs are rifampicin and isoniazid while streptomycin and pyrazinamide have weaker bactericidal action. The other drugs are all bacteriostatic. The most effective combination is rifampicin and isoniazid with the addition of streptomycin or pyrazinamide for the first 3 months. Classical chemotherapy was based on 18 months' treatment with a combination of bactericidal isoniazid and bacteriostatic sodium PAS and streptomycin in addition for the first 3 months of treatment. Since the availability of rifampicin, treatment has changed considerably. Now a 9-month course of rifampicin and isoniazid combined with ethambutol for the first 2 months has been shown to be as effective as classical chemotherapy and is now standard. Recent studies have shown that where regimes contain at least two bactericidal drugs, 6 months' chemotherapy is effective in all but a negligible minority of patients for the treatment of uncomplicated pulmonary tuberculosis.

Wherever possible, anti-tuberculous chemotherapy should be given in one tablet as a combination preparation to ensure that both are taken. Rifampicin and isoniazid; isoniazid and ethambutol; and isoniazid and PAS are available in this form. Where poor compliance with the treatment is a major problem, intermittent chemotherapy with full supervision of all doses is a useful method of treatment in the UK at least: home visiting can provide a useful check that treatment is taken in full. Recently, great interest has been shown in very short-course chemotherapy using the highly effective bactericidal drugs. These provide much shorter treatment periods, but probably have a lower margin of safety as all doses must be taken and therefore, treatment must be fully supervised.

PHYSIOTHERAPY

The place of physiotherapy is discussed in Chapter 21, page 528.

LUNG ABSCESS

A lung abscess is a necrotic cavitating suppurative lesion caused by infection with micro-organisms. It most commonly arises in association with pneumonias especially following infection with *staphylococci* or *klebsiella* but it is also common with tuberculosis. Other less common causes of lung abscesses include obstruction of a bronchus by a foreign body or a benign or malignant tumour. Inhalation of infected material from the upper airways during general anaesthesia or following disturbance of consciousness such as may follow a cerebral vascular accident, or the inhalation of a tooth during dental extraction, can all lead to the occurrence of an infected lung abscess. Other neurological conditions with disturbance of consciousness, and drug overdoses, may lead to inhalation of infected material followed by lung abscess. Here, material lodges in a bronchopulmonary segment leading to a localised infection which then breaks down to form an abscess. Occasionally a pulmonary infarct may become infected and break down with abscess formation.

Rarer causes of lung abscess include infection with actinomycosis, hydatid cyst and amoebic abscess. The latter usually affects the right lower lobe as the result of spread through the diaphragm from the liver. Because of the effects of gravity lung abscesses most commonly develop in the dependent parts of the lung.

Clinical features

There is usually malaise and fever accompanied by cough often with pleuritic pain. A chest radiograph will show a circumscribed opacity usually with a fluid level (Fig. 5/20, p. 150). When the abscess discharges into a bronchus this will lead to the production of large amounts of foul-smelling pus often mixed with blood.

Treatment

This is based upon appropriate antibiotic therapy with accurate postural drainage and physiotherapy. In many incidences bronchoscopy may be indicated to exclude the presence of a foreign body or bronchial carcinoma. Usually antibiotic therapy alone will lead to satisfactory resolution and surgical intervention, drainage and resection of the affected segment are only occasionally necessary.

PHYSIOTHERAPY

See Chapter 21, page 528.

PULMONARY THROMBO-EMBOLIC DISEASE

Pulmonary embolism refers to the impaction within the pulmonary arterial circulation of a venous thrombus arising from systemic veins. A pulmonary infarct is the pathological change which develops in the lungs. Most pulmonary emboli develop in the deep veins of the calves or ileo-femoral vessels but other common sites include the pelvic veins after childbirth and surgery. About 10 per cent may arise from the right atrium in association with atrial fibrillation or a mural thrombus following myocardial infarction. Venous thrombosis is encouraged by venous stasis, trauma to veins and coagulation abnormalities. Pulmonary embolism is common in patients immobilised by confinement to bed, those with a low cardiac output due to heart failure or acute myocardial infarction and compression of calf muscles especially during surgery, prolonged bed rest or following long journeys. In pregnancy, mechanical obstruction of the inferior vena cava by the uterus, and venous dilatation due to hormonal changes are important predisposing factors.

Clinical features

A massive pulmonary embolus usually presents with sudden collapse or fainting with central chest pain and acute breathlessness. Pleuritic pain and haemoptysis occur in a minority of cases. There is pallor, cyanosis, a feeble pulse and low blood pressure with cold peripheries. The jugular venous pressure is raised and a gallop rhythm with third and fourth heart sounds may be present.

Treatment

This should be immediate with oxygen and, where necessary, external cardiac massage. Embolectomy may be life saving with very large pulmonary emboli and this is preceded by pulmonary arteriography. Mortality rates for emergency embolectomy vary from 25 to 50 per cent. Anticoagulant therapy with heparin may be used after embolectomy. Fibrinolytic therapy using streptokinase by intravenous infusion may lead to more rapid resolution of large pulmonary emboli.

Medium-sized pulmonary embolus leading to pulmonary infarction usually also presents suddenly with pleuritic pain which may be referred to the abdomen or shoulder. Breathlessness with tachypnoea and haemoptysis occur in about 50 per cent of patients. Cyanosis and jaundice are less common. There is usually a moderate tachycardia with low grade fever and there may be a pleural friction rub and subsequent signs of a pleural effusion. The chest radiograph may show linear shadows with or without a pleural effusion and elevation of the hemi-diaphragm on the affected side. Treatment is by immediate pain relief with opiates and the administration of oxygen for breathlessness. Anticoagulant therapy should be started at once with heparin followed by warfarin for a further 6 months.

Tumours of the lung

CARCINOMA OF THE BRONCHUS

Carcinoma of the bronchus is the most common primary neoplasm of man in the United Kingdom presenting a twentieth century epidemic in men, and, more recently, there has been a sharp increase in its incidence in women. Three major aetiological factors have been recognised: cigarette smoking, atmospheric pollution and industrial hazards including exposure to uranium, chromates, nickel, arsenic, and radioactive gases. Four main histological types are recognised:

1. Squamous cell carcinomas accounting for 40 to 50 per cent of the total.
2. Anaplastic small cell or oat cell carcinomas for 25 to 33 per cent.
3. Undifferentiated large cell tumours for 10 to 20 per cent.
4. Adenocarcinomas for 4 to 10 per cent and alveolar cell carcinomas less than 1 per cent.

All except adenocarcinomas show a very significant association with cigarette smoking. Squamous and oat cell carcinomas arise from the central bronchi while adenocarcinomas tend to arise more peripherally. The growth rates vary considerably, adenocarcinoma being the slowest growing, oat cell carcinoma the fastest, with undifferentiated large cell and squamous cell occupying intermediate positions. Tumours spread by direct invasion of the lung, chest wall and mediastinum and also by metastases to hilar and mediastinal lymph nodes or via the blood to the liver, adrenal glands, bones and brain. Symptoms may arise by local spread or through secondary metastases and there are also non-metastatic extra-pulmonary manifestations.

Symptoms

Cough is the commonest and may often be neglected. Breathlessness iis usually a late symptom associated with obstruction of a major bronchus, the development of a large pleural effusion, and more rarely by diffuse spread within the lung as lymphangitis carcinomatosa. Haemoptysis may be a first symptom but the haemorrhage is rarely massive. Chest pain presents as three types:

1. A persisting dull ache.
2. Pleuritic pain due to secondary pneumonia with a sympathetic effusion or malignant invasion of the pleura.
3. Chest wall pain from local invasion of the ribs or intercostal nerves.

With left-sided tumours hoarseness often develops due to involvement of the left recurrent laryngeal nerve.

The most common presentations of bronchial carcinoma are seen in middle-aged smokers as:

Pneumonia. Failure to clear with antibiotic treatment or the recurrence of pneumonia in the same segment or lobe should always suggest an underlying tumour; any cigarette smoker beyond early life who develops an unexplained pneumonia should have a bronchoscopy to exclude a tumour.

Lung abscess. Carcinoma of the bronchus may often cavitate and produce appearances on chest radiograph indistinguishable from lung abscess. In addition lung abscess can develop in an area of lung infection distal to obstruction of a bronchus by a bronchial carcinoma.

EMPYEMA

Empyema is the presence of pus within the pleural cavity and usually follows severe bacterial or tuberculous pneumonia or rupture of a lung abscess. It may also occur as a result of chest injury, following surgery or from oesophageal rupture. Clinical signs include continuing fever with marked constitutional upset and signs of pleural involvement. The management includes aspiration of the fluid with massive broad spectrum antibiotic therapy. It may occasionally be necessary to go on to pleural decortication (see p. 372).

SPONTANEOUS PNEUMOTHORAX

Pneumothorax is the presence of air in the pleural space with collapse of the associated lung. This may result from penetrating injuries of the chest wall but more commonly from spontaneous rupture of the visceral pleura with leak of air from the lung. The latter is commonest in young males of tall stature associated with the rupture of subpleural blebs. Less commonly, pneumothorax may complicate asthma, emphysema, pulmonary tuberculosis, cystic fibrosis and lung abscess.

Clinical features

The onset is usually sudden with breathlessness and sharp pleuritic pain which may be referred to the shoulder tip. There may be an irritating cough and breathlessness and tachycardia are common. Cyanosis is unusual unless there is a large, progressing to a tension, pneumothorax with progressive increase in intrathoracic pressure. Chest movement will be diminished on the side of the pneumothorax and there will be resonance to percussion and absent breath sounds. The chest radiograph will show a collapsed lung with peripheral radiolucency and the lung edge is usually visible. Films should always be taken in inspiration and expiration to accentuate small pneumothoraces in the expiration film.

Treatment

The defect in the visceral pleura may close spontaneously and if there is less than about 30 per cent deflation in an otherwise healthy person no intervention is necessary. The patient should be observed while ambulant. With a large pneumothorax, treatment by intercostal drainage with an underwater seal or valve is indicated. A chest radiograph should be taken to check on the position of the tube. If the lung comes up promptly and there is no subsequent deflation after the tube is clamped it can be removed. If the lung fails to re-expand fully within 24 hours of insertion of the catheter with underwater drainage, negative pressure should be applied via a suction pump. If after a further 48 to 72 hours the lung has not come up surgical intervention should be considered (see p. 371). In the typical spontaneous pneumothorax recurrences are common. If the individual has had more than one on the same side then surgical pleurectomy should be advised. This can be carried out through a small thoracotomy and at the same time small blebs or bullae on the surface of the lungs can be resected and ligated. Chemical pleurodesis by instillation of iodised talc or silver nitrate through a cannula is a less satisfactory method for providing pleurodesis.

BIBLIOGRAPHY

Anderson, C. and Goodchild, M. (1976). *Cystic Fibrosis: Manual of Diagnosis and Management*. Blackwell Scientific Publications Limited, Oxford.

Collins, J. V. (1979). *A Synopsis of Chest Diseases*. John Wright and Sons Limited, Bristol.

Crofton, J. and Douglas, A. (1981). *Respiratory Diseases*, 3rd edition. Blackwell Scientific Publications Limited, Oxford.

See also Bibliography on pages 534, 685.

Chapter 21

Applying Chest Physiotherapy in some Conditions

by D. M. INNOCENTI MCSP *and* J. M. ANDERSON MCSP

The physiotherapist does not treat a 'diagnosis' *per se*, but uses the techniques available to her to help solve the patient's problems. These will have been identified by the initial and subsequent assessments. The assessments need not be lengthy, rather should they be an evaluation of a changing situation. This chapter is designed to show the physiotherapist how these problems, once identified, may be treated by a carefully chosen technique suitable for the particular problem.

ASTHMA

Asthma is a condition which can change very quickly and physiotherapists will be asked to treat patients in varying stages of the disease. Treatment may be requested for patients suffering from severe acute asthma, or for those in the recovery stage of an asthmatic attack or those who suffer the occasional mild attack.

Severe acute asthma (status asthmaticus)

On admission the patient is usually very short of breath, due to the bronchospasm and the oedematous mucosal linings of the airways. The effort of trying to move air is exhausting and causes obvious acute anxiety.

Problems may be listed as follows:

1a. Decreased airflow due to bronchospasm.
1b. Anxiety due to difficulty of ventilation.
2. Exhaustion due to increased muscle work of breathing.
3. Disturbed breathing pattern.

TREATMENT PLAN AND MANAGEMENT

1.(a) and (b): If, soon after admission, physiotherapy is requested, then it will be designed both to reassure the patient and to find a comfortable position; this will enable the patient to begin to concentrate on diaphragmatic breathing with relaxation of the upper chest while bronchodilator therapy is being administered.

Relief of bronchospasm is paramount and the prescription of a bronchodilator is the first need. It is usually administered by inhalation of the nebulised fluid using a nebuliser and face mask rather than a mouthpiece as most patients 'mouth-breathe' when they are acutely short of breath.

The dosage of bronchodilator solution often prescribed is 5mg salbutamol (1ml of 0.5% respirator solution). As the patient begins to respond to medical treatment a 2.5mg dose is usually as effective. Terbutaline, which has a similar action to salbutamol, may be prescribed instead of salbutamol: the dose is 7.5mg or 5mg (0.75 or 0.5ml of 1% terbutaline respirator solution). Muscular tremor is a side-effect of both drugs. If a patient complains of shaking, particularly of the hands, the physician may need to reduce the dose of the bronchodilator to a minimum.

If bronchodilation is not produced by either salbutamol or terbutaline, ipratropium bromide (Atrovent) may be prescribed. 2ml Atrovent respirator solution is used and the maximum response may not be reached until 1 hour after inhalation. This inhalation therapy may be repeated 4-hourly during the acute stage and gradually reduced as the patient's condition improves. A peak flow chart provides a useful record of the condition of asthmatic patients (Fig. 21/1). 4-hourly readings are taken by the nursing staff, and the physiotherapist records the peak flow rate before, and 15 minutes after, the completion of inhalation of a bronchodilator. Patients who show a persistent fall in PEFR on awakening, should not have their treatment withdrawn until this 'early morning dip' stabilises. As the bronchodilator takes effect, the patient will be able to breathe more easily and may begin to cough and expectorate tenacious plugs of sputum. At this stage effective huffing using the forced expiration technique can be taught. Periods of relaxed diaphragmatic breathing must be encouraged. Gentle vibrations of the chest on expiration can be carried out in the high side-lying position. This should be discontinued if the patient's airways obstruction is aggravated, or he is unable to expectorate. Often gentle rhythmical percussion is

As soon as coughing results in the expectoration of secretions, vibration and shaking of the chest wall can be carried out with the patient in a suitable comfortable position. The forced expiration technique (FET) can now be used. As the patient's condition improves, modified postural drainage can be started and the foot of the bed tipped if necessary and if it is tolerated. Between attacks, some asthmatic patients have a productive cough and these patients should carry out a regular chest clearance programme of breathing exercises, FET, self-percussion and postural drainage if necessary and if tolerated. Care must be taken to ensure that there are sufficient rest periods of gentle diaphragmatic breathing to prevent any recurrence of bronchospasm. Percussion and shakings should not be too vigorous if the patient has been on high doses of corticosteroids, for there is a tendency for such patients to develop osteoporosis and rib fractures can result.

Patients can be issued with home peak flow meters so they can assess their own problems. Most patients are sensible and will call for help when they are deteriorating. This is often when the bronchodilators are failing to work and they keep taking more puffs of the inhaler. With the peak flow meters, patients can actually see a result, and knowing their own 'danger level', they must call the doctor.

Mild asthmatics

Breathing control and the teaching of appropriate relaxation positions can be helpful in overcoming mild attacks of wheezing, but if bronchospasm is more severe, the physiotherapist should advise on the correct use of a pressurised bronchodilator aerosol or other prescribed inhalation equipment. The treatment should include a chest clearance programme if bronchial secretions are present. Localised basal expansion exercises are taught to assist loosening of secretions during postural drainage and to maintain chest mobility.

Asthma in children

Babies and children respond well to postural drainage, and from the age of three upwards it is possible to teach breathing exercises and effective clearance of bronchial secretions. When teaching the forced expiration technique, it may be necessary to practise by blowing down a tube. Postural drainage can be carried out over a foam wedge or pile of newspapers (Fig. 14/19, p. 349). Instruction should be given to parents in the supervision of the exercises at home, and in assistance to the child during an asthma attack. Children are often more comfortable lying flat during an attack of dyspnoea, either supine with their knees bent, in the side-lying position, or kneeling against a pile of pillows (Fig. 14/5c, p. 334).

Diaphragmatic breathing must be encouraged in these modified relaxation positions. It will be necessary for the child to practise his breathing exercises regularly and carry out daily postural drainage to clear excess secretions. As children develop, the airways increase in size and the narrowing of the airways often becomes less severe. Many children require regular administration of bronchodilator drugs such as salbutamol, prophylactic drugs such as Intal and inhaled corticosteroids, to control their asthma. It is important that both the child and his parents understand the correct use and administration of the various drugs. The physiotherapist can play an important role in the instruction into the correct use of the pressurised aerosol, Rotahaler and Spinhaler, as the drug is ineffective with a poor inhaler technique. Infants or children who are unable to use their inhalers effectively are often prescribed nebulised salbutamol and Intal. For home use a simple nebuliser and electrical compressor will be loaned.

In asthmatic patients, exercise may induce wheezing. Chronic childhood asthma can limit some children in their physical activity, exempting them from physical exercise at school, or from participating in sport or exercise during their leisure time. Consequently this inactivity leads to a reduced capacity for exercise and eventually an inability to keep up with other children. The child loses his self-confidence and becomes frightened of producing an exercise-induced asthma attack. In recent years several physical exercise training programmes have been developed to enable asthmatic children to lead a more active normal life and also help them overcome their fear of producing exercise-induced asthma (Keens, 1979; Graff-Lonnevig et al, 1980). Physiotherapists in the UK are becoming more involved in group exercise training programmes for the asthmatic child. These sessions include general activities or sports, swimming and graduated exercise training schemes. As asthma is less likely to be induced by swimming it is a very effective form of exercise for these patients (Fitch and Morton, 1971).

CHRONIC BRONCHITIS AND EMPHYSEMA

Although physiotherapists have been involved in the treatment of patients with chronic airflow limitation for many years, often doctors do not refer patients until they have fairly severe symptoms. In the early stages of chronic bronchitis, the main problem is hypersecretion of mucus, whereas in the later stages, if secondary emphysema changes have occurred, the patient becomes dyspnoeic and wheezy due to increasing airway closure.

Chronic stage

The problems may be listed as follows:

1. Increased secretions which are difficult to remove. This may lead to sputum retention, which will be a source of localised infection with possible collapse of segments or larger sections of lung tissue.
2. Breathlessness, which is a result of the obstruction to airflow and inability to maintain adequate ventilation.
3. Decreased exercise tolerance.

Unlike asthma, the main aim of treatment is the removal of excessive bronchial secretions. All patients with chronic bronchitis should be given a chest clearance programme which may include postural drainage and be advised to continue at home during the productive phases of the disease. In some cases, where emphysema is predominant, tipping may aggravate dyspnoea and so postural drainage will not be included and all exercises may be carried out in a high side-lying position or lying flat.

TREATMENT PLAN AND MANAGEMENT

1. Chest shaking on expiration will assist in the removal of secretions. Effective huffing and coughing should be interspersed with periods of relaxed diaphragmatic breathing. If oxygen therapy is in progress, it must be continued during treatment and only removed for expectoration. If the patient is unable to clear his secretions adequately, it is sometimes helpful to provide increased ventilation and humidification by IPPB. This, in conjunction with postural drainage, will facilitate expectoration, although IPPB is contra-indicated in the presence of emphysematous bullae because of the risk of causing a pneumothorax.

   A bronchodilator is often prescribed and Vitalograph recordings before and after inhalation will indicate the degree of reversibility of the airways. Some patients with obstructive airways disease show a bronchodilator response to salbutamol or terbutaline, although ipratropium bromide (Atrovent) either given alone or with salbutamol has proved more beneficial to some patients. If reversible bronchospasm is present a bronchodilator may be given prior to chest clearance with a nebuliser, pressurised aerosol, or IPPB.

2. All patients should be taught diaphragmatic breathing and shown how to control their breathing during attacks of dyspnoea (Fig. 14/5, p. 334). They should adopt one of the positions and be encouraged to relax the upper chest and shoulder girdle but should not try to reduce the rate of respiration until their pattern of breathing is more controlled. Many emphysematous patients are unable to reduce their rate of respiration and some are unable to eliminate the use of the accessory muscles. Instruction in how to raise the resting respiratory level (p. 332) is helpful in these situations. It is extremely important to ensure that expiration is completely passive, as any forced, or prolonged, expiration produces a rise in intrathoracic pressure which may cause closure of the airways. Some emphysematous patients automatically use 'pursed-lip' breathing, but unless the patient is doing this spontaneously it is unwise to teach this form of breathing.

3. All breathless patients should be taught to control their breathing when walking on the flat or up stairs and hills (p. 336). Although it is not possible to show any improvement in the patient's respiratory function tests following controlled breathing, many patients find they can walk further distances more comfortably with controlled breathing.

These patients should be as mobile and active as possible. Their exercise tolerance may be increased by gradually increasing the distances walked both on the flat and upstairs or slopes while practising breathing control. A graduated exercise programme can also be given to these patients during the later part of their stay in hospital and should be continued at home (p. 336).

Acute exacerbation

If a patient with long-standing chronic bronchitis develops an acute infection, his condition may deteriorate rapidly. These excessive secretions within the bronchial tree can lead to inadequate gas exchange and the patient may go into hypercapnic respiratory failure, as the P_{O_2} (oxygen tension) of the arterial blood falls and the P_{CO_2} (carbon dioxide tension) of the arterial blood rises. As a result, the patient will become drowsy and confused with rapid shallow breathing. If the secretions can be removed and effective alveolar ventilation restored, the patient's condition will improve. Many of these patients are drowsy and unresponsive.

The problems may be listed as follows:

1. Increased secretions, due to an acute infection, which are superimposed on a chronic situation causing increased difficulty in expectoration.
2. Decreased ventilation leading to respiratory failure.
3. Airways collapse on expiration which leads to increasing muscle work of respiration.

TREATMENT PLAN AND MANAGEMENT

This is designed to remove secretions and improve ventilation as quickly as possible. Oxygen therapy will be prescribed and it must be given continuously, therefore the mask must be kept in place throughout the treatment and only removed for expectoration. If the patient keeps removing the mask, the arterial oxygen tension will fluctuate rapidly. Some consultants now prefer to use nasal cannulae as they provide continuous therapy. The doctor must repeat the blood gases, once the patient starts using the nasal cannulae, as there is no way to judge the percentage of oxygen received by the patient. There is no way of humidifying nasal cannulae, so the patient may need extra saline inhalations, which can be given with a mask over the top of the cannulae. The nebuliser should be run on air in these situations.

If bronchodilator therapy is prescribed, it should be given before physiotherapy. Antibiotics will probably be given to combat the infection. Dehydration can make the expectoration of viscid secretions more difficult. Encouragement to take frequent drinks, together with humidification of the inspired gases will help. Generally, if the patient is prescribed 24% oxygen, there are only 4 litres of dry oxygen mixed with 60–100 litres of room air. In this case, it is probably unnecessary to humidify the oxygen, unless the patient is extremely dehydrated with tenacious secretions. Higher percentages have greater flow rates of oxygen and less room air, so it is more likely to require humidification.

1 and 2. The patient should be turned into side lying. The foot of the bed may be elevated if the patient can tolerate it. Shaking and vibrations should be given on the expiratory phase and often the patient will start to cough and expectorate spontaneously and his colour will improve. Sometimes shaking throughout inspiration and expiration will stimulate deeper breathing and is worth trying. If there has been no cough response after 5 to 10 minutes,

nasopharyngeal suction should be considered. Care must be taken not to overtire the patient and controlled oxygen should be given. Treatment should be carried out for about 20 minutes at 2-hourly intervals for the first 48 hours. If a bronchodilator is being given, this should be used for alternate treatments at 4-hourly intervals.

During the night it is usually possible to cut down the number of treatments, but it is usually necessary for the nursing staff to rouse the patient and encourage him to cough at 2-hourly intervals. After 48 hours many patients will show marked improvement and the number of treatments may be cut down.

If the patient does not improve by the first treatment and IPPB is available, then it may be helpful to use the IPPB with a mask to improve ventilation. This would be contra-indicated if the patient has emphysema as there is a risk of causing a pneumothorax. Help will be required to hold the mask over the patient's face and it may be necessary to hand trigger the IPPB machine. It is important to observe the chest wall movement and the patient's level of consciousness. Vibrations and shaking will be given as above.

The patient should be carefully observed for any signs of increased drowsiness after treatment: if there is, it must be reported to the physician as it may be necessary to run the IPPB machine off air with added controlled oxygen. It is helpful to teach the nurses how to give IPPB during the night.

3. As the patient improves, the treatment plan will follow that of the chronic stage, and re-education of the breathing pattern can begin. If the patient does not improve, the physician will have to decide whether to intubate and ventilate him; many physicians are reluctant to take this step when patients have severe chronic bronchitis. If the patient is intubated treatment will be as described on page 287.

Emphysema (primary)

Although many patients present with the signs and symptoms of both chronic bronchitis and emphysema, a minority of patients with emphysema may have the condition known as 'primary' emphysema. This often develops without any previous history of chest disease and is commonly associated with a familial deficiency in α_1-antitrypsin (see p. 327). The problems are:

1. Extreme dyspnoea.
2. Occasionally there are increased secretions.

OCCUPATIONAL LUNG DISEASE

Damage to the lungs by dusts or fumes or noxious substances inhaled by workers in certain specific occupations is known as 'occupational lung disease' (see pages 472–7).

Coal miners' pneumoconiosis

CLINICAL FEATURES

The diagnosis of pneumoconiosis should be suspected in a man who complains of increasing breathlessness on exertion and who has worked in the coal mines for several years. It is common for the patient to be a cigarette smoker and to have associated chronic bronchitis.

Usually, the problems are:

1. If sputum is present it is usually mucoid but it will become purulent during infective exacerbations. It may become jet black when lesions cavitate.
2. Once progressive massive fibrosis is established the disease is progressive even if the patient is no longer exposed to coal dust. In advanced cases, the patient becomes grossly disabled and death from cor pulmonale is common. Pulmonary tuberculosis may develop as an added complication.

TREATMENT

There is no specific treatment for pneumoconiosis and the most important aspect of its management is prevention. This implies effective dust suppression, the early recognition of dust retention by means of routine radiography and, when necessary, the provision of alternative employment in areas of low dust concentration to prevent progress of the disease.

PHYSIOTHERAPY

Physiotherapy will be similar to that used in the treatment of chronic bronchitis and emphysema. If the patient has an infection every effort should be made to assist in the removal of secretions. If there is extensive fibrosis IPPB may be helpful in assisting the patient to cough. In the advanced stages of the disease, all that the physiotherapist can do is to try to teach the patient to breathe with the minimum amount of effort and to assist in effective coughing.

Silicosis

CLINICAL FEATURES

Usually, symptoms do not develop until after several years of exposure to the dust. Usually, the problems are:

1. Progressive dyspnoea on exertion.
2. Unproductive cough (occasional haemoptysis may occur).
3. Recurrent bouts of bronchitis.

If tuberculosis supervenes there is deterioration in the general condition accompanied by increase in cough and sputum, pyrexia and loss of weight. Eventually the patient becomes very disabled and death occurs from bronchopneumonia, tuberculosis or cor pulmonale.

TREATMENT

There is no specific treatment and since silicosis continues to progress after exposure to the dust has ceased, it is vital to diagnose the disease early and remove the patient from further contact with the dust. All workers exposed to silica dust should have a regular chest radiograph.

PHYSIOTHERAPY

The treatment will be as for chronic bronchitis and emphysema. The aims will be to help in removal of secretions by means of postural drainage and possibly IPPB and to teach the patient to breathe with the minimum amount of effort.

Asbestosis

CLINICAL FEATURES

The main problems are:

1. Cough. Asbestos bodies may be found on microscopy of the sputum.
2. Dyspnoea.

Preventive measures are similar to those used in silicosis.

PHYSIOTHERAPY

This is similar to that described for pneumoconiosis and silicosis.

Various other occupational diseases such as *farmer's lung* and *bird fancier's lung* will be encountered by physiotherapists treating chest disease. Details can be found on pages 475–7. Physiotherapy will be directed towards assistance with expectoration and teaching the patient to breathe with the minimum amount of effort. IPPB may also be of help.

DIFFUSE FIBROSING ALVEOLITIS

This is alternatively known as diffuse interstitial lung disease, diffuse interstitial pulmonary fibrosis, Hamman-Rich syndrome.

It is a condition of unknown aetiology characterised by a diffuse inflammatory process beyond the terminal bronchiole. Essential features are cellular thickening of the alveolar walls showing a tendency to fibrosis and the presence of large mononuclear cells within the alveolar spaces.

Clinically, the outstanding characteristic is progressive and unremitting dyspnoea. In the later stages secondary infection may require treatment. Clubbing of the fingers is common. The disease is often fatal, in the subacute form originally described by Hamman and Rich this may be within six months, in the commonest chronic form within a few years.

The only effective treatment is with corticosteroid drugs. Other treatment is purely palliative. Oxygen is given in high concentrations, as patients with fibrosing alveolitis do not retain carbon dioxide. Heart failure may be temporarily improved with diuretics and digitalis. Appropriate sedation should be given in the terminal stages.

PHYSIOTHERAPY

This will be purely palliative but may be of help during infections when chest vibration may help in the removal of secretions. Positions for dyspnoea and breathing control during walking can also be taught to the patient in the early stages of the disease in the hope that they might help a little.

CYSTIC FIBROSIS

The clinical aspects of cystic fibrosis are discussed on pages 481–3. Physiotherapy plays a vitally important role in the treatment of the cystic fibrosis patient. Physiotherapists will see patients at all stages of the disease; their progression will vary greatly and each patient must be considered individually and treatment adapted accordingly

(Gaskell, 1975). With early diagnosis and improved treatment many patients are now surviving to over the age of 30. As soon as the diagnosis is confirmed, a regime of postural drainage must be instituted and the patient and his family or friends taught how this can be carried out at home for, once started, postural drainage has to continue for life.

The lung condition will be treated by antibiotics and physiotherapy. Although the antibiotic therapy will be varied according to the patient's condition, daily postural drainage will be necessary for life. The length of time required for each treatment session will depend on the amount of secretions present and the areas of the lung that have to be drained. If the radiograph shows that specific areas of the lungs are involved, the appropriate postural drainage positions are used, otherwise the basal and mid-zone areas should be drained each day. At home many patients will need to carry out postural drainage for up to 30 minutes only once or twice a day, but it must be realised that this will need to be increased if they feel unwell or if there is an increase in the sputum volume.

A home postural drainage programme must be worked out for each patient and it is important that drainage is carried out effectively in the shortest possible time. Many patients are able to treat themselves effectively and efficiently without assistance if they are taught postural drainage using the forced expiration technique (p. 339). Pryor et al (1979) showed that cystic fibrosis patients who have been relying on assistance with postural drainage at home could carry out their treatment more efficiently without assistance after being taught the forced expiration technique. Nevertheless, the physiotherapist must realise that patients with an acute exacerbation of their bronchopulmonary infection will need professional assistance, even though the efficiency of assisted postural drainage will be improved by using the forced expiration technique.

A portable tipping frame can be an asset to many patients at home, but it is important that such a frame is designed to fully support the patient in the required postural drainage positions. A frame that is angled in the centre is uncomfortable and only allows the patient to drain the posterior basal segments of the lungs. The families of infants and young children should be shown the postural drainage positions appropriate to the patient as well as being taught the technique of clapping and chest shaking.

Adolescents often become resentful of their condition and frequently rebel against the routine of postural drainage. Great patience must be taken with explanations and persuasion that regular postural drainage is important and, if they can become more independent, added friction within the family may be avoided. The timing of treatment can be varied to fit in with daily commitments. Participation in physical education at school should be encouraged and on leaving school they should continue in activities such as swimming, running and squash. These should continue until such time as vigorous exercise becomes impossible.

Airways obstruction may become a predominant factor in some patients and many develop overinflation of the chest. Breathing control with relaxation of the upper chest should be encouraged during postural drainage. Dyspnoeic patients should be shown relaxation positions (Fig. 14/5, p. 334) and taught the use of controlled breathing in these positions and when climbing stairs, or walking up hills.

With the progression of the disease, many patients develop a rigid lower thoracic cage; therefore exercises to mobilise the trunk and to correct posture, should be included in their treatment programme.

During an exacerbation intensive physiotherapy is essential, for which the patient probably will be admitted to hospital. Physiotherapy may be given up to six times a day: this can be carried out by the physiotherapist four times during the day with the patient giving himself his own late evening and early morning treatment. If several lobes are affected it is often easier to drain one or two areas at one session and the other affected areas at the next session: this will ensure that the patient does not become exhausted. If the patient is not admitted to hospital, and it is difficult to manage his treatment at home, daily outpatient physiotherapy should be arranged.

Patients often find expectoration of tenacious secretions easier after the inhalation of extra humidity from a nebuliser using a mouthpiece. If the patient is being nursed with an oxygen mask, high humidification should be incorporated into the system. The inhalation of hypertonic saline can be beneficial in expectoration of viscid sputum.

If bronchospasm is present it may be relieved by inhalation of a bronchodilator before treatment. In some cases of resistant chest infections, antibiotics may be inhaled directly into the lungs (p. 360). When the patient is prescribed more than one antibiotic, the drugs are inhaled sequentially, as some antibiotics become ineffective if inhaled together in the nebuliser. The inhalation should follow postural drainage.

On rare occasions, if the patient is not in the terminal stages of the disease, IPPB may be of help in the clearance of secretions. Because these patients have a tendency to pneumothorax the inspiratory pressures should be kept low (i.e. below 10cm H_2O). The course of treatment should be short (5 to 14 days) because IPPB has been shown to increase residual volumes in these patients if used for long periods of time (Matthews et al, 1964). Once the acute exacerbation is over IPPB should be discontinued as soon as possible.

Although cystic fibrosis patients do not attend for regular outpatient physiotherapy it is important for the physiotherapist to see them and their relatives at intervals to assess their general condition and to discuss any problems. The most convenient way to do this is for the physiotherapist to be available when they attend the doctor's outpatient clinic. At these visits the physiotherapy regime should be checked and altered as necessary and advice can be given on any problems. It is important to keep regular records of each patient's treatment and progress.

COMPLICATIONS

Complications of cystic fibrosis include haemoptysis and spontaneous pneumothorax. Many patients have mild haemoptyses; if there is only slight streaking of the sputum, postural drainage can be continued avoiding vigorous percussion. If a more severe haemoptysis occurs, postural drainage should be continued, but percussion should not be given until the bleeding lessens. Effective huffing should be encouraged rather than vigorous coughing. If very severe bleeding occurs, postural drainage should be discontinued, but resumed as soon as possible to remove any blood that has accumulated in the lungs.

A spontaneous pneumothorax may occur in the older patient; if it is small it can absorb spontaneously and physiotherapy is continued. A larger pneumothorax may require the insertion of an intercostal drainage tube attached to an underwater seal; physiotherapy is discontinued until the drain has been inserted. Percussion should be avoided over the site of the tube but otherwise treatment can continue. Analgesia may be necessary before treatment.

Breathing exercises should be encouraged to assist re-expansion of the affected lung. If the air leak persists, pleurodesis or pleurectomy may have to be considered (see p. 372). If a thoracotomy is carried out physiotherapy must be resumed as soon as the patient has recovered from the anaesthetic. Postural drainage should be started within a few hours of surgery as the secretions are often thick and tenacious. High humidification can be helpful and it is important to give adequate analgesia particularly before physiotherapy sessions.

Physiotherapy should be continued during the terminal stage of the disease even though it will not be achieving much. As treatment will have become an integral part of the patient's life, he will become

anxious and worried if this is suddenly withdrawn. The physiotherapist should carefully assess the amount of treatment required
and the sessions should not be allowed to cause undue exhaustion.
Nasopharyngeal suction should not be considered as it is an
unpleasant procedure and will serve no useful purpose.

BRONCHIECTASIS

The clinical aspects of this disease are discussed on pages 478–81.
The diagnosis of bronchiectasis is usually confirmed by a bronchogram (see Fig. 5/17, p. 146).

The problems are:

1. A productive cough with purulent sputum and repeated respiratory infections. Haemoptysis of varying severity can occur and,
   in some patients who suffer from 'dry' bronchiectasis, haemoptysis may be the only symptom.
2. Risk of chest deformity.
3. Sometimes there is decreased exercise tolerance.

TREATMENT PLAN AND MANAGEMENT

1. A chest clearance programme is taught.
   As a result of the disease, destruction of the cilia responsible
   for the clearing of secretions will have occurred. Therefore,
   postural drainage is essential for patients with a productive
   cough. They will have to continue postural drainage for the rest
   of their lives and careful home instruction is a vital part of their
   treatment. The correct use of the forced expiration technique (p.
   339) can often help these patients to become more independent.
   During an acute exacerbation of the disease the administration
   of a bronchodilator and high humidity can relieve bronchospasm
   and aid in the expectoration of tenacious secretions. In some
   cases when the patient is too exhausted to cough and clear his
   secretions effectively, IPPB can prove helpful.
2. Breathing exercises to increase ventilation, encourage chest
   expansion and maintain the mobility of the chest must be taught.
3. The participation in general exercise and sport by the younger
   patient can be beneficial and should be encouraged.

For patients with dry bronchiectasis postural drainage will be of
limited value and vigorous coughing may increase the possibility of
haemoptysis. If a mild haemoptysis occurs in productive patients,
postural drainage may be continued, but percussion should be

omitted until the bleeding has ceased. If severe haemoptysis occurs, physiotherapy should be discontinued temporarily until the bleeding has been controlled.

If the disease is localised, surgery may be undertaken; the physiotherapy is discussed in Chapter 15, page 374.

PNEUMONIA

The clinical aspects of the pneumonias are discussed on pages 487–91.

Lobar pneumonia

This type of pneumonia is seen in hospital only occasionally for it responds well to antibiotics. Although consolidation of one or more lobes may be seen on the radiograph, the patient usually has an unproductive cough.

Usually, the problems are:

1. Pain which is due to inflammation of the pleura over the affected lung tissue and is made worse on coughing and deep breathing.
2. Breathlessness.

If physiotherapy is requested, the treatment must not be confused with that given for bronchopneumonia.

TREATMENT PLAN AND MANAGEMENT

1. Ensure that adequate analgesia is given.
2. Breathing exercises will be encouraged, particularly *inspiratory*.

As the consolidation gradually resolves, the pleuritic pain diminishes making coughing less painful. Sputum production is *not* usual: physiotherapists do get concerned about this, but it is a fact that sputum (which will probably be rusty in colour) is rare in lobar pneumonia. If, however, there is sputum then postural drainage may be given for the affected area and, as the pleuritic pain decreases, gentle shaking and vibration may be added. Diaphragmatic breathing and localised basal expansion should be encouraged and treatment carried out as often as necessary.

Bronchopneumonia

This type of pneumonia is very common, particularly in the older patient. It is seen much more frequently than the lobar type, and is

REHABILITATION

Many of these patients are extremely ill and will have a lengthy stay in hospital. It may be necessary to arrange an exercise programme for them, which they can carry out in the gymnasium.

PULMONARY EMBOLISM

A pulmonary embolus most commonly arises from a deep vein thrombosis in the leg or pelvis and the patient may present with the signs of massive pulmonary embolism or pulmonary infarct.

Massive pulmonary embolism

A large pulmonary embolism may cause sudden death; if the embolism is not fatal an emergency pulmonary embolectomy is often performed. (See Chapter 16 for physiotherapy.)

Pulmonary infarction

Small emboli cause pulmonary infarction. Those at greatest risk are the old and obese, the patient with cardiac disease and the postoperative patient.

Frequently, the problems are:

1. Breathlessness.
2. Pleuritic pain.
3. A pleural effusion may develop.

TREATMENT PLAN AND MANAGEMENT

Physiotherapy is mainly prophylactic and all patients at risk should be given active leg exercises and breathing exercises in order to assist the venous return and maintain ventilation. These patients should be encouraged to carry out active foot and leg exercises at frequent intervals during the day and early ambulation is important.

If a pulmonary embolus does occur, physiotherapy may be discontinued until anticoagulant therapy has been established after which treatment is usually re-requested by the physician or surgeon. In many units physiotherapy will continue as it is felt that this is the time when deep breathing should be encouraged to prevent unnecessary collapse/consolidation. If a clot(s) moves it will only do so peripherally and therefore does no more harm. At this stage some patients may expectorate old blood and clot and chest movements may be limited by pleuritic pain. Analgesia is often required before treatment. Localised breathing exercises should be given to the affected area and, occasionally, postural drainage may be necessary. Leg exercises should be continued until the patient is ambulant.

TUMOURS OF THE LUNG

Carcinoma of the bronchus

The clinical aspects are discussed on pages 499–504. Surgical removal of the affected lobe or lung is often the treatment of choice. Pre- and postoperative physiotherapy is discussed in Chapter 15.

If the growth is too extensive or the patient has poor respiratory function, surgical resection may be unsuitable. In these cases, radiotherapy or chemotherapy may be used to reduce the size of the tumour and relieve the bronchial obstruction.

Usually, the problems are:

1. Infection: if there is infection beyond the bronchial obstruction the patient may start to expectorate purulent sputum. This will occur particularly if the tumour is being treated by radiotherapy.
2. Breathlessness, due to pulmonary fibrosis which may result from radiotherapy.

TREATMENT PLAN AND MANAGEMENT

1. Postural drainage and gentle vibrations can aid the removal of secretions. Vigorous shaking or percussion are contra-indicated, because of the poor condition of the patient and the possibility of haemoptysis or the presence of metastases in the spine or ribs.
2. It may be helpful to teach controlled breathing patterns, particularly when walking and during personal daily activities.

As well as treating the lung condition symptoms, the physiotherapist may need to treat other disabilities which can arise from either the primary growth or from metastatic spread. Such effects will include hemiplegia (from cerebral secondaries), paraplegia (from spinal secondaries or lymph node involvement of the para-aortic nodes), generalised neuropathy of the lower limbs or hypertrophic pulmonary osteoarthropathy. It is not unknown for a patient to *present* with any of these signs from which the positive diagnosis of a bronchial carcinoma will be made, although there are no lung symptoms. Physiotherapy for these other conditions will follow the normal treatments for such disabilities, but will require daily modification according to the condition of the patient.

SYMPTOMS (Table 22/1)

Probably the greatest effect of a low carbon dioxide level is a decrease in cerebral blood flow. It is therefore not too surprising that observant people may report that they have lost the ability to concentrate and that they also suffer memory disturbances. Other symptoms include dizziness, fainting, migrainous headache, feelings of depersonalisation, paraesthesiae and the sensation of heaviness 'like lead' in the limbs. There is usually a general lethargy, exhaustion which is unrelated to exercise, muscle pain, tremor and sometimes (but rarely) tetany.

TABLE 22/1   Some symptoms of chronic hyperventilation

Symptom type	Presenting features
Cardiovascular	palpitation, tachycardia, peripheral vasoconstriction
Respiratory	bronchospasm, breathlessness, 'air hunger', excessive sighing, chest pain
Gastro-intestinal	dysphagia, dyspepsia, epigastric pain, 'spastic colon', diarrhoea
Neurological	paraesthesiae, dizziness, lack of co-ordination, disturbance of vision, disturbance of hearing, black-outs
Musculoskeletal	muscle pains, involuntary contractions, tremors, cramps, tetany
General	exhaustion, lethargy, weakness, sleep disturbance, headache, disturbance of concentration and memory, anxiety, panic attacks, phobic states, excessive sweating

Patients who have frequented chest or cardiac clinics without help may complain of shortness of breath or 'breath hunger', bronchospasm, palpitation, tachycardia and chest pain. Patients in this group have often been investigated thoroughly without diagnosis, even to undergoing coronary arteriography and cardiac catheterisation.

Gastro-intestinal symptoms, such as dysphagia, dyspepsia, colonic spasms and diarrhoea, are common. A great number of patients report feelings of excess tension, anxiety, fear, attacks of panic and various phobic states, such as claustrophobia and agoraphobia.

Personality

Why, one may ask, should a group of people respond by overbreathing? One hypothesis is that there is a personality link. The type of person who chronically hyperventilates tends towards the perfectionist personality; one who is striving to fulfil the very high expectations set for self; one who is forever rushing to be on time or meet self-set deadlines. The stress in this type of life is enormous and the primitive reflexes of 'fight or flight' are constantly being stimulated. However, in our Western civilised society there is usually no one to fight and nowhere to flee in the physical sense. Thus an inappropriate pattern of respiratory behaviour is set.

Breathing pattern

The breathing pattern regularly observed is predominantly upper thoracic. There is a typical sternal heave and the accessory muscles of inspiration are seen to be working. The respiratory rate and depth are extremely irregular and the whole pattern is interspersed with excessive sighs (Fig. 22/1).

FIG. 22/1 Diagrammatic representation of a spirometry tracing showing a typically irregular pattern

These patterns vary widely from gross upper thoracic movement with sternomastoid action at a rate of 50 breaths a minute, to minimal upper thoracic movement at a near to normal rate. The degree of lower costal and abdominal movement also varies from almost nil to nearly normal. It is clear that there is a wide range of variants but essentially the patient moves a greater volume of air than that which is demanded by the metabolic rate. There does not seem to be a strict correlation between the abnormality of breathing pattern and the depression of P_{CO_2}.

GUIDE TO PHYSIOTHERAPY

The history should be taken carefully, with understanding and sensitivity. It is not uncommon for the patient to be nervous, frightened and ill at ease because the symptoms may have been misunderstood at many clinics; it helps, therefore, if the patient recognises that the therapist is on his side. During the history taking, note should be made of the breathing pattern and of the manner of speaking.

Record of information

SYMPTOMS

The symptoms should be listed and numbered in order of severity and/or recurrence.

HISTORY

Generally one can elicit from the history that there was a trigger point in the patient's life. It might have been an emotional or physical disturbance. For instance, a great emotional upset such as the death of a close and dear relative or friend, family breakdown, a frightening experience or emotional pressure may have been the precipitating factor. On the other hand, a physical illness such as glandular fever is commonly reported. It would seem that the normal physiological response to these stresses and illnesses persists after recovery, thus becoming abnormal for the recovered situation. If the patient misrepresents the symptoms of an acute short-term episode of stress, a pattern of inappropriate responses may become impressed.

Family history: It is helpful to discover whether parents, siblings, or more distant relatives have experienced similar symptoms, or have a history of respiratory or cardiac disease.

Childhood history: General health, physical ability, exercise tolerance and illness patterns should be discovered.

Recent history: If possible, both medical and social histories should be discussed. This will include a resumé of the occasion when symptoms were first experienced and to what they were attributed. It should be noted whether there is a history of chronic pain.

PHYSICAL EXAMINATION

With the patient undressed note is made of:

(a) the shape of the chest
(b) any physical deformities
(c) the pattern of breathing
(d) auscultation.

PROVOCATION TEST (Hardonk and Beumer, 1979)

This test is done with the patient dressed and sitting comfortably. The test is explained and the patient asked to note any symptoms which are precipitated and whether or not these are recognised as 'their' symptoms. The patient is then requested to breathe as deeply and as quickly as possible for 3 minutes. It will be necessary to encourage this process as it becomes very tiring. Some people cannot complete the 3-minutes' task. The time of recovery is then recorded. Only if the patient becomes very distressed can a re-breathing bag be used to hasten recovery.

Any symptoms which occurred are then noted and discussed. This test is often useful for patients who cannot accept that their symptoms are related to the way they breathe.

Treatment

Treatment is directed towards re-education of the breathing pattern and subsequent physical and mental relaxation. Some therapists concentrate on acquiring a physical relaxation, working towards a mental relaxation or even a mild auto-hypnotic state with ensuing slowing of the respiratory rate. The treatment described here involves conscious control of the breathing pattern. Physical relaxation is usually automatically induced during practice. The aim is to decrease ventilation to raise the resting arterial Pco_2. This is possible by conscious control of the depth, rate and regularity of respiration so that the respiratory centre will eventually accept the higher Pco_2 as its norm. Initially, this is an uncomfortable sensation, but with patient practice it is possible and successful. Until the new pattern becomes the natural, constant, unconscious method of breathing, the patient will continue to experience episodes of the acute symptoms in recognisable situations. That is, some acute local manifestation may continue to be apparent at times of stress, during or after exercise. It is therefore necessary to teach control at these times, so that the sudden lowered Pco_2 may be returned to normality more quickly. It is possible to prevent the intermittent dropping of P_{CO_2} by teaching the patient to recognise the dangerous situations and to take precautionary measures at these times.

In short, the treatment is twofold:

1. Long-term: To re-educate the basic breathing pattern to normality.
2. Short-term: To teach compensatory measures for times of altered breathing patterns which produce local symptoms.

TECHNIQUE

The ideal position for breathing re-education, in a person with no respiratory disease, is lying supported with a pillow or pillows for the head and a pillow under the knees (Fig. 22/2). In this position there is no need for muscular tone to maintain posture and the abdominal muscles can be totally relaxed, thus the natural predominantly 'diaphragmatic' pattern of breathing will not be restricted. When the patient is settled comfortably a brief, simple description of respiration is given so that an understanding is reached of the relationship between the movement of the thorax and abdomen and the movements of air in and out. An explanation of gaseous exchange should also be given in simple terms so that the patient really understands the rationale of the treatment. Breathing awareness must first be learned and can be helped by the physiotherapist

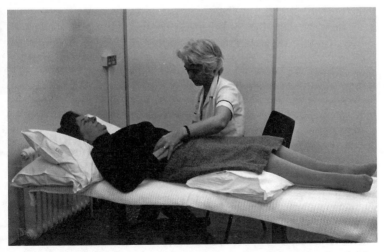

FIG. 22/2 Suggested position for breathing re-education. *Note* the physiotherapist's watch for timing the respiratory rate

placing her hands lightly on the chest and abdomen and at the same time relating what is happening during each phase of the respiratory cycle. This is useful both for patient and physiotherapist.

As soon as one is aware of breathing at the conscious level there is a degree of discomfort or unease. This must be discussed with the patient so that each step is clearly understood. At this stage both patient and therapist should know the rate, depth and rhythm of the breathing cycle. Re-education of a normal, relaxed, predominantly 'diaphragmatic' pattern will begin by directing the patient's attention to the abdomen. Sensory input may be increased if the patient rests both hands over the abdomen and is led to notice the gentle, soft rise and fall of the abdomen during breathing. Care must be taken not to allow a forced movement nor is a large movement to be produced. Guidance can be given breath by breath, and phase by phase, by relating which movement is good, and which is incorrect. Some patients find it remarkably difficult to make any kind of lower costal or abdominal movement during a natural inspiration. It may be necessary to spend many treatments persuading and talking, using different word combinations and different manual pressures on the patient's chest and abdomen to obtain any semblance of a natural pattern of movement. Eventually most patients manage to recognise what is required to change the movement from the upper thorax to the lower thoraco-abdominal region. It is a change from breathing 'in and up' to breathing 'in and down'.

Gradually a new corrected pattern must be found. This will be a very individual pattern. One, two or all three components of the rate, depth and rhythm of breathing may need to be corrected.

Recognition of each phase of breathing can be gained by concentrating on one phase at a time; this is best practised with the eyes closed.

The inspiration should be regarded so that the size and feeling can be recognised.

The expiration is then regarded to experience consciously the gentle movement of air which comes to a spontaneous halt. This point of natural rest (expiratory level) must be recognised.

The point of natural rest is then described so that the patient can begin to feel the relaxation (not tension) of this point in the respiratory cycle. The physiotherapist should have a watch with a second hand available (Fig. 22/2). Although the breathing rate is controlled at the level of the individual breath, it is helpful to make a note of the respiratory rate per minute.

The new breathing cycle may be of two or three phases. A two-phase cycle would consist of a gentle inspiration followed by a slow expiration with the air trickling out to use up the time period. In a three-phase cycle the natural rest point at the end of expiration is used and extended. A gentle inspiration is followed by an easy expiration and then there is a prolonged pause or wait period before the next inspiration is initiated.

The correction can be guided in time by the therapist monotonously counting aloud the phases of each breath cycle, e.g. Inandouttwothreeandinandouttwothreeandin ... A slow, shallow, smooth, regular pattern is sought. There is a multitude of possibilities. It may be necessary to start with a regular, simple Inoutinoutin ... pattern, or a three-phase pattern, e.g. Inoutrelax-inoutrelaxin ... These are shown diagrammatically in Figure 22/3. Once a pattern has been found it must be reinforced in the mind of the patient. This can be achieved by the constant, monotonous counting of the therapist during the breathing cycles. The use of a tape recorder is often invaluable at this stage for those who cannot easily carry the memory of their pattern. The physiotherapist can make a recording of the counting of the pattern during a treatment session. These recorded sessions can then be used at home until the new pattern is accepted.

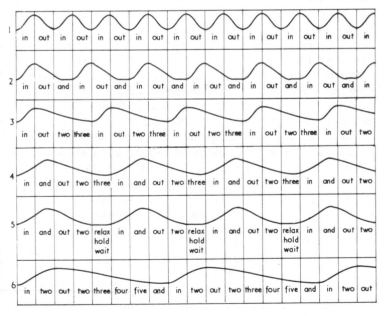

FIG. 22/3 Some suggested patterns of breathing demonstrating inspiratory and expiratory phases

Sooner or later during the practice session the patient will have a growing desire to break away from the control and regularity. At this stage an explanation of what is happening must be made so that the patient is able to participate more fully in the re-education. The desire to breathe is the result of a rising arterial Pco_2 and the natural response is to lower it to acceptable levels. The respiratory centres of patients who live with a low Pco_2 as the norm will respond in the normal way to a rising Pco_2. It is essential that this point of the 'desire to breathe' is reached, because this is a sign that the new pattern is in fact effective in its aim of increasing the circulating CO_2 level. Conscious maintenance of the level must be continued for as long as possible without stress.

The stretch reflexes of the joints and muscles of the chest wall probably also play a part in the degree of discomfort in patients with grossly irregular breathing. The patient will become tense and anxious if the uncomfortable desire to break away from the conscious, regular pattern continues to increase. The situation must therefore be controlled. Simple swallowing may ease the discomfort. If this is not sufficient then the patient must be taught to take a deep, but controlled, slow breath and to compensate for the movement of a large volume of air by extending the period of time, i.e. the breath should be held for 2 or 3 seconds (or a count of five or six) at full inspiration and again at the end of expiration.

In a normal subject the Pco_2 drops as the result of a deep breath and takes anything up to 4 minutes to return to normal, unless compensatory breath-holding procedures are taken. Patients must therefore understand this phenomenon and learn to compensate by breath-holding, preferably at the point of expiration whenever they find themselves deep-breathing or sighing.

The patient should be able to control the breathing pattern while sitting, standing, walking, during and after exercise and at times of stress or individually dangerous situations. Patterns of breathing must be found for these activities and practised at treatment sessions (Figs. 22/4, 22/5).

Tuition is also necessary during a time of breathlessness to enable the patient to control the breathing by doing one thing at a time, i.e. by slowing the rate; then taking smaller breaths; then slowing the rate; and so on until a controlled pattern has been achieved.

SPEECH

Some patients have difficulty in talking and this may be the time that acute local symptoms occur. Teachers or telephone operators may find it very disabling. Control of breathing during speech must be

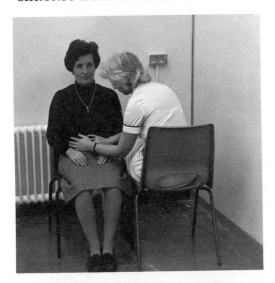

FIG. 22/4 Practice of a new breathing pattern in sitting

FIG. 22/5 Breathing control during exercise

taught to these patients. Generally, large volumes of air are moved especially if one or more sentences are spoken on one breath. Often the expiratory reserve is consumed and the patient is forced to take in a deep breath. The patient is taught to breathe at the commas rather than at alternate fullstops! It is important to keep an adequate reserve of air in the lungs to prevent too rapid a loss of CO_2. Training therefore consists of reading aloud to obtain proficiency in using more small, smooth breaths per sentence and to articulate each word more slowly and softly.

COMPENSATORY PROCEDURES

The short-term or first aid measure is a conscious compensation for the movement of large volumes of air. Whether this movement is from frequent sighing, deep breathing or a resort to the bad habit of irregularity the compensation is similar, i.e. compensatory breath-holding which is so planned that a natural breathing pattern is subsequently possible. This procedure must be practised in treatment sessions.

Intermittent breath-holding is a useful treatment to be practised throughout the day. This breath-holding is not prepared for by a deep breath; rather, the breathing is stopped, anywhere in the cycle, for a count of three, or such time that does not provoke a deeper inspiration to follow. It can be linked to an everyday activity which is frequently performed, such as walking through a doorway, into a lift, or (if the patient is an office worker) every time the telephone rings.

PLANNED RE-BREATHING

There is a small group of people who, for one reason or another, cannot manage to control their pattern unaided. They are able to control their pattern for most of the time but not at times of particular stress. The careful, controlled use of a face mask, paper or polythene bag may be taught for this group. At times of acute distress a polythene bag of approximately 25cm × 30cm may be used as a re-breathing apparatus. The bag must be shaken out so that it is full of room air. The open end of the bag is then placed over the nose and mouth so that the patient can breathe freely (naturally, not deeply) in and out of the bag full of air (Fig. 22/6). Re-breathing of expired gases will then take place, thus raising the patient's P_{CO_2}. After about 12 breaths there will not be sufficient oxygen left in the bag, so it must be removed from the face and re-shaken to re-fill the bag with another supply of fresh air. Care must be taken not to breathe deeply during this time. This procedure should continue

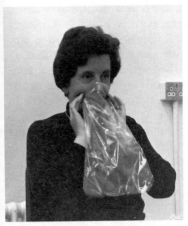

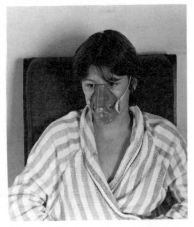

FIG. 22/6 Re-breathing using a
polythene bag

FIG. 22/7 Re-breathing using a
face mask

until the acute presenting symptoms are controlled or until the
patient feels able to control the breathing pattern spontaneously.

An ordinary oxygen therapy face mask may be used for patients
who are unable to control the breathing pattern sufficiently or for
those who, as a result of their hyperventilation, are house-bound and
are unable to do household or personal chores. The plastic face mask
should be worn, possibly for long periods of time or at least for the
duration of the task, so that the Pco_2 is artificially raised by the re-
breathing function of the face mask. Generally all vent-holes are left
open so that normal room air can be drawn in to maintain sufficient
oxygen concentration (Fig. 22/7).

It is unwise to use bags or masks too freely as some patients
become dependent on the aid and never learn self-control. They
must only be used when all other avenues have been investigated and
the patient's personality and situation understood.

HOME PROGRAMME

Practice sessions should be as often as possible and for as long as
possible but common sense must prevail and an acceptable
programme be worked out by the patient and physiotherapist. It
may only be practicable to practise twice a day for 5 minutes, but three
or four times a day for 20 or 30 minutes is obviously more beneficial.

Suggested programme: It is good to start the day with a period of
conscious control of the breathing pattern. It is suggested that
between 10 and 25 minutes is spent in practice before getting up.

Travelling is time well spent in conscious breathing control, whether it be on public transport or, for car drivers, while waiting at traffic lights. Coffee, lunch and tea breaks could afford a few moments of practice. About 15 minutes should be put aside to relax and control the breathing pattern when arriving back home after work or shopping. A longer period is advised at this time as the evening can be more enjoyable if adequate time has been given to correct the system. The last period of practice can be done having retired to bed for the night. The position of choice would be the favourite sleeping position.

Compensatory breath-holding, intermittent breath-holding and general mental and physical relaxation should become part of the normal day and a more regular breathing pattern will eventually take place.

FREQUENCY OF TREATMENT

Treatment sessions may take up to 1 hour at the beginning. In-patients will be treated daily at first, while out-patients' appointments need only be weekly. As the patient progressess, treatment sessions become less frequent. Some patients need merely two or three sessions; others 12 or 14, spaced out over 6 to 12 months. At the time of discharge it is important for the patient to know where to telephone for advice and that he can return for a 'refresher session' if in trouble.

GENERAL EXERCISE

Some patients may need extra help with general relaxation, exercise or fitness programmes. As a result of the disordered breathing many patients have been unable to exercise and so have become unfit, thus compounding their problem. Swimming is also an excellent form of free exercise to advise, as breathing, by necessity, is controlled and synchronised with movement.

GROUP THERAPY

Some centres have arranged self-help groups, where people can exchange ideas and exercise together. These group sessions can be very beneficial after an individual pattern of breathing control has been mastered and the patient is progressing to breathing control during exercise. Fitness training can also be carried out in a group, although each person will be following an individual scheme of progression. These group sessions must be monitored carefully to avoid them becoming centres for 'swapping symptoms'.

Conclusion

Patience and perseverance are needed for the long-term re-education of the breathing pattern, which aims at slowly increasing the resting Pco_2 to more normal levels. This comprises the practice of a conscious control of breathing into a slow, shallow, smooth, and regular pattern. This pattern should eventually become the new, natural, unconscious, constant pattern.

Chronic habitual hyperventilators are often gifted and interesting people: their condition is a challenging one for the physiotherapist. A high proportion of sufferers are greatly helped or cured by a systematic, individual treatment and by an intelligent and sympathetic approach to the syndrome.

REFERENCE

Hardonk, H. J. and Beumer, H. M. (1979). In *The Handbook of Clinical Neurology*, (eds. Vinker, P. J. and Bruyn, G. W.), **38**, 309–60. North Holland Publishing Co, Amsterdam.

BIBLIOGRAPHY

Bass, C. and Gardner, W. N. (1985). Respiratory and psychiatric abnormalities in chronic symptomatic hyperventilation. *British Medical Journal* (Clin. Res.), **290**, 1387–90.

Bass, C. and Gardner, W. N. (1985). Diagnostic issues in the hyperventilation syndrome (letter). *British Journal of Psychology*, **146**, 101–2.

Clark, T. J. H. and Cochrane, G. M. (1970). Effect of personality on alveolar ventilation in patients with chronic airways obstruction. *British Medical Journal*, **1**, 273–5.

Cluff, R. A. (1985). Chronic hyperventilation and its treatment by physiotherapy. *Physiotherapy*, **71**, 7, 301–6.

Evans, D. W. and Lum, L. C. (1977). Hyperventilation: an important cause of pseudo-angina. *Lancet*, **1**, 155–7.

Kraft, A. R. and Hoogduin, A. L. (1984). The hyperventilation syndrome. A pilot study on the effectiveness of treatment. *British Journal of Psychiatry*, **145**, 538–42.

Lewis, B. I. (1959). Hyperventilation syndrome. A clinical and physiological evaluation. *California Medicine*, **91**, 121.

Lum, L. C. (1976). The syndrome of habitual chronic hyperventilation. *Modern Trends in Psychosomatic Medicine*, **3**, 196–229.

Tenney, S. M. and Lamb, T. W. (1965). Physiological consequences of hypoventilation and hyperventilation. *Handbook of Physiology*, Section 3, vol 2, 979–1003. American Physiology Society.

Chapter 23

Respiratory Failure due to Skeletal and Neuromuscular Disorders

by J. M. SHNEERSON MA, DM, FRCP, W. KINNEAR MB, MRCP
and L. BROWN MCSP

INTRODUCTION

Patients with normal, or relatively normal, lungs may develop respiratory failure when there is a failure of the pump mechanism which draws air in and out of the lungs. This pump depends on the respiratory muscles to provide the power; the ribs to provide a firm framework for the expanding lungs; and the nervous system to regulate the pump.

Respiratory failure may develop when the respiratory muscles are weak, such as in muscular dystrophy; when the rib cage is abnormal, e.g. in scoliosis; after surgery, such as thoracoplasty; when the respiratory centres are diseased, e.g after encephalitis; or in primary or central alveolar hypoventilation (Ondine's curse).

In many patients respiratory failure is the result of a combination of abnormalities of these muscles, rib cage and the nervous system. The respiratory muscles have to work harder to expand the rib cage and lungs when the ribs, pleura(ae) or lungs are abnormally stiff, and they may eventually become fatigued and weak. The chronic hypoventilation which results leads to a high arterial carbon dioxide level. The brain's respiratory centres become adjusted to this and hypoxia becomes the main biochemical stimulus to respiration. For this reason, patients with chronic hypoventilation should *not* be given high concentrations of oxygen since the hypoxic drive will be removed and apnoea may result.

The control of respiration is shown diagrammatically in Figure 23/1. The motor output to the respiratory muscles depends on the input to the medullary respiratory centres and the spinal cord from the receptors in the lungs and chest wall and on the activity of these

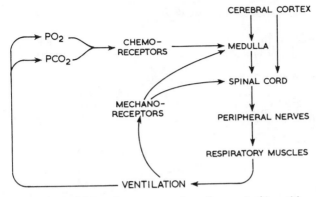

FIG. 23/1 Schematic representation of control of breathing

respiratory centres and the influence of the cerebral cortex. During sleep the activity of the respiratory centres and cerebral cortex decreases and consequently abnormalities of the control of respiration usually first appear during sleep. There may be a diminution in tidal volume (hypopnoea) or prolonged apnoeic periods. The latter may be due to lack of respiratory drive and therefore to an absence of respiratory movements (central apnoea) (Fig. 23/2). Alternatively, it can result from obstruction to the airway, usually at pharyngeal level, during inspiratory efforts because of lack of muscle tone

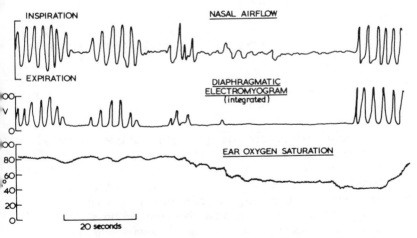

FIG. 23/2 Sleep study of central apnoea. Cessation of diaphragmatic activity is associated with absence of airflow and falling oxygen saturation

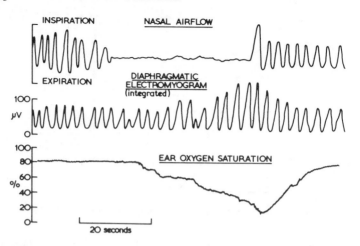

FIG. 23/3 Sleep study of obstructive apnoea. Airflow ceases and oxygen saturation falls despite persistence of diaphragmatic activity

holding the pharynx open (mixed and obstructive apnoeas) (Fig. 23/3). This distinction is important because the treatment of these two types of apnoea is different (Chapter 24). In general, treatment of respiratory failure due to chest wall and neurological diseases is often extremely effective since the lungs are fundamentally normal and able to carry out gas exchange adequately if mechanical assistance to ventilation can be provided.

CONDITIONS PREDISPOSING TO RESPIRATORY FAILURE

Skeletal diseases

SCOLIOSIS

Scoliosis is a lateral curvature of the spine and this is nearly always associated with rotation of the spine as well. It is the rotation which causes most of the respiratory problems because of the gross distortion of the costovertebral joints and consequent mechanical inefficiency of rib movement. Unfortunately, it is very difficult to measure the degree of rotation of the spine and the angle of lateral curvature is usually measured instead. It is important to realise that it is only spinal curvatures affecting the thoracic spine which have cardiac and respiratory consequences. Lumbar scolioses may cause backache and problems with posture, but do not affect the functioning of the lungs.

TABLE 23/1   Causes of structural scoliosis

1	Idiopathic – infantile, juvenile or adolescent
2	Congenital bony abnormalities, e.g. hemivertebrae
3	Neuropathic, e.g. poliomyelitis, spinal muscular dystrophy
4	Muscle diseases, e.g. muscular dystrophies
5	Unilateral lung and pleural diseases, e.g. pulmonary fibrosis, chronic pleural thickening
6	Iatrogenic, e.g. thoracoplasty
7	Miscellaneous, e.g. neurofibromatosis, Marfan's syndrome

There are many causes of scoliosis (Table 23/1). The commonest is idiopathic scoliosis in which no cause can be found for the abnormality. This may become apparent in infancy and often progresses, particularly at puberty, to result in a severe deformity and eventually respiratory failure. However, the more common form of idiopathic scoliosis appears around puberty and rarely becomes as severe as the infantile form. The vast majority of these patients do not develop any respiratory problems although their spinal curvature may be severe enough for them to require spinal fusion. It is still uncertain whether spinal fusion prevents the development of respiratory problems in the long term. Scoliosis may also be due to congenital bone abnormalities. These usually affect the spine, e.g. hemivertebrae, but occasionally may be confined to the ribs. Congenital abnormalities of other parts of the body are common and the scoliosis may be severe. These spinal deformities usually become apparent early in life but are not necessarily noted immediately after birth. A third important group of scolioses is that due to muscular weakness (paralytic scoliosis). In the past this was most commonly due to poliomyelitis (see below) but now that new cases of this infection are extremely uncommon in developed countries because of effective immunisation, the chronic myopathies and muscular dystrophies are becoming more important.

Scoliosis due to muscular weakness usually affects a long length of the spine and, in addition to causing problems with sitting, it may diminish lung function. However, the weakness of the respiratory muscles is usually the major factor in determining whether or not these patients develop respiratory failure. There are also a large number of rarer conditions which can cause scoliosis, including neurofibromatosis, Marfan's syndrome and osteogenesis imperfecta, in which the scoliosis may be due to an abnormality in the collagen or other constituents of the connective tissue.

Scoliosis affects respiratory function mainly because the abnormal shape of the thoracic cage increases the work which the respiratory muscles have to perform to achieve any given amount of ventilation. If the scoliosis is present from an early age, the development of the alveoli is also hindered and certainly the lung volumes are diminished in proportion to the severity of the scoliosis. In general, the smaller the lungs the more limited is the exercise ability of these patients. Respiratory failure may occur at any age and is more frequent if the spinal curvature is severe. However, it depends on other factors as well, particularly the respiratory drive and the presence or absence of other conditions such as chronic bronchitis or asthma which appears to be particularly common in scoliotics. Chest infections are no more common in patients with scoliosis than normal persons but they are more serious, particularly if the deformity is marked and there is respiratory muscle paralysis which weakens the patient's cough.

Cardiac problems also frequently occur in scoliosis. Congenital heart disease is common, particularly in congenital scoliosis but also in idiopathic scoliosis. Pulmonary arterial hypertension occurs, particularly if the lung volumes are severely diminished such that the vital capacity is less than about 1 litre. In these patients the pulmonary vascular bed is too small to accommodate the cardiac output, particularly during exercise, without presenting a resistance which requires a high pressure to drive the blood through the lungs. The other major cause of pulmonary hypertension is hypoxia which results in vasoconstriction in the pulmonary circulation and thereby increases the pulmonary vascular resistance and pulmonary artery pressure. Hypoxia may be due to sub-optimal ventilation/perfusion matching but the major factor is usually hypoventilation. This occurs particularly when the patient is asleep, especially during rapid eye movement sleep and may be much more severe than would be anticipated from the waking blood gases.

SEQUELAE OF TUBERCULOSIS

Tuberculous infections nowadays are readily treated by combination chemotherapy and it is unusual for damage to the lungs to be so extensive that respiratory failure ensues. However, in the era before effective chemotherapy this was commonly the case. A variety of

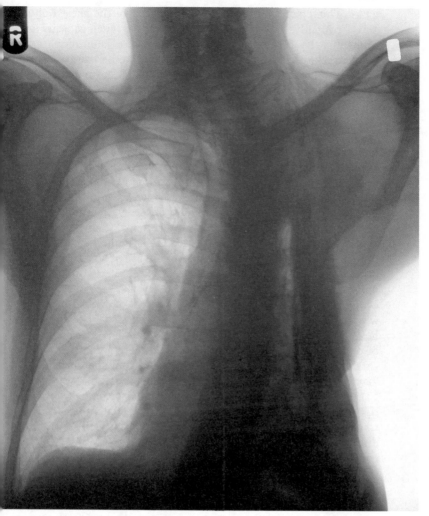

FIG. 23/4 Chest radiograph showing deformity due to thoracoplasty

surgical procedures were carried out in order to close the tuberculous cavities and arrest the disease and many of these, although effective in treating the tuberculosis, had deleterious long-term consequences. This is particularly true of the operation of *thoracoplasty* in which long sections of several ribs were excised in order to enable the chest wall to collapse in over the damaged lung (Fig.

23/4). This operation destroyed the integrity of the chest wall and also frequently led to scoliosis. The fall in vital capacity and, probably, the risk of respiratory failure as a late complication, increase with the number of ribs removed. In other patients *phrenic nerve crush* or *avulsion* was carried out in order to paralyse the hemidiaphragm. *Artificial pneumothoraces* were induced by injecting air into the pleural cavity and were often maintained for several years. Extensive pleural calcification frequently resulted and this causes a restrictive ventilatory defect. *Plombage operations*, in which material was inserted between the chest wall and the pleura caused less alteration in lung function than thoracoplasties, and *pneumoperitoneum*, in which air was injected into the peritoneum to elevate the diaphragm, had no long-term consequences at all. Resection of infected lung also led to remarkably little deterioration probably because it was already virtually non-functional.

Many of these procedures were carried out in the 1940s and 1950s so that these patients are nearly all over the age of 50. Many are now developing respiratory failure or right-sided heart failure. It is important to be sure that their symptoms are due to these complications rather than to a reactivation of their tuberculosis which, of course, would require conventional chemotherapy. Respiratory failure may be severe and is often due to a combination of parenchymal lung damage due to the tuberculosis itself and the surgical treatments. Hypoventilation is most marked at night and may be amenable to treatment by assisted ventilation (see Chapter 24). Pulmonary hypertension is frequent and develops slowly so that right ventricular hypertrophy and failure frequently appear. These complications require treatment with diuretics as well as treatment directed to relief of the hypoxia itself.

ANKYLOSING SPONDYLITIS

In this condition the intervertebral and costovertebral joints become fixed and expansion of the thoracic cage may be completely abolished. As a result inspiration can only be achieved by abdominal expansion due to depression of the diaphragm. The diaphragm is normally strong enough to compensate and respiratory failure is remarkably rare. However, if the diaphragm is damaged in any way, for example by injury to the phrenic nerve, or if there is increased resistance to expansion of the abdomen as in pregnancy, ascites or after a laparotomy, respiratory failure may develop. Ankylosing spondylitis can occasionally cause apical lung fibrosis and pleural effusions and thickening, but these are rarely severe enough to cause respiratory failure.

PECTUS EXCAVATUM AND PECTUS CARINATUM

These two conditions affecting the sternum can lead to marked cosmetic deformities. In pectus excavatum the sternum is depressed (funnel chest) and in pectus carinatum it is unusually prominent (pigeon breast). However, in neither of these abnormalities is respiratory function affected to any significant degree and neither cardiac nor respiratory failure occur. Surgery is for cosmetic reasons only.

Pleural disease

Pleural thickening can develop insidiously and lead to chronic respiratory failure. The thick pleura prevents expansion of the lungs and a restrictive ventilatory defect is seen. These complications occur especially if the pleural thickening is bilateral and extensive. The management of choice is to remove the thickened pleura surgically (decortication) but occasionally this may not be possible and long-term mechanical ventilatory assistance is required.

Neuromuscular diseases

BRAINSTEM ABNORMALITIES

There are a variety of conditions which can affect the respiratory centres and their associated pathways in the medulla. These include multiple sclerosis, syringomyelia, tumours, encephalitis and poliomyelitis. There is also an idiopathic condition (central alveolar hypoventilation or chronic central hypoventilation) in which there is virtually no ventilatory response to an elevated arterial Pco_2. This results eventually in chronic hypoventilation with an elevated Pco_2 and a lowered arterial Po_2 although, initially, the blood gases may be completely normal while the patient is awake and these abnormalities only seen during sleep. There is a wide variation in the normal ventilatory response to a rising Pco_2 and these patients may well represent the unresponsive end of the normal range. Breathlessness during exertion is uncommon and the chest radiograph may be normal. Right ventricular hypertrophy and polycythaemia develop because of the chronic hypoxia. Voluntary control of ventilation is retained and blood gases can return virtually to normal during voluntary hyperventilation. The condition is commoner in men but is only rarely familial. It is more frequent in adults between the ages of 20 and 50 but it can occur in infancy. This congenital form has a very poor prognosis unless adequate assisted ventilation is provided and this may be difficult to achieve. Adults respond better to ventilatory treatment (see Chapter 24).

CERVICAL CORD TRAUMA AND SURGERY

The cell bodies of the nerve fibres in the phrenic nerves supplying the diaphragm originate in the C3–C5 segments of the spinal cord. Damage at, or above, this level may therefore paralyse the diaphragm and cause respiratory failure. This occurs particularly with traumatic damage to the spinal cord either surgically in the operation of cordotomy or as part of a severe injury resulting in quadriplegia.

The operation of cordotomy has been performed frequently in the past in order to relieve intractable pain. Unfortunately, the ascending pain pathways in the spinothalamic tracts are intimately mingled with the descending paths from the medullary respiratory centres to the phrenic nerve nuclei. Damage to these almost invariably results if adequate analgesia is obtained. Respiratory failure occurs particularly if the cordotomy is carried out bilaterally and simultaneously but may develop with unilateral cordotomy if there is pre-existing lung disease. Apnoeas, particularly during sleep, appear within the first few days postoperatively and death during sleep is common.

Traumatic damage to the spinal cord severe enough to cause quadriplegia is becoming increasingly frequent. When the damage is at, or above, the origin of the phrenic nerve (C3–C5), all the respiratory muscles will be paralysed and the patient will be completely dependent on ventilatory support. With injuries below this level in the cervical cord, the diaphragm will continue to function but the intercostal and abdominal muscles will be paralysed. Paradoxical inward movement of the lower thoracic cage occurs but abdominal expansion due to diaphragmatic contraction is normal. Ventilation is remarkably well preserved and chronic respiratory failure is rare. The expiratory muscles are paralysed and consequently the patient's cough is weak. Chest infections are, therefore, frequent and may be fatal.

LOWER MOTOR NEURONE DISORDERS

There are three important conditions in this group.

Spinal muscular atrophy.   This unusual condition becomes apparent in infancy and may be rapidly progressive, leading to death within the first two years of life. However, a more benign form occurs and is associated with generalised hypotonia and the development of a marked scoliosis. These patients may live to adult life but respiratory failure develops insidiously due partly to the scoliosis but particularly to respiratory muscle weakness.

Guillain-Barré syndrome. In this condition there is a widespread radiculitis effectively leading to a combination of lower motor neuron weakness and sensory symptoms. This weakness may involve the respiratory muscles to the extent that mechanical ventilation is required. Bulbar function is also often compromised and aspiration pneumonias are common. Autonomic damage may lead to instability of the blood pressure and pulse. These complications are transitory and, if supportive treatment is successful, a complete or almost complete recovery occurs after a period of weeks or months.

Poliomyelitis. This infection, once very common in this country, is now extremely rare because of the introduction of effective immunisation. It affects the lower motor neurones in a patchy manner, and any of the cranial nerves or spinal nerves can be involved. Respiratory failure is common in poliomyelitis epidemics largely because of respiratory muscle weakness, but occasionally because the respiratory centres themselves are affected. Bulbar involvement is also common and is easily recognisable by the inability to swallow effectively and the presence of coughing while eating or drinking. Aspiration of pharyngeal secretions and food into the tracheobronchial tree is frequent and often fatal unless recognised. Bulbar involvement is a medical emergency requiring endotracheal intubation and ventilation (see Chapter 9) but fortunately most patients make a good recovery if adequate support can be provided in the acute phase.

Some patients, however, are left with severe respiratory muscle weakness which may make it impossible for them to be weaned from assisted ventilation. In other cases the respiratory muscles improve sufficiently for an independent life to be led for many years before respiratory failure appears. These patients often have abnormalities of the respiratory centre and respiratory muscle weakness. Severe respiratory failure and cor pulmonale may present as long as 20 or 30 years after acute poliomyelitis. Assisted ventilation is effective (see Chapter 24).

MUSCLE DISORDERS

Weakness of the respiratory muscles often occurs in conjunction with other conditions such as central hypoventilation and skeletal disorders, and contributes to the development of respiratory failure. There are several important, although uncommon, muscular disorders which may weaken the respiratory muscles sufficiently to lead to respiratory failure in the absence of any other condition.

Dystrophia myotonica. This autosomal dominantly inherited condition is characterised by myotonia (inability of muscle to relax quickly) and muscle weakness and atrophy. It is, however, a systemic disease with other features such as frontal baldness, cataracts and testicular atrophy. The respiratory muscles may be disproportionately weak compared to other muscles and a restrictive defect ensues. It may occur in young children, and even in neonates, as well as in adults and lead to severe respiratory failure at any age. The myotonia itself does not appear to be of any respiratory significance but some of these patients do have a diminished respiratory drive. This is sometimes associated with hypersomnia due presumably to a widespread abnormality in the recticular formation in the brainstem.

Patients with dystrophia myotonica present an increased operative risk because sedation may precipitate respiratory failure. Pharyngeal and oesophageal function is often disturbed and aspiration pneumonias are common postoperatively. Cardiac dysrhythmias also occur.

Duchenne's muscular dystrophy. This sex-linked muscular dystrophy occurs only in boys and runs a very rapid course so that they are unable to walk by the age of about 10 and death usually occurs around the age of 20. Respiratory muscle involvement becomes apparent at about the stage when walking becomes difficult and as a consequence breathlessness on exertion is uncommon. Respiratory drive is normal and the fall in vital capacity and maximal inspiratory and expiratory pressures is due to weakness of the respiratory muscles and the development of scoliosis. These patients have a poor cough because of expiratory muscle weakness and chest infections are common. They may be fatal unless prompt treatment is given. Death also occurs from chronic respiratory failure although this usually appears only when muscle weakness is severe. Assisted ventilation may be effective in prolonging life once respiratory failure has become established (see Chapter 24). These patients also have cardiac abnormalities including left ventricular dysfunction and conduction defects.

Motor neurone disease. This is a rapidly progressive degenerative disease affecting both the upper and lower motor neurones. As a result, muscle weakness is the cardinal symptom and, although this usually affects the hand and other limb muscles first, occasionally the diaphragm is particularly affected and respiratory failure is the presenting feature. In the majority of patients, however, respiratory muscle weakness appears when other muscle weakness is already marked and in this situation respiratory failure occurs as a pre-terminal event. The major respiratory problem is usually aspiration of secretions into the tracheobronchial tree because of bulbar dysfunction. This is a serious complication and death usually follows from pneumonia before long. Ventilatory assistance is of value in selected patients (see Chapter 24).

Myasthenia gravis. This condition is characterised by fatiguability of the muscles due to circulating antibodies which interfere with activation of muscle fibres by acetylcholine. The facial and extra-ocular muscles are most commonly affected but this process may extend to the respiratory muscles. Respiratory failure is usually intermittent rather than chronic and may be precipitated by intercurrent illnesses, particularly infections (myasthenic crisis), over-dosage with anticholinergic drugs (cholinergic crisis) or surgery, particularly thymectomy. A fall in vital capacity to around 1 litre is a serious sign and indicates that assisted ventilation will probably be required. This is usually only needed for a few days while the appropriate treatment is instituted but episodes of acute respiratory failure may recur.

Other myopathies. Respiratory abnormalities are common in several of the myopathies but rare in others. The myopathies are a heterogenous group and there is no satisfactory classification. Some are congenital and may be associated with detectable abnormalities of the skeletal muscle. These may be biochemical (e.g. acid maltase deficiency), structural (e.g. nemaline myopathy) or both (e.g. mitochondrial myopathy). In other cases inflammation of muscle is present. Polymyositis is the most important of this group and may be associated with malignancy or collagen diseases. Metabolic abnor-malities are also associated with myopathies particularly thyrotoxi-cosis, Cushing's syndrome and steroid therapy.

Respiratory consequences occur especially in the myopathies which affect principally the proximal muscles. Respiratory muscle weakness may present neonatally as failure to take the first few breaths after birth and mechanical ventilation may be required. In other cases the myopathy progresses during childhood or adult life and respiratory complications develop as the muscles become progressively more weak. Slowly progressive respiratory failure occurs particularly if the diaphragm is affected. In addition, there may also be congenital abnormalities of the respiratory drive which magnify the effects of the respiratory muscle weakness. Weakness of the trunk may lead to a scoliosis which will contribute to a deterioration in the lung function.

Chest infections are common in myopathies and are largely due to a weak cough. This may be due to weakness of the respiratory muscles or of the larynx. However, involvement of the bulbar musculature is also common and aspiration of pharyngeal secretions may follow.

CLINICAL PRESENTATION

Most of the conditions described above are fairly obvious and the first step in suspecting that respiratory failure may have occurred is to realise that the patient has one of these high-risk diagnoses. Respiratory failure in these conditions presents in a different way to that of chronic lung disease and is often unrecognised. Symptoms arising in the lungs themselves are almost invariably absent. Breathlessness is often not present and wheeze, cough and haemoptysis are not a feature of these diseases. The symptoms which do occur are those related to the blood gas abnormalities themselves. The blood gases are most abnormal at night and consequently sleep abnormalities such as frequent nightmares, snoring and snorting during sleep, frequent waking and early morning headaches (due to carbon dioxide retention) are common. Because of the sleep abnormalities patients sleep frequently during the day and feel drowsy, and they may undergo a personality change with loss of memory. Multiple car crashes may occur due to falling asleep while driving. These symptoms are exacerbated by sedatives such as night sedation or alcohol and may be exaggerated by obesity or acute illness such as upper respiratory infections or asthma.

Examination may reveal central cyanosis indicating severe hypoxaemia and there may be signs of carbon dioxide retention, such as a flapping tremor of the hands, warm peripheries with a rapid high volume pulse, absent tendon reflexes, constricted pupils and confusion. Confusion may also be due to hypoxia. Careful examination of the thorax is essential. The exact site of any scoliosis and its severity should be recorded together with any abnormalities of the rib cage or sternum. Bilateral diaphragmatic weakness is revealed by paradoxical inward movement of the abdomen during inspiration and an inability of the patient to lie flat without becoming breathless. Intercostal muscle weakness is less easily demonstrated but expansion of the chest should be carefully observed. The extent of the use of accessory muscles such as the sternomastoid muscles should be noted and if ventilatory impairment has been present for some time these muscles will be hypertrophied. Right-sided heart failure may be present and a raised jugular venous pulse, ankle oedema, enlarged liver and ascites should be looked for. Signs of pulmonary hypertension and right ventricular hypertrophy may also be present.

INVESTIGATIONS

The following investigations may be useful:

Haemoglobin. Polycythaemia due to erythropoietin production by the kidneys in response to hypoxia is common. Red cell mass and plasma volume estimations may be required to confirm the presence of polycythaemia.

Chest radiograph. This may be normal but it may show a spinal deformity or thoracoplasty and cardiac enlargement or chest infection due to aspiration or other cause. Special views of the thoracic spine may be required.

Electrocardiogram. This may show right atrial or right ventricular hypertrophy. Occasionally an echocardiogram or even cardiac catheterisation may be needed to exclude other causes of pulmonary hypertension or to show its severity.

Arterial blood gases. Mild hypoxaemia may be due to sub-optimal ventilation/perfusion matching and be associated with a normal P_{CO_2}, but most of these conditions lead to ventilatory failure with a rising P_{CO_2} and marked hypoxia. This can often be detected by an arterial blood gas estimation while the patient is awake but a much more sensitive measurement is of the blood gases when the patient is asleep. This poses obvious technical difficulties but with the modern non-invasive continuous monitors of oxygen and carbon dioxide, adequate readings during sleep can be obtained. Oxygenation can be assessed either by measuring the oxygen saturation or transcutaneous P_{O_2} but for carbon dioxide only the transcutaneous method is available. These readings can be displayed continuously on a recorder (Fig. 23/5) and, if necessary, other measurements such as air flow at the nose or the volume change in the chest and abdomen individually can also be continuously recorded (Figs. 23/2, 23/3). Transient hypoxic dips are common in normal elderly patients, particularly males, but in most of the conditions described above,

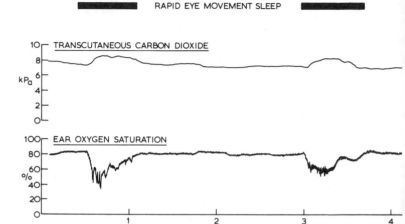

FIG. 23/5 Overnight sleep study showing fall in oxygen saturation and rise in carbon dioxide during rapid eye movement sleep

prolonged periods of hypoxia with a raised CO_2 occur during sleep. During these hypoxic episodes both the pulmonary artery pressure and the systemic blood pressure may rise. Demonstration of hypoventilation at night indicates that assisted ventilation may be of benefit.

Measurement of lung volumes. Most of the conditions described in this chapter lead to a restrictive ventilatory defect. The total lung capacity and vital capacity are decreased. The residual volume may be increased because respiratory muscle weakness prevents full deflation of the lungs. FEV_1/FVC is normal and there is usually no evidence for air flow obstruction.

Tests of respiratory muscle function. Although a diminished vital capacity is quite a sensitive test for respiratory muscle weakness, an earlier sign is a fall in the maximal inspiratory and expiratory mouth pressures. An endurance test for the respiratory muscles is the maximal voluntary ventilation test during which the patients have to breathe as rapidly and deeply as they can for 15 seconds. The ventilation achieved may be disproportionately low in relation to the vital capacity because of an inability to sustain maximal ventilation for this length of time. Endurance can also be tested by the ability to sustain an inspiratory or expiratory mouth pressure of 80 per cent of the maximal pressure.

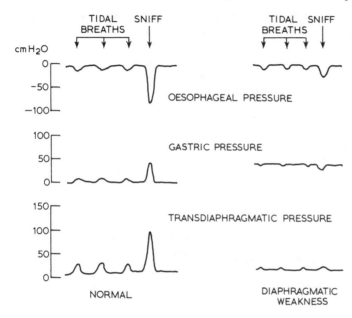

FIG. 23/6 Transdiaphragmatic pressure during sniffs in a normal subject and a patient with diaphragmatic weakness. The patient has a low transdiaphragmatic pressure and is unable to generate a positive gastric pressure

Diaphragmatic function is traditionally assessed by screening the diaphragm radiographically. However, if both halves of the diaphragm are paralysed, this method may be misleading and measurement of the pressure difference across the diaphragm (transdiaphragmatic pressure) is more reliable (Fig. 23/6). This can be coupled with measurement of the volume changes of the abdomen and chest during inspiration which may show paradoxical inward movement of the diaphragm during inspiration. Bilateral diaphragmatic weakness causes a fall in the vital capacity of about 50 per cent when the patient lies supine because the abdominal contents cannot be prevented from entering the chest by gravity and compressing the lungs.

Tests of overall respiratory function.   The distance(s) walked in 6 or 12 minutes are of value in assessing progress during treatment.

More complex tests such as *measurement of the lung* and *chest wall compliance* are of use in selected subjects. Estimation of the *ventilatory response to a rising* Pco_2 is important if an abnormality of the respiratory centres is suspected (Fig. 23/7).

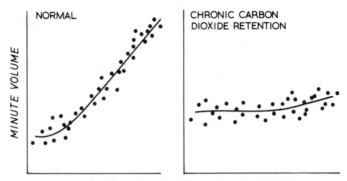

FIG. 23/7 Ventilatory response to rising inspired carbon dioxide concentration: a normal subject and a patient with chronic hypercapnia. The normal increase in ventilation is not seen in the hypercapneic patient

BIBLIOGRAPHY

See page 582.

Chapter 24

Management of Respiratory Failure in Patients with Skeletal and Neuromuscular Disorders

by W. KINNEAR MB, MRCP, L. BROWN MCSP
and J. M. SHNEERSON MA, DM, FRCP

Many patients with skeletal deformities of the chest and respiratory muscle diseases present for the first time to a respiratory unit with acute life-threatening respiratory failure. Others are referred for assessment on account of gradually worsening respiratory symptoms, and some with potential problems, but no current respiratory disability, are assessed at regular intervals.

ACUTE HYPOVENTILATION

Patients admitted with acute life-threatening hypoventilation will often have been fairly stable for a number of years until a respiratory tract infection precipitates respiratory failure, or else inappropriate sedation or oxygen is administered resulting in depression of the respiratory centres with consequent hypoventilation.

The decision to institute artificial ventilatory support in patients with chronic respiratory failure often depends on the condition of the patient prior to the acute deterioration, particularly in patients with chronic airflow obstruction whose prognosis is poor and in whom weaning from ventilatory support may be difficult. In patients with skeletal deformities of the chest, vigorous efforts should be made to resuscitate them even when moribund on arrival in hospital since the prognosis for them is much better than for patients with chronic airflow obstruction. In patients with progressive neuromuscular disorders whose quality of life prior to the onset of respiratory failure has been poor, energetic therapy may be inappropriate. In others, short- or long-term respiratory support may prolong survival with a good quality of life, and in cases where the previous condition is not known then resuscitation should be attempted while enquiries are made.

Artificial ventilation will usually be IPPV via an endotracheal tube; where a tank respirator is available there are considerable advantages in that sedation and paralysis are not necessary and assisted ventilation can be alternated with spontaneous respiration thus lessening the difficulties of weaning from ventilatory support ultimately.

Physiotherapy has an important part to play in the treatment of such acute episodes, in conjunction with antibiotics and respiratory stimulants (see Chapter 11). Oxygen therapy may be hazardous since it abolishes the hypoxic stimulus to respiration on which most of these patients depend, and usually it can be used only in conjunction with artificial ventilatory support.

CHRONIC HYPOVENTILATION

On recovery from an acute episode of respiratory failure, it will be necessary to consider whether long-term respiratory therapy is appropriate and what form it should take. This will be important also for those patients with respiratory failure of gradual onset who are referred in a stable state. Physiological assessment involves investigation of respiratory muscle function, respiratory drive and oxygenation during sleep (see Chapter 23). Most patients will require instruction in breathing exercises, and nocturnal ventilatory support will be necessary in patients with sleep hypoxia. Adequate ventilation during sleep returns the sleep pattern to normal, and in patients with respiratory muscle weakness results in improvement in daytime respiratory muscle strength, ventilation and arterial blood gases.

In addition to physiological assessment, consideration of the patient and his environment will influence the therapeutic options which are chosen. For many patients with skeletal or neuromuscular disorders, referral for assessment of respiratory failure is almost the last straw. They often have considerable problems coping with the activities and relationships of daily life before the onset of respiratory failure, and the prospect of using any sort of 'breathing apparatus', particularly where this increases their dependence on outside help, may cause disproportionate anxiety. Nevertheless, help with respiratory symptoms may have been hard for them to find and most respond well to a positive and encouraging approach to their disability.

Assessment is best made as an in-patient, and during the first few days and nights when the patient will be undergoing physiological assessment, the opportunity must be taken to get to know him, gain his confidence, appreciate his expectations and anxieties, assess the home situation and consider which therapeutic options he is likely to be able to manage in his own home. For instance, it may soon become apparent that a patient is unlikely to learn glossopharyngeal respiration and that since he lives alone and is relatively immobile he is unlikely to cope with a jacket respirator. Time may then be spent concentrating on IPPB or cuirass respirators.

METHODS OF TREATMENT

Breathing exercises

Patients with chronic respiratory failure who are being considered for assisted ventilation in the long term may derive considerable benefit from simpler forms of respiratory therapy. The breathing pattern is usually abnormal in these patients and can be improved by breathing exercises and relaxation techniques. Chest vibrations, shaking and forced expiratory manoeuvres will aid expectoration of secretions. Voluntary hyperinflation, like involuntary sighs, will help maintain inflation in areas of lung underventilated during tidal breathing which are liable to collapse. The effect of hyperinflation on areas of micro-atelectasis and on alveolar surface tension results in increased lung compliance which persists for several hours. The work of breathing is therefore reduced and the likelihood of lower respiratory tract infection is reduced. General mobility exercises can also benefit chronic respiratory patients and simple exercise regimes such as staged walking targets will improve exercise performance and may also improve respiratory failure.

Incentive spirometry

Hyperinflation may be aided by the use of a device which indicates to the patient the volume inspired during such manoeuvres. Incentive spirometers consist of inspiratory flow indicators and by timing the interval for which any flow can be maintained give an indication of volume inspired. This can be practised by the patient at home without any outside help.

Glossopharyngeal respiration

For many patients with respiratory muscle weakness deep inspiration may not be possible. The vital capacity may, however, be augmented by recruiting other muscles not normally used in respiration in the technique known as *glossopharyngeal respiration*. This may be considered as 'auto-assisted' positive pressure breathing. The mouth, lips, tongue, soft palate, pharynx and larynx are used in a pump-like action to squeeze air into the lungs, and the resemblance of this swallowing action to a gulping frog has led to the name 'frog breathing' for this technique. A volume of approximately 60ml of air is trapped in the pharynx with the mouth and nasopharynx closed. The constricting action of the pharyngeal muscles in conjunction with upward movement of the tongue forces air through the open larynx. The larynx and pharynx then prevent escape of the air which has been gulped into the lungs. Each gulping cycle lasts about 0.6 sec and is repeated 10 times or more. In teaching patients to breathe in this manner it is useful to describe the movement of the Adam's apple which is held down while the floor of the mouth is relaxed and the nose is blocked off in a gulping action.

Using glossopharyngeal respiration, patients with weak respiratory muscles can inspire a much larger volume of air than when breathing conventionally. Sudden release of this air aids expectoration of secretions and has the same beneficial effects on lung compliance as hyperinflation produced by the conventional respiratory muscles or by assisted ventilation (Fig. 24/1). Patients with generalised neuromuscular disease who are otherwise dependent on other people may find glossopharyngeal respiration a considerable psychological boost, since it requires no outside assistance.

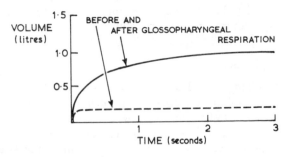

FIG. 24/1 Forced vital capacity recording of a patient with respiratory muscle weakness after a conventional breath and after a glossopharyngeal respiration assisted breath

Muscle training

Muscle training can be used to improve both the power and endurance of the respiratory muscles. Strength training involves inspiring against a resistance which requires near maximal inspiratory effort to achieve adequate ventilation. Although it improves respiratory muscle strength in normal subjects, it carries the danger of rapidly inducing fatigue in patients with respiratory disease. Endurance training involves generating smaller inspiratory pressures for longer periods of time. Although narrow inspiratory holes may be used, it is preferable to have an inspiratory valve with a variable weight attached, since once the opening pressure is reached high flow rates can be generated with little further increase in inspiratory pressure. 30 minutes' training each day over a number of months improves inspiratory muscle endurance, and on cessation of training endurance gradually reverts to the pre-training level. The use of such devices in chronic airflow obstruction results in greater inspiratory muscle endurance, particularly in patients in whom a pre-training inspiratory muscle endurance test induces electromyographic evidence of inspiratory muscle fatigue. In cystic fibrosis inspiratory muscle endurance improves with endurance training, but similar improvement can be obtained with vigorous daily exercise. Quadriplegic patients can endurance train their diaphragms and, although experimental evidence is lacking, it is possible that some patients with skeletal deformities of the rib cage may benefit from carefully supervised inspiratory muscle endurance training. Great care must be taken to avoid inducing fatigue. It is debatable whether training will improve the endurance of patients with neuromuscular disorders of the respiratory muscles.

Intermittent positive pressure breathing (IPPB)

IPPB is fully discussed in Chapter 11. There are several distinct ways in which IPPB can be used in the therapy of patients with skeletal thoracic disorders and neuromuscular disease affecting the respiratory muscles. First, patients with complete respiratory muscle paralysis who spend most of the time being ventilated in a tank respirator, cuirass or jacket respirator, rocking bed or diaphragm pacing device can use IPPB as temporary ventilatory assistance during periods of nursing care, or, in the case of diaphragm pacing, to prevent diaphragmatic damage from prolonged electrical stimulation.

Second, IPPB can be used to achieve hyperinflation in the same way as simpler measures like incentive spirometry. The increase in pulmonary compliance after a short period of IPPB persists for several hours. Third, IPPB can be used to rest the respiratory muscles. When used in this context, it is important to ensure that the patient relaxes and allows the ventilator to perform as much of the work of inflating the lungs as possible. When the patient-triggered mode of operation is employed, care must be taken to set the trigger such that the minimum additional effort is expended by the patient. If IPPB cannot be tolerated for sufficiently long periods to allow recovery from respiratory muscle fatigue then alternative ventilatory support must be considered. Fourth, IPPB may be administered with bronchodilators prior to chest physiotherapy to aid expectoration of secretions.

Intermittent positive pressure ventilation (IPPV)

IPPV is fully discussed in Chapters 10 and 11. It may be employed in the long term in patients with skeletal deformities or neuromuscular disease for continuous or nocturnal ventilatory support and is capable of producing effective ventilation even in patients with severe restrictive defects. A patent airway is maintained in patients with upper airway obstruction, and if a cuffed tube is used then aspiration of food into the lungs in patients with swallowing incoordination is prevented. The ventilators employed are generally simpler than those used in the intensive therapy unit, with batteries providing emergency power in the event of mains failure or to permit mobility. A tracheostomy is necessary and the patients or their attendants must be educated in tracheostomy care to minimise the risk of lower respiratory tract infection. Patients may be taught how to suction secretions from the lower respiratory tract through their tracheostomy, but this procedure is associated with a risk of cardiac dysrhythmias and, if possible, is best avoided. Complications from the tracheostomy itself are rare.

TANK RESPIRATORS

Whereas IPPB and IPPV inflate the lungs by exerting positive pressure on the airways, the same end result may be achieved by lowering the pressure around the patient's chest and abdomen. This was the principal means of artificial ventilation in the first half of this century, and many of the devices still in use were first introduced during poliomyelitis epidemics 30 years ago. The most familiar external negative pressure respirator is the cabinet or tank respirator

(Fig. 24/2). Although these were initially made from wood, subsequent models were constructed in metal and the term 'iron lung' came into use. The patient is enclosed in an airtight cabinet from the neck downwards, and a fan or bellows pump cyclically lowers the pressure inside the cabinet approximately 30cm of water below atmospheric pressure. Since there is no restriction of expansion of the chest wall or abdomen, larger tidal volumes are produced at any suction pressure than with smaller external negative pressure devices, and it is usually possible to maintain adequate ventilation in patients with severe chest wall deformities even when their compliance is reduced still further by respiratory tract infection.

When a patient is to be ventilated in an iron lung, it is important to explain to them in appropriate terms the principle by which it works. To lessen their anxiety it may be helpful for a member of staff to be placed in the iron lung for demonstration purposes. The patient lies supine in the iron lung with the lid open and, if the patient is orthopnoeic, with the feet tilted down. The lid is then closed, the neck and portholes are fastened securely so that an adequate suction pressure can be obtained. The breathing cycle is explained to the patient so that he can co-ordinate his own inspiratory efforts with the negative pressure phase of the cycle. In general, the lowest (most negative) pressure which can be attained should be used, this usually being in the range of -30 to -40cm of water. It is particularly important to use a strong suction pressure in patients who are unable to co-ordinate their own respiratory efforts with the pump cycle.

Physiotherapy is usually carried out with the lid of the tank open (Fig. 24/2b). Depending on the model of tank in use, it may be possible to tip or roll the patient into different positions for physiotherapy. In severely ill patients it is possible to perform physiotherapy through the portholes of the tank without interrupting ventilatory assistance, but additional help is usually necessary in order to stabilise the patient. Patients who are completely paralysed can be nursed in a Kelleher rotating tank respirator, and it is then possible to perform physiotherapy through the removable posterior panel while the patient is ventilated temporarily with a mouthpiece.

CUIRASS RESPIRATORS

Cuirass respirators work on the same principle as the iron lung in that a negative pressure is created around the outside of the thoracic

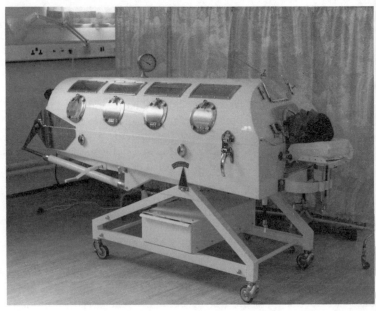

(a)

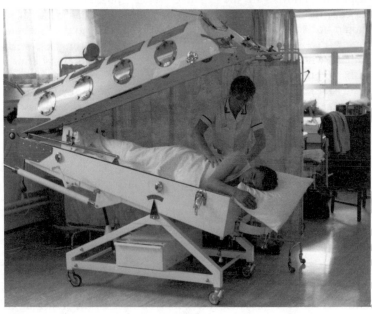

(b)

FIG. 24/2 (a) Patient being ventilated using a tank respirator; (b) Patient receiving physiotherapy between periods of assisted ventilation; (c) A trial of spontaneous breathing between periods of assisted ventilation

cage, but the cuirass shell covers only the anterior portion of the chest and abdomen. The shell has padded edges to produce an airtight seal to the patient and there is sufficient room inside the shell for the chest and abdomen to move outwards when negative pressure is applied. A pressure cycled pump is used to create the negative pressure. The pressure inside the shell falls to approximately 30cm of water below atmospheric pressure and this suction causes the rib cage and abdomen to move outwards and expand the lungs. Expiration occurs passively as the pressure inside the shell returns to atmospheric. Standard shells are available in a variety of sizes and can be used in patients with normal chest shapes such as those with neuromuscular disorders. For patients with chest wall deformities it is necessary to mould a shell for each patient from a plaster cast of their chest. In making the cast attention must be paid to several factors.

MAKING THE CAST

1. The cast must be long enough to include the abdomen.

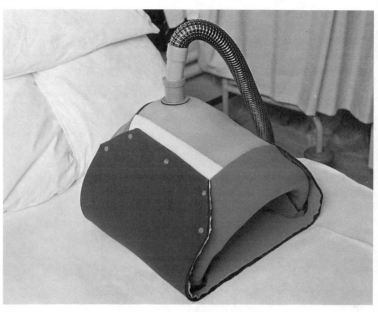

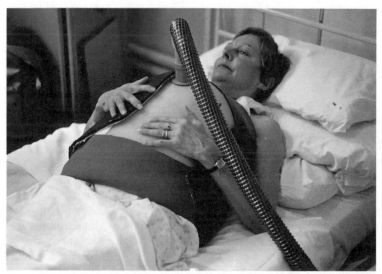

FIG. 24/3 (*above*) Cuirass shell and connecting tubing; (*below*) Patient using cuirass for assisted ventilation

2. The sides of the cast should extend down to the side of the bed so that when the cuirass descends during inspiration as a result of the negative pressure, as much of the weight as possible is borne by the bed.
3. Care must be taken to accurately cast any bony prominences so that the final cuirass shell is comfortable for the patient.

When hard, the cast is removed from the patient and built up anteriorly at least 7cm to allow expansion of the chest wall. Additional plaster is also applied over the site of any bony prominences or areas of tenderness to ensure that the cuirass will not touch them.

A shell is then moulded using a suitable thermoplastic material, trimmed to fit the patient and then padded along the edges with foam covered in airtight material (Fig. 24/3). The design of the cuirass is such that the pattern of respiration is predominantly abdominal, since the upper border of the cuirass will restrict rib cage expansion anteriorly. In patients with diaphragmatic weakness, paradoxical motion of the diaphragm when lying flat is corrected when the cuirass is in place, since negative pressure is applied over both the chest and the abdomen (Fig. 24/4). When the patient is able to relax and allow the cuirass to breathe for them, electromyographic studies show a reduction in the activity of inspiratory muscles, thus relieving them of their load overnight and permitting the muscles to rest. A further sleep study is necessary when the patient is accustomed to the cuirass, in order to determine if the cuirass is effective in maintaining adequate ventilation even when inspiratory muscle activity is either absent or inco-ordinate. Correction of nocturnal hypoxic dips by the cuirass leads to a return to normal of the sleep pattern. This improves the function of the respiratory muscles, reverses right-sided heart failure and leads to a considerable improvement in the quality of life.

In the first few hours of use, encouragement and instruction how to breathe with the cuirass is vital. The amount of time the patient spends in the cuirass is gradually increased until he is able to spend most of the night in it. Air leaks along the edges may require adjustment of the padding; patients should be taught how to adjust the position of the cuirass and apply additional padding as necessary to obtain a good seal in a comfortable sleeping position.

The basic principle of the cuirass and pump, should be explained to all patients and their families. They should also be told what to do in the event of problems arising. The aim is that patients should become as independent as possible, yet they must be aware that support is available in an emergency.

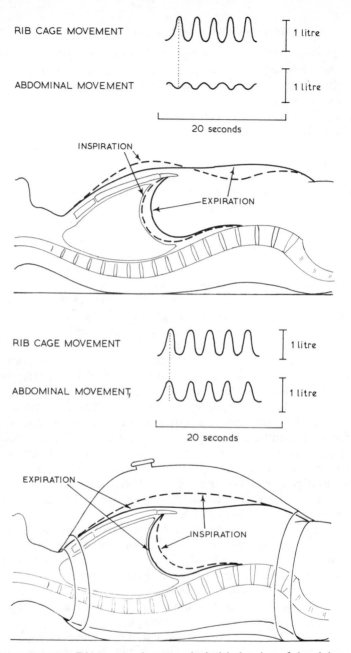

FIG. 24/4 *upper*: Diagram to show paradoxical indrawing of the abdomen during inspiration in a patient with diaphragmatic weakness when supine; *lower*: Paradoxical movement is abolished during assisted ventilation with the cuirass

JACKET RESPIRATORS

Jacket respirators work on the same principle as cuirass respirators, but restriction of expansion of the chest is overcome by the use of a larger shell which does not touch the patient. An airtight garment fits over the shell and forms a seal round the arms, neck and waist (Fig. 24/5). Several designs are available commercially using either plastic or metal shells, and the manufacture of a shell and jacket tailored to the individual patient is possible in the physiotherapy department. The pumps used are the same as for cuirass respirators. The major problems are that the jackets are often cumbersome and difficult for the patient to apply unaided, and considerable leakage may occur, particularly round the waist. This results in loss of pressure and is uncomfortable for the patient. The advantages are that the tidal volumes obtained are greater than with cuirass respirators and that a suitable size selected from a standard range can be used without further adjustment for the majority of patients.

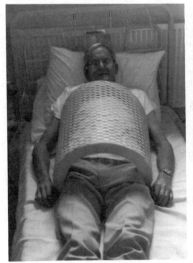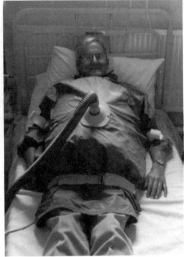

FIG. 24/5 (a) Rigid internal shell of jacket respirator in place over patient; (b) The patient being ventilated using the complete jacket respirator

POSITIVE ABDOMINAL PRESSURE

In contrast to external negative pressure ventilation, positive pressure applied on to the abdomen forces the abdominal contents up into the chest. The pneumobelt is the most familiar device used for external positive pressure ventilation. It is used in the standing or sitting position and compression of the abdomen is used to assist expiration, with inspiration occurring by descent of the abdominal contents by gravity. It can be used for daytime respiratory support in patients with neuromuscular disease and diaphragmatic weakness but tends to be ineffective in the presence of deformity of the chest.

ROCKING BED

For nocturnal ventilatory support, patients with diaphragmatic weakness or central hypoventilation may benefit from the use of a rocking bed which also utilises the movement of the abdominal contents. The bed rocks rhythmically up and down through an arc of approximately 60° (Fig. 24/6). When the bed is in the feet down position, the abdominal contents descend into the abdomen and pull the diaphragm down to produce inspiration. On return to the horizontal, the abdominal contents move up into the chest and produce expiration. Again this technique is generally unsuccessful in the presence of thoracic deformity.

ELECTROPHRENIC RESPIRATION (diaphragm pacing) ·

Patients with either impaired central respiratory control such as central hypoventilation, or interrupted nerve supply to the diaphragm, such as following cervical cord injury may be ventilated by electrical stimulation of the diaphragm. After the phrenic nerve and diaphragm have been shown to function normally a small cuff is inserted surgically round the phrenic nerve. A lead connects this stimulation cuff to a subcutaneous receiver box, and during artificial diaphragmatic stimulation a transmitter box is placed externally over the receiver which controls the rate and intensity of the electrical stimulus. Each phrenic nerve can only be used for a maximum of 12 hours otherwise damage to the diaphragm may occur; if full time respiratory support is needed bilateral implants will be required or else unilateral pacing can be alternated with other means of support.

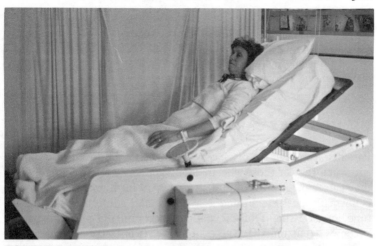

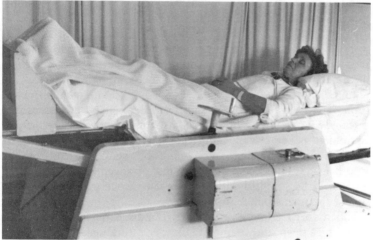

FIG. 24/6 (*above*) Patient on the rocking bed in the head-up position; (*below*) Patient on the rocking bed in the head-down position

Electrophrenic respiration does not usually produce adequate ventilation in the presence of thoracic deformity.

NASAL CONTINUOUS POSITIVE AIRWAY PRESSURE

Patients with obstructive sleep apnoea may be treated with continuous positive pressure applied to the nose. This technique uses either modified cuffed endotracheal tubes inserted into the nose or a nasal mask. Air blown up the nose creates a positive pressure in the pharynx. This will maintain the patency of the pharynx and prevent obstruction at this level. Patients in whom the obstruction is laryngeal will require a tracheostomy.

DOMICILIARY CARE

Patients are ready for discharge when their condition has stabilised and when they or those who are looking after them are confident that they can manage any equipment necessary for home use. Discharge is normally possible around 2–3 weeks after admission; during this time an assessment of the patient is completed and the patient becomes accustomed to the equipment. It is essential that instruction is given to the patient on the practical aspects of the apparatus thereby increasing his confidence with it.

A multidisciplinary team consisting of nursing staff, social workers, community liaison personnel, occupational therapists and physiotherapists is helpful in co-ordinating the discharge arrangements and post-discharge care. If further community services are required these can be arranged via the appropriate member of the team. Home visits prior to, or shortly after, discharge are essential to assess the patient in his home. It is also important to ensure that the equipment is being safely and effectively used.

When a patient is discharged home with ventilatory support the Fire Brigade should be notified, so that arrangements can be made for him to be supplied with an emergency generator, if necessary, should the mains power supply fail.

Patients are readmitted 1–2 weeks after discharge for reassessment including a sleep study to monitor oxygen saturation and Pco_2. They should then be routinely reassessed at gradually lengthening intervals. During these admissions any adjustments or repairs can be carried out to the cuirass or other equipment.

BIBLIOGRAPHY

Banaszak, E. F., Travers, H. and Frazier, M. (1981). Home ventilator care. *Respiratory Care*, **26**, 1262–8.

Bergofsky, E. H. (1979). Respiratory failure in disorders of the thoracic cage. *American Review of Respiratory Diseases*, **119**, 643–69.

Cohen, C. A., Zagelbaum, G., Gross, D. et al (1982). Clinical manifestations of inspiratory muscle fatigue. *American Review of Respiratory Disease*, **73**, 308–16.

Dail, C. W., Affeldt, J. E. and Collier, C. R. (1955). Clinical aspects of glossopharyngeal breathing. *Journal of the American Medical Association*, **158**, 445–9.

de Troyer, A. and Deisser, P. (1984). The effects of intermittent positive pressure breathing on patients with respiratory muscle weakness. *American Review of Respiratory Diseases*, **124**, 132–7.

Evans, T. W. and Howard, P. (1984). Whistle for your wind? *British Medical Journal*, **289**, 449–50.

Fischer, D. A. and Prentice, W. S. (1982). Feasibility of home care for certain respiratory-dependent restrictive or obstructive lung disease patients. *Chest*, **82**, 739–43.

Frith, R. W. and Cant, B. R. (1985). Severe obstructive sleep apnoea treated with long-term continuous positive airway pressure. *Thorax*, **40**, 45–50.

Gilmartin, M. and Make, B. (1983). Home care of ventilator dependent persons. *Respiratory Care*, **28**, 1490–7.

Glenn, W. W. L., Holcomb, W. G. and Shaw, R. K. (1976). Long-term ventilatory support by diaphragmatic pacing in quadriplegics. *Annals of Surgery*, **183**, 566–77.

Glenn, W. W. L. (1980). Treatment of respiratory paralysis by diaphragm pacing. *Annals of Thoracic Surgery*, **30**, 106–9.

Goldberg, A. I. (1984). The regional approach to home care for life-supported persons. *Chest*, **86**, 345–6.

Goldberg, A. I., Faure, E. A. M., Waigh, C. et al (1984). Home care for life-supported people – an approach to program development. *Journal of Pediatrics*, **104**, 785–95.

Goldberg, A. I. (1983). Home care for a better life for ventilator dependent people. *Chest*, **84**, 365–6.

Goldberg, A. I. and Faure, E. A. M. (1984). Home care for life-supported persons in England – the responaut program. *Chest*, **86**, 910–14.

Goldberg, A. I., Kettrick, R. and Buzdygen, A. (1980). Home ventilation for infants and children. *Critical Care Medicine*, **8**, 283.

Gross, D., Ladd, H. W., Riley, E. J. et al (1980). The effects of training on strength and endurance of the diaphragm in quadriplegia. *American Journal of Medicine*, **68**, 27–35.

Guilleminault, C., Cummiskey, J. and Dement, W. C. (1980). Sleep apnoea syndrome: recent advances. *Advances in Internal Medicine*, **26**, 347–72.

Kinnear, W. J. M. and Shneerson, J. M. (1985). Assisted ventilation at home: is it worth considering? *British Journal of Diseases of the Chest*, **4**, 313–51.

Leggett, R. J., Cooke, N. J. and Clancy, L. (1976). Long-term domiciliary oxygen therapy in cor pulmonale complicating chronic bronchitis and emphysema. *Thorax*, **31**, 414–18.

Make, B., Gilmartin, M., Brody, J. S. et al (1984). Rehabilitation of ventilator-dependent subjects with lung disease. *Chest*, **86**, 358–65.

Martin, R. J., Rogers, R. M. and Gray, B. A. (1980). The physiological basis for the use of mechanical aids to lung expansion. *American Review of Respiratory Diseases*, **122**, 105–7.

Mezon, B. L., West, P., Israels, J. et al (1980). Sleep breathing abnormalities in kyphoscoliosis. *American Review of Respiratory Diseases*, **122**, 617–21.

Robert, D., Gerard, M., Leger, P. et al (1982). Long-term intermittent positive pressure ventilation at home of patients with end-stage chronic respiratory insufficiency. *Chest*, **82**, 258–9.

Sivak, E. D., Cordasco, E. M., Gipson, W. T. et al (1983). Clinical considerations in the implementation of home care ventilation: observations in 24 patients. *Cleveland Clinical Quarterly*, **50**, 219–25.

Sivak, E. D., Cordasco, E. M. and Gipson, W. T. (1983). Pulmonary mechanical ventilation at home. A reasonable and less expensive alternative. *Respiratory Care*, **28**, 42–9.

Sonne, L. J. (1984). Respiratory muscle training. *Chest*, **86**, 939–40.

Splaingard, M. L., Frates, F. C., Harrison, G. M. et al (1983). Home positive pressure ventilation. Twenty years' experience. *Chest*, **84**, 376–82.

ACKNOWLEDGEMENTS

The authors wish to thank Miss B. A. Webber MCSP for advice on the glossopharyngeal breathing technique.

They also thank their patients for allowing themselves to be photographed for inclusion in this chapter.

Chapter 25

Assisted Ventilation – A Patient's Viewpoint

by EDNA WARD

I remember during the polio epidemic of the 1950s, looking with horror at newspaper pictures of patients imprisoned in iron lungs and feeling thankful that this would never happen to me because I had recovered from childhood polio and was living a fully mobile and active life.

That impaired ventilation as well as kyphoscoliosis was my legacy from polio was not apparent until many years later when increasing breathlessness became a problem. Logically, with age, both aspects could only get worse but I was enjoying my job and my leisure, and while I was fully occupied such depressing thoughts could be pushed into the background.

After several spells in a London hospital where treatment consisted of an ever-changing cocktail of drugs, I eventually became alarmingly weak – walking was virtually impossible, a handbag was too heavy to carry and I had difficulty in keeping awake in the afternoons. I was admitted to hospital too weak to move from any position in which I was left – an uncomfortable and frustrating predicament. I was completely dependent, sleeping heavily and feeling detached from the world around me. After 5 weeks of tests, drugs and continuous oxygen I began to suspect that this time I would not recover. I was not, I remember, afraid of dying but I was frightened by the thought that this unreal, uncomfortable existence might continue.

At this point I was told of a respiratory unit at St Thomas's Hospital, London, where they were having excellent results by using mechanical aids for old polio patients who had breathing problems. My case was discussed with the unit and thought to be suitable for their specialised help. I felt a wave of enormous relief, although I was reluctant to leave familiar surroundings. No one seemed willing to explain *how* these mechanical aids differed from the various breathing machines available at other hospitals and my imagination covered tubes thrust down the throat (I hoped not), or up the nose, machinery pressing on the chest. . . . Iron lungs were not mentioned and did not enter my mind.

I arrived at the unit on a dreary October day and was taken to a long ward where great open crocodile mouths stood in regimented order on either side of a wide gangway. One was shut and from the end protruded a head as though laid face up on the guillotine – the very picture I had seen in the newspapers 30 years before! A disconcerting thought went through my mind? – was this the mechanical aid? – but, reassuringly, I was taken past and put to bed at the other end of the ward. I was welcomed, cossetted and visited, and it was some hours before the thought returned, made sense, and had to be faced.

Next day the consultant explained with patience, clarity and charm the cause of respiratory failure, what he would have to find out, and what he hoped to do. Polio patients from the 50s and before were reaching middle-age and showing the effects of impaired ventilation. The iron lung had restored a number to a full and useful life. He believed it could do the same for me. Would I be able to go back to work? Yes, he was sure I would. How long would it take? I was disappointed but not at all surprised to know that it would mean at least 6 weeks in the iron lung and a few weeks after that to assess what respiratory aid I would need on leaving hospital. I was left with a greater understanding of the facts and with hope and confidence. A few months would be a reasonable price to pay for restoration to an active life.

Nevertheless, the thought of incarceration in an iron lung was a chilling one and I waited apprehensively for the arrival of Heather, the physiotherapist, who was to make the introduction. She was a charming, gentle girl who talked factually about how the iron lung worked, what it did, how I could be made comfortable, how the bell at my hand would summon staff immediately, and how I would be able to watch television in the mirror. The moment came to be lifted into the gaping jaws and to lie there while Heather made a number of adjustments. Solid and immovable though it looks, the iron lung has a surprising number of variables – its body can be tilted to left or right, head up or head down, the mattress on the floor of the body can be raised or lowered, the head rest can be raised or lowered, and the footrest can be moved forward or backward according to the length of the occupant. Careful adjustments add substantially to the comfort of the patient.

The adjustments made, the top was brought menacingly down and, with sickening thuds, the clamps at each side were locked. I was imprisoned and all I could see in front of me was a wall of plain metal. Reassurances were forgotten, my stomach turned over, I wanted to escape. Then the mirror was pulled forward and I had a limited view of a bed and a window and through the window a tree and a building. This much relieved the first claustrophobic effect. The pump had been switched on at low pressure and for a while I lay comfortably in a gentle draught of air – until the closing of the collar! The heavy flaps fell over my face before being pulled tightly across the front of the neck and fixed under chromium bars which were screwed down. I would surely choke. I had always hated anything falling across my mouth or tight round my neck. Surprisingly, I didn't choke, I was still breathing. The palpitations quietened and after a while Heather left me 'to try it out'. Now I could review the situation. I could move arms, legs and body to a limited extent. My neck was cold and in a vice. I was very conscious of my own breathing and the 'breathing' of the machine. When the nursing staff came at frequent intervals to check that I was all right, I found it difficult to talk – the words came in jerks and only when the machine (and I) breathed out. It was strange, it was not pleasant, but it was not unbearable, I *would* be able to cope with it.

During the next few days, two problems manifested themselves and caused me great anxiety. Severe pains in the chest suggested to me that perhaps my heart would not stand up to 'tanking'. If it would not, what then? It was in fact a temporary reaction to the unaccustomed stretching of the lungs. Then I began to feel sore as a result of lying comparatively still on my back. A pressure sore might make tanking impossible. What then? A plaster cast was suggested, made and tried out but I found it exceedingly uncomfortable and restricting. Heather spent hours cutting it down but I still found it unacceptable – cheerfully and without rancour she agreed that it be abandoned, and sought other ways of relieving the pressure with blocks of foam rubber and small pillows. I was immensely thankful that both problems appeared to have been resolved and that tanking could go ahead.

The aim was to achieve a total of 19 hours in the iron lung each day. This entailed a careful watch on the clock each time the tank was opened. At first it was easy. I was too weak to do anything for myself and only too anxious to get back to resting and sleeping which still came readily, but as my condition improved the 19 hours in the tank seemed to get longer and the 5 hours out shorter.

Draughts, cold, boredom and the frustration of not being independent are lasting impressions of the weeks that followed. Draughts and cold were brought under control by the gradual acquisition of scarves, bedjackets, bedsocks and experience. Boredom was less easily controlled. Visitors provided the best antidote: family and friends ensured that the antidote was applied almost every day. The nursing staff, and particularly the student set at that time, were thoughtful and unselfish in giving freely of any spare moments to chat and divert. I tried reading a book placed on an overhead Perspex shelf but waiting for someone to come and turn each page made this too slow and laborious for enjoyment. On the other hand, talking books, together with radio and television, provided hours of pleasure. However, seeing and hearing selected programmes depended upon someone plugging in, changing channels, adjusting the aerial, or fixing and refixing earphones in ears seemingly reluctant to retain them. But should one ring the bell for such a purpose? In common with most other patients I did not want to be demanding and in spite of reassurances from the nursing staff and their willing gratification of one's every request, I was reluctant to use the bell for other than essential reasons. And how about ringing for a nurse to rub one's nose or face? An itch that cannot be scratched can drive one to distraction and it did not help to remember a television programme about the invisible life on the skin which showed pictures of greatly magnified translucent insects taking their young for a walk in the forest of eyebrows! However, I discovered that if you can hold on the itch often, though not always, disappears.

It was during these weeks that blood gases, of which I had only vaguely been aware, assumed the utmost importance. The aim of tanking was to take the oxygen content up and bring the carbon dioxide content down. So one waited anxiously for the result each time the blood gases were taken. Fortunately the results were encouraging, the oxygen was going up, while the carbon dioxide, though more slowly, was going down. Everyone was pleased. The treatment was working.

Soon I was getting up for meals and in due course was able to bath myself. After all that dependence, a great relief. At the end of 6 weeks the blood gases were much improved and tanking hours were gradually reduced until I was up for most of the day – something I had eagerly looked forward to. Yet, unexpectedly, the time dragged. Tanking had been a positive act towards recovery; sitting about filling up the hours with trivial pursuits was not, and seemed a waste of time. Sadly, the blood gases deteriorated. I had been optimistically convinced that on leaving hospital I would need only a Cape Minor pump to exercise and stretch the lungs two or three times a day as I had been taught, but it was obvious that I was going to need some breathing aid at night. So during the last days before my release I was introduced to the Tunnicliffe. This consists of an anorak, which ties tightly at waist, sleeves and neck, over a Perspex frame fitted round the back and domed across the chest. In the middle of the frame is a hole into which is inserted the end of a flexible hose attached to a portable pump which pushes air into and pulls air out of the, hopefully, airtight jacket.

I would not like to repeat my first nights in that contraption – freezing draughts were everywhere and the pressure on the chest far more uncomfortable than tanking. A made-to-measure jacket and frame, an electric over-blanket, the application of tips from other Tunnicliffe users and adaptations from my own experience eventually produced a modicum of comfort but even after 6 years I derive no pleasure from the thought of going to bed at night. Dressing up, tying up, wrapping up and time-consuming efforts – often frustrated – to eliminate draughts make it a performance to be deferred as long as possible.

Nevertheless, it was the Tunnicliffe, reinforced with occasional nights, days or weeks in the iron lung, that enabled me to return full-time to my job for the four years until retirement and that now enables me to live at home and enjoy a full and active retirement. I have a part-time voluntary job. I can't walk far but my car is in constant use for business and pleasure and provides a taxi service for ageing relatives and friends. I can no longer climb to my favourite amphitheatre seats: instead I watch ballet and theatre from the stalls excusing the extravagance on the grounds of a generous retirement gift from colleagues. No longer possible are trips to foreign parts or overnight stops as the mood dictates. Holidays are confined to Britain and France. All journeys are made by car which carries the breathing equipment and avoids the need to walk or queue. While the rhythm of the pump lulls *me* to sleep, understandably it has the opposite effect on other people, so accommodation must be booked in advance to ensure a single, reasonably soundproof room and the provision of manpower to carry the equipment from and to the car. Visiting historic houses and gardens is an activity which has been affected considerably by breathlessness. I still visit but the extent of the exploration is limited. Would that all gardens provided, as does Wisley, a Bactricar, but maybe one day I will acquire a scooter and a winch to get it in and out of the boot.

Impaired ventilation, respiratory failure – frightening words when I first knew they applied to me – are now facts of life to be accommodated as conveniently as possible. Life is a matter of luck – good and bad. I am glad of the good luck which introduced me to the unit that has given me – to date – 6 years of extended life; which ordained that my home would be within easy reach of the unit, now a second home; which led me, as a challenge to the onset of middle-age, to learn to drive; which stimulated interest in non-physical pursuits, gave me a supportive family and friends and a career which was enjoyable and fulfilling. Can one ask for more? Yes, one can – but maybe one should not.

Chapter 26

Clinical Aspects of Acute Myocardial Infarction

by D. BOYLE MD, FRCP

DEFINITIONS

Coronary disease   This can refer to all possible abnormalities, e.g. congenital, inflammatory, of the coronary arteries. Atheromatous disease of the coronary arteries and its sequelae so outnumber other causes that only it will be considered in this chapter.

Ischaemic heart disease   Any condition in which the oxygen supply to the heart is inadequate whether at rest or under stress. Atheromatous coronary disease is the commonest cause.

Angina pectoris   Transient chest pain felt by the patient when his heart muscle is ischaemic. It may occur when (a) a coronary artery is permanently narrow (due to atheroma) and oxygen requirement of the heart increases, e.g. due to exercise or emotion; or (b) the coronary artery narrows by temporary spasm reducing blood flow.

Myocardial infarction   The death of myocardial muscle cells: it occurs when myocardial ischaemia is sufficiently severe and prolonged to cause irreversible damage.

Coronary thrombosis   The occlusion of a coronary artery by thrombosis. It is only one of the ways of producing myocardial infarction but in lay usage the term is often used interchangeably with myocardial infarction.

Acute coronary attack   When the heart becomes ischaemic it may cause sudden death, angina or myocardial infarction. Acute coronary attack can refer to any or all of these.

Arrhythmia   The ischaemic heart can develop abnormal rhythms (see Chapter 6). Some of these are benign (e.g. ventricular ectopic beats). Some worsen ischaemia by reducing coronary blood flow and increasing oxygen demand (e.g. ventricular tachycardia). Some cause sudden death by stopping the pumping action of the heart (e.g. ventricular fibrillation).

EPIDEMIOLOGY AND PREVENTION

Coronary disease is the commonest cause of death in England and Wales – 30 per cent of all male and 23 per cent of all female deaths. In the last 20 years, mortality for coronary disease has remained stable in England and Wales, has risen in Scotland and Northern Ireland, but has fallen in USA and Australia.

Risk factors

Coronary disease remains an epidemic cause of death. About 40 per cent of patients die within 4 weeks of acute myocardial infarction, and about half of these die from rhythm disturbance in the first hour of the attack, usually before help can be summoned.

Prevention of a coronary attack will potentially save more lives than emergency methods to deal with an acute attack or more traditional methods of coronary management.

Epidemiological work has clearly established risk factors or markers which allow us to recognise communities and individuals at high risk of coronary disease.

FAMILY HISTORY

It you have one or both parents who have suffered coronary disease under the age of 55 years your own risk is increased. This increased risk is in part genetic and in part environmental, and is largely due to an associated increase in other risk factors.

SERUM LIPIDS

The higher the concentration of cholesterol in the blood the higher the risk of coronary disease. Lipids can be divided into separate classes by ultra-filtration. One fraction – high density lipoprotein – paradoxically is associated with a reduced risk.

There remains much debate about the importance of diet in preventing coronary disease. However, communities eating a 'prudent diet', that is one that is low in fat, animal fat and refined carbohydrate and with a high intake of fibre and fish tend to have lower mean serum cholesterol values and a lower incidence of coronary disease. Many individuals switching to the 'prudent diet' will show a fall in serum cholesterol but there is a wide variation in the reduction achieved and in some people no reduction is obtained.

BLOOD PRESSURE

Like serum cholesterol, the higher the blood pressure the greater the risk. While lowering high blood pressure undoubtedly reduces the risk of stroke, it has not been conclusively shown to reduce the risk of coronary attack.

TOBACCO SMOKING

The more cigarettes smoked the greater the risk. Stopping smoking reduces the risk (e.g. stopping smoking 20 cigarettes a day reduces the risk of dying from heart attack by two-thirds).

OTHER FACTORS

(a) Physical activity in leisure or at work is associated with a reduced risk of coronary attacks.

(b) Personality: Men and women with Type 'A' personality are at increased risk. They are aggressive, competitive, tend to set themselves deadlines and speak in a characteristic rapid and staccato manner.

(c) Stress – which is hard to define – may be significant. The risk of acute myocardial infarction in men after bereavement or divorce is higher than normal.

(d) Clotting factors: The concentration of certain clotting factors in the blood, e.g. plasma fibrinogen is predictive of coronary attack.

(e) Obesity does not seem to be an important risk factor for coronary disease.

These risk factors only explain about half the coronary events. Many other minor factors have been described and unrecognised risk factors must exist.

Prevention

A recent report by COMA (DHSS, 1984) on diet and cardiovascular disease has been accepted by the British Government as a basis for action to reduce coronary morbidity and mortality. It recommends a multifactorial community approach with reduction in tobacco smoking, better control of hypertension and dietary modification. This community approach should be combined with screening to identify very high risk individuals who require special management.

A recent 10-year report of such an intervention programme in North Karelia, Finland, gives convincing evidence of the benefits of this approach.

PATHOPHYSIOLOGY

Damage to the intima of the coronary arteries with the deposition of lipids, fibrous tissue and calcification may be initiated by platelet deposits. The lesion produced is called atheroma.

Coronary artery spasm can occur in normal arteries, but is usually associated with atheroma. The precipitating factors for spasm are not known. They may be many and may include thromboxane B – a chemical liberated from damaged platelets. Sudden occlusion of the coronary artery may occur from thrombosis (again started and maintained by platelet activity) or, more rarely, bleeding into the atheroma making it swell in size.

CLINICAL PICTURE

Sixty per cent of patients suffering acute myocardial infarction complain of being unwell in the weeks preceding the attack. Complaints of fatigue, irritability, indigestion, shortness of breath, and chest pain are common. They may have recently noticed angina, or, if they were already sufferers, the angina may have become more frequent and severe.

Presentation

The commonest presentation is chest pain which is similar to angina in character and site – in the centre of the chest and radiating to the jaw, arms or back. The pain may be trivial or severe. If severe, it may be associated with pallor and sweating. Since ischaemic muscle is stiff, filling pressure of the heart rises and the patient may complain of breathlessness. Blood pressure may fall as a result of the damage to the heart muscle, or because of an abnormal cardiac rhythm. Lethal arrhythmia can cause sudden death even without pain and this is most likely to occur in the first 4 hours of the attack.

DIAGNOSIS

Myocardial infarction is diagnosed by the clinical picture, electrocardiographic change and finding elevated serum levels of certain enzymes liberated by necrotic heart muscle.

NATURAL HISTORY

About 40 to 50 per cent of patients die within 4 weeks of their first coronary attack and of these, 50 per cent die within about one hour of the attack, mainly from rhythm disturbance. Survivors of acute myocardial infarction may be symptom free. Others may have angina or shortness of breath. Most are able to return to work and normal activities, but all remain at increased risk of coronary death over the ensuing years.

Predictably, prognosis is less good in patients who show (1) a large mass of muscle necrosis; (2) impaired function of the heart pump; or, (3) severe and extensive coronary artery narrowing.

Causes of death in the acute attack are:

1. Lethal arrhythmias such as ventricular fibrillation. The risk is highest in the first hour, but can occur at any time.
2. Heart failure. Pulmonary oedema occurs when back pressure to the lung rises.
3. Shock occurs when the heart is unable to maintain an adequate cardiac output.
4. Rupture of the heart. The free wall may rupture leaking blood into the pericardium. The septum may rupture causing a shunt of blood from left to right ventricle. Papillary muscle may rupture causing mitral regurgitation which can precipitate pulmonary oedema or shock.
5. Thrombo-embolism. Clot may form on the endocardium overlying the necrosed muscle, and emboli may escape to cause damage elsewhere, for example stroke. Clot may also form in the leg and pelvic veins and cause pulmonary emboli.

MANAGEMENT OF THE PATIENT

The aims of treatment are:

1. To keep the patient alive.
2. To return him to his normal place in society with as few symptoms and as good a prognosis as possible.

To keep the patient alive we must prevent or reverse lethal rhythm change. We must reduce the amount of necrosis to a minimum. We must also ensure the maximal physical fitness that his cardiac function will permit and ensure a state of mind to allow him to exploit this fitness to the maximum. His family, friends, employers, etc., must permit the patient to exploit his capacity to work and play. We must try to reduce the risk of further coronary attack – through lifestyle, drugs, and, possibly, surgery.

MANAGEMENT OF THE EARLY STAGE OF ATTACK
(0–4 hours approx)

In this stage the patient is normally in severe pain. He is at the highest risk of sudden death. For much of the time he will not be in hospital and many of those around him may be in a state of panic. The patient's needs are:

1. Reassurance that he can be helped.
2. Relief of pain (usually with diamorphine by intravenous injection or similar opiate).
3. Possibly, other drugs to reduce pulmonary congestion (e.g. a diuretic or isosorbide dinitrate).
4. Possibly, drugs to maintain circulation (particularly blood pressure and heart rate) to minimise myocardial necrosis (e.g. atropine or beta-blockers).
5. Monitoring rhythm so that arrhythmias that threaten life or heart function can be recognised and abolished.
6. Re-establishment of coronary arterial flow (e.g. using intravenous streptokinase).
7. Administration of oxygen. If heart failure is present oxygen concentration in the blood is low.
8. If there is cardiac arrest – external cardiac massage and artificial respiration until the cause of the arrest is diagnosed (e.g. ventricular fibrillation) and corrected (e.g. electric conversion with a defibrillator) (see Chapter 8).

Points 1 and 8 are probably the most important and these can be carried out by any trained person – lay or otherwise. All health professionals should be familiar with the techniques of cardio-pulmonary resuscitation and may well have opportunities of saving lives (see Chapter 8).

Points 2 to 7 require a trained team. Since time is short it is logical to use Mobile Coronary Care Units which can reach the patient without delay and these have been shown to reduce community mortality. Such teams may or may not include doctors.

Even in the early phase of management it is important to remember the long-term target of return to a normal lifestyle.

Patients and family must understand what is happening. If possible, a provisional estimate of length of stay in hospital and the expected date of return to work should be given and this should produce an optimistic outlook.

MANAGEMENT OF HOSPITAL PHASE (4 hours–9 days approx)

Treatment of suspected acute myocardial infarction is best conducted in a coronary care unit. Home management, however, can be considered in the following circumstances:

(1) If the coronary care unit is geographically distant.
(2) If the patient is seen late, e.g. 12 hours or more after the onset of pain.
(3) If the patient is pain free and stable haemodynamically and in normal cardiac rhythm.
(4) If the patient and family prefer the patient to stay at home.
(5) If the primary care team are willing to undertake home care.

Treatment in hospital offers:

(1) Treatment of arrhythmic complication.
(2) Treatment of failure of the heart's function as a pump (heart failure and shock).
(3) Avoidance of other complications.
(4) Preparation for home convalescence.

The length of stay in hospital has diminished markedly over the last 40 years from 3 months to 9 days. Good risk patients are allowed home from most units less than a week from admission.

Arrhythmia

Routine anti-arrhythmic drug administration has not been proven to reduce mortality. Lethal arrhythmia cannot be predicted. However, constant monitoring of the heart rhythm allows instant recognition of ventricular fibrillation and its electric conversion using direct current shock. Paddles are placed on the front and the back of the chest and a current is passed through the chest, usually about 300 Joules. Anti-arrhythmic drugs are normally given after electrical conversion – usually an intravenous infusion of lignocaine, and in some centres this is followed by oral anti-arrhythmic drugs such as quinidine, mexiletine or flecainide. Probably the only other ventricular arrhythmia requiring treatment is rapid and prolonged ventricular tachycardia. In this, the origin of the heart rhythm lies in the ventricle. It may degenerate into ventricular fibrillation and it both reduces cardiac output (and hence coronary flow) and increases oxygen consumption of the heart. It can be treated purely by drugs (the same as for ventricular fibrillation) or by electrical conversion followed by drugs.

Rapid rhythms arising from the atria or from around the atrioventricular node – atrial fibrillation, atrial flutter, supraventricular tachycardia – usually reflect some degree of heart failure and tend to exacerbate the heart failure. They are often transient, but if they cause haemodynamic deterioration they can be abolished by drugs (e.g. verapamil) or by electric shock.

Heart block, in which the impulse cannot spread from the atria to the ventricle, can be complete or incomplete. Complete heart block is associated with a slow heart rate and reduced cardiac output. It is normally managed by passing a wire through a peripheral vein into the right ventricle. This is done under radiographic screening and the tip of the wire is made to lie touching the apex of the right ventricle. Small electric impulses from the wire can make the heart beat at any rate desired. Early in an attack, heart block may respond to atropine. If pacing is not available the heart rate may also be increased by intravenous infusion of isoprenaline.

Treatment of heart failure

If the pump action of the heart fails the clinical picture can be (1) failure of an adequate cardiac output with low blood pressure, and poor flow to vital organs such as the brain, kidneys and the heart muscle itself; (2) a rise in the filling pressure of the heart which acts on the lungs causing dyspnoea; or, (3) both features.

Treatment is difficult. Diuretics can reduce breathlessness by lowering the filling pressure of the heart. Forward flow can be improved by drugs which make the heart beat more strongly (e.g. digitalis, dobutamine) or drugs reducing peripheral resistance (nitrates, angiotensin-converting enzyme inhibitors).

Occasionally counterpulsation is used when a long balloon is placed in the aorta. It is inflated during diastole, increasing arterial pressure and coronary perfusion. It is deflated during systole, reducing systolic pressure and hence reducing the work of the heart (see p. 391).

Despite treatment, most patients with shock die in hospital.

When heart failure is caused by rupture of the ventricular septum or by rupture of the papillary muscle, surgical repair can be attempted.

Thrombo-embolism

Clotting in a coronary artery may precipitate a coronary attack. Coronary artery clotting is not affected by oral drug intervention. Streptokinase and similar agents which activate plasminogen to plasmin and dissolve fibrin clot can be given by intra-coronary or intravenous infusion. There is good evidence that this can reduce mortality by about 20 per cent but there is a significant risk of inducing haemorrhage. There is still debate on which patients should be given such treatment. Clotting in a peripheral vein is common – perhaps 30 per cent of patients. When it occurs in thigh or pelvic veins pulmonary embolism may occur. The risk is higher in heart failure, with extensive infarction, or in patients with varicose veins. The risk should be reduced by early mobilisation and leg exercises. Anticoagulation with heparin and warfarin reduces the risk, and is used in some units either generally or in high risk patients.

Clotting over the endocardium damaged by the infarction may lead to systemic embolism. Anticoagulation may reduce this risk.

Postural hypotension, deconditioning and morale

Bed rest reduces physical fitness and impairs the reflexes that prevent an undue fall of blood pressure when we assume the upright position. General weakness and dizziness induced by bed rest are wrongly attributed by the patient to the severity of his heart attack. Regular exercise and altering the posture of the patient, even in the early days of the heart attack, help to overcome these problems and improve patient morale. Most patients should be able to sit up in a chair and take a few steps within 24 hours of a coronary attack. Such procedures need to be monitored to avoid producing a rapid heart rate. As the days in hospital pass, exercise increases but the patient must avoid undue tachycardia. Most patients sleep upstairs at home. Before discharge, they should climb stairs in hospital, accompanied by a member of staff so that both the patient and the hospital team can be confident.

Pericarditis

Inflammation of the lining of the heart often occurs after infarction. This is painful and patients should be reassured that they are not having a further heart attack. The pain is controlled by drugs (e.g. aspirin, indomethacin or prednisone).

Frozen shoulder

Older texts quote this complication in up to 10 per cent of coronary patients. Since arm and shoulder movements have been encouraged it is now seen only occasionally.

MANAGEMENT IN LATE PHASE (10 days onwards)

Patients leaving hospital should have a clear understanding of the diagnosis, of drugs prescribed and the reasons for taking them, the level of exercise and activity permitted at home and the expected date of return to work.

Drugs

There is good evidence that some patients may benefit from beta-blocking drugs, e.g. atenolol. If tolerated, beta blockade reduces mortality, particularly sudden death. Digitalis, diuretics and vaso-dilator drugs may be needed to reduce heart failure. Warfarin anticoagulation may reduce thrombo-embolic complications. Patients with recurring arrhythmia may require anti-arrhythmic drugs.

Smoking

Keeping off cigarettes reduces the risk of sudden death and re-infarction.

Exercise

Regular exercise improves the exercise tolerance of patients, increases their confidence and well-being. Regular exercise classes under supervision have proved economical and useful. It has been claimed that such exercise in selected patients may reduce the risk of sudden death and re-infarction, but this is disputed. However, it is safe, and the limited object of patient well-being is well worthwhile.

Surgery

Some patients with angina after a coronary attack may benefit from coronary artery surgery in which a vein is made to by-pass regions of arterial narrowing. Sometimes the area of narrowing can be widened by inflating a balloon in the coronary artery and splitting the atheromatous plaque (percutaneous transluminal angioplasty). This can be done without subjecting the patient to thoracotomy. If there is a localised scar interfering with heart function (ventricular aneurysm) this can be excised.

Social support

Most patients are fit to work and resume their place in family and society. Support may be needed to allow them to do so because of prejudice and mistrust of these patients by the general public, employers, trade unions and by family and friends.

REFERENCE

DHSS (1984). *Diet and Cardiovascular Disease*. Report on Health and Social Subjects, 28, Committee on Medical Aspects of Food Policy. HMSO. London.

BIBLIOGRAPHY

Davies, M. (1985). Ischaemic heart disease – the pathological basis. *Medicine International*, 2, 20, 821–5.

Hampton, J. (1985). Prognosis in ischaemic heart disease. *Medicine International*, 2, 20, 832–6.

Norris, R. M. (1985). The management of acute myocardial infarction. *Medicine International*, 2, 20, 842–3.

Shaper, A. G. (1985). Ischaemic heart disease – epidemiology and possibilities for primary prevention. *Medicine International*, 2, 20, 826–31.

ACKNOWLEDGEMENT

The author wishes to acknowledge the advice and assistance he has received from Mrs P. McCoy MCSP.

Chapter 27

Rehabilitation Following Coronary Thrombosis

by P. McCOY BA, MCSP, DipTP, CertEd

INTRODUCTION

Rehabilitation following coronary thrombosis should start from the beginning of the patient's illness and should continue until the patient has reached his maximum physical potential commensurate with his clinical condition. Thus the aim of the coronary care team will be to enable the patient return to work and normal activities as soon as his clinical state allows. It is important that all members of the team adopt a realistic and forward looking attitude to the patient's rehabilitation. It should be remembered that the patient's family and colleagues also play an important part in his road to recovery. Inevitably, some patients will not be able to resume work or participate in any strenuous physical activity because of the severity of the cardiac muscle damage or other complications following myocardial infarction.

Generally, the policy of 3 weeks bed rest followed by very restricted physical activity has been replaced in most units by a programme of more rapid mobilisation and earlier discharge from hospital. This policy has been found to aid the psychological well-being of the patient as well as shorten the period of hospitalisation. The time scale of mobilisation and the level of physical activity will vary widely between hospitals. The physiotherapist must always follow the policy of the physician responsible for the patient.

INTENSIVE CORONARY CARE – FIRST 48 HOURS

The patient will probably be admitted to an intensive care bed in a coronary care ward. He will be nursed there for the initial 48 hours which is the crucial period following a coronary thrombosis. During this time the patient's ECG is monitored continuously so that potentially dangerous arrhythmias can be treated as they arise thereby minimising the risk of sudden arrhythmic death. Other observations which will be recorded regularly include blood pressure, heart rate, respiratory rate, temperature and fluid intake and output. This information will be used in the patient's regular medical assessment.

During the intensive care stage the patient will be nursed in the semi-recumbent position in bed. A patient in cardiogenic shock or with low blood pressure will probably be nursed in a supine position with one pillow if the condition is stable. Some doctors will permit the patient to sit up in a chair by the bedside for an hour in the later part of the first day. This will be extended to 2 hours in the second day if clinical stability is maintained. Some patients may be permitted to have short walks around the bed while still attached to the electrocardiograph monitor.

Factors which would prevent early mobilisation include tachycardia, ventricular arrhythmias, increased ST segment elevation, decreased systolic blood pressure, cyanosis, persistent chest pain and congestive heart failure.

Physiotherapy in the first 48 hours

The main aim of physiotherapy during this early period is preventive. It is important to prevent accumulation of secretions in the lungs which may predispose to chest infection and its possible complications. Stasis in the deep veins of the legs should be prevented and so lessen the danger of deep venous thrombosis and its possible complications.

Deep breathing exercises should be taught and the patient should be asked to repeat them at least every hour. Patients who have a history of respiratory disease such as chronic bronchitis, or present with chest infection may need other physiotherapy measures such as postural drainage. Foot and ankle exercises should be repeated regularly by the patient to increase blood flow in the legs.

THIRD DAY UNTIL DISCHARGE FROM HOSPITAL

If the patient's condition has remained stable during the first 48 hours he is moved out of the acute monitoring area. He will now be allowed to be more active and will probably be encouraged to have frequent short walks within the ward. Early mobilisation helps to prevent the deleterious effects of immobility and the complications associated with prolonged bed rest. The practice of including supervised exercises in the mobilisation programme is becoming more widespread. This enables staff to monitor progress by recording the duration and type of activity *and* the patient's response. Speed of mobilisation may be modified if the patient develops symptoms. Occasionally, clinical deterioration will require a return to acute monitoring.

Recording of information

In order to record a patient's response to activity it will be necessary to divide the mobilisation programme into stages. An example of a possible mobilisation programme is set out below.

Stage I   Monitoring; bed rest; patient washed and fed if necessary.
Physiotherapy: breathing exercises. Foot and ankle exercises.

Stage II   Monitoring; sit up in chair for 1 hour; patient feeds and washes himself; may use commode.
Physiotherapy: as Stage I.

Stage III   Monitoring; sit up in chair for 2 hours, morning and afternoon.
Physiotherapy: as Stage I

Stage IV   Off monitor; walk to toilet and bathroom.
Physiotherapy: bed-end exercises – 5 repeats of each exercise.

Stage V   As Stage IV, plus 6 repeats of bed-end exercises.

Stage VI   As Stage IV, plus 7 repeats of bed-end exercises.

Stage VII   As Stage IV, plus 8 repeats of bed-end exercises.

Stage VIII   As Stage IV, plus walk up and down 1 flight of stairs.

Bed-end exercises

Starting position. Patient stands facing the end of his bed.

1. Double knee bending.
2. Arm abduction to shoulder level.
3. Alternate leg swinging.
4. Finger tips on shoulders, arm circling.

Figure 27/1 illustrates a chart which could be used to record the patient's response to the various stages of mobilisation. This chart may be kept at the patient's bed so that it is readily available to

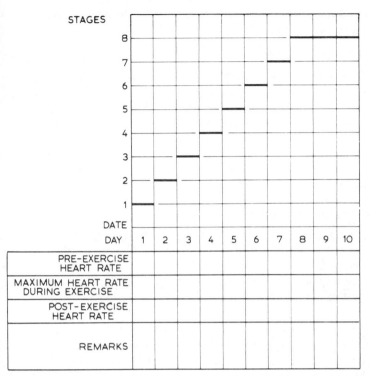

FIG. 27/1 Chart showing a patient's response to mobilisation following coronary thrombosis (ward use)

physiotherapy, nursing and medical staff. The post-infarct day and the date are recorded on the horizontal axis, and the various stages are displayed along the vertical axis. The appropriate line can be ticked to indicate the Stage the patient is at. The pre-exercise heart rate and the maximum and post-exercise heart rates can be recorded. Symptoms which arise during exercise should be noted in the remarks column.

Indications for stopping exercise are shortness of breath, chest pain, irregularities of the pulse, tachycardia (heart rate above 100 beats per minute) and decreased systolic blood pressure.

The patient should be accompanied on the flight of stairs, and if facilities are available the ECG should be monitored by telemetry.

The length of time that patients spend in hospital following a coronary thrombosis will vary between 6 days and 4 weeks depending on the policy of the cardiologist.

Physiotherapy in some early complications which may follow coronary thrombosis

CHEST INFECTIONS

Physiotherapy and antibiotic therapy are usually prescribed. Modified postural drainage may be carried out but it is probably advisable to treat the patient in high side lying as vital capacity is reduced when the patient is lying flat or in a tipped position. This occurs because the volume of blood in the pulmonary vessels is increased and these factors will lead to an increase in work for the heart. Medical advice should be taken before vigorous chest physiotherapy is carried out.

CEREBRAL EMBOLISM

The signs and symptoms will vary with the size and site of the blocked vessel. If the patient develops a hemiplegia then physiotherapy treatment should be undertaken in the usual way. It will be necessary to modify the treatment in the early days so as not to overtire the patient.

LIMITATION OF MOVEMENT IN LEFT SHOULDER GIRDLE

If the patient has had his left arm immobilised because a temporary pacing catheter has been in situ he may have some limitation of shoulder movements. Shoulder movement should be checked after removal of the catheter and mobilising exercises can be taught if necessary. If limitation of the glenohumeral joint persists, then mobilising techniques not involving isometric muscle work can be used. Maitland mobilising techniques are suitable.

Convalescence following discharge from hospital

On discharge from hospital most patients are able to return home but some will spend a few weeks at a convalescent unit for social or other reasons. The first week at home is spent indoors. The patient is advised to have 8 to 10 hours' rest at night and 1 or 2 hours' rest in the afternoon. Most patients will be able to climb stairs once or twice daily. Inevitably some patients with extensive cardiac damage and severe heart failure will not be able to climb stairs. Their exercise tolerance will be low and their activity will be limited by shortness of breath and fatigue. By the second week at home the patient will be able to have short walks out of doors in the garden. After the third week the daily walk can be gradually extended so that by the sixth week following discharge the patient is walking 3 or 4 miles daily. The time scale may vary according to the policy of the physician.

Driving a car is usually forbidden for at least 6 weeks following a coronary thrombosis. Air travel is usually not advised for about 3 months.

Clinical review

Patients are usually reviewed at the hospital outpatient department within a month or two of discharge from the ward. The doctor can then assess the patient's ability to return to work, normal life, or embark on an exercise programme. Most patients will be medically fit to return to their former employment within 3 months of their illness. Some patients may have to take a lighter job because of the inability to do heavy work. Government regulations will debar those who need Heavy Goods Vehicle or Public Service Vehicle licences from their former employment because of coronary thrombosis. These patients will need advice from the social worker as early as possible in their illness so that if possible suitable alternative employment can be found. There are wide variations in medical practice with regard to length of time off work and level of physical activity advised after coronary thrombosis.

REHABILITATION EXERCISE PROGRAMME

Many hospitals now offer facilities for selected patients to attend exercise courses in the physiotherapy department. Not all post-coronary thrombosis sufferers will be clinically fit to attend so it will be necessary to have criteria for selection. The criteria may vary in different centres and the ultimate decision will be the responsibility of the physician.

Aims of rehabilitation programme

1. To reduce the frequency and severity of myocardial infarction.
2. To provide the psychological benefits of exercise.
3. To increase exercise tolerance.
4. To return the patient to work and normal activity as early as possible after the infarction.
5. To restore the patient's confidence in his ability to lead a normal life.

Criteria for selection for exercise class

1. Normally aged 65 years and under.
2. Reasonable cardiovascular function based on heart size, radiographic evidence of heart failure and previous history.
3. No serious locomotor disability or concurrent disease.
4. Acceptance of the concept by the patient.

Testing exercise tolerance

Exercise testing before training provides guidelines for exercise prescription. Ideally patients should be tested on a treadmill to determine their functional physical capacity and to prescribe physical activity. If treadmill facilities are not available then exercise tolerance can be tested on a static cycle ergometer. If monitoring facilities are available the patient should have his ECG monitored throughout the test. The blood pressure and resting heart rate are recorded before the test. The heart rate can be observed continuously throughout the test by means of a finger pulsimeter. The resistance on the ergometer is increased by increments at each completed minute provided the patient does not show signs of distress. The precise length of time of an exercise test will depend on the physician. The test should always be stopped if any of the following symptoms occur:

Chest pain
Severe shortness of breath
Fatigue
Premature ventricular beats
ST segment depression
Dizziness
Muscle cramp
Bradycardia
Heart rate in excess of the maximum recommended for the patient
   (see Table 27/1)
Exertional hypotension (blood pressure drops below pre-exercise
   level)
Blood pressure is disproportionately high in relation to work load.

There are a great variety of exercise training programmes in operation. To some extent the actual choice of exercises and equipment will depend on the available resources. Many centres, particularly in Scandinavia and the United States of America, have sophisticated gymnasium facilities available for rehabilitation. In

TABLE 27/1 Maximal heart rate related to age (Astrand et al, 1977)

Age (years)	Heart Rate (bpm)
20–29	170
30–39	160
40–49	150
50–59	140
60–69	130

the UK some hospitals offer an exercise programme supervised by a physiotherapist. The hospital-based facility has the advantage that medical help is readily available should a crisis arise.

The duration, intensity and frequency of exercise sessions will depend on the policy of the cardiologist and resources available. Some centres ask patients to attend two or three times weekly for 3 months. Exercising the patients in a group using an exercise circuit has several advantages over individually supervised exercise sessions:

1. Better utilisation of the physiotherapist's time and gymnasium space.
2. The group therapy effect of patients working together. This includes mutual support, increased motivation, and better adherence to the programme.
3. Opportunity for patients to discuss common problems with each other and with staff.

Within a class it will be necessary to have a system where patients' individual exercise tolerance is catered for. This can be achieved by altering (a) the speed of repetitions; (b) the time allowed for each exercise; (c) the number of repetitions to be done in the allotted time; and (d) the resistance against which the patient is working.

The patient's natural inclination to compete and compare performance should be discouraged. Exercises should be arranged so that the competitive element is eliminated as far as possible.

Types of activity suitable for training post-coronary thrombosis patients

Endurance-building physical activity is preferable to strength-building exercises. Activities should be enjoyable and adherence to the exercise is encouraged by variety.

In order to produce a training effect a target heart rate of about 70 per cent of the maximum heart rate achieved during exercise testing should be reached and maintained for at least 5 minutes during the exercise class, provided of course that the patient does not develop other symptoms which would indicate that exercise should be stopped. Some authors recommend that patients who have evidence of myocardial disease should not exceed 140 heart beats per minute. This is because the period of diastole is reduced at the higher heart rate thus limiting ventricular filling time and consequently reducing coronary blood flow.

Calisthenics can be used during a warm-up period at the beginning of the exercise session before proceeding to heavier work. A circuit of exercises can be used, alternating arm, leg and trunk work to prevent muscle fatigue. Apparatus used in the circuit may include static bicycle, rowing machine, shoulder wheel, stools for step-ups, weighted pulleys for arm exercises, medicine balls of various weights, skipping ropes and light balls for bouncing. Exercise should be rhythmical, isotonic and involve the large muscle groups.

EXAMPLE OF EXERCISE FOR POST-CORONARY THROMBOSIS PATIENTS

A. Warm-up Exercises
1. Arm swinging
2. Trunk side flexion
3. Alternate leg swinging
4. Trunk rotation with arm swinging
5. Knee bends

B. Circuit
1. Shoulder wheel   3 min
2. Rowing machine   3 min
3. Westminster pulley for arm extension using weights   3 min
4. Step-ups on low stool   3 min
5. Sitting; raising and lowering 5lb medicine ball
   above head   3 min
6. Static bicycle   6 min

C. Group Activity
Volley ball

These activities are an example of an exercise class. Any similar exercises or group activity could be used to provide variety.

The resting pulse should be recorded before exercise is commenced. In order to monitor progress, the pulse can be recorded throughout the static bicycle exercise in a similar way to the recording of the exercise tolerance test. If facilities are available BP and ECG should also be recorded. It is not necessary to record the pulse before and after every single exercise. The patient should be advised to stop exercising if he develops any of the symptoms which were described above as indications for stopping the exercise tolerance test. The patient should rest until symptoms subside. If chest pain persists the patient should be seen and examined by the doctor.

Emergency equipment

It would seem prudent when exercising cardiac patients to have an emergency trolley available in the physiotherapy department. The trolley should have a DC fibrillator; suction apparatus; oxygen cylinder and mask; ECG leads and portable oscilloscope. The physiotherapy staff should be trained to deal with a patient in the event of a cardiac arrest (see Chapter 8). As time is of vital importance, the physiotherapist should be able to initiate external cardiac massage and artificial respiration. Medical help must be summoned immediately and most hospitals will have a cardiac arrest team to deal with such eventualities.

Home exercises

In addition to exercising once or twice weekly in the physiotherapy department, the patients should exercise daily at home. The exercises developed by the Royal Canadian Air Force (1970) provide a very suitable progressive scheme of exercises for men and women. Alternatively a list similar to that shown below could be given.

A. Lying
1. Raise both arms above head to touch floor behind the head
2. Alternate straight leg raising
3. Bend up both knees, feet resting on floor; raise pelvis and lower
4. Bend up both knees, feet resting on floor; drop both knees to one side then to the other side
5. Prone lying, elbow push-ups

B. Standing
6. Trunk side flexion
7. Double knee bending

Exercises 1–7: Start with six repeats of each exercise. Progress by adding two more repeats each week until a maximum of 20 repeats is reached.

C. Walking

Walking is an excellent form of exercise for developing cardiorespiratory endurance. The patient can progress the daily walk until he can walk for about 30–45 minutes at 4 mph. If the terrain is hilly or the weather inclement then the distance and rate should be reduced.

Jogging has similar benefits in developing cardiorespiratory endurance. It is important that it is started at a very low level and gradually increased. Adequate warm-up should always precede a jogging session. Jogging is known to increase musculo-skeletal problems but the wearing of good shock absorbent running shoes and avoidance of hard surfaces should help reduce the risk.

EFFECTS OF EXERCISE

Regular physical activity undertaken by a normal healthy individual produces an improvement in the physical working capacity. This results in a lower resting heart rate, lower heart rate at submaximal work load, increase in stroke volume, and increase in the maximal cardiac output. The difference in oxygen levels between arterial and venous blood $(a-\bar{v}O_2)$ also becomes greater as skeletal muscles become more efficient in extracting oxygen.

Exercise probably plays some role in adapting the heart to cope better with the effects of ischaemic heart disease (Sanne et al, 1970). The changes described above are, probably, more marked in younger patients than in older patients.

The theory that regular exercise promotes the development of coronary collateral vessels in these subjects remains to be proven conclusively. Post-mortem studies of animals who had coronary arterial vessels blocked artificially and were then subjected to regular controlled exercise, demonstrated that the coronary collateral vascularisation had improved. Froelicher et al (1980) using radionuclide ventriculography technique, demonstrated an improvement in both myocardial perfusion and function in a small number of ischaemic heart disease patients who had exercised regularly. Regular exercise promotes a feeling of general well-being and assists in the maintenance of ideal body-weight and adherence to prudent living habits. A number of studies have shown that participation in an organised rehabilitation programme following coronary thrombosis has resulted in lower anxiety levels and a reduction in the number of emergency referrals for false suspicion of recurrent infarction (Hill and Cox, 1983; Singh et al, 1977; Sanne et al, 1970).

Data will have to be collected on subjects over a long period of study under controlled conditions, before claims that regular exercise following coronary thrombosis reduces the incidence of subsequent re-infarction or enhances longevity can be made. But it can probably be said that a programme as described here improves the quality of life for the patient and his family, thus at least adding life to years.

Leisure activities

The patients who fulfil the criteria for exercise class selection will be able to take part in numerous sporting activities. Competitive sport is usually not recommended as this introduces the stress factor. Swimming, bowls, walking, jogging, badminton, volley ball, cycling, golf, gardening, dancing and horse riding are among the long list of activities in which patients can be encouraged to participate, depending on their preferences. Outdoor games should be avoided on cold windy days as the vasoconstriction caused by the cold puts an extra heavy load on the circulation.

Heavy isometric work such as shovelling snow in the cold, lifting or pushing very heavy weights, such as a car, are contra-indicated in patients with coronary heart disease.

REFERENCES

Astrand, P. O. and Rodahl, K. (1977). *Textbook of Work Physiology*, 2nd edition. McGraw Hill Book Company, New York.

Froelicher, V., Jensen, D., Atwood, E. et al (1980). Cardiac rehabilitation: evidence for improvement in myocardial perfusion and function. *Archives of Physical Medicine and Rehabilitation*, **61**.

Hill, D. A. and Cox, T. (1983). Behavioural style, cardiac responsiveness and myocardial infarction. Included in *Stress and Tension Control*, volume 2. Plenum Publishing Co Ltd, London. (Proceedings of the Second International Conference of the Society for Stress and Tension Control, Sussex University September, 1983.)

Royal Canadian Air Force (1970). *Physical Fitness*. Penguin Books, Harmondsworth. This title has been reissued (1986) by Penguin as 2 volumes: *5 Bx Plan for Physical Fitness for Men* and *5 Bx Plan for Physical Fitness for Women*.

Sanne, H., Grimby, G. and Wilhelmsen, L. (1970). Physical training during convalescence after myocardial infarction. Included in the *Proceedings of the Symposium of Coronary Heart Disease and Physical Fitness*, Copenhagen, 1970.

Singh, N., Ferguson, J. R., Barber, J. M. and Boyle, D. McC. (1977). Exercise after myocardial infarction. *Journal of the Irish Medical Association*, **70**, 2.

BIBLIOGRAPHY

Amundsen, L. R. (ed.) (1981). *Cardiac Rehabilitation*. Churchill Livingstone, Edinburgh.

Gentry, W. G. et al (1979). *Psychological Aspects of Myocardial Infarction and Coronary Care*. C. V. Mosby Co, St Louis.

Naughton, J. and Hellerstein, H. K. (1973). *Exercise Testing and Exercise Training in Coronary Heart Disease*. Academic Press, London.

Peterson, L. H. (1983). *Cardiovascular Rehabilitation: A Comprehensive Approach*. Collier Macmillan Publishers, West Drayton, England.

Shephard, R. J. (1981). *Ischaemic Heart Disease and Exercise*. Croom Helm, Beckenham, England.

Vyden, J. K. (1983). *Post-myocardial Infarction Management and Rehabilitation*. Marcel Dekker Inc, New York.

ACKNOWLEDGEMENTS

The author wishes to record her thanks to all the staff of the Coronary Care Unit, the Ulster Hospital, Dundonald, Belfast. Her special thanks go to Dr D. Boyle MD and Miss S. E. Robinson MCSP, who initially stimulated her interest in Cardiac Rehabilitation.

Chapter 28

Some Cardiac Disorders

by D. BOYLE MD, FRCP

HYPERTENSION

Raised blood pressure predisposes to damage of the arterial wall. The higher the pressure the greater the risk of damage. This is true equally for systolic and diastolic levels of blood pressure. It therefore greatly increases the risk of coronary arterial disease – causing sudden death, myocardial infarction or angina – and cerebrovascular disease – causing stroke by cerebral infarction, cerebral haemorrhage or transient ischaemic episodes. Damage to peripheral vessels can cause intermittent claudication – ischaemic pain usually in the calf muscle brought on by exercise – and gangrene. Damage to renal vessels can cause kidney failure. High blood pressure demands extra work from the heart and can cause left ventricular hypertrophy and heart failure.

In many cultures blood pressure remains similar from early adulthood to old age but in Western civilisation blood pressure tends to rise with age. Blood pressure fluctuates widely in both normal people and in patients. Blood pressure can rise acutely due to stress, e.g. due to having it measured, excitement, discomfort or position, exercise, especially isotonic muscle contraction, cold atmosphere, full urinary bladder. Blood pressure measured by a doctor in the surgery or hospital tends to be higher than when it is measured by the patient or his spouse at home.

Diagnosis

Bearing these factors in mind it is clear that it is difficult to define hypertension. Patients with hypertension are the upper range of a statistically normally distributed frequency curve.

In practice a patient with a blood pressure consistently in excess of 160/95 can be considered hypertensive. There is evidence that treatment of pressure greater than 170/110 will reduce subsequent morbidity and mortality but there is continuing dispute about the value of drug therapy in patients with milder hypertension.

Aetiology

A primary cause of high blood pressure can be found in less than 20 per cent of all patients. Causes include:

1. Renal disease:
    (a) Parenchymal disease, e.g. pyelonephritis
    (b) Renal vascular disease, e.g. renal artery stenosis
2. Endocrine disease
    (a) Excess cortisol – Cushing's syndrome
    (b) Excess aldosterone – Conn's syndrome
    (c) Excess catecholamine – phaeochromocytoma
    (d) Pregnancy associated hypertension
    (e) Acromegaly
3. Coarctation of aorta
4. Drugs: Carbenoxolone; non-steroidal anti-inflammatory analgesics; corticosteroids; contraceptive pill; liquorice

In the remaining patients no primary cause can be found and the term *essential hypertension* is used. A positive family history is often found.

RENIN ANGIOTENSIN SYSTEM

Renin is a hormone largely arising from the kidney which acts by converting a pro-hormone in the blood – angiotensinogen – to angiotensin I. This in turn is converted to angiotensin II which is not only a very powerful vasoconstrictor but also stimulates the production of the salt retaining hormone aldosterone by the adrenal gland. It can, therefore, raise blood pressure by both these actions. An acutely ischaemic kidney will excrete more renin. Much research is currently taking place to define the importance of the renin angiotensin system in both secondary and essential hypertension. The concept of the renin angiotensin system has already influenced thinking on therapy.

Assessment

In assessing patients we look for evidence of damage already caused by the high blood pressure (Table 28/1) and associated factors which might facilitate vascular damage (Table 28/2).

TABLE 28/1   Evidence of damage of end-organ

1	Clinical, radiographic and ECG evidence of left ventricular hypertrophy
2	Vascular bruits
3	Clinical evidence of myocardial, cerebral and peripheral ischaemia
4	Kidney damage
5	Vascular changes in the retina seen using an ophthalmoscope
	a Arterial narrowing
	b Apparent obstruction of veins by arteries
	c Exudates and haemorrhages in the retina
	d Papilloedema or oedema of the optic cup

The finding of 5 c and d is called *accelerated hypertension*; and that of 5d *malignant hypertension*. Without treatment the outlook for the patients in these groups is very poor.

TABLE 28/2   Associated factors

1	Smoking
2	Hyperlipidaemia
3	Diabetes mellitus

Investigation

Investigation required for a patient with high blood pressure normally includes urine analysis, chest radiograph, blood urea and electrolytes, serum cholesterol and ECG. More complex investigations – intravenous pyelogram, renal arteriography, CT scans, isotope test of kidney function, and measurement of blood renin activity are occasionally needed to assess renal and adrenal involvement. Measurement of circulating levels of hormones are rarely needed.

Treatment

If a primary cause can be found it can often be treated, usually by appropriate surgery. In essential hypertension, or if surgery is not appropriate for secondary hypertension, treatment can be:

Non-pharmacological: This includes dietary modification of calories, fat and salt, relaxation techniques and yoga. In mild hypertension this may be all that is needed.

Pharmacological intervention: Many classes of drugs are used. Common drugs include:

1. Diuretics in low dose, e.g. bendrofluazide
2. Calcium antagonists, e.g. nifedipine
3. Beta-adrenergic blocking drugs, e.g. atenolol
4. Alpha-adrenergic blocking drugs, e.g. prazosin
5. Angiotensin-converting enzyme inhibitors, e.g. captopril
6. Centrally (CNS) acting drugs, e.g. methyldopa, clonidine
7. Vasodilators, e.g. hydralazine

Certain patient groups tend to respond to some drugs better than others, for example young patients to beta-blocking drugs and angiotensin-converting enzyme inhibitors, and older patients to calcium antagonists and diuretics. However, drug therapy is largely determined by trial and error and may involve the combination of drugs. Patients with uncomplicated hypertension are normally asymptomatic. Therapy is usually life long so that efficacy of control and avoidance of side-effects is paramount. It is important not to restrict a patient's activities. Regular exercise – isotonic and isometric – is generally well tolerated.

Treatment of associated risk factors: Stopping smoking is probably more important than lowering blood pressure, in reducing the patient's risk of premature death.

HEART FAILURE

Physiology

The circulation is a complex closed system ensuring the adequate delivery of blood to the various organs to supply their constantly varying metabolic demands. The force to move the blood comes from the ventricles of the heart which are pulsatile muscle pumps, running in series. The pulsatile flow is converted to a more continuous flow by the elastic properties of the big arteries. Flow to individual organs is controlled by varying the resistance to flow in small arteries and arterioles, which in turn is influenced by the local chemical environment and vasoconstrictor activity of sympathetic nerves and circulating hormones such as noradrenaline. Transfer of metabolites is made at capillary level.

Venous return is controlled by residual pressure from the heart remaining after passage of blood through capillaries; massage of the veins by voluntary muscle action in the limbs (facilitated by venous valves); and the tone of the venous wall.

Resistance to inflow to the ventricle arises from the stiffness of the ventricular wall and, in disease, by narrowing of the mitral and tricuspid valves.

Atrial contraction increases ventricular filling with only a transient increase of filling pressure immediately before ventricular contraction.

The pressure and flow from the heart to the arteries depends on the volume of blood in the ventricle at the onset of contraction, the force of contraction, and the resistance to flow in the arterial system. Blood pressure is directly proportional to both cardiac output and peripheral resistance.

Cardiac output can be increased by increasing the heart rate. This is the most important mechanism in normal activity. It can also be increased by increasing ventricular contraction. The more that heart muscle is stretched the harder it contracts, so that increased filling of a ventricle will increase contraction. Contraction is also increased by hormonal and sympathetic nervous activity. The control of the circulation depends on a very complex set of inter-related systems of controls including the autonomic nervous system, hormonal system and the physical property of its constituent parts.

A failure of this system can be called *heart failure*. In practice 'heart failure' is a clinical syndrome recognised clinically rather than being measured by markers of haemodynamic function.

Compensation

As the heart begins to fail it attempts to compensate.

1. Increase of heart rate to increase the cardiac output. This also increases the metabolic demands of the heart.
2. Increase in the filling pressure of the heart by fluid retention and change in venous capacity. This works by stretching the heart muscle fibres to increase the force of contraction. However, fluid retention also causes congestion in organs downstream, for example the lungs in left ventricular failure, and the liver and kidneys in right ventricular failure. The increased filling pressure also makes coronary perfusion of the myocardium more difficult.
3. Increased peripheral resistance to maintain blood pressure when the cardiac output falls. This however increases heart work.

It can be seen that the effects of compensation is often self-defeating by increasing heart work and producing symptoms in its own right.

Clinical picture

In left ventricular failure the patient is dyspnoeic. Breathing is easier sitting up than lying down flat. There may be signs of cardiac enlargement and there will be a loud filling sound (3rd heart sound) heard. If filling pressure is sufficiently high there will be pulmonary oedema. In right ventricular failure systemic venous pressure is raised. The liver is engorged and there is peripheral oedema.

In many cases left and right ventricular failure co-exist. Malfunction of organs, for example the liver and kidney, is due both to reduced blood supply and venous congestion.

Treatment

Ideally the cause of failure is treated, for example surgery for valve disease and intracardiac septal defects. Occasionally, medical therapy will effectively treat the cause as in hypertension, severe anaemia and rhythm disturbance. If treatment of the cause is impossible or inadequate certain strategies can be tried.

1. *Stimulate* the heart to beat more strongly, for example by giving digoxin, beta-adrenergic stimulants, and amrinone.
   (This strategy has been likened to 'flogging a dying horse' and is often ineffective.)
2. *Diuretic therapy.* This reduces congestion of the lungs and systemic organs and can give great symptomatic relief. However, by reducing ventricular filling pressure it tends to lower cardiac output further. Diuretics include bendrofluazide and frusemide. These both tend to lower serum potassium which in turn can damage the heart. Vasodilator drugs, for example isosorbide dinitrate, also reduce filling pressure of the heart, and are of particular value in acute left ventricular failure.
3. *Vasodilator therapy.* If peripheral resistance or 'after-load' can be reduced, cardiac output can be increased without increasing heart work. This can improve symptoms dramatically in some patients, but it is not clear if life expectancy is increased. If the peripheral resistance falls too low, or the heart fails to respond, dangerous hypotension can be provoked. Probably the most successful drugs are the angiotensin-converting enzyme inhibitors.

When all else fails cardiac transplantation can be considered for younger patients.

COR PULMONALE

Right ventricular hypertrophy and particularly right ventricular failure on the basis of primary lung disease can be called cor pulmonale.

Aetiology

The mechanism of cor pulmonale is the creation of pulmonary hypertension, that is higher pressure in the pulmonary artery than normal. In primary lung disease this is due to an increase in resistance to flow. Obstruction can come from constriction of pulmonary arterioles, obliteration of arterioles (as in embolic hypertension), destruction of lung tissue including the arterioles and, very rarely, occlusive disease affecting the small pulmonary veins.

The commonest cause of cor pulmonale in the UK is chronic bronchitis mainly of the 'blue bloater' variety in which poor ventilation produces anoxia which in turn acts as a stimulant for pulmonary arteriolar constriction. Commonly heart failure is precipitated by sudden worsening of lung function usually by infection.

Treatment

Treatment of heart failure is ideally that of the cause as, for example, in exacerbation of chronic bronchitis: by physiotherapy to clear bronchial secretion, antibiotics for chest infection and careful use of oxygen to reduce anoxia. Postural drainage is usually well tolerated even when the patient is very symptomatic. Therapy for heart failure – inotropic drugs, diuretics and vasodilators – are relatively inefficient, though diuretics in particular are widely used and may give symptomatic help.

When the heart failure is more chronic there is good evidence that oxygen administered on long-term basis – 15 hours a day – will gradually reduce the pulmonary hypertension.

Treatment of less common causes of cor pulmonale is often difficult. Where severe chest deformity causes ventilatory problems with the potential for cor pulmonale, surgery to correct the skeletal abnormality may occasionally help.

Thrombo-embolic hypertension due to multiple small pulmonary emboli may be helped by warfarin anticoagulation. Certain forms of pulmonary arteritis, for example in systemic lupus erythematosus, may be helped by steroids or immunotherapy.

BIBLIOGRAPHY

Kincaid-Smith, P. (1985). The investigation of hypertension. *Medicine International*, 2, 19, 786–91.
Poole-Wilson, P. A. (1985). Heart failure. *Medicine International*, 2, 21, 866–71.
Rajagopalan, B. (1985). Primary pulmonary hypertension and cor pulmonale. *Medicine International*, 2, 19, 813–17.
Simpson, F. O. (1985). Epidemiology of hypertension. *Medicine International*, 2, 19, 781–5.
Swales, J. D. (1985). Management of hypertension. *Medicine International*, 2, 19, 792–6.

ACKNOWLEDGEMENT

The author thanks Mrs P. McCoy MCSP for her advice and help in preparation of this chapter.

Chapter 29

Peripheral Vascular Disease – Pathology, Distribution and Symptoms

by P. A. E. HURST BSc, MS, MRCP, FRCS

Arterial disease is becoming more common as living standards improve and other diseases are eradicated. *Atherosclerosis* is now the commonest cause of death in the Western world, and it affects all major arteries. When it affects the coronary arteries it causes angina pectoris and myocardial infarction. When atherosclerosis affects the aorta and its major branches it causes considerable pain and disability and may ultimately result in gangrene of the limbs requiring amputation. If the arteries supplying the brain are affected this may lead to stroke with hemiplegia or death.

Most patients, in fact, develop atherosclerosis to varying degrees in the coronary, cerebrovascular and peripheral arterial systems simultaneously. Thus, as a group, such persons have a reduced life expectancy and may suffer considerable pain and disability. The aim of vascular surgery is to treat the symptoms and prevent the complications of arterial disease. In the USA the most frequently performed surgical operation is coronary artery bypass grafting which is effective in treating angina and may prevent subsequent death from infarction. In the UK this is usually performed by cardiac surgeons while peripheral vascular surgeons operate on the abdominal aorta and its branches, together with the carotid and subclavian vessels.

ATHEROSCLEROSIS

This is the disease process in which the arterial wall is damaged by the deposition of atheroma. (It is sometimes called arteriosclerosis.) Atheroma is the lipid-rich substance found in the walls of diseased arteries. Streaks of atheroma are present in the wall of the aorta from an early age and are seen at post-mortem in young people killed in accidents. Atherosclerosis is very much more common among people eating a typical Western diet rich in saturated fats and sugars than in persons from underdeveloped regions eating a diet rich in fibre with fewer lipids. The Framingham study (1968) strongly implicates diet as a major cause of arterial disease, and has been borne out by the reduction in mortality from myocardial infarction in the USA following widespread changes in dietary intake avoiding dairy products and sugar.

Further evidence (1983) that fats are involved in arterial disease comes from the fact that patients suffering from a group of hereditary disease known as the hyperlipidaemias suffer from very severe atherosclerosis which may develop at an early age. In these diseases fat metabolism is abnormal and there are high levels of circulating cholesterol and lipoproteins. Similarly, diabetics who also have high levels of cholesterol in the blood suffer from accelerated atherosclerosis (as well as a different form of arterial disease affecting the small vessels supplying the digits).

Cigarette smoking is irrefutably associated with the development of atheroma. It is unusual for non-smokers to suffer from arterial disease and most severe arteriopaths are heavy smokers. Giving up smoking can reduce the risk. This has been shown by comparison of a group of doctors who have given up smoking compared with their colleagues who continued to smoke. The incidence of coronary artery disease was much reduced in those who gave up cigarettes. There is also good evidence that patients do less well after arterial reconstruction if they continue to smoke (Greenhalgh, 1981). Since failed reconstructive surgery may leave the patient worse off than before, it may be unwise to operate on patients who refuse to, or are unable to, stop smoking. It is surprising how many patients fail to heed advice about smoking while their disease inexorably progresses.

Histological and biochemical analysis of atheroma shows it to consist of lipids, cholesterol and excessive numbers of smooth muscle cells. The precise details of how and why atheroma is deposited in the arterial wall is still open to debate. The most likely theory is that damage to the arterial wall (possibly caused by shearing forces resulting from turbulent blood flow) initiates platelet deposition. Platelets themselves are rich in lipid and liberate various biological substances such as prostaglandins which may then induce smooth muscle cell multiplication and other local reactions which together result in the development of atheroma. Another school of thought believed that the development of atheroma is the result of abnormalities of lipid handling and clearance by the arterial wall (Fredrickson et al, 1967). A less likely explanation is that atheroma is a form of benign neoplasia of smooth muscle cells.

Although certain diets may be of use in long-term prevention of arterial disease there is little evidence that dieting can reverse already established arterial disease.

Atherosclerosis is much more common in men than women below the age of the menopause, after which the risk to women approaches that in man. The loss of both ovaries accelerates the development of atherosclerosis and thus oestrogens are thought to offer a protective effect.

Whatever the exact cause of atheroma the result is that plaques of lipid-rich material form in the arterial wall. Figure 29/1 is a diagram of a cross-section of the wall of a medium-sized artery. It is seen to consist of three layers: the external *adventitia*, the *media* – consisting of smooth muscle and elastic tissue – and the *intima* which itself is lined by a delicate layer of endothelial cells. The integrity of the endothelium is crucial to the maintenance of normal blood flow through the vessel. Atheroma is laid down beneath the intima and in the media and this causes stenosis (narrowing) of the lumen of the artery. Atheroma does not develop uniformly throughout the arterial tree, but tends to occur as localised plaques in specific areas (Fig. 29/2a). It may occur in one or several of these sites in each patient and indeed in either limb. The reason for the localisation of atheromatous plaques is probably related to disturbance in the pattern of blood flow particularly at sites where arteries branch. The symptoms produced by this arterial stenosis depend on its severity and location. Because of the complex physics governing blood flow (haemodynamics) an artery has to be very severely narrowed before blood flow through it is restricted and symptoms develop. The

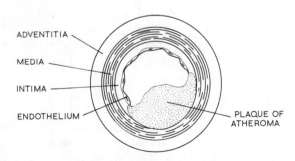

FIG. 29/1 Medium sized artery with narrowed lumen due to atherosclerosis

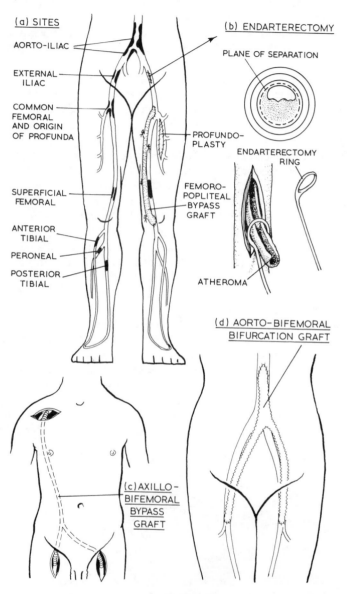

FIG. 29/2 (a) Common sites of arterial stenosis with common surgical procedures; (b) endarterectomy; (c) axillo-bifemoral bypass graft; (d) aorto-bifemoral bifurcation graft

effects of such a narrowing are usually not noticeable at rest but become evident during exercise when a greater blood flow through the artery is required to supply the active muscles, and this increased flow cannot pass through the narrowed vessel.

Intermittent claudication

This is the symptom produced by a significant narrowing of arteries supplying the limb, most commonly the superficial femoral and/or the iliac vessels.

As the stenosis develops, initially the patient will not suffer any symptoms. If, however, the stenosis progresses (and particularly if there is also narrowing at another site, such as the common iliac artery) the patient will notice *pain* in the calf muscles when he has walked a certain distance (or hurried an even shorter distance).

The pain is due to the build-up of the products of anaerobic metabolism in the muscles which are starved of oxygen due to the restriction of arterial inflow. Typically, the patient is forced to rest, whereupon the pain slowly resolves as these metabolites (e.g. lactic acid) are cleared. This pattern of pain on exercise which is relieved by rest is known as *intermittent claudication* (from the Latin *claudicare* – to limp).

Usually arterial stenosis occurs gradually and reaches a point where blood flow is so slow that thrombosis occurs totally blocking the vessel. This, however, does not have the disastrous effect that the sudden blockage of a healthy artery would have, because of the development of collateral channels by the linking up of arterial branches proximal and distal to the block (Fig. 29/3).

These collateral vessels maintain blood supply to the limb, but because they are of narrow calibre their resistance to flow is very

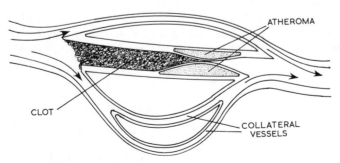

FIG. 29/3 Blocked artery with collateral vessels

great and thus claudication still occurs. With the development of collaterals the distance the patient can walk may improve markedly and since ischaemia (oxygen starvation) may be a stimulus to collateral formation, exercising 'through the pain' should be encouraged. The natural history of claudication is often benign and is not usually an indication for vascular reconstruction unless the symptoms are preventing a patient from working or very severely affecting his lifestyle.

Rest pain

Although most patients who develop claudication either improve or their symptoms remain static, a proportion of patients with widespread disease reach a stage where the arterial perfusion of their limbs is not adequate even at rest. These patients usually first experience pain in bed, the reason being that when they are lying horizontal they do not have the benefit of gravity, that is the hydrostatic pressure of a column of blood to increase flow through the high resistance vessels. In fact most sufferers learn that they can relieve the pain by hanging the affected limb out of the bed thereby using gravity to improve flow. Rest pain is an agonising experience for the patient and usually is the harbinger of the development of gangrene (tissue necrosis) in the limb. It is thus an absolute indication that arterial investigations should be conducted with a view to vascular reconstruction in order to save the limb.

Gangrene

If the tissues receive insufficient blood supply and thus oxygen, cell death (necrosis) will occur. This usually happens in the digits which eventually mummify and become black. This is *dry gangrene*. If superadded infection occurs this is *wet gangrene*. If an entire limb becomes gangrenous the life of the patient is at risk as the chemical by-products of necrosis may cause renal failure. Overwhelming sepsis may also occur. A limb with established gangrene *must* be amputated.

DISTRIBUTION OF VASCULAR DISEASE (Fig. 29/2)

Aorto-iliac disease

The aorta, because of its wide lumen, does not often become significantly stenosed, but it may be blocked by thrombosis spreading up from the iliac vessels which themselves may have become blocked. This thrombosis may extend proximally to the level of the renal arteries, where the high flow to the kidneys prevents extension of the clot.

The iliac vessels are often severely diseased and this may be sometimes unilateral.

Le Riche syndrome

Named after the Frenchman who first described it, this consists of buttock claudication and impotence. It results from occlusion of the distal aorta and the common, external and internal iliac arteries.

Femoro-popliteal disease

Atheroma commonly affects this segment of the arterial tree, particularly in the superficial femoral artery as it passes beneath the adductor muscles. Plaques also occur diffusely in the distal vessels below the trifurcation.

Aneurysm

The development of atheroma usually results in progressive stenosis of the affected arteries. There is, however, a group of patients in whom atheroma leads to a weakening of the vessel wall causing it to dilate under arterial pressure. Localised dilatation of an artery is known as an *aneurysm*. Atheromatous aneurysms occur most commonly in the abdominal aorta (Fig. 29/4) but may also affect the iliac, femoral and popliteal arteries. It is not clear why some individuals react in this way to atheroma; in some cases both dilating disease and stenosing disease can occur in the same patient at different sites.

Clinical diagnosis of an aneurysm depends on the finding of a pulsatile swelling. Unfortunately, they often remain undiagnosed until a major complication occurs.

False aneurysm

Following needle puncture or injury to an artery, or at an arterial surgical anastomosis, leakage of blood may occur forming a haematoma. This haematoma may then organise to form a false aneurysm the lumen of which is in communication with the arterial system and the wall of which is composed of clot (Fig. 29/5).

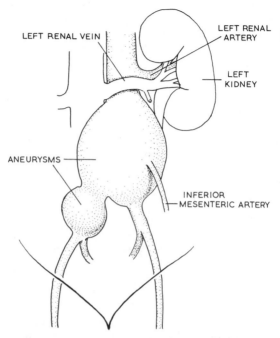

FIG. 29/4 Fusiform aneurysm of aorta and right common iliac artery

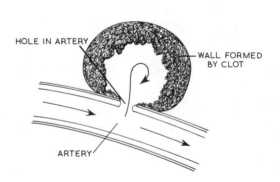

FIG. 29/5 False aneurysm

Diabetic vascular disease

Diabetics suffer major problems with lipid as well as carbohydrate metabolism. This leads to the development of atherosclerosis at an earlier age than in non-diabetics. As well as this accelerated vascular disease affecting large vessels, diabetes also affects the smaller vessels producing ischaemic ulcers and isolated necrosis of digits. These effects are made worse by an increased susceptibility to infection, and peripheral neuropathy leading to anaesthesia.

Treatment is modified for diabetics since conservative excision of necrotic tissue (e.g. amputation of a digit) with vigorous control of infection and blood sugar may achieve satisfactory results.

Buerger's disease

This disease results in inflammation of the neurovascular bundle (artery, vein and nerve). It affects predominantly small distal vessels and occurs only in heavy smokers. It results in sequential necrosis of digits in both upper and lower limbs. More severe ischaemia may necessitate multiple amputations. The tragic young bilateral amputee who continues to hold a cigarette between his few remaining fingers is familiar to all vascular clinics.

Vascular disease in the upper limb

For reasons which are poorly understood the arteries of the upper limb are seldom affected by severe atherosclerosis.

Thoracic outlet syndrome

An abnormal rib which has developed on the 7th cervical vertebra or a tough fibrous band attached to the 1st rib may press upon the subclavian artery thereby stenosing it. An aneurysm commonly forms distal to the narrowing and, together with pressure on the nerves of the brachial plexus, will cause tingling and weakness in the forearm and Raynaud's syndrome in the hand.

Raynaud's syndrome

This is an abnormal sensitivity to cold resulting in intense vasoconstriction in the cutaneous vessels of the fingers and, sometimes, the toes. On exposure to cold the hands become white; on warming they become blue and then red and painful. Primary

Raynaud's disease occurs predominantly in young women. Treatment is usually conservative with advice about wearing gloves – electrically heated ones are now available. Cervical sympathectomy gives temporary relief.

The same symptoms occur in secondary Raynaud's disease, although more severe problems including necrosis and ulceration are common. An older age-group is affected, again predominantly women, and there is an underlying collagen disease present, for example scleroderma, systemic lupus erythematosus or rheumatoid arthritis.

Arterial embolus

A piece of thrombus or atheroma may become dislodged and travel in the bloodstream to become lodged in a vessel downstream from where it formed. This is known as an *embolus* and if it blocks the vessel this will have serious consequences as it will totally cut off the blood supply. Arterial emboli most commonly originate from the heart, either from the left atrium which is fibrillating due to mitral valve disease, or from the left ventricular wall after myocardial infarction (mural thrombus). Emboli can also be dislodged from atheroma in the aorta. Small emboli coming from atheromatous plaques in the carotid arteries cause short-lived neurological symptoms known as transient ischaemic attacks (TIAs), and may herald the development of a stroke.

A large embolus can lodge in the distal aorta blocking both common iliac arteries. Because of its shape this is termed a 'saddle' embolus and affects both legs. More commonly the embolus lodges in the femoral or politeal artery, whereupon the affected limb will suddenly become Painful, Pulseless, Pale and Paralysed. Gangrene may ensue if the embolus is not quickly removed (embolectomy). This operation has been simplified by the development by an American surgeon, Dr Fogarty, of the embolectomy catheter. This is passed down the affected vessel past the clot. A balloon at the end of the catheter is then inflated and as the device is withdrawn it pulls back the embolus thus clearing the vessel. In some cases anticoagulants are indicated to prevent further thrombosis and embolisation.

REFERENCES

Framingham Study (1968). *An Epidemiological Investigation of Cardiovascular Disease*, section 10. US Government Printing Office (September).

Fredrickson, D. S., Levy, R. I. and Lees, R. S. (1967). Fat transport in lipoproteins: an integrated approach to mechanisms and disorders. *New England Journal of Medicine*, **276**, 34, 94, 148, 215, 273.

Greenhalgh, R. M. (ed.) (1981). *Smoking and Arterial Disease*. Pitman, London.

Proceedings of the International Symposium on Epidemiology and Prevention of Arteriosclerotic Disease (1983). *Preventive Medicine*, **11**, 1–234.

BIBLIOGRAPHY

See page 653.

Chapter 30

Peripheral Vascular Disease – Assessment and Treatment

by P. A. E. HURST BSc, MS, MRCP, FRCS

THE ASSESSMENT OF VASCULAR STENOSIS

Patients presenting with symptoms suggestive of arterial disease must be carefully assessed: (1) to rule out other diseases which might cause the same symptoms; (2) to determine the extent of their vascular disease and any co-existent cardiorespiratory disease; and (3) to decide on an appropriate treatment plan.

Assessment starts by taking a careful history. Pain in the legs on walking which stops on resting is typical of arterial stenosis. Very similar pain can, however, be caused by orthopaedic problems affecting the lumbo-sacral spine, for example a prolapsed intervertebral disc particularly if this is causing stenosis of the spinal canal thereby reducing the blood supply to the spinal cord. Arthritis of the hip and/or knee joints may also be confused with claudication.

A careful examination usually rules out these other problems since the cardinal feature of arterial disease is the loss of palpable pulses distal to the site of a complete arterial block, or reduction of the volume of the pulse distal to a critical stenosis. Pulses are normally easily palpable over the femoral arteries in the groins; in the popliteal arteries behind the knees; in the dorsalis pedis arteries on the front of the feet; and in the posterior tibial arteries below the medial malleoli. If, for instance, the femoral pulse is palpable but the popliteal pulse is absent this indicates a block in the superficial femoral artery; if the femoral artery pulse on one side is much weaker than on the other side this indicates a stenosis proximal to the femoral artery on that side (in the iliac vessels).

Stenosis in a vessel disturbs the flow through it causing turbulence, and this can be heard by listening over the vessel with a stethoscope (the swishing sound which is heard is termed a *bruit*).

Limbs affected by chronic arterial disease have a typical appearance. They are pale and cold particularly when the foot is elevated. When the foot is then hung down the foot slowly becomes dusky blue as the blood flow (such as it is) returns. The hair on the calves is often lost and if the disease is severe there may be ischaemic ulcers on the toes or heels.

A careful examination of the chest and heart is also made and the blood pressure and pulse rate are recorded.

Thus, a very accurate assessment of the patient, his disability and the extent of his vascular disease can be made on the history and clinical examination.

INVESTIGATIONS

Non-invasive tests

These are so-called because they do not involve needles and are safe. Nowadays, they mostly involve the use of Doppler ultrasound machines. These work on the principle that a moving stream of blood in a vessel will reflect and change the frequency of ultrasonic sound waves which can be detected by a special microphone. The simplest Doppler machine consists of a pen-sized probe which, when placed on an artery, produces an audible pulsatile sound heard in an earpiece like a stethoscope (Fig. 30/1). If a blood pressure cuff is then inflated on the limb above the Doppler probe the sound will disappear when the cuff pressure exceeds the pressure in the artery (Fig. 30/2). Arterial stenosis will markedly lower the pressure in the artery as compared to the systemic blood pressure measured in the arm. More sophisticated Doppler machines can provide detailed information about blood flow thereby helping to distinguish the importance of disease in one arterial site compared to another, and are helpful in planning surgery. Ultrasound can also be used to image blood vessels so that a computer produced facsimile of the artery is shown on a screen thus revealing if disease is present. The

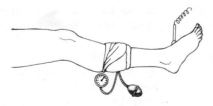

FIG. 30/1 Diagram to show Doppler technique of measuring ankle pressure

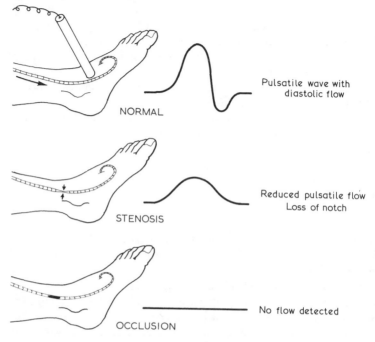

FIG. 30/2 Diagram of the wave form using a Doppler flow probe on the dorsalis pedis artery

latest generation of Doppler vascular laboratory equipment is the Duplex scanner which combines the facility of imaging the artery with the ability to assess blood flow.

Arteriography

If, after clinical examination and laboratory investigation, it is felt that the patient's disease requires surgical treatment an arteriogram is usually required. In order to use x-rays to visualise the arterial tree, a substance which is opaque to x-rays must be injected directly into an artery.

Translumbar aortograms provide good visualisation of the aorta, iliac and femoral vessels. The technique requires the insertion of a needle in the lumbar region into the abdominal aorta. A general anaesthetic is usually required. Dye is then injected under pressure and radiographs are taken in rapid succession as the dye passes down into the leg vessels as the patient is automatically moved by the apparatus.

Similar results may be obtained by introducing a catheter into the femoral artery in the groin and advancing it into the aorta. The method used is known as the Seldinger technique and involves the insertion of a needle into the artery through which a guide wire is inserted. The catheter is then pushed over the guide wire and when it is in the desired place (as seen on the x-ray screen) the wire is removed. The catheter may be guided into the orifices of the major arterial branches of the aorta thereby allowing selective arteriograms (e.g. coronary, mesenteric or renal) to be taken. Selective catheter-isation of these vessels allows the dye to be injected at greater concentration locally, allowing better visualisation.

If information about the vessels in one leg only is required the dye may be injected through a needle directly into the femoral artery.

These techniques give very good visualisation of the arterial system and show up blocks and stenoses. They allow the precise planning of operations. They are, however, unpleasant for the patient and have a variety of complications which include local damage to the vessels caused by needles and catheters and the production of emboli due to the dislodging of atheroma or clots. Allergy to iodine (which is contained in radio-opaque dye) occasion-ally gives rise to severe and even fatal anaphylactic reactions. Renal failure may ensue following injection under pressure into the kidneys. In view of these problems arteriograms are *only* ordered *after* the decision that surgery is required has been made. They are *not* used as a diagnostic screen.

As radiological techniques improve these problems are being overcome. A particularly exciting new development is that of Digital Subtraction Angiography (DSA) also known as Digital Vascular Imaging. This involves the computerised removal of unwanted detail on the radiograph, such as bones and soft tissues, thereby enhancing the visualisation of the blood vessels. It enables the dye to be injected into a peripheral vein at a much lower dose than in conventional arteriography. DSA may thus be used as a screening technique even before a surgical procedure has been planned. It also provides a useful method for follow-up after vascular reconstructions. Another new promising development is Nuclear Magnetic Resonance (NMR) which holds exciting future prospects of safe and very detailed visualisation of blood vessels.

Assessment of aneurysmal disease

Clinical examination will usually make the diagnosis of an aneurysm even though the history in most cases will be negative unless complications have occurred.

Conventional arteriography should be avoided as needle insertion into an aneurysm might cause rupture or embolisation. In fact, arteriography is not particularly helpful since the lumen of the aneurysm sometimes appears of normal calibre because the aneurysm sac is filled with clot. DSA may be useful in delineating the state of vessels distal to the aneurysm.

Ultrasound of the abdomen can measure accurately the size of an aneurysm and can be used serially to identify expansion which might indicate the need for early surgery.

Computerised axial tomography (CT scan) is also very helpful as it provides a cross-sectional view of the aneurysm and will identify or exclude small early retroperitoneal leaks. It will also identify inflammatory aneurysms.

Table 30/1 summarises the findings on examination relative to the different sites of obstruction.

THE SURGICAL TREATMENT OF PERIPHERAL VASCULAR DISEASE

The specialty of vascular surgery is a relatively new one although operations on blood vessels have been reported in the past – John Hunter (1728–93) experimented in animals and actually ligated a popliteal aneurysm in a patient. Only during the last 40 years, with the development of advanced anaesthesia and radiology together with advances in the manufacture of prosthetic grafts, has it been possible to offer patients with vascular disease the possibility of surgery.

Sympathectomy

Blood vessels in the skin are supplied with sympathetic vasoconstrictor nerve fibres whose role is to control blood flow to the skin by opening or closing arterio-venous pre-capillary shunts. These are important in temperature control. Emotion has a profound effect on skin blood flow: we are all familiar with blushing, and the expression 'white with anger or fear' relates to skin vasoconstriction which

TABLE 30/I   A summary of how to recognise sites of obstruction

SIGNS AND SYMPTOMS	BIFURCATION OF AORTA	BIFURCATION OF ILIAC ARTERY	BIFURCATION OF COMMON FEMORAL ARTERY	TRIFURCATION OF POPLITEAL ARTERY
Pain	Mainly whole of lower extremities	Mainly whole of lower extremities	Foot and leg below knee	Foot, calf, ankle
Numbness	Legs, thighs	Leg, thigh	Foot, ankle	Foot, ankle, lower $\frac{1}{3}$ of leg
Cold as symptom	Entire lower extremity (bilateral)	Entire lower extremity	Leg, lower part of thigh	Leg
Paraesthesia	Legs	Leg	Foot, ankle	Foot, ankle, calf
Pulses	None below aorta	None below aorta on affected side	None below common femoral artery	None below femoral artery
Mottling Pallor	Both extremities, lower abdomen, trunk	Lower extremity to groin	Lower extremity to upper $\frac{1}{3}$ of thigh	Foot, ankle, leg
Cold as sign	Groins	To groin	Nearly to knee	Knee
Hyperaesthesia	Legs	Leg	Foot and sometimes ankle	Foot, ankle, lower $\frac{1}{3}$ of leg
Weakness	Hips, lower extremities	Lower extremity	Foot, ankle	Foot, ankle, knee
Paralysis	Thighs, legs, feet	Leg and foot	Toes, sometimes foot or ankle	Toes and foot

under stressful conditions diverts blood to muscles where it is most needed for 'fight' or 'flight'. Sympathetic nerve fibres also supply sweat glands – this is the basis of the lie detector which is a device which measures electrical conductance across the skin. Telling a lie evokes a response in the skin changing its conductance.

Interruption of the sympathetic nerve supply produces marked vasodilatation and also prevents sweating. The latter is a permanent result of sympathectomy but unfortunately the vasodilatation is short-lived, lasting usually only two to three years.

CERVICAL SYMPATHECTOMY

Cervical sympathectomy may be used to improve the circulation in the hand in Raynaud's disease. It is initially effective but the improvement wears off after some years. It is thus usually held in reserve until the problem becomes very severe in which case sympathectomy may heal necrotic lesions on the fingers.

Cervical sympathectomy prevents sweating from the hands permanently and is used for hyperhidrosis if it is severe enough for the patient to require surgery. It is possible to interrupt the sympathetic nerve supply to the hands and arms by removing the 1st, 2nd and 3rd thoracic ganglia from the sympathetic chain.

Method: Cervical sympathectomy is performed under general anaesthesia. The usual approach is through an incision just above the clavicle. The subclavian artery and phrenic nerve must be retracted and care taken to avoid damage to the brachial plexus. The pleura is pushed down to reveal the sympathetic ganglia lying deeply crossing the neck of the ribs, and the appropriate segment of the sympathetic chain is removed. Damage to the 8th cervical ganglion produces Horner's syndrome with pupillary constriction, drooping of the eyelid and loss of sweating on the face. If the pleura is damaged a pneumothorax will occur.

Cervical sympathectomy may also be performed through an incision in the axilla. The chest is opened and the lung collapsed allowing access to the sympathetic chain. The advantage of this approach is that it avoids an obvious scar in the neck, but, *bilateral* procedures cannot be performed at one operation.

LUMBAR SYMPATHECTOMY

Lumbar sympathectomy brings permanent relief for hyperhidrosis of the feet. It is also useful in the treatment of ischaemic vascular disease in the feet either as an adjunct to reconstructive surgery or alone if reconstruction is not possible.

Method: Lumbar sympathectomy is performed under a general anaesthetic through an incision in the loin. The lumbar sympathetic chain is exposed without opening the peritoneum and the 2nd, 3rd and 4th ganglia are removed.

Phenol sympathectomy has largely replaced surgical lumbar sympathectomy in the elderly atherosclerotic patient. A long needle is inserted, under radiographic control, through the back alongside the spine and an injection of phenol is made adjacent to the sympathetic chain thereby destroying it. This technique may be effective in healing small ischaemic lesions and reducing ischaemic pain, probably by interrupting the pain fibres which run alongside the sympathetic nerves.

Lumbar sympathectomy is of no value in treating intermittent claudication.

Endarterectomy

It is possible to remove the atheromatous deposits from within arteries by the technique of endarterectomy. This involves mobilisation of the affected artery from the surrounding structures. Heparin is then given intravenously in order to prevent distal vessels from clotting up while the operation is performed. Clamps are applied across the artery above and below the diseased segment; the artery is then incised longitudinally, whereupon it is possible to identify a plane of cleavage between the atheroma containing intima and media and the relatively normal adventitia (Fig. 29/2b, p. 626). This plane is developed with the use of instruments, and the diseased layer is cored out. (This procedure is sometimes termed a re-bore or disobliteration.) Care must be taken at the distal end of the artery that a flap of tissue is not left behind as this might block the lumen. The remaining vessel wall consisting of the adventitia plus some media is sutured together – although thin, this layer is strong and takes stitches well. The arterial clamps are then removed and blood flow restored. This technique can be applied in a variety of situations.

AORTO-ILIAC ENDARTERECTOMY

The aorta below the renal arteries together with both common iliac arteries may all be treated by endarterectomy. This is a difficult procedure technically and is not appropriate if the external iliac vessels are severly diseased. It may cause impotence due to division of autonomic nerves crossing the aortic bifurcation. It has the advantage of avoiding the use of implanted foreign material and a graft may still be performed if disease redevelops later.

ILIAC/COMMON FEMORAL ENDARTERECTOMY

These vessels may also be treated by endarterectomy, the iliacs being exposed by retracting the peritoneum (extra-peritoneal approach).

PATCH ANGIOPLASTY

This consists of the insertion of a patch (consisting of a segment of vein or prosthetic material) into a longitudinal arteriotomy. Angioplasty may be performed in conjunction with endarterectomy, thereby removing disease and enlarging the vessel. Profundoplasty is a useful technique (Fig. 29/2) particularly if there is occlusion of the superficial femoral artery and the popliteal artery is unsuitable for anastomosis of a bypass graft. Atheroma commonly stenoses the origin of the profunda artery but more distally the vessel is patent. Endarterectomy and patch angioplasty markedly increases flow into the profunda and is usually sufficient to reverse rest pain and allow ischaemic tissue (even in the foot) to heal.

Bypass procedures

If an artery is blocked along one segment, but is patent proximally and distally to the block, it may be possible to bypass the blockage by anastomosing a graft to the vessel above and below the block.

The bypass will remain open if the pressure and volume of blood flow (usually termed the 'run-in') is sufficiently high. This will be the case only if there is no significant vascular disease proximal to the graft. Patency will be maintained only if there are adequate vessels distal to the graft to receive the increased flow ('run-off').

Provided the run-in and run-off are adequate, the other limitation to patency is clotting of the graft. Normal blood vessels have elaborate intrinsic mechanisms to prevent blood clotting within them under normal physiological circumstances. The best material to use for vascular grafts is a natural blood vessel and the saphenous vein is most commonly used. This is suitable to bypass the femoral vessels but is of too small a calibre to be of use to replace the abdominal vessels. Attempts at the use of preserved human cadaveric artery grafts have proved unsuccessful and this technique is no longer used. There has been enormous research into the development of an effective artificial prosthetic vessel. Dacron (Terylene) grafts are now available in a variety of designs. They remain patent for long periods in the aorto-iliac situation where blood flow is great but are much less useful in the leg.

REVERSED SAPHENOUS VEIN FEMORO-POPLITEAL GRAFT

This operation is commonly used to overcome the effects of an atherosclerotic occlusion of the superficial femoral artery. As stated above, for long-term patency there should be no significant proximal arterial disease as judged clinically by the femoral pulse; by non-invasive Doppler assessment of the pulse wave; and by arterio-graphy. Similarly, there must be a good run-off, i.e. patent calf and foot vessels. This is more difficult to judge since in the presence of disease in the femoral vessels it may be impossible to obtain radiographs of the distal vessels. If the operation is being performed for intermittent claudication the surgeon will stick rigidly to these criteria, but for limb salvage he may perform an exploratory procedure and attempt a bypass in sub-optimal conditions in order to save the limb. Even if the bypass is not patent long term, it may preserve the limb long enough for new collaterals to develop.

Method: The operation is performed under a general anaesthetic. The saphenous vein is dissected, its branches tied and, after ligation at its junction with the femoral vein, is removed. It is then gently distended with fluid to check for any leaks. The vein is then reversed since it contains valves which normally allow blood flow only towards the heart. These valves do not affect flow through the vein after it is reversed.

The common femoral artery is then dissected, as is the popliteal artery distal to the diseased segment. A tunnel is made deep to the muscles and the prepared vein is passed through it. Heparin is then given, the vessels are clamped and arteriotomies are made at both sites. The vein is then anastomosed to the common femoral artery above and the popliteal artery below. Prolene sutures are normally used because of their good handling characteristics. On removal of the clamps a good pulse should be palpable in the graft and in the vessels beyond the distal anastomosis. Postoperatively, pulses should have returned in the feet and these are regularly checked. If they suddenly disappear in the early postoperative period this indicates clotting of the graft. The cause is usually a technical one and early re-exploration is normally required to sort out the problem. Patients are confined to bed routinely for 24 hours and then allowed to sit in a chair. Slow mobilisation begins on the 3rd postoperative day. Skin sutures are removed at 10 days and the patient discharged soon after. Long-term results from this operation are good. An average of 75 per cent of grafts will still be working after five years, and as previously stated some 30 to 40 per cent of patients with arterial disease will have died during this period from coronary or cerebrovascular occlusion.

IN SITU FEMORO-POPLITEAL VEIN GRAFT

This technique has recently been revived. Instead of removing the saphenous vein it is left in situ, and the valves are destroyed using a special instrument which is passed up the vein after the upper anastomosis has been constructed. Since blood at arterial pressure is held up by the valves the instrument is able to cut them without damaging the vein. This operation has the advantage that the larger proximal end of vein is sutured to the large femoral artery while the small distal end of the vein is sutured to the small popliteal artery. Because of this it may be used in so-called *femoro-distal* bypasses where the popliteal artery is diseased and the distal anastomosis is constructed on to the posterior or anterior tibial vessels or occasionally the peroneal artery.

Short-term results, as in all vascular surgery, are dependent on technical expertise. Long-term patency, however, depends on the state of the vessels and the progression of the disease.

FEMORO-POPLITEAL BYPASS WITH PROSTHETIC GRAFTS

As previously stated the most effective bypass conduit is the patient's own saphenous vein (Darling and Linton, 1972). This might, however, not be available due to previous varicose vein surgery, or, it might be unsuitable since it itself has become varicose or is of too small a diameter. Under these circumstances an artificial graft must be used and as yet none give as good results as natural vein. Dacron grafts which are used to replace vessels in the leg tend to occlude, since blood clots within these small diameter tubes if flow rates are not very high. Polytetrafluoroethylene (PTFE) grafts may give somewhat better results due to the very smooth character of their walls. Human umbilical veins processed with glutaraldehyde to prevent rejection have been developed in the USA by Dr Dardik and these grafts have, in some series, given good long-term results (Dardik et al, 1979; Robison et al, 1983). The ideal 'off the shelf' vascular prostheses are still awaited. Bypass procedures using prostheses are quicker since the vein does not need to be dissected. Infection of artificial grafts remains a problem.

AORTO-ILIAC OR AORTO-BIFEMORAL BYPASS GRAFTS

Atheromatous disease in the abdominal aorta and in the iliac vessels may be treated using a prosthetic graft to bypass the affected segments of artery. Endarterectomy may be preferred for localised disease or in young patients (since there is some reluctance to implant prostheses which may have to function long term). Nowadays, aortic bypass procedures are most commonly performed and in this large vessel and high flow situation long-term patency rates are excellent (Crawford et al, 1981). In view of these good results surgeons are more ready to undertake aortic bypass than femoral procedures and indications include claudication if severe enough to markedly restrict the patient's lifestyle. Rest pain and pre-gangrene are absolute indications for reconstruction of the aorta if this is the site of severe disease. The risks of aortic reconstruction are greater than procedures on the limb alone, although with modern anaesthesia and intensive care facilities it may be undertaken even in elderly patients with co-existent respiratory or cardiac disease.

Dacron is used for the manufacture of the majority of aortic prostheses. The actual mode of construction varies. The Dacron fibres may be woven producing an impermeable graft, or knitted in which case the graft must be pre-clotted (washed with non-heparinised blood) before insertion. Knitted grafts have theoretical advantages in that cells introduced between the fibres during the pre-clotting procedure may develop into a more natural pseudo-intima lining the graft. In practice, there is no major difference and the choice is largely made on the handling characteristics of the graft.

If disease is confined to the aorta then an aorto-iliac bypass may suffice. Usually disease also affects the external iliac vessels and an aorto-bifemoral graft must be inserted (Fig. 29/2d). The aorta is exposed through a long abdominal incision either mid-line or transverse, and dissected free from surrounding fat and lymphatics just below the origin of the renal arteries. The iliac or femoral vessels are similarly controlled as appropriate. A tunnel must be developed beneath the inguinal ligaments through which the limbs of the graft are passed to reach the femoral arteries. The inferior mesenteric artery, if still patent, is preserved. Heparin is given and the aorta and distal vessels (iliacs or femorals) are clamped. The aorta may be divided completely and an end-to-end anastomosis with the graft performed, or, alternatively, the graft may be sutured on to an arteriotomy made in the front wall of the aorta. Prolene suture material is commonly used. The distal anastomosis can also be end-to-end or end-side as appropriate. It is important to re-establish flow into at least one internal iliac artery and in the case of aorto-bifemoral reconstructions the internal iliac vessels are perfused by backflow from the femoral anastomosis up the external iliac vessels.

Occasionally, it may be necessary in the presence of aortic disease and blockage of the superficial femoral arteries in the leg to perform an aorto-bifemoral bypass and then a femoral-popliteal bypass at the same operation. In this situation it is often very difficult to decide which area of disease is most significant. Since distal bypasses will block without good inflow it is usual to reconstruct the aorta. Sometimes the graft is sutured to the profunda arteries which may be relatively healthy and this procedure may re-vascularise the limb despite superficial femoral artery occlusion.

EXTRA-ANATOMIC BYPASS

It is usual to place bypass grafts in the same anatomical situation as the diseased arteries. It is possible, however, to route prosthetic grafts beneath the skin and subcutaneous fat, thereby simplifying the operation. An axillo-femoral bypass (Fig. 29/2c) may be used to re-vascularise the limbs if the aorta is blocked, without the need to open the abdomen. This has obvious advantages if the patient is elderly and a poor operative risk. The axillary artery is exposed on one side and the femoral arteries are mobilised. A tunnelling device is then passed from the axillary incision beneath the skin to the groin and a graft routed down. A further tunnel takes one limb of the graft to the other groin. Anastomoses are constructed in the usual fashion. An axillo-femoral graft may be used if a previously inserted aortic graft becomes infected and has to be removed.

If one iliac artery is healthy and the other blocked, a femoro-femoral cross-over graft may be used to take blood from the well-perfused femoral artery into the ischaemic limb.

Patients with subcutaneous grafts must avoid tight belts or clothing which might constrict the graft. New grafts with rigid plastic encircling rings are now available to avoid this problem.

Abdominal aortic aneurysm

Aneurysms are potentially dangerous: they continue to expand and may ultimately rupture. A leaking aortic aneurysm (Fig. 30/3) is one of the most urgent surgical emergencies – if the aneurysm bursts into the peritoneal cavity (B) the patient may die rapidly due to catastrophic blood loss. If, however, the tear in the aneurysm wall occurs at the back (A), the initial haemorrhage will occur into the retroperitoneal tissues and may be contained initially. The patient will experience agonising back pain and on examination will be found to have a tender pulsatile abdominal mass. Resuscitation with blood transfusion and immediate surgery may save his life.

Method: The abdomen is opened and the aorta above the aneurysm

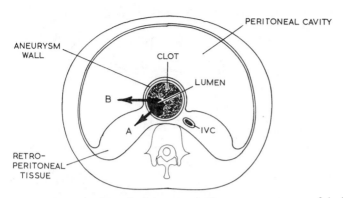

FIG. 30/3 Cross-section of abdomen to illustrate two types of leaking aneurysm: (a) Contained leak into retroperitoneal tissues; (b) Free rupture into peritoneal cavity

is clamped, thereby arresting the bleeding. Rarely, the aneurysm involves the origins of the renal arteries making aortic replacement much more difficult. The aneurysmal aorta is then replaced with a prosthetic graft (usually woven Dacron), which is sutured into place using polypropylene stitches. Figure 29/4, p. 630, shows an aortic aneurysm also involving the right common iliac artery. Figure 30/4 shows the aneurysm replaced by a Dacron 'trouser' graft sutured to the normal left common iliac artery and to the right common femoral artery in the groin replacing the aneurysmal iliac vessel.

Most aneurysms should be detected on physical examination before they get too large. If they are operated on under routine 'cold' conditions the mortality is low, whereas emergency repair carries a high mortality particularly as most sufferers are elderly and have co-existent cardiorespiratory disease. Aneurysms usually contain a large quantity of clot surrounding a lumen equivalent to the size of a normal vessel. Pieces of this clot may embolise producing patchy occlusion in distal vessels particularly in the digital arteries of the toes causing painful blue toes. Sometimes, an aneurysm may thrombose spontaneously.

Popliteal aneurysm

Aneurysms of the popliteal artery also commonly go unnoticed until complications occur. Thrombosis is particularly dangerous in popliteal aneurysms since there has been no previous stimulus to collateral formation and the limb may be lost.

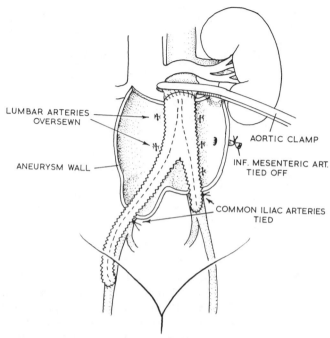

FIG. 30/4 Replacement of aneurysm with a Dacron 'trouser' graft

Femoro-popliteal bypass with ligation of the aneurysm is the treatment of choice. Since the condition is often bilateral both limbs may require arterial reconstruction.

Amputation (Fig. 30/5)

Unfortunately, it is not possible to re-vascularise all ischaemic limbs and a proportion of vascular surgical procedures are unsuccessful and amputation becomes necessary. Patients inevitably become demoralised in this situation particularly if the amputation stump fails to heal and a second more proximal ablation is required. A below-knee amputation, by preserving the knee joint, allows quicker more complete rehabilitation on a prosthetic limb. This procedure will only heal if the blood supply to the flaps is adequate. The long posterior flap technique (Fig. 30/5a) is most often used although some centres favour the skew-flap operation.

The decision to proceed directly to an above-knee amputation is sometimes difficult, but it is far better to recognise that a below-knee

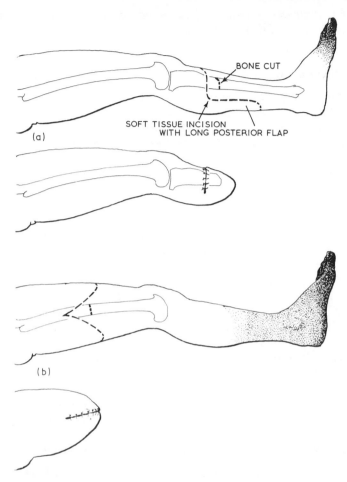

FIG. 30/5 Amputation sites in the lower limb: (a) Below knee showing line of excision and division of the tibia, with postoperative stump (the knee joint is preserved); (b) Above knee, showing the equal flap procedure with a postoperative stump

stump would not heal than have to re-operate after many days of pain and anxiety for the patient. It might be possible to predict stump healing with the use of transcutaneous oxygen electrodes or laser Dopplers to assess skin blood flow at the proposed site. Anaerobic infection is always likely in ischaemic tissues and all amputations are covered by prophylactic antibiotics. The physiotherapist plays a central role in the rehabilitation of the amputee (see

Cash's Textbook of General Medical and Surgical Conditions for Physiotherapists, Chapter 18).

Carotid artery disease

The arteries supplying the brain may be affected by atherosclerosis, indeed the deterioration in mental ability with age is largely due to cerebrovascular disease. These effects are usually gradual except if a sudden cerebrovascular accident (stroke) occurs. Strokes may result from (a) cerebral haemorrhage, often associated with hypertension; (b) cerebral infarction due to occlusion of a major artery; or (c) embolisation to the brain. Whatever the cause the result of the stroke depends on the area of the brain which is damaged. If vital areas of the brain are destroyed this may cause sudden death. Most commonly the opposite side of the body to that of the brain damage becomes paralysed (hemiplegia). Confusion, dysarthria, visual defects, faecal and urinary incontinence and a variety of other problems may occur. These effects may be permanent although some improvement is usual and complete recovery may sometimes occur. The patient is at risk in the early stages from pneumonia and later from pressure sores.

Since many strokes result from disease in the arteries supplying the brain, vascular surgery has a role to play. Experience has shown that surgery has little to offer once the stroke has occurred. The vertebral arteries, because of their anatomical position within a canal in the cervical vertebrae, do not lend themselves to surgery. However, reconstruction of the diseased carotid arteries may prevent a stroke from occurring. The main problem is identifying those patients who are at risk and who would benefit from this procedure.

Carotid stenosis: This may be diagnosed if a bruit is heard over the vessel. However, in view of the bifurcation in to the internal carotid artery supplying the brain and the external carotid supplying the face and scalp, the bruit might originate from a harmless stenosis in the external carotid.

The extent and position of any carotid atheroma is best shown by arteriography but conventional techniques have a significant morbidity, digital subtraction angiography (DSA) provides adequate visualisation of the carotid vessels and is very safe. Non-invasive Doppler techniques which are now available also provide good anatomical and functional information about carotid disease.

Whether carotid surgery should be offered to patients with asymptomatic carotid bruits is still a matter of debate. At present it is routine practice in many clinics in the USA and Europe but most surgeons in the UK feel it is unjustified.

Transient ischaemic attacks (TIAs)

Small clumps of platelets from plaques of atheroma (usually at the origin of the internal carotid artery) may embolise into the brain and retina causing short-lived neurological symptoms known as transient ischaemic attacks (TIAs).

The retinal artery is one of the terminal branches of the internal carotid artery and during such an attack it is sometimes possible by viewing the retina through an ophthalmoscope to actually see the platelet emboli in the retinal vessels. While these emboli are within the vessels they render the retinal cells ischaemic causing fleeting attacks of blindness (amaurosis fugax). The patient typically perceives this as being like a curtain passing over the vision in one eye. The affected eye will be on the same side as the diseased carotid artery.

Emboli may also pass to the cerebral motor and sensory cortex causing tingling and weakness in the opposite limbs, or, commonly, only in the arm. The symptoms are short lived because the emboli, being very small, disperse or dissipate into the capillaries having little or no permanent effect.

TIAs are unpleasant symptoms to suffer and may herald the development of a complete stroke when a larger embolus breaks off and permanently blocks an important cerebral vessel, or the carotid artery thromboses and becomes totally occluded. The effects of carotid occlusion are unpredictable because normally the brain may still be adequately supplied by the contralateral carotid artery and the vertebral arteries. These vessels may, however, also be diseased.

Most neurologists would investigate fully any patient with TIAs; some would treat carotid disease using antiplatelet drugs such as aspirin and dipyridamole, while others would refer all such cases for surgical treatment. Many trials are in progress at present in an attempt to clarify the position but since carotid surgery can now be undertaken with very low risk it is more and more commonly performed (*BMJ*, 1983).

The usual operative procedure is a carotid endarterectomy. Usually under general anaesthesia (although some surgeons favour local anaesthesia) the carotid vessels are exposed through an incision along the anterior border of the sternomastoid muscle. The vessels are carefully dissected to avoid dislodging emboli. Care must be taken to avoid damage to the vagus and hypoglossal nerves. After

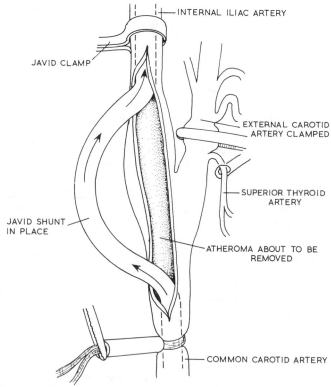

FIG. 30/6 Shunt in position for performance of carotid endarterectomy

heparinisation, the common, internal and external carotid arteries are clamped: at this point many surgeons insert a shunt to preserve cerebral blood suppy (Fig. 30/6). Shunting may be avoided if cross-flow from the other vessels is assessed as adequate by measuring the pressure in the internal carotid above the clamp. The endarterectomy is performed in the usual fashion and the vessel sutured, the shunt being removed as the last few stitches are placed. Sometimes a patch graft may be used to prevent narrowing of the vessel.

REFERENCES

Crawford, E. S., Bomberger, R. A., Glaeser, D. H. et al (1981). Aorto-iliac occlusive disease: factors influencing survival and function over a 25-year period. *Surgery*, **90**, 1055–67.

Dardik, H., Ibrahim, I. M., Sussman, B. et al (1979). Glutaraldehyde-stabilised umbilical vein prosthesis for re-vascularisation for the legs. *American Journal of Surgery*, **138**, 234–7.

Darling, R. C. and Linton, R. R. (1972). Durability of femoro-popliteal reconstructions. *American Journal of Surgery*, **123**, 472–9.

Robison, J. G., Brewster, D. C., Abbott, W. M. and Darling, R. C. (1983). Femoropopliteal and tibioperoneal artery reconstruction using human umblical vein. *Archives of Surgery*, **118**, 1039–42.

Variation in the use of angiography and carotid endarterectomy by neurologists in the UK TIA/aspirin trial. (1983). *British Medical Journal* (Clinical Research), **286**, 514–17.

BIBLIOGRAPHY

Bergan, J. and Yao, J. (jt. eds.) (1980). *Operative Techniques in Vascular Surgery*. Grune and Stratton, New York.

Eastcott, H. H. G. (1973). *Arterial Surgery*. Pitman, London.

Fogarty, T. J. and Cranley, J. J. (1965). Catheter technique for arterial embolectomy. *Annals of Surgery*, **161**, 325–30.

Greenhalgh, R. M. (ed.) (1981). *Smoking and Arterial Disease*. Pitman, London.

Greenhalgh, R. M. (ed.) (1982). *Extra-anatomic and Secondary Arterial Reconstruction*. Pitman, London.

Chapter 31

Venous and Lymphatic Disease – Assessment and Treatment

by P. A. E. HURST BSc, MS, MRCP, FRCS

The veins of the leg consist of a superficial group beneath the skin and a deep system beneath the fascia.

Superficial veins (Fig. 31/1)

The long saphenous vein passes up the medial side of the leg, in front of the medial malleolus, behind the knee and through a defect in the fascia to join the femoral vein in the groin. The short saphenous vein passes up the lateral side of the back of the calf and through the fascia to join the popliteal vein behind the knee. These superficial veins drain blood from the skin. Their walls have smooth muscle which is under the control of the autonomic nervous system and plays an important role in temperature regulation, constricting to conserve heat and dilating to lose excess body heat.

Deep veins (Fig. 31/2)

There are three groups of veins accompanying the arteries in the calf, and large venous sinuses within the calf muscles. These all drain into the popliteal, then femoral, veins, and finally into the iliac veins which join to form the vena cava. The deep veins drain the muscles.

The two systems are separate and divided by the deep fascia. They communicate at the sapheno-femoral junction in the groin, the sapheno-popliteal junction at the knee and, sometimes, at mid-thigh level through a vessel known as a Hunterian perforator. Other perforator veins indirectly join the superficial veins, particularly at three sites above the ankle (sometimes known as Cockett's perforators).

Very careful assessment and investigation of such a limb should be carried out. Non-invasive tests can indicate the state of the deep and superficial veins. Sometimes radiographic examination of the veins (phlebograms) will need to be obtained by injecting radio-opaque dye into the vein. Surgical treatment is based on these investigations. Incompetent perforating veins may be ligated but this requires an incision through the chronically affected skin and may be slow to heal.

Most venous ulcers will heal with a period of bed rest and elevation which reverses the venous hypertension. The ulcer is usually locally infected; culture swabs should be taken but antibiotics should be used *only* if cellulitis is present. The ulcer may be cleansed with a mild antiseptic but the application of other potions should be avoided as they encourage local sensitivity reactions. When clean, skin grafts may be applied to the ulcer to speed healing.

Although the majority of ulcers may be healed in this way it is time consuming and expensive. Outpatient ambulatory methods may save time and money. Similar results may be obtained by bandaging the leg with impregnated paste bandages applied directly over the ulcer; these are left untouched initially for a week and then for longer periods. Very good control of oedema is obtained and venous hypertension is counteracted. Frequent dressing of the ulcer which removes healing tissues is avoided and most ulcers heal.

Whatever method of healing the ulcer is used, and after appropriate surgery if indicated, all patients with the post-phlebotic limb must wear firm specially designed support hose to prevent recurrence. Poor patient compliance invariably results in re-ulceration, but if stockings are worn, long-term results are good.

There are an infinite number of regimes available for the treatment of venous ulceration. Many of them have never been subjected to adequate scientific evaluation and most are probably without major benefit. The policy enumerated above is the most consistently effective, and is the one used by most vascular surgeons in the United Kingdom.

PHLEBITIS (Superficial thrombophlebitis)

Superficial primary varicose veins, or dilated superficial secondary varicose veins, may become thrombosed and inflamed causing local erythema and pain. Treatment is by firm bandaging and anti-inflammatory drugs such as indomethacin. When the phlebitis resolves the underlying venous problem is treated appropriately.

DEEP VEIN THROMBOSIS (DVT)

Thrombosis in the deep veins of the leg is a common problem. It may be associated with reduced blood flow, changes in the vessel wall or changes in the coagulability of the blood.

Normally, high flow occurs in the deep veins particularly during exercise; when recumbent, this flow is reduced and pressure on the calves may encourage thrombosis. Thus patients are at risk during prolonged bed rest, while anaesthetised (when they do not move their legs at all) or during long journeys.

Some drugs, notably the contraceptive pill, encourage thrombosis.

Deep vein thrombosis causes pain and swelling in the calf. It is a hazard because some of the clot may become dislodged and embolise to the lung. Massive pulmonary embolus can be fatal. Deep vein thrombosis also causes long-term problems with the post-phlebotic limb. Because of these dangers every effort must be made both to prevent a DVT from occurring and to diagnose and treat it adequately if it does.

Prevention

Early postoperative mobilisation is the most important factor in DVT prophylaxis and has markedly reduced the incidence of pulmonary embolism; the physiotherapist plays a vital role. The wearing of anti-embolism stockings while confined to bed may also be beneficial by diverting flow into the deep veins.

Where possible, predisposing risk factors should be removed – the contraceptive pill should be stopped several weeks before planned surgery.

Anticoagulants may be given pre-operatively – subcutaneous low dose heparin has been found to be effective at the cost of slightly increased peri-operative bleeding. Dextran may be administered intravenously during surgery thus reducing the blood viscosity which, in turn, reduces the risk of thrombosis.

The blood flow in the leg veins may be stimulated during surgery by enclosing the calves in a pneumatic compression boot.

These techniques may be used on all surgical patients; those at special risk from DVT, such as the obese, the elderly, those with malignant disease and those with a past history of thrombosis, may need a combination of these methods.

Diagnosis

The clinical diagnosis depends on the finding of tenderness and swelling of the calf sometimes associated with a mild pyrexia. If dorsiflexion of the foot exacerbates the calf pain this is suggestive of DVT (Homan's sign). A Doppler probe may be used to assess flow in the femoral vein – when the calf is squeezed a rush of blood is normally heard but if the calf veins are thrombosed no flow is produced.

Differential diagnosis includes rupture of the tendon of the plantaris muscle and other musculoskeletal problems, and phlebitis in superficial veins.

Since the treatment is prolonged and carries some risk it should only be started after the diagnosis has been confirmed by phlebography which, since the development of new contrast media, is very safe.

Treatment

Initial treatment is with an intravenous heparin infusion usually using a pump. This produces immediate anticoagulation but is quickly reversible (if required) by intravenous protamine. The affected limb is firmly bandaged. Oral anticoagulants, most commonly warfarin, are then started. The effects are monitored by measuring the prothrombin time and when adequate anticoagulation is achieved the heparin is stopped. Oral coagulation with regular monitoring is usually continued on an outpatient basis for six months to reduce the risk of subsequent DVT.

Occasionally phlebograms show a segment of loose clot in the leg veins and surgery may be required to remove it. Alternatively, a metal filter may be inserted through the jugular vein into the inferior vena cava to entrap any clots before they reach the lungs.

PULMONARY EMBOLUS

A sudden sharp pain in the chest made worse by breathing and haemoptysis are often the first signs of a small pulmonary embolus. A pleural rub may be heard on auscultation. The chest radiograph may show a wedge-shaped shadow. Massive pulmonary embolus causes sudden collapse with hypotension, chest pain, severe dyspnoea and signs of right heart failure including fullness of neck veins. ECG and chest radiographic changes are often marked.

Cardiac arrest may occur requiring emergency resuscitation. The diagnosis is confirmed by pulmonary angiography; if a large embolus is found to be blocking the pulmonary artery emergency surgery is required (see p. 404). Mortality is high since many cases never reach theatre.

Drugs, such as streptokinase, which encourage clot dissolution may be given intravenously. Such drugs although effective may be difficult to control and severe bleeding may occur.

Pulmonary embolus following simple surgery in young patients is a disaster – hence the need for vigorous prophylactic and diagnostic regimes for DVT.

LYMPHOEDEMA

Lymphoedema occurs when the lymphatics are unable to remove protein-rich fluid from the tissues. Normally, protein passes through the walls of the arterioles and fluid is re-absorbed into the venules

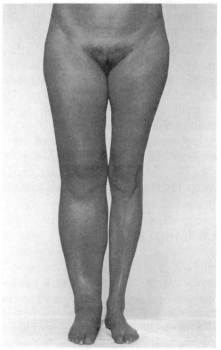

FIG. 31/4 Lymphoedema of the right leg

while the lymphatic tubules absorb the protein through pores. Although some contractility may occur in lymphatics most fluid movement is passive due to squeezing of the lymph vessels by adjacent muscle contractions. Valves within the lymphatics prevent back flow.

The lymph vessels from the lower limb drain to lymph nodes in the groin. Further lymphatics take the flow to iliac and then para-aortic nodes. Lymphatics draining the gut join those from the legs at the cisterna chyli from which the lymphatic duct travels up through the chest alongside the vertebral column. Lymphatics from the arms then join the system which ultimately drains into the left subclavian vein. The negative intrathoracic pressure aids lymph flow.

Any malfunction of the lymphatic system allows protein molecules to collect in the limbs and, because of osmotic forces, these retain fluid thereby producing oedema. Chronic fibrosis tends to occur together with skin changes to produce the typical appearance of oedema (Fig. 31/4). Lymphoedema is hard and tends not to pit on pressure, although this cannot invariably be used to distinguish it from other forms of oedema.

Primary lymphoedema

This is caused by a primary abnormality in the lymph system. Often, only one limb is severely affected although the other limbs may be involved subclinically and oedema of the genitals may also occur. It is sometimes hereditary and Milroy's disease refers to a familial and congenital type of lymphoedema. Some congenital diseases, such as Turner's syndrome and the 'yellow nail' syndrome, may also be associated with lymphoedema.

Most cases occur without any apparent hereditary factor. They are classified according to their age of onset: *congenital lymphoedema* is apparent at birth; *lymphoedema praecox* manifests itself at puberty. It is likely that the underlying lymphatic defect cannot cope with the changes in tissue protein handling resultant upon the hormonal changes involved. *Lymphoedema tarda* occurs in later life possibly as a result of deterioration in a barely adequate lymph system.

Lymphoedema is commoner in women than men.

The late Professor John Kinmonth (1952) added much to the study of lymphoedema by developing lymphangiography enabling radiographic examination of the lymphatics (see Chapter 5, p. 119). Using this method Kinmonth classified lymphoedema into aplastic, or hypoplastic if no lymphatics or very few lymph vessels were found. He also found a distinct group in which the lymphatics are hyperplastic with incompetent valves allowing backflow of lymph, causing leakage from the skin and sometimes into the chest producing pleural effusion and into the abdomen causing ascites. In these cases the lymph is mixed with fat absorbed by the gut lymphatics and is termed chyle.

Secondary lymphoedema

In these cases the previously normal lymphatics have been damaged. Worldwide, the commonest cause is filariasis caused by infection through mosquito bites with filarial worms. These parasites make their way up lymphatics thereby blocking them causing massive oedema to develop. In endemic tropical areas it is not uncommon to see massively swollen limbs in which the skin is severely affected with large warty lymph vesicles giving rise to the appearance known as elephantiasis. Scrotal lymphoedema is also common.

Most other secondary lymphoedema results from surgical removal of lymph nodes and/or irradiation in the treatment of malignant disease. The most commonly seen example is post-mastectomy oedema of the arm following radical mastectomy for breast cancer. Block dissection for malignant melanoma may also produce lymphoedema.

Treatment of lymphoedema

Surgical treatment is appropriate in some cases. Excisional operations may be performed: these are plastic surgical procedures in which the oedematous skin and subcutaneous tissue are excised and the residual skin flaps sutured together (Homan's operation); or the defects covered with split-thickness skin grafts (Charles operation). Alternatively, operations designed to improve the lymph drainage have been developed: these include the microsurgical anastomosis of lymph vessels or nodes to veins, or the construction of a bridge of lymphatic-bearing tissue (e.g. the mesentery) which is sutured to lymphatics distal to the blockage.

The majority of cases are best managed conservatively, and the physiotherapist can play an active part in this treatment. Good results have been obtained using intermittent compression machines to reduce oedema (see p. 680). The mainstay of treatment, however, is specially fitted heavy elastic stockings worn at all times (except in bed) to prevent the accumulation of oedema.

COMPLICATIONS OF LYMPHOEDEMA

The commonest problem is cellulitis due to the entry of organisms through small skin defects and superinfection of interdigital fungal lesions. Antifungal treatment is important and bacterial infection must be treated quickly with appropriate antibiotics.

Malignant change in long-standing lymphoedematous tissue may very rarely occur resulting in lymphangiosarcoma (Stewart-Treves syndrome).

REFERENCE

Kinmonth, J. B. (1952). Lymphangiography in man. A method of outlining lymphatic trunks at operation. *Clinical Science*, 11, 13–20.

BIBLIOGRAPHY

Dodd, H. and Cockett, F. B. (1976). *The Pathology and Surgery of the Veins of the Lower Limb*, 2nd edition. Churchill Livingstone, Edinburgh.

Kinmonth, J. B. (1982). *The Lymphatics: Surgery, Lymphography and Diseases of the Chyle and Lymph Systems*. Edward Arnold, London.

Negus, D. (1981). The peripheral venous system. In *Operative Surgery and Management*, pp. 533–60 (ed. Keen, G.). John Wright and Co, Bristol.

Chapter 32

Peripheral Vascular Disease – The Place of Physiotherapy

by R. WHITTAKER MCSP, DipTP

PREVENTIVE TREATMENT

Preventive medicine and health education are terms which are used freely in the medical and daily press. Arterial disease in particular and vascular disease in general are prime targets for the practice of preventive medicine. No member of a health care team can escape having a role in this, and physiotherapists, particularly those working in the community, must be prepared to endorse the teaching of nurses, doctors and others. The following section is a summary of points relative to prevention in the context of peripheral vascular disorders.

Diet

Many people may be living a sedentary life and may be overweight. These patients will benefit from a reducing diet in which the fat intake is limited (a high cholesterol level is thought to affect the course of the disease). There is strong evidence that the elevation of the plasma fat concentration, primarily triglycerides and cholesterol, contributes to the formation of atherosclerosis (Fredrickson and Levy, 1972). Therefore, patients should reduce animal fat intake, and when plasma concentration levels are elevated drug treatment can be instituted.

Smoking

Only about 10 per cent of non-smokers suffer from intermittent claudication. A reduction in smoking by only 20 per cent could result in roughly 4000 fewer deaths each year from cardiovascular disease. Vasoconstriction of the terminal vessels occurs during smoking. It is clear, therefore, that in vascular disease smoking should be avoided since a limb surviving on a limited blood supply would be at an even greater risk in a patient who smokes.

Hygiene

The patient will need to be advised to be extremely careful with his personal care, particularly frequent washing and inspection of the skin of the feet and legs, and the wearing of clean socks which should be well fitting as should the shoes. He should understand why it is important to keep the feet (and hands) clean and dry in all weather conditions, especially if the sensation is poor and the skin is showing signs of trophic changes. Patients should be encouraged to seek out a qualified chiropodist for attention to their nails, corns or callosities; and to take professional advice in the treatment of blisters and minor skin lesions. They should be careful of trauma however small, since lesions can be slow to heal and may easily lead to the precipitation of gangrene.

They should be particularly careful of hot objects, for example hot water bottles, hot radiators, cookers and hot food spillage. A domiciliary visit is helpful to identify potential danger sites and offer remedial advice, particularly if the patient is elderly and infirm, yet independent.

Activity

The patient's exercise tolerance should be carefully assessed, and he should be encouraged to exercise frequently within the limits of claudication and/or breathlessness. Some may be able to improve gradually on their walking distances by a carefully graded increase in activity together with other remedial measures. This will help to build up an improved collateral circulation and keep as much blood as possible circulating through the vascular field, thus retarding the progress of trophic changes and limiting muscle wasting. The patient should be advised not to lie in bed, sit or stand still for long periods of time as this will contribute to venous stasis and further devitalise tissues.

Drugs (*see also* Chapter 7, p. 186)

Vasodilators and anticoagulants have both been tried with varying success. If vasodilators are given orally their effect is general over the whole body with the normal vessels dilating more easily than those which are diseased, and diverting blood from the areas where it is most needed.

If large arteries are blocked there is little benefit to be obtained from dilating a distal vessel, for however much the arterial bed is opened up the blood will not flow through in an increased amount. Injecting vasodilators directly into an affected artery is too dangerous a procedure to be carried out regularly. If these drugs could give relief then a sympathectomy would be preferable to avoid the regular use of drugs.

Anticoagulants may help to prevent deep vein thrombosis and pulmonary emboli. It is still unproven as to whether they prevent the formation of arterial thrombi. There is also the risk that if the patient is on long-term therapy then even minor surgery such as dental extractions, and trauma such as cuts and bruises, could become serious when the clotting time is lengthened.

PHYSIOTHERAPY

Some patients may be referred for physiotherapy though its specific value is limited in peripheral arterial disease, and certain treatments and rigorous handling are contra-indicated. Special care should be taken with patients who may be referred for the treatment of other disorders, for example a fracture or a rheumatological condition, if peripheral vascular disease is present.

Heat or cold therapy

Extreme heat or cold therapy is usually contra-indicated in peripheral arterial disease, since sensation is commonly impaired, the vascular response is obviously abnormal, and the skin devitalised. A minor lesion produced on heating or cooling would be difficult, or at least slow, to heal. Occasionally, contrast bathing with warm and cool water may be helpful.

Exercise

Exercising to improve muscle power and maintain joint range may be possible and, for example, can be taught for a relatively unaffected lower limb, should amputation be contemplated on the other one. *Buerger's exercises* are occasionally tried in an attempt to improve the blood supply and venous drainage in some conditions, particularly if the patient is likely to be in bed for some time. The routine involves three positional changes of posture in order that the effect of gravity on blood flow is felt.

1. The patient is comfortably supported in lying with the limbs elevated some 45° and the limb colour observed until blanching occurs; the time should be noted for the change to occur, and a further 2 minutes added.
2. The patient is then placed in a high sitting position with the limbs dependent until full filling of the superficial veins is observed, and a further 3 minutes added.
3. The patient then lies completely flat (supine) if possible, for approximately 5 minutes

The times are noted, and the sequence repeated four or five times per treatment session; the patient should continue the routine at home, not less than three times per day.

When giving any treatment extreme care should be taken in handling the ischaemic limb and, when changing position, great care should be observed to avoid contact against furniture or equipment. Relatively trivial contact can easily cause trauma with swelling and possible infection.

Surgery

Surgical techniques and postoperative routines will vary (a) according to the region involved; (2) according to the particular surgeon; and (3) the patient's individual requirements. Many cases will be emergency procedures and in these cases pre-operative routines will be minimal. The postoperative management will vary from that provided in an intensive care unit after, for example, major surgery to the aorta, to minimal requirements and early ambulation, as in chemical sympathectomy.

PRE-OPERATIVE

If it is possible to see the patient pre-operation, he should be taught breathing exercises including expansion and expiratory techniques, area breathing control, unilateral respiratory excursions, 'huffing' and coughing techniques and expectoration. (The early postoperative management of this is taught pre-operatively.) According to the surgery, and the likely incisional site, particular attention is paid to those areas known to be at risk, especially if it is anticipated that drainage tubes will be used in the surgical procedure.

The physiotherapist should explain to the patient, the passive, active-assisted and active exercises which might be used to maintain or improve the circulation after surgery.

The patient should be taught the importance of posture and postural awareness; it helps if the physiotherapist can explain the importance of this in relation to the positions into which patients may be placed both during and after surgery.

According to the operative procedure, the patient may be shown the method of lifting or turning into modified postural drainage positions, and shown the vibration, shaking or percussion manipulations which may be necessary. This reduces the fear of unknown procedures, since the patient will be aware of what is happening. Again, according to the procedure, the patient should be taught simple exercise routines designed to maintain muscle power and joint range. This is more important if a relatively longer period in bed, and convalescent stage is anticipated following surgery.

POSTOPERATIVE

Postoperatively, the main aims are to prevent respiratory and circulatory complications, while maintaining the integrity of the surgical procedure. The whole treatment team should be familiar with possible complications of the particular procedure and observe carefully for any signs and symptoms which could indicate an impending problem. For a patient who has undergone major surgery the physiotherapist should arrange to make frequent, short visits to him, and to co-ordinate treatment with nursing procedures such as position change, bed-making, dressings, etc. Postural drainage, particularly after surgery on the aorta, should only be given after discussion with the surgeon.

Breathing exercises which have been taught previously are practised and the patient should be given maximum support and assistance while doing this and while coughing. Circulatory exercises are practised regularly within the limits of the condition. A progressive scheme of exercise and activity may be started, taking care of any drainage tubes, catheters and intravenous infusions.

Subsequently, the patient is taught to transfer from bed to chair, chair to standing, walking and re-education of gait and posture, gradually increasing the normal day to day activities, and increasing his exercise tolerance.

VENOUS ULCERS

Physiotherapy for venous ulcers has its critics! There are many surgeons who would not consider referring patients with venous ulcers preferring to leave their management to the nursing staff, community or hospital. Where physiotherapy is prescribed the following sections outline the assessment, objectives of treatment, possible specific treatments and general management which could be carried out.

In general, the aim of treatment is to establish, as near as possible, a normal circulation at the ulcer site and in the limb as a whole. Only when an adequate blood flow is restored can infection be controlled, and healing proceed. The co-operation of the patient, and his/her relatives, are vitally important, as is the active involvement of the whole treatment team.

Examination

The patient's history is most important, particularly any predisposing and maintaining causes. Note is taken of present and previous occupation, previous thrombosis, previous pregnancy, trauma, surgery and family history.

The limbs are examined, noting size, shape and the nature and extent of any oedema. Ranges of movement are carefully measured at all lower limb joints, and any reasons for lack of range are recorded. An estimate of muscle power is made and charted. The peripheral pulses, posterior tibial and dorsalis pedis arteries, should be palpated, and the digital capillary pressure tested by mild compression and release. The presence of varicose veins, signs of phlebitis, cellulitis or thrombosis should be carefully assessed. The presence of pain or discomfort is taken into consideration, and a note made of how this varies with rest, position, movement and exercise.

A tracing of the ulcer outline is taken as follows: a piece of clear cellophane is sterilised (with the normal cleansing agent used) and placed over the ulcer; a second piece of cellophane is laid over the first and a tracing made. The first piece of cellophane is discarded, and the second piece bearing the trace may be retained as a record. It can be placed over graph paper and be used to measure the area of the ulcer; or it may be used as an outline from which to make a mask for use in ultraviolet irradiation. Subsequent tracings may be made at intervals thus recording progress (and the efficacy of treatment).

A visual assessment is made of the lesion, noting the tissue changes in the floor of the ulcer and the surrounding skin. It is important to make note of the cleanliness/infective state of the ulcer, the presence of granulation tissue, the filling in of the floor, and the formation of a healing, spreading or indolent edge, in order that subsequent progression or regression of the ulcer healing becomes obvious, and the treatment varied accordingly.

Objectives of treatment

REDUCTION OF OEDEMA

The presence of oedema inhibits the circulation, and hence local metabolism and the repair process. It may, by its tension, thrombose minute blood vessels in the skin and subcutaneous tissues causing further degeneration and tissue breakdown. Oedema may limit movement, particularly if it becomes organised and adhesions form; because of the tension there could be pain. It may be a culture medium for bacteria leading to a spread of infection.

CONTROL OF INFECTION

Infection not only maintains the ulcer but also leads to it spreading; it also causes pain. Any infection requires strict asepsis and may contra-indicate some physiotherapy procedures.

MOBILISATION OF THE TISSUES IN THE FLOOR AND EDGES OF THE ULCER

This helps to soften and increase the vascularity of the tissues, and, possibly, hastens the more rapid, non-adherent healing of the ulcer.

MOBILISE STIFF JOINTS

An attempt should be made to mobilise any joints which have limited movement, and then to maintain this range of movement. It may well be that the patient has limited range of movement due to the oedema, and/or because of the necessity of supporting bandaging to maintain dressings and control the oedema over a considerable period of time. It is essential to maintain joint range in the long term in order to utilise the muscle pump drainage mechanism effectively, and to be able to walk normally.

INCREASE MUSCLE STRENGTH

Muscle bulk and power may be considerably diminished because of oedema, pain, joint stiffness, continued use of support bandaging, faulty gait, and general lack of normal use. This also reduces the effectiveness of the muscle pump. An attempt should be made to improve muscle strength while bearing in mind the patient's ability to tolerate an exercise programme.

RE-EDUCATION OF GAIT AND POSTURE

Many patients have adopted a faulty gait and posture, and they should be advised to improve these progressively as part of the restoration of normal function within the limit of the patient's capability, as the condition improves.

RELIEF OF PAIN

This will result from the realisation of the above objectives.

ADVICE TO PATIENTS AND RELATIVES

Effective sustained results are difficult to achieve without the full co-operation of both the patient and his relatives. This applies to both the overall management of the condition, and the subsequent care should full healing occur, in order to prevent recurrence.

Physiotherapy methods

A combination of the following methods may be of value in the treatment of this condition. The reader is advised to keep abreast of current trends and development of techniques.

REDUCTION OF OEDEMA

The following methods are available to augment normal physiological methods of venous and lymphatic drainage.

Faradic-type current under pressure: The patient is supported comfortably with the limb in elevation. Tight, constrictive clothing should be removed or loosened. The infra- and retro-malleolar fossae should be packed with shaped plastic foam or felt, and padding applied over the course of varicose veins. Electrodes are placed over the antero-lateral tibial groups and dorsum of foot; the current output is turned up, movement tested and then turned off. Similarly, electrodes are placed over the proximal end of the calf and the plantar aspect of the foot; the current output is turned up, this movement tested and then turned off. An outer elasticated bandage is now applied over the electrodes and packing material. A Bisgaard (blue- or red-line) bandage is commonly used, and should be applied at approximately half stretch to the foot and ankle areas and successively less firmly as the spiralling turns of bandage ascend the limb. The bandage should be applied proximal to the upper limit of the oedema and include the whole calf. The anterior electrode leads are then connected to the apparatus and a long slow surging current applied for up to 10 minutes sufficiently strong to produce a firm contraction. After a rest, the posterior electrode leads are connected to the apparatus and up to 10 minutes slow surging current applied to the plantar flexors. Capilliary pressure testing on the tips of the digits should be carried out before, and frequently during, the treatment to ensure that the bandaging/packing is not too tight so as to obstruct circulation. It is essential to keep the area of the ulcer dry throughout the treatment as well as ensuring that this method does not disturb the dressing on the ulcer itself. This treatment may be more effective if the patient is encouraged to participate actively in the contraction produced by the current during the surge of current. Increasing discomfort requires the immediate removal of the bandaging.

An alternative method of application is to place both electrodes over the nerve trunks above the level of the bandaging, that is over the common peroneal nerve in one application, and over the tibial nerve in the other.

Air compression: Various intermittent pulsating machines are in more common use. The patient is supported comfortably with the limb in elevation. The limb is placed in a double skinned plastic tube which is alternately inflated and emptied of air. The machine allows for control of pressure up to 100mgHg, with a compression and rest phase. This method has the advantages of being quick and easy to apply; the limb can be maintained dry throughout and the dressings undisturbed. The treatment reduces oedema mechanically, and may be of additional benefit if the patient is able to practise static muscle contractions during the pressure phase.

Exercises in the pressure support bandage or elasticated support stockings: With the limb in elevation and the malleolar hollows and the ulcer filled to surface level, the limb is firmly bandaged. The patient is taught vigorous, repeated, toe, foot, ankle and knee exercises within pain-free range. The exercises should follow a distal to proximal pattern. The more rapid exercises should be punctuated with slow sustained contraction of the calf and anterior tibial muscles. The patient should be well instructed in the exercise routines, and encouraged to practise frequently at home. Muscle contraction and joint movement, within the constraints of a tight bandage, plus elevation, effectively augment the normal muscle pump drainage of the limb. Care must be taken to ensure, at least initially, that the bandaging is not so firm as to occlude the circulation; should the oedema be reduced during the treatment session, the bandaging should be removed and re-applied.

High elevation: The patient is asked to practise this method frequently for periods of 20 minutes at least twice daily. It can be practised as an in-patient or outpatient. The patient should lie on the bed, or floor, with the legs vertical, supported by the wall. It is difficult for some patients to get into this position and modifications will have to be considered and the positioning varied. Resting in this position may reduce oedema by removing the gravitational effect and reducing venous hypertension.

Massage: Massage, though time consuming, may be effective in reducing oedema if the patient can tolerate firm application of pressure. Slow, firm effleurage starting proximal to the oedema and gradually moving distally. Slow deep kneading and squeeze kneading is used to soften the oedema, punctuated by effleurage in an attempt to express the fluid proximally. Thumb and finger kneading manipulations are used below and behind the malleoli, sole of the foot, dorsum of foot and toes. Care must be taken to avoid the ulcer itself and its surrounding skin if in poor condition. It may be helpful to apply effleurage against a background of underlying muscle contraction or passive movement.

Massage is used frequently in the area of the ulcer and surrounding skin in order to soften the oedema and mobilise the skin and connective tissue, and to gain and retain mobility and flexibility of soft tissues. This is aimed to accelerate healing and produce a supple non-adherent scar. Strict asepsis must be observed when handling the scar with the therapist wearing sterile gloves, while performing small finger kneading, skin rolling and thumb kneading manipulations. This technique is discontinued in the presence of haemorrhage, or if it is found to produce discomfort.

Other electrotherapy: Ultrasound therapy may be of value in treating the surround to the ulcer to soften oedema, but not in the presence of haemorrhage. It is usually used in pulsed mode at low output and at the highest available frequency. Careful cleansing of the treatment head and skin surround are essential after treatment.

[The reader is advised to follow developments in the use of pulsed high frequency energy in the management of this condition. Much research remains to be done into the effectiveness of this treatment method as a means of reducing oedema, improving circulation, relieving pain and accelerating healing.]

Bandaging (Fig 32/1): Correct bandaging is very important in the management of this condition, reducing oedema, augmenting the muscle pump mechanism, and supporting distended veins. Some patients are intolerant of this method, and possibly allergic to the materials used.

Local pressure should be applied by well-shaped pads to the malleolar hollows, the ulcer, and over varicose veins. These are held in place by a crêpe or conforming bandage, which should be retained undisturbed between treatment sessions and at night. An elasticated bandage is applied over the conforming bandage in a careful pattern, and this should be retained when the limb is dependent. The bandages should be cut to a precise length to fit the patient, otherwise a 'garter' effect may be produced by too many circular turns applied at the proximal end of the pattern. The patient, or relative, should be taught carefully how to apply the bandage, in pattern, and with the correct tension. The bandage should be removed and replaced several times during the day in order to vary the pressure imprint of the pattern of the bandage on the skin. The patient should have at least three bandages issued – one on – one spare – and one in the wash. The heavier gauge bandages should never be applied directly on to the skin, as sensitive areas could be abraded along its edges. The bandage should be applied from the webs of the toes to the tibial tubercle. Applied firmly over the foot and ankle at approximately half stretch, the bandage is applied with successively less tension as the pattern ascends the leg.

Alternative bandaging materials are in frequent use according to individual preference. Some are of the medicated type such as Viscopaste, Calaband, Caltopaste and supported by an outer bandage such as crêpe, Elastocrêpe, Lestroflex, Elastoplast or Poroplast. The non-extensible medicated bandages must be applied without tension, cut and adjusted to conform to limb shape as necessary.

The patient should be taught to practise exercises within the bandaging, and not to sit, or stand still for long periods of time. In keeping the muscles and joints moving within the bandage the patient is, in effect, performing auto massage.

CONTROL OF INFECTION

In the presence of acute or sub-acute infection, active physiotherapy to the ulcer and surround is usually discontinued, and resumed only at the discretion of the doctor in charge of the case. In less acute condition, ultraviolet irradiation (UVR) may be used in an attempt to sterilise the surface of the ulcer and improve the blood supply. The lamp chosen should include UVC (i.e. less than 280nm) in its output in order to maximise the bactericidal effect.

Subsequent to skin tolerance testing, an intense dose of irradiation

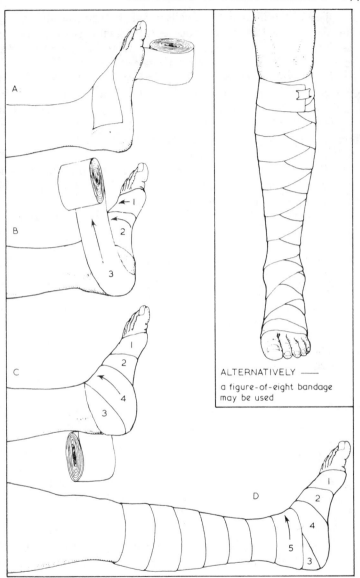

ALTERNATIVELY ——

a figure-of-eight bandage
may be used

FIG. 32/1 The application of the support bandage

is applied to the ulcer only, usually a fourth degree erythema (E_4) equivalent – or a double fourth degree ($2E_4$) – taking extreme care to mask the surrounding skin. A mask may be made from a tracing as previously described, or the skin is protected by placing sterile Tulle Gras to the skin up to the edges of the ulcer. The same dose may be repeated once or twice a week if the ulcer remains infected. The irradiation is discontinued as healing occurs; it may be continued in the presence of healing if the UVC and UVB (less than 315nm) are filtered out with the use of a *blue uviol* filter and a first degree erythema (E_1) equivalent dose given.

An E_1 or E_2 dose may be given to the surrounding skin in some cases in an attempt to maintain an improved blood supply to the surrounding skin and subcutaneous tissues.

It is essential that strict aseptic techniques are used in the handling and dressing of the ulcer.

MOBILISATION OF SKIN AND CONNECTIVE TISSUE

This is achieved primarily by massage using skin rolling, finger kneading as previously stated. Low dosage ultrasonic therapy may be used either alone or in conjunction with massage, particularly if the massage produced pain. Sterile gloves must be used for the massage. Both methods are stopped should bleeding occur.

STIMULATION OF THE ULCER FLOOR AND EDGES

If the ulcer becomes chronic or indolent it may need stimulating to produce healing. In this case an E_2 equivalent dose is often used to the floor of the ulcer and the surrounding skin. As the ulcer becomes cleaner, and of more healthy appearance, the dose is reduced to a sub-erythemal one ($\frac{1}{2}E_1$) and/or the blue uviol filter used to screen UVB and UVC irradiation.

The application of ultrasound therapy may also help with an ulcer in this state; using pulsed, low output, at 3MHz to the surrounding area to soften oedema and increase vascularity of the skin and subcutaneous tissue.

Pulsed high frequency treatment may prove to be of value in this stimulation and acceleration of healing.

First aid: Anyone concerned with the management of patients with venous ulcers, including the patient, should be acquainted with basic first aid should bleeding occur from the bed of the ulcer. *Tourniquets must not be used in any circumstances*. The treatment is to elevate the limb and apply a pressure pack and bandage over the site. The pressure applied should only be in the order of venous pressure, and light pressure from the hand is sufficient while medical help is sought. It is important to adhere to these simple methods as it is possible to lose a considerable amount of blood from a bleeding varicose ulcer.

MOBILISATION OF JOINTS AND STRENGTHENING MUSCLES

The patient should be on an active programme of exercises compatible with his ability. The joints may become increasingly stiff, with adaptive shortening of muscles, and possible contraction of peri-articular structures. Muscles will atrophy due to disuse and impoverished blood supply. Full range movement and reasonable muscle power are essential in the long-term management of the condition, particularly when the supportive bandage is to be progressively discarded. The exercises should be performed in pain-free ranges.

Passive anatomical and accessory movements are used to gain and maintain range. Active exercises are practised – free and resisted to the intrinsic muscles of the foot, leg and thigh, using such techniques as hold-relax, slow reversals, rhythmic stabilisations and pivoting. The patient should have a positive, well taught routine of exercises to practise at home. Much time will need to be spent on re-education of gait and the carrying out of activities of daily living.

ADVICE TO PATIENTS

The patient should fully understand the rationale of the methods being used in his treatment. A detailed regime is taught, and the patient should be able to carry out the exercises to a numbered and timed routine. Most of all he should know not to sit or stand still for long periods of time with the limb dependent; he must understand that an increase in pain or discharge from the ulcer requires prompt referral back to the department. It is important to explain to the patient, and his family, that help and reassurance are available if they should have problems.

Occasionally, it may be necessary to remove surgically the avascular fibrous base on which the ulcer lies and graft skin on to normally vascularised tissue which will sustain the vitality of the graft. Physiotherapists may be involved in the pre- and postoperative care, but this will depend upon the individual surgeon.

LYMPHOEDEMA

In some units lymphoedema is treated by pneumatic compression and this method is now fully described.

Pneumatic compression treatment

Over the last three decades, compression treatments have been used in an attempt to control or alleviate lymphoedema of the limbs, with varying degrees of success. Originating in the USA where the early machines were maufactured, indeed are still manufactured, by the Jobst Institute Inc, Toledo, intermittent compression was largely used for treating lymphoedema following mastectomy. Today, there are a number of firms making such machines both in the UK as well as the USA and Europe. Basically, there are two types of compression available – intermittent and sequential.

PRINCIPLES OF WORKING

The apparatus consists of a pneumatic pump with a series of controls which regulate the sequence of inflation/deflation, the amount of pressure applied and the time ratio of inflation/deflation. The pressure garment, either arm or leg, consists of a double layered, sealed polyurethane (or similar material) sheath. If for intermittent compression the sleeve will be a continuous single compartment; if for sequential compression then the sleeve will consist of a number of compartments which can be inflated/deflated in sequence depending on the setting. Sequential apparatus usually has 10 or 12 cells, although there are small portable ones of 1 or 3 cells for use in the home.

Intermittent compression: In this method the sleeve inflates and compresses at the chosen pressure (mmHg) and then deflates. The whole limb is therefore compressed at the same time.

Sequential compression: In this method, like a Ripple bed, the cells inflate sequentially – as one set deflates so another set inflates allowing for a ripple or sequential effect upon the tissues.

(All machines have detailed instruction sheets which the therapist should read carefully, and machines should be tested by the therapist with a colleague acting as a patient so that she is aware of the pressure(s) and timing ratios, before treating a patient.)

USES OF COMPRESSION TREATMENT

In addition to lymphoedema of the limbs (primary or secondary), post-traumatic oedema may also be treated. Compression treatment is being used also to aid the reduction of flexion deformities and in spasticity. It is not proposed to discuss the latter conditions.

CONTRA-INDICATIONS TO TREATMENT

The following conditions would be absolute contra-indications to treatment either being commenced or for immediate cessation should treatment have begun. Cellulitis of the limb; thrombophlebitis; atrial congestion; abdominal and/or thoracic venous occlusion; ischaemia of the extremities; dermatitis; carcinoma affecting the limb under treatment. Patients with any degree of cardiac failure should not have two limbs treated simultaneously.

In any cases of doubt treatment should not be started until the patient has been assessed by a doctor. If, during treatment, the patient complains of pain or discomfort, the machine should be switched off immediately and treatment stopped.

METHOD OF TREATMENT

Treatment may be given as an in-patient or as an outpatient. It may subsequently be continued as a home treatment, with the patient being lent a suitable home model.

When the patient first attends for treatment he/she should receive a full explanation from the therapist as to the purpose of the treatment, what it will feel like and of what he should be aware. The question of wearing a graduated support garment when not having treatment should be considered and, where necessary, arrangements made for the supply of one.

The therapist should note the history of the swelling: if post-mastectomy whether radiotherapy has been given, what type of mastectomy; if primary lymphoedema how long the swelling has been present and whether it was precipated by anything particular.

Assessment: Before starting treatment measurements should be taken to allow for comparison to be made. This may be by the volumetric displacement method, or by simple girth measuring using a centimetre calibrated tape at points on the limb adjacent to fixed bony points. It helps if the same therapist can carry these out regularly throughout treatment. In addition the feel of the oedema should be noted – Does it pit? Is it brawny? Is there pain? Is the skin stretched? Mobility of adjacent joints and muscle strength should also be noted.

Preparation of the patient: The limb to be treated should be completely bared, shoulder straps lowered or pants removed. Any rings, bracelets, watch, splint or bandages must be removed. If the wedding ring is constricting the finger it may have to be removed by a jeweller.

The limb is then placed in a cotton gauze sleeve – Tubigauze is very suitable – before being put into the compression sleeve. (This is necessary because the limb will sweat.) The sleeve is then connected by plastic/rubber tubing to the machine which is then switched on.

Position for treatment: Because the treatment time is lengthy it is essential that the patient is positioned in a comfortable manner. The limb must be treated in some elevation supported by pillows or a foam wedge placed on a plinth, chair arm or table. It pays to take time to achieve maximum comfort.

Duration of treatment: This will depend upon the type of lymph-oedema, whether the patient is an in- or outpatient. On average an in-patient would receive three sessions of 3 hours' each for 5–14 days. This would almost certainly be used only for severe cases. An outpatient would receive daily treatment of $1-1\frac{1}{2}$ hours possibly combining it with additional home treatment. If daily treatment is not possible, then twice weekly treatment is given but this would certainly have to be combined with home treatment.

Timing of compression: If intermittent compression is being given the ratio of inflation/deflation would be around 3:1, given that the time sequence is 60 seconds this would mean 45 seconds compression and 15 seconds deflation. These are only average figures and the therapist must work out her own ratios for the individual patient. The pressure (in mmHg) should start low and increase to about 60mmHg. Again this will be individually tailored. While it is seldom necessary to go above 60mmHg, there are occasions when considerably higher pressures may be used (Zelikovski et al, 1980).

The time ratio in sequential compression varies according to the number of cell compartments and again will need to be tailored to the individual patient.

Home treatment: In all cases where home treatment is desirable, full and careful instructions must be given, not only to the patient but also to a relative. Treatment should be for a minimum of 2 hours daily, divided if more convenient. Periodic checks must also be kept on the continuing efficacy of the treatment. Because the pump is run off electricity, the patient should be reassured that the cost of this is no more than burning a 60 watt light bulb.

PRESSURE BANDAGING

In-patients should wear correctly applied pressure bandages or a support garment at all times when they are not receiving treatment. *Outpatients* should be encouraged to do so, also.

All patients receiving treatment for lymphoedema should also be taught exercises in elevation, and they should be encouraged to do them regularly through the day while wearing the bandages.
Note: Pressure garments are effective only when the pressure is graduated from high to low distally to proximally.

In addition to compression treatment, the following points relating to other forms of treatment should be considered:

Exercises

The patient must have an effective and progressive regime of exercises to strengthen muscles and improve joint range in order to increase the effectiveness of the muscle pump on venous and lymphatic drainage over a period. Exercises are also essential to obtain the maximum functional use of the limb as the oedema reduces. The patient should be encouraged to practise circulatory exercises in elevation with and without the supporting bandage or stocking.

Massage

Massage, if used, should consist of slow, deep, rhythmical effleurage and kneading, squeeze kneading, wringing, and picking up manipulation. Finger kneading and frictions may be utilised over local pockets of firm oedema.

Electrotherapy is of little value in extensive oedema.

Surgery

Depending on the surgeon's wishes pre-operative physiotherapy will follow the plans previously described. In addition circulatory exercises are stressed, in preparation for the immediate postoperative phase of recovery.

Postoperatively, breathing, coughing and expectoration is encouraged as necessary together with appropriate 'bed' maintenance exercises. Early ambulation is usually encouraged, and depending on the patient, active physiotherapy may be required together with re-education of gait, posture and the functional use of the part. Later, the physiotherapist may be asked to use a combination of massage, ultrasound, pulsed high frequency and exercise to assist in the mobilisation of any postoperative scarring.

REFERENCES

Fredrickson, D. S. and Levy, R. I. (1972). Diseases characterised by evidence of abnormal lipid metabolism. In *The Metabolic Basis of Inherited Disease*, (eds. Stanbury, J. B., Wyngaarden, J. B. and Fredrickson, D. S.). McGraw–Hill Book Co., New York.

Zelikovski, A. et al (1980). The 'Lymphapress'. A new pneumatic device for the treatment of lymphoedema: clinical trial and results. *Folia Angiologica*, **28**, 165–90.

BIBLIOGRAPHY

Beninson, J. (1961). Six years of pressure gradient therapy. *Angiology*, **12**, 1, 38–44.

Hazarika, E. Z., Knight, M. T. N. and Frazer-Moodie, A. (1979). The effect of intermittent compression on the hand after fasciectomy. *Hand*, **2**, 3, 309–14.

McNair, T. J., Martin, I. J. and Orr, J. D. (1976). Intermittent compression for lymphoedema of arm. *Clinical Oncology*, **2**, 339–42.

Raines, J. K., O'Donnell Jr, T. F., Kallsher, L. and Clement Darling, R. (1977). A selection of patients with lymphoedema for compression therapy. *American Journal of Surgery*, **133**, 430–7.

Swedborg, I. (1977). Voluminometric estimation of the degree of lymphoedema and its therapy by pneumatic compression. *Scandinavian Journal of Rehabilitation Medicine*, **9**, 131–5.

Swedborg, I. (1980). Effectiveness of combined methods of physiotherapy for post-mastectomy lymphoedema. *Scandinavian Journal of Rehabilitation Medicine*, **12**, 77–85.

Zelikovski, A., Deutsch, A. and Reiss, R. (1983). The sequential pneumatic compression device in surgery for lymphoedema in the limbs. *Journal of Cardiovascular Surgery*, **24**, 2, 122–6.

Available from Dr C. Regnard, Sir Michael Sobell House, Churchill Hospital, Oxford OX3 7LJ are a paper and leaflet entitled:
Lymphoedema Clinic Results 1983–85 and Lymphoedema Advice on Treatment.
(A large stamped addressed envelope should be enclosed.)

ACKNOWLEDGEMENT

The author and the book's editor are indebted to Mrs A. Thomson MCSP for contributing the section relating to compression treatment.

Select Bibliography

In addition to the references and bibliography at the end of most of the chapters, the following is a select list of books and papers which could be used for further in-depth reading. They all have additional reference material to enable follow-up of interesting points.

In the case of book titles, the current editions are listed; most textbooks are regularly up-dated and the reader should check whether there has been a new edition. This can be ascertained by asking the librarian at the hospital or postgraduate centre library, or by checking in Whittaker's *Books in Print* which is to be found in the reference section of all public libraries.

BOOKS

ABC of Hypertension (1981). British Medical Association, London.

ABC of Resuscitation (1986). British Medical Association, London.

Baddekey, H. (1984). *Radiological Investigations: A Guide to the Use of Medical Imaging in Practice*. John Wiley, Chichester.

Breathing Control for Asthma and Emphysema, 10th edition. (1974). Asthma Research Council, London.

Brenwald, E. (ed.) (1984). *Heart Disease. A Textbook of Cardiovascular Medicine*, 2nd edition. W. B. Saunders Co, Philadelphia.

Brooker, M. J. (1986). *Computed Tomography for Radiographers*. MTP Press, Lancaster.

Chapman, S. and Nakielny, R. (1981). *A Guide to Radiological Procedures*. Ballière Tindall, London.

Comroe, J. H. (1974). *Physiology of Respiration: An Introductory Text*, 2nd edition. Year Book Medical Publisher, Chicago.

Comroe, J. H. (1976). *Pulmonary and Respiratory Physiology*. Hutchison Ross/Academic Press, London.

Conway, N. (1981). *A Colour Atlas of Cardiology*. Wolfe Medical Publications Limited, London.

Davies, P. M. (1978). *Medical Terminology in Hospital Practice*, 3rd edition. William Heinemann Medical Books Limited, London.

Downie, R. S. and Calman, K. C. (1987). *Healthy Respect: Ethics in Health Care*. Faber and Faber, London.

Duncan, A. S., Dunstan, G. R. and Wellborn, R. B. (eds.) (1981). *Dictionary of Medical Ethics*, 2nd edition. Darton, Longman and Todd, London.

Gorowitz, S., Macklin, R., Janeton, A. et al (eds.) (1983). *Moral Problems in Medicine*, 2nd edition. Prentice Hall, Englewood Cliffs, N. J.

Hampton, J. R. (1983). *Cardiovascular Disease*. William Heinemann Medical Books Limited, London.

Harris, J. (1985). *The Value of Life*. Routledge and Kegan Paul, London.

Hart, J. T. (1980). *Hypertension*. Churchill Livingstone, Edinburgh.

Horton, R. E. (1980). *Vascular Surgery*. Hodder and Stoughton, London.

James, D. G. and Studdy, P. R. (1981). *A Colour Atlas of Respiratory Disease*. Wolfe Medical Publications Limited, London.

Johnson, N. M. (1986). *Respiratory Medicine: Pocket Consultant*. Blackwell Scientific Publications Limited, Oxford.

Jonsen, A. R., Siegler, M. and Winslade, S. J. (1982). *Clinical Ethics*. Ballière Tindall, London.

Kennedy, I. (1983). *The Unmasking of Medicine*. Granada Books, London.

Mason, J. K. and McCall Smith, R. A. (1983). *Law and Medical Ethics*. Butterworths, London.

Moghissi, K. (1986). *Essentials of Thoracic and Cardiac Surgery*. William Heinemann Medical Books Limited, London.

Morgan, K. W. and Seaton, A. (eds.) (1984). *Occupational Lung Disease*, 2nd edition. Holt-Saunders, Eastbourne.

Neutze, J. M., Moller, C. T. and Harris, E. A. (1982). *Intensive Care of the Heart and Lungs: A Text for Nurses and Other Staff in the Intensive Care Unit*. Blackwell Scientific Publications Limited, Oxford.

Occupation Asthma (1986). Cmnd 9717. HMSO, London.

Op't Holt, T. B. (1986). *Assessment-Based Respiratory Care*. Wiley, New York.

Page, G., Mills, K. and Morton, R. (1986). *A Colour Atlas of Cardiopulmonary Resuscitation Techniques*. Wolfe Medical Publications Limited, London.

Rees, J. (1984). *ABC of Asthma*. British Medical Association, London.

Sturridge, M. F. and Treasure, T. (1985). *Belcher's Thoracic Surgical Management*, 5th edition. Ballière Tindall, London.

The SI for the Health Professions (1977). World Health Organisation, Geneva.

Tinker J. and Jones, S. N. (1986). *A Pocket Book for Intensive Care: Data, Drugs and Procedures*. Edward Arnold, London.

Watson, H. (1984). *Disorders of Cardiac Rate, Rhythm and Conduction*. Beaconsfield Publishers Limited, Beaconsfield, England.

Wright, P. and Treacher, A. (eds.) (1982). *The Problem of Medical Knowledge: Examining the Social Construction of Medicine*. Edinburgh University Press, Edinburgh.

Young, S. W. (1984). *Nuclear Magnetic Resonance Imaging: Basic Principles*. Raven Press, New York.

PAPERS

Brooks, R. G. et al (1985). Infectious complications in heart-lung recipients. *American Journal of Medicine*, **79**, 4, 412–22.

Burke, C. M., Theodore, J., Baldwin, J. C. et al (1986). Twenty-eight cases of human heart–lung transplantation. *Lancet*, **1**, 517–19.

Connellan, S. J. and Gough, S. E. (1982). The effects of nebulised salbutamol on lung function and exercise tolerance in patients with severe airflow obstruction. *British Journal of Diseases of the Chest*, **76**, 135–42.

Editorial (1986). High frequency ventilation. *Lancet*, **1**, 477–9.

Gillon, R. (1985). Telling the truth and medical ethics. *British Medical Journal*, **291**, 1556–7.

Gillon, R. (1985). Consent. *British Medical Journal*, **291**, 1700–1.

Jenkins, S. C. and Soutar, S. A. (1986). A. survey into the use of incentive spirometry following coronary artery by-pass graft surgery. *Physiotherapy*, **72**, 10, 492–3.

Leading Article (1986). Mechanical ventilation of the newborn. *British Medical Journal*, **292**, 575.

Leading Article (1986). PEEP and CPAP. *British Medical Journal*, **292**, 643.

Lipkin, D. P., Scriven, A. J., Crake, T. and Poole-Wilson, P. A. (1986). Six minute walking test for assessing exercise capacity in chronic heart failure. *British Medical Journal*, **292**, 653–5.

Luksza, A. R. (1982). A new look at asthma. *British Journal of Diseases of the Chest*, **76**, 11–14.

Marsh, B. (1986). A second chance. (Personal Paper.) *British Medical Journal*, **292**, 675–6.

Useful Organisations

Action on Smoking and Health (ASH)
5–11 Mortimer Street
London W1N 7RH   01-637 9843

Asthma Research Council
300 Upper Street
London N1 2XX   01-226 2260

The British Heart Foundation
102 Gloucester Place
London W1H 4DH   01-935 0185

The British Thoracic Society
30 Britten Street
London SW3 6NN   01-352 2194

Cardiac Spare Parts Club
c/o National Westminster Bank Limited
2 High Street
Olney
Bucks MK46 4BB

The Chest, Heart and Stroke Association
Tavistock House North
Tavistock Square
London WC1H 9JE   01-387 3012

The Chest, Heart and Stroke Association
   (Scotland)
65 North Castle Street
Edinburgh EH2 3LT   031-225 6527

The Cystic Fibrosis Research Trust
5 Blyth Road
Bromley
Kent BR1 3RS   01-464 7211

The Raynaud's Association Trust
40 Bladon Crescent
Alsager
Cheshire ST7 2BG   0936 35167

Scoliosis Self-Help Group
380–384 Harrow Road
London W9 2HU   01-289 5652

Index